AWS for Solutions Architects

Third Edition

Design and scale secure AWS architectures with GenAI strategies and real-world patterns

Saurabh Shrivastava

Neelanjali Srivastav

Dhiraj Thakur

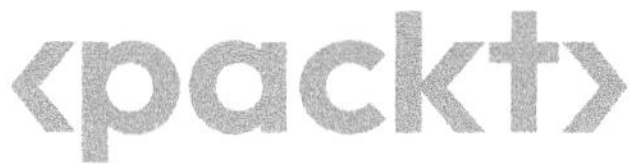

AWS for Solutions Architects

Third Edition

Portfolio Director: Kartikey Pandey

Relationship Lead: Aaron Tanna

Project Manager: Sonam Pandey

Content Engineer: Sayali Pingale

Technical Editor: Simran Ali

Copy Editor: SafisE diting

Indexer: Hemangini Bari

Proofreader: Sayali Pingale

Production Designer: Ganesh Bhadwalkar

Growth Lead: Shreyans Singh

First published: January 2021

Second edition: April 2023

Third edition: July 2025

Production reference: 2120825

Published by Packt Publishing Ltd.

Grosvenor House

11 St Paul's Square

Birmingham

B3 1RB, UK.

ISBN 978-1-83664-193-3

www.packtpub.com

To our loving kids, Shubh and Sanvi, who bring immeasurable happiness and joy to our lives.

– Saurabh and Neelanjali

Forewords

"You can't build a reputation on what you are going to do."

—*Henry Ford*

In today's cloud-driven world, action is everything. Innovation rewards the bold—those who move quickly, architect thoughtfully, learn from their failures, and never stop learning. The role of a solutions architect has never been more critical to that momentum, and yet also never more complex. You're expected to make decisions across a fast-evolving landscape of services, patterns, use cases, and priorities, all while aligning technology to business strategy.

This book, *AWS for Solutions Architects*, is built for that reality.

It is not just a reference manual—it's a blueprint for how to think, evaluate, and build on AWS with confidence and clarity. Whether you are designing multi-account landing zones, implementing a data lake strategy, modernizing applications, or scaling AI workloads, this book is your guide to doing it the right way.

Over the past two decades—and especially in my current role at AWS—I've seen firsthand that successful architecture isn't about choosing a single service. It's about an end-to-end solution. It's about making informed trade-offs, optimizing for agility and cost, and integrating across domains such as security, automation, data, and performance. This book mirrors that complexity with structure and purpose.

You'll find deep insights into foundational cloud principles, the Well-Architected Framework, and real-world strategies for enterprise transformation. But it doesn't stop there. The content dives into modern, high-impact topics such as AI-led transformation, DevOps pipelines, storage patterns, event-driven systems, ML integration, and cloud-native security and compliance. It culminates in practical, hands-on implementation guidance—because the best ideas are the ones you actually bring to life.

One of this book's greatest strengths is its relevance. It doesn't just focus on *how* AWS works—it shows you *why* certain architectural decisions matter. It also arms you with the language, frameworks, and mental models to lead, influence, and build resilient systems in an environment that never stands still.

As you read through these pages, I encourage you to do more than absorb information. Challenge assumptions. Experiment boldly. Think not just as an engineer but as an innovator. Because what we architect today becomes the foundation of what's possible tomorrow.

If you're preparing for a certification, this book will sharpen your edge. If you're deep in the trenches of enterprise modernization, it will be your tactical guide. If you're mentoring the next generation of cloud builders, it will help you teach them to design not just for scale but for impact.

The cloud rewards those who build with intention. So, dive in. Think bigger. Build smarter. Architect the future.

Kamal Arora

Director, Solutions Architecture – AWS

Inventor | Author | Cloud & AI Strategy Leader

As organizations continue their digital transformation journeys, **Amazon Web Services (AWS)** remains at the core of cloud innovation, empowering teams to build faster, scale globally, and reduce operational complexity. Today, designing solutions in the cloud isn't just about deploying services; it's about making informed, cost-effective, and secure decisions that align with business objectives. This makes the role of a solutions architect more vital than ever. Architects must understand the full AWS ecosystem and how to leverage it strategically to deliver measurable value.

With over 20 years of experience in mentoring technology professionals, I consider *AWS for Solutions Architects* an essential guide for those aiming to master the AWS platform. This updated edition is especially timely, as it reflects the latest advancements in cloud architecture, security, FinOps, and AI, including the rise of agentic AI.

A standout update in this edition is its coverage of Amazon Q Developer and AWS Transform, two of AWS's most powerful new tools designed to modernize how we build in the cloud. These are not just productivity enhancers; they are agentic AI services—tools that actively assist you in planning, developing, troubleshooting, and even optimizing cloud workloads through real-time, intelligent interactions. This shift from passive tools to active AI agents is redefining how cloud professionals work, and this book helps you understand and prepare for that future.

The book also addresses the rising need for cost-aware architectures, teaching you how to balance performance with cost-efficiency using services such as AWS Budgets, Savings Plans, and resource tagging strategies. It provides clear guidance on topics such as security, data engineering, serverless patterns, and multi-account strategy, making it a practical reference for real-world scenarios.

Whether you are aiming to pass the AWS Certified Solutions Architect – Associate or Professional exams or are working toward a long-term career as a cloud architect, this book provides the foundational and advanced knowledge you need. The real-world case studies, hands-on design patterns, and certification-aligned content make it especially valuable for learners at all levels.

Having seen one of the authors, Saurabh, grow from a passionate learner into a thought leader and author, I am confident this book will serve as a powerful tool for IT professionals, developers, and decision-makers alike. If you are looking to build a career in cloud architecture, stay current with GenAI trends, and prepare for AWS certifications, this book will be your trusted companion.

Congratulations to the authors for delivering a resource that is both comprehensive and future-ready.

Dr. Siddhartha Choubey, Ph.D.

Head of Department, Computer Science & Engineering, SSTC-SSGI Bhilai

Contributors

About the authors

Saurabh Shrivastava is an accomplished technology leader and author with more than two decades of experience in the IT industry. He is currently a global solutions architect leader at AWS, where he helps AWS customers and partners on their cloud journeys. Saurabh has also led the global technical partnerships team at AWS, playing a key role in launching several strategic initiatives and AWS agentic AI services.

In addition to his work at AWS, Saurabh is the co-author of Packt's best-selling book *Solutions Architect's Handbook*, and has authored several blogs and whitepapers on various topics, such as advanced analytics, generative AI, machine learning, and cloud computing. He is passionate about the latest innovations and how they can impact our daily lives. Saurabh holds a patent in cloud platform automation and has worked as an enterprise solutions architect, software architect, and software engineering manager in Fortune 50 enterprises, start-ups, and global product and consulting organizations. With his vast experience and expertise, Saurabh is a valuable resource for anyone looking to learn about cloud computing and its various applications.

Neelanjali Srivastav has extensive experience in the software industry as a technology leader, product manager, and agile coach, and she brings a wealth of knowledge to the field. Currently, she leads the IT and security portfolio at Aya Healthcare. Before that, she worked as senior product manager at AWS, where she evangelized and guided AWS customers and partners in AWS database, analytics, and machine learning services.

Neelanjali is also the co-author of Packt's best-selling book *Solutions Architect's Handbook*, which is a valuable resource for those looking to kick-start their careers as solutions architects. With her experience leading teams of software engineers, solutions architects, and systems analysts to modernize IT systems and develop innovative software solutions for large enterprises, Neelanjali is well equipped to provide insights into the challenges and opportunities in the field.

Neelanjali's expertise in enterprise application management, agile coaching, cloud service management, and orchestration makes her a sought-after speaker and thought leader in the industry. She is dedicated to helping others learn and grow in their careers, and her contributions to the field are sure to make a lasting impact.

Dhiraj Thakur currently works at **Amazon Web Services (AWS)** as a global solutions architect, enabling AWS partners and customers on their journey to the cloud. With a passion for innovation, Dhiraj has dedicated his career to exploring the latest advancements in technology and their impact on society and daily life.

He has authored several books, whitepapers, and blog posts. With a robust background in AI/ML, GenAI, data analytics, IoT, SAP, cloud technology, and application development, Dhiraj has helped numerous enterprise and public sector clients across various industries. His work has been widely recognized and respected in the industry, and he is a sought-after speaker and thought leader in the field of technology.

About the reviewer

Kishore Vinjam is a principal solutions architect at AWS and a recognized thought leader in cloud operations and governance. With over 1,500 LinkedIn followers and extensive technical publications, he specializes in helping enterprises navigate complex cloud transformations while maintaining security and compliance. His work has significantly impacted how organizations implement scalable cloud foundations. Passionate about cloud technologies and building customer solutions, Kishore ensures to maintain a work-life balance through family time and activities such as hiking, volleyball, and ping-pong.

Table of Contents

Chapter 2: Understanding the AWS Well-Architected Framework and Getting Certified 27

Chapter 3: Leveraging the Cloud for Enterprise Transformation 73

Chapter 7: Selecting the Right Database Service 279

Part 3: AWS Cloud Security and Monitoring 343

Chapter 8: Best Practices for Application Security, Identity, and Compliance 345

Part 4: AWS Advance Analytics, ML, and GenAI Service Offerings 447

Chapter 10: Data Engineering and Big Data Analytics in AWS 449

Part 5: Applying Architectural Patterns and Reference Architectures 563

Chapter 12: Data Lake Patterns: Integrating Your Data Across the Enterprise 565

Part 6: Hands-On Labs 665

Chapter 14: Hands-On Guide to Building an App in AWS 667

Preface

The adoption of cloud technologies is accelerating at a pace never seen before. Today, the question is no longer *if* cloud computing will dominate, but *how fast* companies—large and small—can leverage it to gain a competitive edge. **Amazon Web Services (AWS)**, the leader in cloud computing, empowers millions of customers worldwide with a vast array of services to build, deploy, and manage modern, scalable, and secure applications.

This book is tailored for AWS solutions architects, developers, and IT professionals looking to build expertise across the AWS ecosystem. It guides you through the critical building blocks of cloud infrastructure, encompassing compute, storage, networking, security, databases, analytics, and more. You'll explore how AWS enables organizations to build high-performance applications with robust architectural best practices.

Each chapter is organized to align with a practical, architecture-first approach, explaining core AWS services through real-world use cases from companies such as Netflix, Airbnb, Capital One, and Moderna, to help you understand how to apply these technologies effectively in your environment. Whether it's running containerized microservices with Amazon ECS and EKS, automating workloads using AWS Lambda, or architecting globally resilient applications, you'll see how cloud services translate to real impact.

The book also explores advanced domains, including **machine learning** (**ML**) and **Generative AI**. You'll get hands-on guidance using services such as Amazon SageMaker for model training, Amazon Bedrock for building generative applications, and AWS-managed services such as Comprehend and Rekognition to infuse AI into your solutions without managing infrastructure. You will learn how to use agentic AI services like AWS Transform to rapidly modernize legacy workloads. These sections will help you design intelligent applications that adapt to user behavior and automate decision-making.

Security, identity management, and compliance are woven throughout the chapters, including in-depth coverage of IAM, AWS Organizations, CloudTrail, and GuardDuty.

You'll also explore the AWS Well-Architected Framework and its six pillars—including the Sustainability pillar—to evaluate and optimize your workloads.

By the end of this book, you'll have a solid foundation to design and implement AWS-based solutions that are not just technically sound but also cost-effective, secure, and aligned with your organization's business goals.

Who this book is for

This book is designed for a broad audience looking to harness the power of AWS—from technical professionals to decision-makers:

- **Solutions architects**: Whether you're new to AWS or preparing for the AWS Solutions Architect certification, this book is your go-to guide. It dives deep into essential AWS services, architecture best practices, and the AWS Well-Architected Framework, helping you design scalable and secure cloud applications.
- **Developers and IT professionals**: If you're building, deploying, or managing cloud-based applications, this book walks you through AWS services in compute, storage, networking, databases, analytics, security, and emerging tech such as machine learning and generative AI. You'll gain the technical know-how to solve complex business problems using AWS.
- **Business executives and technology leaders**: For decision-makers seeking a deeper understanding of cloud capabilities, this book offers insight into how AWS can drive innovation, reduce costs, and support digital transformation. Real-world use cases help bridge the gap between business goals and technical execution.

No matter your background or experience level, if your goal is to build reliable, cost-effective, and scalable solutions using AWS, this book is for you.

What this book covers

Chapter 1, Understanding AWS Cloud Principles and Key Characteristics, gets things started with cloud basics, AWS's position in the market, and why it has become the platform of choice for start-ups and enterprises. You'll learn about AWS fundamentals, including elasticity, security, and faster provisioning cycles.

Chapter 2, Understanding the AWS Well-Architected Framework and Getting Certified, dives into the six pillars of the Well-Architected Framework—Security, Reliability, Performance Efficiency, Cost Optimization, Operational Excellence, and Sustainability. You'll also learn how to build your career path with AWS certifications across domains such as security, networking, ML, AI, data engineering , solutions architecture, and more.

Chapter 3, Leveraging the Cloud for Enterprise Transformation, explores how AWS supports digital transformation with cloud migration strategies (7Rs), enterprise transformation use cases, and large-scale deal considerations using the **AWS Cloud Adoption Framework** (**CAF**).

Chapter 4, Networking in AWS, covers the AWS global infrastructure and services, including VPC, Route 53, CloudFront, Direct Connect, and AWS Cloud WAN, that enable you to architect secure and performant network layers.

Chapter 5, Storage in AWS: Choosing the Right Tool for the Job, compares storage options, including EBS, EFS, S3 (with its various tiers), and hybrid storage solutions. You'll also learn best practices around performance, cost optimization, and data protection.

Chapter 6, Harnessing the Power of Cloud Computing, helps you understand EC2 instance families, AWS Lambda, Fargate, HPC, and hybrid compute using Outposts. You'll learn how to optimize workloads based on application demands.

Chapter 7, Selecting the Right Database Service, explores relational and NoSQL databases, including RDS, DynamoDB, Neptune, Timestream, and Amazon DocumentDB, and how to migrate, manage, and tune databases on AWS.

Chapter 8, Best Practices for Application Security, Identity, and Compliance in AWS, helps you learn about IAM, AWS Organizations, GuardDuty, WAF, Macie, and encryption strategies. This chapter will help you design compliant, secure cloud architectures using AWS-native tools.

Chapter 9, Driving Efficiency with Cloud Operation Automation and DevOps in AWS, looks at the CloudOps model using tools such as CloudTrail, CloudFormation, AWS CDK, and monitoring with CloudWatch, X-Ray, and other services.

Chapter 10, Data Engineering and Big Data Analytics in AWS, explores how to ingest, catalog, process, and secure big data and streaming data using services such as Glue, EMR, MSK, Kinesis, and Athena.

Chapter 11, Machine Learning and Generative AI in AWS, covers building ML pipelines with Amazon SageMaker AI, implementing MLOps best practices, and creating Generative AI apps using Amazon Bedrock, SageMaker Jumpstart, and Amazon Q.

Chapter 12, Data Lake Patterns: Integrating Your Data Across the Enterprise, looks at the architecture and best practices of data lakes, lakehouses, and data mesh. You'll discover how AWS Lake Formation, S3, and analytics tools work together to deliver enterprise-scale insights, enabling the use of ML and GenAI.

Chapter 13, Building Microservices and Event-Driven Architectures in AWS, explores microservice architecture patterns, API Gateway, event-driven models, **domain-driven design** (**DDD**), and AWS services that support modular, scalable app design.

Chapter 14, Hands-On Guide to Buildling an App in AWS, puts theory into practice by designing and building the AWSome store using Lambda, IAM, DynamoDB, API Gateway, and monitoring tools. You'll go through setup, deployment, security, and optimization guided by the Well-Architected Framework.

To get the most out of this book

To fully benefit from this book, you should have a foundational understanding of cloud computing concepts. Familiarity with general IT terminology—such as networking, storage, compute, and databases—will help you navigate the topics with ease.

We recommend setting up your own AWS account and exploring the AWS Management Console alongside the examples and hands-on labs provided in the chapters. This practical engagement will reinforce your learning and provide real-world context for the services discussed.

For a smooth learning path, consider progressing through the book sequentially. Each chapter builds upon concepts introduced earlier, helping you develop a holistic view of AWS architecture and services. Make sure to spend time on the hands-on chapter at the end, where you will apply everything you've learned to build a real-world application using AWS tools.

To deepen your knowledge, take advantage of the rich ecosystem of AWS resources:

- AWS documentation and whitepapers
- AWS training and certification
- AWS Skill Builder and Learning Paths
- AWS events, re:Invent sessions, and webinars

Finally, stay connected by engaging with the AWS community through forums such as AWS re:Post, local AWS User Groups, LinkedIn, and GitHub. Interacting with fellow cloud professionals and sharing insights will not only keep you up to date but also enrich your learning journey.

Conventions used

There are a number of text conventions used throughout this book.

`CodeInText`: Indicates code words in text, database table names, folder names, filenames, file extensions, pathnames, dummy URLs, user input, and Twitter handles. For example: "You need to replace `<function-name>` with the name of your Lambda function, `<handler>` with the name of your function's handler, `<role-arn>` with the ARN of the execution role for your Lambda function, and `<namespace>` with the namespace for your CloudWatch metrics."

A block of code is set as follows:

```
const AWS = require('aws-sdk');
class Order {
  constructor(orderId, customerId, orderDate, items, payment) {
    this.orderId = orderId;
    this.customerId = customerId;
    this.orderDate = orderDate;
    this.items = items;
    this.payment = payment;
  }
```

Any command-line input or output is written as follows:

```
aws cognito-idp create-user-pool --pool-name awsomestore-pool
```

Bold: Indicates a new term, an important word, or words that you see on the screen. For instance, words in menus or dialog boxes appear in the text like this. For example: "Open the **Amazon CloudWatch Logs** console, select the log group for **VPC Flow Logs**, and run a query to filter logs where the destAddr field is **10.0.2.0/24** and the srcAddr field is **198.51.100.10**."

Warnings or important notes appear like this.

Tips and tricks appear like this.

If You Enjoyed This Book...

You may also enjoy "*Solutions Architect's Handbook: Kick-start your career as a solutions architect by learning architecture design principles and strategies, 3rd Edition.*"

Available on Amazon: `https://www.amazon.com/dp/1835084230/`

This companion book provides a comprehensive exploration of the role of a solutions architect, from foundational design principles to advanced strategies for building resilient, scalable, and cost-optimized systems in the cloud. Covering real-world scenarios, enterprise use cases, and architecture patterns, it is a practical guide for both aspiring and experienced architects. Whether you're preparing for certification or leading cloud transformation initiatives, this book will help sharpen your architecture mindset and delivery skills.

Let's keep the conversation going!

Join our Discord community to connect with other readers, ask questions, or chat about the topics in this book: `https://discord.gg/kbFRRSB2Qs`.

Get in touch

Feedback from our readers is always welcome.

General feedback: If you have questions about any aspect of this book or have any general feedback, please email us at `customercare@packt.com` and mention the book's title in the subject of your message.

Errata: Although we have taken every care to ensure the accuracy of our content, mistakes do happen. If you have found a mistake in this book, we would be grateful if you reported this to us. Please visit `http://www.packt.com/submit-errata`, click **Submit Errata**, and fill in the form.

Piracy: If you come across any illegal copies of our works in any form on the internet, we would be grateful if you would provide us with the location address or website name. Please contact us at `copyright@packt.com` with a link to the material.

If you are interested in becoming an author: If there is a topic that you have expertise in and you are interested in either writing or contributing to a book, please visit `http://authors.packt.com/`.

Your Book Comes with Exclusive Perks - Here's How to Unlock Them

Unlock this book's exclusive benefits now

UNLOCK NOW

Scan this QR code or go to `packtpub.com/unlock`, then search this book by name. Ensure it's the correct edition.

Note: Keep your purchase invoice ready before you start.

Enhanced reading experience with our Next-gen Reader:

- **Multi-device progress sync**: Learn from any device with seamless progress sync.
- **Highlighting and notetaking**: Turn your reading into lasting knowledge.
- **Bookmarking**: Revisit your most important learnings anytime.
- **Dark mode**: Focus with minimal eye strain by switching to dark or sepia mode.

Learn smarter using our AI assistant (Beta):

- **Summarize it**: Summarize key sections or an entire chapter.
- **AI code explainers**: In the next-gen Packt Reader, click the **Explain** button above each code block for AI-powered code explanations.

Note: The AI assistant is part of next-gen Packt Reader and is still in beta.

Learn anytime, anywhere:

Access your content offline with DRM-free PDF and ePub versions—compatible with your favorite e-readers.

Unlock Your Book's Exclusive Benefits

Your copy of this book comes with the following exclusive benefits:

- Next-gen Packt Reader
- AI assistant (beta)
- DRM-free PDF/ePub downloads

Use the following guide to unlock them if you haven't already. The process takes just a few minutes and needs to be done only once.

How to unlock these benefits in three easy steps

Step 1

Keep your purchase invoice for this book ready, as you'll need it in *Step 3*. If you received a physical invoice, scan it on your phone and have it ready as either a PDF, JPG, or PNG.

For more help on finding your invoice, visit `https://www.packtpub.com/unlock-benefits/help`.

Note: Did you buy this book directly from Packt? You don't need an invoice. After completing Step 2, you can jump straight to your exclusive content.

Step 2

Scan this QR code or go to `packtpub.com/unlock`.

On the page that opens (which will look similar to Figure 1 if you're on desktop), search for this book by name. Make sure you select the correct edition.

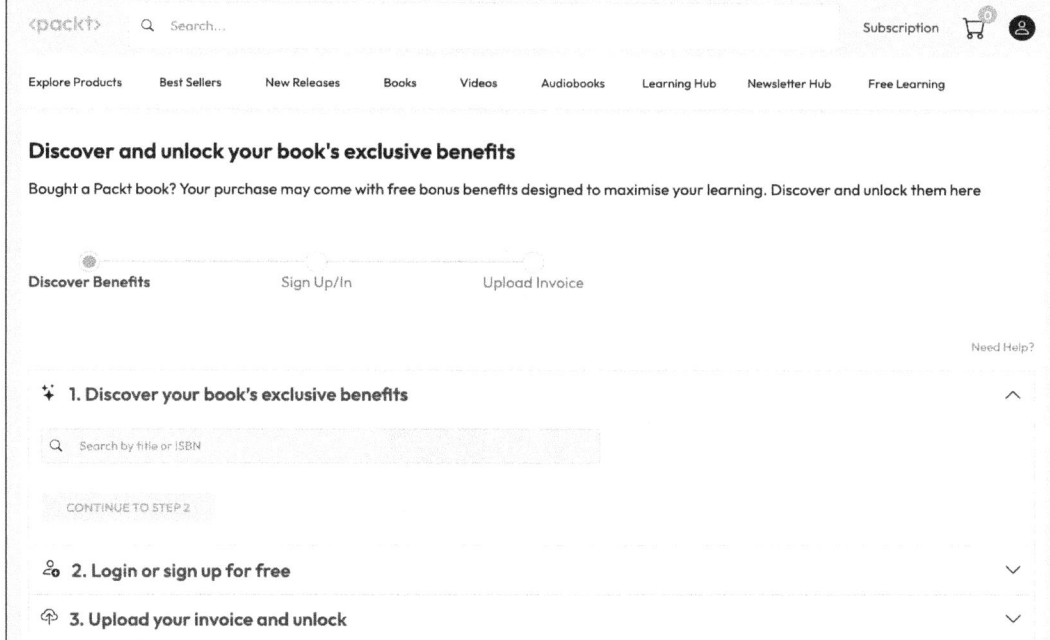

Figure 1: Packt unlock landing page on desktop

Step 3

Sign in to your Packt account or create a new one for free. Once you're logged in, upload your invoice. It can be in PDF, PNG, or JPG format and must be no larger than 10 MB. Follow the rest of the instructions on the screen to complete the process.

Need help?

If you get stuck and need help, visit `https://www.packtpub.com/unlock-benefits/help` for a detailed FAQ on how to find your invoices and more. The following QR code will take you to the help page directly:

Note: If you are still facing issues, reach out to `customercare@packt.com`.

Share your thoughts

Once you've read *AWS for Solutions Architects, Third Edition*, we'd love to hear your thoughts! Scan the QR code below to go straight to the Amazon review page for this book and share your feedback.

`https://packt.link/r/1836641931`

Your review is important to us and the tech community and will help us make sure we're delivering excellent quality content.

Part 1

Exploring AWS

In this part, you'll build a strong foundation in AWS and cloud computing. You'll start by understanding why AWS is the leading cloud provider and how its core principles, such as elasticity, scalability, and security can transform how your organization builds and runs applications. You'll then explore the AWS Well-Architected Framework, learning how to apply its six pillars to design better systems. This part will also help you prepare for AWS certifications with a clear overview of certification paths and tips for exam readiness. Finally, you'll discover how enterprises approach digital transformation using AWS services, tools, and migration strategies.

This part of the book includes the following chapters:

- *Chapter 1, Understanding AWS Cloud Principles and Key Characteristics*
- *Chapter 2, Understanding AWS Well-Architected Framework and Getting Certified*
- *Chapter 3, Leveraging the Cloud for Enterprise Transformation*

1

Understanding AWS Cloud Principles and Key Characteristics

The last decade has revolutionized the IT infrastructure industry; cloud computing was introduced, and now it is everywhere, from small start-ups to large enterprises. Nowadays, the cloud is the norm. It all began in 2006, with Amazon launching a cloud service called **Amazon Web Services** (**AWS**), which included a couple of services.

Netflix started migration to AWS in 2008 and became a market disruptor. After that, there was no looking back, and there were many industry revolutions led by cloud-born start-ups such as Airbnb in hospitality, Robinhood in finance, Lyft in transportation, and many more. The cloud rapidly gained market share, and now big names such as Coca-Cola, Starbucks, Sony, Goldman Sachs, and Toyota are all accelerating their digital journey with cloud adoption.

Even though the term "cloud" is widespread today, it continuously evolves with new offerings such as advanced analytics, machine learning, and generative AI.

This chapter explores the cloud landscape and highlights how AWS is leading the way. You'll gain insight into the widespread adoption and growing influence of cloud technologies, with a focus on AWS.

Here's what you'll learn in this chapter::

- What is cloud computing?
- What is **Amazon Web Services** (**AWS**)?
- The market share, influence, and adoption of AWS
- Basic cloud and AWS terminology
- Why is AWS so popular?

Let's get started, shall we?

What is cloud computing?

What exactly is cloud computing? It's a term that many people hear often, but not everyone fully understands. Some may even wonder what it means. Having your infrastructure in the cloud doesn't mean your servers are floating in the sky! Let's break it down clearly.

Cloud computing involves outsourcing a company's hardware and software infrastructure to a third party. At its core, it provides on-demand access to IT resources, such as servers, storage, and databases, over the Internet, eliminating the need to manage physical infrastructure. Instead of maintaining their own data centers, businesses leverage someone else's.

There are numerous advantages of cloud computing:

- **Economies of scale**: By sharing resources, companies benefit from reduced costs, similar to buying in bulk
- **Pay-as-you-go**: Businesses only pay for the time and resources they use, measured in minutes or seconds
- **Scalability**: One of the most powerful features is the ability to easily scale up, out, down, or in, adapting to changing business needs seamlessly

Cloud computing's flexibility and cost-effectiveness make it a game-changer for organizations of all sizes.

When using cloud computing, you are not buying the equipment but leasing it. Equipment leasing has been around for a long time, but not at the speeds cloud computing provides. Cloud computing makes it possible to start a resource within minutes, use it for a few hours, minutes, or even seconds, and then shut it down. You will only pay for the time you use it. Furthermore, with *serverless* computing, such as AWS Lambda services, there is no need to provision servers. You can simply call a Lambda function and pay by the function call.

The idea of being able to *scale out* and *in* is often called **elasticity** or **elastic computing**. This concept allows companies to treat their computing resources as just another utility bill and only pay for what they need at any moment.

The best way to understand the cloud is to take the electricity supply analogy. Flip a switch on to get light in your house and electric bulbs light up your home. In this case, you only pay for your electricity when needed; when you switch off electric appliances, you do not pay anything. Imagine if you needed to power a couple of appliances and had to set up an entire powerhouse. It would be costly. It would involve the costs of maintaining the turbine and generator, and building the whole infrastructure. Utility companies make your job easier by supplying electricity in the quantity you need. They maintain the entire infrastructure to generate electricity, and they can keep costs down by distributing electricity to millions of houses, which helps them benefit from mass utilization. Here, the utility companies represent cloud providers such as AWS, and the electricity represents the IT infrastructure available in the cloud.

While consuming cloud resources, you pay for IT infrastructure such as computing, storage, databases, networking, software, machine learning, and analytics in a pay-as-you-go model. Here, public clouds such as AWS do the heavy lifting to maintain IT infrastructure and provide you with on-demand access over the internet. As you generally only pay for the time and services you use, most cloud providers can provide massive scalability, making scaling services up and down easy. While, traditionally, you would have to maintain your servers on-premise to run your organization, now you can offload that to the public cloud and focus on your core business.

In the past, launching a start-up required substantial upfront funding to get your product to a beta stage. This often involved purchasing expensive server racks and high-memory servers and securing a network infrastructure. This required a significant financial investment to support a basic user base, making it nearly impossible for many solo entrepreneurs to start. However, the game has completely changed with the cloud's pay-as-you-go model. Now, entrepreneurs can launch without worrying about hefty upfront costs. Programs such as **AWS Activate** even offer start-up support, including credits, to help turn ideas into reality and quickly get MVPs in front of their target users. Many cloud-born start-ups have thrived because there is no longer a need for large initial investments.

You can learn more about the AWS Activate program at `https://aws.amazon.com/startups?lang=en-US` and see how countless successful cloud-native companies have benefited from this accessible model. As we discussed, the cloud is not just about hardware infrastructure but also has substantial software offerings. Let's look at some examples.

Software offerings in the cloud

Despite our efforts to narrow it down, cloud is still a broad term. For example, we specified that the cloud could offer software, which is a general term. In our definition, the software includes video conferencing, virtual desktops, email services, contact centers, and document management.

When AWS started, it only offered a few core services, such as compute (Amazon EC2) and basic storage (Amazon S3). AWS has continually expanded its services to support virtually any cloud workload. As of 2025, it has more than 200 fully featured services for compute, storage, databases, networking, analytics, machine learning, artificial intelligence, generative AI, Internet of Things, mobile, security, hybrid, media, application development, and deployment. As a fun fact, as of 2025, Amazon **Elastic Compute Cloud** (**EC2**) alone offers over 750 types of compute instances.

From the software offering perspective, you can see some examples given in the following table:

Category	AWS Offering
Video conferencing	Amazon Chime
Virtual desktops	AWS WorkSpaces
Email services	Amazon WorkMail
Contact Center	Amazon Connect
Virtual desktop streaming	Amazon AppStream 2.0
Customer engagement platform	Amazon Pinpoint
Business intelligence	Amazon QuickSight
Workflow automation	AWS Step Functions
Enterprise resource planning (**ERP**)	AWS for SAP
Email sending	**Amazon Simple Email Service** (**SES**)
Push notifications	**Amazon Simple Notification Service** (**SNS**)
Content delivery network	Amazon CloudFront
Media services	AWS Elemental

Table 1.1: AWS software offerings example

Not all cloud services are intertwined with their cloud ecosystems. For example, you may use Amazon SageMaker for machine learning projects, but you may use the TensorFlow package in SageMaker even though Google maintains TensorFlow. Similarly, you may be using Amazon Bedrock to build your generative AI application, but access the foundation model Llama2 models provided by Meta.

Similarly, you can use AWS CodePipeline to automate the **Continuous Integration and Continuous Deployment (CI/CD)** process, but you can integrate Jenkins for pipeline orchestration and GitHub as the source code repository.

You may also opt for a cloud-agnostic strategy; however, it has pros and cons. You want to distribute your workload between cloud providers to have competitive pricing and keep your options open, like in the old days. However, each cloud has different networking needs, and connecting distributed workloads between clouds to communicate with each other is a complex task. Also, each major cloud provider, such as AWS, Azure, and GCP, has a breadth of services, and building a workforce with all three skill sets is another challenge.

Finally, clouds such as AWS provide an economy of scale, which means the more you use, the more the price goes down, which may not benefit you if you choose multi-cloud. Again, it doesn't mean you cannot choose a multi-cloud strategy, but you must think about logical workload isolation. It would not be wise to run the application layer in one cloud and the database layer in another, but you can think about logical isolation, running the analytics workload and application workload in a separate cloud.

In this section, you learned about cloud computing at a very high level. Now let's learn about the difference between public and private clouds.

Private versus public clouds

A private cloud is a service dedicated to a single customer; it is like your on-premises data center, which is accessible to one large enterprise. A private cloud is a fancy name for a data center managed by a trusted third party. This concept gained momentum to ensure security as, initially, enterprises were skeptical about public cloud security, which is multi-tenant. However, having your infrastructure in this manner diminishes the value of the cloud, as you have to pay for resources even if you are not running them.

Let's use an analogy to further understand the difference between private and public clouds. The gig economy has great momentum. Everywhere you look, people are finding employment as contract workers. One of the reasons contract work is getting more popular is that it enables consumers to contract services that they may otherwise not be able to afford. Could you imagine how expensive it would be to have a private chauffeur? However, with Uber or Lyft, you almost have a private chauffeur who can be at your service and call within a few minutes of you summoning them.

A similar economy of scale happens with a public cloud. You can access infrastructure and services that would cost millions of dollars if you bought them on your own. Instead, you can access the same resources for a small fraction of the cost.

Private clouds are generally expensive to run and maintain compared to public clouds. For that reason, many of the resources and services offered by the major cloud providers are hosted in a shared tenancy model. In addition, you can securely run your workloads and applications on a public cloud: you can use best practices and sleep well at night knowing that you use AWS's state-of-the-art technologies to secure sensitive data.

Additionally, most major cloud providers' clients use public cloud configurations. That said, there are a few exceptions, even in this case. For example, the United States government's intelligence agencies are big AWS customers. With these government agencies, AWS will often set up the AWS infrastructure and dedicate it to the government workload. For example, AWS launched two top-secret regions accredited to operate workloads at the top-secret US security classification level.

Region Name	Region Code	Launch Year	Availability Zones	Endpoint
GovCloud (US-West)	`us-gov-west-1`	2011	3	`rds.us-gov-west-1.amazonaws.com`
GovCloud (US-East)	`us-gov-east-1`	2018	3	`rds.us-gov-east-1.amazonaws.com`

Table 1.2: AWS GovCloud region in the USA

The preceding AWS GovCloud regions are designed for US government agencies and contractors to run sensitive workloads in a highly secure cloud environment. These regions are isolated from other AWS regions, ensuring compliance with strict regulations such as FedRAMP, ITAR, and DoD SRG. Access is restricted to verified US persons only. The launch of the GovCloud (US-East) region in 2018 added customer redundancy and resiliency options. GovCloud offers many of the same AWS services as commercial regions but with enhanced security, allowing government entities to meet regulatory and security requirements while leveraging the cloud.

Public cloud providers such as AWS provide you with choices to adhere to compliance needs, as government or industry regulations require. For example, AWS offers Amazon EC2 dedicated instances, which are EC2 instances that ensure that you will be the only user for a given physical server. Further, AWS offers AWS Outpost, where you can order server racks and host workloads on-premise using the AWS control plane.

Dedicated instance and outpost costs are significantly higher than on-demand EC2 instances. On-demand instances are multi-tenant, which means the physical server is not dedicated to you and may be shared with other AWS users. However, just because physical servers are multi-tenant doesn't mean that anyone else can access your server, as there will be dedicated virtual EC2 instances accessible to you only.

Now that we have a better understanding of cloud computing in general, let's get more granular and learn about how AWS does cloud computing.

What is Amazon Web Services (AWS)?

With over 200 fully featured services available worldwide, **Amazon Web Services** (**AWS**) is the most widely used cloud platform globally. The growth of AWS and its features has been tremendous each year. As of 2025, AWS offers over 240 fully featured services worldwide. In the first quarter of 2024, AWS achieved an annual revenue run rate of $100 billion. The company continues to make significant investments in emerging technologies, with a particular focus on areas such as artificial intelligence and data security, further solidifying its position as a leader in cloud computing.

There is no doubt that the number of offerings will continue to grow at a similar rate for the foreseeable future. Gartner has named AWS as a leader for the 14th year in a row in the 2024 Gartner Magic Quadrant for Cloud Infrastructure & Platform Services. AWS is innovating fast, especially in new areas such as machine learning and artificial intelligence, **Generative AI**, advanced analytics, serverless computing, blockchain, and even quantum computing.

The following are some of the key differentiators for AWS in a nutshell:

AWS strengths	Key details
Oldest and most experienced cloud provider	AWS was the first major public cloud provider (it was founded in 2006), and since then, it has gained millions of customers worldwide.
The fast pace of innovation	AWS has 240+ fully featured services to support any cloud workload.
Continuous price reduction	Since its inception in 2006, AWS has reduced prices across various services 135+ times to improve the **Total Cost of Ownership** (**TCO**).

Community of partners to help accelerate the cloud journey	AWS has a large Partner Network of 130,000+ partners across 200+ countries. 70% of these partners are headquartered outside of the United States. These partners include large consulting partners and software vendors. In AWS Marketplace, there are over 4,000 **Independent Software Vendors (ISVs)** offering more than 15,000 products across 70 categories.
Security and compliance	AWS provides security standards and compliance certifications to fulfill your local government and industry compliance needs.
Global infrastructure	As of 2025, AWS has 114 Availability Zones within 36 geographic regions, 42 Local Zones, 29 Wavelength Zones, and 700+ Points of Presence. AWS also operates 135 Direct Connect locations, providing services in 245 countries and territories. For the latest information, refer to `https://aws.amazon.com/about-aws/global-infrastructure/`.

Table 1.3: AWS differentiators

While not all workloads can be moved to the cloud, AWS provides a broad set of hybrid capabilities in the areas of networking, data, access, management, and application services. For example, suppose you want to run your workload on-premises. In that case, AWS Outposts enables you to utilize native AWS services, infrastructure, and operating models in almost any data center, co-location space, or on-premises facility if you prefer to run your workload on-premises. You will learn more details about hybrid cloud services later in this book.

This is just a small sample of the many AWS services you will see throughout this book. Before we proceed, let's learn about the basic cloud and AWS terminology.

Basic cloud and AWS terminology

Cloud providers provide the core functionality for a wide variety of customer needs, but they all feel compelled to name these services differently, no doubt in part to try to separate themselves from the rest of the pack. As an example, every major cloud provider offers compute services. In other words, it is simple to spin up a server with any provider, but they all refer to this compute service differently:

- AWS uses **Elastic Compute Cloud (EC2)** instances
- Azure uses **Azure Virtual Machines**
- GCP uses **Google Compute Engine**

While the naming conventions differ, these services all provide similar core functionality – allowing users to spin up and manage virtual machines in the cloud. Each provider offers various instance types, sizes, and configurations to meet different computing needs. The different names reflect each company's branding and product strategies, but the underlying concept of providing scalable, on-demand compute resources in the cloud remains consistent across all major providers. Here's a non-comprehensive table comparing some of the core services offered by AWS, Azure, and GCP, along with their respective names:

Service Category	**AWS**	**Azure**	**Google Cloud (GCP)**
Compute	EC2 (Elastic Compute Cloud)	Virtual Machines (VMs)	Compute Engine
Serverless Compute	Lambda	Azure Functions	Cloud Functions
Container Orchestration	ECS/EKS (Elastic Kubernetes Service)	Azure Kubernetes Service (AKS)	Kubernetes Engine (GKE)
Object Storage	S3 (Simple Storage Service)	Blob Storage	Cloud Storage
Block Storage	EBS (Elastic Block Store)	Managed Disks	Persistent Disks
Relational Database	RDS (Relational Database Service)	Azure SQL Database	Cloud SQL
NoSQL Database	DynamoDB	Cosmos DB	Firestore / Datastore
Data Warehousing	Redshift	Synapse Analytics (SQL Data Warehouse)	BigQuery
Networking	VPC (Virtual Private Cloud)	Virtual Network (VNet)	Virtual Private Cloud (VPC)
Content Delivery Network	CloudFront	Azure CDN	Cloud CDN
Load Balancer	Elastic Load Balancing (ELB)	Azure Load Balancer	Cloud Load Balancing
Identity & Access Management	IAM (Identity and Access Management)	Azure Active Directory (Azure AD)	Cloud Identity / IAM
Monitoring & Logging	CloudWatch	Azure Monitor	Stackdriver / Cloud Monitoring

Message Queue	SQS (Simple Queue Service)	Azure Queue Storage / Service Bus	Pub/Sub
API Management	API Gateway	API Management	API Gateway
Machine Learning	SageMaker	Azure Machine Learning	Vertex AI

Table 1.4: Cloud provider terminology and comparison

The preceding table summarizes the terminology that is used by each cloud provider for similar services, which will help to navigate the differences between AWS, Azure, and GCP as you explore and go through the cloud ecosystem.

The next section will explain why cloud services are becoming popular and why the adoption of AWS is prevalent.

Why is AWS so popular?

MarketsandMarkets expects the market to grow from USD 626.4 billion in 2023 to USD 1.27 trillion by 2028. This implies a **Compound Annual Growth Rate (CAGR)** of around 15.1% for the period.

There are multiple reasons why the cloud market is growing so fast. Some of them are listed here:

- Elasticity and scalability
- Security
- Availability
- Faster hardware cycles
- System administration staff

In addition to the preceding, AWS provides access to emerging technologies and faster time to market. First, let's look at the most important reason behind the popularity of cloud computing (and, in particular, AWS).

Elasticity and scalability

The concepts of *elasticity* and *scalability* are closely tied. Elasticity refers to the ability of a system to automatically scale resources up or down in response to real-time demand, ensuring efficient resource utilization. Scalability, on the other hand, is the system's capability to handle increasing workloads by adding more resources, either vertically (scaling up) or horizontally (scaling out). Let's start by understanding scalability. In the context of computer science, *scalability* can be used in two ways:

- An application can continue to function correctly when the volume of users and transactions it handles increases. The increased volume is typically handled by using bigger and more powerful resources (scaling up) or adding more similar resources (scaling out).
- A system can function well when rescaled and fully utilized. For example, an application is scalable if it can be refactored to microservices handling a bigger use workload. It can take full advantage of the more modular architecture, achieving greater performance, processing transactions faster, and handling more users.

Scalability can be tracked over multiple dimensions:

- **Administrative scalability**: Increasing the number of users of the system
- **Functional scalability**: Adding new functionality without altering or disrupting existing functionality
- **Heterogeneous scalability**: Adding disparate components and services from a variety of vendors
- **Load scalability**: Expanding capacity to accommodate more traffic and/or transactions
- **Generation scalability**: Scaling by installing new versions of software and hardware
- **Geographic scalability**: Maintaining existing functionality and SLAs while expanding the user base to a larger geographic region

IT organizations worldwide encounter scalability challenges daily. Demand and traffic for many applications, especially internet-facing applications, are difficult to predict. Therefore, it is difficult to predict how much storage capacity, compute power, and bandwidth will be needed.

There are two methods for scaling resources: scaling up (vertical scaling) and scaling out (horizontal scaling).

Scaling up is achieved by getting a bigger boat. For example, AWS offers a range of different-sized instances, including nano, micro, small, medium, large, and 2x, 4x, 8x, 16x, and 32x large. If you are running a job on a medium instance and the job starts hitting the performance ceiling for that size, you could swap your work to a large or large instance. This could happen because a database needs additional capacity to perform at a prescribed level. The new instance would have a better CPU, more memory, more storage, and faster network throughput. Scaling up can also be achieved using software – for example, allocating more memory or overclocking the CPU.

Scaling up is achieved by using more powerful nodes, while scaling out is achieved by adding more nodes. Scaling out can be achieved in the following ways:

- Adding infrastructure capacity by adding new instances or nodes on an application-by-application basis
- Adding additional instances independently of the applications
- Adding more processes, connections, or shards with software

Scaling out is particularly valuable for multi-tiered architectures where each tier has a well-defined responsibility. It allows you to modify just one resource where a bottleneck exists and leave the other resources alone. For example, if you are running a multi-tiered architecture and discover that an application server is running at 95% CPU, you can add additional application servers to help balance the load without modifying your web server or database server.

These scaling options can also be used simultaneously to improve an application. For example, in addition to adding more instances to handle traffic, more significant and capable instances can be added to the cluster.

Suppose you finally launch a site you've been working on for months and, within a few days, you begin to realize that too many people are signing up and using your service. While this is an excellent problem, you'd better act fast, or the site will start throttling, and the user experience will go down or be non-existent. But the question now is, how do you scale? When you reach the limits of your deployment, how do you increase capacity? If the environment is on-premises, the answer is *very painfully*. You will need approval from the company leadership. New hardware will need to be ordered. Delays will be inevitable. In the meantime, the opportunity in the marketplace will likely disappear because your potential customers will bail to competitors that can meet their needs. Being able to deliver quickly may mean more than just getting there first. It may differ between getting there first and not getting there in time.

If your environment is on the cloud, things become much simpler. You can spin up an instance that can handle the new workload (correcting the size of a server can even be as simple as shutting down the server for a few minutes, changing a drop-down box value, and restarting the server). You can *scale* your resources to meet increasing user demand.

The cloud's scalability exponentially improves the time to market by accelerating the time it takes for resources to be provisioned. In addition to making it easy to scale resources, AWS and other cloud operators allow you to quickly adapt to shifting workloads due to their elasticity. Elasticity is defined as the ability of a computing environment to adapt to changes in workload by *automatically* provisioning or shutting down computing resources to match the capacity needed by the current workload.

These resources could be a single database instance or a thousand copies of the application and web servers used to handle your web traffic. These servers can be provisioned within minutes. In AWS and the other main cloud providers, resources can be shut down without being terminated completely, and the billing for resources will stop if the resources are shut down.

The ability to quickly shut down resources and not be charged for that resource while it is down is a very powerful characteristic of cloud environments. If your system is on-premises, once a server is purchased, it is a sunk cost for the server's useful life. In contrast, whenever we shut down a server in a cloud environment, the cloud provider can quickly detect that and put that server back into the pool of available servers for other cloud customers to use the newly unused capacity.

This distinction must be emphasized more. The only time absolute on-premises costs may be lower than cloud costs is when workloads are extremely predictable and consistent, and you don't need any scaling. Computing costs in a cloud environment on a per-unit basis may be higher than on-premises prices. Still, the ability to shut resources down and stop getting charged for them makes cloud architectures cheaper in the long run – often quite significantly.

The following examples highlight how useful elasticity can be in different scenarios:

- **Web storefront**: A famous use case for cloud services is to use them to run an online storefront. Website traffic in this scenario will be highly variable depending on the day of the week, whether it's a holiday, the time of day, or other factors; almost every retail store in the USA experiences more than a 10x user workload during Thanksgiving week. The same goes for Boxing Day in the UK, Diwali in India, Singles' Day in China, and almost every country has a shopping festival. This kind of scenario is ideally suited for a cloud deployment. In this case, we can set up resource auto-scaling that automatically scales up and down compute resources as needed. Additionally, we can set up policies that allow database storage to grow as needed.
- **Big data workloads**: As data volumes are increasing exponentially, the popularity of Apache Spark and Hadoop continues to grow in analyzing GBs and TBs of data. Many Spark clusters don't necessarily need to run consistently. They perform heavy batch computing for a period and then can be idle until the next batch of input data comes in. A specific example would be a cluster that runs every night for 3 or 4 hours and only during the working week. In this instance, you need decoupled compute and data storage to shut down resources that may be best managed on a schedule rather than by using demand thresholds. Or, we could set up triggers that automatically shut down resources once the batch jobs are completed. AWS provides that flexibility where you can store your data in Amazon **Simple Storage Service (S3)** and spin up an Amazon **Elastic MapReduce (EMR)** cluster to run Spark jobs and shut them down after storing results back in decoupled Amazon S3.

- **Employee workspace**: In an on-premises setting, you provide your development team with a high-configuration desktop/laptop and pay for it 24 hours a day, including weekends. However, considering an eight-hour workday, they use one-fourth of the capacity. AWS provides workspaces accessible by low-configuration laptops, and you can schedule them to stop during off-hours and weekends, saving almost 70% of the cost.

Another common technology use case is file and object storage. Some storage services may grow organically and consistently, and the traffic patterns can also be consistent. This may be one example of how using an on-premises architecture may make sense economically. In this case, the usage pattern is consistent and predictable.

Elasticity is by no means the only reason the cloud is growing rapidly. The ability to easily enable world-class security for even the simplest applications is another reason the cloud is becoming pervasive.

Security

The perception that *on-premises* environments were more secure than cloud environments was a common reason companies, large and small, would not migrate to the cloud. However, more and more enterprises now realize that it is tough and expensive to replicate the security features provided by cloud providers such as AWS. Let's look at a few of the measures AWS takes to ensure the security of its systems.

Physical security

AWS data centers are highly secured and continuously upgraded with the latest surveillance technology. Amazon has had decades to perfect its data centers' design, construction, and operation.

AWS has been providing cloud services for over 18 years, and they have an army of technologists, solution architects, and some of the brightest minds in the business. They leverage this experience and expertise to create *state-of-the-art* data centers. These centers are in nondescript facilities. You could drive by one and never know what it is. Getting in would be extremely difficult if you found out where one is. Perimeter access is heavily guarded. Visitor access is strictly limited, and they must always be accompanied by an Amazon employee.

Video surveillance, motion detectors, intrusion detection systems, and other electronic equipment monitor every corner of the facility. Amazon employees with access to the building must authenticate themselves multiple times before stepping on the data center floor.

Only Amazon employees and contractors with a legitimate right to be in a data center can enter. Any other employee is restricted. Whenever an employee does not have a business need to enter a data center, their access is immediately revoked, even if they are only moved to another Amazon department and stay with the company. Lastly, audits are routinely performed and are part of the normal business process.

Encryption

AWS makes it extremely simple to encrypt data at rest and data in transit. It also offers a variety of encryption options. For example, for encryption at rest, data can be encrypted on the server side, or it can be encrypted on the client side. Additionally, AWS can manage the encryption keys, or you can use keys that you manage using tamper-proof appliances such as a **Hardware Security Module (HSM)**. AWS provides you with a dedicated cloud HSM to secure your encryption key if you want one. You will learn more about AWS security in *Chapter 8, Best Practices for Application Security, Identity, and Compliance*.

AWS supports compliance standards

AWS has robust controls to allow users to maintain security and data protection. We'll discuss how AWS shares security responsibilities with its customers, but the same is true of how AWS supports compliance. AWS provides many attributes and features enabling compliance with standards established in different countries and organizations. By providing these features, AWS simplifies compliance audits. AWS allows the implementation of security best practices and many security standards, such as the following:

- STAR
- SOC 1/SSAE 16/ISAE 3402 (formerly SAS 70)
- SOC 2
- SOC 3
- FISMA, DIACAP, and FedRAMP
- PCI DSS Level 1
- DOD CSM Levels 1-5
- ISO 9001 / ISO 27001 / ISO 27017 / ISO 27018
- MTCS Level 3
- FIPS 140-2
- I TRUST

Additional important standards and regulations supported by AWS include the following:

- GDPR
- NIST 800-53
- ITAR
- FIPS 140-3 (the successor to FIPS 140-2)
- CSA STAR
- C5 (Cloud Computing Compliance Criteria Catalogue)
- HITRUST CSF
- PIPEDA

In addition, AWS enables the implementation of solutions that can meet many industry-specific standards, such as these:

- **Criminal Justice Information Services** (**CJIS**)
- **Family Educational Rights and Privacy Act** (**FERPA**)
- **Motion Picture Association of America** (**MPAA**)
- **Health Insurance Portability and Accountability Act** (**HIPAA**)

The preceding is not a full list of compliance standards; according to industries and local authorities worldwide, AWS meets many more compliance standards.

AWS provides a shared responsibility model for security and compliance. While AWS manages the security "of" the cloud (infrastructure, hardware, software, facilities), customers are responsible for security "in" the cloud (customer data, platform, applications, identity, and access management). AWS offers various tools and services to help customers meet these compliance standards, such as AWS Config, AWS Security Hub, AWS Audit Manager, and AWS Artifact for accessing compliance reports. It's important to note that while AWS provides the infrastructure and tools to enable compliance, achieving and maintaining compliance is ultimately the responsibility of the customer using AWS services.

Another important aspect of the cloud that can explain its meteoric rise is the ability to create high-availability applications without paying for the additional infrastructure needed to provide them. Architectures can be crafted to start additional resources when other resources fail. This ensures that we only use additional resources when necessary, keeping costs down. Let's analyze this important property of the cloud in a deeper fashion.

Availability

Intuitively and generically, the word *availability* conveys that something is available or can be used. To be used, it needs to be up and running and functional. For example, if your car is in the driveway, it is working, and it is ready to be used, then it meets some of the conditions of availability. However, to meet the technical definition of *availability*, it must be turned on. A server that is otherwise working correctly but is shut down will not help run your website.

Often, high availability is confused with fault tolerance. A system can be 100% available but 50% fault-tolerant. For example, you need four servers to handle your application load and provide the required performance. You have built redundancy by putting two servers in two different data centers. In that case, your system is 100% available and 100% fault-tolerant. However, one of the data centers has gone down for some reason. Your system is still 100% available but running at half capacity, which may impact system performance and user experience, reducing fault tolerance to 50%. To achieve 100% fault tolerance, you must put eight servers, positioning four in each data center.

In mathematical terms, the formula for availability is simple:

Imagine you're checking how much time a system in your company was up and running in a month. It ran for 732 hours but had 4 hours of unexpected downtime and 8 hours for scheduled maintenance, totaling 12 hours of downtime. To find its availability, you calculate:

Availability = 732 hours (running time) / 744 hours (total time, including downtime). This equals about 98.38%.

It does not matter if your computing environment is on your premises or in the cloud, availability is paramount and critical to your business.

When we deploy infrastructure in an on-premises environment, we have two choices. We can purchase enough hardware to service the current workload or ensure enough excess capacity to account for failures. This extra capacity and eliminating single points of failure is more complex than it may seem. There are many places where single points of failure may exist and need to be eliminated:

- Compute instances can go down, so we need a few on standby
- Databases can get corrupted

- Network connections can be broken
- Data centers can flood or be hit by earthquakes

In addition to eliminating single points of failure, you want your system to be resilient enough to automatically identify when any resource fails and automatically replace it with an equivalent resource. For example, you are running a Hadoop cluster with 20 nodes, and one of the nodes fails. In that case, a recommended setup immediately replaces the failed node with another well-functioning node. The only way this can be achieved on a pure *on-prem* solution is to have excess capacity servers sitting ready to replace any failing server nodes.

In most cases, the only way to achieve this is by purchasing additional servers that may never be used. As the saying goes, *it's better to have and not need than to need and not have.* The price that could be paid if we don't have these resources when required could be orders of magnitude greater than the hardware price, depending on how critical the system is to your business operations.

Using the cloud simplifies the *single point of failure* problem and makes it easy to provision resources. We have already determined that provisioning software in an on-premises data center can be long and arduous. However, cloud services such as AWS allow you to start up resources and services automatically and immediately when you need them, and you only get charged when you start using these newly launched resources. So, we can configure minimal environments, knowing that additional resources are a click away.

AWS data centers are built in different regions worldwide. All data centers are *always on* and deliver services to customers. Their extremely sophisticated systems automatically route traffic to other resources if a failure occurs. Core services are always installed in an `N+1` configuration. In the case of a complete data center failure, there should be the capacity to handle traffic using the remaining available data centers without disruption.

AWS enables customers to deploy instances and persist data in more than one geographic region and across various data centers within a region. Data centers are deployed in fully independent zones. They are constructed with enough separation between them that the likelihood of a natural disaster affecting two of them simultaneously is very low. Additionally, data centers are not built in flood zones.

To increase resilience, data centers have discrete **Uninterruptable Power Supplies (UPSes)** and onsite backup generators. They are also connected to multiple electric grids from various independent utility providers. Data centers are connected redundantly to multiple tier-1 transit providers. Doing all this minimizes single points of failure and improves availability. You will learn more details about AWS global infrastructure in *Chapter 4, Networking in AWS*.

Faster hardware cycles

When hardware is provisioned on-premises, it becomes obsolete from the instant it is purchased. Hardware prices have been on an exponential downtrend since the first computer was invented, so the server you bought a few months ago may now be cheaper, or a new version of the server may be out that's faster and still costs the same. However, waiting until hardware improves or becomes more affordable is not an option. A decision needs to be made at some point to purchase it.

Using a cloud provider instead eliminates all these problems. For example, whenever AWS offers new and more powerful processor types, using them is as simple as stopping an instance, changing the processor type, and starting the instance again. In many cases, AWS may keep the price the same or even cheaper when better and faster processors and technology become available, especially with their own proprietary technology, such as the Graviton chip.

The cloud optimizes costs by building virtualization at scale. Virtualization underpins resource efficiency and cost optimization in the cloud by enabling multiple **virtual machines (VMs)** to run on a single physical server, thereby maximizing hardware utilization. By leveraging virtualization, cloud providers offer multi-tenancy, where multiple users share the same physical resources while maintaining isolation. This reduces idle capacity, improves operational efficiency, and lowers costs by optimizing infrastructure usage. Applications running on virtual machines are unaware that they are not running on a dedicated machine and share resources with other applications on the same physical machine.

A **hypervisor** is a computing layer that enables multiple operating systems to execute in the same physical compute resource. The operating systems running on top of these hypervisors are **Virtual Machines (VMs)** – a component that can emulate a complete computing environment using only software, but as if it were running on bare metal. Hypervisors, also known as **Virtual Machine Monitors (VMMs)**, manage these VMs while running side by side. A hypervisor creates a logical separation between VMs. It provides each of them with a slice of the available compute, memory, and storage resources. It allows VMs not to clash and interfere with each other. If one VM crashes and goes down, it will not make other VMs go down with it. Also, if there is an intrusion in one VM, it is fully isolated from the rest.

AWS uses its own proprietary Nitro hypervisor. AWS's next-generation EC2 instances are built on AWS Nitro System, a foundational platform that improves performance and reduces costs. Typically, hypervisors secure the physical hardware, while the BIOS virtualizes the CPU, storage, and networking, providing advanced management features. AWS Nitro System enables the segregation of these functions, transferring them to dedicated hardware and software, and delivering almost all server resources to EC2 instances.

System administration staff

An on-premises implementation may require a full-time system administration staff and a process to ensure that the team remains fully staffed. Cloud providers can handle many of these tasks by using cloud services, allowing you to focus on core application maintenance and functionality without worrying about infrastructure upgrades, patches, and maintenance.

By offloading this task to the cloud provider, costs can come down because the administrative duties can be shared with other cloud customers instead of having a dedicated staff. You will learn more about system administration in *Chapter 9, Driving Efficiency with Cloud Operation Automation and DevOps in AWS*.

This ends the book's first chapter, providing a foundation for the cloud and AWS. As you move forward with your learning journey, in subsequent chapters, you will dive deeper and deeper into AWS services, architecture, and best practices.

Knowledge check

Let's start with some questions to test your knowledge. In this first chapter, we will focus on basic concepts, but as you progress through future chapters and become more familiar with AWS services, you will encounter more complex questions. These questions will help you prepare for AWS certifications at various levels and equip you for AWS Solutions Architect interviews. Let's dive in!

1. Your client is a medium-sized digital marketing firm operating across five countries. They want to migrate their legacy application stack from on-premises data centers to AWS. They face challenges such as unpredictable traffic spikes during promotional campaigns, long lead times for provisioning new infrastructure, and underutilized hardware during off-peak times. Their main goals are to improve agility, lower operational costs, and scale automatically as demand changes.

   Which AWS cloud benefit best addresses the core challenges this company faces?

   a. Global infrastructure capabilities that allow hosting data in multiple AWS Regions and Availability Zones to ensure data sovereignty.

   b. Elasticity and scalability offered by AWS services, which dynamically adjust infrastructure based on workload demand without manual intervention.

   c. Access to managed services such as Amazon RDS and DynamoDB reduces the need for database administration and backup scripting.

   d. **High-performance computing** (**HPC**) options in AWS, such as EC2 HPC clusters, are designed for large-scale simulations and scientific workloads.

Answer: b.

Explanation:

a. Incorrect. This is helpful, but focuses more on data locality than the elasticity issue.

b. **Correct.** AWS's elasticity allows the company to automatically handle traffic spikes during marketing campaigns without overprovisioning.

c. Incorrect. Amazon RDS and DynamoDB helps with database management, but it's not the central problem here.

d. Incorrect. HPC is for niche use cases and does not solve the company's scaling and cost concerns.

2. A fintech start-up has just secured funding and wants to go to market quickly with its new mobile banking application. They are evaluating AWS for hosting the application backend, data storage, and real-time analytics. Their key requirements include rapid provisioning, minimal upfront investment, and the ability to scale globally in the future.

Which of the following AWS cloud characteristics are best suited to support this start-up's requirements? (Choose two.)

a. A pay-as-you-go pricing model that enables resource consumption billing without upfront infrastructure purchase.

b. Tight integration with proprietary on-premises vendor stacks that support legacy mainframe systems and batch processing.

c. Global presence through AWS Regions and edge locations that ensure low latency and scalability as the customer base expands.

d. Emphasis on manual scaling of compute and storage, providing full control over every infrastructure element.

e. AWS Marketplace enables the deployment of third-party software tools for financial compliance.

Answers: a. and c.

Explanation:

a. **Correct**. The pay-as-you-go model ensures no capital expense, which is critical for start-ups.

b. Incorrect. AWS encourages modern architectures, not mainframe legacy setups.

c. **Correct**. AWS's global infrastructure helps reduce latency and supports global customer growth.

   d. Incorrect. This is outdated, as AWS offers auto-scaling and abstracted infrastructure management.
   e. Incorrect. It is useful but not core to the question's requirements.

3. An enterprise retailer is comparing AWS to traditional data centers. Their leadership team is skeptical about cloud adoption due to perceived risks and loss of control. As an AWS solutions architect, you're tasked with explaining the long-term business value of moving to AWS.

   Which of the following arguments is the strongest to convince the team of AWS's cloud value proposition?

   a. AWS offers full control over hardware procurement and data center rack space for each client.
   b. AWS allows deployment of custom routers and firewalls, offering the same control level as traditional data centers.
   c. AWS removes the need to over-provision for peak usage, ensuring that resources are used efficiently and cost-effectively throughout the year.
   d. AWS limits access to root user privileges, reducing the risks of user-level misconfiguration.

   Answer: c.

   Explanation:

   a. Incorrect. AWS removes the need to manage hardware or custom networking.
   b. Same as option a.
   c. **Correct**. Cloud removes overprovisioning, which is a major cost in traditional IT setups.
   d. Incorrect. This option focuses on security, which is important but secondary in this context.

4. A public health analytics firm is developing a COVID-19 tracking app and must handle real-time data ingestion from thousands of devices. The system needs to scale rapidly during health surges and should ensure high availability even during system failures. They are considering moving this system to AWS.

   Which of the following AWS features and design principles will best support their system requirements? (Choose two.)

a. Multi-AZ deployment and regional failover options in AWS services such as RDS and S3 for high availability.
b. Ability to scale vertically using AWS Lambda memory adjustments and adding EC2 instances with more CPU.
c. Auto Scaling groups and **Elastic Load Balancing** (**ELB**) that help automatically distribute and adjust traffic across healthy servers.
d. Custom physical server deployment per customer to ensure complete isolation and maximum hardware usage.
e. Dedicated bandwidth provisioning for each Lambda function execution to guarantee a predictable response time.

Answers: a. and c.

Explanation:

a. **Correct**. Multi-AZ and regional failover ensure app resilience and uptime.
b. Incorrect. This option oversimplifies vertical scaling, which isn't as elastic as AWS horizontal scaling promotes.
c. **Correct.** ELB and Auto Scaling are designed to handle rapid demand changes.
d. Incorrect. This is not scalable or aligned with AWS's cloud model.
e. Incorrect. AWS Lambda does not offer dedicated bandwidth per function execution.

5. A manufacturing enterprise is considering a cloud-first strategy. Their CIO is concerned about security, compliance, and cost transparency in the cloud. You need to design an AWS architecture that ensures security and cost control without compromising agility.

   Which approach best addresses the CIO's concerns using AWS capabilities?

   a. Provision dedicated data centers for each department to isolate workloads and assign separate budgets.
   b. Use AWS Organizations with **Service Control Policies** (**SCPs**), consolidated billing, and AWS Config to manage access, compliance, and cost tracking centrally.
   c. Set up a decentralized AWS architecture where each team provisions its own resources and controls billing.
   d. Build custom security services on EC2 and use third-party firewalls for complete control over networking.

   Answer: b.

Explanation:

a. Incorrect. This option is traditional and doesn't leverage AWS capabilities.
b. **Correct.** AWS Organizations + SCPs + consolidated billing + AWS Config provide centralized control, security, and visibility for cost and compliance.
c. Incorrect. It lacks governance, which the CIO is concerned about.
d. Incorrect. It increases complexity and doesn't use managed services.

Summary

This chapter gathered many of the technologies, best practices, and AWS services we cover in the book. As fully featured as AWS has become, it will certainly continue to provide more services to help enterprises, large and small, simplify information technology infrastructure.

In this chapter, you learned about cloud computing and the key differences between the public and private cloud. This led to learning more about the largest public cloud provider, AWS, and its market share and adoption.

One of the main reasons for the cloud's popularity is the concept of elasticity, which we explored in detail. You also learned about AWS's key differentiators from other cloud providers. Further, you explored AWS terminology compared to other key players such as Azure and GCP. Finally, you learned about the benefits of AWS and the reasons behind its popularity. You ended the chapter with a knowledge check.

Under its Well-Architected Framework, AWS provides some of the industry's best architecture practices. In the next chapter, we will learn more about it.

2

Understanding the AWS Well-Architected Framework and Getting Certified

In the previous chapter, you saw AWS's innovation pace and broad service offerings. As a solutions architect, you might wonder how these services come together to address various parameters of your IT workload needs. You may also wonder how to ensure your architecture follows best practices while achieving your business needs. For that purpose, AWS provides architecture guidance in a cloud-native way using its **Well-Architected Framework** (**WAF**).

In this chapter, you will learn details about the WAF and how to apply best practices for every component of your cloud application. You will go through the six pillars of the WAF and the AWS Well-Architected Lenses for specific workloads such as serverless, analytics, IoT, and so on. You will learn about using the AWS Well-Architected tool to validate your architecture against AWS-recommended best practices by conducting a **Well-Architected Review** (**WAR**), which is very useful to ace the AWS certification in addition to building real-world applications.

Further, you will then learn how we can take a slice of the cloud pie and build your credibility by becoming certified. Finally, towards the end of the chapter, we will look at some tips and tricks you can use to simplify your journey to obtain AWS certifications. We will also look at some frequently asked questions about the AWS certifications.

In this chapter, we will cover the following topics:

- The AWS Well-Architected Framework
- The six pillars of the Well-Architected Framework
- AWS Well-Architected Lenses
- Building credibility and getting certified
- Learning tips and tricks for obtaining AWS certifications
- The best way to get certified
- Some frequently asked questions about the AWS certifications
- How to land a job as an AWS Solutions Architect

Let's get started by looking at a holistic architecture approach in AWS.

The AWS Well-Architected Framework

As a solutions architect, you may question architecture optimization for reliability, scaling, high availability, performance, and security even before starting with various AWS services. You may ask how the AWS cloud will accommodate those needs and compare it with your existing on-premises architecture practice.

AWS built the WAF to address those needs. The framework provides customers with access to AWS's Well-Architected content, which is based on extensive architectural reviews with clients. This content helps to identify and mitigate potential architectural risks while promoting best practices.

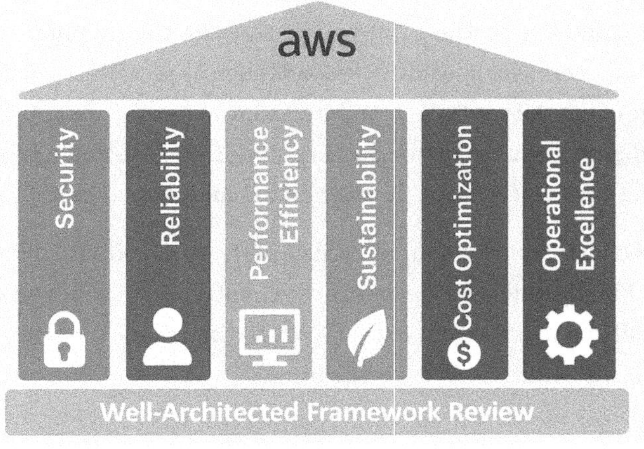

Figure 2.1: Well-Architected Operational Excellence

The preceding diagram illustrates the AWS WAF, which helps you design and operate reliable, secure, efficient, and cost-effective systems in the cloud. It is built around six key pillars: Security, Reliability, Performance Efficiency, Sustainability, Cost Optimization, and Operational Excellence. Each pillar represents a critical area of cloud architecture and provides best practices for achieving success on AWS.

AWS created the **Well-Architected Review (WAR)** to help customers have better outcomes when building architectures on AWS. You can identify areas for improvement in your architecture, allowing you to address persistent issues and focus on value-adding activities. As you go through the review process, you can learn about new capabilities to add value to your application and drive better outcomes to build and operate workloads on the cloud. With this, you can get the following benefits:

- Learn strategies and best practices for architecting in the cloud
- Measure your architecture against best practices
- Improve your architecture by addressing any issues

AWS has six Well-Architected pillars covering the breadth and depth of architecture, along with the WAR to validate them. Let's learn more about it.

The six pillars of the WAF

The cloud, in general, and AWS are so popular because they simplify the development of well-architected frameworks. If there is one *must-read* AWS document, it is *the AWS Well-Architected Framework*, which spells out the six pillars of the Framework.

The full document can be found here: `https://docs.aws.amazon.com/wellarchitected/latest/framework/welcome.html`.

AWS provides the Well-Architected tool, which offers prescriptive guidance about each pillar to validate your workload against architecture best practices and generate a comprehensive report.

Please find a glimpse of the tool here:

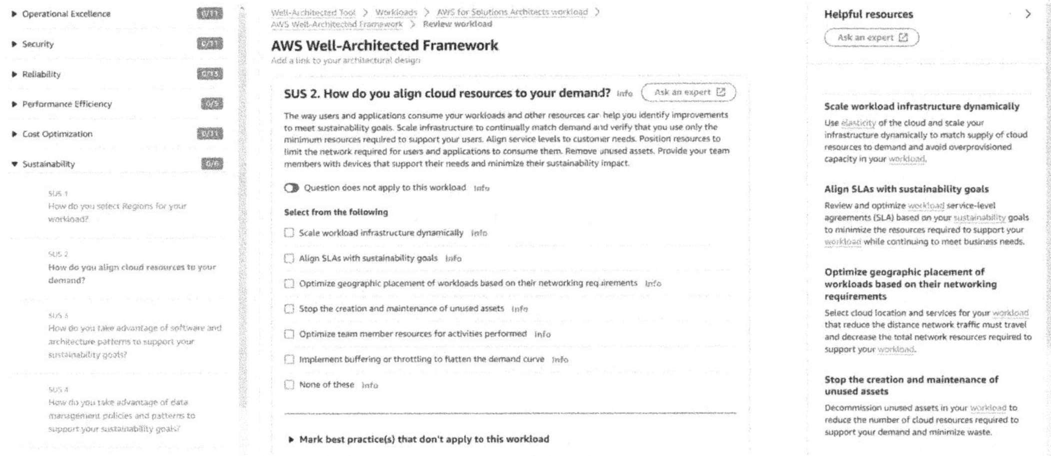

Figure 2.2: AWS Well-Architected tool

Quick tip: Need to see a high-resolution version of this image? Open this book in the next-gen Packt Reader or view it in the PDF/ePub copy.

The next-gen Packt Reader is included for free with the purchase of this book. Scan the QR code OR go to `packtpub.com/unlock`, then use the search bar to find this book by name. Double-check the edition shown to make sure you get the right one.

To kick off a WAR for your workload, you must create an AWS account and open the Well-Architected tool. To start an architecture review per the gold standard defined by AWS, you need to provide workload information such as the name, environment type (production or pre-production), AWS workload hosting regions, industry, reviewer name, and so on. After submitting this information, you will see (as in *Figure 2.2*) a set of questions about each Well-Architected pillar, with the option to select what is most relevant to your workload. AWS provides prescriptive guidance and various resources for applying architecture best practices to questions within the right-hand navigation.

As AWS has provided detailed guidance for each Well-Architected pillar in their document, let's look at the main points about the six pillars of the WAF.

The first pillar – Security

Security should always be a top priority in both on-premises and cloud architectures. All security aspects should be considered, including data encryption and protection, access management, infrastructure security, network security, monitoring, and breach detection and inspection.

To enable system security and guard against nefarious actors and vulnerabilities, AWS recommends these architectural principles:

- Implement a strong identity foundation
- Maintain traceability
- Apply security at all levels
- Automate security best practices
- Protect data in transit and at rest
- Keep people away from data
- Prepare for security events

You can find the security pillar checklist from the Well-Architected tool here, which has 11 questions with one or more options relevant to your workload:

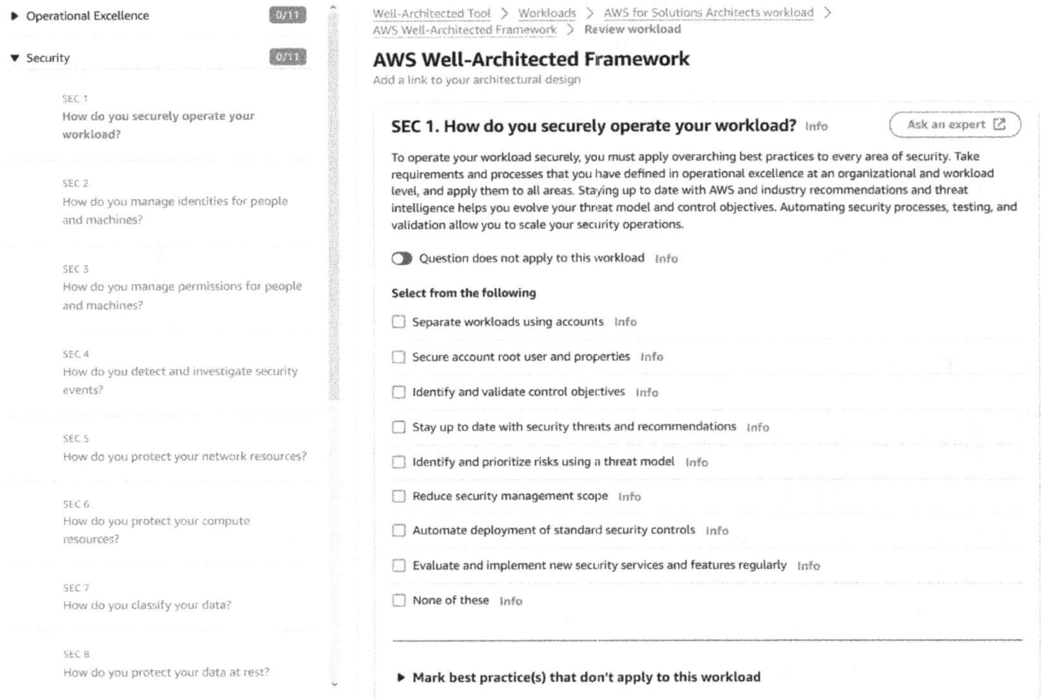

Figure 2.3: AWS Well-Architected security pillar

In the preceding screenshot, in the left-hand navigation, you can see questions related to security best practices, and for each question, there will be multiple options to choose from, as per your workload. Answering these questions will help you determine the current state of your workload security and highlight any gaps in the WAR report, such as **high-risk issues (HRIs)**. You can find more details on the security pillar by referring to the AWS WAF user document: `https://docs.aws.amazon.com/wellarchitected/latest/security-pillar/welcome.html`.

To gain practical experience in implementing optimal security practices, it is advisable to complete the Well-Architected security labs. You can find details on the labs here: `https://www.wellarchitectedlabs.com/security/`.

The next pillar, reliability, is almost as important as security. You want your workload to perform its business functions consistently and reliably.

The second pillar – Reliability

Before discussing reliability in the context of the WAF, let's first get a better understanding of reliability as a concept. Intuitively, a resource is said to have *reliability* if it often works when we try to use it. You will be hard-pressed to find an example of anything that is perfectly reliable. Even the most well-manufactured computer components have a degree of *unreliability*. Using a car analogy, if you go to your garage and you can usually start your car and drive it away, it is said to have high *reliability*. Conversely, if you can't trust your vehicle to start (maybe because it has an old battery), it is said to have low *reliability*.

Reliability is the probability of a resource or application meeting a certain performance standard and continuing to perform for a certain period. Reliability is leveraged to gain an understanding of how long the service will be up and running in the context of various real-life conditions.

Reliability and availability are sometimes erroneously used interchangeably. To continue with the car analogy, for your car to be available, it must be functional, ready for use, turned on, and ready to go. These conditions make it highly available. For your car to have high reliability, it must start most of the time – you can depend on it being able to function.

Reliability is the measurement of how long a resource performs its intended function. In contrast, availability measures how long a resource is in operation as a percentage of the total time it was in operation and not in operation (see the *Availability* section of the previous chapter for more information). For example, a machine may be available 90% of the time but have a reliability of 75%. The two terms are related but different and have different meanings. They have different objectives and can have different costs to maintain certain service levels.

It can take time to measure an application's reliability. There are a couple of methods to measure reliability. One is to measure the probability of failure of the application components that may affect the availability of the whole application.

More formally, we can calculate the **Mean Time Between Failures** (**MTBF**).

MTBF represents the time elapsed between component failures in a system. The metric used to measure time in MTBF is typically hours. Still, it can also be measured in other units of time, such as days, weeks, or years, depending on the specific system, component, or product being evaluated.

Similarly, **Mean Time to Repair (MTTR)** may be measured as a metric representing the time it takes to repair a failed system component. Ensuring the application is repaired on time is essential to meet service-level agreements. Other metrics can be used to track reliability, such as the fault tolerance levels of the application. The greater the fault tolerance of a given component, the lower the susceptibility of the whole application to being disrupted in a real-world scenario.

As you can see, reliability is a vital metric for assessing your architecture. Your architecture should be as reliable as possible, and the WAF recognizes this with its second pillar, reliability. A key characteristic of the reliability pillar is minimizing or eliminating single points of failure. Ideally, every component should have a backup. The backup should be able to come online as quickly as possible and in an automated manner without human intervention.

Self-healing is another important concept to attain reliability. An example of this is how Amazon S3 handles data replication. Before returning a `SUCCESS` message, S3 saves your objects redundantly on multiple devices across a minimum of three **Availability Zones (AZs)** in an AWS Region. This design ensures the system can withstand numerous device failures by rapidly identifying and rectifying any lost redundancy. Additionally, the service conducts regular checksum-based data integrity checks.

The WAF paper recommends these design principles to enhance reliability:

- Automatically recover from failure
- Test recovery procedures
- Scale horizontally to increase aggregate workload availability
- Stop guessing capacity
- Manage changes through automation

You can find the reliability pillar checklist from the Well-Architected tool here:

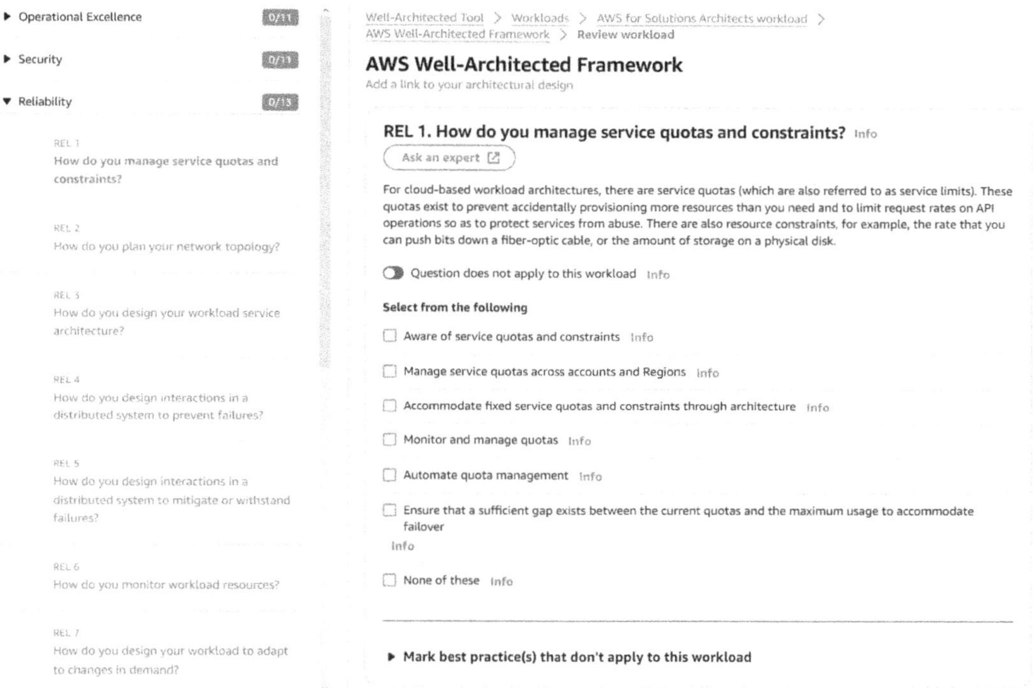

Figure 2.4: AWS Well-Architected reliability pillar

In the preceding screenshot, you can see questions about achieving reliability best practices in the left-hand navigation. Answering these questions will help you determine the current state of your workload reliability and highlight HRIs that you must fix. You can find more details on the reliability pillar by referring to the AWS Well-Architected Framework user doc: `https://docs.aws.amazon.com/wellarchitected/latest/reliability-pillar/welcome.html`.

Reliability is a complex topic that requires significant effort to ensure that all data and applications are backed up appropriately. The Well-Architected labs can be utilized to implement the best reliability practices, providing hands-on experience in applying optimal reliability strategies. You can find details on the labs here: `https://www.wellarchitectedlabs.com/reliability/`

To retain users, your application needs to be highly performant and respond within seconds or milliseconds, depending on the nature of your workload. This makes performance a key pillar when building your application. Let's look at more details on performance efficiency.

The third pillar – Performance efficiency

In some respects, overprovisioning resources is just as bad as not having enough capacity to handle your workload. Launching a constantly idle or almost idle instance indicates a bad design. Resources should not be at full capacity and should be utilized efficiently. AWS provides various features and services to assist in creating efficient architectures. However, we are still responsible for ensuring that our design architectures are suitable and correctly sized for our applications.

When it comes to performance efficiency, the recommended design best practices are as follows:

- Democratize advanced technologies
- Go global in minutes
- Use serverless architectures
- Experiment more often
- Consider mechanical sympathy

You can find the performance efficiency pillar checklist from the Well-Architected tool here, with eight questions covering multiple aspects to make sure your architecture is optimized for performance:

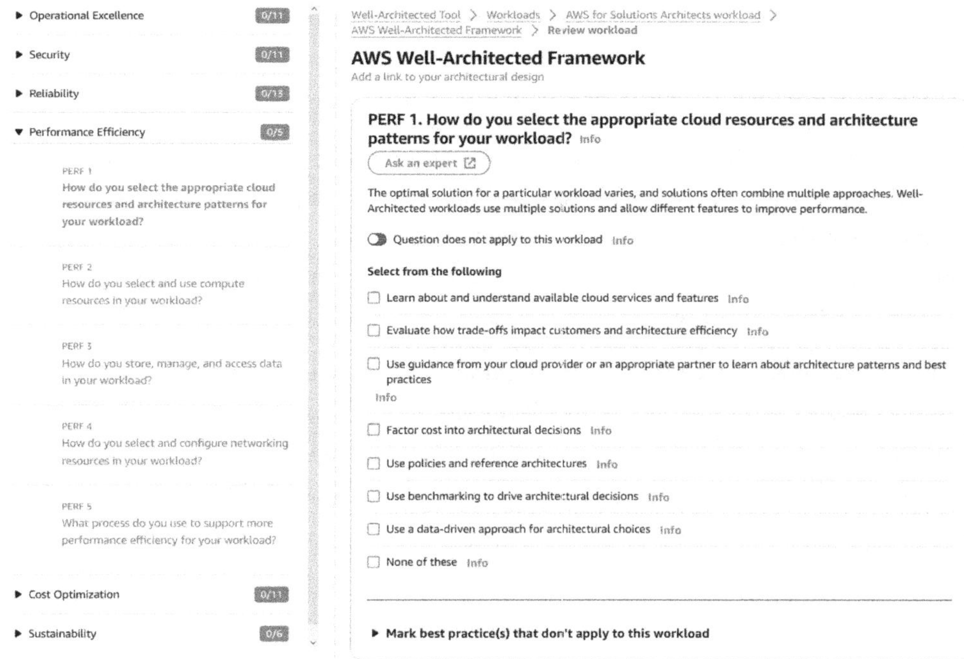

Figure 2.5: AWS Well-Architected performance pillar

In the preceding screenshot, you can see questions related to building performant applications. Answering these questions will help you identify and improve your workload performance. You can find more details on the performance efficiency pillar in the AWS Well-Architected Framework user doc: `https://docs.aws.amazon.com/wellarchitected/latest/performance-efficiency-pillar/welcome.html`.

Monitoring is critical to performance, as it helps identify potential issues within a system and optimize its operation. To effectively monitor your workload for performance, hands-on labs are available that provide practical experience and help implement appropriate monitoring techniques. You can find details on the labs here: `https://www.wellarchitectedlabs.com/performance-efficiency/`.

Cost optimization is one of the primary motivators for businesses to move to the cloud, according to Gartner's *6 Steps for Planning a Cloud Strategy*. You can find details on that here: `https://www.primobonacina.com/gartner-6-steps-for-planning-a-cloud-strategy/`.

The cloud can become expensive if you don't apply best practices and run the cloud workload like on-premises. However, proper cost optimization techniques can save you tons of money. Let's look into the next pillar: cost optimization.

The fourth pillar – Cost optimization

This pillar is related to the third pillar. Suppose your architecture is efficient and can accurately handle varying application loads and adjust as traffic changes.

Additionally, your architecture should be cost-aware, identify when resources are not being used, and allow you to stop them or, even better, stop those unused compute resources for you. In this department, AWS provides autoscaling, which allows you to turn on monitoring tools that will automatically shut down resources if they are not being utilized. We strongly encourage you to adopt a mechanism to stop resources once they are identified as idle. This is especially useful in development and test environments.

To enhance cost optimization, these principles are suggested:

- Implement cloud financial management
- Adopt a consumption model
- Measure overall efficiency
- Stop spending money on undifferentiated heavy-lifting
- Analyze and attribute expenditure

Whenever possible, use AWS-managed services instead of services you need to manage yourself. Managed cloud-native services should lower your administration expenses. You can find the cost optimization pillar checklist from the Well-Architected tool in the following screenshot, with 10 questions covering multiple aspects to make sure your architecture is optimized for cost:

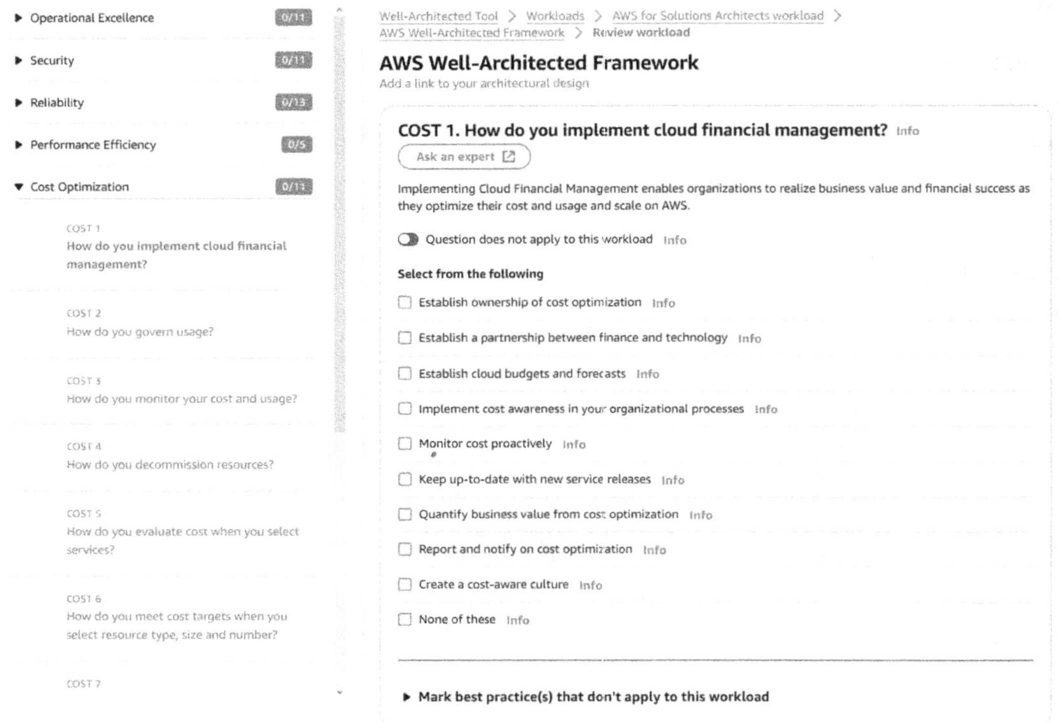

Figure 2.6: AWS Well-Architected cost optimization pillar

In the preceding screenshot, you can see questions about cost optimization best practices, and answering these questions will help you save costs by optimizing your workload for the cloud. You can find more details on the cost optimization pillar by referring to the AWS WAF user doc: `https://docs.aws.amazon.com/wellarchitected/latest/cost-optimization-pillar/welcome.html`.

One of the primary motivations for businesses to move to the cloud is cost savings. Optimizing costs is essential to realizing a return on investment after migrating to the cloud. To learn about the best practices for cost monitoring and optimization, hands-on labs are available that provide practical experience and help implement effective cost management strategies. You can find details on the labs here: `https://www.wellarchitectedlabs.com/cost/`.

Significant work starts after deploying your production workload, making operational excellence a critical factor. You need to ensure that your application maintains the expected performance in production and improves efficacy by applying as much automation as possible. Let's examine more details of the operational excellence pillar.

The fifth pillar – Operational excellence

The operational excellence of a workload should be measured across these dimensions:

- Agility
- Reliability
- Performance

The ideal way to optimize these key performance indicators is to standardize and automate the management of these workloads. To achieve operational excellence, AWS recommends these principles:

- Organize teams around business outcomes
- Implement observability for actionable insights
- Safely automate where possible
- Make frequent, small, reversible changes
- Refine operations procedures frequently
- Anticipate failure
- Learn from all operational events and metrics
- Use managed services

You can find the operational excellence pillar checklist from the Well-Architected tool here, with 11 questions covering multiple aspects to make sure your architecture is optimized for running in production:

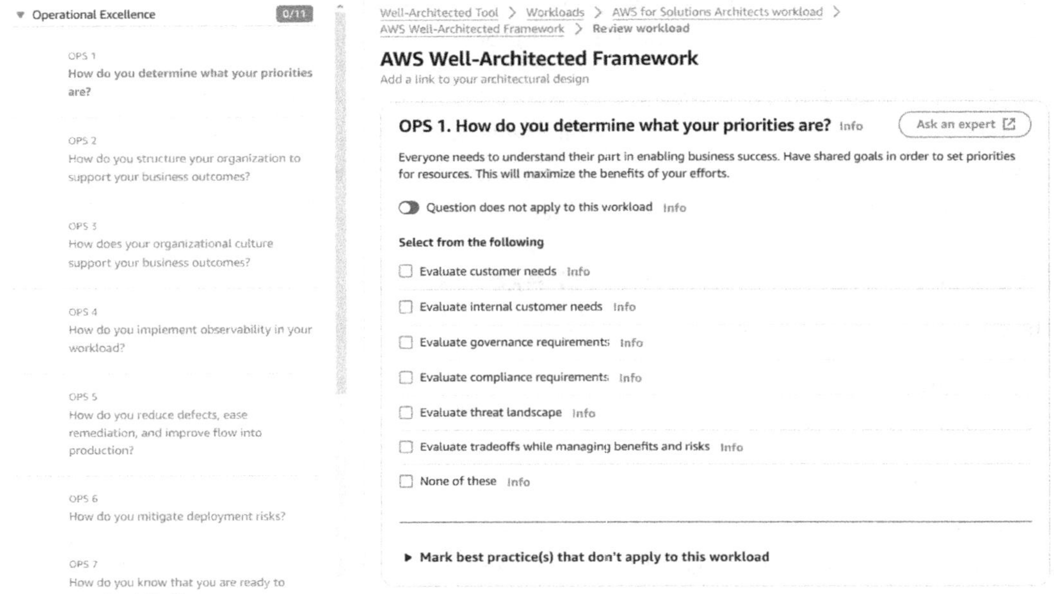

Figure 2.7: AWS Well-Architected operational excellence pillar

In the preceding screenshot, you can see questions about driving operational excellence best practices. Answering these questions will help you achieve efficiency and agility by automating your workload infrastructure, application deployment, monitoring, and alerts. You can find more details on the operational excellence pillar in the AWS WAF user doc: `https://docs.aws.amazon.com/wellarchitected/latest/operational-excellence-pillar/welcome.html`.

Operational excellence is the true value of the cloud, as it enables the automation of production workloads and facilitates self-scaling. Hands-on guidance for implementing best practices in operational excellence is available through the Well-Architected labs, providing practical experience to optimize the operational efficiency of a system. You can find details on the labs here: `https://www.wellarchitectedlabs.com/operational-excellence/`.

Sustainability is now the talk of the town, with organizations worldwide recognizing their social responsibilities and taking the pledge to make business more sustainable. As a leader, AWS was the first cloud provider to launch suitability as an architecture practice at re:Invent 2021. Let's look into more details of the sustainability pillar of the WAF.

The sixth pillar – Sustainability

As more and more organizations adopt the cloud, cloud providers can make the world more sustainable by improving the environment, economics, society, and human life. *The United Nations World Commission on Environment and Development* defines sustainable development as "*development that meets the needs of the present without compromising the ability of future generations to meet their own needs.*" Your organization can have direct or indirect negative impacts on the Earth's environment through carbon emissions or by damaging natural resources such as clean water or farming land. To reduce environmental impact, it's important to talk about sustainability and adopt it in practice wherever possible. AWS is achieving that by adding the sixth pillar to its WAF with the following design principles:

- Understand your impact
- Establish sustainability goals
- Maximize utilization
- Anticipate and adopt new, more efficient hardware and software offerings
- Use managed services
- Reduce the downstream impact of your cloud workloads

You can find the sustainability pillar checklist from the Well-Architected tool here, with six well-thought-out questions covering multiple aspects to make sure your architecture is sustainable:

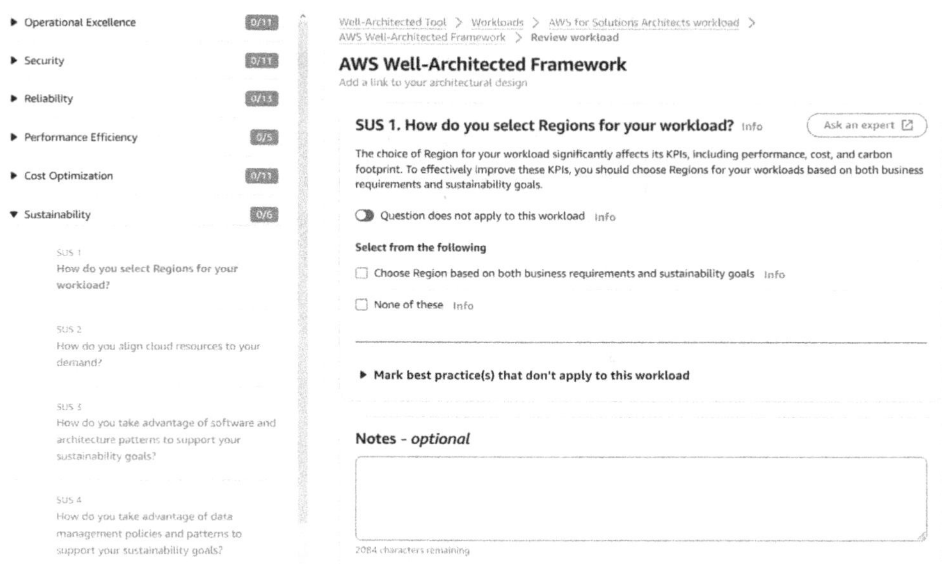

Figure 2.8: AWS Well-Architected sustainability pillar

In the preceding screenshot, you can see questions related to understanding whether your workload is helping you to achieve your sustainability goals and how AWS can help you meet these goals. You can find more details on the sustainability pillar in the AWS WAF user doc: `https://docs.aws.amazon.com/wellarchitected/latest/sustainability-pillar/sustainability-pillar.html`.

Making conscious choices and being aware of your carbon footprint is essential to driving sustainability. AWS provides ways to save energy through its services, and with the help of the Well-Architected labs, workloads can be made sustainable and environmentally aware. You can find details on the labs here: `https://www.wellarchitectedlabs.com/sustainability/`.

While the WAF provides more generic guidance for optimizing your architecture, which is applicable across workloads, specialized workloads require more specific architectural practices. That's why AWS published Well-Architected Lenses to address workload and domain-specific needs. Let's take an overarching view of AWS's Well-Architected Lenses.

AWS Well-Architected Lenses

As of October 2024, AWS has launched 15 Well-Architected Lenses addressing architecting needs specific to technology workloads and industry domains. The following are the important available lenses for AWS's WAF:

- **Migration Lens**: The AWS Migration process comprises three phases: assess, mobilize, migrate & modernize. The WAF's six pillars are overlaid to mitigate cloud migration and implementation risks. When initiating workload migration to the cloud, one of the initial decisions is determining the migration strategy. This strategy outlines the approach for moving applications to the cloud, commonly known as the 7 Rs: retire, retain, rehost, relocate, repurchase, re-platform, and refactor. The Migration Lens specifically focuses on the rehost, relocate, re-platform, and retire migration strategies. The refactor strategy involves modernizing the application during the migration. More information on the design principles is available on the AWS website: `https://docs.aws.amazon.com/wellarchitected/latest/migration-lens/migration-lens.html`

- **Serverless Applications Lens**: Building a serverless workload saves costs and offloads infrastructure maintenance to the cloud. The Serverless Applications Lens provides details on best practices for architecting, designing, and deploying serverless application workloads in the AWS cloud. More information on the design principles is available on the AWS website: `https://docs.aws.amazon.com/wellarchitected/latest/serverless-applications-lens`.
- **Internet of Things (IoT) Lens**: To design an IoT workload, you must know how to manage and secure it on millions of devices that need to connect over the internet. The IoT Lens provides details on designing an IoT workload. More details on design principles are available on the AWS website: `https://docs.aws.amazon.com/wellarchitected/latest/iot-lens`.
- **Data Analytics Lens**: Data is the new gold. Every organization is trying to use its data to gain insights for its customers and improve its business. The Data Analytics Lens provides best practices for building a data pipeline. More details on the design principles are available on the AWS website: `https://docs.aws.amazon.com/wellarchitected/latest/analytics-lens`.
- **Machine Learning (ML) Lens**: ML applies to almost any workload, especially getting future insights from historical data. With the ever-increasing adoption of ML workloads, it is essential to have the ability to put an ML model into production and use it at scale. The ML Lens provides best practices for training, tuning, and deploying your ML model. More details on the design principles are available on the AWS website: `https://docs.aws.amazon.com/wellarchitected/latest/machine-learning-lens`.

Above, we have covered some of the important lenses. Still, I encourage you to explore other industry-focused Well-Architected Lenses such as healthcare, streaming media, finance, and workload-specific lenses, including the SAP Lens, SaaS Lens, Healthcare Industry Lens, Connected Mobility Lens, and Financial Services Industry Lens, to validate your cloud platforms. You can apply various lenses when defining your workload in AWS's Well-Architected tool, as shown here:

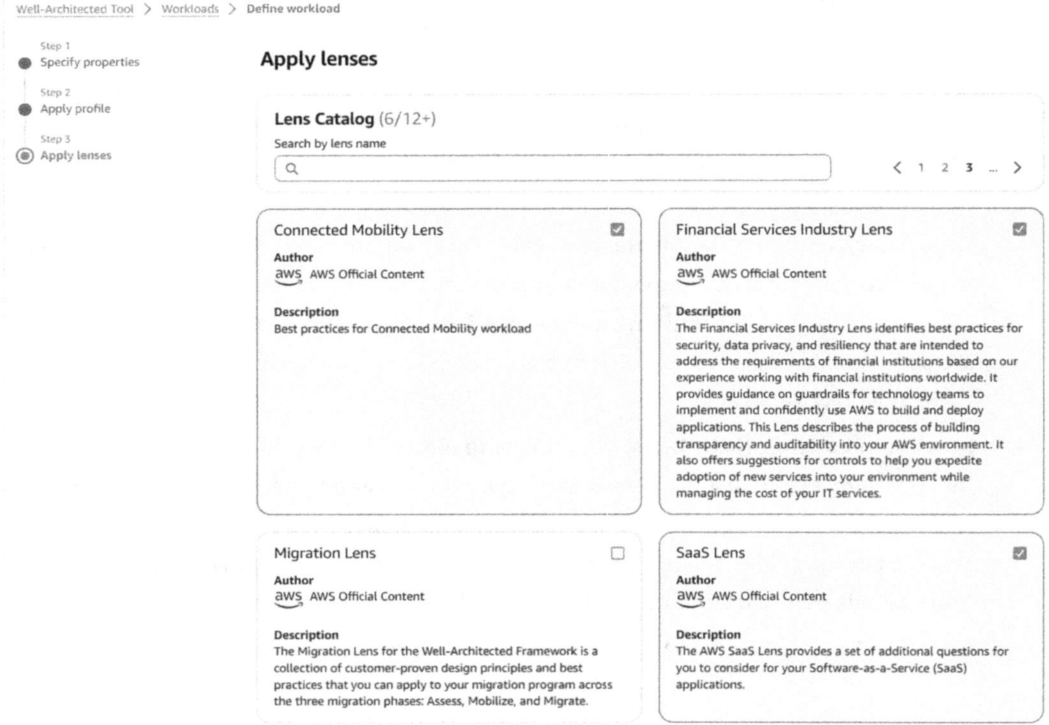
Well-Architected Tool > Workloads > Define workload
Step 1
Specify properties
Step 2
Apply profile
Step 3
Apply lenses
Apply lenses
Lens Catalog (6/12+)
Search by lens name
1 2 3 ...
Connected Mobility Lens
Author
aws AWS Official Content
Description
Best practices for Connected Mobility workload
Financial Services Industry Lens
Author
aws AWS Official Content
Description
The Financial Services Industry Lens identifies best practices for security, data privacy, and resiliency that are intended to address the requirements of financial institutions based on our experience working with financial institutions worldwide. It provides guidance on guardrails for technology teams to implement and confidently use AWS to build and deploy applications. This Lens describes the process of building transparency and auditability into your AWS environment. It also offers suggestions for controls to help you expedite adoption of new services into your environment while managing the cost of your IT services.
Migration Lens
Author
aws AWS Official Content
Description
The Migration Lens for the Well-Architected Framework is a collection of customer-proven design principles and best practices that you can apply to your migration program across the three migration phases: Assess, Mobilize, and Migrate.
SaaS Lens
Author
aws AWS Official Content
Description
The AWS SaaS Lens provides a set of additional questions for you to consider for your Software-as-a-Service (SaaS) applications.

Figure 2.9: AWS Well-Architected Lenses

After applying a lens to your workload, you will get a best practice checklist specific to the domain; for example, the following screenshot shows a Well-Architected checklist for the Financial Services Industry Lens:

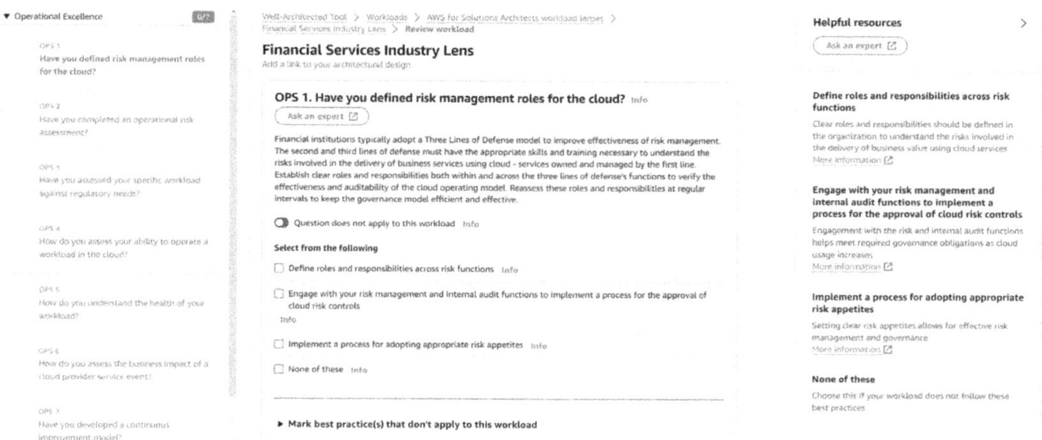

Figure 2.10: AWS Well-Architected Financial Services Industry Lens

As shown in the preceding screenshot, much like AWS's WAR tool, where you saw six pillars in the previous section, each lens has questions related to six pillars to validate workloads and identify HRIs.

AWS users must constantly evaluate their systems to ensure they follow the recommended principles of the AWS WAF and AWS Well-Architected Lenses and comply with and follow architecture best practices. As you must be getting more curious about AWS by now, let's learn how to build your knowledge of the AWS cloud and establish yourself as a subject matter expert.

Building credibility and getting certified

It is hard to argue that the cloud is not an important technology shift. We have established AWS as the clear market and thought leader in the cloud space.

Now, enterprises are eager to adopt cloud technologies because they do not want to fall behind their competition and become obsolete. Hopefully, by now, you are excited to learn more about AWS and other cloud providers, or at the very least, you're getting a little nervous and have a little FOMO yourself.

We will devote the rest of this chapter to showing you the path of least resistance for becoming an AWS guru and someone who can build themselves as an AWS expert. As with other technologies, it is hard to become an expert without hands-on experience, and it's hard to get hands-on experience if you can't demonstrate that you're an expert. The best method to crack this chicken-and-egg problem is to get certified.

Fortunately, AWS offers a wide array of certifications to demonstrate deep AWS knowledge and expertise to potential clients and employers. As AWS creates more services, it continues offering new certificates aligned with these new services. The following are the available AWS certifications listed on the AWS website as of April 2025. Find the website link here: `https://aws.amazon.com/certification/`.

FOUNDATIONAL
Knowledge-based certification for foundational understanding of AWS Cloud.
No prior experience needed.

aws certified
Cloud Practitioner
FOUNDATIONAL
aws certified
AI Practitioner
FOUNDATIONAL
Beta

PROFESSIONAL
Role-based certifications that validate advanced skills and knowledge required to design secure, optimized, and modernized applications and to automate processes on AWS.
2 years of prior AWS Cloud experience recommended.

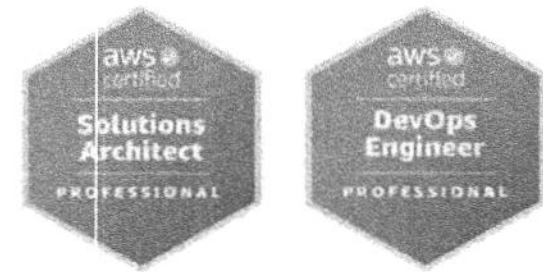
aws certified
Solutions Architect
PROFESSIONAL
aws certified
DevOps Engineer
PROFESSIONAL

ASSOCIATE
Role-based certifications that showcase your knowledge and skills on AWS and build your credibility as an AWS Cloud professional. Prior cloud and/or strong on-premises IT experience recommended.

aws certified
SysOps Administrator
ASSOCIATE
aws certified
Developer
ASSOCIATE
aws certified
Solutions Architect
ASSOCIATE
aws certified
Data Engineer
ASSOCIATE
aws certified
Machine Learning Engineer
ASSOCIATE
Beta

SPECIALTY
Dive deeper and position yourself as a trusted advisor to your stakeholders and/or customers in these strategic areas. Refer to the exam guides on the exam pages for recommended experience.

aws certified
Advanced Networking
SPECIALTY
aws certified
Machine Learning
SPECIALTY
aws certified
Security
SPECIALTY

Beta: These exams are currently beta versions

Figure 2.11: AWS certifications

In the preceding screenshot, you can see that AWS has certifications for everyone. If you are starting or working in a non-tech domain, it's better to go for foundational certifications. To gain further knowledge, you can choose associated certifications and become an expert by gaining specialist and professional certifications.

AWS continuously updates certification exams to accommodate all new services and feature launches. Let's review the available certifications and how they fit into your career aspirations to enhance your current skills in the cloud.

AWS Learning Badges

AWS Learning Badges are digital certificates that show your understanding of specific AWS topics. You can earn these badges by completing free online courses and passing assessments on the AWS Skill Builder platform.

Here's how to earn AWS Learning Badges

1. **Sign Up**: Create a free account on AWS Skill Builder.
2. **Enroll in Courses:** Choose from various learning plans that offer badges upon completion.
3. **Complete Assessments:** After finishing the course, pass the assessment to earn your badge.

Here's a list of some popular AWS Learning Badges:

- **Cloud Essentials:** Understand the basics of AWS cloud computing.
- **Architecting**: Learn how to design applications and systems on AWS.
- **Serverless:** Explore building applications without managing servers.
- **Object Storage:** Dive into storing and managing data using AWS services.
- **Block Storage:** Gain knowledge about block-level storage options.
- **File Storage:** Learn about file storage solutions on AWS.
- **Data Migration:** Understand how to move data to AWS securely.
- **Data Protection & Disaster Recovery**: Learn strategies to protect data and recover from disasters.
- **Networking Core:** Get insights into networking concepts within AWS.
- **Compute:** Explore computing services and how to use them.
- **Amazon Elastic Kubernetes Service (EKS):** Learn about deploying and managing Kubernetes on AWS.
- **Events and Workflows:** Understand event-driven architectures and workflows.

- **Amazon Braket**: Get introduced to quantum computing services.
- **AWS for Games: Cloud Game Development**: Learn how to develop games using AWS services.
- **Media & Entertainment: Direct-to-Consumer and Broadcast Foundations**: Explore AWS solutions for media and broadcasting.

To earn these badges, register for a free AWS Skill Builder account, enroll in the desired learning plan, complete the assessment with at least an 80% score, and claim your badge through Credly.

These badges are free and can be shared on social media or added to your resume, helping you stand out to employers. For a complete and up-to-date list of available badges, visit the AWS Training and Certification page: `https://aws.amazon.com/training/badges/`.

Building a non-tech AWS cloud career

Working with the cloud is a very tech-savvy job. However, that is not always the case. Several cloud roles don't require deep technical knowledge; just a basic understanding will get your foot in the door to start a cloud career. For example, anyone from a sales and marketing background can thrive in cloud marketing, cloud business development, or a cloud sales role without deep technical knowledge. Similarly, program managers are required in any industry where basic cloud knowledge will help you get started in the role. However, building cloud foundation knowledge to prepare yourself better is recommended, which you can gain from an AWS Certified Cloud Practitioner certification. Let's look into more details.

AWS Certified Cloud Practitioner – Foundational

This is the most basic certification offered by AWS. It is meant to demonstrate a broad-stroke understanding of the core services and foundational knowledge of AWS. It is also a good certification for non-technical people who need to be able to communicate using the AWS terminology but are not necessarily going to be configuring or developing in AWS. This certification is ideal for demonstrating a basic understanding of AWS technologies for salespeople, business analysts, marketing associates, executives, and project managers.

The AWS Solutions Architect path

Solutions Architect is one of the most sought-after roles in the cloud industry. Often, Solutions Architects are responsible for designing a workload in the cloud and applying architecture best practices using the AWS WAF. The following AWS certifications can help you kick-start your AWS cloud solutions architect career.

AWS Certified Solutions Architect – Associate

This is the most popular certification offered by AWS. Many technically minded developers, architects, and administrators skip the Cloud Practitioner certification and start by taking this certification instead. If you are looking to demonstrate technical expertise in AWS, obtaining this certification is a good start and the bare minimum to demonstrate AWS proficiency. However, to demonstrate proficiency in architecting IT workloads in the AWS cloud, you should pursue the Solutions Architect – Professional certification as mentioned next.

AWS Certified Solutions Architect – Professional

This certification is one of the toughest to get and at least five to six times harder than the Associate-level certification. Earning this certification will demonstrate to employers that you have a deep and thorough understanding of AWS services, best practices, and optimal architectures based on the particular business requirements for a given project. Obtaining this certification shows potential employers that you are an expert in designing and creating distributed systems and applications on the AWS platform. It used to be that having at least one of the Associate-level certifications was a prerequisite to sitting the Professional-level certifications, but AWS has eliminated that requirement.

For more details on the AWS solutions architect role and to gain in-depth knowledge of building use-case-focused architecture on the AWS platform, refer to Solution Architect's Handbook 3rd Edition, available on Amazon (`https://www.amazon.com/gp/product/1835084230`).

DevOps is one key component for operationalizing any workload. Let's learn more about the DevOps path in AWS.

The AWS Cloud DevOps Engineer path

DevOps is a critical engineering function that makes a development team more agile by automating the deployment pipeline. Automation is key to adopting the cloud and using its full potential, where a DevOps engineer plays an essential role. Gaining the AWS certification can help you navigate the DevOps path with AWS.

AWS Certified SysOps Administrator – Associate

This certification will demonstrate to potential employers and clients that you have experience deploying, configuring, scaling up, managing, and migrating applications using AWS services. You should expect the difficulty level of this certification to be higher than the other associate-level certifications, but also expect quite a bit of overlap in the type of questions that will be asked about this certification and the other associate-level certifications.

AWS Certified DevOps Engineer – Professional

This advanced AWS certification validates knowledge of how to provision, manage, scale, and secure AWS resources and services. This certification will demonstrate to potential employers that you can run their DevOps operations and proficiently develop solutions and applications in AWS. This certification is more challenging than any Associate certification but easier than the AWS Solutions Architect Professional certification.

The AWS Cloud Developer path

Developers are central to any IT application. They are builders who bring life to ideas, making developers vital in the cloud. However, software developers are more focused on programming languages and algorithms, but build software in the cloud; they need to be aware of the various development tools that cloud providers facilitate. The following is the certification to gain the required cloud knowledge for building software in AWS.

AWS Certified Developer – Associate

Obtaining this certification will demonstrate your ability to design, develop, and deploy applications in AWS. Even though this is a developer certification, do not expect coding in any questions during the exam. However, knowing at least one programming language supported by AWS will help you achieve this certification. Expect to see many of the same concepts and similar questions to what you would see in the Solutions Architect certification. AWS doesn't have a professional certification for developers, but it is recommended that you pursue AWS DevOps Engineer certifications to scale and operationalize your software applications in the cloud.

While we have talked about the generalist career path in the cloud, several specialty paths are available where AWS has certifications to validate your knowledge. Let's look at the overview of AWS certifications to see if you have expertise in a specific area.

The AWS Specialty Solutions Architect path

While generalist solutions architects design overall workloads, they need to dive deep into certain areas where more in-depth knowledge is required. In that case, specialist solutions architects come to the rescue; they provide their expertise to apply best practices for a specific domain, such as security, networking, analytics, ML, and so on. In the Well-Architected tool sections, you will see that AWS has domain-specific lenses to optimize specialty workloads and engage specialist solutions architects. The following are AWS certifications to validate your specialty knowledge in the AWS cloud.

AWS Certified Advanced Networking – Specialty

This AWS specialty certification demonstrates that you possess the skills to design and deploy AWS services as part of a comprehensive network architecture and the know-how to scale using best practices. It is one of the hardest certifications to obtain, like AWS Certified Solutions Architect – Professional. You have to put in additional effort to pass the networking specialty exam.

For most exams, you go through online courses on famous learning platforms such as Pluralsight/Udemy and take practice exams before attending. However, the networking specialty certification will not be enough. You need to review other resources such as AWS whitepapers, blogs, and AWS re:Invent videos and take notes. You must review multiple resources until you are clear about concepts and keep revising your notes. We will discuss learning resources in more detail later in this chapter, under the *Learning tips and tricks for obtaining AWS certifications* section.

AWS Certified Security – Specialty

Possessing the AWS Certified Security – Specialty certification demonstrates to potential employers that you are well-versed in AWS and the ins and outs of AWS security. It shows that you know the best security practices for encryption at rest, encryption in transit, user authentication and authorization, and penetration testing, and you can generally deploy AWS services and applications securely that align with your business requirements.

AWS Machine Learning Engineer path

Machine learning and generative AI are among the most sought-after skill sets in the market, and they will remain so for the next several years. If you come from a data and analytics background, it's worth exploring this high-reward career.

AWS Certified Data Engineer – Associate

Data is the foundation for starting a machine learning career path. This AWS certification demonstrates that you possess the skills and knowledge in core data-related AWS services, the ability to ingest and transform data, orchestrate data pipelines while applying programming concepts, design data models, manage data life cycles, and ensure data quality. This certification not only offers you a means to build your confidence and credibility in data engineer, data architecture, and other data-related roles but also provides a solid foundation for an ML engineer career.

AWS Certified AI Practitioner

The AWS Certified AI Practitioner certification validates knowledge in **artificial intelligence (AI)**, **machine learning (ML)**, and generative AI concepts, focusing on fundamental AI/ML technologies and AWS services such as Amazon SageMaker, Amazon Bedrock, Amazon Rekognition, and Amazon Lex. The certification covers AI/ML use cases, responsible AI practices, and security for AI systems. Earning this certification can validate in-demand AI/ML skills, lead to career growth, and help you stay competitive in the evolving field of AI. Unlike AWS Certified Cloud Practitioner, this certification focuses on AI/ML technologies rather than general AWS cloud concepts.

AWS Certified Machine Learning Engineer – Associate

This AWS certification demonstrates that you possess the technical ability to implement and operationalize ML workloads in production. You can boost your career profile and credibility and position yourself for in-demand machine learning job roles. Currently, this certification is in the beta version. AWS Certification uses beta exams to validate the performance of exam questions before the questions are used on standard versions of an exam. An exam can go through the beta process before the exam is launched for the first time. AWS Certification can also complete a beta process when the exam content outline changes. Candidates who pass the beta exam will be among the first to hold the new certification. This certification affirms an individual's ability to effectively design, implement, deploy, and maintain ML solutions using AWS services.

AWS Certified Machine Learning – Specialty

This is an excellent certification in your pocket if you are a data scientist or data analyst building an ML engineer or ML architect career. It shows potential employers that you are familiar with many of the core ML concepts and the AWS services that can be used to deliver ML and artificial intelligence projects. This certification is designed for individuals with experience developing, designing, and deploying AWS ML models. It validates advanced skills in machine learning, including building, training, tuning, and deploying ML models using AWS services. Earning this certification showcases expertise in machine learning, enhances credibility, and can open up advanced career opportunities in the growing field of AI/ML.

Let's learn some tips and tricks for obtaining AWS certifications.

Learning tips and tricks for obtaining AWS certifications

Now that we have learned about the various certifications offered by AWS, let's learn about some of the strategies we can use to get these certifications with the least amount of work possible and what we can expect as we prepare for these certifications.

Focus on one cloud provider

Some enterprises try to adopt a cloud-agnostic or multi-cloud strategy. The idea behind this strategy is not to depend on only one cloud provider. In theory, this is a good idea, and some companies, such as **Databricks**, **Snowflake**, and **Cloudera**, offer their wares to be run using the most popular cloud providers.

However, this agnosticism comes with some difficult choices. One way to implement this strategy is to choose the least common denominator – for example, only using compute instances so that workloads can be deployed on various cloud platforms. Implementing this approach means you cannot use the more advanced services cloud providers offer. For example, using AWS Lambda in a cloud-agnostic fashion is quite tricky.

Another way to implement a multi-cloud strategy is to use more advanced services, but this means that your staff will have to know how to use these services for all the cloud providers you decide to use. To use a common refrain, you will be a *jack of all trades and a master of none.*

Similarly, individually, it isn't easy to be a cloud expert across vendors. Pick one cloud provider and become an expert on that stack. To name the most popular options, AWS, Azure, and GCP offer an immense amount of services that continuously change and get enhanced, and they keep adding more services. Keeping up with one of these providers is not an easy task. Keeping up with all three is nearly impossible. Pick one and dominate it.

Start with Practitioner certifications

To build a strong foundation in cloud computing, it's recommended to begin with Practitioner-level certifications. These certifications, such as the **AWS Certified Cloud Practitioner** or **AWS Certified AI Practitioner**, are designed to help you explore different cloud career paths and understand which direction is right for you. Practitioner certifications provide the essential knowledge needed to grasp the fundamentals of cloud technologies, making them an excellent starting point.

Earning a Practitioner certification establishes a solid base that you can build upon as you advance to more specialized certifications. It equips you with a core understanding of cloud services and concepts, allowing you to move confidently toward intermediate and expert levels as your knowledge and experience grow.

Focus on the Associate-level certifications

As we mentioned before, there is some overlap between the Associate-level certifications. In addition, the jump in difficulty between the Associate-level certificates and the Professional-level ones is quite steep.

It's highly recommended to sit at least two of the Associate-level certifications before attempting the Professional-level certifications. Not only will this method prepare you for the Professional certifications, but having multiple Associate certifications will also make you stand out against others who only have one Associate-level certificate.

Get experience wherever you can

AWS recommends having one year of experience before taking the Associate-level certifications and two years of experience before sitting for the Professional-level certifications. This may seem like a *catch-22* situation. How can you get experience if you are not certified? However, it's a recommendation and not a mandatory requirement. This means you can gain training experience and study for the exam. You can do your project using an AWS Free Tier account with a decent number of services available in the first year and gain good hands-on experience.

The best way to get certified

Before we discuss the best way to get certified, let's examine the worst way. Amazon offers extremely comprehensive documentation. You can find it here: `https://docs.aws.amazon.com/`.

AWS docs are a great place to help you troubleshoot issues you may encounter when you are directly working with AWS services or to size the services you will be using correctly. However, there are better places to study for exams. It will get overwhelming quickly, and much of the material you will learn about will not be covered in the exams.

The better way to get certified is to use the training materials that AWS specifically provides for certification, starting with the learning paths of what will be covered in each certification. These roadmaps are a good first step toward understanding the scope of each exam.

As AWS calls them, you can learn about all these roadmaps or learning paths here: `https://aws.amazon.com/training/learning-paths/`.

You will find free online courses and paid intensive training sessions for these learning paths. While the paid classes may be helpful, they are not mandatory for you to pass the exam.

Before you look at the learning paths, the first place to find out the scope of each certification is the study guides available for each certification. In these study guides, you will learn at a high level what will and won't be covered for each exam. For example, the study guide for the AWS Cloud Practitioner certification can be found here: `https://aws.amazon.com/certification/certified-cloud-practitioner/`.

Now, while the training provided by AWS may be sufficient to pass the exams, and I know plenty of folks who have passed the certifications using only those resources, plenty of third-party companies specialize in training people with a special focus on the certifications. The choices are almost endless. Let's look at a few more resources here.

Getting started in AWS

AWS launched the Skill Builder portal (`https://explore.skillbuilder.aws/`), which enhances AWS's training portal.

AWS Skill Builder has thousands of self-paced digital training sessions and learning paths, as shown here.

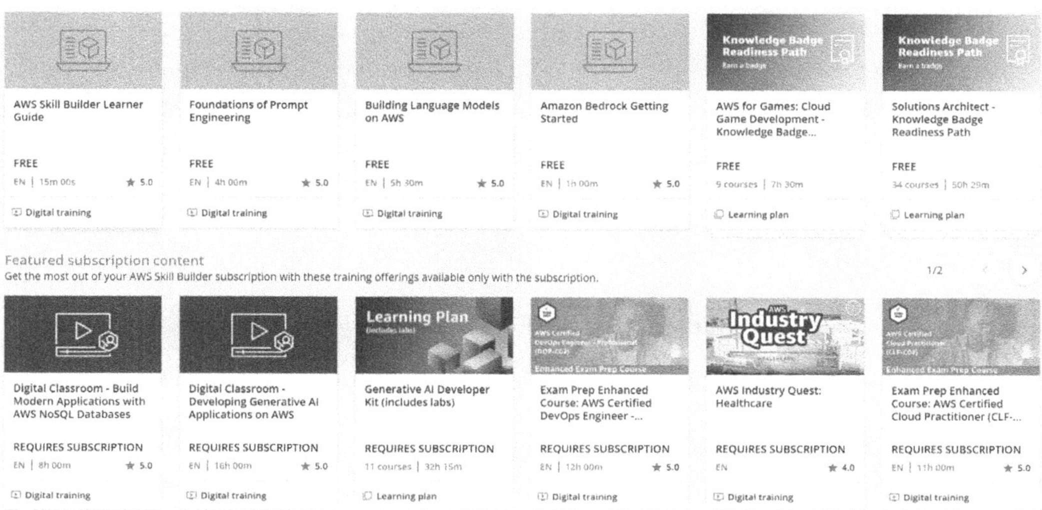

Figure 2.12: AWS Skill Builder learning paths

You can pick any learning path you need and explore related digital courses. If you want classroom training, that is available in the AWS training portal; however, it may come at a price. AWS provides free cloud practitioner training in its Skills Center, where you can register and get instructor-led training for free. AWS has also opened its first free training center in Seattle and plans to expand in the coming months. If you have Skills Centers where you are, you can benefit by registering on the AWS website directly: `https://aws.amazon.com/training/skills-centers/`.

Online courses

In addition to the courses provided by AWS, other training organizations and independent content creators offer excellent courses for obtaining AWS certifications.

Pluralsight

Pluralsight is a top online learning platform offering expert-led AWS certification courses, including video tutorials, hands-on labs, and practice exams. It covers cloud architecture, security, networking, and databases in a self-paced format. With flexible subscription plans, individuals and teams can prepare for AWS certifications at their convenience. Pluralsight also includes A Cloud Guru content, providing the best AWS training in one place. Access training at `https://www.pluralsight.com`.

Packt Publishing

If you're prepping for an AWS certification, Packt has a great set of resources that might be just what you need. They've put together a comprehensive suite of tools, from in-depth study guides to practical walk-throughs, designed to help you build a solid understanding of core AWS services and concepts.

These materials are super handy for reinforcing what you've learned, gaining hands-on experience, and figuring out how ready you are for the actual exam. The structured format really helps you stay on track and confident as you move through your certification journey.

You can check it out here: `https://www.packtpub.com/en-us/cloud-and-networking/tool/aws`.

Udemy courses

As of February 2025, several independent instructors on Udemy continue to offer high-quality AWS certification courses. Stephane Maarek's *Ultimate AWS Certified Solutions Architect Associate* course has over 1,092,419 students and 249,605 ratings, maintaining a 4.7 out of 5-star rating. Jon Bonso provides comprehensive practice exams for various AWS certifications, including the Solutions Architect Associate and Developer Associate exams. These resources are valuable for learners aiming to achieve AWS certification.

You can also explore other training providers such as Cloud Academy and Coursera. However, you don't need to sign up for multiple course providers.

YouTube videos

As always, YouTube is an excellent source of free learning. AWS has its own YouTube channel with nearly 600,000 subscribers and 14,000 videos. These videos cover AWS services by AWS product managers and solutions architects. AWS uploads all Re:invent and AWS Summits videos on the YouTube channel, which is the best resource for diving deep into any service. You can find several playlists people have created to prepare for certifications.

Books

If you are a book reader, multiple AWS certification-related books are available on Amazon, which you can refer to to prepare for the exam. If you are preparing for the AWS Solutions Architect exam and are solidifying concepts, refer to the *Solution Architect's Handbook* (`https://www.amazon.com/dp/1835084230`). It explains multiple architectural patterns using the AWS platform and goes deep into using each Well-Architected pillar to apply architectural best practices.

Get your hands dirty with practice labs

To clear AWS certifications, hands-on experience is essential. Engaging in hands-on labs gives you a deeper understanding of cloud services and provides a competitive edge during interviews by equipping you with practical knowledge and real-world experience. AWS offers several hands-on resources, with one of the most valuable being the AWS Skill Builder Labs (`https://aws.amazon.com/training/digital/aws-builder-labs/`), which include over 200 self-paced labs. These labs offer step-by-step instructions to develop cloud skills in a safe, sandbox AWS environment. This allows you to experiment without incurring costs and focus on specific areas you need to strengthen. AWS Hands-On Tutorials (`https://aws.amazon.com/getting-started/hands-on/`) is another great resource, offering free guided instructions to help users launch their first applications on AWS. Also, it's worth exploring the AWS architecture website: `https://aws.amazon.com/architecture/`. Additionally, third-party practice labs from platforms such as Pluralsight (`https://www.pluralsight.com/resources/blog/cloud/10-fun-hands-on-projects-to-learn-aws`), Udemy, and other course providers offer access to a real AWS environment where you can work through guided scenarios involving key services such as Amazon S3, EC2, and VPC. Hands-on practice is critical for certification success, as it reinforces theoretical concepts with practical applications, prepares you for scenario-based questions, and helps identify gaps in your knowledge. Combining practical labs with study materials ensures thorough preparation for certification exams and real-world cloud roles.

Practice exam websites

It doesn't matter how much you read or how many courses you watch; there are always knowledge gaps, and practice exams are the best sources for identifying and focusing on weak areas. Let's look at some practice exam resources.

AWS practice question sets

AWS recently launched practice question sets for all its Skill Builder portal certifications. These are the official AWS certification practice question sets, featuring 20 questions developed by AWS to demonstrate the style of AWS certification exams. These exam-style questions include detailed feedback and recommended resources to help you prepare for your exam. They are an excellent source for understanding exam patterns and difficulty levels.

The following is a sample list, which you can access using the link `https://explore.skillbuilder.aws/learn` and select the filter **Exam Preparation** under **Training Category**.

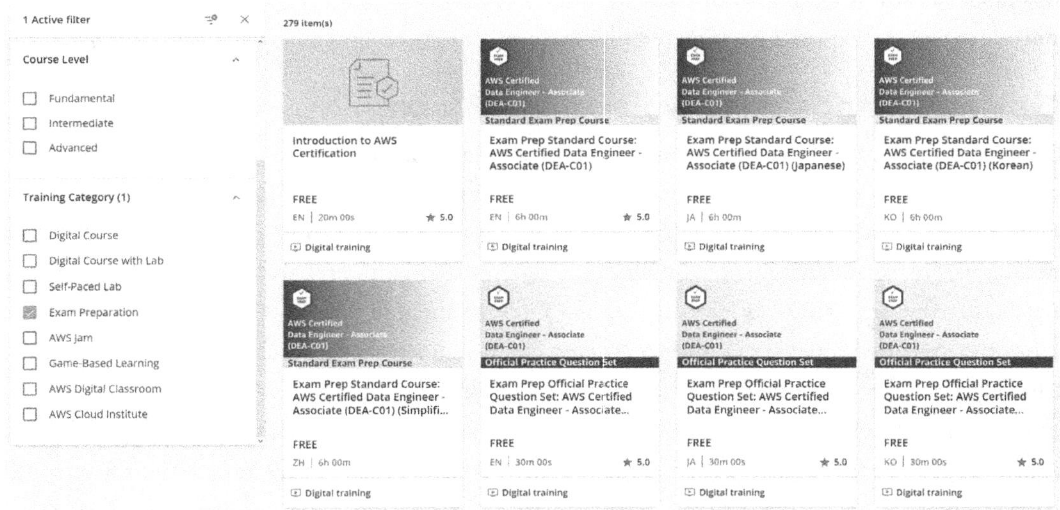

Figure 2.13: AWS certification practice question sets

There are free practice exams available for almost all available certifications. Let's look at more third-party resources for more practice exam choices.

Whizlabs

Whizlabs (`https://www.whizlabs.com/`) is suitable for Associate-level certification and testing your knowledge in multiple areas to find weak points. Whizlabs also provides answers with detailed explanations and associated resources that can help you fill any knowledge gaps by exploring related content against questions you got wrong.

Whizlabs divides the charges for their training between their online courses and their practice tests. One disadvantage of Whizlabs is that, unlike the exam simulator with A Cloud Guru, where they have a bank of questions and randomly combine them, the Whizlabs exam questions are fixed and cannot be shuffled to create a different exam.

They also have a free version of their practice exams for most certifications, with 20 free questions.

BrainCert

Like Whizlabs, you can use BrainCert for AWS Professional and Specialty level certification (`https://www.braincert.com`). They have a perfect set of questions that are similar to the exam's difficulty level, with detailed explanations for each answer. While Whizlabs practice exams have lifetime validity, BrainCert provides only one year.

Tutorials Dojo

Tutorials Dojo is another good practice exam website. You can access it by visiting `https://tutorialsdojo.com/`. It has recently received great reviews from the certification community and has good-quality questions for AWS Specialty certification exams.

As mentioned before, the same strategy can be used with Whizlabs or BrainCert. You don't need to sign up for multiple vendors for the more straightforward exams, but you can combine a couple for the harder exams.

Certification preparation approach

Video courses such as Udemy and Pluralsight are used the most to prepare for certifications. The following are recommendations for tackling the training:

- Unless you have previous experience with the topics covered, watch all the training videos at least once. If you feel comfortable with a topic, you can play the videos at a higher speed, and then you will be able to watch the full video faster.
- For video lessons that you find difficult, watch them again. You don't have to watch all the videos again – only the ones you found difficult.

- Make notes of topics that seem to be pretty new to you. Writing notes always clears your thoughts.
- Get to the hands-on lab and solidify your knowledge as much as possible.
- Make sure to take any end-of-section quizzes, wherever available.
- Once you finish watching the videos, the next step is to attempt some practice exams.

The preceding recommendations remain true if you choose books for your exam preparation in which you want to take notes and revisit chapters where the topic is new to you.

Finally, keep taking practice exams until you feel confident and consistently correctly answer a high percentage of the questions (anywhere between 80% and 85%, depending on the certification).

The questions provided in the exam simulator will not be the same as the ones from the exam, but they will be of a similar difficulty level, in the same domains, and often about similar concepts and topics.

By using the exam simulator, you will achieve a couple of things. First, you can gauge your progress and determine whether you are ready for the exam. Keep taking the exam simulator tests until you consistently score at least 85% or above. Most real certifications require you to answer 75% of the questions correctly, so consistently scoring a little higher should ensure that you pass the exam.

Some exams, such as the Security – Specialty exam, require a higher percentage of correct answers, so you should adjust accordingly. Using the exam simulator will also enable you to figure out which domains you are weak in. After taking a whole exam in the simulator, you will get a list detailing exactly which questions you got right and which were wrong, and they will all be classified by domain.

So, if you get a low score in a certain domain, you know that's the domain you need to focus on when you review the videos again. Lastly, you can learn new concepts by taking the tests in the exam simulator.

Now, let's address some of the questions that frequently arise while preparing to take these certifications.

Some frequently asked questions about the AWS certifications

While preparing for certifications, you may have questions such as where to start and how to finish. The following sections will list frequently asked questions that often come to mind.

How long will it take to get certified?

A question frequently asked is how many months you should study before sitting down for the exam. Look at that in terms of hours instead of months.

As you can imagine, you will be able to take the exam a lot sooner if you study for 2 hours every day instead of only studying for 1 hour a week. If you decide to take some AWS-sponsored intensive full-day or multi-day training, that may go a long way toward shortening the cycle.

One way to optimize your time is to listen to videos instead of watching them, in the car or while on the train going into the city. Even though watching them is much more beneficial, you can still embed key concepts while listening to them, and that time would have been dead time anyway.

You don't want to have too much time between study sessions. If you do that, you may find yourself in a situation where you start forgetting what you have learned. The number of hours it will take you depends on your experience. If you are working with AWS for your day job, that will shorten the number of hours needed to complete your studies.

The following subsections will give you an idea of the amount of time you should spend preparing for each exam.

The Cloud Practitioner certification

Preparing for this certification typically takes between 15 and 25 hours. Achieving this credential will help you develop skills and acquire critical knowledge related to implementing cloud initiatives.

Associate-level certifications

If you don't have previous AWS experience, plan to spend between 70 and 100 hours preparing. Also, keep in mind that there is considerable overlap between the other certifications once you pass one of the Associate certifications. Obtaining the second and third certifications will not take another 70 to 100 hours. As mentioned in this chapter, taking the two other Associate-level certifications is highly recommended soon after passing the first one.

If you don't wait too long to take the two remaining certifications after passing the first one, you can expect to spend another 20 to 40 hours studying for them.

Professional-level certifications

There is quite a leap between the Associate-level certifications and the Professional-level certifications. The domain coverage will be similar, but you will need to know how to use the AWS services covered in much more depth, and the questions will certainly be harder. Assuming you took at least one of the Associate-level certifications, expect to spend another 70 to 100 hours watching videos, reading, and taking practice tests to pass this exam.

AWS removed the requirement of having to take the Associate-level certifications before being able to sit for the Professional-level certifications. However, taking at least some Associate exams before taking the Professional-level exams is a good idea.

As is the case with the Associate-level exams, once you pass one of the Professional-level exams, it should take much less study time to prepare for another Professional exam, as long as you don't wait too long to take the second exam and forget everything.

Specialty certifications

I am lumping all the Specialty certifications under one subheading, but there is significant variability in the difficulty level between all the Specialty certifications. If you have a background in networking, you will be more comfortable with the Advanced Networking certification than with the Data Science certification.

When it comes to these certifications, you may be better off focusing on your area of expertise unless you are collecting all certifications. For example, the Machine Learning – Specialty certification and Analytics certification may be your best bet if you are a data scientist.

Depending on your experience, expect to spend the following amounts of time:

- Security – Specialty: 40 to 60 hours
- Machine Learning – Specialty: 50 to 70 hours
- Advanced Networking – Specialty: 50 to 70 hours

Time management and focus tips for AWS Pro and Specialty certification exams

Preparing for AWS Professional or Specialty certification exams requires more than just technical knowledge; you also need solid time management and focus strategies. These exams often contain long, complex scenario-based questions that can easily eat up your time if you're not careful. A good way to manage your time is to follow a three-pass strategy: use the first 60 minutes to tackle easy questions quickly, the next 50 minutes to revisit and work through the challenging ones, and the final 20 minutes to review and polish your answers.

To handle lengthy questions efficiently, try reading the last sentence first to understand what's being asked, then identify keywords such as "high availability" or "cost-effective" to guide your thinking. Rephrasing the question in your own words can also help you stay focused and reduce confusion. To maintain concentration during the exam, practice with full-length tests that mimic real conditions. Use scratch paper or the exam's digital notepad to break down tricky questions, and don't hesitate to take short mental resets, such as deep breathing or quick stretches, if you feel your focus slipping. With these habits, you'll be better equipped to stay sharp and on pace throughout the exam.

One of the best ways to improve both time management and focus is to simulate real exam conditions. Platforms such as Whizlabs and BrainCert offer timed practice exams that mimic the actual test experience. Taking these exams under timed conditions will help you get used to managing your time and focusing under pressure.

How to request additional exam time

An additional 30 minutes can make a lot of difference between passing and failing exams, especially when sitting for more challenging exams such as AWS Professional and Specialty certifications. An essential tip for **non-native English speakers** is that you can request an extra 30 minutes to complete the exam. Take the following steps to get an additional 30 minutes:

1. Click on the home page of your CertMetrics account: `https://www.certmetrics.com/amazon/`.
2. On the right, click the **Request Exam Accommodations** button.

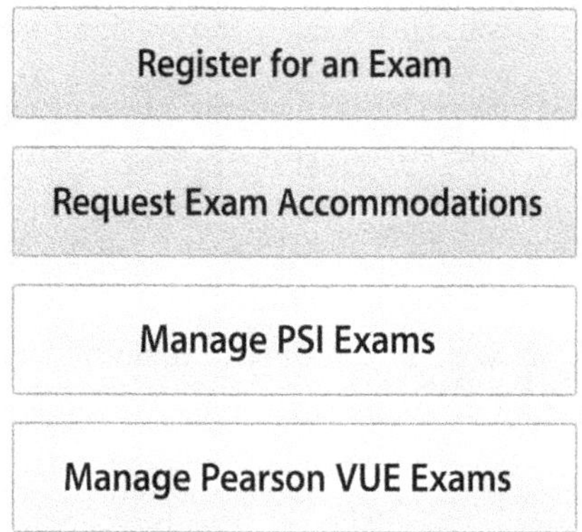

Figure 2.14: Request Exam Accommodations button

3. Click the **Request Accommodation** button.

4. Select **ESL +30 Minutes** from the accommodation dropdown.
5. Click **Create**, and you will see the following approval request available under the **Exam Registration** tab.

Accommodation	Status	Expires	Download Documentation	
ESL +30 MINUTES	Approved			Edit

Figure 2.15: Exam Registration tab

Make sure to apply for the accommodation before scheduling your exam, as it won't apply to already scheduled exams. It's a one-time activity that applies to all future exam registrations after approval.

What are some last-minute tips for the day of the exam?

AWS offers two exam modes: remote and on-site at an AWS-authorized exam center. When taking an AWS certification exam at a testing center, the on-site staff will help with check-in and exam access on test center computers and answer any questions. On the other hand, with online exam proctoring, you can take the same exam with the same allotted time as you would in a testing center, but on your computer. During the exam, a proctor will remotely monitor your progress.

A decent half-marathon time is about 90 minutes, which is how long you get to take the Associate-level exams, and a good marathon time is about 3 hours, which is how long you get to take the Professional-level exams.

Keeping focus for that amount of time is not easy. Therefore, you should be well-rested when you take the exam. It is highly recommended that you take the exam on a day when you don't have too many other responsibilities; I would not take it after working a full day. You will be too burned out.

Ensure you have a light meal before the exam – enough so you are not hungry during the test and feel energetic, but not so much that you feel sleepy from digesting all that food.

Just as you wouldn't want to get out of the gate too fast or too slow in a race, pace yourself during the exam. You also want to avoid being beholden to the clock, checking it constantly. The clock will always appear in the top-right part of the exam, but you want to avoid looking at it most of the time. I recommend writing down on the three sheets you will receive where you should be after every 20 questions, and checking the clock against these numbers only when you have answered 20 questions. This way, you will be able to adjust if you are going too fast or too slow, but you will not spend excessive time watching the clock. Consider flagging the questions in doubt and using any leftover time to review them at the end.

The preceding is just a recommendation; everyone has their own strategy, which you can build when practicing the exam. Apply whatever strategy best fits your style. Now you've got certified, but your overall goal is to get an AWS cloud job. Let's explore that path.

How to land a job as an AWS Solutions Architect

Getting an AWS Solution Architect job can be very competitive and require detailed preparation. Key strategies include preparing for technical interviews by studying AWS services and architectures in depth, practicing the design of scalable, secure, and cost-effective solutions, and being able to explain your architectural decisions and trade-offs. Developing soft skills is also important; you need strong communication skills to explain complex concepts, problem-solving abilities to address customer needs, and leadership qualities to guide teams effectively. The good news is that you have that resource now, crafted by solutions architecture working in AWS with a consolidated 1000+ interview experience. You can grab a copy of the AWS Solutions Architect book on Amazon using this link: `https://www.amazon.com/gp/product/B0D3B73KS4/`. This book serves as a valuable resource.

Hands-on experience is crucial, so work on personal AWS projects, participate in workshops and hackathons, and contribute to open source AWS-related projects. Earning AWS certifications is another important step, starting with AWS Certified Solutions Architect – Associate and progressing to the Professional level or relevant specialty certifications. Networking is also key – attend AWS events, join user groups, and stay updated by following AWS blogs and whitepapers. Finally, tailor your resume to highlight AWS projects and certifications, and practice mock interviews using resources such as Exponent's Solutions Architect Interview Course. Combining technical skills with real-world experience and communication proficiency will help you succeed in landing an AWS SA role.

Now, let's explore some questions that can help you to crack certifications.

Knowledge check

The following sample questions align with the difficulty and scope typically found in the AWS certification exams. Please do not just concentrate on explaining the correct answers when taking the practice tests. Instead, it will be helpful if you start reviewing the explanations for incorrect answers, which can provide deeper insights into the concepts and help you identify areas for improvement.

1. You are tasked with designing a highly available and fault-tolerant architecture for a critical web application. The application must handle dynamic traffic patterns with occasional spikes in user requests. Which of the following approaches would you recommend to meet the scalability and reliability requirements while adhering to the AWS WAF's best practices?

    a. Deploy the application on a single EC2 instance with Auto Scaling enabled to handle traffic spikes.

    b. Use an Auto Scaling group with multiple **Availability Zones (AZs)** and an **Elastic Load Balancer (ELB)** to distribute traffic across the instances.

    c. Use Amazon EC2 Reserved Instances to ensure consistent performance and cost optimization.

    d. Leverage Amazon ElastiCache for caching frequently accessed data and offloading the application's database.

    Answer: b.

    Explanation:

    a. Incorrect. Deploying the application on a single EC2 instance with Auto Scaling would not provide high availability or fault tolerance since a single instance is a single point of failure.

    b. **Correct**. According to the AWS WAF's Reliability and Performance Efficiency pillars, the recommended approach to build a highly available and fault-tolerant architecture is to use an Auto Scaling group with multiple AZs and an ELB to distribute traffic across the instances. Using multiple AZs, your application can withstand the failure of an entire AZ without disrupting service. AZs are physically separate data centers within an AWS Region, ensuring fault tolerance and redundancy. Auto Scaling groups automatically adjust the number of EC2 instances based on defined scaling policies, allowing your application to handle dynamic traffic patterns and occasional spikes in user requests. The ELB distributes incoming traffic across the healthy EC2 instances in the Auto Scaling group, ensuring efficient load distribution and failover in case of instance failures. Auto Scaling groups allow you to scale resources up or down based on demand, optimizing costs by only running the required number of instances.

c. Incorrect. Using Amazon EC2 Reserved Instances can provide cost optimization for consistent workloads, but it does not directly address high availability, fault tolerance, or scalability requirements.
d. Incorrect. Leveraging Amazon ElastiCache for caching can improve performance and offload the application's database, but it does not address the core requirements of high availability, fault tolerance, and scalability.

2. Which of the following best defines the **Operational Excellence (Ops)** pillar of the AWS WAF?
   a. Ensuring that the system is designed to handle failures automatically and recover quickly.
   b. Enabling efficient and effective management and operation of systems to deliver business value.
   c. Protecting information, systems, and assets while delivering business value through risk assessments and mitigation strategies.
   d. Ensuring that the architecture is designed to efficiently use computing resources to meet requirements.
   e. Providing a consistent customer experience across all applications and platforms.

   Answer: b.

   Explanation:

   a. Incorrect. Ensuring that the system is designed to handle failures automatically and recover quickly is related to the Reliability pillar.
   b. **Correct**. The **Operational Excellence (Ops)** pillar of the AWS WAF focuses on efficient and effective system management and operation to deliver business value.
   c. Incorrect. Protecting information, systems, and assets while delivering business value through risk assessments and mitigation strategies is related to the Security pillar.
   d. Incorrect. Ensuring that the architecture is designed to efficiently use computing resources to meet requirements is related to the Cost Optimization pillar.
   e. Incorrect. Providing a consistent customer experience across all applications and platforms is not directly related to any specific pillar, but can be considered a general design principle.

3. Which of the following statements accurately describes the principles of the AWS WAF's Cost Optimization pillar? (Select three.)

    a. Implement cloud financial management to maximize cost-saving opportunities.
    b. Use managed services to reduce operational overhead and improve resource utilization.
    c. Continuously monitor and optimize resource usage to avoid over-provisioning.
    d. Prioritize cost optimization over performance, reliability, and security.
    e. Avoid using reserved instances and savings plans to maintain flexibility.

    Answer: a., b., and c.

    Explanation:

    a. **Correct**. The Cost Optimization pillar recommends implementing cloud financial management practices to identify cost-saving opportunities, optimize spending, and maximize the value of cloud investments.
    b. **Correct**. Leveraging managed services can help reduce operational overhead and improve resource utilization, leading to cost savings. Managed services offload responsibilities such as patching, scaling, and maintenance to AWS.
    c. **Correct**. Continuously monitoring resource usage and optimizing resources based on demand patterns can help avoid over-provisioning and reduce unnecessary costs.
    d. Incorrect. The WAF emphasizes that cost optimization should not compromise other pillars such as performance, reliability, and security. It's about optimizing costs while maintaining the desired level of operational excellence.
    e. Incorrect. The Cost Optimization pillar recommends using reserved instances and savings plans when appropriate to take advantage of pricing discounts for long-term commitments and thereby reduce costs.

4. Which of the following practices are recommended by AWS for optimizing performance efficiency in a well-architected system? (Select two.)

    a. Leveraging managed services and serverless architectures to reduce operational overhead.
    b. Implementing aggressive caching strategies across all layers of the application.
    c. Over-provisioning resources to ensure ample capacity during peak loads.

d. Regularly reviewing and adjusting resources to match current demand.
e. Deploying monolithic architectures for simplicity and ease of management.

Answer: a. and d.

Explanation:

a. **Correct.** This practice aligns with the AWS WAF's recommendation to use managed services and serverless architectures to offload operational responsibilities. By doing so, you can focus on product innovation rather than infrastructure management, which improves performance efficiency.
b. Incorrect. While caching can improve performance, this answer is too broad and may not be applicable in all scenarios. The WAF emphasizes making data-driven decisions based on workload patterns and requirements.
c. Incorrect. Over-provisioning resources can lead to underutilized capacity and increased costs, which goes against the Performance Efficiency pillar's principle of matching supply to demand.
d. **Correct.** This practice aligns with the WAF's recommendation to monitor and adjust resources based on workload demand continuously. It helps optimize resource utilization and costs, contributing to performance efficiency.
e. Incorrect. Monolithic architectures can be challenging to scale and maintain, which contradicts the Performance Efficiency pillar's principle of using modern architectural patterns that promote horizontal scaling and agility.

5. According to the AWS Well-Architected Framework, which of the following are key design principles for security in the cloud? (Select three.)

   a. Protect data in transit and at rest.
   b. Apply the principle of least privilege across all layers of the architecture.
   c. Rely solely on AWS-managed security services for comprehensive protection.
   d. Automate security event response and remediation whenever possible.
   e. Prioritize performance over security to ensure optimal application responsiveness.

Answer: a., b., and d.

Explanation:

a. **Correct.** Classify your data into sensitivity levels and use mechanisms such as encryption, tokenization, and access control where appropriate, which is a key design principle.

b. **Correct**. Applying the principle of least privilege is a recommended security practice, where users, services, and applications are granted only the minimum necessary permissions to perform their intended functions.

c. Incorrect. While AWS-managed security services are valuable, relying solely on them is not recommended. Organizations should implement a multi-layered security approach that includes both AWS-managed and customer-managed security controls.

d. **Correct**. Automating security event response and remediation is a key design principle for security, as it can help reduce the risk of human error and improve the overall security posture.

e. Incorrect. Prioritizing performance over security is generally not advisable, as it can increase the risk of security vulnerabilities and potential breaches. A balanced approach that considers both security and performance is recommended.

Summary

This chapter pieced together many technologies, best practices, and AWS services covered in the book. We weaved it all together into AWS's WAF, which you should be able to leverage and use for your projects.

You learned about AWS's WAF and how to use the AWS Well-Architected tool to validate your architecture against AWS-provided best practices. All workloads are not the same, and you learned about AWS's Well-Architected Lenses, focusing on specific workloads.

After reviewing the architecture best practices, you have hopefully convinced yourself to hop aboard the cloud train. One of the easiest ways to build credibility is to get certified. We learned that AWS offers 12 certifications, including one beta version. We learned that the most basic one is AWS Cloud Practitioner and that the most advanced certifications are Professional-level certifications. In addition, as of October 2024, we learned that there are three Specialty certifications for various domains. We also covered some of the best ways to obtain these certifications. You also explored various resources to clear certifications and land a job as a cloud solutions architect.

Finally, we hope you are now curious enough to get some of AWS's certifications. I hope you are excited about the possibilities that AWS can bring.

The next chapter will cover how the AWS infrastructure is organized and how you can leverage the cloud to drive digital transformation initiatives.

Join us on Discord

For discussions around the book and to connect with your peers, join us on Discord at `https://discord.gg/kbFRRSB2Qs` or scan the QR code below:

3

Leveraging the Cloud for Enterprise Transformation

Organizations are continuously seeking ways to innovate to stay competitive and grow their user base. Many large enterprises are leveraging the cloud to scale their operations as their business needs change. Retail giants such as Amazon utilize AWS to manage inventory and customer data, while media companies such as Netflix depend on AWS for content delivery and data analytics. General Electric uses AWS in manufacturing for data monitoring and predictive analytics in various sectors.

Financial institutions, including JP Morgan Chase and Capital One, have moved significant parts of their operations to AWS for risk analysis, customer relationship management, and secure data handling. Similarly, Expedia leverages AWS to manage global travel bookings and optimize travel experiences, showcasing how AWS supports diverse industry needs. These organizations lead in their fields due to innovations fueled by AWS technology.

AWS provides essential infrastructure services, enabling businesses to focus on their core activities and growth. By managing the complex IT backend, AWS allows companies of all sizes – from start-ups to large enterprises – to drive transformation and stay ahead in competitive markets.

In this chapter, you will begin by understanding various cloud computing models, such as **Software as a Service (SaaS)**, **Platform as a Service (PaaS)**, and **Infrastructure as a Service (IaaS)**, and how AWS complements each model with its services and infrastructure. You will also learn how today's businesses use AWS to transform their technology infrastructure, operations, and business practices completely.

In this chapter, you will learn about the following topics:

- Exploring the various cloud computing models
- Understanding the cloud migration strategies
- Driving enterprise transformation using the cloud
- Implementing an enterprise transformation program
- The AWS Cloud Adoption Framework
- Building large deals in AWS
- Architectures to provide high availability, reliability, and scalability

Without further ado, let's get down to business and learn about terms commonly used to specify how much of your infrastructure will live in the cloud versus how much will stay on-premises.

Exploring the various cloud computing models

Cloud computing allows organizations to focus on their core business and offload unwanted work, such as IT infrastructure capacity planning, procurement, and maintenance, to cloud providers.

As cloud computing has grown exponentially in recent years, different models and strategies have surfaced to help meet the specific needs of organizations and their user bases. Each type of cloud computing model provides additional flexibility and management.

There are many ways to classify cloud services, and understanding the differences helps you decide what set of services is suitable for your application workload. In this section, you will learn a common classification. Cloud services can be categorized as follows:

- IaaS
- PaaS
- SaaS

As the names indicate, each model provides a service at a different stack level.

Each of these solutions has its advantages and disadvantages. It is essential to fully understand these trade-offs to select the best option for your organization:

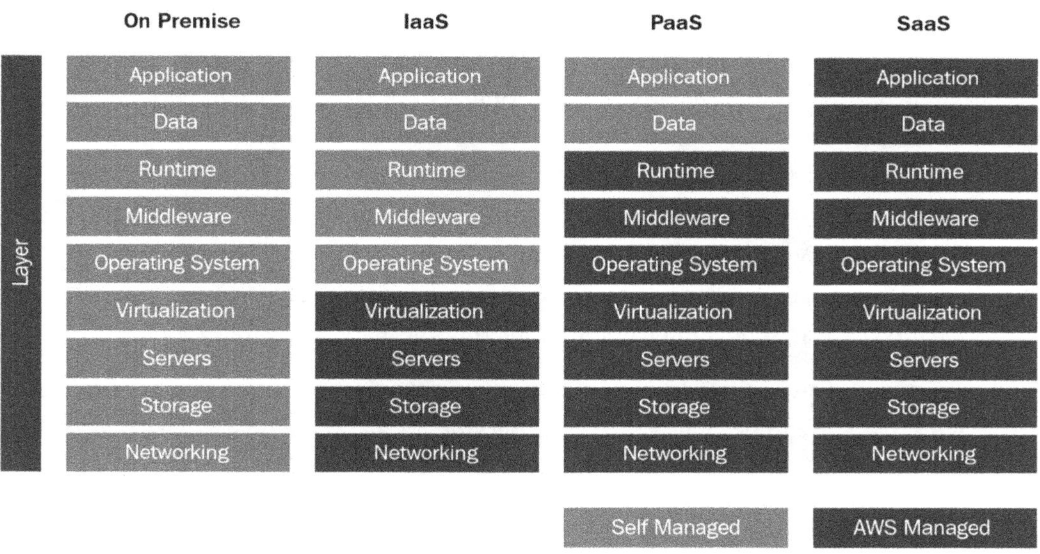

Figure 3.1: Cloud service classification

As you can see in the preceding figure, the number of services managed by you or AWS determines how the stack will be classified. On one extreme, we have an on-premises environment where all the infrastructure is in your **data center** (**DC**). Conversely, we have a SaaS architecture where all the infrastructure is on the cloud. In an **on-premises** model, the organization has full control and manages everything. With **IaaS**, AWS manages the infrastructure layers (networking, storage, servers, and virtualization) while the organization controls the operating system and above. In **PaaS**, AWS manages the platform (infrastructure, operating system, middleware, and runtime), leaving the organization to handle only the applications and data. Finally, in **SaaS**, AWS manages the entire stack, and the organization uses the application without managing any underlying components.

The following sections will explore the advantages and disadvantages of using each and provide examples of services under each classification.

On-premises

In an on-premises model, the organization manages all technology stack layers, from physical infrastructure to application. This means handling networking, storage, servers, virtualization, the operating system, middleware, runtime, data, and applications on their premises.

This setup doesn't use AWS services directly. However, organizations may use AWS tools such as **AWS Outposts** to integrate some AWS capabilities with their on-premises infrastructure, allowing them to manage on-premises data with the flexibility of the cloud. Also, backup and **Disaster Recovery (DR)** are other common use cases where on-premises customers use the cloud.

IaaS

In the IaaS model, AWS manages the core infrastructure layers, including networking, storage, servers, and virtualization. The organization controls and customizes everything from the operating upwards to the next, including middleware, runtime, data, and applications.

AWS provides services such as **Amazon Elastic Compute Cloud (EC2)** for computing power, **Amazon Simple Storage Service (S3)** for scalable storage, and **Amazon Virtual Private Cloud (VPC)** for networking. With these services, AWS takes care of the hardware, while the organization is responsible for configuring the operating system, applications, and data. This model is popular for companies that want control over their operating environment without handling the physical infrastructure.

PaaS

In the PaaS model, AWS manages more of the technology stack, taking responsibility for everything from networking to runtime. The organization only needs to manage data and the application.

AWS offers **AWS Elastic Beanstalk**, a PaaS service that allows organizations to deploy and manage applications without managing the underlying infrastructure, operating systems, or runtime. With Elastic Beanstalk, AWS handles everything up to the runtime layer so developers can focus solely on their application code and data. This model is ideal for companies that want to develop applications quickly without managing servers, operating systems, or runtime environments.

SaaS

In the SaaS model, AWS handles the entire stack, from networking to the application. The organization uses the software without managing any infrastructure, operating system, or application environment.

Examples of AWS SaaS offerings are **Amazon WorkSpaces** (for virtual desktops), **Amazon Chime** (for video conferencing), and **Amazon WorkMail** (for email services). These services allow businesses to use software applications directly without worrying about maintenance, updates, or any underlying infrastructure. This is ideal for companies that want to use ready-made applications without handling any IT management.

Let's do a side-by-side comparison of the pros and cons of each model:

Cloud Model	Pros	Cons
On-premises	• Full control over all layers • Maximum customization and optimization • Physical control over data and security • Lower latency for local data access	• High upfront costs for hardware and infrastructure • Requires dedicated IT staff for maintenance • Limited scalability, slower to adapt to demand changes • Complex disaster recovery setup needed
IaaS	• High flexibility for application needs • Fast provisioning of resources • Complete control over infrastructure • Scalable and fault-tolerant	• Security responsibility for operating system and apps • Complex migration of legacy systems • Staff training needed for infrastructure management • Potential cost overruns due to pay-as-you-go model
SaaS	• Minimal maintenance required • AWS handles upgrades and security patches • Quick setup and accessibility • Reduced operational complexity	• Limited customization and control • Complex integration with on-premises systems • Compliance challenges in highly regulated industries • Dependency on AWS for feature updates and functionality

PaaS	• Cost-effective development and testing • High availability and scalability • Reduced maintenance workload • Simplified security policies	• Integration complexity with legacy systems • Data security concerns due to third-party environment • Limited customization of infrastructure • Runtime restrictions on supported languages and frameworks

Table 3.1: Pros and cons for each cloud model

The preceding table outlines on-premises, IaaS, SaaS, and PaaS in detail, focusing on how AWS services support each model and their advantages and disadvantages. It helps organizations understand the different responsibilities and considerations for choosing a cloud model based on their needs.

Choosing between SaaS, PaaS, and IaaS

As you learned in the previous section, each cloud model, including the on-premises model, has advantages and disadvantages, and the choice between them depends on your business requirements, the specific features you need, and the skill set of your staff. For instance, if you require an out-of-the-box solution with a fast time to market, SaaS might be ideal, despite its higher costs, as it minimizes setup and maintenance efforts. On the other hand, if you operate in a regulated industry where full control over the environment is essential, you may need IaaS or even on-premises solutions to comply with regulatory constraints. AWS offers robust assurances around **Service-Level Agreements** (**SLAs**) and **compliance certifications** for each model. Still, the more of the stack you choose to manage, the greater your responsibility to ensure regulatory compliance across those components.

A general best practice is to let AWS manage as much of the infrastructure as possible, reducing your workload and focusing your resources on core business functions. Only take over management responsibilities when necessary. For example, implementing advanced load balancing or container orchestration can be resource-intensive. Instead of building and maintaining these from scratch, AWS provides **Application Load Balancing** (**ALB**) and **Elastic Kubernetes Service** (**EKS**), which offer these functionalities out of the box.

Let's take scenarios where IaaS or PaaS is preferable over SaaS:

- **Specialized requirements:** Some use cases require specific software or databases that AWS SaaS solutions don't support. For instance, if your organization already uses **Tableau** for business intelligence and has invested in licenses and custom reports, running Tableau on EC2 instances using IaaS may be more efficient than switching to a SaaS BI solution such as **Amazon QuickSight**.
- **Cost considerations:** In some cases, an application's **Total Cost of Ownership (TCO)** might be lower with IaaS or PaaS. For example, running thousands of queries daily on **Amazon Athena** (a SaaS solution) can become costly, so some users find deploying **Apache's Presto** on EC2 instances as an IaaS solution is more cost-effective. Similarly, **Amazon Redshift** as a PaaS model might be more economical than Athena for high query volumes. It's essential to calculate the TCO comprehensively, considering all relevant costs, including staffing, support, and infrastructure, beyond software fees.

Choosing between SaaS, PaaS, IaaS, and on-premises models requires balancing control, costs, and compliance. AWS solutions provide flexibility to adopt the model that best suits your needs, allowing you to hand over management to AWS wherever feasible and focus on critical business priorities. As you continue to explore AWS's offerings, understanding these options will be foundational to making the right choices in cloud architecture.

Moving forward, let's dive into cloud migration strategies to understand how to transition to these models effectively.

Understanding the cloud migration strategies

The proportion of IT spending shifting to the cloud is accelerating as system infrastructure, application software, and more are moving from traditional solutions.

Migrating to the AWS cloud makes your organization more innovative by enabling it to experiment and be agile. Your company's cloud migration truly depends on your ability to move quickly and achieve business value for your users.

By migrating your digital assets to the cloud, you can gain insights from your data, innovate faster, modernize aging infrastructure, scale globally, and restructure organizational models to create better customer experiences. Often, cost reduction is one of the primary drivers of migrating workloads to the cloud. In practice, organizations regularly see the value of migration going well beyond the cost savings from retiring legacy infrastructure.

As you have started to discover, there are other tasks you can perform in addition to migrating workflows to the cloud. What tasks should be performed and when they should be done will depend on the available budget, staff technical expertise, and leadership buy-in.

Creating distinct cohorts to classify these tasks takes a lot of work since they are done on a large scale. So, without further ado, let's attempt to create a classification. Keep in mind that this classification is not presented as conclusive. You may run into other ways to classify this migration. Additionally, you can mix and match the approaches, depending on your needs. For example, your CRM application may be moved over without changing it, but your accounting software was built in-house, and now you want to use a vendor-enabled solution such as **QuickBooks Online**.

Let's review the migration patterns, also known as "the 7 Rs," for migrating to the cloud and learn when to pick one over the others.

Cloud migration patterns – The 7 Rs

There is more than one way to handle migration. The following are the 7 Rs of cloud migration defined by AWS:

1. Rehost
2. Replatform
3. Refactor
4. Repurchase
5. Relocate
6. Retain
7. Retire

Creating a detailed strategy identifying the patterns within your workloads is essential to accelerating your cloud journey and achieving your desired business objectives. The following diagram shows the 7 Rs cloud migration model.

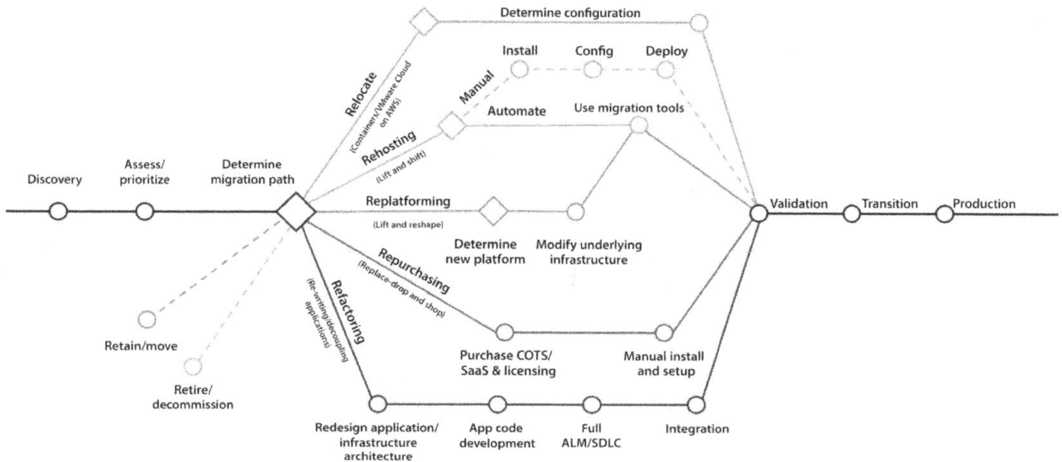

Figure 3.2: 7 Rs of AWS cloud migration (source: https://aws.amazon.com/blogs/enterprise-strategy/new-possibilities-seven-strategies-to-accelerate-your-application-migration-to-aws/)

Let's fully summarize the 7 Rs and what each migration pattern brings.

Rehost in the cloud

This method is also commonly known as *lift and shift*. With this method, you perform the least work to move your workloads to the cloud by rehosting your application in the cloud. Applications are rehosted as they are in a different environment. Services are migrated. Let's say, for example, that you are hosting a simple three-tier application on your on-premises environment that is using the following:

- A web server
- An app server
- A database server

Using the lift-and-shift strategy, you would set up three similar servers on the cloud, install the applicable software on each server, and migrate the necessary data. Therefore, this approach will have the lowest migration costs. However, this simplicity comes at a price. Any problems with the existing applications will come up during the migration. If the current applications are obsolete and suboptimal, they will remain obsolete and suboptimal.

Have you ever had to move from one house to another? It's a painful process. In broad strokes, there are two ways that you can pack for the move:

- You can just put everything in a box and move it to the new house
- You can be judicious and sort through what you have, item by item, and decide whether to toss, sell, recycle, or take the thing with you

Packing everything and going is quick because you avoid sorting through everything, but it can be more expensive because you will be moving more things, and it is painful because you may realize later that you should not have moved some items.

The move to the cloud is similar. Using the lift-and-shift strategy is good if you are confident that your processes and workflows are solid and do not need to be changed, but this is rarely the case. This approach takes everything from the on-premises DC to the cloud. However, additional work is still required, such as preparing servers, creating VPCs, and managing user access. You can automate most rehosting with AWS-provided tools such as AWS **Application Migration Service (MGN)**. You can learn more about AWS MGN here: `https://aws.amazon.com/application-migration-service/`.

The lift-and-shift approach may not always allow us to optimize the desired cost. However, it is the first step toward the cloud and is still a highly cost-effective option for many organizations. This approach is often the best choice if you want to start the migration process while getting a feel for cloud benefits. Let's look into other methods.

Replatform in the cloud

Replatforming your services to run in the cloud entails migrating the applications and changing the underlying infrastructure architecture. However, the code for higher-level services will remain the same. This way, you can leverage the existing code base, languages, and frameworks that you are currently using. It may be a good balance between taking advantage of some of the properties of the cloud, such as elasticity and scalability, without making wholesale changes to your existing applications. For example, while migrating to the cloud, you can upgrade Windows-based applications running on an older version, such as Windows Server 2008, to the latest version, such as Windows Server 2022.

It is advisable to use this method when you are comfortable with your current set of applications but want to take advantage of certain cloud advantages and functionality. For example, you can add failover to your databases without buying the software to run this setup reliably.

If you were implementing this functionality *on-premises*, you would have to own all the infrastructure. A specific example is **Oracle Data Guard**, which allows you to implement this failover, but not without having to install the product, and you need enough expertise to ensure that the product is configured correctly. Instead, when you are in a cloud environment, you can leverage the virtualization nature of the cloud, and costs can be shared with other cloud customers.

Refactor in the cloud

Refactoring allows you to rearchitecture your applications. For example, you can change your monolithic apps to a more modular microservice-based architecture and make them cloud-native serverless applications. Refactoring is an advanced approach that adds agility and innovation to your business to meet user demand.

The refactoring approach will enable you to fully utilize all cloud features. This will allow you to use state-of-the-art technologies to create new services and reinvent your existing business workflows. There will be considerable work to accomplish this rewrite. In many cases, especially for established enterprises that new start-ups disrupt, they will soon be relegated to a historical footnote if they don't reinvent themselves.

This approach allows you to make wholesale changes and start from scratch to create new applications and workflows. It is essential to have subject matter experts and business experts involved in the design process because you may want to change how you do business and suspend all your current beliefs about how things should be done. Overall, migration is a long process and requires the involvement of application developers, business stakeholders, infrastructure engineers, security experts, and so on. Collaboration between different teams in organizations is necessary because significant changes to apps and infrastructure are critical for success.

Revise before migrating to the cloud

Another potential strategy is to modify, optimize, and enhance the existing applications and code base before migrating to the cloud in preparation for doing so. Only then do you rehost or refactor the applications to the cloud. This may be a good strategy and provide business continuity and enhancement in the long run. The downside of this approach is the cost associated with changing and testing the code upfront. In addition, changing the code in the on-premises environment may only allow you to take advantage of some of the features that creating the code in the cloud would offer, for example, creating reports using **AWS QuickSight**. AWS QuickSight is an excellent tool for creating dashboards and reports. However, AWS QuickSight can only be used in a cloud environment, not in your on-premises environment, because QuickSight is only supported within AWS.

This method suits you when you know your applications are suboptimal and need revision. You take cloud migration as an opportunity to enhance and fix your applications. Using this approach, you will only need to test your application once. The drawback is that if things go south, it may be challenging to ascertain whether the problems that arise are because of new bugs in the code or because you migrated to the cloud.

Repurchase in the cloud

Repurchase replaces your existing environment and is known as *drop and shop*; you drop legacy applications and purchase more cloud-native software in the repurchase. So, with this method, instead of rebuilding your applications, you get rid of them and replace them with commercially available SaaS alternatives such as **Salesforce**, **Workday**, **ServiceNow**, **Datadog for observability**, or **SAP**. Depending on how deep and skilled your talent pool is and their areas of expertise, this option may be more expensive than rebuilding your application.

Using this option, your software costs will likely be higher, but this will be offset by lower development and maintenance costs. If you decide to rebuild, you will not have to pay for CRM and commercial software licenses, but development cycles will likely be longer. You will have fewer defects, and higher maintenance may apply.

The previous methods of migration implied that all development was done in-house. One difference with the repurchase approach is that you are migrating from in-house systems to software built by professional vendors. As with the other methods, this approach has advantages and disadvantages. One of the advantages is that the learning curve and the development life cycle will be shortened, whereas in other methods, more development will be needed. However, a disadvantage is that the software will require additional licenses and drive the adoption of new solutions that the company may not have used earlier.

Relocate to the cloud

The relocation method allows you to move your applications to the cloud without any changes. For example, you can relocate VMware-based on-premises applications to AWS without any changes. It will also help maintain consistent operations between VMware and the AWS cloud.

Overall, the cloud approach, where you focus on a pay-as-you-go model and reduce CapEx, will help you to reduce the TCO as you move to operational costs from upfront capital investment. After moving to the cloud, you can optimize the cloud resources to utilize the various AWS services. You can add advanced features such as data engineering, machine learning, containerization, and mobility capabilities backed by the power of AWS.

Retain on-premises

The retain method means doing nothing for now and leaving your on-premises workload as is. You may decide to keep your application on-premises because it is nearing the end of its life or because it's too complex to move now. For example, organizations often decide to retain mainframe applications because they have decades of tech debt that no one knows how to migrate, and they need more planning.

Another example is enterprises that want to keep their applications on-premises and near to users due to the need for ultra-low latency or because of compliance regions, especially in the finance industry. In those cases, retaining your application on-premises and working with a hybrid cloud may be the best solution.

Retire

Finally, while analyzing your workload for cloud migration, you may realize that many servers are running unutilized or have decided to replace the existing application with cloud-native software.

The retire method involves decommissioning unwanted portions of your IT workload. During the discovery phase of your migration, you may encounter applications that are no longer being used. By rationalizing your IT portfolio, you can identify assets that are no longer valuable and can be turned off. This will strengthen your business case and direct your team toward maintaining the more widely used resources.

AWS provides prescriptive guidance to help you plan and decide which migration strategy will fit your workload. You can refer to the AWS guide at `https://docs.aws.amazon.com/prescriptive-guidance/latest/application-portfolio-assessment-guide/prioritization-and-migration-strategy.html` to customize the flow for your enterprise on-premises workload while working on migration planning. Let's look into some AWS tools to help you with cloud migration.

AWS cloud migration tools

You don't have to reinvent the wheel as you migrate your workloads and projects from your current environment to the cloud. As you can imagine, many others have already started this journey. AWS and third-party vendors offer various tools to facilitate this process. A few examples of services and tools that are worth exploring are as follows.

AWS Application Migration Services (MGN)

AWS MGN (`https://aws.amazon.com/application-migration-service/`) is a popular service designed for the automated migration of applications to AWS. MGN is a robust solution for migrating applications to AWS with minimal downtime and automation. It simplifies cloud migration by automating much of the process, allowing organizations to move applications without significant changes. For example, a financial institution looking to migrate its on-premises applications to AWS can leverage AWS MGN to replicate workloads in the cloud. By installing the AWS MGN agent on source servers, the bank can ensure real-time data replication. Before the migration, the IT team can test instances to verify application performance before making the final switch.

Migration Evaluator (ME)

ME (`https://aws.amazon.com/migration-evaluator/`) helps assess and plan migrations by providing detailed insights and evaluation tools. ME helps businesses plan and optimize their migration journey by providing detailed assessments of costs and performance before moving to AWS. For example, a retail company wanting to shift its e-commerce platform from an on-premises DC to AWS can use ME to evaluate the cost benefits of different migration strategies. The company can also use ME's application dependency mapping feature to ensure that no critical services are left behind during migration.

Application Discovery Service (ADS) and Migration Hub

ADS (`https://aws.amazon.com/application-discovery/`) and **Migration Hub** (`https://aws.amazon.com/migration-hub/`) help organizations plan and manage migrations with deep insights and centralized control. ADS collects and visualizes data on network dependencies, while Migration Hub offers a unified dashboard to track migration progress. For example, a healthcare provider planning to move patient record systems to AWS can use ADS to visualize network dependencies and Migration Hub to centrally monitor all migration tasks across multiple AWS accounts.

Mainframe Modernization

Mainframe Modernization (`https://aws.amazon.com/mainframe-modernization/`) aims to simplify the migration and modernization of mainframe applications. Mainframe Modernization in AWS enables businesses to transition from traditional mainframe systems to cloud-based architectures. It offers automated tools for assessment, migration, and post-migration enhancements.

For example, a government agency looking to modernize its legacy mainframe systems can leverage AWS Mainframe Modernization to migrate COBOL-based applications to a cloud-native environment. This shift allows for better scalability and integration with modern cloud services such as AI-powered analytics.

AWS Database Migration Service (DMS)

AWS DMS (`https://aws.amazon.com/dms/`) facilitates migrations between on-premises and AWS-based databases. AWS DMS simplifies database migrations by supporting homogeneous (e.g., MySQL to MySQL) and heterogeneous (e.g., Oracle to Amazon Aurora) migrations with minimal downtime. For example, an online travel agency using an Oracle database on-premises wants to transition to Amazon Aurora. AWS DMS can continuously replicate data from Oracle to Aurora, allowing the agency to keep both databases in sync until the final cutover, ensuring no data loss or downtime.

This is a partial list. Many other AWS and third-party services can assist in your migration. The complete list can be found on the AWS migration page: `https://aws.amazon.com/free/migration/`.

AWS Migration Acceleration Program (MAP)

AWS MAP (`https://aws.amazon.com/migration-acceleration-program/`) is a structured, comprehensive program created by AWS organizations to accelerate their migration to the AWS cloud. AWS MAP provides businesses with financial incentives, technical guidance, and expert support to help streamline the migration process, reduce associated risks, and build strong cloud adoption practices. It's particularly beneficial for organizations undertaking large-scale migrations, such as moving entire DCs or critical applications to the cloud.

AWS uses a three-phase approach that integrates modernization into the migration transition. This process and the seven migration patterns help provide the guiding principles for structuring the cloud migration journey so you can quickly realize continuous, quantifiable business value. Let's look at this pattern in the three-phase migration process.

The three-phase migration process

The AWS cloud migration project typically executes in three phases, from discovery to building cloud readiness and finally migrating to the cloud. The following are the three phases of cloud migration:

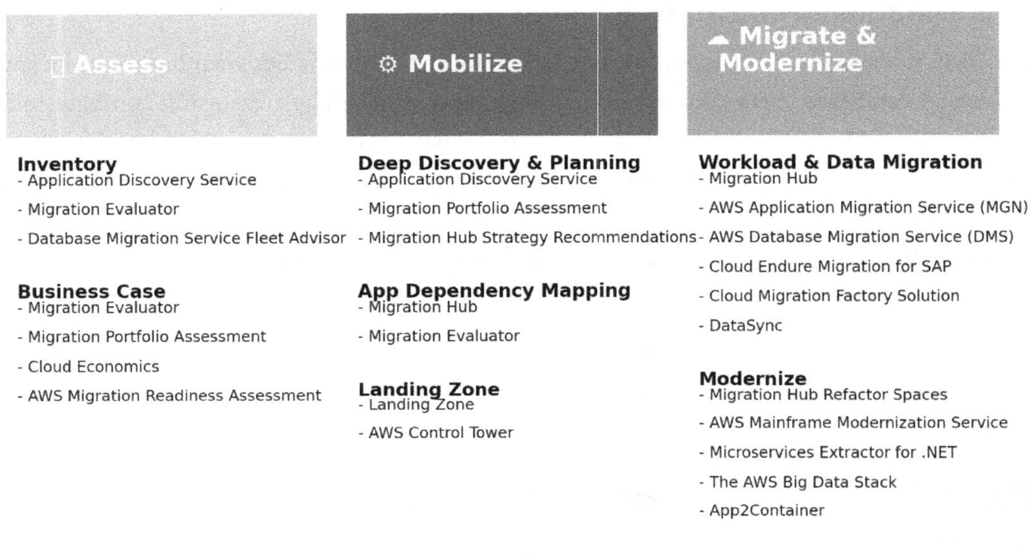

Assess
Mobilize
Migrate & Modernize
Inventory
- Application Discovery Service
- Migration Evaluator
- Database Migration Service Fleet Advisor
Business Case
- Migration Evaluator
- Migration Portfolio Assessment
- Cloud Economics
- AWS Migration Readiness Assessment
Deep Discovery & Planning
- Application Discovery Service
- Migration Portfolio Assessment
- Migration Hub Strategy Recommendations
App Dependency Mapping
- Migration Hub
- Migration Evaluator
Landing Zone
- Landing Zone
- AWS Control Tower
Workload & Data Migration
- Migration Hub
- AWS Application Migration Service (MGN)
- AWS Database Migration Service (DMS)
- Cloud Endure Migration for SAP
- Cloud Migration Factory Solution
- DataSync
Modernize
- Migration Hub Refactor Spaces
- AWS Mainframe Modernization Service
- Microservices Extractor for .NET
- The AWS Big Data Stack
- App2Container

Figure 3.3: AWS MAP phases

The preceding diagram illustrates the three main phases of cloud migration: **Assessment**, **Mobilize**, and **Migrate & Modernize**, which align well with the steps outlined for a comprehensive AWS migration strategy. Here's how each phase in the diagram corresponds to the migration steps:

- **Assessment phase**: The **Assessment** phase in the diagram represents the first critical step in a cloud migration journey. AWS services such as **Migration Evaluator** (originally developed after AWS acquired TSO Logic) and **ADS** are essential in evaluating existing on-premises workloads. These tools gather data about current workloads and calculate projected costs and savings, supporting businesses in defining a clear business case for cloud migration. During this phase, the **Inventory** and **Business Case** categories in the diagram emphasize collecting workload data and projecting costs, which provide the foundational insights needed for the **Migration Readiness Assessment** (**MRA**) and cloud readiness analysis. AWS's **Cloud Adoption Framework** (**CAF**) also fits here, guiding organizations to plan a migration strategy by addressing licensing, server dependencies, and overall cloud feasibility.

- **Mobilize phase**: After building the initial assessment, the **Mobilize** phase focuses on addressing gaps identified in the evaluation, such as cloud skills, account setup, and foundational environments. In this phase, as shown in the diagram, the **App Dependency Mapping** and **Landing Zone** categories represent crucial steps for building a stable cloud environment and structuring user accounts through tools such as **AWS Landing Zone** and **AWS Control Tower**. AWS **Migration Hub** is highlighted in this phase, providing a centralized platform to manage and track migration processes, simplifying application dependencies and migration workflows across multiple tools. This phase is also where AWS's **Cloud Adoption Readiness Tool** (**CART**) supports planning and gap analysis, helping organizations achieve operational cloud readiness.
- **Migrate & Modernize phase**: With a solid cloud foundation from the **Mobilize** phase, the **Migrate & Modernize** phase involves migrating workloads to AWS and optimizing applications for the cloud. The **Workload & Data Migration** category in the diagram represents tools such as AWS MGN and AWS DMS, which facilitate moving applications and databases with minimal downtime. Following the initial migration, the **Modernize** category illustrates services for refactoring and rearchitecting applications to fully leverage AWS's cloud-native benefits, such as serverless computing and microservices. The diagram's approach supports AWS's recommended two-step method: initially performing a lift-and-shift migration and later modernizing workloads by rearchitecting them to unlock additional cloud efficiencies.

AWS provides a structured view of each phase's tools and services, making it clear how AWS supports organizations through each step of the migration process – from initial feasibility assessments to skill-building and foundational setup to executing migrations and modernizing applications. Each phase ensures a seamless and adaptable cloud migration journey on AWS.

You can refer to AWS's prescriptive guidance to learn about the preceding three-phase cloud migration approach in detail: `https://docs.aws.amazon.com/prescriptive-guidance/latest/large-migration-guide/phases.html`. These phases are standard guidelines for successful cloud migration; however, each organization may have varying needs, and these guidelines are not set in stone.

Now that you have reviewed the different ways to migrate to the cloud, let's understand why you might want to do so. You will gain this understanding by learning about the concept of enterprise transformation. Let's dive deeper into how organizations leverage enterprise transformation using the cloud model.

Driving enterprise transformation using the cloud

As a seasoned **Solution Architect (SA)**, your role goes beyond deep technical expertise; you're expected to catalyze enterprise transformation, creating measurable value for the organization through technology solutions. This requires technical understanding and an ability to align diverse business and technical stakeholders, ensuring that cloud adoption drives tangible improvements across the enterprise.

Understanding your key stakeholders is essential when considering cloud-driven transformation for an entire company. Stakeholders may include the following:

- **Technical stakeholders**: Focused on building for scale, ensuring security and compliance, and driving efficient execution
- **Business stakeholders**: Concerned with strategic direction, disciplined execution, and leveraging the cloud to reduce risk and justify the investment of time and resources

Once you've identified and aligned your stakeholders, it's time to understand what enterprise transformation means for the organization. To guide this understanding, ask yourself the following key questions:

- **What is the value creation for my customer?** This question centers on the value that cloud providers such as AWS can deliver to your business and its customers. Value creation should be measurable and resonate with all stakeholders' goals.
- **What drives success?** Identify the factors or patterns that promote success. These could include reliable processes, effective communication, or security measures. From a risk perspective, consider what might obstruct progress if these success drivers are absent.
- **Which business model should we follow?** Success in cloud transformation involves aligning business and technology toward a unified customer focus. Identify and ensure that both business and tech teams operate in harmony, pursuing a shared objective of enhancing the customer experience.
- **How can the cloud help?** What kind of cloud providers have experience and scalability backed by enterprise-level orchestration expertise and tools available to execute transformative initiatives?

Let's dive deeper into how each of these questions shapes enterprise transformation.

Creating value for customers

Creating value for your customers is essential for the success of any business. By focusing on key areas such as customer experience, speed to market, time to revenue, and cost efficiency, you can achieve meaningful results that resonate with your customers:

- **Differentiated customer experiences**: Enhancing how customers interact with your products or services can significantly boost satisfaction and loyalty. For example, **Neiman Marcus**, a luxury retailer, developed Connect, an omnichannel digital selling application using AWS services. This app empowers associates to access personalized customer information, elevating the shopping experience and maintaining high service standards, especially during increased online shopping periods. You can find details here: `https://aws.amazon.com/solutions/case-studies/neimanmarcus-case-study/`.
- **Increased speed to market**: Bringing new products or services to customers quickly is crucial in today's fast-paced market. **Itau**, Latin America's largest bank, improved its speed to market for machine learning models by adopting Amazon SageMaker Studio. This transition reduced deployment times from 6 months to just 3–5 days, allowing the bank to respond swiftly to customer needs and market changes. You can find more details here: `https://aws.amazon.com/solutions/case-studies/itau-ml-case-study/`.
- **Faster time to revenue**: Reducing the time between a customer's decision to purchase and the actual revenue recognition is vital for business growth. **Vanguard**, a leading investment management company, utilized AWS services such as Amazon ECS and AWS Fargate to enhance its application deployment processes. This improvement shortened the development cycle from 3 months to 24 hours, enabling faster delivery of services to clients and quicker revenue generation. You can find more details here: `https://aws.amazon.com/solutions/case-studies/vanguard-ecs-fargate-case-study/`.
- **Improved cost efficiency**: Optimizing operations to reduce costs while maintaining quality is a key aspect of creating value. **Marketing Evolution**, an advertising analytics company, built an innovative measurement and attribution solution on AWS. By utilizing AWS Glue and other serverless solutions, the company achieved an 85% reduction in compute costs and a 40% decrease in labor costs, allowing them to reinvest savings into new product development. You can find more details here: `https://aws.amazon.com/solutions/case-studies/marketing-evolution-case-study/`.

Success factors for enterprise transformation

Achieving successful enterprise transformation in the cloud involves focusing on several key factors. By understanding and implementing these, you can effectively navigate your cloud journey and deliver sustained value to your customers:

- **Customer-focused approach**: Prioritizing your customers' needs is crucial. By centering your initiatives around customer requirements, you can make swift, high-quality decisions that enhance value delivery. For example, Amazon's **Working Backwards** process starts with a press release written as if the product has already been launched, ensuring that development is customer-centric from the beginning.
- **High-quality, rapid decision-making**: Breaking down broad objectives into smaller, manageable initiatives allows for timely decisions aligned with your organization's vision. This approach facilitates incremental value creation and keeps your team focused on strategic goals. At Amazon, small, decentralized "two-pizza" teams (teams small enough to be fed by two pizzas) are empowered to make quick decisions, fostering agility and innovation.
- **Culture of experimentation**: Encouraging experimentation empowers your team to test new ideas and innovate. With a foundation of quality decision-making, manageable experimentation fosters learning and progress through iterative adjustments. Amazon's culture embraces experimentation, understanding that failure is a natural part of innovation, leading to more successful outcomes over time.
- **Embracing failure**: Recognizing that obstacles and setbacks are part of the transformation journey is crucial. Lessons learned from challenges inform better future decisions. By focusing on customer needs and incremental value, your team can address and resolve issues promptly, adopting a "two-way door" concept where reversible decisions allow for quicker course corrections.
- **Organizational agility**: Structuring your enterprise flexibly ensures that all functions contribute to long-term customer value. An agile organization can adapt to changing market conditions and customer demands more effectively, facilitating continuous improvement and responsiveness. Amazon's use of adaptive practices enables "think big" interactions to address complex problems, fostering an environment that supports rapid innovation.
- **Team autonomy**: Empowering small, cross-functional teams representing all necessary departments – such as technology, sales, finance, business operations, and compliance – to work autonomously toward customer-driven objectives supports faster decision-making and greater accountability. This structure enhances your organization's ability to respond swiftly to opportunities and challenges. Amazon's "two-pizza" teams operate with a high degree of autonomy, allowing them to innovate and deliver customer value rapidly.

- **Focus on long-term value**: Concentrating on long-term value for customers sustains the transformation journey. A long-term perspective helps your organization prepare for and navigate both anticipated and unforeseen challenges, including global disruptions. This focus ensures that short-term challenges do not detract from larger objectives, maintaining a steady course toward sustained success. Amazon's emphasis on durable customer needs, such as price, selection, and convenience, has led to innovations such as **Amazon Prime**, continually adding value for customers over time.

Modern business model for customer-centric transformation

In a cloud-enabled enterprise, achieving customer-centric outcomes requires a business model shift that integrates business and technology objectives. You must adopt a **converged business model** that unites business and technology efforts, enabling organizations to make swift, high-quality decisions focused on customer impact.

To fully realize the value of cloud adoption, enterprises need to transform their technology operations and how they organize and deliver value across all business domains. This transformation shifts the focus from activity-based, project-oriented models to customer-centered, outcome-based models. In this setup, IT and business teams collaborate closely to prioritize and deliver customer value.

This transformation is possible through three primary workstreams encompassing the core aspects of enterprise value: **innovation**, **insights**, and **modernization**.

- The **innovation** workstream organizes business and technical teams to deliver meaningful innovations that align closely with customer needs. By employing cross-functional, autonomous teams, companies gain a well-rounded perspective on customer requirements, accelerating the innovation process from ideation through delivery. This approach enables organizations to speed up ideation and product development cycles, deliver compelling new offerings, and reduce the time to market for new products and services. For example, **Metro Retail Stores Group** in the Philippines partnered with AWS to enhance its digital capabilities, leading to improved customer experiences and operational efficiency. You can find more details here: `https://aws.amazon.com/awstv/watch/ecbee1083a0/`.

- The **insights** workstream leverages data to guide strategic decision-making and enhance the customer experience. By transforming into a data-driven enterprise, organizations can ensure that data insights at every level consistently inform decisions. This workstream enables businesses to gain scalable insights into customer behaviors and preferences, ultimately driving greater organizational efficiency through data-driven optimizations. For instance, **Coca-Cola** improved its operational performance by using AWS IoT SiteWise to gain real-time insights into its production processes, leading to better decision-making and efficiency. You can find more details here: `https://aws.amazon.com/solutions/case-studies/innovators/coca-cola/`.
- The **modernization** workstream extends beyond updating the technology stack; it focuses on refining business processes to improve customer service and optimize core operations. Modernization efforts encompass updating workflows, implementing digital solutions that enhance customer interactions, and deploying tools that support core business functions. When possible, AWS's **Solutions Library** is used to accelerate innovation by leveraging pre-built solutions, minimizing the need to start from scratch. For example, **Liberty Mutual** adopted a serverless-first approach using AWS, reducing costs and improving time to market, which enhanced customer experiences. You can find more details here: `https://aws.amazon.com/solutions/case-studies/liberty-mutual-case-study/`.

Together, these three workstreams form the foundation of the cloud transformation approach, empowering organizations to create value for their customers through continuous improvement and operational excellence. Now, let's learn about implementing enterprise digital transformation.

Implementing an enterprise digital transformation program

As you can imagine, digital transformation can be challenging, especially for large enterprises with a long history of using old technologies and making significant investments in them. Deciding to start migrating applications and on-premises services to the cloud is a decision that takes time. A complete migration will likely take years and potentially cost millions of dollars in migration, transformation, and testing costs.

For this reason, important decisions need to be made along the way. Some of the most critical decisions that need to be made are as follows:

- Should you perform the bare minimum of tasks to achieve the migration, or do you want to use this change as an opportunity to refactor, enhance, and optimize your services? Doing the bare minimum (only migrating your workloads to the cloud) will mean that any problems and deficiencies in the current environment will be transferred to the new environment.
- Should the migration be purely technological, or should you use this opportunity to transform current business processes? You could thoroughly assess how your organization does business today and determine how to improve it. This will create efficiencies, cut costs, and increase customer satisfaction. It also sets up the organization to scale for future growth with minimal effort. However, this option will inherently have a higher upfront cost and may not work.

In this section, you will start learning the primary strategies for migration to the cloud and weigh up some of the options. It explains why and how you may want to undertake a digital transformation and the benefits and pitfalls that can come with this.

What exactly is an enterprise digital transformation?

The term "digital transformation" is complex and harder to define because it is overloaded to the point that it has become a nebulous concept. Like many technology trends, it is overhyped and overused.

According to the **International Data Corporation** (IDC), worldwide spending on **Digital Transformation (DX)** is projected to reach almost $4 trillion by 2027, with a **Compound Annual Growth Rate (CAGR)** of 16.2% over the 2022–2027 forecast period. You can find the full IDC report here: `https://www.idc.com/getdoc.jsp?containerId=prUS52305724`.

The term "digital transformation" has become something that means platform modernization, including migrating on-premises infrastructure to the cloud. You can blame CIOs, consultants, and third-party vendors for this confusion. They all try to convince the C-suite that their solution can cover today's enterprise infrastructure and business requirements.

However, savvy high-level executives understand that there is no magic bullet and that a digital transformation will require planning, strategizing, testing, and much effort.

Let's nail it down and define it.

Digital Transformation Definition

Digital transformation involves using the cloud and other advanced technology to create new or change existing business flows. It often involves changing the company culture to adapt to this new business type. The end goal of digital transformation is to enhance the customer experience and to meet ever-changing business and market demand. Now, cloud migration is an essential part of digital transformation.

A digital transformation is an opportunity to reconsider everything, including the following:

- The current structure of teams and departments
- Current business flows
- The way new functionality is developed

For a digital transformation to succeed, it should be broader than one aspect of the business, such as marketing, operations, or finance. It should eventually be all-encompassing and cover the whole gamut of how you engage with your customers. It should be an opportunity to completely transform how you interact with your potential and existing customers. It should go beyond simply swapping one server in one location for another, more powerful or cheaper one in the cloud.

In some regards, start-ups have a big advantage over their more significant, established rivals because they can learn and reimagine their processes. Start-ups have a clean slate that can be filled with anything from AWS's 240+ services and other technologies. Existing players must wipe the slate clean while keeping their existing client base and finding a way to keep the trains running while performing their digital transformations.

Digital transformation goes well beyond changing an enterprise's technology infrastructure. For a digital transformation to be successful, it must also involve rethinking processes, using your staff in new ways, and fundamentally changing how business is done.

Disruptive technological change is usually undertaken to pursue new revenue sources or increase profits by creating efficiencies. Today's customers continue to raise the bar of expectations, driven by so many successful businesses that have delivered on the execution of their digital transformations.

In the next section, you will learn about some of the forces that push companies to adopt digital transformation. The status quo is a powerful state. Most companies will find it challenging to move from what's already working, even though they may realize that the current approach could be better. It usually takes significant pressure to finally bite the bullet and migrate to the cloud.

Enterprise digital transformation examples

Digital transformation, when focused on delivering tangible, positive business outcomes, drives long-term success. Innovation in the business world must connect to measurable improvements, such as increased sales, enhanced efficiency, or greater profitability. Digital transformation is more than just migrating operations to the cloud; it involves rethinking and updating processes and often integrating new technologies such as generative AI, robotics, the **Internet of Things (IoT)**, blockchain, advanced analytics, and machine learning. The following are some of the examples listed by AWS:

- **McDonald's**: McDonald's leverages AWS to drive a cloud-enabled digital transformation. Through AWS services such as **Amazon Redshift** and **Amazon EMR**, McDonald's has scaled its digital capabilities, implementing kiosks, digital menu boards, mobile ordering, and personalized drive-thru experiences. This transformation has improved performance and enhanced customer interactions (`https://aws.amazon.com/solutions/case-studies/mcdonalds/`).
- **Takeda Pharmaceuticals**: Takeda transformed its IT infrastructure by migrating over 600 applications to AWS. This migration allowed the company to close most of its DCs, enhance operational agility, and foster innovation. It included setting up secure, collaborative environments to support initiatives such as the CoVIg-19 Plasma Alliance for COVID-19 treatment (`https://aws.amazon.com/solutions/case-studies/takeda-case-study/`).
- **National Australia Bank (NAB)**: NAB undertook a digital transformation with AWS, migrating hundreds of applications to the cloud and establishing cloud fluency across its workforce. AWS Managed Services, Professional Services, and training programs significantly built NAB's cloud capabilities, resulting in enhanced customer service with high availability and security (`https://aws.amazon.com/solutions/case-studies/national-australia-bank-digital-transformation-case-study/`).
- **Swire Coca-Cola**: Swire Coca-Cola migrated its entire IT infrastructure, including SAP and CRM systems, to AWS. This transformation allowed the company to shut down legacy DCs, reduce resource provisioning times, and adopt new technologies such as IoT and AI, which enhance responsiveness to business demands (`https://aws.amazon.com/solutions/case-studies/swire-coca-cola/`).

These examples highlight how companies leverage AWS for digital transformation, improving efficiency, enhancing customer service, and driving innovation.

What are some best practices when implementing a digital transformation? In the next section, we will help you navigate so that your digital transformation project is successful, regardless of how complicated it may be.

Enterprise digital transformation tips

Digital transformation can take many forms, but some approaches are more effective. Here are actionable tips to streamline implementation and reduce disruption:

- **Ask the right questions**: Don't just focus on doing things faster – consider how to fundamentally change operations to serve customers better. Key questions include: "How can we enhance customer outcomes?", "What processes could we eliminate?", "What are the desired business outcomes?", and "How are our competitors evolving?" A thorough understanding of the customer journey is crucial.
- **Get leadership buy-in**: Transformation efforts are more successful when supported from the top down. Without C-suite commitment, cloud adoption may be confined to isolated departments without enterprise-wide impact. Start with a **proof of concept** in one area, gather results, and then expand to other departments once business outcomes are validated.
- **Delineate clear objectives**: Your transformation goals must remain clear even in agile environments. Define whether the objective is to lift and shift workflows or to merge systems following a merger. Prioritize completing each transformation goal before branching out to new initiatives.
- **Apply agile methodology**: Adopt an agile, adaptive design. This enables quick course adjustments and resource allocation based on impact and avoids long waits to realize results. Focus on small, incremental wins ("singles") rather than massive overhauls ("home runs") to demonstrate early value, gain support, and secure additional resources.
- **Encourage risk-taking**: Foster a culture of "failing fast." Small, manageable risks can help refine ideas quickly without extensive time loss. Early experimentation can deliver valuable insights, allowing you to learn and adapt without derailing the entire project.
- **Use one-way versus two-way door decisions**: Classify decisions as one-way (irreversible) or two-way (reversible). Prioritize two-way door decisions, where you can easily backtrack if needed. Conduct a detailed risk analysis for one-way choices, such as moving a customer-facing platform to the cloud, as reversing this could be highly impactful.

- **Define roles and responsibilities clearly**: Ensure all team members have defined roles and no skill gaps. Seek a balanced team with experts in cloud migration and digital transformation alongside engineers and analysts who can execute the strategy. Roles may include software engineers, cloud specialists, data scientists, SAs, and DevOps administrators. Attracting skilled talent in these areas is critical to your transformation's success.

These tips provide a structured approach to digital transformation that encourages agility, clarity, and alignment across teams. In the next section, we'll explore common pitfalls and strategies to avoid them for a smoother transformation journey.

Enterprise digital transformation pitfalls

There are countless ways for digital transformation initiatives to fail. Recognizing common pitfalls can help avoid missteps along the way. Here are some frequent reasons digital transformations don't succeed:

- **Lack of commitment from the C-suite**: Even when the CEO expresses commitment to transformation, success depends on a clear vision, direction, and resource allocation. Without full backing from leadership, transformation efforts often stall.
- **Not having the right team in place**: It's critical to have skilled personnel who understand the nuances of digital transformation. Engaging people with relevant experience – in-house or through consulting partners such as the **AWS Partner Network** (**APN**) – significantly increases success rates. Attempting to reinvent the wheel or lacking the right expertise can quickly derail an initiative.
- **Internal resistance**: Transformations often bring personnel changes, leading to friction. For instance, moving workloads to the cloud might reduce the need for on-premises administrators, causing resistance from affected staff. Open communication about training, the migration process, and new responsibilities helps alleviate resistance and ensures smoother adoption.
- **Moving too fast**: Moving too quickly can lead to costly mistakes. It's essential to test concepts on a small scale before scaling enterprise-wide. For example, migrating a handful of databases before tackling all of them enables learning and refinement without large-scale risks. Remember to distinguish between "one-way" and "two-way" decisions to mitigate irreversible missteps.
- **Going too slow**: After initial success in specific departments, over-cautious pacing can be equally detrimental. Once a template is proven, accelerate adoption across the organization to maintain a competitive edge. Gradual rollouts can limit agility and allow competitors to gain ground.

- **Outdated rules and regulations:** Regulatory constraints can also hinder transformation. For example, the real estate industry's reliance on physical documents and wet signatures limits the adoption of digital solutions such as blockchain. In other cases, as with some online pharmacies, outdated methods (such as requiring faxed prescriptions) restrict the effectiveness of modern technology investments.

By anticipating and navigating these pitfalls, companies can improve their chances of successful digital transformation. AWS's CAF offers guidance to help organizations start on the right foot and avoid these common traps.

The AWS Cloud Adoption Framework (CAF)

As discussed in the previous section, cloud adoption has some critical pitfalls. Thing may have started well for the organization with the pilot but they could not move it further, or tech leadership may need to be aligned to focus on cloud modernization. In some cases, even if an organization migrates to the cloud, it cannot realize its full value, as replicating the on-premises model to the cloud can fail to reduce costs or increase flexibility. To help customers overcome these pitfalls, AWS designed the CAF by applying their learning across thousands of customers who had completed their cloud migration to AWS.

The AWS CAF is a mechanism for establishing a shared mental model for cloud transformation. It utilizes AWS's experience and best practices to enable customers to build business transformation in the cloud. It further helps validate and improve cloud readiness while evolving your cloud adoption roadmaps.

The CAF helps to identify business outcomes such as risk, performance, revenue, and operational productivity. The following diagram provides a full view of the AWS CAF:

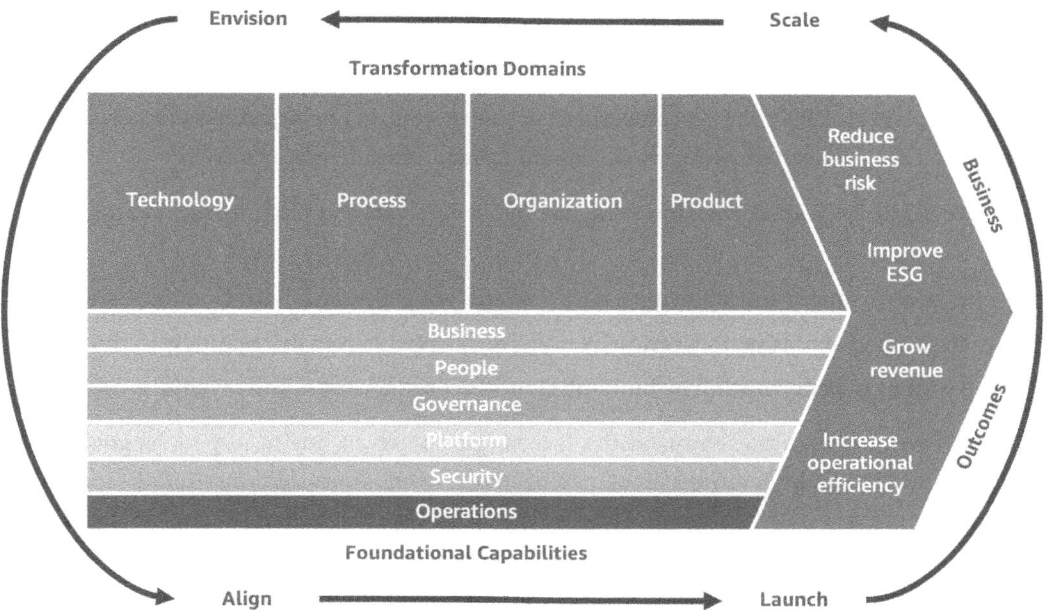

Figure 3.4: AWS CAF (source: https://aws.amazon.com/blogs/aws/aws-cloud-adoption-framework-caf-3-0-is-now-available/)

As shown in the preceding diagram, the AWS CAF proposes four incremental and iterative phases for organizations to succeed in their digital transformation journey:

- **Envision**: Understand business transformation opportunities with your strategic goals and seek buy-in from senior executives to drive change. Define quantified business outcomes to drive value.
- **Align**: Identify gaps and dependencies across the organization to create a plan for cloud readiness and drive stakeholder alignment at all organizational levels.
- **Launch**: Build a proof of concept and deliver impactful, successful pilots that can define future directions. Adjust your approach from pilot projects to build a production plan.
- **Scale**: Scale pilots to take it to production and realize continuous business value.

You can learn more about the AWS CAF by visiting the following page: `https://aws.amazon.com/cloud-adoption-framework/`.

Further, the AWS CAF identifies four transformation domains that help customers accelerate their business outcomes. The following are the digital transformation opportunities:

- **Technology transformation** using a cloud migration and modernization approach in the cloud
- **Process transformation** using a data and analytics approach with cloud technology
- **Organizational transformation** by building an efficient operating model in the cloud
- **Product transformation** by building cloud-focused business and revenue models

The AWS CAF organizes these capabilities into six perspectives: business, people, governance, platform, security, and operations. Each perspective encompasses a distinct set of capabilities managed by various stakeholders involved in the cloud transformation process. By leveraging these capabilities, organizations can improve their cloud readiness and transform their operations effectively.

Every organization's cloud journey is unique. Organizations must define their desired cloud transformation state to succeed in their transformations, understand cloud readiness, and close the gaps. However, driving digital transformation through cloud adoption has been in practice for a while, and many organizations have already implemented it. So, you don't need to reinvent the wheel and can take advantage of the learning offered by AWS.

Building large deals in AWS

When discussing enterprise transformation, the conversation often leads to large, strategic deals ranging from multi-million to billion-dollar engagements for your organization. As an SA, understanding the dynamics of these large deals and effectively crafting solutions that align technical and business objectives can be incredibly valuable.

Large, strategic deals go beyond just implementing technology – they involve reshaping business processes, improving customer outcomes, and achieving measurable results.

What are large deals?

A **large deal** represents a comprehensive integration of technology, processes, and personnel-focused transactions designed to deliver a unified outcome that accelerates a customer's business momentum and addresses their technology debt.

Large deals often encompass IT-managed services, transition services, and IT transformation, focusing on infrastructure, applications, testing, security, and more. These deals are typically executed by **Systems Integrators (SIs)**, who are well positioned to handle large-scale projects from end to end due to their global presence and expertise in delivering domain-centric services.

Components of a large deal

Large deals in AWS go beyond simple technical deployments; they are strategic, comprehensive projects that integrate multiple facets of technology, processes, and people. These deals address intricate infrastructure, application, and business requirements, leveraging AWS's advanced tools and programs to drive seamless transitions, reduce costs, and support long-term business transformation. SAs play a key role in these deals by aligning technical solutions with business objectives, creating proposals that deliver value, and ensuring solutions align with customer priorities.

Here are the main components of a large AWS deal:

- **IT infrastructure migration and modernization**: This includes large-scale initiatives such as DC exits, consolidation, divestitures, and mass migrations. These activities are particularly relevant when a customer intends to vacate an existing IT infrastructure facility, dispose of or refresh physical assets, or consolidate aging DCs. The result often involves migrating workloads to the public cloud (such as AWS) or rehosting in a modernized facility, providing streamlined operations and enhanced cost efficiency. For example, **DXC Technology** partnered with AWS to assist clients in exiting aging DCs in favor of agile, secure, and sustainable cloud technology provided by AWS. DXC also planned to divest some of its existing DCs to interested parties, showcasing a strategic move toward modernization. You can find more details here: `https://dxc.com/us/en/newsroom/11202023`.
- **Application and data migration and modernization**: Large deals frequently encompass application and database replatforming (e.g., containerization or managed databases) and refactoring (e.g., .NET core or Amazon Aurora) after an initial stabilization period of around 18–24 months. Early identification of replatforming strategies allows for improved planning and lower TCO over the deal term. **Thomson Reuters**, for instance, completed a large-scale migration project ahead of schedule on AWS, migrating over 400 applications and 10,000 assets across 7 DCs. This migration improved reliability, availability, and scalability for its customers. You can find more details here: `https://aws.amazon.com/solutions/case-studies/thomson-reuters-migration/`.

- **Mainframe modernization:** Mainframe Modernization is critical for customers aiming to exit DCs, as mainframes can be a major obstacle in migration projects. AWS offers solution patterns to facilitate mainframe migration, including the following:
    - *Replatforming* with tools such as **Micro Focus**, enabling infrastructure modernization with minimal code changes
    - *Automated rearchitecting* using **Blu Age** to modernize the complete software stack, including application code, dependencies, and infrastructure
- **DC divestiture:** Data center divestiture can provide financial and technical support for DC migrations. This program focuses on physical asset divestiture, where a third party may buy the customer's IT facilities. Targeting large deals, DC divestiture can offer the following:
    - **TCO analysis:** Assessing the cost versus benefit of migration to AWS compared to maintaining the current DC
    - **DC purchase and leaseback:** Buying a customer's DC and leasing it back for the migration duration
    - **Colocation divestiture:** Providing financial offsets for ongoing colocation agreements to facilitate migration
    - **IT hardware divestiture:** Selling or leasing back hardware, such as servers, storage, and networking gear, that is no longer needed after migration
    - **IPv4 block purchase:** Purchasing unused IPv4 address blocks to help offset migration expenses

    Somos, a global provider of telephone number and identity information services, sought to securely decommission four on-premises DCs after migrating to AWS. Partnering with ReluTech, an AWS Global Recommended Partner, Somos efficiently decommissioned its DCs, ensuring compliance with security policies and allowing the company to focus on its core business operations. You can find more details here: `https://relutech.com/case-studies/somos-accelerates-aws-migration-and-decommission-data-centers-securely-with-relutechs-it-divest-services`.

These components form the backbone of large AWS deals, aligning with customers' strategic goals and enabling significant business transformation. Through these engagements, AWS supports the migration of complex IT environments and provides flexible financial solutions, operational improvements, and long-term value.

Drivers for large deals

Large deals are typically driven by a combination of business and technology factors that align with a customer's strategic goals. These drivers encourage organizations to invest significantly in cloud solutions and IT transformations to enhance agility, efficiency, and competitiveness.

Key business drivers for large deals

- **Agility and innovation**: Migrating to the cloud enables faster deployment of new technologies, empowering organizations to innovate and adapt more swiftly to evolving market conditions.
- **Global reach and expansion**: Cloud infrastructure allows companies to expand internationally easily, leveraging geographically dispersed DCs without the need for extensive physical setup.
- **Reduced time to market**: Cloud solutions facilitate the quicker development and deployment of new products and services, allowing businesses to capitalize on market opportunities more rapidly.
- **Enhanced user experience**: Cloud services can improve service quality and user experience, fostering customer satisfaction and loyalty.
- **Improved resource management**: Cloud migration and outsourcing enable efficient resource utilization, allowing organizations to pay only for the needed resources, thus reducing waste and optimizing operational efficiency.
- **Sustainability initiatives**: Migrating to the cloud is often more energy-efficient and environmentally friendly than maintaining on-premises DCs, supporting organizations' sustainability goals.

Key technology drivers for large deals

- **Technology modernization**: Many advanced capabilities are not feasible with traditional infrastructure, making cloud migration essential for accessing cutting-edge technologies.
- **DC contract renewal**: Companies may aim to reduce investments in DCs or colocation services, especially when contracts are nearing expiration.
- **Cost savings**: Cloud migration avoids capital investment in replacing outdated hardware and helps control escalating licensing costs, leading to long-term financial benefits.
- **Merger/acquisition**: Mergers or acquisitions often require rapid DC consolidation to meet strict deadlines, making cloud solutions an attractive option.

- **Divestiture**: When entities are separated, they need distinct IT infrastructure and operations. Cloud solutions provide flexibility and scalability to meet the unique requirements of a divested entity.

These business and technology drivers highlight the strategic value of large cloud deals, helping organizations achieve their operational, financial, and growth objectives.

Customer expectations in large deals

In large-scale transformation deals, customers make significant investments and enter long-term commitments, expecting you to deliver solutions that align with their strategic goals. Here's an overview of the core expectations customers have in large deals:

- **Cost**: Customers expect cost transparency and predictability. They look for clear pricing models that allow them to anticipate expenses as their needs grow without surprises. Efficiency is another key expectation, with customers often seeking cost savings through volume discounts, competitive pricing, or cost reduction commitments. These financial considerations are critical for customers to justify their investment in a large transformation project.
- **Contractual flexibility and lock-in**: Customers in large deals need flexibility in contract terms. They want the ability to scale services up or down as business requirements change without being locked into rigid long-term contracts with penalties for early termination. Many customers are also concerned about vendor lock-in; they prefer solutions that aren't overly proprietary, making it easier to switch providers if needed. This independence gives them control over their technology choices in the future.
- **Technical debt management**: Customers expect you to help modernize their IT infrastructure with current, sustainable technologies, avoiding legacy systems that could increase technical debt. Scalability and performance are also high priorities; customers want infrastructure that can scale effortlessly as their business grows, ensuring high performance without requiring frequent overhauls. Addressing these concerns helps organizations stay agile and competitive in a rapidly evolving technology landscape.
- **SLAs**: High availability and uptime are non-negotiable for critical services, and customers expect SLAs that guarantee these metrics. Performance and response times are also crucial, as they directly impact the infrastructure's ability to support business needs. Strong SLAs around security, data protection, and compliance are also vital, especially for customers in regulated industries. SLAs assure customers that their investment is protected and that AWS will meet operational expectations.

- **Support and maintenance:** Reliable customer support is a top expectation in large deals. Customers expect prompt, knowledgeable support to address any issues or inquiries quickly. Regular maintenance, updates, and patch management are essential to keep the infrastructure secure, stable, and up to date. This ongoing support ensures the infrastructure remains resilient and capable of supporting evolving business needs.
- **Transparency and reporting:** Customers expect transparent reporting on service performance, usage, and costs, which helps them monitor the value they receive from the cloud. Access to detailed, timely reports enables customers to make informed decisions, track ROI, and manage budgets effectively. This level of transparency builds trust and reinforces the cloud's role as a reliable partner.
- **Scalability and future-proofing:** Customers expect scalable infrastructure that can easily accommodate business growth without requiring significant reconfiguration. Future-proofing is also essential; customers want assurance that their infrastructure can adapt to emerging technologies and trends without major overhauls. This flexibility is key to sustaining long-term value from their investment.
- **Exit strategy:** Customers value having a clear exit strategy, including provisions for data migration and continuity planning if they decide to move away from the cloud. This includes seamless data transfer, minimal downtime, and a structured transition plan. A defined exit strategy gives customers peace of mind, knowing they have a viable option if their business needs change.

Addressing these expectations can help customers achieve their transformation goals while building trust and fostering long-term partnerships. SAs play a critical role in ensuring these needs are met, delivering solutions that are not only technologically robust but also aligned with the customer's business and operational requirements.

Large deal commercial models

Large deals often require flexible and customized commercial models to address the complex requirements of enterprise transformation. Here are typical commercial constructs used in large deals, each suited to specific project characteristics and customer needs:

- **Fixed-Price Model (FPM):** In this model, customers agree on a fixed price for the entire project or specific services. It works best for projects with a clear scope and stable requirements. The client pays a predetermined amount, regardless of the actual resources used, providing cost certainty. This model is ideal for projects where deliverables and timelines are well defined.

- **Time and Materials (T&M)**: This model allows the client to pay based on actual hours and resources used, with established hourly rates for different skill levels. It offers flexibility for projects with evolving or uncertain requirements, allowing clients to adjust as the project progresses. However, costs can be more challenging to control, as expenses may increase with scope changes.
- **Fixed Price with Milestones (FPWM)**: FPWM combines elements of both FPM and T&M. Payments are made upon reaching predefined milestones or deliverables, with a fixed price for each stage. This model provides some cost predictability while offering flexibility in project execution, balancing certainty and adaptability.
- **Subscription-based model**: In this model, the client pays a recurring fee, usually monthly or annually, for ongoing managed services such as IT support, cloud management, or cybersecurity. It provides a predictable revenue stream for service providers and ensures continuous client support, making it well suited for services requiring long-term, ongoing management.
- **Outcome-based pricing model**: In this model, payment is based on the outcomes or business results achieved, aligning the service provider's incentives with the client's business goals. Rather than focusing on hours or resources, this approach emphasizes the value delivered to the client, making it effective for projects where measurable results are critical.
- **Risk and reward-sharing models**: Risk and reward-sharing models distribute risks and potential rewards between vendors and customers. An example is a gain-sharing model, where any cost savings or performance improvements achieved are shared between the parties. This model encourages collaboration and aligns interests but requires clear metrics for evaluating performance.
- **Cost-plus pricing model**: The customer pays for the vendor's actual expenses plus a predetermined profit margin in the cost-plus model. This approach offers transparency, allowing clients to see the costs and profits directly. It is especially useful for projects where the scope or requirements are expected to change, and transparency is valued.
- **Hybrid models**: Many large deals employ a combination of these models, tailoring the pricing structure to meet the project's unique demands. Hybrid models allow service providers and clients to address a project's fixed and variable aspects, balancing cost certainty with flexibility.

These commercial models provide varied options to align pricing with the project's complexity, scope, and desired outcomes, ensuring the client and service provider have a mutually beneficial arrangement. Each model has unique advantages, making it essential to choose the right structure to support successful execution in large-scale transformations.

Common challenges in large deals

Large deals present unique challenges that complicate the commercial and operational aspects of enterprise transformation. Here are some typical challenges encountered in large-scale deals.

Commercial challenges

- **Increased on-premises costs**: When utilization of on-premises resources declines, fixed costs remain, driving up the unit cost for remaining infrastructure and eroding cost-efficiency.
- **Double bubble and transformation costs**: The combined cost of running legacy infrastructure and transformation efforts can make the business case financially unfeasible.
- **DC exit timing mismatch**: The schedule for exiting DCs often does not align perfectly with the transformation timeline, leading to potential cost and operational inefficiencies.
- **Early termination penalties**: Contracts with existing service providers may involve early termination fees or other liabilities, adding unplanned costs to the transformation budget.

Operational challenges

- **Transitioning legacy platforms**: DCs often house large, core legacy platforms that require careful planning and handling during the migration to minimize disruption.
- **Lack of organizational readiness**: Many customers may not be fully prepared for the shift, as legacy processes and outdated tools may limit their ability to adopt new infrastructure.
- **Decommissioning processes**: Some organizations lack established procedures for handling decommissioned IT assets and DCs, adding complexity to the shutdown process.
- **Complexity of DC decommissioning**: Shutting down a DC is a complex, lengthy process that can reveal unexpected issues. Thorough planning and flexibility are essential to effectively navigate these unforeseen challenges.

These commercial and operational hurdles require proactive management, clear communication, and flexible solutions to ensure the success of large deals. AWS and SAs play a crucial role in identifying these challenges early, collaborating with customers to develop effective strategies for a smooth transition.

Let's combine what you have learned so far and understand how to build a large **IT Outsourcing (ITO)** deal in AWS.

Building large ITO deals using AWS

Building a large ITO deal on AWS involves crafting a solution that addresses a customer's comprehensive IT requirements, often encompassing infrastructure, applications, DCs, and ongoing managed services. AWS provides the tools and flexibility to support complex outsourcing engagements that drive efficiency, innovation, and cost savings. The following diagram demonstrates a framework for constructing a successful large ITO deal with AWS:

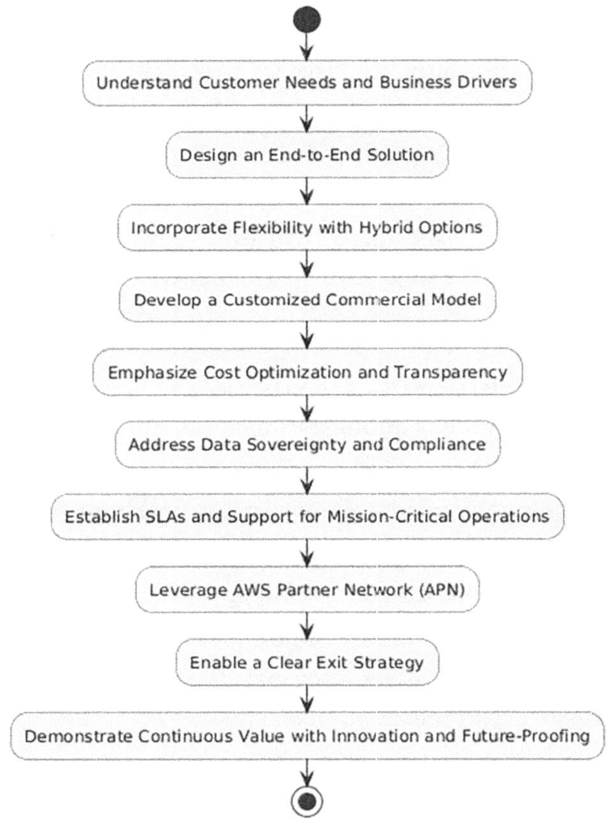

Figure 3.5: ITO deal process

As shown in the preceding diagram, let's look at the flow of a large ITO deal process:

1. **Understand customer needs and business drivers**: Understand the customer's unique business goals, industry challenges, and desired outcomes. Key drivers may include cost optimization, agility, technology modernization, regulatory compliance, and sustainability. Align the deal structure to address these drivers, creating a compelling business case that underscores the value AWS can bring.

2. **Design an end-to-end solution**: An ITO deal on AWS should include all aspects of the customer's IT ecosystem. This often involves the following:

    - **Infrastructure services:** Migrating on-premises infrastructure to AWS with flexible, scalable solutions such as Amazon EC2, Amazon S3, and managed databases (e.g., Amazon RDS).
    - **Application modernization:** Leveraging AWS's serverless technologies (e.g., AWS Lambda), managed container services (e.g., Amazon ECS and EKS), and managed databases to modernize applications.
    - **DC exit and consolidation**: Planning a DC exit or consolidation with AWS solutions to minimize downtime and streamline asset decommissioning.
    - **Managed services and operations**: Offering ongoing management and monitoring using AWS Managed Services, Amazon CloudWatch, AWS Systems Manager, and automated backup and disaster recovery.

3. **Incorporate flexibility with hybrid options**: Large enterprise customers may have complex requirements and existing investments in hybrid or multi-cloud environments. AWS provides hybrid solutions (e.g., AWS Outposts or AWS Direct Connect) and partnerships to enable seamless integration with other environments. This flexibility meets customer interoperability, disaster recovery, and workload distribution needs.
4. **Develop a customized commercial model**: Large ITO deals benefit from tailored commercial models that align with the customer's budget and project requirements:

    - **Fixed price or milestone-based payments** for predictable phases such as migrations.
    - **T&M** for ongoing support or project-based work with evolving requirements.
    - **Outcome-based pricing** for projects focused on achieving specific business metrics.
    - **Hybrid models**, combining these options, can provide optimal flexibility, cost control, and predictability.

5. **Emphasize cost optimization and transparency**: Cost management is critical in large ITO deals. Leverage AWS's tools for cost control, such as AWS Cost Explorer and AWS Budgets, and explore Reserved Instances or **Savings Plans** for further cost savings. Transparency around cost structures, projections, and potential optimizations builds trust and supports long-term sustainability for the deal.

6. **Address data sovereignty and compliance**: Compliance with industry and regional regulations is essential, particularly in sectors such as healthcare, finance, and government. AWS's compliance certifications (e.g., **HIPAA**, **GDPR**, and **SOC**) and tools (e.g., **AWS Artifact** and **AWS Shield**) help with meeting regulatory requirements. Address data sovereignty with AWS's global DC presence and options for data residency.
7. **Establish SLAs and support for mission-critical operations**: Define clear SLAs to meet customer expectations on availability, performance, and security. Use AWS's high availability and disaster recovery options to minimize downtime. To ensure continuous, reliable service, provide ongoing support through AWS Enterprise Support or AWS Managed Services.
8. **Leverage APN**: Collaborate with the APN to bring specialized expertise and resources to the ITO deal. Partners can support specific needs, such as data migrations, application development, or regulatory compliance, strengthening the deal's overall value proposition.
9. **Enable a clear exit strategy**: Customers expect a well-defined exit strategy in large outsourcing deals. AWS offers flexible options to support exit planning, such as data transfer services for data migration and support for data sovereignty requirements. An exit plan reassures customers of AWS's commitment to long-term success beyond the ITO contract.
10. **Demonstrate continuous value with innovation and future-proofing**: Highlight AWS's commitment to continuous improvement by incorporating AI, machine learning, analytics, and IoT into the ITO solution. AWS's innovation services (e.g., Amazon SageMaker or AWS IoT) help customers stay competitive and future-ready, enhancing the long-term value of outsourcing engagement.

Building a large ITO deal on AWS requires a deep understanding of customer objectives and crafting a solution that balances flexibility, cost control, and long-term value. By addressing these elements, AWS can help organizations achieve transformation through secure, efficient, and scalable cloud solutions that support growth and innovation.

Knowledge check

The following scenario-based questions with multiple-choice options offer practical insights for AWS solution architects to handle enterprise-level cloud transformations, cost management, and migration strategies:

1. A fast-growing e-commerce start-up operating across Southeast Asia is struggling with rising infrastructure costs and inconsistent hardware utilization. Their CTO wants to reduce capital expenditures and move toward a more scalable and agile model. You've been asked to assess their infrastructure and recommend a migration strategy to AWS. The primary concern is whether their current CapEx-heavy model is sustainable and how AWS can provide more transparency in spending.

   Which AWS feature most directly supports transitioning from CapEx to OpEx while ensuring financial predictability and elasticity?

   a. Deploying all workloads using EC2 Spot Instances, which are the cheapest and allow bidding on unused capacity.

   b. Shifting to Amazon EC2 Reserved Instances, which offer long-term savings with one- or three-year commitments.

   c. Using AWS Cost Explorer and Budgets to review monthly spending and adjust resource usage accordingly, retroactively.

   d. Migrating to the AWS cloud, which supports an OpEx model by replacing upfront hardware investment with consumption-based billing.

   Answer: d.

   Explanation:

   a. Incorrect. It reduces costs but doesn't guarantee availability or financial predictability due to interruptions.

   b. Incorrect. It helps with cost savings but still requires upfront commitment—closer to CapEx than pure OpEx.

   c. Incorrect. It is reactive, not a structural shift.

   d. **Correct**. AWS enables companies to replace fixed, capital-heavy infrastructure with flexible, consumption-based OpEx.

2. A national logistics company is preparing to move all its workloads to AWS and aims to optimize costs during and after migration. The CIO asks you which tools or models AWS offers to assess current spending and make projections.

   Which AWS services and features can help the company assess **total cost of ownership (TCO)** and manage ongoing cloud costs? (Choose two.)

   a. AWS Pricing Calculator to forecast charges across compute, storage, and networking services based on projected usage.

b. AWS Cost Anomaly Detection to block over-budget spending before it's billed
c. AWS TCO Calculator to compare existing infrastructure costs with potential AWS migration savings.
d. AWS Budgets with hard enforcement, which terminates resources once thresholds are crossed.
e. AWS Simple Monthly Calculator, which is deprecated and no longer recommended for current AWS pricing estimates.

Answers: a. and c.

Explanation:

a. **Correct.** AWS Pricing Calculator helps estimate costs based on services and usage.
b. Incorrect. AWS Cost Anomaly Detection monitors spending but does not prevent it automatically.
c. **Correct.** AWS TCO Calculator compares on-premises versus cloud infrastructure cost models.
d. Incorrect. AWS Budgets sends alerts but doesn't enforce terminations.
e. Incorrect. AWS Simple Monthly Calculator is deprecated and has been replaced by the Pricing Calculator.

3. A financial tech company has workloads that need continuous uptime and consistent compute performance. They've been using On-Demand EC2 instances for flexibility, but the CFO is concerned about long-term costs. The cloud team is exploring alternatives while preserving availability.

   What would be the most cost-effective and suitable AWS pricing model for these stable workloads?

   a. Continue with On-Demand instances for flexibility and avoid lock-in, even at a higher cost.
   b. Purchase Reserved Instances for one or three years, which guarantees capacity and significantly lowers long-term cost.
   c. Migrate all workloads to EC2 Spot Instances, which are available at steep discounts and ideal for long-running tasks.
   d. Use AWS Lambda to run containerized workloads, thus eliminating EC2 costs.

   Answer: b.

Explanation:

a. Incorrect. This is not cost-efficient for steady-state workloads.
b. **Correct**. Reserved Instances offer up to 72% cost savings for predictable usage.
c. Incorrect. This is risky for persistent workloads due to potential termination.
d. Incorrect. This is not viable for workloads requiring persistent compute or long uptime.

4. An edtech start-up wants to explore AWS's free offerings to test several microservices for a new learning platform. They want to evaluate backend compute, database, and storage components over the next three months before deciding on full-scale deployment.

   Which AWS services are included in the Free Tier and would best meet the needs of this start-up? (Choose two.)

   a. Amazon EC2: 750 hours per month of `t2.micro` or `t3.micro` instances for one year.
   b. Amazon RDS: 1 TB of high-performance SSD storage per month for testing purposes.
   c. Amazon S3: 5 GB of Standard storage with 20,000 `GET` and 2,000 `PUT` requests per month.
   d. AWS Fargate: Unlimited compute resource usage under the Always Free plan.
   e. Amazon Aurora: 750 hours per month for Aurora Serverless databases for 12 months.

   Answers: a. and c.

   Explanation:

   a. **Correct**. EC2's Free Tier includes 750 hours of `t2.micro` or `t3.micro` instances for eligible accounts.
   b. Incorrect. RDS's Free Tier includes 20 GB, not 1 TB.
   c. **Correct**. S3's Free Tier includes 5 GB with request limits.
   d. Incorrect. Fargate is not included in the Always Free plan.
   e. Incorrect. It only applies under specific promotional offers and not by default for Aurora Serverless.

5. A global media company running high-traffic streaming workloads on AWS wants to prepare for variable traffic caused by major events. Their goal is to balance performance with cost. You are asked to recommend a compute purchasing strategy that helps reduce costs during normal loads and scales up when needed.

Which AWS pricing strategy best supports this need?

a. Purchase dedicated hosts to run all compute services with high availability guarantees and full hardware visibility.
b. Use a combination of On-Demand and Spot Instances via Auto Scaling groups to optimize cost and responsiveness.
c. Invest in Reserved Instances across all services, which lock compute capacity regardless of usage patterns.
d. Set up separate AWS accounts for each traffic zone and manually reassign compute when demand changes.

Answer: b.

Explanation:

a. Incorrect. Purchasing dedicated hosts is costlier and better for compliance-heavy workloads, not for cost efficiency.
b. **Correct**. Combining On-Demand with Spot Instances in Auto Scaling balances performance and cost using dynamic provisioning.
c. Incorrect. Reserved Instances lack flexibility for unpredictable traffic.
d. Incorrect. Creating separate accounts is inefficient and hard to manage.

Summary

In this chapter, you explored the various cloud computing models, such as IaaS, PaaS, and SaaS, delving into their unique value propositions and understanding how each model can meet different IT workload requirements. This foundation helps identify the most suitable model for your organization's needs.

You then moved on to implementing an enterprise transformation program and migrating to the cloud. Recognizing that cloud migration can catalyze broader organizational changes, you examined cloud migration strategies, in particular, AWS's 7 Rs strategy, to build a comprehensive migration and modernization plan. This approach allows organizations to migrate and improve business processes and workflows during the transition.

The chapter also highlighted drivers for enterprise transformation, along with real-world examples of successful digital transformation efforts. Key tips and potential pitfalls were discussed to help you steer your transformation toward success. You learned how the AWS CAF provides structured guidance to accelerate a smooth and effective transformation journey.

Finally, you explored the components of building large, strategic deals on AWS, understanding the benefits, challenges, and considerations involved in these significant engagements.

In the next chapter, you will learn how AWS's global infrastructure can support your digital transformation objectives. This includes a closer look at AWS networking solutions, which form a foundational aspect of building resilient and scalable architectures on AWS.

Part 2

AWS Core Service Offerings

Here, you'll dive into the core AWS services that form the backbone of cloud solutions. You'll learn how to build secure networks using VPC and other content delivery tools. When choosing storage, you'll see how services such as S3, EBS, and EFS fit different use cases. For compute, you'll compare EC2, Lambda, and container-based services to find the right fit for your workloads. Finally, you'll explore AWS database services, including both relational and NoSQL options, to design efficient and scalable data layers for your applications.

This part of the book includes the following chapters:

4

Networking in AWS

Today, enterprises have become exponentially more agile by leveraging the power of the cloud. In this chapter, we will highlight the scale of AWS Global Infrastructure and teach you about AWS networking foundations.

Networking is the first step for any organization to set up its landing zone, and the entire IT workload is built on top of it. Networking is the backbone of the IT application and infrastructure workload. AWS provides various networking services for building your IT landscape in the cloud, and in this chapter, you will dive deep into AWS networking services.

Every business is now running globally, and organizations need to target global populations with their product. With a traditional on-premises IT workload, scaling globally and providing the same user experience globally becomes challenging. AWS helps solve these problems through edge networking, and you will learn more about deploying your application for global users without compromising their experience. Furthermore, you will learn about network security and building a hybrid cloud.

In this chapter, we will cover the following topics:

- The AWS Global Infrastructure
- AWS networking foundations
- Edge networking
- Building hybrid cloud connectivity in AWS
- AWS cloud network security

Without further ado, let's get down to business.

The AWS Global Infrastructure

AWS's infrastructure is highly secure and reliable. It offers over 240 services, most of which are available in all AWS Regions worldwide, spread across 245 countries and territories. Regardless of the type of technology application you are planning to build and deploy, AWS is sure to provide a service that will facilitate its deployment.

AWS has millions of customers and thousands of consulting and technology partners worldwide. Businesses large and small across all industries rely on AWS to handle their workloads. Here are some statistics to give you an idea of the breadth of AWS's scale. AWS provides the following as its global infrastructure:

- 34 launched Regions
- 108 Availability Zones
- Over 135 Direct Connect locations
- Over 600 CloudFront Points of Presence
- 41 Local Zones
- 29 Wavelength Zones

Important Note

These numbers are accurate as of the time of writing this book. It would not be surprising if they had changed by the time you read this.

For the latest details on AWS's global infrastructure, you can visit the official AWS Global Infrastructure page: `https://aws.amazon.com/about-aws/global-infrastructure/`.

Now that we have covered how the AWS infrastructure is organized at a high level, let's learn about the elements of the AWS Global Infrastructure in detail.

Regions, Availability Zones, and Local zones

How can Amazon provide such a reliable service across the globe? How can they offer reliability and durability guarantees for some of their services? The answer reveals why they are the cloud leaders and why it's difficult to replicate what they offer. AWS has billions of dollars worth of infrastructure deployed across the world. These locations are organized into different Regions and Zones. More formally, AWS calls them the following:

- **AWS Regions**
- **Availability Zones (AZs)**
- **Local Zones (LZs)**

As shown in the following diagram, an AZ comprises multiple distinct data centers, each equipped with redundant power, networking, and connectivity and located in separate facilities.

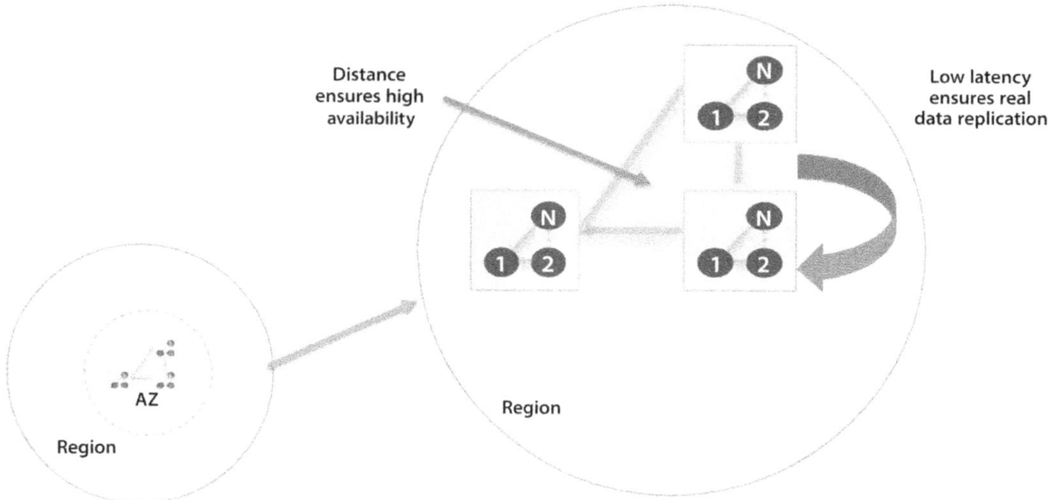

Figure 4.1: AWS Regions and AZs

AWS Regions exist in separate geographic areas. Each AWS Region comprises several independent and isolated data centers (AZs) that provide a full array of AWS services.

AWS continuously enhances its data centers to provide the latest technology. AWS's data centers have a high degree of redundancy. It uses highly reliable hardware, but the hardware is not failure-proof. Occasionally, a failure can happen that interferes with the availability of resources in each data center. Suppose all instances were hosted in only one data center. If a failure occurred with the whole data center, none of your resources would be available. AWS mitigates this issue by having multiple data centers in each Region.

In the following subsection, we will examine AWS Regions in greater detail and explain why they are essential.

AWS Regions

AWS Regions are groups of data centers in one geographic location designed to be independent and isolated. A single Region consists of a collection of data centers spread within that Region's geographic boundary. This independence promotes availability and enhances fault tolerance and stability. While working on the console, you will see AWS services available in that Region. There is a possibility that a particular service is not available in your Region. Eventually, all services will become **generally available (GA)** after their launch; however, the timing of availability may differ between different Regions. Some global services include **Direct Connect Gateway (DXGW)**, **Identity and Access Management (IAM)**, CloudFront, and Route 53. AWS global services operate at a global level and are not limited to a specific AWS Region, allowing you to manage and deploy resources across multiple Regions from a single control point.

Other services are not global but allow you to create inter-Region fault tolerance and availability. For example, services such as **Amazon S3 Cross-Region Replication**, **AWS Global Accelerator**, and **AWS Transit Gateway** can be configured to enable a robust inter-Region architecture.

This combination of global services and inter-Region options helps AWS customers build resilient, scalable, and highly available applications across multiple Regions. One advantage of such an architecture is that resources will be closer to users, increasing access speed and reducing latency.

Another obvious advantage is that you can serve your clients without disruption, even if a whole Region becomes unavailable, by planning your disaster recovery workload to be in another Region. You can recover faster if something goes wrong, as these read replicas can be automatically converted to the primary database if needed.

As of October 2024, there are 34 AWS Regions. The naming convention usually followed is to list the country code, the geographic Region, and the number. For example, the US East Region in Ohio is named as follows:

- **Location**: US East (Ohio)
- **Name**: `us-east-2`

AWS has a global cloud infrastructure, so you can likely find a Region near your user base, with a few exceptions, such as Russia. If you live in Greenland, it may be a little further away; however, you will still be able to connect as long as you have an internet connection.

In addition, AWS has dedicated Regions specifically and exclusively for the US government called **AWS GovCloud**. This allows US government agencies and customers to run highly sensitive applications in this environment. AWS GovCloud offers the same services as other Regions, but it complies explicitly with requirements and regulations specific to the needs of the US government.

The full list of available Regions can be found here: `https://docs.aws.amazon.com/AWSEC2/latest/UserGuide/using-regions-availability-zones.html#concepts-available-regions`.

As AWS continues to grow, do not be surprised if it offers similar Regions to other governments worldwide, depending on their importance and the demand they can generate.

AWS AZs

As we discussed earlier, AZs are components of AWS Regions. The clusters of data centers within a Region are called AZs. A single AZ consists of multiple data centers. These data centers are connected using AWS-owned dedicated fiber optic cables. They are located within a 60-mile radius, far enough to avoid localized failures yet achieve faster data transfer between the data centers. AZs have multiple power sources, redundant connectivity, and redundant resources. All this translates into unparalleled customer service, allowing them to deliver highly available, fault-tolerant, and scalable applications.

The AZs within an AWS Region are interconnected. These connections have the following properties:

- Fully redundant
- High-bandwidth
- Low-latency
- Scalable
- Encrypted
- Dedicated

Depending on the service you are using, if you decide to perform a multi-AZ deployment, an AZ will automatically be assigned to the service. Still, you can designate which AZ is to be used for some services.

Every AZ forms a completely segregated section of the AWS Global Infrastructure, physically detached from other AZs by a substantial distance, often spanning several miles. Each AZ operates on a dedicated power infrastructure, allowing customers to run production applications and databases that are more resilient, fault-tolerant, and scalable compared to relying on a single data center.

High-bandwidth, low-latency networking interconnects all the AZs – but what about fulfilling the need for low-latency bandwidth within a highly populated city? For that, AWS launched LZs. Let's learn more about them.

AWS LZs

While AZs focus on covering larger areas throughout Regions, such as the US-West and the US-East, AWS fulfills the needs of highly populated cities through LZs. AWS LZs are newer components in the AWS infrastructure family. LZs place select services close to end users, allowing them to create AWS applications that deliver single-digit, millisecond responses. An LZ is the compute and storage infrastructure close to high-population areas and industrial centers and offers high-bandwidth, low-latency connectivity to the broader AWS infrastructure. Due to their proximity to the customer, LZs facilitate the delivery of applications that necessitate latency in single-digit milliseconds to end users. As of October 2024, AWS has 41 LZs.

AWS LZs can run various AWS services, such as **Amazon Elastic Compute Cloud (Amazon EC2)**, **Amazon Virtual Private Cloud (Amazon VPC)**, **Amazon Elastic Block Store (Amazon EBS)**, **Elastic Load Balancing (ELB)**, **Amazon FSx**, **Amazon EMR**, **Amazon ElastiCache**, and **Amazon Relational Database Service (Amazon RDS)** in geographic proximity to your end users.

The naming convention for LZs is to use the AWS Region followed by a location identifier, such as `us-west-2-lax-2a`. Please refer to this link for the latest supported services in LZs: `https://aws.amazon.com/about-aws/global-infrastructure/localzones/features/?nc=sn&loc=2`.

Now that you have learned about the different components of the AWS Global Infrastructure, let's examine its benefits.

Benefits of the AWS Global Infrastructure

The following are the key benefits of using AWS's cloud infrastructure:

- **Security**: One of the most complex and risky tasks is maintaining security, especially regarding the data center's physical security. With AWS's shared security responsibility model, you offload infrastructure physical security to AWS and focus on the application security that matters for your business.
- **Availability**: One of the most important factors for the user experience is making sure your application is highly available. This means you need to have your workload deployed in a physically separated geographic location to reduce the impact of natural disasters. AWS Regions are fully isolated, and within each Region, the AZs are further isolated partitions of AWS infrastructure. You can use AWS infrastructure with an on-demand model to deploy your applications across multiple AZs in the same Region or any Region globally.

- **Performance**: Performance is another critical factor in retaining and increasing the user base. AWS provides low-latency network infrastructure by using redundant 100 GbE fiber, which leads to terabits of capacity between Regions. You can also use AWS Edge AZs for applications that require low millisecond latency, such as 5G, gaming, AR/VR, and IoT.
- **Scalability**: When user demands increase, you must have the capacity to scale your application. With AWS, you can quickly spin up resources, deploying thousands of servers in minutes to handle any user demand. You can also scale down when demand decreases, and you don't need to pay for overprovisioned resources.
- **Flexibility**: With AWS, you can choose how and where to run your workloads; for example, you can run applications globally by deploying into any AWS Region and AZs worldwide. You can run your applications with single-digit millisecond latencies by choosing AWS LZs or AWS Wavelength. You can select AWS Outposts to run applications on-premises.

Now that you have learned about the AWS Global Infrastructure and its benefits, the next question that comes to mind is how you are going to use this infrastructure. Don't worry – AWS provides network services that allow you to create your own secure logical data center in the cloud and control your IT workload and applications. Furthermore, these network services help you establish connectivity to your users, employees, on-premises data centers, and content distributions. Let's learn more about AWS's networking services and how they can help you build your cloud data center.

AWS networking foundations

When you set up your IT infrastructure, what comes to mind first? I have the servers now – how can I connect them to the internet and each other so that they can communicate? This connectivity is achieved by networking, without which you cannot do anything.

Networking concepts are the same when it comes to the cloud. In this section, you will learn what networking is and how to set up your private network in the AWS cloud. You will also learn how to establish connectivity between the different servers in the cloud and from on-premises to the AWS cloud. First, let's start with the foundation; the first step to building your networking backbone in AWS is using Amazon VPC.

Amazon VPC

VPC is one of the core services AWS provides. Simply speaking, a VPC is your version of the AWS cloud, and as the name suggests, it is "private," which means that, by default, your VPC is a logically isolated and private network inside AWS.

You can imagine a VPC as the same as your logical data center in a virtual setting inside the AWS cloud, where you have complete control over the resources inside your VPC. AWS resources such as Amazon EC2 and Amazon RDS instances are placed inside the VPC, including all the required networking components to control the data traffic per your needs.

Creating a VPC could be complex, but AWS has made it easy by providing **Launch VPC Wizard.** You can visualize your network configuration when creating the VPC. The following screenshot shows the VPC network configuration across two AZs, **us-east-1a** and **us-east-1b**:

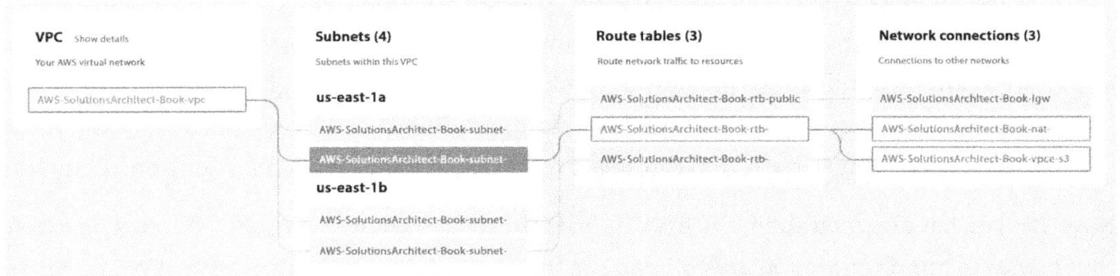

Figure 4.2: AWS VPC configuration with a private subnet flow

Quick tip: Need to see a high-resolution version of this image? Open this book in the next-gen Packt Reader or view it in the PDF/ePub copy.

The next-gen Packt Reader is included for free with the purchase of this book. Scan the QR code OR go to `packtpub.com/unlock`, then use the search bar to find this book by name. Double-check the edition shown to make sure you get the right one.

In the preceding diagram, you can see VPCs spread across two AZs, where each AZ has two subnets – one public and one private. The highlighted flow shows the data flow of a server deployed into a private subnet of the `us-east-1a` AZ. Before going into further details, let's look at key VPC concepts to understand them better:

- **Classless Inter-Domain Routing (CIDR) blocks**: CIDR is the IP address range allocated to your VPC. When you create a VPC, you specify its set of IP addresses with CIDR notation. CIDR notation is a simplified way of showing a specific range of IP addresses. For example, `10.0.0.0/16` covers all IPs from `10.0.0.0` to `10.0.255.255`, providing 65,536 IP addresses to use. All resources in your VPC must fall within the CIDR range.
- **Subnets:** As the name suggests, the subnet is the VPC CIDR block subset. Partitions of the network are divided by the CIDR range within the range of IP addresses in your VPC. A VPC can have multiple subnets for different kinds of services or functions, such as a frontend subnet (for internet access to a web page), a backend subnet (for business logic processing), and a database subnet (for database services).

  Subnets create trusted boundaries between private and public resources. You should organize your subnets based on internet accessibility. A subnet allows you to define clear isolation between public and private resources. The majority of resources on AWS can be hosted in private subnets. You should use public subnets under controlled access and use them only when necessary. As you will keep most of your resources under restricted access, you should plan your subnets so that your private subnets have substantially more IPs available than your public subnets.
- **Route tables:** A routing table contains a set of rules called routes. Routes determine where the traffic will flow. By default, every subnet has a routing table. You can manually create a new route table and assign subnets to it. For better security, use the custom route table for each subnet.
- **Internet gateway (IGW)**: The IGW sits at the edge of the VPC and provides connectivity between your VPC resources and the public network (the internet). By default, internet accessibility is denied for internet traffic in your environment. An IGW needs to be attached to your public subnet through the subnet's route table, defining the rules of the IGW. All of your resources that require direct access to the internet (public-facing load balancers, NAT instances, bastion hosts, and so on) would go into the public subnet.
- **Network address translation (NAT) gateways:** A NAT gateway provides outbound internet access to the private subnet and prevents connections from being initiated from outside to your VPC resources. A private subnet blocks all incoming and outgoing internet traffic, but servers may need outgoing internet traffic for software and security patch installation. A NAT gateway enables instances in a private subnet to initiate outbound traffic to the internet and protects resources from incoming internet traffic. All restricted servers (such as database and application resources) should be deployed inside your private subnet.

- **Security groups (SGs)**: SGs are the virtual firewalls that control inbound and outbound packets for your instances. You can only use `allow` statements in the SG; everything else is denied implicitly. SGs control inbound and outbound traffic as designated resources for one or more instances from the CIDR block range or another SG. As per the principle of least privilege, all incoming traffic must be denied by default, and rules must be created to filter traffic based on TCP, UDP, and **Internet Control Message Protocol (ICMP)**.
- **Network access control list (NACL)**: An NACL is another firewall that sits at the subnet boundary and allows or denies incoming and outgoing packets. The main difference between an NACL and an SG is that the NACL is stateless; therefore, you need rules for incoming and outgoing traffic. With an SG, you need to allow traffic in one direction, and return traffic is, by default, allowed.

  You should use an SG in most places as it is a firewall at the EC2 instance level, while an NACL is a firewall at the subnet level. You should use an NACL where you want to control the VPC level and deny specific IPs, as an SG cannot have a deny rule for network traffic coming from a particular IP or IP range.
- **Egress-only IGWs**: These provide outbound communication from **Internet Protocol version 6 (IPv6)** instances in your VPC to the internet and prevent the inbound connection to your instances on IPv6. IPv6, the sixth iteration of the Internet Protocol, succeeds IPv4 and employs a 128-bit IP address. Like IPv4, it facilitates the provision of unique IP addresses required for internet-connected devices to communicate.
- **DHCP option sets**: These are a group of network information, such as the DNS name server and domain name, used by EC2 instances when they launch.
- **VPC Flow Logs** enables you to monitor traffic flow to your system VPC, such as accepted and rejected traffic information for the designated resource, to understand traffic patterns. Flow Logs can also be used as a security tool to monitor traffic that reaches your instance. You can create alarms to notify you if certain types of traffic are detected. You can also create metrics to help you identify trends and patterns. Additionally, it plays a crucial role in troubleshooting network issues by assisting you in verifying whether traffic is being blocked by NACLs or SGs and pinpointing the source of network disruptions or misconfigurations. Furthermore, VPC Flow Logs serves as a valuable tool for compliance auditing, providing a detailed record of network traffic that can be used to demonstrate adherence to regulatory standards and internal policies. The following diagram shows an example of the default logging format:

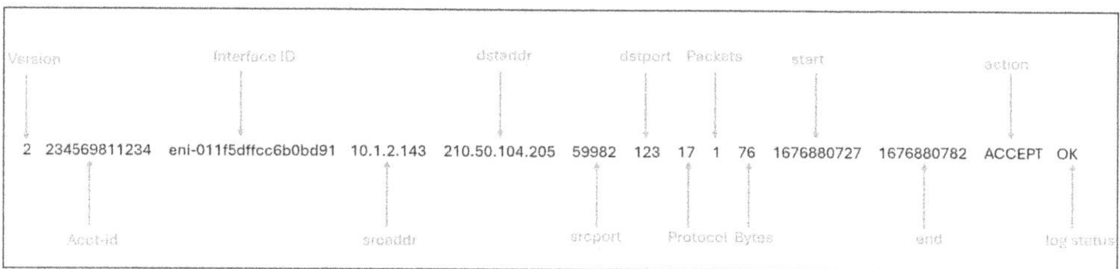

Figure 4.3: AWS VPC Flow Logs

VPC Flow Logs allows the incorporation of additional information, such as VPC ID, instance ID, and TCP flags, into log entries. You have the flexibility to customize the order of these fields. In CloudWatch Contributor Insights, rules are constructed by matching the position of the field in the log event with the field's name or its alias. While the position of the `<interface-id>` field is typically 3 in the default logging format, this may differ if you have configured a customized logging format.

- **Elastic IP addresses:** Elastic IP addresses are static, public IP addresses that can be allocated and associated with instances or network interfaces within an Amazon VPC. They serve as a persistent, unchanging address for communication with resources in the VPC, even if the underlying instance is stopped or terminated. Elastic IP addresses can be remapped to different instances, ensuring continuity of service and minimizing downtime. They are particularly useful for applications that require a fixed IP address, such as web servers, databases, or other internet-facing services.
- **Endpoints:** These provide a dedicated, private connection for accessing AWS services without traversing the public internet, enhancing security and reducing latency. There are two types of endpoints in Amazon VPC: gateway endpoints and interface endpoints. Gateway endpoints enable access to specific AWS services, such as **Amazon S3** or **DynamoDB**. At the same time, interface endpoints allow you to connect to services powered by **AWS PrivateLink**, providing an even higher level of isolation and security.

To access servers in a private subnet, you can create a bastion host, which acts like a jump server. It must be hardened with tighter security so that only appropriate people can access it. To log in to the server, use public-key cryptography for authentication rather than a regular user ID and password method.

A VPC resides only within an AWS Region and can span across one or more AZs within the Region. In the following diagram, two AZs are utilized within a Region. Furthermore, you can create one or more subnets inside each AZ, and resources such as EC2 and RDS are placed inside the VPC in specific subnets. This architecture diagram shows a VPC configuration with a private and public subnet:

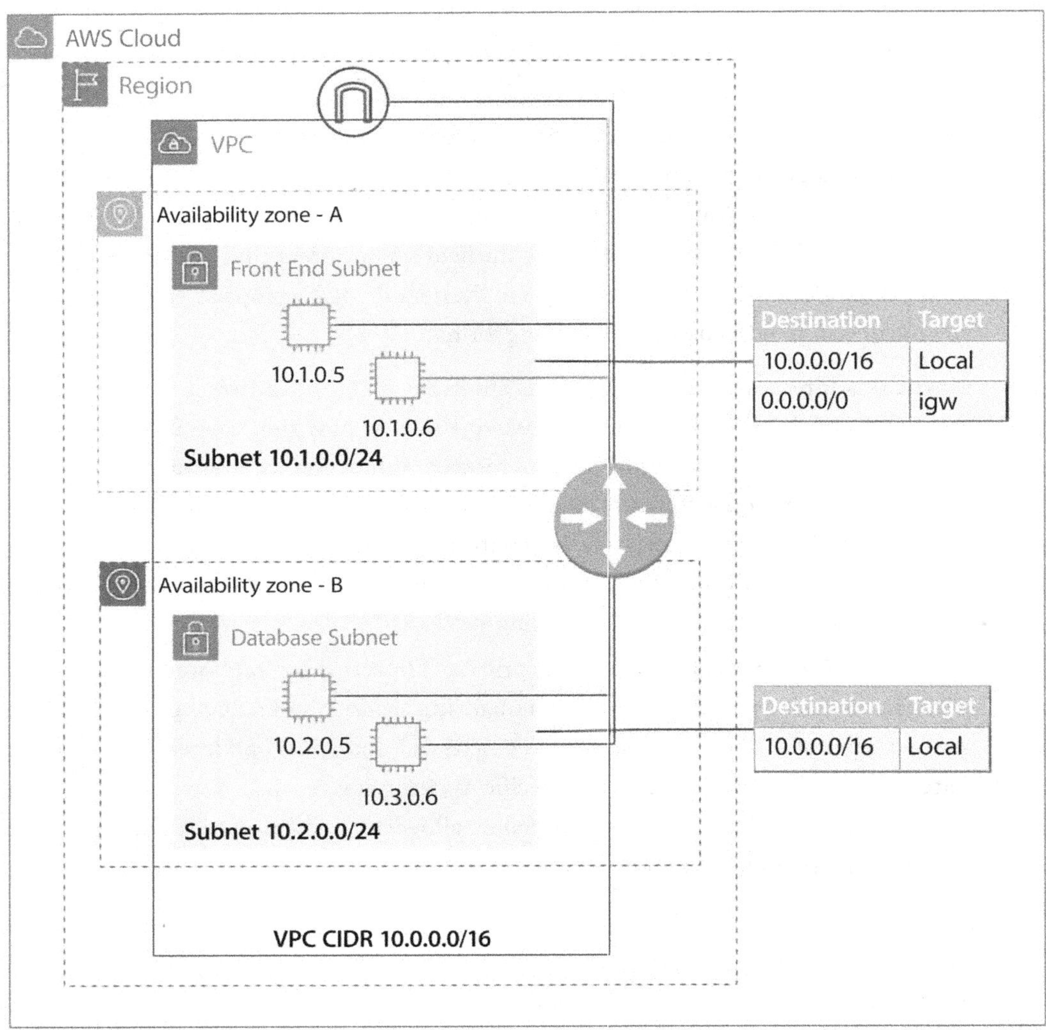

Figure 4.4: Amazon VPC network architecture

This diagram shows that VPC subnets can be private or public. As the name suggests, a private subnet doesn't have access to and from the internet, and a public subnet does. By default, any subnet you create is private; what makes it public is the default route, as in `0.0.0.0/0` via the IGW. However, it is recommended to avoid creating a public subnet to secure your infrastructure and application. Public subnet resources are directly accessible from the internet, increasing the risk of security breaches if not properly protected.

The VPC's route tables comprise directives for packet routing, and a default route table exists. However, unique route tables can be assigned to individual subnets. By default, all VPC subnets possess interconnectivity. This default behavior can be modified with VPC enhancements for more precise subnet routing, which enables the configuration of subnet route tables that direct traffic between two subnets in a VPC through virtual appliances such as intrusion detection systems, network firewalls, and protection systems.

As you can see, AWS provides multiple layers for network configuration and security at each layer to help build and protect your infrastructure. If attackers can access one component, they must restrict access to limited resources by keeping them in their isolated subnet. Due to the ease of VPC creation and the need to build tighter security, organizations tend to create multiple VPCs, which makes things more complicated when these VPCs need to communicate with each other. To simplify this, AWS provides **Transit Gateway** (**TGW**). Let's learn more about it.

AWS TGW and VPC peering

As customers spin more VPCs in AWS, there is an ever-increasing need to connect various VPCs. Before TGW, you could connect VPCs using VPC peering, but VPC peering is a one-to-one connection, meaning that resources within peered VPCs can only communicate. Even with TGW, VPC peering is still good for a few customers, depending on their use case. If multiple VPCs need to communicate with each other, which is often the case, it results in a complex mesh of VPC peering. For example, as shown in the following diagram, you need 10 peering connections if you have 5 VPCs, and for *n* VPCs, the number of required peering connections is *n (n-1)/2*.

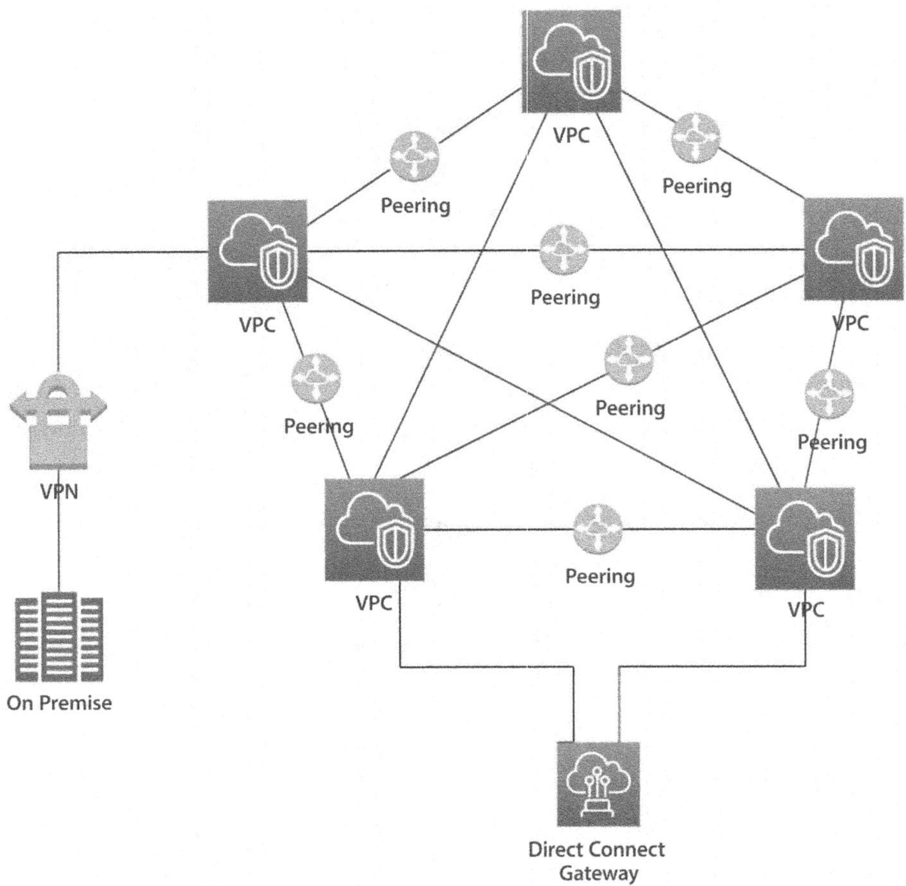

Figure 4.5: VPC connectivity using VPC peering without TGW

As you can see in the preceding diagram, managing so many VPC peering connections will become challenging, and there is also a limit on the number of peering connections per account. Also, VPC peering is not transitive, which means if VPC A peers with VPC B, and VPC B peers with VPC C, VPC A cannot communicate with VPC C through VPC B – you must create a direct peering connection between A and C to allow communication. To overcome this challenge, AWS released TGW. TGW needs one connection called an attachment to a VPC, and you can establish full- or part-mesh connectivity easily without maintaining so many peering connections.

The following diagram shows simplified communication between five VPCs using TGW:

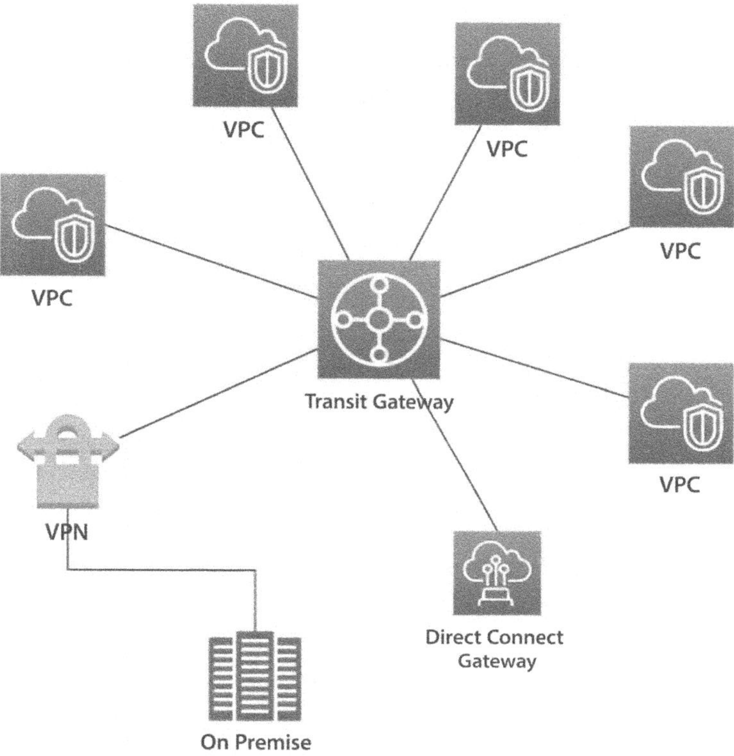

Figure 4.6: VPC connectivity with TGW

AWS TGW is a central aggregation service spanning a Region that can connect your VPCs and on-premises networks. TGW is a managed service that considers your availability and scalability and eliminates complex VPN or peering connection scenarios when connecting with multiple VPCs and on-premises infrastructure. You can connect transit gateways in different Regions by using TGW peering.

Here's a table comparing AWS TGW and VPC peering:

Feature	AWS TGW	VPC peering
Purpose	Central hub for connecting multiple VPCs and on-premises networks	Direct connection between two VPCs
Scalability	Scales to hundreds of VPCs, on-premises networks, and AWS accounts	Primarily used for connecting two VPCs; requires additional peering connections for multiple VPCs

Management complexity	Simplifies management with a hub-and-spoke model	Becomes complex with multiple peerings
Multi-Region support	Supports inter-Region peering for global VPC connectivity	Requires separate peering for each VPC pair across Regions
Routing control	Centralized routing control via TGW route tables	Decentralized, managed within each VPC's route table
Cost	Charged per hour and per GB for data processed	No hourly cost; charged per GB for data transferred
Use cases	Suitable for large, scalable, and centralized network architectures	Simple, low-latency connections between two VPCs
Network segmentation	Supports segmentation with multiple route tables for isolating traffic	Limited to basic route table management within each VPC
Security	Offers enhanced security with AWS Network Firewall integration	Basic network access control between peered VPCs

Table 4.1: Transit Gateway and VPC peering comparison

The preceding table shows that TGW is ideal for complex, large-scale network architectures, especially for multi-VPC and multi-Region environments. At the same time, VPC peering is suitable for simple, low-latency connections between two VPCs, but can become complex and costly for larger networks.

TGW is a Regional entity, meaning you can only attach VPCs to the TGW within the same Region. The bandwidth reserved per VPC is 50 Gbps. However, one TGW can have up to 5,000 VPC attachments.

Best practice

The following are some of the best practices for TGW:

- **Centralize management**: Use TGW to consolidate multiple VPCs and on-premises connections into a hub-and-spoke model. This reduces network sprawl, simplifies routing, and improves security.
- **Enable TGW peering**: For multi-Region architectures, peering two transit gateways between AWS Regions can enhance redundancy and fault tolerance, facilitating disaster recovery.

- **Leverage route tables for segmentation:** Use route tables within TGW to control traffic flow, segment workloads, and isolate sensitive resources, ensuring secure network segmentation.
- **Optimize costs:** Use TGW selectively to minimize data transfer costs, avoiding unnecessary cross-Region or cross-AZ traffic where possible.

Use cases

TGW can be very useful for the following use cases:

- **Enterprise-scale network architectures:** TGW is ideal for organizations managing complex networks with numerous VPCs, providing a unified network management approach.
- **Multi-Region high availability:** Peering transit gateways across Regions allows fault tolerance and low-latency connections, supporting critical applications and disaster recovery setups.
- **Hybrid cloud networking:** TGW simplifies hybrid connectivity for enterprises with on-premises data centers, enabling seamless integration of AWS and on-premises environments through VPNs or AWS Direct Connect.

AWS TGW is a powerful tool for enterprises seeking to manage large-scale, secure, and efficient cloud networks. It ensures flexible connectivity across cloud and on-premises resources.

In this section, you have learned how to establish network communication between VPCs, but what about securely connecting to resources such as Amazon S3 that live outside of a VPC or other AWS accounts? AWS provides PrivateLink to establish a private connection between VPCs and other AWS services. Let's learn more about AWS PrivateLink.

AWS PrivateLink

AWS PrivateLink establishes secure connectivity between VPCs and AWS services, preventing traffic exposure to the internet. PrivateLink allows for the private connection of a VPC with supported AWS services hosted by different AWS accounts.

You can access AWS services from a VPC using the gateway VPC and interface VPC endpoints. Gateway endpoints do not support PrivateLink but allow connection to Amazon S3 and DynamoDB without needing an IGW or NAT device in your VPC. An interface VPC endpoint can be created for other AWS services to establish a connection to services through AWS PrivateLink.

Enabling PrivateLink in AWS requires creating an endpoint network interface within the desired subnet and assigning a private IP address from the subnet address range for each specified subnet in the VPC. You can view the endpoint network interface in your AWS account, but you can't manage it yourself.

PrivateLink essentially provides access to resources hosted in other VPCs or AWS accounts, accessing a service in another VPC privately without full VPC connectivity. This eliminates the need to use any NAT gateway, IGW, public IP address, or VPN. Therefore, it provides better control over your services, which are reachable via a client VPC.

As shown in the following diagram, AWS PrivateLink enables private connectivity between the **service provider** and **service consumer** using AWS infrastructure to exchange data without going over the public internet. To achieve this, the service provider creates an endpoint service in a private subnet.

In contrast, the service consumer creates an endpoint in a private subnet with the service provider's service API as the target.

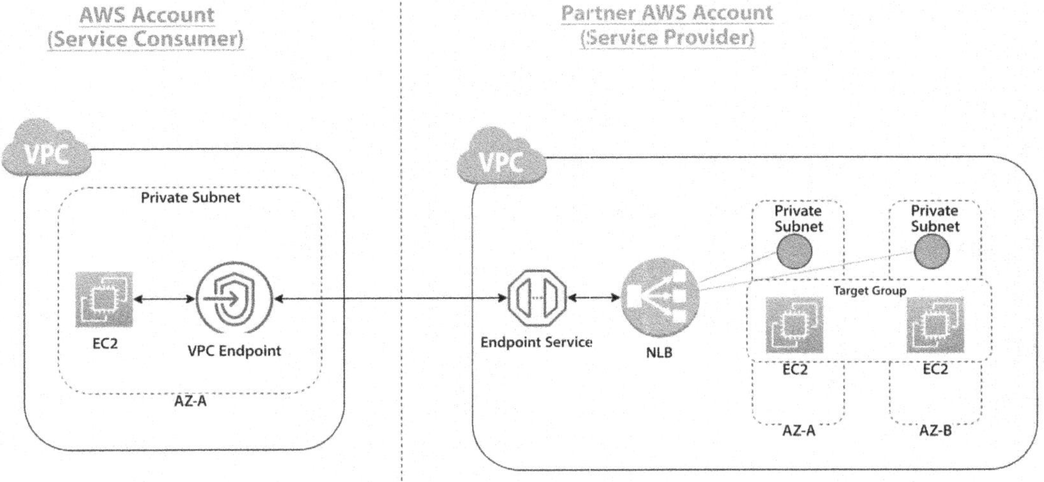

Figure 4.7: PrivateLink between partner service provider and service consumer accounts

The preceding architecture diagram shows that the partner sets up an endpoint service to expose the service running behind the load balancer (NLB). An NLB is created for each private subnet. These services are running on EC2 instances hosted inside a private subnet. The client can then create a VPC endpoint with the target as the endpoint service and use it to consume it.

Let's look at another pattern, shown in the following diagram, which depicts the use of PrivateLink between a service consumer on an AWS account and an on-premises service provider:

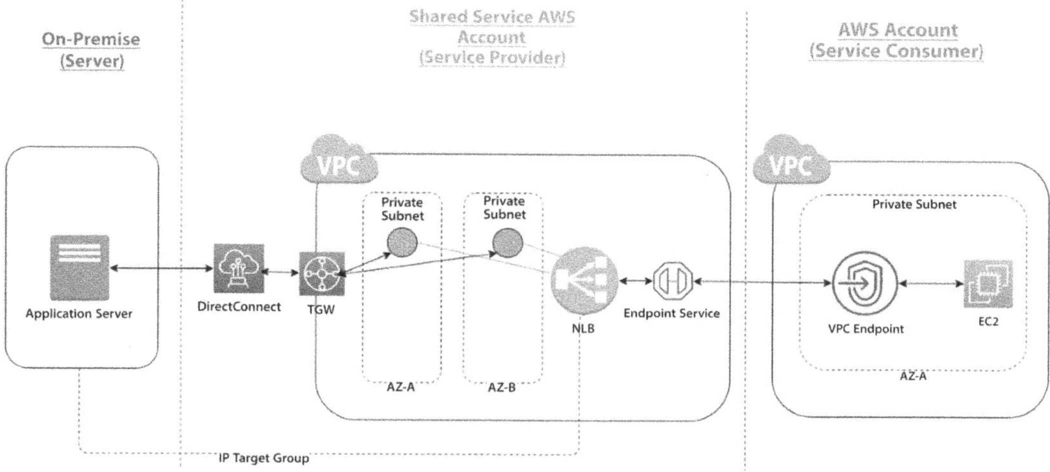

Figure 4.8: PrivateLink between a shared service provider, an on-premises server, and a service consumer account

In this setup, the on-premise servers are the service providers. The NLB in the shared service account is configured with an auto-scaling group with targets referencing the IP addresses of the on-premises servers. The NLB is then exposed as an endpoint service. The service consumer account can consume this endpoint service by creating a VPC endpoint. **Direct Connect** provides a dedicated high-speed fiber-optic line between the on-premises server and AWS Regions. You will learn more about Direct Connect in this chapter in the *Building hybrid cloud connectivity in AWS* section.

Here's a simple comparison table to help you understand when to use AWS PrivateLink versus VPC peering versus TGW, along with clear examples to guide your decision:

Feature	AWS PrivateLink	VPC peering	Transit Gateway
Type	One-way private access to services	Two-way full network connectivity	Centralized hub for connecting multiple VPCs and on-premises networks
Connectivity scope	Service consumer to service provider (specific endpoints)	Direct connectivity between two VPCs	Many-to-many VPC and VPN/Direct Connect attachment

Transitive support	No	No	Yes
Use case	Accessing a service in another VPC privately without full VPC connectivity	When two VPCs need to talk directly (e.g., app to database)	Connecting many VPCs or hybrid networks at scale
Data access direction	One-way (consumer initiates)	Two-way	Two-way
Cross-account support	Yes	Yes	Yes
Billing	Based on data processed via endpoint	No extra cost beyond data transfer	TGW hourly plus data processing fees
Security	Limits exposure to just the endpoint, ideal for sensitive services	Allows access to all subnets (unless restricted)	Provides centralized control with route tables and segmentation
Example	You run a SaaS service and want customers to access it without exposing the VPC	App in VPC A needs direct DB access in VPC B	Large enterprise with many VPCs needing centralized routing and management

Table 4.2: AWS PrivateLink vs. VPC peering vs. TGW

Now, many applications run globally and aim to harness users from every corner of the world to accelerate their business. In such a situation, it becomes essential that your users have the same experience while accessing your application, regardless of their physical location. AWS provides various edge networking services to handle global traffic. Let's learn more about this.

Edge networking

Edge networking is like last-mile delivery in the supply chain world. When you have users worldwide, from the USA to Australia and India to Brazil, you want each user to have the same experience, regardless of the physical location of your server where the application is hosted. There are several components that play their role in building last-mile networking. Let's explore them in detail.

Amazon Route 53

Amazon Route 53 is a fully managed, simple, fast, secure, highly available, and scalable DNS service. It provides a reliable and cost-effective means for systems and users to translate names such as `www.example.com` into IP addresses such as `1.2.3.4`. Route 53 is a domain register where you can register a new domain. You can choose an available domain, add it to the cart from the AWS console, and define contacts for the domain. AWS allows you to transfer your domains to AWS and between accounts.

In Route 53, AWS assigns four name servers for all domains, as shown in the screenshot: one for `.com`, one for `.net`, one for `.co.uk`, and one for `.org`. Why? For higher availability! If there is an issue with the `.net` DNS services, the other three provide high availability for your domains.

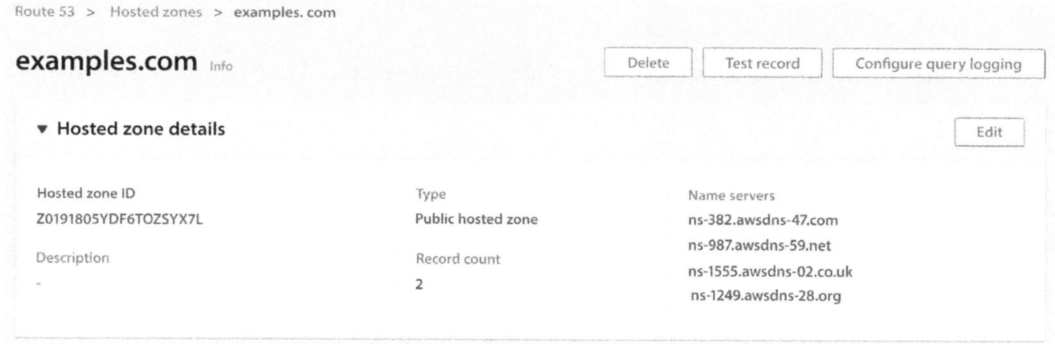

Figure 4.9: Route 53 name server configuration

Route 53 supports both public and private hosted zones. Public-hosted zones have a route to internet-facing resources and resolve from the internet using global routing policies. Meanwhile, private hosted zones have a route to VPC resources and resolve from inside the VPC. It helps to integrate with on-premises private zones using forwarding rules and endpoints.

Route 53 provides IPv6 support with end-to-end DNS resolution, support for IPv6 forward (AAAA) and reverse (PTR) DNS records, and health check monitoring for IPv6 endpoints. For PrivateLink support, when configuring, you can specify a private DNS name, and the Route 53 resolver will resolve it to the PrivateLink endpoint.

Route 53 provides the following eight types of routing policies for traffic:

- **Simple routing policy**: This is used for a single resource (e.g., a web server created for the `www.example.com` website).

- **Failover routing policy**: This is used to configure active-passive failover.
- **Geolocation routing policy**: This routes traffic based on the user's location.
- **Geoproximity routing policy**: Use when you want to route traffic based on the location of your resources and, optionally, shift traffic from resources in one location to resources in another location.
- **Latency routing policy**: This optimizes the best latency for the resources deployed in multiple AWS Regions.
- **IP-based routing**: This allows you to customize your DNS routing based on your knowledge of your network, applications, and clients, enabling you to make optimal DNS routing choices for your end users. This feature provides granular control over routing, allowing you to enhance performance or reduce network expenses by uploading your user-IP-to-endpoint mapping data to Route 53.
- **Multi-value answer routing policy**: This is used to respond to DNS queries with up to eight healthy, randomly selected records.
- **Weighted routing policy**: This policy routes traffic to multiple resource properties as you define (for example, you want to send 80% of traffic to site A and 20% to site B).

You can build advanced routing policies by nesting these primary routing policies into traffic policies; the following diagram shows a nested policy architecture:

Figure 4.10: Route 53 nested routing based on

In the preceding diagram, the geolocation-based policy routes traffic based on the user's location and proximity to the nearest Region. In the second level, a nested policy is defined as a weighted policy within the Region that routes traffic to servers based on the weight you have determined to route traffic to individual application servers.

Advanced routing policies can be built by nesting the seven primary routing policies into traffic policies. You can find more details on this routing policy in the AWS user document here: `https://docs.aws.amazon.com/Route53/latest/DeveloperGuide/routing-policy.html`.

Route 53 Resolver rules tell Route 53 to query a domain, add a forward rule, and point toward the appropriate outbound resolver for DNS zones that should resolve on-premises. Public hosted zones route traffic to internet-facing resources and resolve from the internet using global routing policies. Private hosted zones route traffic to VPC resources and resolve from inside the VPC. Private hosted zones integrate with on-premises private zones using forwarding rules and endpoints.

Route 53 is the only service that AWS offers with a 100% SLA, which means AWS makes its best effort to ensure it is 100% available. You will be eligible for a service credit if Route 53 does not meet the availability commitment.

Amazon Route 53 provides a reliable and scalable domain registration and management service, allowing users to register new domain names or transfer existing domains to AWS. With Route 53, users can manage their domain's DNS records and configure routing based on geographic location, latency, or weighted routing policies to direct traffic to the most appropriate endpoints. Route 53 integrates seamlessly with other AWS services, making linking domains with applications hosted in AWS environments easy. Additionally, Route 53 offers automatic renewal options, ensuring domains stay active without manual intervention. Using Route 53's DNS management capabilities, organizations can streamline their domain and DNS management processes, maintaining high availability and resiliency for their online resources.

While Route 53 helps direct global traffic to your server, there could be latency if you wanted to deliver significant static assets, such as images and videos, to users far from your server's deployment Region. AWS provides CloudFront as a content distribution network to solve these latency problems. Let's learn more about it.

Amazon CloudFront

Amazon CloudFront is a content delivery service that accelerates the distribution of both static and dynamic content, such as image files, video files, and JavaScript, CSS, or HTML files, through a network of data centers spread across the globe. These data centers are referred to as **edge locations**. When you use CloudFront to distribute your content, users requesting content get served by the nearest edge location, providing lower latency and better performance.

As of October 2024, AWS has over 400 high-density edge locations spread across over 90 cities in 48 countries. All edge locations have ample cache storage space and intelligent routing mechanisms to increase the edge cache hit ratio. AWS content distribution edge locations are connected with high-performance 100-GbE network devices and are fully redundant, with parallel global networks with default physical layer encryption.

Suppose you have an image distribution website, `www.example.com`, hosted in the USA, which serves art images. Users can access the URL `www.example.com/art.png`, and the image is loaded. If your server is close to the user, the image load time will be faster. Still, suppose users from other locations, such as Australia or South Africa, want to access the same URL. In that case, the request has to cross multiple networks before delivering the content to the user's browser. The following diagram shows the HTTP request flow with Amazon CloudFront:

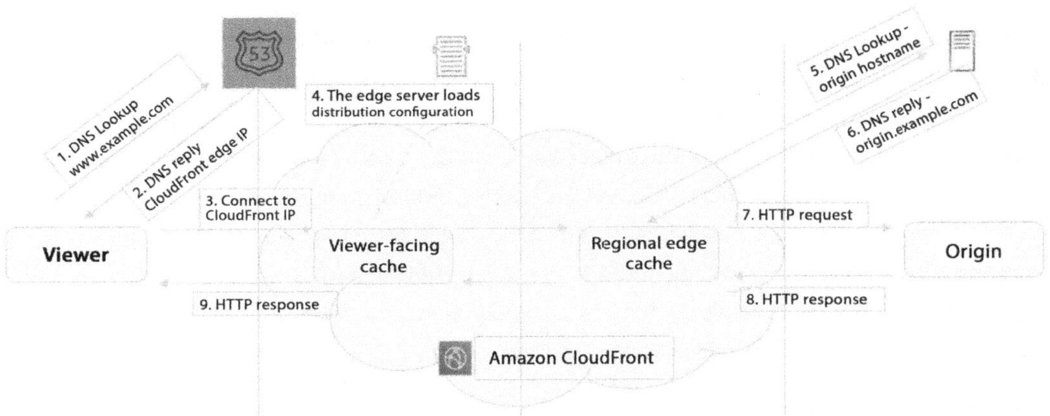

Figure 4.11: HTTP request flow with Amazon CloudFront

As shown in the preceding diagram, when a viewer requests access to page content from the origin server – in this case, `www.example.com` – Route 53 replies with the CloudFront edge IP and redirects the user to the CloudFront location. CloudFront uses the following rules for content distribution:

- If the requested content is already in the edge data center, it is a "cache hit" and will be served immediately.
- If the content is not at the edge location (a "cache miss"), CloudFront will request the content from the original location (the web server or S3). The request flows through the AWS backbone, is delivered to the customer, and a copy is kept for future requests.
- Using CloudFront also provides an extra layer of security since your origin server is not directly exposed to the public network.

CloudFront eliminates the need to go to the origin server for user requests, and content is served from the nearest location. CloudFront provides security by safeguarding the connection between end-users and the content edge and between the edge network and the origin. By offloading SSL termination to CloudFront, application performance is improved since the burden of processing the required negotiation and SSL handshakes is removed from the origins.

Caching strategies

Optimizing caching strategies in CloudFront is crucial to balance performance, cost, and content freshness. Here are some key caching strategies used with Amazon CloudFront:

- **Cache-Control headers**: You can control how long objects are cached at CloudFront edge locations by setting `Cache-Control` and `Expires` headers in the origin responses. For static content that doesn't change often, setting a longer cache duration reduces the frequency of origin requests, lowering costs and improving load times.
- **Dynamic content caching**: CloudFront can cache dynamic content based on query strings, headers, and cookies. By configuring CloudFront to cache different versions of content based on these attributes, you can reduce the load on your origin server while delivering personalized or frequently updated content to users.
- **Time-to-live (TTL) settings**: CloudFront allows fine-grained TTL settings, which dictate how long objects are cached at edge locations before checking back with the origin for updates. Shorter TTLs ensure fresher content but may increase requests to the origin. Setting a longer TTL can be more cost-effective for content that changes infrequently.
- **Invalidate cache for updates**: When content changes and needs to be refreshed, you can use cache invalidations to remove specific objects from the CloudFront cache. This strategy ensures that users receive updated content without waiting for TTLs to expire, although it can incur additional costs.
- **Origin Shield**: Origin Shield is an additional caching layer within CloudFront that helps reduce the origin load by consolidating requests at a regional cache before they reach the origin. This strategy is particularly useful for lowering origin costs and ensuring that only one request per Region returns to the origin, minimizing bottlenecks.

Improving the cache hit ratio

When you're using Amazon CloudFront to deliver content, improving the cache hit ratio is one of the most effective ways to boost performance and reduce costs. A higher cache hit ratio means more content is served directly from CloudFront edge locations, reducing the need to fetch data from your origin servers.

To optimize this, start by setting longer TTL values for static content such as images, JavaScript, CSS, and fonts. This tells CloudFront to keep these objects cached longer, avoiding repeated trips to the origin. Be careful with query strings, headers, and cookies; CloudFront treats requests with different values for these as separate cache entries. By forwarding only what's necessary using cache and origin request policies, you can avoid unnecessary cache misses.

Caching strategies in CloudFront can optimize content delivery performance, reduce latency, and minimize the load on origin servers, resulting in faster response times and a better user experience. CloudFront is a vast topic, and you can learn more about it here: `https://aws.amazon.com/cloudfront/features/`.

In this section, you learned how CloudFront improves performance for cacheable content such as static images and videos. To address global user traffic from edge locations, AWS provides **AWS Global Accelerator** (**AGA**), which improves the availability and performance of your applications with local or global users. Let's learn more about it.

AWS Global Accelerator

AGA enhances application availability and performance by offering fixed static IP addresses as single or multiple entry points to AWS Regions, including ALBs, NLBs, and EC2 instances. AGA utilizes the AWS global network to optimize the path from users to applications, thereby improving the performance of TCP and UDP traffic. AGA continuously monitors the health of application endpoints and promptly redirects traffic to healthy endpoints within one minute in the event of unhealthy endpoint detection.

AGA and CloudFront are distinct services that employ the AWS global network and its edge locations. While CloudFront accelerates the performance of both cacheable (e.g., videos and images) and dynamic (e.g., dynamic site delivery and API acceleration) content, AGA enhances the performance of various applications over TCP or UDP. Both services are compatible with AWS Shield, protecting against DDoS attacks. You will learn more about AWS Shield in *Chapter 8, Best Practices for Application Security, Identity, and Compliance.*

AGA automatically reroutes your traffic to the nearest healthy endpoint to avoid failure. AGA health checks will react to customer backend failure within 30 seconds, in line with other AWS load-balancing solutions (such as NLB) and Route 53. AGA raises the bar with its ability to shift traffic to healthy backends in as short a timeframe as 30 seconds, whereas DNS-based solutions can take minutes to hours to change the traffic load. Some key reasons to use AGA are as follows:

- **Accelerate your global applications**: AGA intelligently directs TCP or UDP traffic from users to the AWS-based application endpoint, providing consistent performance regardless of their geographic location.
- **Improve global application availability**: AGA constantly monitors your application endpoints, including, but not limited to, ALBs, NLBs, and EC2 instances. It instantly reacts to changes in their health or configuration, redirecting traffic to the next closest available endpoint when problems arise. As a result, your users experience higher availability. AGA delivers **inter-Region** load balancing, while ELB provides **intra-Region** load balancing.

  ELB in a Region is suitable for AGA as it evenly distributes incoming application traffic across backends, such as Amazon EC2 instances or ECS tasks, within the Region. AGA complements ELB by expanding these capabilities beyond any single Region, enabling you to create a global interface for applications with application stacks in a single Region or multiple Regions.
- **Fixed entry point**: AGA provides a set of static IP addresses for use as a fixed entry point to your AWS application. Announced via Anycast and delivered from AWS edge locations worldwide, these eliminate the complexity of managing the IP addresses of multiple endpoints and allow you to scale your application and maintain DDoS resiliency with AWS Shield.
- **Protect your applications**: AGA allows you to serve internet users while keeping your ALBs and EC2 instances private.

AGA allows customers to run global applications in multiple AWS Regions. Traffic destined for static IPs is globally distributed. End user requests are ingested through AWS's closest edge location and routed to the correct regional resource for better availability and latency. This global endpoint supports TCP and UDP and stays the same, even as customers move resources between Regions for failover or other reasons (i.e., client applications are no longer tightly coupled to the specific AWS Region an application runs in). Customers will like the simplicity of this managed service.

As technology becomes more accessible with the high-speed networks provided by 5G, there is a need to run applications such as connected cars, autonomous vehicles, and live video recognition with ultra-low latency. AWS provides a service called AWS Wavelength, which delivers AWS services to the edge of the 5G network. Let's learn more about it.

AWS Wavelength

AWS Wavelength is designed to reduce network latency when connecting to applications from 5G-connected devices by providing infrastructure deployments within the Telco 5G network service providers' data centers. It allows application traffic to reach servers running in Wavelength Zones and AWS compute and storage services. This eliminates the need for traffic to go through the internet, which can introduce latency of up to 10 milliseconds and limit the full potential of 5G's bandwidth and latency advancements.

AWS Wavelength allows for creating and implementing real-time, low-latency applications, such as edge inference, smart factories, IoT devices, and live streaming. This service enables the deployment of emerging, interactive applications that require ultra-low latency to function effectively.

Some key benefits of AWS Wavelength are as follows:

- **Ultra-low latency for 5G**: Wavelength combines the AWS core services, such as compute and storage, with low-latency 5G networks. It helps you build applications with ultra-low latencies using the 5G network.
- **Consistent AWS experience**: You can use the same AWS services you use daily on the AWS platform.
- **Global 5G network:** Wavelength is available in popular Telco networks such as Verizon, Vodafone, and SK Telecom worldwide, including the USA, Europe, Korea, and Japan, enabling ultra-low latency applications for a global user base.

Mobile edge computing use cases for AWS Wavelength include the following:

- **Augmented reality/virtual reality (AR/VR)**: It enables immersive experiences by reducing the time data travels between devices and processing servers.
- **Autonomous vehicles:** It allows vehicles to receive real-time data processing for navigation and hazard detection.
- **Smart cities and IoT**: It supports IoT applications in smart cities, where sensors and devices require real-time data processing.
- **Gaming**: It enhances mobile gaming with low-latency, high-performance compute resources near the user, enabling smooth and responsive gameplay.

AWS Wavelength empowers developers to deliver innovative, latency-sensitive mobile applications, transforming the potential of 5G technology with cloud computing at the mobile edge.

Wavelength Zones are connected to a Region and provide access to AWS services. Architecting edge applications using a hub-and-spoke model with the Region is recommended for scalable and cost-effective options for less latency-sensitive applications.

Here's a comparison table to help you decide when to use AGA, Route 53 latency-based routing, Amazon CloudFront, or AWS Wavelength for latency-sensitive applications:

Feature	AWS Global Accelerator	Route 53 latency-based routing	Amazon CloudFront	AWS Wavelength
Primary purpose	Directs traffic to the optimal AWS endpoint via the AWS backbone	Routes DNS queries to the Region with the lowest latency	Delivers cached content through global edge locations	Brings AWS compute to the edge of 5G networks
Latency optimization level	Global low latency via static IP and intelligent routing	Latency-based DNS routing across AWS Regions	Reduces latency for web content by caching close to users	Ultra-low latency (single-digit ms) for edge 5G applications
Best for	Multi-Region apps needing static IPs and TCP/UDP optimization	Apps deployed in multiple AWS Regions	Static and dynamic web content (images, video, and APIs)	Real-time apps: AR/VR, gaming, and live video
Transports supported	TCP and UDP	DNS-level only	HTTP and HTTPS	Any low-latency compute at the 5G edge
Cross-Region support	Yes, automatically routes to the closest healthy Region	Yes, routes based on DNS response	Not applicable (focuses on content delivery)	No, local to Telco edge zones
Static IP support	Yes	No	No	No
Content caching	No	No	Yes	No
Integration use case	Gaming, VoIP, financial apps, and global APIs	Regional routing for web or app traffic	Media delivery, e-commerce, and software distribution	AR/VR, connected vehicles, and industrial IoT

Real-world Example	A global financial app using static IPs for reliable routing	Media streaming services directing traffic by geography	E-commerce platform caching images and assets globally	Live AR experience at sports events using 5G edge zones

Table 4.3: Comparison between AWS options

As enterprises adopt the cloud, moving all IT workloads to the cloud will not be possible. Some applications need to run on-premises and still communicate with the cloud. Let's learn about AWS services for setting up a hybrid cloud.

Building hybrid cloud connectivity in AWS

A hybrid cloud comes into the picture when you must keep some of your IT workloads on-premises while creating your cloud migration strategy. You may have decided to keep them out of the cloud for various reasons, such as compliance and the unavailability of out-of-the-box cloud services, such as a mainframe, when you need more time to re-architect them, or when you are waiting to complete your license term with an existing vendor. In such cases, you need highly reliable connectivity between your on-premises and cloud infrastructure. Let's learn about the various options available from AWS to set up hybrid cloud connectivity.

AWS Virtual Private Network (VPN)

AWS VPN is a networking service that establishes a secure connection between AWS, on-premises networks, and remote client devices. There are two variants of AWS VPN: Site-to-Site VPN and AWS Client VPN. AWS Site-To-Site VPN establishes a secure tunnel between on-premises and AWS virtual private gateways or AWS transit gateways.

It offers fully managed and highly available VPN termination endpoints at AWS Regions. You can add two VPN tunnels per VPN connection, secured with an IPsec Site-to-Site tunnel with AES-256, SHA-2, and the latest DH groups. The following diagram shows the AWS Site-to-Site VPN connection.

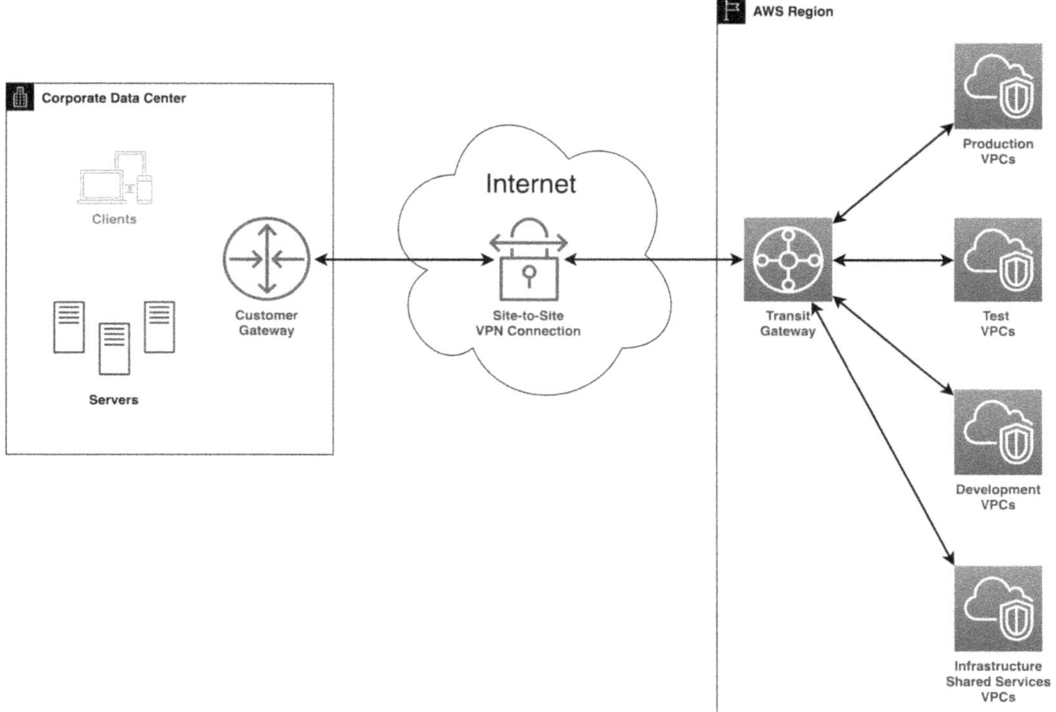

Figure 4.12: AWS Site-to-Site VPN with TGW

As depicted in the preceding diagram, a connection has been established from the customer gateway to AWS TGW using a Site-to-Site VPN, which is further connected to multiple VPCs.

AWS Client VPN can be used with OpenVPN-based VPN client software to access your AWS and on-premises resources from anywhere in the world.

AWS Client VPN also supports a split tunneling feature, which can be used only to send traffic destined to AWS via Client VPN and the rest of the traffic via a local internet breakout.

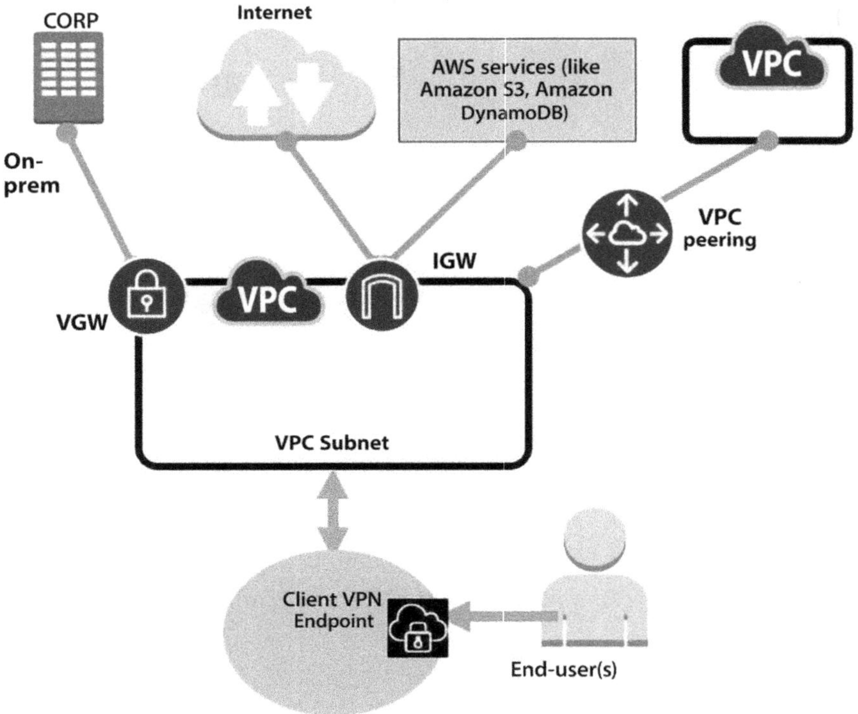

Figure 4.13: AWS Client VPN

AWS Client VPN provides secure access to any resource in AWS and on-premises from anywhere using OpenVPN clients. It seamlessly integrates with existing infrastructure, such as Amazon VPC and AWS Directory Service.

AWS Direct Connect

AWS Direct Connect is a low-level infrastructure service that enables AWS customers to set up a dedicated network connection between their on-premises facilities and AWS. Using AWS Direct Connect, you can bypass any public internet connection and establish a private connection linking your data centers with AWS. This solution provides higher network throughput, increases connection consistency, and, counterintuitively, can often reduce network costs.

There are two variants of Direct Connect: dedicated and hosted. A dedicated connection is made through a single customer's 1 Gbps, 10 Gbps, or 100 Gbps dedicated Ethernet connection. Hosted connections are obtained via an AWS Direct Connect Delivery Partner, which provides the connectivity between your data center and AWS via the Partner's infrastructure.

However, it is essential to note that AWS Direct Connect does not provide encryption in transit by default. Suppose you want to have encryption in transit. In that case, you have two choices – you can either use AWS Site-To-Site VPN to provide IPsec encryption for your packets, or you can combine AWS Direct Connect with AWS Site-to-Site VPN to deliver an IPsec-encrypted private connection while, at the same time, lowering network costs and increasing network bandwidth throughput.

The other option is to activate the MACsec feature, which provides line-rate, bi-directional encryption for 10 Gbps and 100 Gbps dedicated connections between your data centers and AWS Direct Connect locations. MACsec is done at the hardware; hence, it provides better performance. To encrypt the traffic, you can also use an AWS technology partner as an alternative solution to encrypt this network traffic.

AWS Direct Connect uses the 802.1q industry standard to create VLANs. These connections can be split into several **virtual interfaces (VIFs)**. This enables us to leverage the same connection to publicly accessible services such as Amazon S3 using an IP address space and private services such as EC2 instances running in a VPC within AWS. The following are AWS Direct Connect interface types:

- **Public virtual interface**: You can use this interface to access any AWS public services globally, accessible via public IP addresses such as Amazon S3. A public VIF can access all AWS public services using public IP addresses.
- **Private virtual interface**: You can connect to your VPCs using private VIFs and IP addresses. You can connect to the AWS Direct Connect gateway using a private VIF, connecting you to up to 10 VPCs globally with a single VIF, unlike connecting a private VIF to a virtual private gateway associated with a single VPC.
- **Transit virtual interface**: A transit VIF is connected to your TGW via a Direct Connect gateway and is supported for a bandwidth of 1 Gbps or higher.

The following diagram shows various AWS Direct Connect interfaces, highlighting how to use various interfaces while designing your hybrid cloud connectivity:

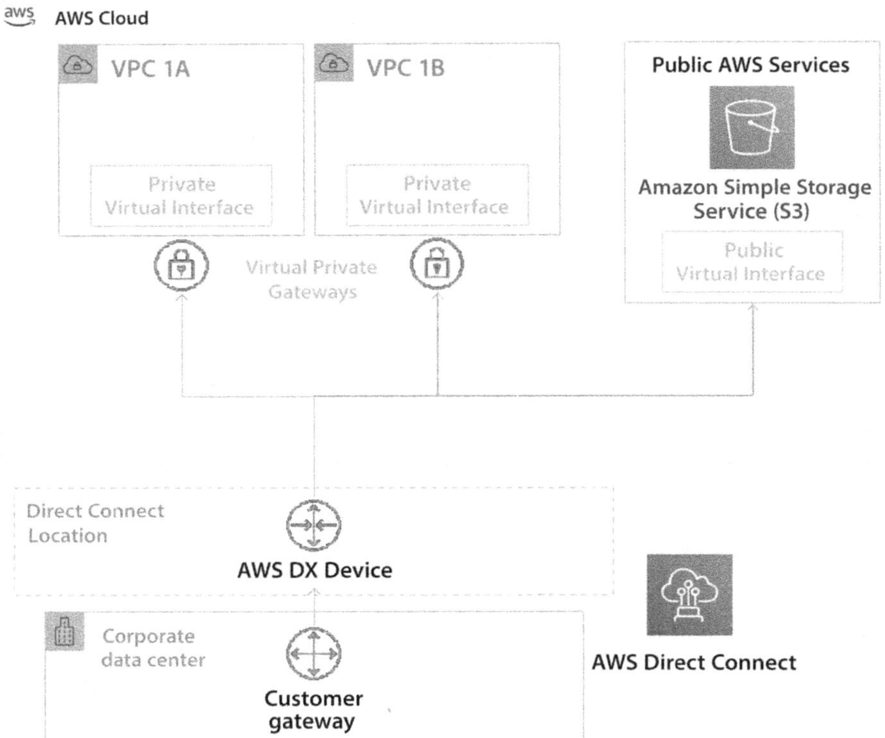

Figure 4.14: AWS Direct Connect interface types

The preceding diagram shows the corporate data center connected to the AWS cloud using the Direct Connect location. Most of your application workloads, such as the web server, app server, and database server, run inside the VPC under a private restricted network, so a private VIF connects to VPCs across different AZs. Conversely, Amazon S3 is in the public domain, where you might host static pages, images, and videos for your applications connected through a public VIF.

AWS Direct Connect can reduce costs when workloads require high bandwidth. It can reduce these costs in two ways:

- It transfers data from on-premises environments to the cloud, reducing cost commitments to **internet service providers** (**ISPs**).
- The costs of transferring data using a dedicated connection are billed using the AWS Direct Connect data transfer rates, not the internet data transfer rates, which are lower.

Network latency and response to requests can be highly variable. Workloads that use AWS Direct Connect have much more homogeneous latency and a consistent user experience. Direct connection comes with a cost; you may only occasionally need such high bandwidth, and want to optimize costs better. For such cases, you may want to use AWS VPN, as discussed in the *AWS Virtual Private Network (VPN)* section.

You have learned about different patterns of setting up network connectivity within an AWS cloud and to or from an AWS cloud, but connecting multiple data centers, office locations, and cloud resources can be a very tedious task for a large enterprise with branch offices or chain stores. AWS provides **Cloud WAN** to simplify this issue. Let's learn more about it.

AWS Cloud WAN

How many of you would be paged if your entire network suddenly dropped? Let's take an example: Petco, which has over 1,500 locations. Imagine what happens on a network like that on any given day. One way to connect your data centers and branch offices is to use fixed, physical network connections. These connections are long-lived and not easy to change quickly.

Many use AWS Site-to-Site VPN connections to connect their locations to AWS. Alternatively, you can bypass the internet and use AWS Direct Connect to create a dedicated network link to AWS. Some use broadband internet with SD-WAN hardware to create virtual overlay networks between locations. Inside AWS, you build networks within VPCs and route traffic between them with TGW. The problem is that these networks all take different connectivity, security, and monitoring approaches. As a result, you are faced with a patchwork of tools and networks to manage and maintain.

For example, to keep your network secure, you must configure firewalls at every location. However, you are faced with many different firewalls from many different vendors, each configured slightly differently. Ensuring your access policies are synced across the entire network quickly becomes daunting. Likewise, managing and troubleshooting your network is difficult when the information you need is kept in many different systems.

Every new location, network appliance, and security requirement makes things more and more complicated. We see many customers need help to keep up. To solve these problems, network architects need to unify their networks so there is one central place to build, manage, and secure their network. They need easy ways to make and change connections between their data centers, branch offices, and cloud applications, regardless of what they're running on today. And they need a backbone network that can smoothly adapt to these changes.

AWS Cloud WAN is a global network service enabling you to create and manage your infrastructure globally in any AWS Region or on-premises. Consider it a global router that you can use to connect your on-premises networks and AWS infrastructure. AWS Cloud WAN provides network segmentation to group your network or workloads, which can be located across any AWS Region. It takes care of the route propagation to connect your infrastructure without manually maintaining the routing.

AWS Cloud WAN provides network segmentation, which means you can divide your global network into separate and isolated networks. This helps you to control the traffic flow and cross-network access tightly. For example, a corporate firm can have a network segment for invoicing and order processing, another for web traffic, and another for logging and monitoring traffic.

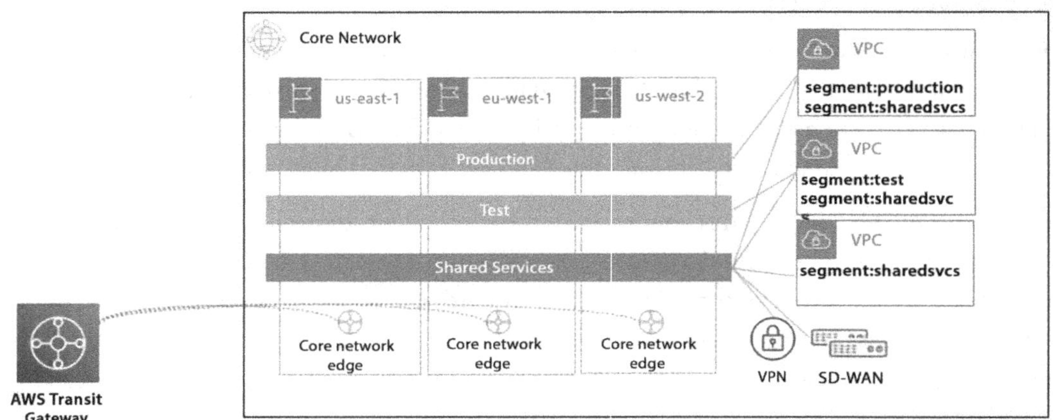

Figure 4.15: AWS Cloud WAN architecture

When using Cloud WAN, you can see your entire network on one dashboard, giving you one place to monitor and track metrics for your whole network. Cloud WAN lets you spot problems early and respond quickly, which minimizes downtime and bottlenecks while helping you troubleshoot problems, even when data comes from separate systems.

A great real-world example of this is from **Miro**, a visual collaboration platform. As Miro scaled globally, its infrastructure became complex, with multiple VPCs and static routes managed by a small engineering team. By adopting AWS Cloud WAN, Miro was able to centralize network control, automate configurations, and reduce deployment times from days to under 30 minutes. This made it easier for Miro's teams to roll out new infrastructure quickly and maintain performance across Regions, all while reducing operational overhead. You can learn more about the Miro case study here: `https://aws.amazon.com/solutions/case-studies/miro-cloud-wan-case-study/`.

As you learned about various networking components, AWS also offers very high-speed networking for specific use cases. Let's look at it in detail.

High-speed networking with AWS Elastic Fabric Adapter

AWS Elastic Fabric Adapter (**EFA**) is a network interface designed for **high-performance computing** (**HPC**) and machine learning applications requiring high inter-node communication levels at ultra-low latency. EFA is particularly effective in environments where applications must communicate rapidly across multiple instances, such as scientific simulations, financial modeling, and large-scale deep learning models.

EFA integrates with Amazon EC2 instances to deliver network speeds comparable to on-premises HPC clusters. Unlike standard EC2 network interfaces, EFA uses the AWS **Scalable Reliable Datagram** (**SRD**) protocol, which reduces network latency and improves packet loss resilience, enabling faster communication and higher data throughput. This makes it possible to run tightly-coupled workloads that require frequent data exchange between instances with minimal latency. The following are the key benefits of AWS EFA:

- **Ultra-low latency**: EFA significantly reduces latency, enabling applications to achieve microsecond-level response times. This is essential for HPC applications that require real-time data processing and fast communication between nodes.
- **High bandwidth**: EFA offers bandwidth of up to 100 Gbps on supported EC2 instances, allowing large volumes of data to be transferred quickly between instances. You can find more details here: `https://docs.aws.amazon.com/AWSEC2/latest/UserGuide/efa-acc-inst-types.html`.
- **Scalability**: With EFA, users can scale HPC applications across hundreds or thousands of nodes on AWS, achieving performance comparable to traditional HPC on-premises setups.
- **MPI compatibility**: EFA is compatible with **message passing interface** (**MPI**) libraries, which are widely used in HPC environments. This enables applications developed with MPI to leverage EFA seamlessly.

Here are some of the use cases where you should opt for EFA:

- **Scientific simulations**: Applications in genomics, weather forecasting, and physics simulations benefit from EFA's low-latency, high-bandwidth capabilities.
- **Financial modeling**: EFA enables faster computation for complex financial analyses, such as Monte Carlo simulations and risk modeling.

- **Machine learning and deep learning:** EFA accelerates distributed training for large models across multiple instances, significantly reducing the training time for machine learning workloads.
- **Computational fluid dynamics (CFD):** EFA supports large-scale CFD applications, providing the necessary speed and bandwidth for real-time simulations.

For more information about the AWS EFA and its capabilities, you can visit the official AWS EFA page: `https://aws.amazon.com/hpc/efa/`.

By leveraging AWS EFA, organizations can achieve high-speed networking crucial for demanding applications, enabling them to meet performance benchmarks that were traditionally only possible with dedicated, on-premises HPC clusters.

Security is the top priority, and throughout this chapter, you have learned about the security aspect of network design. Let's go into more detail to learn about network security best practices.

AWS cloud network security

Security is always a top priority for any organization. Generally, you must protect every infrastructure element individually and as a group – as the saying goes, "Dance as if nobody is watching and secure as if everybody is." AWS provides various managed security services and a well-architected pillar to help you design a secure solution.

You can implement a secure network infrastructure by creating an allowed list of permitted protocols, ports, CIDR networks, and SG sources and enforcing several policies on the AWS cloud. An NACL is used to explicitly block malicious traffic and segment the edge connectivity to the internet, as shown in the following diagram:

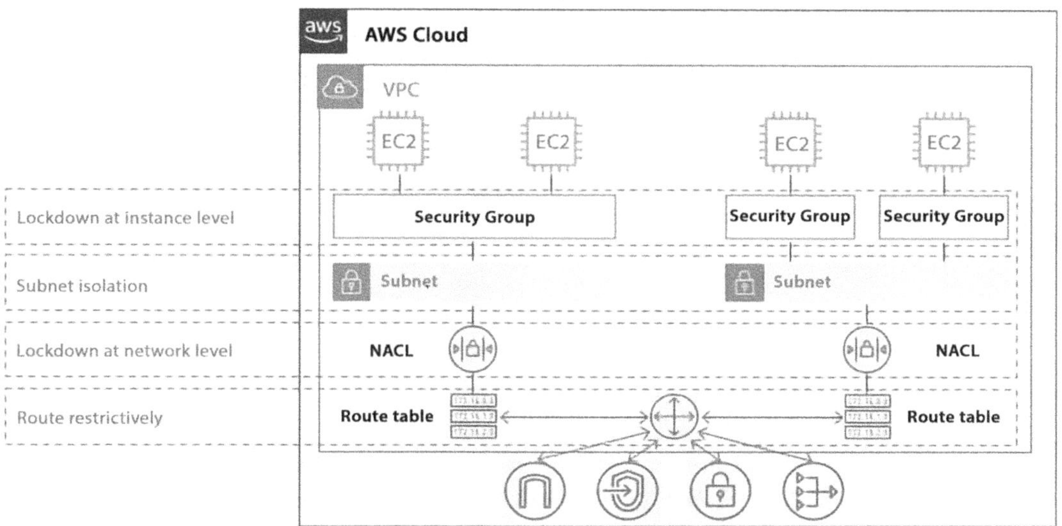

Figure 4.16: SGs and NACLs in network defense

As shown in the preceding diagram, SGs are the host-level virtual firewalls that protect your EC2 instance from the traffic coming or leaving from a particular instance. An SG is a stateful firewall, meaning you must create a rule in one direction only, and the return traffic will automatically be allowed. An NACL is a virtual firewall at the subnet boundary, regulating traffic in and out of one or more subnets. Unlike an SG, an NACL is stateless, which means you need both inbound and outbound rules to allow specific traffic.

The following table outlines the difference between SGs and NACLs:

SG	NACL
The SG is the first layer of defense, which operates at the instance level.	An NACL works at the subnet level inside an AWS VPC.
You can only add "allow" security rules.	You can explicitly add a "deny" rule in addition to allow rules. For example, you can deny access to a specific IP address.
The SG is stateful, which means once you add an inbound allow rule, it automatically adds an outbound allow rule. For example, for a CRM server to respond, you have only to allow a rule to accept traffic from the IP range.	An NACL is stateless, meaning that if you add an inbound allow rule, you must add an explicit allow rule. For a CRM server to respond, you should add both allow and deny rules to accept traffic from the IP range.

If you have added multiple rules in the instance, the SG will validate all rules before deciding whether to allow traffic.	In an NACL, you define rule priority by assigning values, such as `100` or `200`. The NACL processes the rules in numerical order.
As an SG is at the instance level, it applies to an instance only.	As an NACL is at the subnet level, it automatically applies to all instances in the subnets it's linked to.

Table 4.4: Comparison between SGs and NACLs

While the SG and NACL provide security inside the VPC, let's learn more about AWS network security best practices overall.

AWS Network Firewall (ANFW)

ANFW is a highly available, fully redundant, and easy-to-deploy managed network firewall service for your Amazon VPC. It offers a service-level agreement with an uptime commitment of 99.99%. ANFW scales automatically based on your network traffic, eliminating the need for capacity planning, deployment, and management of the firewall infrastructure.

ANFW supports open source Suricata-compatible rules for stateful inspection. It provides fine controls for your network traffic, such as allowing or blocking specific protocol traffic from particular prefixes. ANFW also supports third-party integration to source-managed intelligent feeds.

ANFW also provides alert logs that detail a particular rule that has been triggered. Its native integration with Amazon S3, Amazon Kinesis, and Amazon CloudWatch can act as the destination for these logs.

You can learn about various ANFW deployment models from the detailed AWS blog here: `https://aws.amazon.com/blogs/networking-and-content-delivery/deployment-models-for-aws-network-firewall/`.

Let's learn more about network security patterns and anti-patterns, keeping SGs and NACLs in mind.

AWS network security patterns – Best practices

Several patterns can be used when creating an SG and NACL strategy for your organization, such as the following:

- **Create the SG before launching the instance(s), resource(s), or cluster(s)**: This will force you to determine whether a new SG is necessary or whether an existing SG should be used. This enables you to predefine all the rules and reference the SG at creation time, especially when creating these programmatically or via a CloudFormation/Landing Zone pipeline. Additionally, you should not use the default SG for your applications.
- **Logically construct SGs into functional categories based on their application tier or the role they perform**: Consider the number of distinct tiers your application has, and then logically construct the SGs to match those functional components. For a typical three-tier architecture, a minimum of three SGs should be used (e.g., a web, app, and database tier).
- **Configure rules to chain SGs to each other**: In an SG rule, you can authorize network access from a specific CIDR address range or another SG in your VPC. Either option could be appropriate, depending on your environment. Generally speaking, organizations can "chain" the SGs together between application tiers, thus building a logical flow of allowed traffic from one SG to another. However, an exception to this pattern is described in the following pattern.
- **Restrict privileged administrative ports (e.g., SSH or RDP) to internal systems (e.g., bastion hosts)**: As a best practice, administrative access to instances should be blocked or restricted to a small number of protected and monitored cases – sometimes referred to as bastion hosts or jump boxes.
- **Create NACL rule numbers with the future in mind**: NACL rules are evaluated in numerical order based on the rule number, and the first rule that matches the traffic will be used. For example, if there are 10 rules in an NACL and rule number 2 matches `DENY SSH traffic` on port 22, the other 8 rules never get evaluated, regardless of their content. Therefore, when creating NACL rules, it is best practice to leave gaps between the rule numbers – `100` is typically used. So, the first rule has a rule number of `100`, and the second rule has a rule number of `200`.

  If you have to add a rule between these rules in the future, you can add a new rule with rule number `150`, which still leaves space for future planning.
- **In well-architected, high-availability VPCs, share NACLs based on subnet tiers**: The subnet tiers in a well-architected, high-availability VPC should have the same resources and applications deployed in the same subnet tiers (e.g., the web and app tiers). These tiers should have the same inbound and outbound rule requirements. In this case, it is recommended to use the same NACL to avoid making administrative changes in multiple places.

- **Limit inbound rules to the minimum required ports and restrict access to commonly vulnerable ports**: As with hardware firewalls, it is important to carefully determine the minimum baseline for inbound rules needed for an application tier to function. Reducing the ports greatly reduces the overall attack surface and simplifies the management of the NACLs.
- **Finally, audit and eliminate unnecessary, unused, or redundant NACL rules and SGs**: As your environment scales, you may find that unnecessary SGs and NACL rules were created or mistakenly left behind from previous changes.

AWS network security anti-patterns

While the previous section described patterns for using VPC SGs and NACLs, there are several ways you might attempt to configure or utilize your SGs and NACLs in non-recommended ways. These are referred to as "anti-patterns" and should be avoided:

- The default SG is included automatically with your VPC. Launching an EC2 instance or any other AWS resource in your VPC is linked to the default SG. Using the default SG does not provide granular control. You can create custom SGs and add them to instances or resources. You can create multiple SGs per your applications' needs, such as a web server EC2 instance or an Aurora database server.
- If you already have SGs applied to all instances, *do not* create a rule referencing these in other SGs. By referencing an SG applied to all instances, you are defining a source or destination of all instances. This is a wide-open pointer to or from everything in your environment. There are better ways to apply least-privileged access.
- Multiple SGs can be applied to an instance. Within a specific application tier, all instances should have the same set of SGs applied to them. However, ensure that tier instances are uniform. Suppose web, application, and database servers co-mingle in the same tier. In this case, they should be separated into distinct tiers and have tier-specific SGs applied. *Do not* create unique SGs for related instances (one-off configurations or permutations).
- Refrain from sharing or reusing NACLs in subnets with different resources. Although the NACL rules may be the same now, there is no way to determine future rules required for the resources. Since the resources in the subnet differ (e.g., between different applications), resources in one subnet may need a new rule that isn't required for the resources in the other subnet. However, since the NACL is shared, opening up the rule applies resources in both subnets. This approach does not follow the principle of least privilege.

- NACLs are stateless, so rules are evaluated when traffic enters and leaves the subnet. You will need an inbound and outbound rule for each two-way communication. Evaluating large, complex rule sets on traffic in and out of the subnet will eventually lead to performance degradation.

It is recommended to periodically audit SGs and NACLs rules that are unnecessary or redundant and delete them. This will reduce complexity and help prevent accidentally reaching the service limit.

AWS network security with third-party solutions

You may not always want to get into all the nitty-gritty details of AWS security configuration and look for more managed solutions. AWS's extensive partner network builds managed AWS solutions to fulfill your network security needs. Some of the most popular network security solutions provided by **integrated software vendor** (**ISV**) partners in AWS Marketplace are as follows:

- **Palo Alto Networks**: Palo Alto Networks has introduced a Next-Generation Firewall service that simplifies securing AWS deployments. This service enables developers and cloud security architects to incorporate inline threat and data loss prevention into their application development workflows.
- **Aviatrix**: The Aviatrix Secure Networking Platform is made up of two components: the Aviatrix controller (which manages the gateways and orchestrates all connectivity) and the Aviatrix Gateways that are deployed in VPCs using AWS IAM roles.
- **Check Point**: Check Point CloudGuard Network Security is a comprehensive security solution designed to protect your AWS cloud environment and assets. It provides advanced, multi-layered network security features such as a firewall, IPS, application control, IPsec VPN, antivirus, and anti-bot functionality.
- **Fortinet**: This provides firewall technology to deliver complete content and network protection, including application control, IPS, VPN, and web filtering. It also provides more advanced features such as vulnerability management and flow-based inspection work.
- **Cohesive Networks**: Cohesive's VNS3 is a software-only virtual appliance for connectivity, federation, and security in AWS.
- **CrowdStrike**: CrowdStrike Falcon provides endpoint protection and advanced threat detection, leveraging AI-driven threat intelligence for proactive security. It's particularly valuable for real-time visibility into AWS workloads, detecting and responding to threats across environments.

In addition, many more solutions are available through partners such as Netskope, Valtix, IBM, and Cisco. You can find the complete network security solutions available in the AWS Marketplace using this link: `https://aws.amazon.com/marketplace/search/results?searchTerms=network+security`.

AWS cloud security has multiple components, starting with networking as a top priority. You can learn more about AWS security by visiting their security page at `https://aws.amazon.com/security/`.

Knowledge check

The following are sample questions that are appropriate for the difficulty and scope of the AWS Certification exam:

1. Your company has enabled VPC Flow Logs for its VPC to monitor network traffic. The VPC has a CIDR block of `10.0.0.0/16`, with two subnets: `10.0.1.0/24` (public) and `10.0.2.0/24` (private). You have observed an unusual amount of traffic destined for the private subnet from an IP address, `198.51.100.10`, which is not part of your organization's IP address ranges. You need to investigate whether this traffic is legitimate or potentially malicious. Which of the following steps should you take to investigate this traffic using VPC Flow Logs?

    a. Open the **Amazon CloudWatch Logs** console, select the log group for **VPC Flow Logs**, and run a query to filter logs where the `destAddr` field is `10.0.2.0/24` and the `srcAddr` field is `198.51.100.10`.

    b. Open the **AWS CloudTrail** console, select the log group for **VPC Flow Logs**, and run a query to filter logs where the `dstAddr` field is `10.0.2.0/24` and the `srcAddr` field is `198.51.100.10`.

    c. Open the **Amazon CloudWatch Logs** console, select the log group for **VPC Flow Logs**, and run a query to filter logs where the `dstAddr` field is `198.51.100.10` and the `srcAddr` field is `10.0.2.0/24`.

    d. Open the **AWS CloudTrail** console, select the log group for **VPC Flow Logs**, and run a query to filter logs where the `destAddr` field is `198.51.100.10` and the `srcAddr` field is `10.0.2.0/24`.

    Answer: a.

Explanation:

a. **Correct.** VPC Flow Logs are captured and stored in Amazon CloudWatch Logs, not AWS CloudTrail. To investigate the traffic destined for the private subnet (`10.0.2.0/24`) from the external IP address (`198.51.100.10`), you should open the **Amazon CloudWatch Logs** console, select the log group for VPC Flow Logs, and run a query to filter logs where the `destAddr` field is `10.0.2.0/24` (the private subnet CIDR block) and the `srcAddr` field is `198.51.100.10` (the external IP address). This query will retrieve all the **VPC Flow Logs** entries that match the specified source and destination IP addresses, allowing you to analyze the traffic and determine if it is legitimate or potentially malicious.

b. Incorrect. VPC Flow Logs are not stored in AWS CloudTrail. AWS CloudTrail is a service that records AWS API calls made within your account, while VPC Flow Logs capture network traffic information, which is stored in Amazon CloudWatch Logs.

c. Incorrect. It reverses the source and destination IP addresses. The question states that you need to investigate traffic destined for the private subnet (`10.0.2.0/24`) from the external IP address (`198.51.100.10`). Therefore, the `destAddr` field should be `10.0.2.0/24` (private subnet), and the `srcAddr` field should be `198.51.100.10` (external IP address).

d. Incorrect. VPC Flow Logs are not stored in AWS CloudTrail, and this option reverses the source and destination IP addresses, similar to option C.

2. You are designing a highly available and fault-tolerant architecture for a web application hosted on AWS. The application requires a private subnet with resources that can communicate with the internet for software updates and patches. What is the recommended AWS service or configuration to achieve this requirement while ensuring high availability and scalability?

    a. Configure a NAT gateway in a public subnet and route traffic from the private subnet through the NAT gateway.

    b. Configure an NLB in a public subnet and route traffic from the private subnet through the NLB.

    c. Configure a bastion host in a public subnet and use SSH tunneling to access resources in the private subnet.

    d. Configure a NAT instance in a public subnet and route traffic from the private subnet through the NAT instance.

Answer: a.

Explanation:

a. **Correct.** A NAT gateway is an AWS-managed service that allows resources in a private subnet to communicate with the internet or other AWS services. Still, it prevents the internet from initiating connections with those resources. By configuring a NAT gateway in a public subnet and routing traffic from the private subnet through the NAT gateway, resources in the private subnet can access the internet for software updates and patches while remaining isolated from direct internet access. NAT gateways are highly available and scalable and require minimal administration effort, making them the recommended solution for this scenario.

b. Incorrect. An NLB distributes incoming traffic across multiple targets, such as EC2 instances. It is not designed to provide internet access for resources in a private subnet.

c. Incorrect. While a bastion host (a hardened EC2 instance in a public subnet) can be used to access resources in a private subnet through SSH tunneling, it does not provide a direct mechanism for resources in the private subnet to access the internet for software updates and patches.

d. Incorrect. While a NAT instance can also be used to enable internet access for resources in a private subnet, it is a single EC2 instance. It does not provide the same level of high availability and scalability as a NAT gateway. Additionally, NAT instances require more administrative effort for maintenance and failover than the managed NAT gateway service.

3. A company has a multi-account AWS environment managed by AWS Organizations. They have a shared services VPC in the organization's management account, which hosts various shared services such as Active Directory Domain Controllers and NAT gateways. Each of the company's development teams has its own AWS account within the organization, with separate VPCs for their applications. The teams need to access the shared services in the management account's VPC from their respective VPCs. Which of the following solutions would you recommend to allow secure communication between the development teams' VPCs and the shared services VPC while minimizing operational overhead?

    a. Use VPC peering between each development team's VPC and the shared services VPC.

    b. Implement AWS Transit Gateway with a single transit gateway across all VPCs.

    c. Establish AWS Site-to-Site VPN connections between each development team's VPC and the shared services VPC.

d. Deploy a managed AWS Direct Connect connection from each development team's VPC to the shared services VPC.

Answer: b.

Explanation:

a. Incorrect. While VPC peering can establish communication between VPCs, it requires setting up and managing peering connections between each development team's VPC and the shared services VPC. As the number of VPCs grows, the operational overhead of managing multiple peering connections increases significantly, making this solution less scalable and more complex to manage.
b. **Correct**. AWS Transit Gateway serves as a hub for routing traffic between VPCs, on-premises networks, and AWS resources. By implementing a single transit gateway across all VPCs, including the shared services VPC, you can establish secure communication between the development teams' VPCs and the shared services VPC without complex VPC peering or VPN connections. Transit Gateway simplifies network management and reduces operational overhead by providing a centralized routing mechanism.
c. Incorrect. Using Site-to-Site VPN connections would require setting up and managing VPN connections between each development team's VPC and the shared services VPC. Like VPC peering, this approach becomes increasingly complex and operationally intensive as the number of VPCs grows, making it less suitable for a large multi-account environment.
d. Incorrect. AWS Direct Connect is a dedicated connection between your on-premises network and AWS. While it provides a high-bandwidth and low-latency connection, deploying a Direct Connect connection from each development team's VPC to the shared services VPC would be an expensive and overkill solution for internal communication within the AWS environment. Additionally, it would require managing multiple Direct Connect connections, increasing operational overhead.

4. You have an application hosted on AWS that serves traffic from multiple Regions. The application needs to route traffic to the closest AWS Region based on the client's geographic location to minimize latency. Which Amazon Route 53 routing policy should you use to achieve this?

a. Weighted routing policy

b. Geolocation routing policy

c. Latency routing policy

d. Failover routing policy

Answer: c.

Explanation:

a. Incorrect. The weighted routing policy allows you to distribute traffic across multiple resources based on the weight (a percentage) assigned to each resource. This policy is useful for load balancing and traffic splitting scenarios, but it does not consider the user's geographic location or latency.

b. Incorrect. The geolocation routing policy routes traffic based on the user's geographic location but does not consider latency. With this policy, you can define geographic locations (e.g., countries, states, or continents) and map them to specific resources (e.g., EC2 instances or Elastic Load Balancers). While this policy ensures that users are served from the designated geographic location, it does not guarantee the lowest latency.

c. **Correct.** The latency routing policy in Amazon Route 53 is designed to route traffic to the AWS resource (e.g., EC2 instance, Elastic Load Balancer, etc.) that provides the lowest latency or best performance for the end user based on their geographic location. This policy can route traffic across multiple AWS Regions, and it works by estimating the latency between the user's location and the different AWS Regions where your resources are hosted. Route 53 then routes the traffic to the Region with the lowest latency, providing the best performance for the user.

d. Incorrect. The failover routing policy creates an active-passive failover configuration for your resources. It routes traffic to a primary resource (e.g., an EC2 instance or Elastic Load Balancer) and automatically fails over to a secondary resource if it becomes unavailable. This policy does not consider latency or geographic location; its purpose is to provide failover capabilities for high availability.

5. You have an Amazon VPC with public and private subnets. Your application, hosted in the private subnets, must access an Amazon S3 bucket to store and retrieve data. You want to ensure that the traffic between your application and the S3 bucket remains within the AWS network and does not traverse the public internet. Which of the following solutions would you choose to achieve this?

a. Create a VPC endpoint for Amazon S3 and associate it with the private subnets where your application is hosted.

b. Create an internet gateway and configure a route table for the private subnets to route traffic destined for Amazon S3 through the internet gateway.

c. Create a NAT gateway in the public subnet and configure a route table for the private subnets to route traffic destined for Amazon S3 through the NAT gateway.

d. Create an egress-only internet gateway and configure a route table for the private subnets to route traffic destined for Amazon S3 through the egress-only internet gateway.

Answer: a.

Explanation:

a. **Correct.** The correct solution is to create a VPC endpoint for Amazon S3 and associate it with the private subnets where your application is hosted. A VPC endpoint provides a secure and scalable way to access AWS services, such as Amazon S3, from within your VPC without traversing the public internet. When you create a VPC endpoint for Amazon S3, traffic between your application in the private subnets and the S3 bucket remains within the AWS network, ensuring data privacy and reducing network costs.

b. Incorrect. Creating an internet gateway and routing traffic destined for Amazon S3 through it would not achieve the desired goal of keeping the traffic within the AWS network. An internet gateway enables communication between resources in your VPC and the public internet. By routing the traffic through the internet gateway, your data would traverse the public internet, which is not secure, and would incur additional data transfer costs.

c. Incorrect. Creating a NAT gateway in the public subnet and routing traffic destined for Amazon S3 would also not achieve the desired goal. A NAT gateway enables instances in private subnets to access the internet or other AWS services. However, in this case, the traffic would still traverse the public internet, which is not secure and would incur additional data transfer costs.

d. Incorrect. Creating an egress-only internet gateway and routing traffic destined for Amazon S3 is not a valid solution. An egress-only internet gateway is used to allow resources in a private subnet to access the internet or other AWS services while preventing the internet from initiating connections to those resources. However, it does not provide a direct, private connection to AWS services such as Amazon S3, and the traffic would still traverse the public internet.

Summary

In this chapter, you started with learning about the AWS Global Infrastructure and understanding the details of AWS Regions, AZs, and LZs. You also learned about the various benefits of using the AWS Global Infrastructure.

Networking is the backbone of any IT workload, whether in the cloud or on-premises network. To start your cloud journey in AWS, you must have good knowledge of AWS networking. When you start with AWS, you create your VPC within AWS. You learned about using an AWS VPC with various components, such as an SG, an NACL, a route table, an IGW, and a NAT gateway. You learned how to segregate and secure your IT resources by putting them into private and public subnets.

With the ease of creating VPCs in AWS organizations, multiple VPCs tend to be made, whether it is intentional to give each team their own VPC or unintentional when the development team creates multiple test workloads. Often, these VPCs need to communicate with each other; for example, the finance department needs to get information from accounting. You learned about setting up communication between multiple VPCs using VPC peering and TGW. You learned to establish secure connections with services on the public internet or other accounts using AWS PrivateLink.

Furthermore, you learned about AWS edge networking to address the global nature of user traffic. These services include Route 53, CloudFront, AGA, and AWS Wavelength. You then learned about connecting an on-premises server and an AWS cloud. Finally, you closed the chapter with the network security best practices, patterns, and anti-patterns, and third-party managed network security solutions available via the AWS Partner network.

AWS provides various types of storage to match your workload needs. In the next chapter, you will learn about storage in AWS and how to choose the right storage for your IT workload needs.

Join us on Discord

For discussions around the book and to connect with your peers, join us on Discord at `https://discord.gg/kbFRRSB2Qs` or scan the QR code below:

5

Storage in AWS: Choosing the Right Tool for the Job

Storage is a critical and foundational service for any cloud provider. If this service is not implemented in a durable, available, efficient, low-latency manner, it doesn't matter how many other excellent services are offered, your system will not perform at full capacity. Among all the different kinds of storage, file, block, and object storage are at the foundation and core of many applications. In *Chapter 7, Selecting the Right Database Service*, you will learn about other storage services focused on databases.

In this chapter, you will learn the difference between block and object storage. After that, you will learn how these types of storage work in the AWS platform, including Amazon **Elastic Block Store** (**EBS**), Amazon **Elastic File System** (**EFS**), and Amazon **Simple Storage Service** (**S3**). You will also dive deeper into versioning in Amazon S3 and explore Amazon S3 best practices.

In this chapter, you will learn about the following topics:

- Understanding local storage with Amazon EBS
- Investigating file storage with Amazon EFS
- Learning about Amazon S3
- Versioning in Amazon S3
- Choosing the right cloud storage type
- Exploring Amazon S3 best practices
- Understanding Amazon S3 analytics and metrics
- Building hybrid storage with AWS Storage Gateway and AWS Backup

Moving storage workloads to the cloud has been one of the main ways to address strategic priorities, such as increasing an organization's agility, accelerating its ability to innovate, strengthening security, and reducing costs. Let's learn how all of this can be achieved in AWS.

Understanding Amazon EBS

Block storage is a foundational technology that has existed since the early days of computing. It is the basis for the hard drive in your laptop, the memory in your mobile phone, and all other forms of data storage, from USB thumb drives to storage arrays that organizations place in their data centers.

Persistent block storage that can be used with Amazon EC2 instances is provided by Amazon EBS. When using EC2, you have the option to use local instance storage or EBS for block storage:

- **Instance storage** is great for high-performance (over 80K IOPS and 1,750 MB/s throughput) and low-latency (under 1 ms) applications. However, instance storage is ephemeral, meaning that when you stop, hibernate, or terminate an EC2 instance, every storage block in the instance store is reset. Therefore, do not rely on instance storage for valuable, long-term data.
- **EBS volumes** provide excellent performance and persistent storage. EBS allows your customer to correctly size their instance for the memory and CPU they need, relying on EBS for their storage, which they can independently size on capacity, IOPS, or throughput.

  With EBS io2 Block Express, you can achieve SAN-like performance in the cloud.

In simple terms, Amazon EBS is a hard drive for an AWS server. One advantage of Amazon EBS over many typical hard drives is that you can easily detach it from one server and attach it to another using software commands. Usually, with other servers outside of AWS, this would require physically detaching the hard drive and physically attaching it to another server.

When using Amazon EBS, data is persisted. This means that data lives even after the server is shut down. Like other services, Amazon EBS provides high availability and durability.

Amazon EBS should not be confused with the instance store available in EC2 instances. EC2 instance stores deliver ephemeral storage for EC2 instances. One of the use cases for EC2 instance stores would be any data that does not need to be persisted, such as the following:

- Caches
- Buffers
- Temporary files

If data needs to be stored permanently, the following Amazon EBS options are available.

Parameter	General-Purpose SSD (gp2)	General-Purpose SSD (gp3)	Provisioned IOPS SSD (io1)	Provisioned IOPS SSD (io2)	Throughput Optimized HDD (st1)	Cold HDD (sc1)
Use Case	Virtual desktops, development, and staging environments	Virtual desktops, development, and staging environments	Business applications and critical production databases	Business applications and critical production databases	Big data, log processing, and streaming applications	Large datasets and infrequently accessed data
Volume Size	1 GiB–16 TiB	1 GiB–16 TiB	4 GiB–16 TiB	4 GiB–64 TiB	125 GiB–16 TiB	125 GiB–16 TiB
IOPS	Up to 16,000	Baseline: 3,000 Scalable: 16,000	Up to 64,000	Up to 256,000 (500 IOPS/GB)	500 IOPS per volume	250 IOPS per volume
Throughput	Up to 250 MiB/s	Baseline: 125 MiB/s Scalable: 1,000 MiB/s	Up to 1,000 MiB/s	Up to 4,000 MiB/s	Baseline: 40 MiB/s per TB Max: 500 MiB/s	Baseline: 12 MiB/s per TB Max: 250 MiB/s
Cost Efficiency	Balanced cost and performance	20% lower cost than gp2; more throughput	Higher cost for critical workloads	Improved performance at a similar cost to io1	Lower cost for high-throughput applications	Lowest cost for infrequent access
Performance Scalability	Fixed	Independent scaling of IOPS, throughput, and size	Scales with provisioned size	Scales with provisioned size	Scales with volume size	Scales with volume size

Special Features	Default SSD option	Higher throughput with customizable performance	Low latency for intensive IOPS applications	Enhanced durability and Block Express for io2	High throughput for sequential workloads	Optimized for cost with infrequent access

Table 5.1: EBS volume types and their comparison

As you are looking for more performance-efficient storage, the good news is AWS has expanded the capabilities of io2 volumes with Block Express, supporting volume sizes up to 64 TiB and delivering up to 256,000 IOPS and 4,000 MiB/s throughput. Find more about EBS volume in the AWS docs link here: `https://aws.amazon.com/ebs/features/`. Also, with real-time visibility into metrics such as I/O operations and latency, you can monitor the health and performance of your storage resources. You can find more details in AWS's official announcement: `https://aws.amazon.com/about-aws/whats-new/2024/11/amazon-ebs-performance-statistics-ebs-volume-health`.

This would be a good time to note that EC2 instances are virtualized, and there isn't a one-to-one relationship between servers and EC2 instances. Similarly, when you use EBS storage, a single physical storage device is not assigned to you by AWS; instead, you get a slice of several devices that store the data in a distributed fashion across data centers to increase reliability and availability.

Amazon EBS volumes are, by default, highly available, durable, and reliable. This redundancy strategy and multiple server replication are built into the base price of Amazon EBS volumes. Amazon EBS volume files are mirrored across multiple servers within an **Availability Zone** (**AZ**), minimizing data loss. For data loss to occur, more than one device must fail simultaneously. If a disk fails, Amazon EBS volumes will also self-heal and bring in additional healthy resources.

In addition, Amazon EBS volumes are replicated transparently by design. Therefore, setting up RAID or other redundancy strategies is unnecessary to provide extra redundancy. We have learned about many EBS volumes; now, let's understand how to choose the right one.

Choosing the right EBS volume

As you learned in the previous section, EBS offers volume types in two buckets: SSD and HDD. The first step in helping you size your storage is to understand whether your workload is sequential or random I/O:

- **SSD** (gp2, gp3, io1, io2, and io2 Block Express) is great for random I/O applications such as boot volumes and databases (MySQL, SQL, PostgreSQL, Oracle, Cassandra, MongoDB, SAP, etc.). Performance is measured on disk I/O (IOPS).
- **HDD** (st1 and sc1) is great for sequential I/O applications such as EMR/Hadoop, Kafka, Splunk, media streaming, logs, and any cold data infrequently accessed. Performance is measured on throughput (MB/s).

From there, you can use AWS documentation (`https://aws.amazon.com/ebs/volume-types/`) to help decide which specific volume will best suit your needs and give the best price for performance. Here is a decision tree to assist in the process:

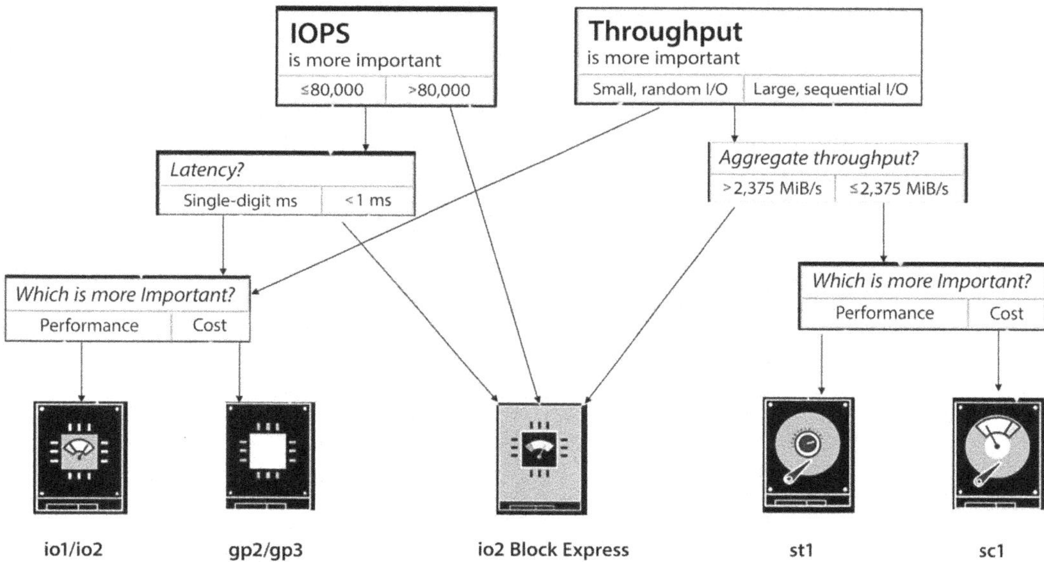

Figure 5.1: Decision tree to select the EBS volume

To understand the approach for choosing the right EBS volume, let's dive deeper into the SSD-backed products, gp3 and io2. The **gp3** volume type is designed to meet the performance needs of 70–80% of workloads, making it a versatile and cost-effective choice for general-purpose storage. gp3 satisfies nearly all workloads and is designed to be a general-purpose volume. That's why it has the name *general purpose*, so if you don't know which volume type to use, it is highly recommended that you start with gp3. Additionally, with gp3, you can provision more IOPS and throughput when needed without being dependent on storage size.

The low latency of gp3, measured in single-digit milliseconds, makes it well suited for applications sensitive to latency, such as interactive applications, boot volumes, development and testing environments, burst databases, and various other use cases. But what about sub-millisecond latency? Now, if you are looking for very high performance and low latency, use **io2 Block Express** volumes, which offer 4 times the performance of io1, up to 256,000 IOPS, 4GB/s of throughput, and you can provision up to 4x more storage – up to 64 TiB.

Now, we move on to the media workload for your rendering farms, transcoding, encoding, and any streaming product. Here, you typically have a higher throughput requirement, mostly sequential and fairly sustained, especially when you have a substantial render job. Throughput Optimized HDDs (also known as st1s) might be a good fit for these kinds of workloads. These are good for large blocks, high throughput, and sequential workloads.

sc1 is a low-cost storage option ideal for storing infrequently accessed data, such as data accessed once a month or less. It is a good choice for cold storage or data that is not accessed very often. st1, on the other hand, is a low-cost storage option designed for storing frequently accessed data, such as data accessed daily or weekly. It is a good choice for data accessed frequently but not in real time.

The main difference between sc1 and st1 is their intended use cases. sc1 is designed for infrequently accessed data, while st1 is designed for frequently accessed data.

In a nutshell, with EBS, you get persistent storage, which enables you to stop and start your instances without losing your storage and build cost-effective point-in-time snapshots of the volumes you are storing in S3. EBS provides built-in encryption for security, so you don't need to manage your own. For monitoring, EBS has better volume monitoring with Amazon CloudWatch metrics. EBS io2/io3 is designed for 99.999% availability and is highly durable, with an annual failure rate of 0.001%.

Having a backup of this storage is a common way of replicating the environment. Let's learn about EBS snapshots.

Amazon EBS snapshots

Amazon EBS snapshots provide an efficient and cost-effective way to back up your EBS volumes. Snapshots enable incremental backups, where only the data that has changed since the last snapshot is stored. This reduces storage costs while ensuring comprehensive backups, making them a vital data protection and recovery tool.

Creating the first EBS snapshot captures all the data in the EBS volume (e.g., 100 GB). Subsequent snapshots only store changes made since the last snapshot. For example, if 5 GB of new data is added, only 5 GB will be included in the next snapshot. This incremental approach minimizes storage usage while maintaining the ability to restore full volumes. Snapshots are stored as Amazon S3 objects, accessible through the EBS API but not directly accessible as S3 files. These snapshots are foundational for creating **Amazon Machine Images (AMIs)**, which enable seamless restoration or replication of EC2 instances.

Amazon EBS snapshots have seen several advancements to improve security, cost efficiency, and automation. The **Snapshot Lock** feature allows snapshots to be locked for a defined period to prevent accidental or malicious deletion. Locking can be set in two modes: **Governance Mode** (allowing authorized modifications) or **Compliance Mode** (preventing all changes). Another significant enhancement is the **EBS Snapshots Archive**, a cost-effective storage tier ideal for long-term retention, reducing costs by up to 75%. Snapshots in the Archive tier can be restored to the standard tier within 72 hours. You can attach an EBS volume to an EC2 instance in the same AZ only; however, you can use a snapshot to create multiple volumes and move across AZs.

AWS also introduced **Backup support for EBS Snapshots Archive**, enabling automated migration of infrequently accessed snapshots to the Archive tier. To enhance security, AWS now allows blocking public sharing of EBS snapshots on a per-region, per-account basis, mitigating risks of unintentional data exposure. These enhancements ensure better customer cost optimization, compliance, and data protection.

Best practices for EBS cost optimization

When you're using EBS to provide storage for your EC2 instances, managing costs effectively is crucial. One key strategy is to right-size your EBS volumes. This means ensuring that the storage capacity and performance you provision match your actual workload requirements. Over-provisioning leads to unnecessary expenses, while under-provisioning can cause performance issues. AWS provides tools such as **AWS Compute Optimizer** to help you analyze your volume usage and recommend optimal configurations. By adjusting your EBS volumes based on these insights, you can achieve significant cost savings. You can refer to the details available here: `https://aws.amazon.com/blogs/storage/cost-optimizing-amazon-ebs-volumes-using-aws-compute-optimizer/`.

Another effective practice is to monitor and delete unused snapshots. Snapshots are incremental backups of your EBS volumes, and while they are essential for data protection, retaining unnecessary snapshots can accumulate costs over time. Regularly reviewing and removing outdated or redundant snapshots helps control storage expenses. To automate this process, you can use **Amazon Data Lifecycle Manager**, which allows you to set policies for snapshot retention and deletion, ensuring that only relevant backups are kept.

Tagging your EBS resources is another best practice that enhances cost management. By assigning meaningful tags to your volumes and snapshots, such as "production," "development," or "archive," you can easily identify and manage resources based on their purpose. This organization facilitates the application of specific policies and helps in tracking usage and costs associated with different projects or environments.

Regularly monitoring and analyzing your EBS costs is essential to identify trends and inefficiencies. Utilize tools such as **AWS Cost Explorer**, **AWS Budgets**, and **AWS Trusted Advisor** to gain insights into your storage usage and expenses. These tools can help you detect underutilized resources, forecast future costs, and set up alerts for budget thresholds, enabling proactive cost management.

This concludes our discussion of the Amazon EBS service. Let's move on to another important service: Amazon EFS.

Investigating Amazon EFS

Amazon EFS implements an elastic, fully managed **network file system** (**NFS**) that can be leveraged by other AWS cloud services and on-premises infrastructure. Amazon EFS natively integrates with the complete family of AWS compute models and can scale as needed to provide parallel, shared access to thousands of Amazon EC2 instances as well as AWS container and serverless compute models from AWS Lambda, AWS Fargate, Amazon **Elastic Container Service** (**ECS**), and Amazon **Elastic Kubernetes Service** (**EKS**).

The main difference between EBS and EFS is that an EFS volume can be mounted to multiple EC2 instances simultaneously, while an EBS volume can be attached to only one EC2 instance. Amazon EFS provides shared file storage that can adjust on demand to expand or shrink depending on your workload's required space. It can grow and shrink as you add and remove files. Other than that, the structure will be like it is with Amazon EBS. Amazon EFS provides a typical file storage system where files can be organized into directories and subdirectories.

Common use cases for EFS volumes include the following:

- Web serving and content management systems for WordPress, Drupal, Moodle, Confluence, and OpenText.
- Data science and analytics for TensorFlow, Qubole, and Alteryx.
- Media processing includes video editing, sound design, broadcast processing, studio production, and rendering. It often depends on shared storage to manipulate large files.
- Database backups for Oracle, Postgres, Cassandra, MongoDB, CouchDB, and SAP HANA.
- Hosting CRM applications that require hosting within the AWS data center but need to be managed by the AWS customer.

The following are the key benefits of using EFS:

- EFS is **elastic**, automatically scaling up or down as you add or remove files, and you pay only for what you use. Your performance automatically scales with your capacity. By the way, EFS file systems scale to petabytes in size.
- EFS is also highly available and designed to be highly durable. AWS offers a four 9s availability SLA (99.99% availability) and is intended for 11 9s of data durability (which means it delivers 99.999999999% durability across multiple AZs).
- To achieve these levels of availability and durability, all files and directories are redundantly stored within and across multiple AZs. EFS file systems can withstand the full loss of a single AZ while still providing the same quality of service as the other AZs.
- EFS is serverless; you don't need to provision or manage any infrastructure or capacity. As your workload scales up, so does your file system, automatically accommodating any additional storage or connection capacity you need.
- EFS file systems support thousands of concurrent clients, regardless of type. These could be traditional EC2 instances, containers running in one of your self-managed clusters, or in one of the AWS container services (ECS, EKS, and Fargate), or a serverless function running in AWS Lambda. You can also access your EFS file systems on-premises through AWS Direct Connect and AWS VPN.
- Regarding performance, EFS file systems provide low, consistent latencies (in the single-digit millisecond range for active file system workloads). They can scale to tens of GB/s of throughput and support over 500,000 IOPS.
- Finally, EFS storage classes automatically optimize costs and help you achieve an optimal price/performance blend for your workloads. Files you aren't using frequently will be automatically moved from the Standard storage class to the lower-cost EFS **Infrequent Access (IA)** storage class, which is completely transparent to users and applications. IA costs 92% less than EFS Standard storage.

Amazon EFS offers two performance modes, General Purpose and Max I/O, designed to cater to different workload requirements:

Feature	General Purpose Mode	Max I/O Mode
Use Case	Suitable for most file system workloads	Ideal for highly parallelized, large-scale workloads
Performance	Balanced mix of latency, throughput, and IOPS	Optimized for higher throughput and IOPS
Latency	Low latency	Higher latency compared to General Purpose Mode
Best for Applications	Applications requiring consistent performance	**High-performance computing (HPC)**, media processing, and large-scale data processing
Workload Characteristics	Designed for moderate I/O and throughput requirements	Handles massive parallel I/O operations effectively
Scalability	Scales automatically with moderate workloads	Scales automatically with high-performance workloads

Table 5.2: EFS performance mode comparison

The preceding table helps clarify the trade-offs and best use cases for selecting the appropriate EFS performance mode based on workload needs.

To optimize EFS performance, it's crucial to understand your workload characteristics and choose the appropriate performance mode accordingly. Additionally, you can leverage features such as file system bursting, which allows you to temporarily scale up your file system's throughput and IOPS for short periods to handle burst workloads. Furthermore, implementing best practices such as distributing workloads across multiple AZs, using appropriate EC2 instance types, and optimizing your application's I/O patterns can significantly improve the overall performance of your EFS deployments.

You can learn more about EFS by visiting the AWS website: `https://aws.amazon.com/efs/`.

While EFS provides generic file system storage, file system-specific storage is needed to optimize the workload for a particular file system. For that, AWS provides Amazon FSx.

Using Amazon FSx to manage file systems

Amazon FSx is a fully managed file storage service offered by AWS that supports industry-standard protocols, including NFS and **Server Message Block** (**SMB**).

FSx is designed to provide high performance and availability for file storage, making it a good choice for applications requiring fast access to files or data. It supports many workloads, including big data analytics, content management, and video editing. Amazon FSx lets you choose between four widely used file systems: NetApp ONTAP, OpenZFS, Windows File Server, and Lustre.

Here's a comparison table for Amazon FSx file system options:

Feature	NetApp ONTAP	OpenZFS	Windows File Server	Lustre
File System	NetApp ONTAP	OpenZFS	Microsoft Windows File Server	Lustre
Protocol Support	NFS, SMB, and iSCSI	NFS (v3, v4, v4.1, v4.2)	SMB	Lustre protocol and POSIX
Best for Workloads	Applications requiring ONTAP's advanced data management capabilities	Linux-based workloads leveraging OpenZFS features	Applications requiring seamless Windows integration	HPC, **machine learning** (**ML**), and analytics workloads
Performance	High performance with advanced caching and management	High throughput and low-latency access	Optimized for Windows-based applications	Low latency for high-performance workloads
Use Cases	Shared storage, database applications, and disaster recovery	Media processing, analytics, and Linux workloads	Windows-based applications and Active Directory integration	HPC, AI/ML, and data analytics
Key Features	Snapshots, data deduplication, and replication	Built-in data compression and snapshots	Native integration with Active Directory	Integration with S3 for large-scale data processing
Integration	Supports hybrid deployments (on-premises and cloud)	Built for OpenZFS use cases in cloud environments	Windows-native integration for seamless management	Tight integration with compute-intensive workloads

Table 5.3: Amazon FSx option comparison

Overall, Amazon FSx is a fully managed file storage service that provides high performance and availability for file storage, making it a good choice for applications requiring fast access to files or data.

How do you choose between EFS and FSx? They are both fully managed file storage services in AWS, but they are designed for different use cases and performance needs. Amazon EFS is ideal when you need shared file storage for Linux-based workloads that can scale automatically and be accessed by multiple EC2 instances at the same time. On the other hand, Amazon FSx provides high-performance file systems optimized for specific workloads – FSx for Windows File Server is best for Windows applications requiring SMB protocol, and FSx for Lustre is great for high-speed processing tasks such as ML and big data.

In addition, Amazon EFS supports access from on-premises servers, allowing you to mount EFS file systems using NFS v4.1 via AWS Direct Connect or VPN. This is useful for hybrid workloads such as backups and migrations. Similarly, Amazon FSx for Windows File Server supports integration with Microsoft **Active Directory** (**AD**), AWS Managed AD, and self-managed AD, enabling seamless user authentication and file access control based on existing AD credentials. These capabilities make EFS and FSx well-suited for hybrid cloud environments where secure and centralized file storage is needed.

Till now, you have learned about Amazon EFS/FSx file storage, which can be compared to **network-attached storage** (**NAS**) in the on-premises data center. Further, you went into detail about Amazon EBS, which is block storage and can be compared with **storage area network** (**SAN**) in an on-premises environment. Let's now learn about the object storage system in AWS called Amazon S3.

Learning about Amazon S3

Amazon S3 was the first AWS service launched 19 years ago on Pi Day, March 14, 2006. After the launch of S3, AWS also launched many other services to complement S3. S3 is durable, highly available, and very scalable online storage. S3 comes in various tiers, including the following:

- S3 Standard
- Amazon S3 Intelligent-Tiering
- Amazon S3 Standard-IA
- S3 Express One Zone
- S3 One Zone-Infrequent Access (S3 One Zone-IA)
- Amazon S3 Glacier Instant Retrieval
- Amazon S3 Glacier Flexible Retrieval
- Amazon S3 Glacier Deep Archive
- Amazon S3 on Outposts

While we will explore each of the preceding tiers in detail in the following subsections, let's briefly explore some of the more common attributes that apply to multiple S3 service tiers:

- **Durability**: Data is stored with 11 9s across at least 3 AZs to provide resiliency against an AZ failure for S3 Standard, S3 Intelligent-Tiering, and S3 Standard-IA. S3 One Zone-IA has 11 9s across 1 AZ. This means that if you stored 10K objects, on average, you would lose one object every 10 million years with S3.
- **Availability**: S3 Standard is designed for 99.99% availability, with monetary penalties introduced at 99.9% per the S3 SLA. S3 Intelligent-Tiering and S3 Standard-IA are built to be 99.9% available, while S3 One Zone-IA is built to be 99.5% available. These three classes are backed by a 99% availability SLA. There are no scheduled maintenance windows – the service is maintained, upgraded, and scaled as it operates. 99.99% availability means the service is down for less than 52 minutes a year.
- **Utility pricing**: There is no upfront capital expenditure and pay-for-what-you-use pricing (100% utilization). Volume discounts as usage scales.
- **Scalability**: Instant scalability for storage and delivery.

Let's analyze the various S3 tiers in detail.

S3 Standard

When Amazon launched the S3 service, it was called Amazon S3. Since Amazon now offers various object storage services, all of which use the S3 moniker, Amazon has renamed Amazon S3 as Amazon S3 Standard.

S3 Standard delivers highly performant, available, and durable storage for data that will be accessed frequently. S3 Standard has low latency, high performance, and high scalability. S3 Standard is suited for a long list of use cases, including the following:

- **Websites with static content**: You can host website HTML pages in S3 and directly attach them to your domain, which is very low-cost, as you don't need a server to host your website. Further, you can supplement your website with high-quality content such as videos and images by putting them into S3.
- **Distribution of content**: To make your website fast for a global audience, you can host your content in S3, which will be cached in an edge location by AWS's content distribution network service, Amazon CloudFront.

- **Data analytics and processing:** You can host a large amount of data and scale it on demand for your analytics and ML needs.
- **Mobile and gaming applications**: You can supplement your application by storing all application-heavy data, such as images and videos, in S3 and loading them on demand to improve application performance.

S3 Standard can persist in many objects, such as plaintext, HTML, JSON, XML, AVRO, Parquet, and ORC files. It is one of the most popular services, addressing many use cases. You can learn more about S3 by visiting the AWS page here: `https://aws.amazon.com/s3/`.

Let's now look at another service in the S3 family, Amazon S3 Intelligent-Tiering, and let's learn what makes it intelligent.

Amazon S3 Intelligent-Tiering

The S3 Intelligent-Tiering storage service can reduce expenses by systematically moving files to the most cost-effective way to store data without impacting operations or performance. It can do this by keeping the files in two tiers:

- An optimized tier for frequent access
- An optimized tier for infrequent access that has a lower cost

Optimize storage costs by automatically moving data to the most cost-effective deep archive access tier.

Amazon S3 constantly scans the access patterns of files and transfers files that have not been accessed. If a file has not been accessed for 30 days straight, it is moved to the IA tier. If a file in the IA tier is retrieved, it is again transferred to the frequent access tier.

The Amazon S3 Intelligent-Tiering storage class offers multiple access tiers – Frequent, Infrequent, and Archive Instant Access – all with the same low-latency and high-throughput performance as S3 Standard. By moving data to the IA tier, you can save up to 40% on storage costs, while the Archive Instant Access tier offers up to 68% in savings. For rarely accessed data over time, you can opt in to asynchronous archive capabilities. The Archive Access and Deep Archive Access tiers deliver performance comparable to S3 Glacier Flexible Retrieval and S3 Glacier Deep Archive, allowing you to save up to 95% on storage costs for long-term, infrequently accessed data.

With the S3 Intelligent-Tiering storage class, the additional cost comes from the monitoring charge. There are no retrieval fees, and there are no additional file transfer fees when objects are transferred between the tiers. S3 Intelligent Tiering is a good solution when we know that data will be needed for a long time, but are uncertain about how often this data will be accessed.

S3 services can be enabled granularly up to the object level. For example, a given bucket can have one object that uses S3 Standard, another using S3 Intelligent-Tiering, one more with S3 Standard-IA, and one with S3 One Zone-IA (we will cover these two other services in the next few sections).

> To take advantage of the auto-tiering capability, it is recommended to aggregate objects smaller than 128 KB to meet the minimum size requirement. This enables the objects to be automatically tiered and reduces storage costs while improving performance. Smaller objects that are not monitored are always charged at the rates of the Frequent Access tier without any additional monitoring or automation charges.

To learn more about S3 intelligent tiering, you can refer to the AWS docs here: `https://aws.amazon.com/s3/storage-classes/intelligent-tiering/`.

So, what if we know that the data we create and store will be infrequently accessed? Amazon offers a service that is ideally suited for that and cheaper than Amazon S3 Standard.

Amazon S3 Standard-IA

Depending on your data's use case, this storage class might be the ideal solution. The data can be accessed at the same speed as S3 Standard, with some trade-offs on the data's resiliency. For example, storing monthly payroll data will be accessed most in the last week of each month, so it's better to use S3 Standard-IA to save costs.

S3 Standard-IA offers a similar profile to the Standard service but with a lower storage cost and a retrieval fee billed per GB. Combining low cost with high performance makes S3 Standard-IA a well-suited option for use cases such as backups, snapshots, long-term storage, and a file repository for disaster recovery. S3 Lifecycle policies could automatically move files between storage classes without any coding needed.

You should configure your Amazon S3 to manage your items and keep them cost-effectively stored throughout their lifecycle. An S3 Lifecycle configuration is a set of rules that specify how Amazon S3 handles a collection of objects. Using S3 Lifecycle configuration rules, you can instruct Amazon S3 to transition objects to more cost-effective storage classes or archive, or delete them automatically after a specified period.

You can learn more details on setting up the S3 Lifecycle by visiting the AWS user document here: `https://docs.aws.amazon.com/AmazonS3/latest/userguide/how-to-set-lifecycle-configuration-intro.html`.

So, what if your data is not that critically important, and you are willing to give up some availability in exchange for a cheaper alternative? Amazon has a service that fits that criterion. We'll learn about it in the next section.

Amazon S3 Express One Zone

Amazon S3 Express One Zone is a high-performance storage class designed for applications that require extremely fast data access. It offers data retrieval speeds up to 10 times faster than the standard S3 storage class, providing consistent single-digit millisecond latency. Additionally, it reduces request costs by 50%, making it a cost-effective solution for performance-critical workloads.

S3 Express One Zone is designed for applications that require single-digit millisecond data access with low latency, all within a single AWS AZ. This storage class offers the same high durability of 99.999999999% as other Amazon S3 storage classes, and ensures 99.95% availability. It's ideal for latency-sensitive workloads where rapid data retrieval is critical, and it comes with no minimum storage duration and no retrieval fees. Express One Zone provides a cost-effective solution for use cases such as real-time analytics and media processing, where high performance and fast access are essential.

With S3 Express One Zone, you can choose to store your data in a specific AZ within an AWS Region. This allows you to co-locate your storage and compute resources, such as Amazon EC2 instances, in the same zone, further optimizing performance by reducing latency between your application and its data.

This storage class is particularly beneficial for applications that demand high-speed data processing, such as ML training, real-time analytics, and HPC tasks. For example, Pinterest integrated S3 Express One Zone with their MemQ system and observed over a 10x improvement in data processing speeds. This enhancement enabled faster data consumption and more frequent experimentation, significantly boosting their operational efficiency

S3 Express One Zone uses a different bucket type known as **directory buckets**, which can handle hundreds of thousands of requests per second. This capability ensures that your applications can scale seamlessly without the need to manage multiple storage systems. Moreover, the storage automatically adjusts to your usage patterns, scaling up or down based on your needs, thereby eliminating the complexities associated with manual storage management.

Amazon S3 One Zone-IA

A better name for S3 Standard-IA might be *S3 Standard-IA*; that is not critical. Like the previous service, S3 Standard-IA, S3 One Zone-IA can be used for files that need to be retrieved less frequently but need rapid access. This service is cheaper than S3 Standard because instead of storing data in three AZs, S3 One Zone-IA persists data in only one AZ with the same durability.

S3 One Zone-IA is a good solution for use cases that don't need the reliability of S3 Standard or S3 Standard-IA and, therefore, get a lower price. The reliability is still high, and there is still duplication, but this duplication is not done across AZs. It's a suitable option for storing files such as backup files and data that can be quickly and easily recreated. It can also be a cost-effective way to store data copied from another AWS Region with S3 **Cross-Region Replication** (**CRR**).

Remember that these files will be unavailable and potentially destroyed if an AZ goes down or is destroyed. So, it should only be used with files that are not mission-critical.

S3 One Zone-IA delivers similar high throughput, durability, and speed to S3 Standard, coupled with an inexpensive retrieval cost; however, it is lower in availability (99.5%) due to single AZ data storage.

So far, we have looked at services that allow us to access the data immediately. What if we are willing to give up that immediate accessibility in exchange for an even cheaper service? Amazon S3 Glacier fits that bill. We'll learn about it in the next section.

Amazon S3 Glacier

When it's known that a file will not be needed immediately, S3 Glacier is a good option. S3 Glacier is a secure, durable class for data archiving. It is significantly cheaper than S3 Standard, but retrieving an S3 Glacier file will take longer. Data can be stored on S3 Glacier at a cost that would be competitive with an on-premises solution. Within S3 Glacier, the options and pricing are flexible.

Amazon S3 Glacier storage classes are tailored for long-term data archiving, providing cost-effective options with varying retrieval speeds to suit different use cases. These storage classes provide virtually unlimited scalability and 11 9s of data durability, ensuring the safety and reliability of your data over the long term.

S3 Glacier provides three storage classes:

- S3 Glacier Instant Retrieval
- S3 Glacier Flexible Retrieval
- S3 Glacier Deep Archive

S3 Glacier Flexible Retrieval is the base storage class of S3 Glacier and is designed for long-term storage of data that is accessed infrequently. It is a low-cost storage option ideal for storing data accessed once a year or less. You can use this option to retrieve data in minutes to 12 hours. **S3 Glacier Deep Archive** is the lowest-cost storage class of S3 Glacier and is designed for long-term data storage that is accessed once a year or less and does not need to be retrieved quickly. You can use this option if you can wait for 12 to 24 hours to retrieve data. **S3 Glacier Instant Retrieval** is a storage class that allows you to query and analyze data stored in S3 Glacier without retrieving the entire dataset. You can use the Amazon **S3 Glacier Select** feature, which allows you to run SQL-based queries directly on data stored in S3 Glacier without having to restore the entire archive. This means you can retrieve only the specific data you need, which reduces cost and speeds up access to archived content. You should use this option to retrieve data immediately in milliseconds. However, the faster data retrieval time comes with a higher cost. These storage classes are designed for different use cases and provide low-cost options for storing infrequently accessed data. You can choose them as per your workload requirements.

S3 Glacier Deep Archive is Amazon S3's cheapest option for object storage. It enables long-term storage and is suited for files that will only be retrieved occasionally. It is designed for customers who are required to keep data for seven years or longer to meet regulatory compliance regulations, such as those in the financial, healthcare, and government agencies industries.

Heavy penalties can often accrue if these rules are not adequately followed. Other good use cases are backup and disaster recovery. Many customers are using this service instead of magnetic tape systems. S3 Glacier Deep Archive can be used with Amazon S3 Glacier, allowing data to be retrieved faster than the Deep Archive service.

In the following figure, we have a summary of the profiles of storage classes and how they compare to each other:

Feature	S3 Standard	S3 Intelligent-Tiering	S3 Standard-IA	S3 One Zone-IA	S3 Glacier Instant Retrieval	S3 Glacier Flexible Retrieval	S3 Glacier Deep Archive
Use Case	Frequently accessed data	Data with unpredictable access	Infrequently accessed data	Infrequently accessed data	Archival with low latency	Flexible retrieval for archives	Long-term archive storage
Availability	99.99%	99.9% – 99.99%	99.9%	99.5%	99.9%	99.99%	99.99%
Availability Zones	3	3	3	1	3	3	3
Min. Storage Duration Charge	None	None	30 days	30 days	90 days	90 days	180 days
Retrieval Charge	None	None	Per GB retrieved	Per GB retrieved	Per GB retrieved	Per GB retrieved	Per GB retrieved
First Byte Latency	Milliseconds	Milliseconds	Milliseconds	Milliseconds	Milliseconds	Minutes to hours	Select hours

Figure 5.2: Summary of storage class features

In the preceding summary, storage costs get cheaper as we move from left to right. This means that S3 Standard has the highest storage cost, while S3 Glacier Deep Archive is the most affordable. You can get more details on the comparison between all S3 classes by referring to the link here: `https://docs.aws.amazon.com/AmazonS3/latest/userguide/storage-class-intro.html#sc-compare`.

In this section, you have learned that AWS has many offerings for your storage use cases. Depending on how quickly the data needs to be retrieved and how durably it needs to be stored, the costs will vary and allow for savings if high durability and fast retrieval are not required. Sometimes, you want to change data at runtime. For that, AWS launched a new feature called **S3 Object Lambda**. Often, there is a need for on-premise storage due to latency and compliance requirements. To achieve that, AWS provides S3 on Outposts.

Amazon S3 on Outposts

Amazon S3 on Outposts is a service designed to bring Amazon S3's robust object storage capabilities to your on-premises AWS Outposts environment. It allows organizations to store and retrieve data locally while leveraging the same S3 APIs and features available in AWS Regions. S3 on Outposts ensures high performance and supports data residency requirements by keeping data close to on-premises applications. Its key features include the following:

- **Local object storage**: Stores data directly on AWS Outposts, enabling low-latency access to data for on-premises applications.
- **Single storage class**: The `OUTPOSTS` storage class redundantly stores data across multiple devices and servers within the Outposts rack for durability and reliability.
- **Seamless integration**: Works with the same S3 APIs and features, ensuring a consistent experience with AWS Region-based S3 services.
- **Data residency**: Ideal for workloads requiring strict local data residency to meet compliance or regulatory requirements.
- **High performance**: Reduces latency by keeping data close to compute resources on-premises, which is critical for time-sensitive applications.

The following are some of the use cases:

- **Data residency compliance**: Organizations with regulatory or compliance requirements to keep data within specific physical locations can benefit from S3 on Outposts.
- **Low-latency applications**: Workloads such as media processing, industrial IoT, and ML can achieve faster performance by accessing data locally.
- **Hybrid cloud storage**: S3 on Outposts enables a seamless hybrid cloud environment where local data interacts with AWS cloud-based services.
- **Edge computing**: It supports edge-based applications that require immediate data access and processing close to the data source.

A great example scenario where AWS Outposts would be the best fit is when you need to run low-latency applications in locations with limited or no AWS Region availability, but still want the same infrastructure, services, and tools that AWS provides in the cloud. Imagine you're building a real-time trading platform for a financial firm that operates in a country where there's no AWS Region nearby. Financial trading applications are extremely latency-sensitive, every millisecond counts. If your application had to communicate with an AWS Region several hundred miles away, network latency could slow down transactions and impact competitiveness.

In this case, AWS Outposts allows you to install AWS infrastructure directly inside your own data center or colocation facility. You can run services such as EC2, EBS, RDS, and ECS/EKS locally while still integrating with your broader AWS cloud environment. This setup gives you the performance of on-premises infrastructure with the consistency and manageability of AWS.

Amazon S3 on Outposts combines the flexibility and scalability of Amazon S3 with the local residency and performance of AWS Outposts, making it an ideal solution for hybrid cloud architectures and edge workloads. Let's learn about some best practices to manage S3 storage.

Best practices to manage Amazon S3 storage

Amazon S3 is one of the simplest services in AWS, yet it is also one of the most powerful and scalable. We can easily scale our Amazon S3 applications to process thousands of requests per second while uploading and retrieving files. This scalability can be achieved "out of the box" without providing resources or servers.

Some AWS customers are already leveraging Amazon S3 to host petabyte-scale data lakes and other applications storing billions of objects and performing billions of requests. With little optimization, these applications can upload and retrieve multiple terabytes of data per second.

Other customers with low latency requirements have used Amazon S3 and other Amazon file storage services to achieve consistent low latency for small objects. Being able to retrieve this kind of object in 100 to 200 milliseconds is not uncommon.

For bigger objects, it is possible to achieve similar low-latency responses for the *first byte* received from these objects. As you can imagine, the retrieval time to receive the complete file for bigger objects will be directly proportional to object size.

Managing data with S3 Object Lambda

Amazon S3 Object Lambda is a feature of Amazon S3 that allows users to run custom code on objects stored in S3. S3 Object Lambda is designed to transform and process data as it's retrieved from Amazon S3. These actions can perform various tasks, such as automatically resizing images, creating thumbnails, or transcoding videos.

To use S3 Object Lambda, you first need to write custom code that defines the actions you want to perform. This code can be written in various languages, such as Node.js, Python, or Java, and run on AWS Lambda, a serverless compute service.

Once you have written your custom code, you can create a Lambda function and attach it to an S3 bucket. When objects are created, updated, or deleted in the S3 bucket, the Lambda function will be triggered and perform the actions defined in your code.

S3 Object Lambda is a powerful feature that can automate a variety of tasks and improve the management of data stored in S3. It allows you to perform custom actions on objects in S3 and saves time and effort when working with large amounts of data.

Sometimes, you want to create multiple copies of an object, in which case S3 allows versioning.

Versioning in Amazon S3

Amazon S3 can optionally store different versions of the same object. Have you ever been working on a document for hours and suddenly made a mistake where you deleted all of the content, or have you made a big mistake and wanted to return to a previous version? Many editors, such as Microsoft Word, offer the ability to undo changes and recover from some of these mistakes. However, once you save, close, and open the document again, you may be unable to undo any changes.

What if you have a document where multiple people make revisions, and you want to keep track of who made what changes?

Amazon S3 offers versioning capabilities that can assist with these use cases. So, what is versioning? Put simply, **versioning** is the ability to keep incremental copies. For example, if you store an important proposal document in S3, the first version of the document may have the initial architecture and statement of work, and the subsequent version may have evolved to look at future architecture, which increases the scope of the work. If you want to compare these two versions, it is easy to view and recover the previous version, which has the original work statement.

As you can imagine, keeping multiple versions of the same document can get expensive if there are many changes. This is especially true if you have a high volume of documents. To reduce costs, we can implement an S3 Lifecycle policy in which older versions are purged or moved to a cheaper storage option, such as Amazon S3 Glacier.

The exact logic of implementing the S3 Lifecycle policy will depend on your requirements. Some possibilities are setting up your policy based on document age, the number of versions, or other criteria. By the way, S3 Lifecycle policies are not limited to just older document versions. They can also be used for any document that persists in Amazon S3.

Due to S3's high availability, durability, and unlimited scalability, enterprises often use this to host critical workloads that may need backing up to other regions. Let's learn about S3 multi-destination replication, which allows users to distribute multiple copies to different environments.

Amazon S3 multi-destination replication

Amazon S3 multi-destination replication is a feature of Amazon S3 that allows users to replicate objects across multiple Amazon S3 buckets or AWS accounts. With multi-destination replication, you can define a replication rule that specifies which objects should be replicated and where they should be replicated.

To use multi-destination replication, you must create a replication rule in the Amazon S3 console. This rule defines the source bucket where objects are stored, the destination buckets where objects should be replicated, and the prefixes or tags that identify which objects should be replicated.

Once the replication rule is created, Amazon S3 will automatically replicate objects that match the specified criteria to the destination buckets. This replication is performed asynchronously, so the source and destination buckets do not have to be online simultaneously.

S3 multi-destination replication is useful for users who need to replicate objects across multiple S3 buckets or AWS accounts. It allows you to replicate objects easily and can be used to improve the availability and durability of your data. To learn more, visit `https://docs.aws.amazon.com/AmazonS3/latest/userguide/replication-metrics.html`.

Performance is key for any storage, so let's learn more about it.

Enhancing Amazon S3 performance

One simple way to enhance performance is to know where most of your users are and where your Amazon S3 bucket is. Amazon S3 buckets must be unique globally, but files will be stored in a given AWS Region. When you architect your solution, this is considered in your design. It will help reduce the time it takes to transfer files and minimize data transfer costs.

One more way to scale Amazon S3 is to scale S3 connections horizontally. Amazon S3 allows you to connect to any given bucket and access thousands of files per second. Highly scalable performance can be achieved by issuing multiple concurrent requests. Amazon S3 is designed to support high-performance levels and can handle many requests per second. While the exact number of requests per second that the service can handle will depend on various factors, it can support at least 3,500 requests per second to add data and 5,500 requests per second to retrieve data per prefix. You can think of Amazon S3 as a highly distributed system, not just a single endpoint with only one server to support the workloads.

There are several ways that users can enhance the performance of Amazon S3, including the following:

- **Choose the right storage class**: S3 offers several different storage classes, each optimized for different use cases. Choosing the right storage class for your data can help improve performance and reduce latency.
- **Use caching:** S3 uses caching techniques to improve the performance of frequently accessed data. Enabling caching for your data can help increase the number of requests per second the service can handle and reduce the time it takes to retrieve data.

- **Use object partitioning**: S3 uses a partitioning scheme to distribute data across multiple servers and storage devices, which can help increase the number of requests per second the service can handle.
- **Use regional buckets**: S3 allows you to store data in regional buckets, which can help reduce latency and improve performance by storing data closer to users.

Overall, there are many ways that users can enhance Amazon S3's performance and improve the speed and reliability of their data storage and retrieval. By choosing the right storage class, using caching, object partitioning, and regional buckets, users can maximize Amazon S3's performance for their specific use case.

In the previous section, we mentioned that Amazon S3 files could be retrieved with sub-second performance. However, suppose this level of performance is not enough, and you are looking to achieve single-digit millisecond performance. In that case, you can use Amazon CloudFront to store data closer to your user base to achieve even higher performance or Amazon ElastiCache to cache the data in memory and reduce data load time.

Amazon CloudFront

You learned about CloudFront in *Chapter 4, Networking in AWS*. Amazon CloudFront is a **content delivery network** (**CDN**) that can cache content stored in Amazon S3 and distribute it across dispersed geographic regions with thousands of **Points of Presence** (**PoPs**) worldwide. Amazon CloudFront enables these objects to be cached close to those using these resources.

Amazon S3 Transfer Acceleration

Yet another way to achieve single-digit millisecond responses is to use Amazon S3 Transfer Acceleration. This AWS service uses CloudFront edge locations to accelerate data transport over long distances. It is ideally suited to transferring a large amount of data (gigabytes or terabytes) that needs to be shared across AWS Regions.

It would help if you considered using Amazon S3 Transfer Acceleration in the following cases:

- Application requirements call for uploading files to a central location for many places around the globe
- There is a need to regularly transfer hundreds of gigabytes or terabytes worth of data across AWS Regions
- The available bandwidth must be fully utilized and leveraged when uploading to Amazon S3

The benefits of Amazon S3 Transfer Acceleration are as follows:

- It will allow you to transfer files faster and more consistently over long distances
- It can reduce network variability usage
- It can shorten the distance traveled to upload files to S3
- It will enable you to maximize bandwidth utilization

One critical consideration when using Amazon S3 is ensuring that the data stored is accessible only by parties that need to access the data. Everyone else should be locked out. Let's learn about AWS's capabilities to assist in data protection and data security.

Choosing the right S3 bucket/prefix naming convention

S3 bucket names must be unique, meaning no two buckets can have the same name. Once a bucket is deleted, its name can be reused, although there are some exceptions to this, and it may take some time before the name becomes available again. It is, therefore, recommended that you avoid deleting a bucket if you want to reuse its name.

To benefit from new features and operational improvements, as well as virtual host-style access to buckets, it is recommended that bucket names comply with DNS naming conventions, which are enforced in all regions except US East. When using the AWS Management Console, bucket names must comply with DNS naming conventions in all regions.

Here are some best practices for differentiating between file and bucket key names when uploading a large number of objects to S3:

- Avoid using the same key name for different objects. Each object should have a unique key name to avoid overwriting existing objects with the same name.
- Use a consistent naming convention for object key names. This will make it easier to locate and manage objects later on.
- Consider using a hierarchical naming structure for your objects. For example, you could use a directory structure in your object key names to help organize objects into logical groups.
- Use a delimiter, such as a slash (/), to separate the directory structure in your object key names. This will help you navigate the structure and organize and manage your objects more easily.
- Avoid using special characters in your key names, which can cause compatibility issues with different systems and applications.
- Choose key names that are descriptive and easy to understand. This will make it easier for others to navigate and understand your objects.

To ensure workload efficiency, avoiding sequential key names (or adding a random prefix) is recommended if a workload is expected to exceed 100 requests per second. This can help evenly distribute key names across multiple index partitions, improving the workload distribution and overall system performance.

All of the preceding best practices apply to S3 bucket naming. Amazon S3 stores bucket names as part of key names in its index. Security is key for data storage; let's learn about the best security practices in detail.

Security best practices to protect your data in Amazon S3

Amazon makes it extremely easy to provision an Amazon S3 bucket and quickly allows you to distribute the data worldwide by simply providing a URL pointing to files in the bucket. The good news is that this is so easy to do. The bad news is that this is so easy to do.

There have been many documented cases of sensitive data in publicly accessible endpoints in S3 and other people accessing this data. "Leaky" Amazon S3 buckets are a perfect example of how AWS's shared responsibility security model works.

AWS provides a fantastic array of security services and protocols, but data can still be exposed if not used correctly, and breaches can occur. By default, each bucket is private, but you need to configure your Amazon S3 buckets and object security with the least privilege principle when providing access.

The good news is that, as easy as it is to make the bucket public and leave it open to the world, it is almost as simple to lock it down and restrict access only to the required individuals and services.

Some of the features that Amazon S3 provides to restrict access to the correct users are as follows.

Blocking Amazon S3 public access to buckets and objects whenever possible

Starting with the principle of least privilege, AWS blocks public access to any newly created S3 bucket by default. Amazon S3 provides a bucket policy that allows you to define who can access this S3 resource. Amazon S3 **access control lists (ACLs)** provide granular control at the object level. You can learn more about S3 ACLs by visiting the AWS user document here: `https://docs.aws.amazon.com/AmazonS3/latest/userguide/acl-overview.html`. Now, AWS is moving away from ACLs, and it is disabled by default for new buckets.

Further, AWS provides S3 Access Points, which simplify management for shared bucket access by many teams. For example, a data lake bucket where you want to store all your organization's data as a single source can be accessed by the finance, accounting, and sales teams. As shown in the following figure, you can use S3 Access Points to restrict each team's access to their data only based on a defined prefix.

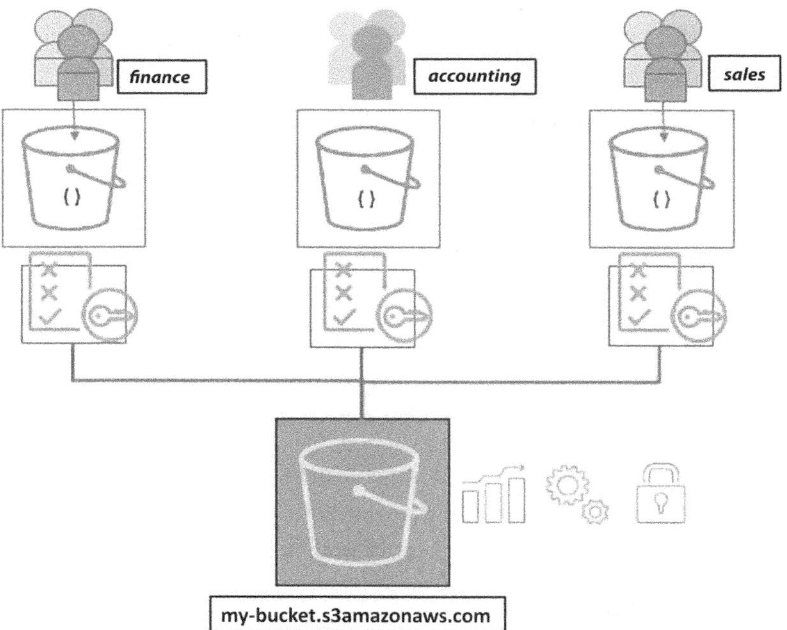

Figure 5.3: Amazon S3 Access Points

As shown in the preceding diagram, users are segmented into distinct groups, and each group is given its own S3 access point through the specific policies applied to the group. This helps centrally manage access policies across multiple users. The following is an example of the segregation of read and write access in a bucket:

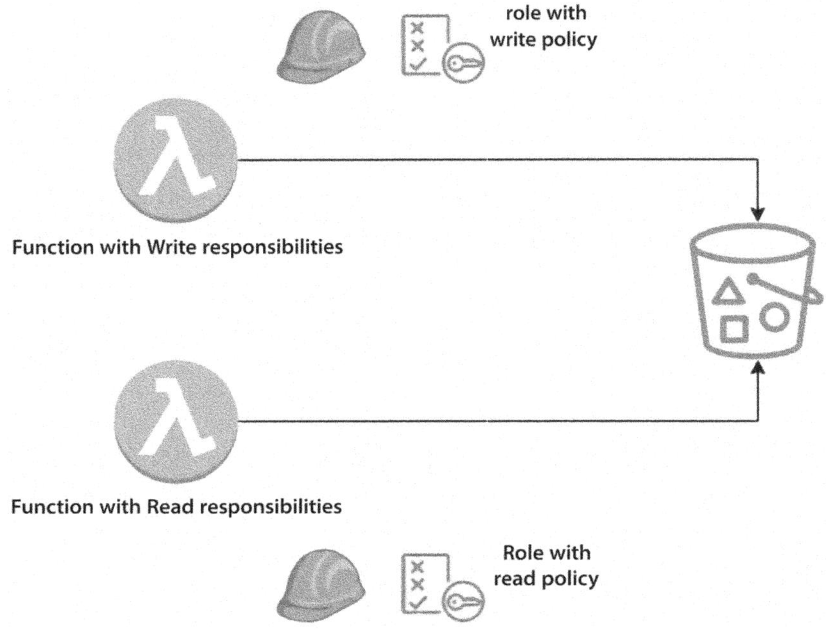

Figure 5.4: Amazon S3 access policy segregation

Quick tip: Need to see a high-resolution version of this image? Open this book in the next-gen Packt Reader or view it in the PDF/ePub copy.

The next-gen Packt Reader is included for free with the purchase of this book. Scan the QR code OR go to `packtpub.com/unlock`, then use the search bar to find this book by name. Double-check the edition shown to make sure you get the right one.

Leveraging Amazon S3 to block public access, Amazon S3 bucket administrators can configure a way to control access in a centralized manner and limit public access to Amazon S3 buckets and objects. This feature can deny public access regardless of how objects and buckets are created in Amazon S3.

Avoiding wildcards in policy files

Policy files allow a powerful syntax where you can use a wildcard character (*) to specify policies. Even though wildcards are permitted, they should be avoided whenever possible, and instead, names should be spelled out explicitly to name resources, principles, and others. The following is a sample policy with no wildcards:

```
{
   "Version":"2012-10-17",
   "Statement":[
      {
         "Effect":"Allow",
         "Action":[
            "s3:PutObject",
            "s3:GetObject",
            "s3:GetObjectVersion",
            "s3:DeleteObject",
            "s3:DeleteObjectVersion"
         ],
         "Resource":"arn:aws:s3:::DOC-EXAMPLE-BUCKET1/Mary/*"
      }
   ]
}
```

Figure 5.5: Sample policy with no wildcards

The same wildcard rule applies to Amazon S3 bucket ACLs. ACLs are files that can be used to deliver read, write, or full access to users, and if wildcards are used, they can leave the bucket open to the world.

Leveraging the S3 API

Like other AWS services, Amazon S3 provides hundreds of APIs you can use through the AWS **Command Line Interface** (**CLI**) or call the API from your application code. For example, the `ListBuckets` API can scan Amazon S3 buckets in an AWS account. `GetBucketAcl` returns the ACL of a bucket, and `GetBucketWebsite` returns the website configuration for a bucket. `GetBucketpolicy` commands can monitor whether buckets are compliant and whether the access controls, policies, and configuration are properly set up, only to allow access to authorized personnel. You can refer to AWS user docs to get the list of all the APIs and how to use them through the CLI or application; you can find the user docs here: `https://docs.aws.amazon.com/AmazonS3/latest/API/Welcome.html`.

Leveraging IAM Access Analyzer to inspect S3

AWS **Identity and Access Management** (**IAM**) Access Analyzer for S3 can generate comprehensive findings if your resource policies grant public or cross-account access. It continuously identifies resources with overly broad permissions across your entire AWS organization. It resolves results by updating policies to protect your resources from unintended access before it occurs, or archives findings for intended access.

IAM Access Analyzer continuously monitors for new or updated policies. It analyzes permissions granted using policies for your Amazon S3 buckets, AWS **Key Management Service** (**KMS**) keys, AWS IAM roles, and AWS Lambda functions. It generates detailed findings about who can access what resources from outside your AWS organization or AWS account.

If the resource access level is not intended, modify the resource policy to restrict further or expand access to the resource. If the access level is correct, you can archive the finding. IAM Access Analyzer provides comprehensive results that can be accessed through the AWS IAM, Amazon S3, and AWS Security Hub consoles and APIs. This service delivers detailed findings, allowing users to easily view and analyze access-related issues and take appropriate action to address them.

Enabling AWS Config

Another way to verify your security configuration is to deploy a continuous monitoring system using `s3-bucket-public-read-prohibited` and `s3-bucket-public-write-prohibited` and manage the configuration using AWS Config rules. You can look at the full list of Config rules here: `https://docs.aws.amazon.com/config/latest/developerguide/managed-rules-by-aws-config.html`.

AWS Config is a service that can monitor and evaluate how resources are configured in your AWS setup. AWS Config continuously audits the environment to comply with pre-established desired configurations. If a configuration deviates from the expected standards, alerts can be generated, and warnings can be issued. As you can imagine, it doesn't apply only to Amazon S3 but to all AWS services. You will learn more about AWS Config in *Chapter 8, Best Practices for Application Security, Identity, and Compliance.*

AWS greatly simplifies the monitoring of your environment, enhances troubleshooting, and ensures that established standards are followed.

Implementing S3 Object Lock to secure resources

S3 Object Lock allows storing objects with **write once, read many** (**WORM**) models. It assists in preventing the accidental or nefarious deletion of important information. For example, it can be used to ensure the integrity of AWS CloudTrail logs.

Implementing data at rest encryption

AWS provides multiple encryption options for S3, as explained here:

- **Server-side encryption with Amazon S3 managed keys (SSE-S3)**: To use SSE-S3, you need to enable the feature for your S3 bucket, and Amazon S3 will automatically encrypt and decrypt your data using keys that are managed by the service.

  SSE-S3 uses **256-bit Advanced Encryption Standard (AES-256)** encryption, one of the most secure encryption algorithms. SSE-S3 is a convenient and safe way to encrypt data at rest in Amazon S3. It automatically encrypts and decrypts your data using keys managed by Amazon S3, providing a simple and secure way to protect it without any additional cost.

- **Server-side encryption with AWS KMS (SSE-KMS)**: SSE-KMS is similar to SSE-S3 but has some additional benefits and charges. AWS managed keys for S3 (`aws/s3`) come with no extra charges, while **customer master keys (CMKs)** will have a cost. AWS KMS is a fully managed service that enables the creation and management of CMKs, which are the keys used for encrypting your data. For using a CMK, there are different permissions available that provide extra security against unauthorized access to your Amazon S3 objects. Using the SSE-KMS option, an audit trail can be created that indicates when and by whom the CMK was used. The option also enables you to create and manage customer-managed CMKs or use AWS-managed CMKs exclusive to your service, Region, and you.
- **Server-side encryption with customer-provided keys (SSE-C)**: In SSE-C, you manage the encryption keys, while Amazon S3 is responsible for encryption during the write-to-disk process and the decryption process when accessing your objects.
- **Client-side encryption**: You can encrypt data before sending it to Amazon S3. You can choose your own encryption method, but you are responsible for managing the encryption key.

Enabling data-in-transit encryption

Amazon S3 supports HTTPS (TLS) to prevent attacks that would nefariously access or modify the traffic between your users and the Amazon S3 buckets. It is highly recommended that you modify your Amazon S3 bucket policies only to permit encrypted connections that use the HTTPS (TLS) protocol.

Implementing a rule in AWS Config that enables continuous monitoring controls using `s3-bucket-SSL-requests-only` is also recommended.

Turning on Amazon S3 server access logging

By default, access is not logged. This ensures that you are not charged for the storage space these logs will take. However, it's relatively easy to turn on logging. Logging will give you a detailed record of any traffic in Amazon S3 and help determine who accessed your buckets and when.

This will help not only from a security perspective but also to assess traffic patterns and control costs. You can also enable AWS CloudTrail to log all activity related to S3.

S3 server access logging allows users to log requests made to their S3 bucket. With server access logging, you can capture detailed information about every request made to your S3 bucket, including the requestor's IP address, the request type, the response status, and the request time.

To turn on server access logging for your S3 bucket, you must first create a target bucket where the logs will be stored. This bucket can be in the same AWS account as your source bucket or in a different account.

Once you have created the target bucket, you can enable server access logging for your source bucket. When server access logging is enabled, Amazon S3 will automatically log requests to your bucket and store the logs in the target bucket. You can view the logs by accessing the target bucket in the Amazon S3 console or by using the Amazon S3 API.

Considering the use of Amazon Macie with Amazon S3

Amazon Macie leverages the power of ML to automatically ensure that sensitive information is not mishandled when using Amazon S3. Amazon Macie can locate and discern sensitive data in Amazon S3 and provide data classification. Macie can recognize **personally identifiable information (PII)**, intellectual property, and similar sensitive information. Amazon Macie has instrumentation panels, reports, and warnings to show how data is used. You can integrate findings with AWS Security Hub to have a full picture in one place.

Implementing monitoring leveraging AWS monitoring services

Monitoring is a critical component of any computing solution. AWS provides various services to consistently and reliably monitor Amazon S3, such as CloudWatch, which offers various metrics for Amazon S3, including the number of `put`, `get`, and `delete` requests.

Using VPC endpoints to access Amazon S3 whenever possible

Using **Virtual Private Cloud (VPC)** endpoints with Amazon S3 enables Amazon S3 to be used without traversing the internet and minimizes risk. A VPC endpoint for Amazon S3 is an artifact within an Amazon VPC that only allows connections from Amazon S3. To allow access from a given Amazon VPC endpoint, an Amazon S3 bucket policy can be used.

The following is the VPC endpoint policy:

```
{
  "Version": "2012-10-17",
  "Id": "Access-to-bucket-using-specific-endpoint",
  "Statement": [
    {
      "Sid": "Access-to-specific-VPCE-only",
      "Effect": "Deny",
      "Principal": "*",
      "Action": "s3:*",
      "Resource": ["arn:aws:s3:::bucket_name",
                   "arn:aws:s3:::bucket_name/*"],
      "Condition": {
        "StringNotEquals": {
          "aws:sourceVpce" : "vpce-1a2b3c4d"
        }
      }
    }
  ]
}
```

Figure 5.6: VPC endpoint policy

Here is the S3 bucket policy to accept a request from the VPC endpoint:

```
{
  "Version": "2012-10-17",
  "Id": "Access-to-bucket-using-specific-endpoint",
  "Statement": [
    {
      "Sid": "Access-to-specific-VPCE-only",
      "Effect": "Deny",
      "Principal": "*",
      "Action": "s3:*",
      "Resource": ["arn:aws:s3:::example_bucket",
                   "arn:aws:s3:::example_bucket/*"],
      "Condition": {
        "StringNotEquals": {
          "aws:sourceVpce" : "vpce-1a2b3c4d"
        }
      }
    }
  ]
}
```

Figure 5.7: S3 bucket policy

VPC endpoints for Amazon S3 use two methods to control access to your Amazon S3 data:

- Controlling the requests made to access a given VPC endpoint
- Controlling the VPCs or VPC endpoints that can make requests to a given S3 bucket by taking advantage of S3 bucket policies

Data exfiltration can be prevented by leveraging a VPC without an internet gateway.

To learn more, please check the following link: `https://docs.aws.amazon.com/AmazonS3/latest/dev/example-bucket-policies-vpc-endpoint.html`.

After security, cost is the most important aspect of storage, especially when storing huge amounts of data. Let's learn some cost optimization best practices.

Amazon S3 cost optimization

You should configure Amazon S3 to manage your items and keep them cost-effectively stored throughout their lifecycle. You can use an S3 Lifecycle configuration to make S3 move data from S3 Standard to S3 Glacier after it hasn't been accessed for a certain period. This can help you reduce storage costs by storing data in the most cost-effective storage class. Additionally, you can use the following to reduce costs further:

- **Data transitions**: Using Amazon S3 storage classes, define when objects transfer from one storage class to another. For example, one year later, archive it to the S3 Glacier storage class.
- **Data expirations**: Specify when objects will expire. On your behalf, Amazon S3 deletes expired objects. When you choose to expire items, the lifetime expiration costs vary. If you transfer intermittent logs to a bucket, your application might require them for a week or a month. After that, you might need to erase them. Some records are habitually written for a restricted period. After that, they are rarely accessed.
- **Archiving**: At some point, you may no longer be accessing data, but your organization might require you to archive it for a particular period for administrative compliance. S3 Glacier is a proper choice for enterprises that only need to reference a data group once or twice a year or for backup purposes. Glacier is Amazon's most affordable storage class. Compared to other Amazon storage offerings, an organization can store large amounts of data at a much lower cost. S3 Standard is suitable for frequently accessed data, while S3 Glacier is better suited for infrequently accessed data, tolerating longer retrieval times. Choosing the right storage class can help you save money by only paying for the storage and retrieval performance you need.

- **Automated cost saving:** S3 Intelligent-Tiering automatically stores objects in three access tiers:
    - A Frequent Access tier is available if you want to access data more often
    - An IA tier has a 40% lower cost than the Frequent Access tier (the object is not accessed for 30 consecutive days)
    - The new Deep Archive IA tier has a 68% lower cost than the Infrequent Access tier (object is not accessed for 90 consecutive days)

S3 Intelligent-Tiering monitors access patterns and moves objects that have not been accessed for 30 consecutive days to the IA tier and, after 90 days of no access, to the new Archive IA tier.

Let's say you have an S3 bucket that contains many objects, some of which are accessed frequently and some of which are accessed infrequently. If you used the S3 Standard storage class to store all these objects, you would pay the same price for them, regardless of their access patterns.

With S3 Intelligent Tiering, however, you can take advantage of the cost savings offered by the IA tier for the less frequently accessed objects. For example, let's say you have a set of log files accessed frequently during the first 30 days after they are created but only occasionally after that. With S3 Intelligent Tiering, these log files would be automatically moved to the IA tier after 30 days of inactivity. This would result in cost savings compared to storing them in the Frequent Access tier for the entire time.

The movement of objects between tiers in S3 Intelligent Tiering is fully automated and does not require any management or intervention from the user. You are charged a small monitoring and automation fee in addition to the storage and data transfer fees associated with the storage class.

Note that by opting into asynchronous archive capabilities for rarely accessed objects, you can realize storage cost savings of up to 95%, with the lowest storage cost in the cloud.

You can use S3 Transfer Acceleration to reduce data transfer costs. S3 Transfer Acceleration allows you to transfer large amounts of data to S3 over long distances more quickly and cheaply than using the internet alone. This can help you save on data transfer costs, especially if you transfer a lot of data between regions, AWS, and your on-premises data centers.

Using S3 batch operations

S3 batch operations reduce the number of requests made to the service, and allow you to perform multiple operations on your data in a single request. This can help you reduce the number of requests you make to the service and save on request fees.

Many application workloads on-premises today either can't be moved to the cloud or are challenging. Some common application examples include genomic sequencing, media rendering, medical imaging, autonomous vehicle data, seismic data, and manufacturing. AWS provides AWS Storage Gateway to connect those applications to the cloud.

When you're building applications that store and retrieve data in Amazon S3, it's important to understand how storage consistency works. Storage consistency means how soon you can reliably read the data after writing or updating it. Let's learn about it in detail.

Storage consistency in Amazon S3

Amazon S3 automatically offers strong read-after-write consistency for all applications. This means that after you write or update an object, any subsequent read request will immediately receive the latest version of that object. Additionally, S3 provides strong consistency for list operations, ensuring that any changes to the objects in a bucket are immediately reflected in the listing. Before December 2020, S3 only provided eventual consistency. The change to strong consistency was a significant upgrade by AWS, where no action is required from users to enable this feature. This feature simplifies the migration of on-premises analytics workloads, eliminates the need for additional infrastructure for consistency, and is provided at no extra cost without compromising performance or availability.

Amazon S3 Tables

Amazon S3 Tables is a new fully managed feature that helps you store and query large datasets in a tabular format using the open source Apache Iceberg table format. It is designed for developers and data teams who want to build scalable data lakes and lakehouses without spending time on manual optimization. With S3 Tables, you don't need to manage the underlying infrastructure – AWS takes care of tasks such as data compaction, snapshot management, and schema evolution. You can query your data directly using services such as Amazon Athena, Amazon EMR, Amazon Redshift, or even third-party engines such as Apache Spark, Trino, and Flink. According to AWS, S3 Tables can deliver up to 3x faster query performance compared to unmanaged Iceberg tables and 10x higher transaction throughput, helping you process and analyze your data more efficiently. You can refer to the details in the AWS launch announcement here: `https://aws.amazon.com/about-aws/whats-new/2024/12/amazon-s3-tables-apache-iceberg-tables-analytics-workloads/`.

To get started, you create a new type of S3 bucket called a table bucket, which is designed specifically to store Iceberg tables. These buckets support table-level permissions, giving you better access control.

S3 Tables work well with Amazon SageMaker and the Lake Formation lakehouse architecture, making it easier to run ML and analytics workloads on top of tabular data. For example, a data engineering team working on retail sales analytics can create a table in S3 Tables and allow data scientists to run SQL queries through Athena with faster response times, without worrying about optimizing file layout or compaction. This makes S3 Tables a powerful tool if you're building modern data platforms and want better performance, cost savings, and less operational overhead.

Understanding Amazon S3 analytics and metrics

When you're using Amazon S3 to store large amounts of data, it's important to understand how your storage is being used. **Amazon S3 Storage Lens** is a tool that gives you a clear view of your storage usage and activity across all your accounts and buckets. It provides more than 60 metrics, such as the number of objects, total storage size, and how often data is accessed. With this information, you can find areas where you might reduce costs or improve data protection. For example, if you notice that certain data isn't accessed often, you might move it to a less expensive storage class, such as S3 Glacier. You can learn more about it from the AWS page: `https://aws.amazon.com/s3/storage-analytics-insights/`.

A real-world example of using S3 Storage Lens involves a digital marketing agency that stored data in multiple S3 buckets for different clients. Over time, as projects ended, some buckets remained unused. By using S3 Storage Lens, the agency identified large, unmonitored buckets containing outdated campaign data. They proceeded to delete this unnecessary data, which significantly reduced their storage costs.

Another helpful feature is the **S3 Inventory**, which provides a daily or weekly report of all objects in your buckets, including details such as size, storage class, and encryption status. This is useful for tracking your data and ensuring compliance with regulations. For instance, a company can use the S3 Inventory to verify that all sensitive data is properly encrypted.

To monitor the performance of your S3 requests, you can use **Amazon CloudWatch**. It tracks metrics such as the total number of requests, latency, and errors. By using these tools, you can better understand and manage your S3 storage. This helps you optimize costs, maintain performance, and ensure your data is stored securely and efficiently.

Now that we have covered Amazon EBS, Amazon EFS, and Amazon S3, we will spend some time understanding the difference between the services and when it's appropriate to use one versus the other.

Choosing the right cloud storage type

So far, this chapter has taught you about three different kinds of cloud storage. First, Amazon EBS stores data in blocks; you can also use this as a SAN in the cloud. Second, Amazon EFS is a cloud file storage system, a NAS in the cloud. Finally, Amazon S3 stores data as objects. So, now that we have covered all these storage services, the obvious question is which one is better. The following table should help you decide which service is best for your use case:

Service	Performance	Cost	Availability	Storage Limits	File Size Limits	Use Cases
Amazon S3	Supports at least 3,500 PUT/COPY/POST/DELETE and 5,500 GET/HEAD requests per second per prefix	Starts at $0.023 per GB/month for S3 Standard	Designed for 99.99% availability	No limit on the number of objects; individual objects can be up to 5 TB	Maximum object size is 5 TB	Object storage for backups, content delivery, data lakes, and analytics
Amazon EBS	Provisioned IOPS SSD (io2) volumes support up to 256,000 IOPS and 4,000 MB/s of throughput	Pricing varies by volume type; for example, io2 starts at $0.125 per GB/month	Designed for 99.999% availability	Each volume can be up to 16 TB; multiple volumes can be used for larger storage needs	Maximum volume size is 16 TB	Block storage for databases, transactional systems, and persistent storage for EC2 instances
Amazon EFS	Supports up to 1.5 GB/s of throughput per client and up to 10 GB/s of throughput per file system with Provisioned Throughput mode	Standard storage pricing starts at $0.30 per GB/month	Designed for 99.99% availability	Scales automatically to petabytes	Maximum file size is 52.6 TB	File storage for content management systems, big data analytics, and shared storage for containers

Table 5.4: Choosing the service based on your use case

An EBS volume is always attached to a single EC2 instance, so when you need high-performance, persistent storage, always use an EBS volume. If you need shared file storage between multiple EC2 instances, then you want to use EFS. S3 is your choice to store any amount of data in any format for big data analytics, backups, and even large-volume content for your application.

As you will use S3 frequently for your day-to-day large volume (from GBs to PBs) of data storage needs, let's learn some best practices for managing S3.

Building hybrid storage with AWS Storage Gateway

While working on cloud migration, some applications will be more complex when moving to the cloud. Those apps might need to stay on-premises for performance or compliance reasons, or they may need to be simplified to move into the cloud quickly. Some apps, such as mainframe or legacy applications that must meet licensing requirements, may need to remain on-premises indefinitely. To address these use cases, you must explore hybrid cloud storage solutions that provide ready access for on-premises apps to data stored in AWS.

AWS Storage Gateway

AWS Storage Gateway acts as a bridge to provide access to almost unlimited cloud storage by connecting applications running on-premises to Amazon storage. The following diagram shows that Storage Gateway allows customers to connect to and use key cloud storage services such as Amazon S3, Amazon S3 Glacier, Amazon FSx for Windows File Server, and Amazon EBS. Additionally, Storage Gateway integrates with AWS services such as AWS KMS, AWS IAM, AWS CloudTrail, and Amazon CloudWatch.

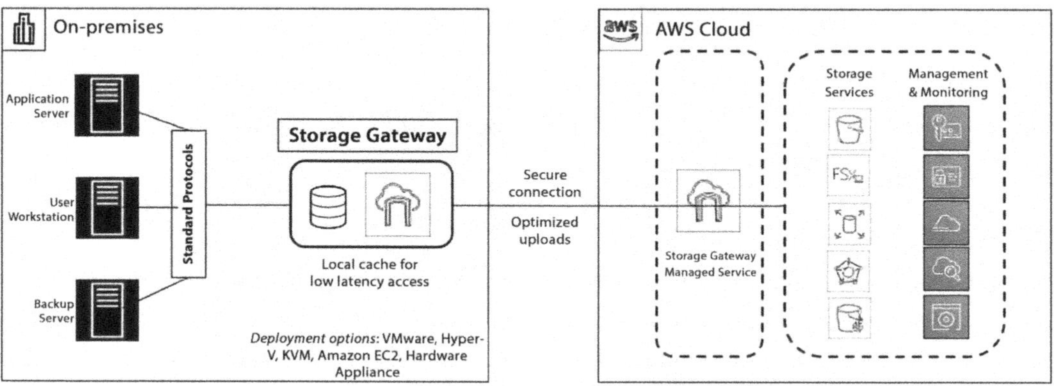

Figure 5.8: AWS Storage Gateway

Storage Gateway quickly deploys on-premises as a preconfigured hardware appliance. There is also a virtual machine option that supports all the major hypervisors. Storage Gateway provides a local cache to access frequently accessed data with low-latency access. Storage Gateway supports access via standard storage protocols (NFS, SMB, and iSCSI VTL), so no changes to customers' applications are required. There are four types of Storage Gateway.

Amazon S3 File Gateway

Amazon S3 File Gateway is a service that allows you to store and retrieve files from Amazon S3 using the file protocol (i.e., NFS and SMB). This means you can use S3 File Gateway as a file server to access your S3 objects as if they were files on a local file system. This can be useful for applications that require access to files stored in S3 but don't support object storage directly. You can see the data flow in the following diagram.

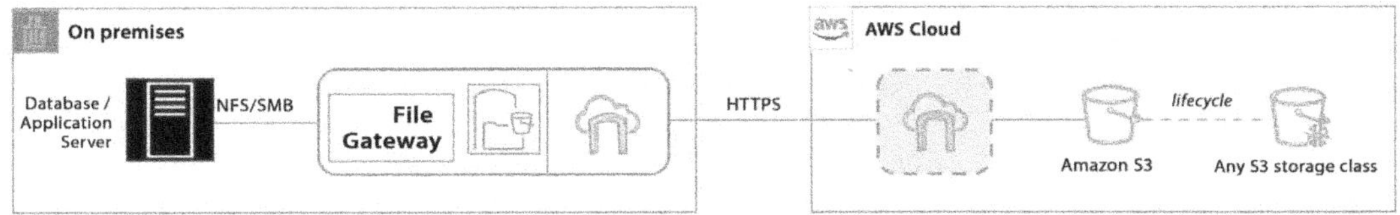

Figure 5.9: Amazon S3 File Gateway

To use S3 File Gateway, you create a file share and configure it to store files in your S3 bucket. You can then access the file share using the file protocol from within your Amazon VPC or over the internet. This lets you easily integrate S3 File Gateway with your pre-existing applications and workflows.

Overall, S3 File Gateway is a useful service for applications that require file storage but want to take advantage of S3's scalability, durability, and cost-effectiveness.

S3 File Gateway supports various features such as versioning, deduplication, and tiering. It also integrates with other AWS services, such as AWS Backup, IAM, and AWS KMS, allowing you to use these services with your S3 objects.

Amazon FSx File Gateway

Amazon FSx File Gateway is a hybrid cloud storage solution that provides on-premises applications with seamless, low-latency access to file shares hosted by Amazon FSx for Windows File Server. You deploy it as a virtual or hardware appliance connected via VPN or AWS Direct Connect. It caches frequently accessed data locally, while storing files in a resilient, cloud-managed Windows file system. This lets you offload on-premises NAS and file servers to AWS without changing your applications. Here's an example of how Amazon FSx File Gateway works:

Suppose you have an on-premises file server to store important files and data. As your storage needs grow, you run out of space on your local file server. Instead of purchasing additional storage or upgrading your hardware, you can use Amazon FSx File Gateway to extend your storage to the cloud seamlessly, as follows:

1. First, you deploy a virtual machine on your on-premises infrastructure and install the Amazon FSx File Gateway software. This virtual machine is a gateway between your on-premises file server and Amazon S3 or Amazon FSx. Next, you create an Amazon S3 bucket or an Amazon FSx file system to store your files in the cloud. You can choose different S3 storage classes and lifecycle policies to manage your cloud storage costs.
2. Then, you create a file share on the Amazon FSx File Gateway virtual machine and connect it to your on-premises file server using standard protocols such as SMB or NFS. You can use your existing file server permissions and AD to manage file access.
3. Finally, when you save a file on your on-premises file server, it is automatically backed up to the cloud using Amazon FSx File Gateway. You can also access the files in the cloud directly from the file server without any additional steps.

Amazon FSx File Gateway also provides features such as caching, multi-protocol access, and file-level restore, making it an ideal solution for backup and disaster recovery, content distribution, and data archiving. It allows you to use your existing on-premises file servers to store and access files on the cloud, providing virtually unlimited storage capacity without additional hardware or complex software configurations.

Tape Gateway

Amazon Tape Gateway is a service that allows you to store data on tapes using the tape protocol (i.e., **Linear Tape-Open** (**LTO**) and **virtual tape library** (**VTL**)). This means that you can use Tape Gateway as a tape library, allowing you to access your data as if it were stored on tapes in a local tape library. This can be useful for applications requiring access to data stored on tapes but not directly supporting tapes.

Tape Gateway supports various features, such as data deduplication, tiering, and encryption. It also integrates with other AWS services, such as AWS Storage Gateway, AWS Backup, and AWS KMS, allowing you to use these services with your data on tapes.

To use Tape Gateway, you create a tape virtual device and configure it to store data on tapes in your tape library. You can then access the tape virtual device using the tape protocol from within your VPC or over the internet. This lets you easily integrate Tape Gateway with your existing applications and workflows. Overall, Tape Gateway is a useful service for applications that require tape storage but want to take advantage of the scalability and durability of AWS.

Volume Gateway

Amazon Volume Gateway is a service that allows you to store data on cloud-backed storage volumes using the iSCSI protocol. You can use Volume Gateway as a storage device, allowing you to access your data as if it were stored on a local storage volume. This can be useful for applications that require access to data stored on a storage volume but don't support cloud storage directly.

Volume Gateway supports two storage modes: cached and stored. In cached mode, data is stored on your local storage volume and asynchronously backed up to Amazon S3, allowing you to quickly access your most frequently accessed data while still providing long-term durability. In stored mode, data is directly stored on Amazon S3, allowing you to store large amounts without needing local storage.

To use Volume Gateway, you create a storage volume and attach it to your on-premises or Amazon EC2 instance. You can then access the storage volume using the iSCSI protocol from within your Amazon VPC or over the internet. This lets you easily integrate Volume Gateway with your existing applications and workflows. Overall, Volume Gateway is a useful service for applications that require storage volumes but want to take advantage of AWS's scalability and durability.

Storage Gateway offers customers the advantages of hybrid cloud storage by providing a seamless migration path to the cloud. Customers experience a fast deployment, which enables them to leverage the agility and scale of the cloud quickly. Storage Gateway doesn't require any application changes. It easily integrates with standard storage protocols on-premises.

AWS Storage Gateway comparison

Here's a side-by-side comparison table for AWS Storage Gateway types:

Feature	Amazon S3 File Gateway	Amazon FSx File Gateway	Tape Gateway	Volume Gateway
Description	Provides file-based access to Amazon S3 using NFS/SMB protocols	Extends on-premises file servers to Amazon S3, and FSx for Windows File Server	Enables backup to VTLs in AWS, simulating physical tape storage	Provides iSCSI-based cloud-backed storage volumes, accessible as local storage devices
Protocols Supported	NFS, SMB	SMB	LTO and VTL	iSCSI

Storage Modes	S3 objects, accessible as files	Direct integration with on-premises NAS for cloud-based extensions	Virtual tapes stored in Amazon S3, with optional tiering to Glacier for long-term archiving	Cached (local cache with cloud backing) and stored (entire data stored in cloud)
Use Cases	File storage for analytics, media processing, and backup	Extending on-premises file servers for unlimited cloud storage, backup, disaster recovery, and archiving	Tape-based backup and archiving; replacing physical tape libraries	Storage for databases, virtual machines, and file servers with scalable cloud-backed storage
Caching	Local cache for frequently accessed files	Local cache to reduce latency for frequently accessed data	N/A	Cached mode provides local access to frequently used data; stored mode directly writes to the cloud
Integration with AWS Services	Integrates with S3, IAM, KMS, CloudWatch, and Backup	Integrates with S3, FSx for Lustre, FSx for Windows File Server, IAM, KMS, CloudWatch, and Backup	Integrates with AWS Backup, S3, Glacier, and KMS	Integrates with S3, CloudWatch, IAM, and KMS
Performance	Low-latency access for cached files; ideal for bursty workloads	Seamless, high-throughput access to cloud storage	Optimized for backup and archival workflows; supports deduplication and tiering to Glacier	Low-latency access to frequently accessed data in cached mode; durable cloud storage in stored mode

Storage Limits	Unlimited in Amazon S3	Unlimited in Amazon S3, FSx for Lustre, or FSx for Windows File Server	Scales with the number of virtual tapes stored	Each volume supports up to 32 TB; multiple volumes can scale storage
Data Residency	Data is backed up to Amazon S3 in the cloud	Data is stored in Amazon S3 or FSx for Lustre/ Windows File Server	Data is backed up to Amazon S3; can be archived in Amazon Glacier	Data can reside locally in cached mode or entirely in Amazon S3 for stored mode
Best Use Cases	Applications requiring file system integration with cloud scalability	Seamless hybrid storage for on-premises file servers, enabling cloud backups and disaster recovery	Organizations migrating away from physical tapes or needing long-term archival at reduced costs	Scalable cloud storage for workloads such as databases and file servers while retaining on-premises accessibility
Key Features	Versioning, deduplication, and data tiering	Caching, multi-protocol access, and file-level restore capabilities	Deduplication, encryption, and tiering to Glacier	Cached and stored modes with robust backup and disaster recovery options

Table 5.5: Key differences between the Storage Gateway types

AWS Storage Gateway is managed centrally via the AWS console. It integrates with various AWS services such as CloudWatch, CloudTrail, and IAM to provide customers with visibility and control over the solution. You often want to back up your data for various reasons, such as disaster recovery. In such cases, you need an easy option to back up your data facilitated by AWS: using AWS Backup.

AWS Backup

AWS Backup is a service that centralizes backup management and enables a straightforward and economical means of backing up application data across multiple AWS services to help customers comply with their business continuity and backup requirements. It automates backup scheduling and retention management and provides a centralized way for configuring and auditing the resources that require backup.

Additionally, it monitors backup activity and alerts you in case of any issues. AWS Backup integrates with CloudTrail and AWS Organizations for governance and management, giving customers many options to help meet their recovery, restoration, and compliance needs.

AWS Backup enables centralized configuration and management of backups for various AWS resources, including Amazon EC2 instances, Amazon EBS volumes, Amazon **Relational Database Service** (**RDS**) databases, Amazon DynamoDB tables, Amazon EFS file systems, and other resources. You can learn more about the supported applications by referring to this link: `https://docs.aws.amazon.com/aws-backup/latest/devguide/whatisbackup.html#supported-resources`. You will learn about all the database services mentioned in *Chapter 7, Selecting the Right Database Service*. Some of the use cases where you may want to use AWS Backup are as follows:

- Compliance and disaster recovery
- Unifying backup solutions to avoid the complexity of cloud backups being done by different groups
- Creating audit and compliance alerts, reports, and dashboards across all backups

To use AWS Backup, you create a backup plan and specify the AWS resources you want to back up. AWS Backup will automatically create backups according to your specified schedule and store them in your selected storage location. You can restore your backups as needed, either to the original location or a new one. This allows you to easily manage your backups and recover from data loss in a disaster. Overall, AWS Backup is a useful service for businesses that want to ensure the durability and availability of their critical data on AWS.

In this section, you learned about various Storage Gateway options for building a hybrid cloud by storing data in the AWS cloud and using AWS Backup to provide a cloud-native option for data backup. Now, let's learn about best practices for storage assessment.

Approach and best practices for AWS storage assessment

A robust storage assessment is a critical step in transitioning to the cloud. You can take a structured approach to assess, optimize, and migrate on-premises storage to its scalable, cost-effective services, such as Amazon S3, Amazon FSx, Amazon EBS, and Amazon EFS. Let's learn more about it.

Key challenges in data migration

Migrating your data to AWS can bring significant benefits, but it's essential to address several challenges to ensure a smooth transition. One major challenge is understanding your current storage usage. Before moving to AWS, analyze your existing data by asking questions:

- How much storage do you use?
- How often do you access different datasets?
- What are your performance needs regarding speed and responsiveness?

For example, if you have a customer database that requires quick access, you'll need to choose AWS storage options that offer low latency.

Another critical challenge is categorizing your data. Not all data is the same; some is accessed frequently (active data), while other data is rarely used (archival data). For instance, daily transaction records might be active data, whereas old compliance documents could be archival. AWS provides various storage classes tailored for different access patterns. Storing active data in high-performance storage such as Amazon FSx ensures quick access, while archival data can be placed in cost-effective options such as Amazon S3 Glacier. This strategy optimizes your storage costs without compromising on accessibility.

Predicting and managing costs during migration is also important. Unexpected expenses can arise from data transfer fees, temporary storage needs, or extended timelines. Tools such as the AWS Pricing Calculator and Migration Evaluator can help you estimate costs accurately. For example, if you are migrating TBs of data, use these tools to forecast expenses and adjust the migration plan to stay within budget.

Aligning your workloads with the appropriate AWS services is another challenge. AWS offers a wide range of storage solutions, each designed for specific use cases. For example, Amazon EBS is ideal for applications requiring block storage, while Amazon S3 suits object storage needs. If you are migrating a vast library of images and videos to Amazon S3, you can benefit from S3's scalability and durability.

AWS storage assessment approach

When you plan to move your storage systems to AWS, a clear assessment process makes everything smoother and more cost-effective. The AWS storage assessment approach helps you understand your current setup, evaluate the right AWS services, and build a strong business case for migration.

The first step is to define the scope of your assessment. This means identifying which applications, storage systems (such as NAS, SAN, and object storage), and business goals are in focus. You'll want to break down your data into two groups:

- Frequently accessed data (active or hot data)
- Infrequently accessed data (cold or archival)

This helps you figure out the right mix of high-performance and low-cost storage options.

Next, you move into the data collection phase. AWS offers tools that make this process easy and secure without needing agents. For example, you can use AWS DataSync Discovery, Migration Hub, or Migration Evaluator to gather information about your storage environment. Ideally, collect metrics over 7 to 14 days to get an accurate performance baseline. You may want to look at things such as how much capacity is used, IOPS, latency, and access protocols (such as NFS, SMB, or iSCSI). If your system uses deduplication or compression, include those savings in your analysis.

Once you've collected the data, it's time to analyze and map your workloads to the most suitable AWS services. Here's how this typically looks:

- Use **Amazon FSx** for Windows or Lustre if you're running high-performance workloads such as SQL databases or engineering simulations
- Choose **Amazon S3** for storing large amounts of unstructured or archival data
- Go with **Amazon EBS** when you need high-performance block storage, especially for transactional workloads
- Pick **Amazon EFS** for scalable file storage that's shared across multiple compute resources

Then, divide your data into storage tiers. Store hot data on faster services such as Amazon FSx or EBS, and move cold data to more affordable options such as S3 Glacier.

Now you're ready to build a business case. This involves comparing your current infrastructure costs with what you'll spend on AWS. Highlight how moving from CapEx (buying servers and hardware) to OpEx (pay-as-you-go cloud pricing) can save money. Also, include how using AWS can reduce your carbon footprint since AWS data centers are more energy efficient. Add a clear **return on investment (ROI)** calculation to help your stakeholders understand the long-term value.

Finally, you move to implementation and validation. Start with a **proof of concept (PoC)** to test performance and identify any issues. Validate your assumptions, tweak your mappings if needed, and make sure your AWS solution truly meets both technical and business needs. By following this structured approach, you can migrate your storage to AWS with confidence. It helps you match the right storage type to your workloads, reduce costs, and scale more easily in the future.

Best practices for AWS storage migration

Migrating your storage to AWS is more than just moving files; it's about planning strategically so your data is secure, your costs stay under control, and your systems run efficiently. One of the best ways to do this is by using automated tools. Services such as AWS DataSync help you transfer data from on-premises systems to AWS automatically and securely. You can also use AWS Backup to manage backup policies across your AWS services. These tools reduce manual work and lower the risk of human error during migration.

Another important step is to optimize your costs using storage tiering. With Amazon S3 Intelligent-Tiering, AWS automatically moves your data between storage classes based on how often it's accessed. This means you're not paying high prices to store files that no one uses regularly. For data you rarely need such old records or compliance logs; you can move it to Amazon S3 Glacier or S3 Glacier Deep Archive, which are much cheaper and still meet long-term retention needs.

You should also focus on cleaning up unused data, often called "zombie data." This includes outdated backups, test data, or duplicated files that no one touches anymore, especially in dev/test environments. By tagging and deleting these during migration, you'll cut down on storage waste and only move what matters.

It's also crucial to validate performance. Not all workloads need the same storage speed. For example, a transactional database might need high IOPS and low latency, which you can get with Amazon FSx for NetApp ONTAP. On the other hand, static files or archived logs can go into Amazon S3 or EBS gp3 volumes. Testing your workloads in their new environment ensures that they continue to run smoothly.

In addition to these, there are a few critical planning elements that you should not overlook:

- **Network bandwidth planning**: Ensure that your network can handle data transfer volumes within migration timelines. Use AWS Direct Connect or Snowball for large datasets where applicable.
- **Rollback planning**: Always plan for contingencies. Keep the original data intact until migration validation is complete.
- **Change management**: Coordinate with IT and business teams to avoid disruptions, and follow governance protocols for scheduled changes.
- **Pilot testing**: Before a full-scale migration, run pilot tests with non-critical data or applications to uncover potential issues early.

- **Disaster recovery planning:** As you migrate, define disaster recovery strategies in AWS. Use AWS services such as Amazon S3 CRR and AWS Backup Vault Lock to ensure business continuity.
- **Post-migration monitoring**: Use tools such as Amazon CloudWatch, AWS CloudTrail, and AWS Config to track performance, access, and configuration changes after the migration.

Finally, you can't ignore governance and compliance. Use lifecycle rules to move data between storage tiers automatically and define how long it should be kept. Protect your data with AWS KMS for encryption, and monitor access and changes using AWS CloudTrail. This helps you stay aligned with industry standards such as HIPAA, GDPR, or SOC 2. These steps help you align with your business goals while taking full advantage of AWS's scalable, secure storage options.

Knowledge check

The following are sample questions that align with the difficulty and scope of the *AWS Certified Solutions Architect - Professional* exam:

1. You have a web application hosted on AWS that serves static content such as images, CSS files, and JavaScript files from an Amazon S3 bucket. The application has experienced rapid growth, and you need to ensure that the static content is delivered with low latency to users globally. Which combination of AWS services and features would you implement to meet this requirement? (Select two.)

    a. Enable Amazon S3 Transfer Acceleration
    b. Configure Amazon CloudFront with the S3 bucket as the origin
    c. Enable Amazon S3 Cross-Region Replication
    d. Configure Amazon Route 53 to use latency-based routing with the S3 bucket endpoint
    e. Enable Amazon S3 byte-range fetching

    Answer: b. and d.

    Explanation:

    a. Incorrect. Amazon S3 Transfer Acceleration accelerates the transfer of data to and from Amazon S3 over long distances, but it does not improve content delivery for static website hosting.

- b. **Correct.** Amazon CloudFront is a **content delivery network (CDN)** service that caches and serves static content from edge locations worldwide, providing low latency and high data transfer rates for end-users globally.
- c. Incorrect. Amazon S3 Cross-Region Replication replicates data across different AWS Regions for compliance or disaster recovery purposes, but it does not directly address low-latency content delivery.
- d. **Correct.** Configuring Amazon Route 53 with latency-based routing and using the S3 bucket endpoint as the target allows Route 53 to route traffic to the S3 bucket through the AWS edge location, providing the lowest latency for the user's location.
- e. Incorrect. Amazon S3 byte-range fetching optimizes the delivery of partially cached content, but it does not address the global delivery of static content with low latency.

2. You are designing a highly available and fault-tolerant architecture for a mission-critical application that requires consistent, low-latency access to persistent storage. The application will be deployed across multiple **Availability Zones (AZs)** in the same AWS Region. Which of the following EBS volume types should you choose to meet these requirements?

   - a. Amazon EBS Provisioned IOPS SSD (io2) volumes
   - b. Amazon EBS General Purpose SSD (gp3) volumes
   - c. Amazon EBS Throughput Optimized HDD (st1) volumes
   - d. Amazon EBS Cold HDD (sc1) volumes

   Answer: a.

   Explanation:

   - a. **Correct.** Amazon EBS Provisioned IOPS SSD (io2) volumes are designed for mission-critical applications that require sustained high random **input/output operations per second (IOPS)** performance and consistent low-latency access to storage. They are suitable for applications with demanding performance requirements, such as databases, and are recommended for use cases that require high IOPS and low-latency storage. By deploying the application across multiple AZs and using Amazon EBS Provisioned IOPS SSD (io2) volumes, you can achieve high availability, fault tolerance, and consistent, low-latency access to persistent storage, meeting the requirements of the mission-critical application.

   b. Incorrect. While Amazon EBS General Purpose SSD (gp3) volumes are suitable for many workloads, they may not provide the consistent low-latency performance required for mission-critical applications with demanding performance requirements.
   c. Incorrect. Amazon EBS Throughput Optimized HDD (st1) volumes are designed for workloads requiring high throughput and are not optimized for low-latency access, making them unsuitable for the given requirements.
   d. Incorrect. Amazon EBS Cold HDD (sc1) volumes are designed for infrequently accessed workloads and are not recommended for low-latency or high-performance use cases, making them an incorrect choice for the given requirements.

3. You have been tasked with designing a highly available and scalable file storage solution for a web application running on **Amazon Elastic Kubernetes Service (Amazon EKS)**. The application requires shared access to a file system from multiple Kubernetes Pods across multiple Availability Zones. Which AWS service would you recommend to meet these requirements?

   a. Amazon EFS
   b. Amazon EBS
   c. Amazon S3
   d. AWS Storage Gateway

   Answer: a.

   Explanation:

   a. **Correct**. Amazon EFS is a scalable and highly available file system that can be mounted concurrently by multiple Amazon EC2 instances or Amazon EKS Pods across multiple Availability Zones. It provides a shared file system that can be accessed from multiple compute resources, making it a suitable choice for the given requirements.
   b. Incorrect. Amazon EBS provides block-level storage volumes for EC2 instances but cannot be shared concurrently by multiple instances or Pods across Availability Zones.
   c. Incorrect. Amazon S3 is an object storage service that doesn't provide a traditional file system interface, which is required for the given use case.
   d. Incorrect. AWS Storage Gateway is a hybrid cloud storage service that enables on-premises applications to use AWS cloud storage seamlessly. Still, it doesn't provide a shared file system for multiple compute resources in AWS.

4. You have an application that generates large amounts of data that needs to be stored durably and cost-effectively. However, you also need the ability to retrieve a subset of this data for occasional analysis quickly. Which of the following Amazon S3 storage classes would be the most appropriate choice?

    a. S3 Standard

    b. S3 Glacier Instant Retrieval

    c. S3 Glacier Flexible Retrieval

    d. S3 Glacier Deep Archive

    Answer: b.

    Explanation:

    a. Incorrect. S3 Standard is designed for frequently accessed data and would not be cost-effective for large amounts of infrequently accessed data.

    b. **Correct**. S3 Glacier Instant Retrieval is designed for long-term data archiving and can retrieve objects within milliseconds, making it suitable for occasional analysis of a subset of data.

    c. Incorrect. S3 Glacier Flexible Retrieval is designed for long-term data archiving but has retrieval times ranging from minutes to hours, which may not be suitable for occasional analysis requiring quick retrieval.

    d. Incorrect. S3 Glacier Deep Archive is designed for long-term data archiving with the lowest storage cost. However, it has the longest retrieval times, typically within 12 hours, which would not meet the requirement for occasional quick analysis.

5. You are a solutions architect working for a company with a large on-premises data center that wants to leverage AWS for backup and disaster recovery. They have a requirement to store their frequently accessed data on-premises while keeping the infrequently accessed data in AWS. Which AWS Storage Gateway mode would you recommend to meet this requirement?

    a. File Gateway

    b. Volume Gateway in cached volume mode

    c. Volume Gateway in stored volume mode

    d. Tape Gateway

    Answer: b.

Explanation:

a. Incorrect. File Gateway stores flat files in Amazon S3 and accesses them through an NFS or SMB file system interface.

b. **Correct.** In Volume Gateway in cached volume mode, the entire dataset is stored in Amazon S3, and a cache of frequently accessed data is maintained on-premises for low-latency access. This mode suits scenarios where you must keep frequently accessed data on-premises while storing the entire dataset in AWS.

c. Incorrect. In Volume Gateway in stored volume mode, the entire dataset is stored on-premises, and asynchronous backups are taken and stored in Amazon S3. This mode is suitable for scenarios where you must keep the whole dataset on-premises while maintaining backups in AWS.

d. Incorrect. Tape Gateway stores backup data on virtual tapes in AWS and replaces existing on-premises tape backup infrastructure.

Summary

In this chapter, you learned about storage area networks in the cloud with Amazon EBS. You learned about various EBS options and how to choose the right EBS volume per your workload. You further learned about network-attached storage in the cloud with Amazon EFS and file system-specific workloads with Amazon FSx.

With the ever-increasing amount of data, you need scalable storage to store petabytes of data, and AWS provides Amazon S3 to fulfill that need. You learned about the various tiers of Amazon S3, including S3 Standard, Intelligent Tiering, Infrequent Access-IA, One Zone-IA, and S3 Glacier. You further learned about S3 versioning to save a copy of your file and build multi-destination replication.

Later in the chapter, you learned about Amazon S3's best practices and optimized your S3 storage for performance, cost, and security. Finally, you learned about building a hybrid cloud with AWS Storage Gateway and a cloud-native backup option with AWS Backup.

In the next chapter, you will learn how to harness the power of the cloud to create powerful applications. We will also deep-dive into another important AWS service: Amazon EC2.

6

Harnessing the Power of Cloud Computing

Technology is transforming the world, yet a substantial portion of enterprise IT budgets continues to be allocated toward maintaining existing infrastructure. According to Mechanical Orchard, 60–80% of IT budgets are recurrent costs used to "keep the lights on" in the IT department (`https://www.mechanical-orchard.com/insights/1-14-trillion-to-keep-the-lights-on-legacys-drag-on-productivity`). In data centers, servers are at the core of any IT workload and consume most of the IT effort and budget. To run any application, you need computing. Even though the cloud brings the concept of serverless computing, there are still servers in the background managed by cloud vendors. Further, these computing costs could vary depending on the business and organization. The other significant IT costs include networking infrastructure, storage systems, software licenses, personnel, facilities, and energy costs.

The AWS compute platform helps you shift your budgets from maintaining existing infrastructure to driving innovation. You will learn about some of the basic computing services available in AWS and how these services came to be. In addition, you will learn about serverless compute and hybrid compute. You will also learn how AWS handles the fundamental services of computing.

In this chapter, we will discuss the following topics:

- Compute in AWS
- Amazon EC2
- Amazon EC2 best practices
- Containerization in AWS

- Amazon Elastic Load Balancing
- Serverless compute with AWS Lambda and Fargate
- High-performance computing
- Hybrid compute
- Tips for choosing the right compute option in AWS

By the end of this chapter, you will be familiar with the various compute options available in AWS and be able to choose the right compute option for the right workload. Let's dive deep into the world of AWS compute.

Compute in AWS

The cloud has changed the way we see compute today. A decade ago, there was no such word as **compute**, and **server** was the most commonly used terminology. Running your application code or database was about servers with CPUs. These servers could be dedicated to physical bare-metal machines or **virtual machines** (**VMs**) hosted on physical machines. The cloud started with the same concept of providing on-demand servers, which are VMs hosted in cloud providers' data centers. In AWS terminology, **Amazon Elastic Compute Cloud** (**EC2**) servers are on-demand VMs based on a per-second billing model.

With EC2, AWS takes care of the physical server, but a maintenance overhead is still involved in patching and securing the underlying OS in these EC2 instances. Also, cloud providers such as AWS are looking to provide more optimized solutions and help you focus on the coding part to build business logic. AWS launched a serverless computing service called **AWS Lambda** to reduce OS maintenance overhead in 2014. It was the first offering where you write and run a piece of code using the service without worrying about servers and clusters, which generated the term **function-as-a-service** (**FaaS**). Lambda pointed the entire IT industry toward building computing services without servers. However, Lambda still runs on servers behind the scenes, but that is abstracted from the end user, resulting in the term **serverless compute**.

Initially, Lambda was used to run small functions, mainly automating operations such as spin-up infrastructure and triggering CI/CD pipelines. However, AWS Lambda became more powerful, and organizations built complex applications such as dynamic e-commerce websites using Lambda. It's become a low-cost and scalable option for new businesses, and it helps them succeed. For example, in 2017, *A Cloud Guru* built an entire training content distribution website using Lambda, which scales to 300,000 students at a meager cost. Read this SiliconANGLE article to find out more: `https://siliconangle.com/2017/08/15/a-cloud-guru-uses-lambda-and-api-gateway-to-build-serverless-company-awssummit/`.

Further down the line, customers started using serverless compute services to run their container workloads. This resulted in AWS Fargate, launched in 2017 for **Elastic Container Service (ECS)**, allowing customers to run their Docker containers in AWS without a server. Later, in 2019, Fargate launched **Elastic Kubernetes Service (EKS)** to enable customers to run Kubernetes serverless.

Now, AWS is going all-in on serverless. In 2021, they launched various serverless options for analytics services, such as Amazon Redshift Serverless for building petabyte-scale data warehouses in the cloud without a server, **Elastic MapReduce (EMR)** Serverless for transforming terabytes of data using a serverless Hadoop system in the cloud, and **Managed Streaming for Kafka (MSK)** Serverless for running Kafka workloads in the cloud without worrying about the server. You will learn about these serverless compute services throughout this book.

So, now you know why the term is not called *server* but *compute*. *Server* only refers to a physical server or VM, while *compute* is much more than that, with AWS Lambda and serverless compute. AWS provides choices in how you consume compute to support existing applications and build new applications that suit your business needs, whether in the form of instances, containers, or serverless compute. Let's dive into the computing world and start with AWS's core service, EC2.

Amazon EC2

As you learned in the previous section, Amazon EC2 is AWS's way of naming servers. It's nothing but VMs hosted on a physical server residing inside the AWS data center in a secure environment. It is all about standardizing infrastructure management, security, and growth, and building an economy of scale to quickly meet client demand for services in minutes and not months. AWS takes full advantage of virtualization technologies and can slice one computer to act like many computers. When using AWS, you can shut off access to resources with the same speed and agility as when you requested and started the resources, with an accompanying reduction in the billing.

EC2 was first developed to be used in Amazon's internal infrastructure. It was the idea of Chris Pinkham, who was head of Amazon's worldwide infrastructure from around 2003. Amazon released a limited beta test of EC2 to the public on August 25, 2006, providing limited trial access. In October 2007, Amazon expanded its offerings by adding two new types of instances (large and extra large). In May 2008, two additional instance types were added to the service (high-CPU medium and high-CPU extra large).

Amazon EC2 is the most essential and critical service on the AWS cloud computing platform. If you are trying to create something using AWS, and no other service offers the functionality you desire, you will probably be able to use EC2 as the foundation for your project. You can think of the EC2 service as a computer of almost any size and capability that you can turn on or off at any point and stop being charged when you shut it down.

We briefly mentioned that EC2 allows various computer sizes and capabilities. Let's revisit that idea and see how many choices are available. Amazon EC2 offers a comprehensive selection of over 750+ instance types. Each type addresses different needs and is optimized to fit a specific use case. Instance types are defined by a combination of their memory, CPU, GPU, storage, and networking capabilities. Each different type can provide a sweet spot for your individual use case. Each EC2 instance type Amazon provides has a different size, allowing you to match the right instance size with your target workload.

As better CPU cores and memory chips become available, AWS continually improves its EC2 offerings to take advantage of these new components. The Amazon EC2 service is constantly improving, and staying on top of the constant changes can be quite challenging.

For example, when the *T* instance types were launched, AWS called them *T1*, but better instances, such as *T4* instances, are now available as AWS keeps evolving its offerings. To see the complete list of instance types AWS offers, visit the *EC2 instance families* section later in this chapter.

In general terms, the EC2 instance types and their classifications have remained unchanged, but each type's models and sizes continue to evolve. What used to be the *top-shelf* offering last year might be a medium-level offering this year due to improvements to the underlying components. Depending on budgetary constraints and workload needs, different models and sizes might offer the optimal solution for your project.

AWS supports various processors for its EC2 instances, such as Intel, AMD, ARM, NVIDIA, and its own homegrown processor, Graviton. Let's take a quick peek at the Graviton processor.

AWS Graviton

AWS supports many CPU options, offering flexibility for diverse workloads. Intel processors have been a foundational choice since AWS launched in 2006, powering general-purpose, compute-intensive, and memory-intensive workloads. In 2018, AWS introduced AMD-based instances, which provide a cost-effective alternative, and debuted its own Graviton processors, ARM-based chips designed for optimized price performance. The latest Graviton3 processors enhance compute efficiency, delivering higher performance and energy savings.

One of the essential things that keeps AWS ahead of the game is its innovation. When AWS launched its processor in 2018, it was a big leap that helped it gain a lead over other cloud providers. Graviton is an ARM chip from Annapurna Labs, a chip design company in Israel that AWS acquired in 2015.

The most important thing about having your own Graviton processor is that it is custom-built to suit your needs. To complement the Graviton processor, AWS launched a Nitro hypervisor as the backbone, and now they have an entire infrastructure system optimized for cloud-native workloads. This resulted in an added advantage for AWS, as they can offer low prices and high performance for workload-focused custom instances.

AWS Graviton processors have significantly advanced cloud computing by delivering cost-effective, high-performance solutions for various workloads. Here's a detailed breakdown of their evolution:

- **Graviton (first generation)**: Launched in 2018, the first generation of Graviton processors powered EC2 *A1* instances, which provided up to 16 vCPUs, 10 Gbps enhanced networking, and 3.5 Gbps EBS bandwidth. Graviton processors offered a cost-effective solution for entry-level performance needs, enabling customers to manage workloads efficiently without breaking the budget.
- **Graviton2 (second generation)**: Introduced in 2019, Graviton2 processors marked a significant leap forward with up to 64 compute cores, delivering up to 7x better performance than their predecessors. These processors were designed to handle compute-heavy tasks, such as **machine learning** (**ML**), video processing, and **high-performance computing** (**HPC**). Instances powered by Graviton2, such as the *M6g*, *C6g*, and *R6g* families, offered up to 40% better price-performance than x86-based instances. This made Graviton2 the go-to choice for workloads such as web applications, data analytics, and microservices.
- **Graviton3 (third generation)**: Released in 2021, Graviton3 processors introduced significant advancements in performance and efficiency, delivering up to 25% better compute performance than Graviton2. They featured up to 2x faster floating-point performance, making them ideal for HPC and scientific applications. Additionally, Graviton3 processors achieved up to 3x better ML performance with support for `bfloat16`, a key feature for deep learning tasks. Graviton3 processors are highly energy-efficient, using up to 60% less energy for equivalent workloads, aligning with sustainability goals. Instances such as the *C7g*, *M7g*, and *R7g* families leverage Graviton3 for superior performance in real-time analytics, ML, and HPC.

AWS Graviton processors, from the foundational Graviton to the advanced Graviton3, showcase AWS's commitment to delivering cutting-edge, cost-effective solutions. These processors provide the flexibility, performance, and efficiency needed to power modern cloud workloads while optimizing costs and sustainability.

Graviton processors are not available for all EC2 instances, but it is recommended to use Graviton-backed instances wherever possible for better price and performance.

AWS compute for AI/ML

AWS offers a wide range of GPU-accelerated instances to support workloads such as ML, HPC, graphics rendering, and generative AI. AWS has gained recognition for its Graviton processors in CPU-based computing, and subsequently launched its silicon for GPU workloads, such as **AWS Inferentia** and **Trainium**.

For customers using popular ML frameworks such as TensorFlow or PyTorch, AWS provides a variety of NVIDIA GPU instances. These include *G4* and *G5* instances, which are well-suited for inference and graphics workloads, and *P4* instances, designed for deep learning training and large-scale compute tasks. For example, the *P4d* instance delivers up to 2.5x higher deep learning performance compared to the previous generation, making it ideal for training **large language models** (**LLMs**) or processing image recognition workloads.

AWS also offers AMD GPU-based instances, such as the *G4ad series*, which provide a balance between performance and cost. These are especially useful for graphics-heavy applications such as game streaming, 3D rendering, and virtual desktop environments. For customers looking to optimize their budget while maintaining solid graphics capabilities, these instances offer a smart alternative.

In addition to third-party GPUs, AWS has developed its own chips. AWS Inferentia, launched in 2019, powers *Inf1* and *Inf2* instances and is tailored specifically for ML inference. Companies such as Snap Inc. use Inferentia to reduce inference latency and costs for applications such as content recommendation and image moderation. On the training side, AWS Trainium, available in *Trn1* and *Trn2* instances, is designed to train deep learning models at scale. According to AWS, Trainium offers up to 50% better price performance for training compared to equivalent GPU instances.

AWS also offers custom hardware specialized compute instances for AI/ML workloads, such as *F1* and *FE1* instances. *F1* instances are equipped with **field-programmable gate arrays** (**FPGAs**), allowing you to build custom hardware accelerations for applications such as genomics, video processing, and high-frequency trading. In contrast, *FE1* instances are purpose-built for generative AI inference and powered by AWS Inferentia2 chips. These are optimized for deploying LLMs with high performance and cost efficiency: *F1* for custom acceleration and *FE1* for scalable, low-latency AI inference, giving you the flexibility to choose the right compute for your ML solution.

With this wide selection of GPU-based instances, ranging from NVIDIA and AMD to AWS-designed chips, you can pick the right compute engine for your workload, whether it's building a GenAI chatbot, running complex simulations, or serving real-time inference at scale. This flexibility helps you balance performance needs with cost, making AWS a powerful platform for developers building the future of intelligent applications.

Now, let's look at EC2 instance families in more detail.

EC2 instance families

As of April 2025, AWS offers over 750 EC2 instance types grouped into families designed for different workloads:

- **General Purpose** (e.g., *M7g, T4g*): Best for web servers, development, and general applications
- **Compute Optimized** (e.g., *C7g, C6i*): Ideal for HPC, such as simulations or ML training
- **Memory Optimized** (e.g., *R7i, X2idn*): Designed for memory-heavy apps such as real-time analytics or in-memory databases
- **Accelerated Computing** (e.g., *P5, Inf2, Trn1*): Uses GPUs and custom chips for ML, graphics, and AI workloads
- **Storage Optimized** (e.g., *I4i, D3en*): Tailored for large-scale data processing and storage-heavy workloads
- **HPC Optimized** (e.g., *Hpc7a, Hpc6id*): Built for tightly coupled workloads such as weather forecasting or scientific modeling

AWS regularly updates these families to support performance, scalability, and cost-efficiency across all major use cases. You can look at all version instances in each family by visiting `https://aws.amazon.com/ec2/instance-types/`.

AWS instance naming conventions

AWS uses a systematic naming convention for its EC2 instance types to convey information about the instance's characteristics, generation, and size. This structured approach simplifies understanding and selecting instance types that align with specific workload requirements. The following are the key naming components of EC2:

- **Family prefix**: The first letter(s) indicate the instance family, which defines the instance's general purpose or specialization:
    - *c*: Compute Optimized
    - *m*: General Purpose
    - *r*: Memory Optimized
    - *g*: Graviton Powered
    - *p*: GPU Powered

    - *i*: I/O Optimized
    - *f*: FPGA Powered
- **Generation number**: The number following the family prefix indicates the instance generation. A higher number represents the latest generation with improved performance, efficiency, or capabilities. For example, *7* represents the 7th generation.
- **Additional capabilities**: Letters following the generation number provide details about unique features or optimizations:
    - *a*: Indicates AMD processors
    - *g*: Denotes AWS Graviton processors
    - *i*: Refers to Intel processors
    - *d*: Specifies instance store volumes
    - *n*: Highlights network optimization
    - *b*: Refers to block storage optimization
    - *e*: Indicates extra storage or memory
    - *z*: Represents high-frequency processors
- **Instance size**: The part of the name after the period indicates the instance size, represented as a number followed by a descriptor (e.g., *8xlarge*). This specifies the relative performance and resources (vCPU, memory, and storage) allocated to the instance. Larger sizes offer more capacity.

  For example, let's break down the *c7g.8xlarge* instance type:
    - *c*: Compute Optimized family
    - *7*: 7th generation
    - *g*: Graviton-based processor
    - *8xlarge*: Instance size, offering a specific combination of vCPUs, memory, and storage

AWS's naming convention provides clarity and consistency, enabling users to make informed decisions when selecting instance types. Let's look at AWS's five instance families in more detail.

AWS General Purpose instances

AWS General Purpose instances offer a balanced combination of CPU, memory, and networking resources, making them versatile for a wide range of workloads.

They are ideal for web hosting, microservices, development environments, and small databases. AWS consistently updates these instances to ensure optimal performance and cost-efficiency. The following table summarizes the latest instance types and their specific features.

Instance family	Processor	Instance types	Key features	Ideal use cases
T4g	AWS Graviton2	`t4g.nano` to `t4g.2xlarge`	Burstable performance with CPU credits Energy-efficient Lower cost	Web servers, small databases, and development environments
T3	Intel Xeon	`t3.nano` to `t3.2xlarge`	Burstable performance Balance of compute, memory, and networking resources	Microservices, caching fleets, and small business applications
T3a	AMD EPYC	`t3a.nano` to `t3a.2xlarge`	Cost-effective option with burstable performance, similar to T3 instances	Cost-sensitive workloads and low-traffic applications
M7g	AWS Graviton3	`m7g.medium` to `m7g.metal`	Up to 25% better compute performance and 60% energy efficiency compared to M6g	Application servers, gaming servers, and backend microservices
M8g	AWS Graviton4	`m8g.medium` to `m8g.metal`	Fixed performance Up to 3x more vCPU and memory over M7g	Web applications, enterprise applications, and API backends
M6i	Intel Xeon	`m6i.large` to `m6i.metal`	Higher memory bandwidth Support for more vCPUs per instance	Backend systems, database servers, and ERP systems
M6a	AMD EPYC	`m6a.large` to `m6a.48xlarge`	Cost-efficient fixed performance with high compute capacity	Balanced workloads requiring cost optimization and scalability

A1	AWS Graviton	`a1.medium` to `a1.4xlarge`	First Graviton-based instances Optimized for scale-out workloads ARM architecture	Open source applications, containerized workloads, and web servers
Mac	Apple Silicon M1/ M2	`mac2.m2pro .metal`	macOS environment for development, testing, and signing applications with Apple Xcode	iOS/macOS app development, testing, and deployment

Table 6.1: The General Purpose instance family

The General Purpose instance family provides a starting point for most workloads, delivering a seamless balance of resources to drive business outcomes effectively. For specialized workloads, AWS also offers Compute Optimized, Memory Optimized, and Storage Optimized instance families to meet every need. Let's continue our journey through the different instance types offered by AWS.

AWS Compute Optimized instances

AWS's Compute Optimized instances are tailored for applications that demand high computational power. They offer a high ratio of CPU to memory to efficiently handle compute-intensive tasks. These instances are ideal for HPC workloads, video encoding, ML inference, scientific modeling, dedicated gaming servers, and ad server engines.

The following table provides an overview of the latest Compute Optimized instance families, their processors, instance types, key features, and ideal use cases:

Instance family	Processor	Instance types	Key features	Ideal use cases
C8g	AWS Graviton4	`c8g.medium` to `c8g.metal`	Larger instance sizes with up to 3x more vCPUs and memory than C7g instances	HPC, ad serving, video encoding, gaming, scientific modeling, and distributed analytics

C7g	AWS Graviton3	`c7g.medium` to `c7g.metal`	Up to 25% better performance and 60% less energy usage than C6g Enhanced networking	HPC, ML inference, and scientific modeling
C7a	AMD EPYC	`c7a.medium` to `c7a.48xlarge`	High performance with cost efficiency Suitable for compute-bound applications	Batch processing, ad serving, and high-performance web servers
C7i	Intel Xeon	`c7i.large` to `c7i.metal`	Advanced networking capabilities Optimized for compute-intensive tasks	Video encoding, gaming servers, and CPU-based ML
Hpc6a	AMD EPYC	`hpc6a.48xlarge`	Optimized for HPC workloads Up to 100 Gbps networking with Elastic Fabric Adapter (EFA)	Molecular dynamics, weather forecasting, and computational fluid dynamics

Table 6.2: Compute Optimized instance families

AWS continues to innovate by offering a variety of Compute Optimized instances powered by different processors, including AWS Graviton3, AMD EPYC, and Intel Xeon. This allows customers to select the most suitable instance type for their specific compute-intensive workloads. The `hpc6a` instances, for example, are specifically designed to deliver cost-effective high performance for HPC applications, providing up to 100 Gbps of networking throughput for efficient inter-node communication.

Let's learn about another popular instance type: the Accelerated Computing family of instances.

AWS Accelerated Computing instances

AWS Accelerated Computing instances are designed to handle computationally intensive workloads requiring specialized hardware accelerators such as GPUs, FPGAs, or custom chips. These instances deliver unparalleled performance for tasks such as ML training and inference, generative AI model development, HPC, video processing, encryption, and compression. AWS provides a broad portfolio of Accelerated Computing instances, each tailored to specific workloads.

Instance family	Processor	Instance types	Key features	Ideal use cases
P5	NVIDIA H100 Tensor Core GPUs	`p5.2xlarge` to `p5.48xlarge`	Up to 8 GPUs per instance Industry-leading GPU performance High-throughput networking	Deep learning training, HPC applications, and generative AI models
G5	NVIDIA A10G Tensor Core GPUs	`g5.xlarge` to `g5.48xlarge`	Up to 8 GPUs per instance Cost-effective for graphics and inferencing workloads	ML inference, generative AI chatbots, 3D rendering, and graphics modeling
F2	Virtex UltraScale+ HBM VU47P FPGAs	`f2.6xlarge`, `f2.12xlarge`, and `f2.48xlarge`	Custom hardware acceleration Programmable FPGAs for specialized tasks	Genomics research, financial analytics, real-time video processing, big data search and analysis, and security
Inf2	AWS Inferentia2	`inf2.xlarge` to `inf2.48xlarge`	High-performance ML inference Up to four Inferentia2 chips per instance	Generative AI inference, natural language processing, and computer vision

Trn2	AWS Trainium	`Trn2.48xlarge` and `trn2u.48xlarge`	Optimized for ML training Up to 16 Trainium chips per instance High interconnect bandwidth	Training generative AI models such as GPT, NLP models, and recommender systems
DL1	Habana Gaudi accelerators	`dl1.24xlarge`	Cost-effective deep learning training High networking throughput	Deep learning training, generative image and text models, and object detection
VT1	Xilinx Alveo U30 media accelerators	`vt1.3xlarge` to `vt1.24xlarge`	Optimized for low-cost, real-time video transcoding	Live video streaming, video conferencing, and real-time transcoding

Table 6.3: Accelerated Computing instance families

AWS Accelerated Computing instances are at the forefront of enabling generative AI applications. For example, *P5* instances can train LLMs such as GPT and BERT faster, reducing development cycles for conversational AI or content generation platforms. *G5* and *Inf2* instances power real-time inferencing for chatbots, voice assistants, and personalized recommendation engines. *Trn1* instances support scalable training for next-generation AI models, providing cost-effective solutions for companies driving innovation in AI.

The next instance type family we will learn about is Memory Optimized instances.

AWS Memory Optimized instances

AWS offers a range of Memory Optimized instances designed to deliver fast performance for workloads that process large datasets in memory. These instances are ideal for real-time big data analytics, in-memory databases, and enterprise-class applications requiring significant memory resources. These instances enable rapid processing and transformation by loading entire datasets into memory.

The following table provides an overview of the latest Memory Optimized instance families, their processors, instance types, key features, and ideal use cases:

Instance family	Processor	Instance types	Key features	Ideal use cases
R6i	Intel Xeon Scalable	`r6i.large` to `r6i.metal`	Up to 1,024 GiB memory High EBS and network bandwidth	In-memory databases, real-time analytics, and big data processing
R8g	AWS Graviton4	`r8g.medium` to `r8g.metal`	Up to 1,536 GiB memory Cost-effective ARM-based processing	Memory-intensive applications, open source databases, in-memory caches, and real-time big data analytics
R7iz	Intel Xeon Scalable	`r7iz.large` to `r7iz.metal-32xl`	High-frequency CPUs Up to 1,024 GiB memory	Electronic design automation (EDA), financial modeling, and CPU-bound relational databases
X2idn	Intel Xeon Scalable	`x2idn.16xlarge` to `x2idn.metal`	High memory-to-vCPU ratio Up to 1,952 GiB memory	High-performance databases, in-memory analytics, and SAP HANA
X2gd	AWS Graviton2	`x2gd.medium` to `x2gd.metal`	Up to 1,024 GiB memory NVMe SSD storage options	Memory-intensive ARM-based workloads and real-time big data analytics
High Memory (U-24tb1)	Intel Xeon Scalable	`u-6tb1.metal` to `u-24tb1.metal`	Up to 24 TiB memory Ideal for large in-memory databases	SAP HANA, large-scale enterprise applications, and extensive in-memory databases

z1d	Intel Xeon Scalable	`z1d.large` to `z1d.metal`	Sustained all-core frequency up to 4.0 GHz High compute and memory	EDA, financial simulations, and CPU-intensive applications requiring high single-thread performance

Table 6.4: Memory Optimized instance families

AWS's diverse range of Memory Optimized instances enables businesses to select the most appropriate instance type for their specific memory-intensive workloads, ensuring optimal performance and cost efficiency. Let's look at the next category of instance families.

AWS Storage Optimized instances

AWS offers a variety of Storage Optimized instances tailored for workloads that require high, sequential read-and-write access to large datasets in local storage. These instances are ideal for distributed filesystems, data warehousing, and high-frequency **online transaction processing (OLTP)**.

The following table provides an overview of the latest Storage Optimized instance families, their processors, instance types, key features, and ideal use cases:

Instance family	Processor	Instance types	Key features	Ideal use cases
I8g	AWS Graviton4 processors	`I8g.large` to `i8g.metal-24xl`	Up to 45 TB instance storage and 1.5 TB RAM	Relational databases, real-time databases, NoSQL databases, and real-time analytics
I7i	3.2 GHz Intel Xeon	`I7i.large` to `i7i.metal-48xl`	Up to 45 TB instance storage and 1.5 TB RAM	Search engines, relational and real-time databases, NoSQL databases, and real-time analytics

H1	Intel Xeon E5-2686 v4 (Broadwell)	`h1.2xlarge` to `h1.16xlarge`	Up to 16 TB HDD storage Optimized for high disk throughput and sequential I/O	Big data workloads, MapReduce-based applications, distributed filesystems, and log or data processing applications
D3	Intel Xeon Scalable	`d3.xlarge` to `d3.8xlarge`	Up to 48 TB HDD storage High disk throughput 45% faster read/write than D2	Distributed filesystems, data warehousing, and big data processing
I4i	Intel Xeon Scalable (Ice Lake)	`i4i.large` to `i4i.metal`	Up to 30 TB NVMe SSD storage AWS Nitro SSDs with up to 60% lower I/O latency	High-performance databases, NoSQL databases, and transactional workloads requiring low latency and high IOPS
Im4gn	AWS Graviton2	`im4gn.large` to `im4gn.16xlarge`	Up to 30 TB NVMe SSD storage Cost-effective ARM-based processing	I/O-intensive workloads, large-scale data processing, and real-time analytics
Is4gen	AWS Graviton2	`is4gen.medium` to `is4gen.8xlarge`	Up to 30 TB NVMe SSD storage Optimized for storage-intensive applications	File storage workloads, distributed filesystems, and data lakes

Table 6.5: Storage Optimized instance families

AWS's diverse range of Storage Optimized instances enables businesses to select the most appropriate instance type for their specific storage-intensive workloads, ensuring optimal performance and cost-efficiency.

AWS HPC Optimized instances

AWS offers a range of HPC Optimized instances designed to handle complex, compute-intensive workloads efficiently. These instances are ideal for computational fluid dynamics, molecular dynamics, weather forecasting, and large-scale scientific simulations.

The following table provides an overview of the latest HPC Optimized instance families, their processors, instance types, key features, and ideal use cases:

Instance family	Processor	Instance types	Key features	Ideal use cases
Hpc6a	3rd Gen AMD EPYC	`hpc6a.48xlarge`	Up to 96 vCPUs 384 GiB memory 100 Gbps networking with EFA Optimized for tightly coupled HPC workloads	Computational fluid dynamics, finite element analysis, and seismic reservoir simulations
Hpc6id	3rd Gen Intel Xeon Scalable (Ice Lake)	`hpc6id.32xlarge`	Up to 128 vCPUs 1,024 GiB memory 7.6 TB local NVMe storage 200 Gbps networking with EFA Optimized for data-intensive HPC workloads	Structural simulations, genomics, and financial risk modeling

Hpc7a	4th Gen AMD EPYC	`hpc7a.12xlarge` to `hpc7a.96xlarge`	Up to 384 vCPUs 1,536 GiB memory 300 Gbps networking with EFA Enhanced performance for tightly coupled HPC applications	Weather forecasting, molecular dynamics, and computational chemistry
Hpc7g	AWS Graviton3E	`hpc7g.4xlarge` to `hpc7g.16xlarge`	Up to 64 vCPUs 128 GiB memory 200 Gbps networking with EFA Cost-effective ARM-based processing with high performance	CFD simulations, numerical weather prediction, and seismic imaging

Table 6.6: HPC Optimized instance families

AWS's diverse HPC Optimized instances enable organizations to select the most suitable instance types for their specific HPC needs, ensuring optimal performance and cost-efficiency.

Amazon will likely continue to enhance its EC2 service by offering new instance types and improving the current ones. You can use AWS's new **EC2 Instance Type Explorer** to update you on new EC2 instance offerings. EC2 Instance Type Explorer helps you navigate and discover the right instances for your customers. Use filters to quickly narrow down the instance family by category or hardware configuration. You can access it by going to `https://aws.amazon.com/ec2/instance-explorer`.

You have now learned about the various EC2 types. As cost is one of the main factors in the cloud, let's learn more about the EC2 pricing model.

EC2 pricing model

While the standard cloud price model is the pay-as-you-go model, AWS provides multiple options to optimize your costs further. As servers are a significant part of any IT infrastructure, it is better to understand all the available cost options to get the most out of your dollar. The following are the four different ways to purchase compute in AWS:

- **On-Demand**: Pay for compute capacity by the second without any long-term commitment. This option is best suited for fluctuating workloads, such as stock trading or e-commerce website traffic. It is the default choice when you spin up an instance and is suitable for quick experiments.
- **Reserved Instance** (**RI**): You can commit to 1 or 3 years for a specific EC2 instance family and receive a significant discount of up to 72% off On-Demand prices. This is best for a steady workload you know will not fluctuate much, such as an internal HR portal. An RI is like a coupon: you pay in advance, which applies automatically when your spin-up instance belongs to the same EC2 instance family for which you pay the RI price. AWS also provides **Convertible RIs**, where you can exchange one or more Convertible RIs for another Convertible RI with a different configuration, including instance family, operating system, and tenancy. The new Convertible RI must be of an equal or higher value than the one you're exchanging. You can find details on Reserved Instance pricing in AWS at `https://aws.amazon.com/ec2/pricing/reserved-instances/pricing/`.
- **Savings Plan**: This is like an RI, but monetary commitment and computing can be used across Fargate, EC2, and AWS Lambda. In a Savings Plan, you don't have to make commitments to specific instance configurations, but commit to a spending amount. You can get significant savings, up to 72% off On-Demand instance prices, with the flexibility to apply it across instance families. AWS has two types of Savings Plans: **EC2 Instance Savings Plans**, which provide the highest savings (up to 72%) when you commit to a specific instance family, Region, and operating system, and **Compute Savings Plans**, which offer more flexibility across instance types, families, and even services such as AWS Fargate and Lambda, with slightly lower savings (up to 66%).
- **Spot Instances**: These are the same as the pay-as-you-go pricing model of On-Demand, but at up to 90% off. EC2 can reclaim Spot Instances with a 2-minute warning. They are best for stateless or fault-tolerant workloads. You can leverage the scale of AWS at a fraction of the cost with a simplified pricing model. A Spot Instance is only interrupted when EC2 needs to reclaim it for On-Demand capacity. You don't need to worry about your bidding strategy. Spot prices gradually adjust based on long-term supply and demand trends.

- **Dedicated Hosts**: You pay for a physical server fully dedicated to your use. This option allows you to bring and use your existing per-socket, per-core, or per-VM software licenses, which can help reduce overall costs, especially for enterprise applications such as Oracle or Microsoft SQL Server.
- **Dedicated Instances**: These are EC2 instances that run on hardware dedicated to you, but unlike Dedicated Hosts, you're charged per instance hour rather than for the entire host. It ensures your instances don't share physical hardware with others.
- **Capacity Reservations**: You can reserve capacity for your EC2 instances in a specific Availability Zone. This is useful when you need to guarantee availability during peak times or for disaster recovery planning.

As shown in the following diagram, the given purchasing options use the same underlying EC2 instances and AWS infrastructure across all Regions. You can combine multiple options to optimize the cost of your workload, and you can use auto-scaling to use all four options to optimize cost and capacity.

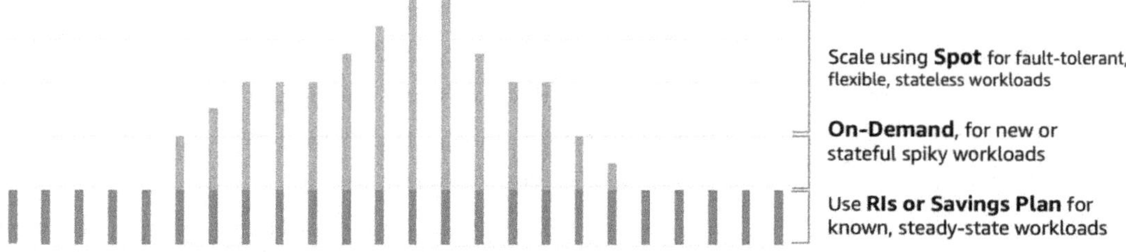
Scale using **Spot** for fault-tolerant, flexible, stateless workloads
On-Demand, for new or stateful spiky workloads
Use **RIs or Savings Plan** for known, steady-state workloads

Figure 6.1: EC2 pricing model to optimize cost

The preceding diagram shows a smart way to manage EC2 costs using a blended purchasing strategy. It helps you balance flexibility and cost by combining three EC2 pricing models: Savings Plans or RIs, On-Demand Instances, and Spot Instances, each serving a specific purpose in your infrastructure.

At the bottom, the blue bars represent your base usage, which includes workloads that run consistently, such as a web server or backend processing system. You can cover this base layer using RIs or Savings Plans, which offer big discounts (up to 72%) compared to On-Demand pricing. These are ideal for workloads you can predict and commit to over 1 or 3 years.

The green bars in the middle show variable workloads; these might increase during business hours, special events, or feature rollouts. On-Demand instances work best here because they let you scale up quickly without any long-term commitment.

For example, if you launch a marketing campaign and expect more traffic, On-Demand gives you the flexibility to handle the spike without overcommitting resources.

Finally, the orange bars at the top represent burst capacity that comes and goes. For this layer, you can use Spot Instances, which let you tap into unused EC2 capacity at up to 90% lower cost. Spot is great for fault-tolerant or stateless workloads such as video encoding, ML model training, or data processing jobs that can handle interruptions.

In short, to get the best out of EC2 and control costs, use RIs or Savings Plans for your always-on base, On-Demand for flexible scaling, and Spot for additional, short-term capacity. This approach gives you performance when you need it, and savings when you don't.

Let's take an example of an e-commerce website's workload. As shown in the preceding diagram, you can use an RI for daily traffic patterns, with which you can save up to 72% compared to On-Demand instances. But if you run a deal, such as 20% off Apple products, and get a sudden spike, auto-scaling spins up On-Demand instances to handle the spike. At the end of the day, when you are processing orders for fulfillment, you can use a Spot Instance to expedite the order queue with 90% savings compared to an On-Demand instance.

There are so many choices in EC2 that you can easily get confused, and to address that problem, AWS provides Compute Optimizer.

AWS Compute Optimizer

AWS Compute Optimizer is a service that helps you select the most appropriate AWS resources for your workloads to reduce costs and improve performance. It analyzes your resource configurations and utilization metrics using ML models trained on millions of workloads. Compute Optimizer provides recommendations for various AWS resources, including the following:

- Amazon EC2 instances
- EC2 Auto Scaling groups
- Amazon **Elastic Block Store** (**EBS**) volumes
- AWS Lambda functions
- Amazon ECS services on AWS Fargate
- Amazon RDS DB instances and storage
- Commercial software licenses that run on Amazon EC2

Compute Optimizer identifies whether your resources are under-provisioned or over-provisioned by evaluating your workload's configuration, resource utilization, and performance data. It then offers up to three recommended options for each analyzed resource, allowing you to choose configurations that best fit your workload requirements. These recommendations include projected utilization metrics, enabling you to assess performance before implementing changes.

To enhance recommendation quality, you can activate features such as enhanced infrastructure metrics, which extend the analysis period to three months and provide deeper insights into usage patterns. Compute Optimizer also supports the ingestion of external metrics from observability products such as Datadog, Dynatrace, Instana, and New Relic, allowing for more comprehensive analysis.

Consider a rapidly growing design platform such as **Canva**, which experienced significant increases in compute demand due to user growth and new feature launches. To manage costs effectively while maintaining performance, Canva utilized AWS Compute Optimizer alongside other AWS cost optimization tools. This strategic approach enabled Canva to reduce compute costs by 46% in less than 2 years, demonstrating the practical benefits of implementing Compute Optimizer's recommendations in a dynamic, large-scale environment. You can find more details on the case study here: `https://aws.amazon.com/solutions/case-studies/canva-cost-optimization-case-study/`.

For more detailed information on AWS Compute Optimizer, refer to the user guide here: `https://docs.aws.amazon.com/compute-optimizer/`.

When you spin up an EC2 instance, the first thing you select is an **Amazon Machine Image (AMI)** to decide which operating system to use. Let's learn more about AMIs.

Amazon Machine Images

When you launch an EC2 instance in AWS, you need to select an AMI. Think of an AMI as a pre-packaged template that contains everything your instance needs to run, such as the operating system, application server, software, and configurations. Using an AMI helps you deploy multiple instances with the same setup, which is very useful when you're scaling an application or keeping development, testing, and production environments consistent.

Each AMI has a few key parts. The operating system is the base layer; AWS supports several popular ones, such as Ubuntu, Amazon Linux, Windows Server, Red Hat, SUSE, Debian, and even macOS for Apple development on Mac-dedicated EC2 instances. Then, there's the processor architecture, which determines what type of CPU your instance can use. For example, you can choose from 64-bit ARM, 64-bit or 32-bit x86, or Mac architecture, depending on your application's needs.

AMIs also have launch permissions that control who can use them. You can keep your AMI private (only you can use it), share it with specific AWS accounts (explicit), or make it public so anyone can launch instances with it. This is helpful if you're building a reusable application template for others. The root device storage defines where the instance's root volume lives – either on Amazon EBS, which is persistent and survives reboots, or the instance store, which is temporary storage tied to the host hardware.

For example, a start-up building a mobile app backend might use a custom AMI that includes Ubuntu, a preconfigured Node.js server, and monitoring tools. They can launch new servers with this AMI in minutes, ensuring that all servers are exactly the same. This saves time and avoids manual configuration errors.

AWS offers thousands of AMIs, including official ones from AWS, community-built images, and those provided by trusted vendors through **AWS Marketplace**. AWS maintains dozens of official AMIs, while many more are available from vendors in AWS Marketplace and the community. Whether you're launching a simple web server or a compliance-certified enterprise app, you can find an AMI that matches your needs or create your own to meet specific requirements.

You have learned about the many options available when creating and launching Amazon EC2 instances. Now, let's explore the best practices to optimize the Amazon EC2 service.

Amazon EC2 best practices

How you use and configure EC2 will depend on your use case. However, some general EC2 best practices will ensure the security, reliability, durability, and availability of your applications and data. Let's delve into the recommended practices for handling security, storage, backup management, and so on.

Access management

Securing access to your Amazon EC2 instances is critical for protecting your workloads. Start by applying strong credential management policies: rotate access keys regularly, automate credential handling where possible, and avoid sharing long-term credentials. Always use IAM roles instead of IAM users for granting temporary access to applications or services, following the principle of least privilege to give only the permissions needed.

To prevent unauthorized access, avoid exposing SSH (port 22) directly to the internet. Instead, use secure options such as **AWS Systems Manager Session Manager** or connect through a VPN. These methods provide safer ways to access your instances while keeping them off the public internet.

Lastly, remember that *you are responsible for maintaining the EC2 operating system and installed software*. This includes regularly patching the OS, updating applications, and monitoring for vulnerabilities. Keeping your system up to date is essential for maintaining performance and protecting against security threats.

Storage management

Storage management is a crucial aspect of optimizing Amazon EC2 instances. When you launch an EC2 instance, most instances are EBS-backed by default. That means that your root volume (and any additional volumes you attach) are EBS volumes. These provide durable, persistent storage independent of the lifespan of your instance. However, the data in an instance store is not persistent and will be lost when the instance is stopped or terminated. This makes instance stores ideal for temporary or cache-based workloads but unsuitable for storing critical data.

To retain data even after shutting down an instance, it is recommended to use EBS volumes. EBS volumes are network-attached and provide persistent storage, making them reliable for critical data needs. They offer flexibility and durability, although their performance may be slightly lower than instance stores due to their network-backed nature. For better organization and performance, using a dedicated EBS volume for your operating system and separate volumes for application or data storage is best. Additionally, EBS-optimized instances can be leveraged to maximize throughput and minimize latency.

For workloads requiring backup or large-scale data storage, Amazon S3 can be used. It ensures high durability and availability, making it suitable for archiving and backup needs.

You can effectively meet your storage requirements by strategically combining instance stores, EBS volumes, and Amazon S3 while optimizing performance, reliability, and cost.

Resource management

When launching an EC2 instance, AWS can include instance metadata and custom resource tags. These **tags** can be used to classify and group your AWS resources.

Instance metadata is data specified for an instance that can then be used to customize, label, and maintain the instance. Instance metadata can be classified into topics such as the following:

- The name of the host
- Events
- Security groups
- Billing tags
- Department or organizational unit tags

The following diagram illustrates the basics of tagging your EC2 instances:

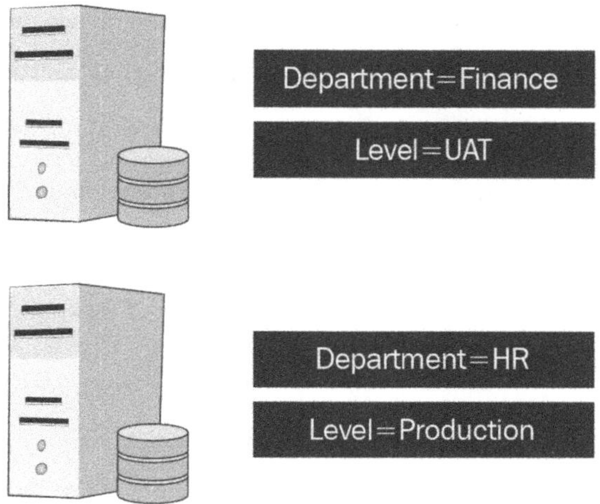

Figure 6.2: EC2 instance tags

In this example, two tags are assigned to each one of the instances – one tag is given the key **Department**, and another is given the key **Level**. In this example, you can identify and consolidate the HR and finance department workloads for billing and automation or apply tag-based security. You can learn more about tag strategies using the AWS docs at `https://docs.aws.amazon.com/general/latest/gr/aws_tagging.html`.

Tags are a powerful yet simple way to classify EC2 instances. They can help in development, code testing, environment management, and billing. Every tag also has a corresponding value.

Managing Amazon EC2 limits

AWS enforces service limits to safeguard against unintentional over-provisioning, ensure resource availability, and mitigate potential security risks. These limits, referred to as **quotas**, are designed to provide customers with control over their usage while maintaining the reliability and availability of AWS's shared infrastructure.

By understanding these limits, you can proactively plan when to request increases before they become bottlenecks. AWS offers two types of quotas:

- **Soft limits**: Adjustable limits that can be increased by submitting a request through the AWS Management Console or the **Service quotas** interface
- **Hard limits**: Fixed limits that cannot be increased and are typically related to architectural constraints

Here are some of the default soft limits for an AWS account:

- Twenty EC2 instances per Region (this may vary based on account type and Region)
- Five Elastic IP addresses per Region, including unassigned Elastic IPs

To request a limit increase for soft quotas, follow these steps:

1. Navigate to the **Service quotas** console in your AWS Management Console, as shown here:

Quota name	Applied account-level quota value	AWS default quota value	Utilization	Adjustability
All DL Spot Instance Requests	0	0	0	Account level
All F Spot Instance Requests	0	0	0	Account level
All G and VT Spot Instance Requests	0	0	0	Account level
All Inf Spot Instance Requests	0	0	0	Account level
All P4, P3 and P2 Spot Instance Requests	0	0	0	Account level
All P5 Spot Instance Requests	0	0	0	Account level
All Standard (A, C, D, H, I, M, R, T, Z) Spot Instance Requests	32	5	0	Account level
All Trn Spot Instance Requests	0	0	0	Account level
All X Spot Instance Requests	0	0	0	Account level
Amazon FPGA images (AFIs)	Not available	100	Not available	Account level
AMI sharing	1,000	1,000	Not available	Account level
AMIs	50,000	50,000	Not available	Account level

Figure 6.3: Amazon EC2 quota limit per account

2. Select the service (e.g., EC2 instances or Elastic IPs).
3. You can submit a request for a higher limit using the **Request increase at account level** button. AWS typically reviews these requests within a few hours to a few days.

For updated quotas and details, refer to the AWS documentation on service quotas at `https://docs.aws.amazon.com/general/latest/gr/aws_service_limits.html`. It is crucial to regularly monitor your account's resource usage and plan for anticipated growth to avoid operational disruptions due to quota constraints.

EC2 backup, snapshots, and recovery

Ensuring the availability and durability of your data and applications in Amazon EC2 requires a robust **backup and recovery** strategy. The primary components for EC2 backups are EBS volumes and AMIs.

EBS snapshots enable periodic backups of EBS volumes. These snapshots are stored incrementally, meaning only the data that has changed since the last snapshot is saved, reducing storage costs. Regularly scheduled snapshots help maintain consistent backups and ensure recoverability in case of data loss.

AMIs can be created from existing instances to preserve their configurations. AMIs are templates for launching new instances with identical setups, making them vital for scaling and disaster recovery.

Deploying application components across multiple **Availability Zones** (**AZs**) enhances durability and availability. Replicating data and application configurations across AZs ensures resilience during hardware failures or natural disasters. Combining this strategy with **Elastic Load Balancing** (**ELB**) improves reliability by automatically distributing traffic among healthy instances.

Assign an **Elastic IP** (**EIP**) for failover readiness to backup instances. EIPs provide a static, public IP address that can be remapped between instances in case of primary instance failure. Using **elastic network interfaces** (**ENIs**) offers further flexibility by allowing seamless attachment and detachment to instances without reconfiguring the network setup. Testing failover configurations is crucial to ensure smooth transitions during outages. Now, let's look at another popular compute technology container.

Containerization in AWS

In today's cloud landscape, there is a constant race to optimize both cost and resources. While Amazon EC2 remains one of the most widely used and foundational services in AWS, it operates on a traditional model, typically designed for running one application per server or instance. This setup can lead to underutilized compute resources and higher operational costs, especially when applications have variable workloads. That's where containers come into play. **Containers** allow you to run multiple lightweight, isolated applications on the same infrastructure, making better use of compute resources. This leads to improved efficiency, faster deployment times, and a more scalable approach to application management – an ideal fit for modern cloud-native and microservices architectures.

Unlike traditional virtualization, containers share the host operating system's kernel, making them lightweight, faster to start, and highly portable across environments. This is especially beneficial in cloud-native and microservices-based architectures, including those involving ML and GenAI workloads. Containers help ensure that your application behaves the same regardless of where it runs – whether on a developer's laptop, a test environment, or in production. They are ideal for breaking down monolithic applications into modular microservices, scaling applications dynamically, and deploying ML models in a consistent and repeatable way.

Core container technologies

There are multiple tools available to implement container-based applications, including Containerd, Podman, and Buildah. However, in this chapter, we'll focus on the two most widely adopted technologies that form the foundation of most containerized workloads:

- **Docker**: This is the most popular containerization platform, allowing you to package applications and their dependencies into portable, lightweight containers. A Docker image acts as a blueprint containing everything needed to run an application, while a container is the live, running instance of that image. Docker greatly simplifies testing, deploying, and moving applications across environments.
- **Kubernetes**: This is a powerful, open source container orchestration system designed to automate the deployment, scaling, and management of containerized applications. It's ideal for managing large-scale, distributed systems with high availability and resilience. Kubernetes also supports features such as rolling updates, service discovery, and auto-healing, making it the standard for production-grade container orchestration.

Now, let's explore how AWS supports and enhances these core container technologies through its managed services.

Container services in AWS

AWS offers a comprehensive suite of container services designed to cater to diverse use cases, operational models, and levels of control. Whether you're looking for simplicity, serverless flexibility, or full orchestration power, AWS has a solution that fits your needs:

- **Amazon ECS**: ECS is a fully managed container orchestration service that enables you to run and scale Docker containers effortlessly. It abstracts away the complexity of managing your orchestration engine and integrates deeply with core AWS services such as IAM, CloudWatch, ELB, and Auto Scaling. ECS is ideal for organizations that prefer AWS-native solutions and want fast, seamless deployments without needing Kubernetes expertise. You can run ECS on either EC2 (self-managed compute) or Fargate (serverless).
- **AWS Fargate**: Fargate is a serverless compute engine for containers that works with both ECS and EKS. With Fargate, you no longer have to provision, scale, or manage the underlying EC2 instances – AWS does it for you. You define your task definitions and resource requirements, and Fargate handles the rest. This is especially useful for teams that want to focus on building applications without worrying about infrastructure. It also provides better cost control by charging only for the exact CPU and memory resources used. You will explore more about Fargate under the *Serverless compute* section later in this chapter.

- **Amazon EKS**: EKS provides a **managed Kubernetes control plane** that enables you to run Kubernetes applications on AWS or on-premises. It gives you full access to the Kubernetes ecosystem while offloading control plane management to AWS. EKS is suited for organizations that already use Kubernetes or need granular control over container scheduling, networking, and policy enforcement. It supports GPU workloads, **custom resource definitions** (**CRDs**), and advanced networking through CNI plugins.

Each of these services is designed to support different operational models. If you want AWS to manage most of the orchestration with minimal overhead, go with ECS. If you wish to offload infrastructure management completely, Fargate is your best option. If you need maximum flexibility and want to leverage Kubernetes-native tooling, EKS gives you full control. By combining these services, AWS provides you with the flexibility to select the optimal deployment model for each application or workload within your organization.

Containerization is particularly useful for ML workflows. You can package training scripts, dependencies, and model artifacts into containers, enabling consistent training and inference across development and production environments. Tools such as Amazon SageMaker support bringing your containers for training and hosting models. You can also deploy ML inference services in ECS or EKS, or use Fargate for serverless scaling. You can learn more about containers in AWS by referring to this AWS user guide: `https://aws.amazon.com/containers/`.

To handle traffic demands effectively, leverage AWS load balancers to manage and distribute requests across EC2 instances or containers deployed in ECS, Fargate, or EKS. You can safeguard your applications against downtime and ensure continuous operations. Let's learn about load balancing in detail.

Amazon Elastic Load Balancer

Elastic Load Balancer (ELB) in AWS allows you to assemble arrays of similar EC2 instances to distribute incoming traffic among these instances. ELB can distribute this application or network traffic across EC2 instances or containers within the same AZ or across AZs.

In addition, to help with scalability, ELB also increases availability and reliability. A core feature of ELB is the ability to implement health checks on the managed instances. An ELB health check determines the *health* or availability of registered EC2 instances and their readiness to receive traffic. A health check is simply a message or request sent to the server, and the response that may or may not be received. If the instance responds within the `200` range, everything is fine. Any other response is considered *unhealthy*.

If an instance does not return a healthy status, it is considered unavailable, and ELB will stop sending application traffic to that instance until it returns to a healthy status. To learn more about return statuses, see `https://docs.aws.amazon.com/elasticloadbalancing/latest/classic/ts-elb-http-errors.html`.

Before we discuss the different types of ELB services in detail, let's first understand some fundamental concepts.

Load balancer rules

Load balancer rules are typically comprised of one or more conditions and one or more actions. The **conditions** specify the criteria that must be met for the rule to be applied, while the **actions** define what should be done with the request if the rule's conditions are met.

For example, a listener rule may have a condition that requires traffic to be received on a specific port and protocol and an action that directs that traffic to a particular target group. Similarly, a path-based routing rule may have a condition that requires a request's path to match a specific value and an action that directs that request to a different target group.

In some cases, you may also specify a priority for your rules, which determines the order in which they are evaluated. This can be important if you have multiple rules that apply to the same traffic and must ensure that the correct rule is used in a specific order. Let's go into more detail about the parts that make up a rule:

- **Conditions**: A condition is a regular expression indicating the path pattern that needs to be present in the request for the traffic to be routed to a certain range of backend servers.
- **Target groups**: A target group is a set of instances. Whenever a condition is matched, traffic will be routed to a specific target group to handle requests. Any of the instances in the group will handle the request. Target groups define a protocol (HTTP, HTTPS, FTP, and others) and a target port. A health check can be configured for each target group. There can be a one-to-many relationship between ALBs and target groups. Targets define the endpoints. Targets are registered with the ALB as part of a target group configuration.
- **Priorities**: Priorities specify in which order the ALB will evaluate the rules. A rule with a low priority number will have higher precedence than a high one. As the rules are evaluated by priority, the rules are evaluated. Whenever a pattern is matched in a rule, traffic is routed to a target group, and the evaluation stops.

Like many other AWS services, an ELB can be created and configured via the AWS console, the AWS CLI, or the Amazon API. Let's look at some specific ELB rules in this table:

Rule type	Description	Conditions	Actions	Use cases
Listener rules	Define how incoming traffic is forwarded to a target group based on protocol and port.	Protocol (e.g., HTTP or HTTPS) and port (e.g., `80` or `443`)	Forward traffic to a specific target group	Forward HTTP traffic on port `80` to a target group of web servers
Target group rules	Determine how traffic is distributed across targets within a target group based on specific criteria such as response time or connection count.	Criteria such as response time, connection count, and so on	Distribute traffic evenly across instances in the group to balance load	Optimize web application performance by distributing traffic across instances with the lowest response times
Host-based routing	Route traffic based on the host field in the HTTP headers, allowing multiple domains or services on a single load balancer.	Hostname in the request URL	Redirect traffic to a specific target group based on the hostname	Route `api.example.com` to API servers and `www.example.com` to web servers
Path-based routing	Route traffic to specific instances or containers based on substrings in the URL path.	Path patterns such as `/es/*` or `/en/*`	Forward traffic to language-specific servers or containers based on URL paths	Route `/en/*` to English servers, `/fr/*` to French servers, and scale dynamically based on language-specific traffic demand
Query string rules	Route traffic based on query string parameters in the URL, enabling dynamic routing based on key-value pairs.	Query string parameters such as `category=books` or `category=movies`	Route traffic to specific target groups based on the query string value	Route requests with `category=books` to book servers and `category=movies` to movie servers for a tailored user experience

Priorities	Specify the order in which rules are evaluated. Rules with lower numbers have higher precedence.	Rule priority number	Stop evaluation once a condition matches and traffic is routed	Ensure specific rules (e.g., secure traffic routing) are evaluated before more general rules

Table 6.7: Amazon ELB rules and use cases

Understanding and leveraging ELB rules allows you to create highly customizable traffic routing strategies that align with your application requirements. Whether distributing traffic evenly across instances, directing requests based on hostnames or paths, or managing priorities to ensure the correct rules are applied, ELB rules provide the flexibility needed for robust and efficient load balancing. These best practices and regulations ensure high availability, seamless scalability, and optimal application performance.

Elastic load balancer types

In August 2016, AWS launched a new service called **Application Load Balancer** (**ALB**). This service allows users to direct traffic at the application level.

The old ELB service offering can still be used, but it was renamed **Classic Load Balancer** (**CLB**), which is now deprecated. Later, more types of ELBs were launched, such as the **Network Load Balancer** (**NLB**) and **Gateway Load Balancer** (**GWLB**). This section will try to understand their differences and when to use one versus the other.

Classic Load Balancers (CLBs)

CLBs are considered legacy technology within AWS. They are being phased out in favor of newer and more advanced load-balancing solutions such as ALBs and NLBs. These modern load balancers offer enhanced features. In a later section, we will summarize CLBs and go deeper into ALBs and NLBs. The following are the traffic routing methods for CLBs:

- **Round robin**: Traffic is evenly distributed across all registered instances sequentially. This default algorithm works best when all instances have similar capacities.
- **Least connections**: Traffic is routed to the instance with the fewest active connections, ensuring optimal resource utilization for workloads with variable instance capacities.
- **IP hash**: Traffic from the same client IP is consistently routed to the same instance. This method is ideal for stateful applications requiring session persistence.

CLBs can route traffic based on protocols (e.g., HTTP, HTTPS, or TCP) and ports while performing health checks to ensure only healthy instances receive traffic. However, they lack advanced features such as host-based or path-based routing and operate at Layer 4 of the OSI model, routing traffic based solely on IP and port. Additionally, static port mapping requirements make CLBs less flexible for containerized environments.

With the emergence of ALBs and NLBs offering advanced routing, scalability, and modern protocol support, CLBs are best suited for legacy environments. AWS recommends transitioning to ALBs or NLBs for new and evolving applications. Let's learn about ALBs in detail.

Application Load Balancers (ALBs)

An ALB is a load-balancing solution in AWS that provides advanced routing capabilities for modern web applications. It operates at the application layer (Layer 7) of the OSI model, allowing it to route traffic based on the content of the request rather than just the source and destination IP addresses and ports. Unlike CLBs, ALBs offer modern routing capabilities optimized for containerized and microservices-based architectures. Here are some key features of ALBs:

- **Advanced routing**: ALBs allow traffic to be routed based on URL paths, query strings, HTTP headers, methods, hostnames, and source IPs. This enables fine-grained control and sophisticated traffic distribution rules.
- **Content-based routing**: ALBs support routing decisions based on the requested content, such as user agents, MIME types, or Accept-Language headers. This is ideal for serving personalized content to clients or routing traffic to specific microservices.
- **Dynamic load balancing**: Incoming traffic can be evenly distributed across targets, such as EC2 instances, IP addresses, Lambda functions, or containers, using advanced algorithms such as round-robin or least outstanding requests.
- **SSL/TLS termination**: ALBs can offload SSL/TLS encryption at the load balancer level, reducing the computational overhead on backend servers while ensuring secure client-server communication.
- **Sticky sessions**: ALBs support session persistence (sticky sessions), ensuring that requests from the same client are consistently routed to the same target during a session.
- **Host-based and path-based routing**: ALBs can route traffic to multiple services or endpoints using hostnames or specific URL paths, making it easy to manage complex multi-service architectures.

The ALB is integrated with other AWS services, such as AWS Certificate Manager, AWS CloudFormation, and AWS Elastic Beanstalk, making deploying and managing your applications easier. It is ideal for modern web applications that use microservices and container-based architectures, as it provides advanced routing and load-balancing capabilities optimized for these applications.

ALBs also easily integrate with ECS by enabling a *service load balancing* configuration. Doing so allows the dynamic mapping of services to ports. This architecture can be configured in the ECS task definition. In this case, several containers point to the same EC2 instance, executing multiple services on multiple ports. The ECS task scheduler can seamlessly add tasks to the ALB.

ALBs are versatile and well-suited for various use cases, particularly in modern application architectures. They are ideal for microservices architectures, as they can direct traffic to specific microservices running in containers or EC2 instances based on sophisticated routing rules, streamlining service discovery and traffic management. ALBs also excel in modern web applications that require advanced routing features such as host-based or path-based routing, ensuring efficient traffic distribution. ALBs seamlessly integrate with AWS Lambda for hybrid workloads, allowing serverless backend processing and hybrid scenarios involving containers and instances. Additionally, ALBs are invaluable in multi-tenant environments, where host-based rules can route tenant-specific traffic to isolated application stacks, ensuring secure and efficient resource allocation.

Network Load Balancers (NLBs)

The NLB is a robust AWS load-balancing solution designed to operate at the OSI model's transport layer (Layer 4). At this layer, the NLB focuses solely on the TCP layer and network values for routing traffic without inspecting request headers or application-specific details. The key features of NLB include the following:

- **Layer 4 routing**: The NLB forwards traffic without analyzing headers or content, relying purely on IP protocol data. This makes it ideal for high-speed routing but limits its ability to distinguish between traffic for different applications sharing the same port.
- **Health checks**: The NLB determines target availability through basic mechanisms such as **Internet Control Message Protocol** (**ICMP**) pings or completing a three-way TCP handshake. This ensures that traffic is routed only to healthy targets.
- **High throughput and low latency**: Designed for workloads requiring high throughput and low latency, the NLB is well-suited for applications such as web applications, media streaming, and gaming. It efficiently handles millions of requests per second with minimal latency.

- **Flow-based load balancing:** The NLB uses a flow-based algorithm, consistently routing traffic from a particular client to the same target within a session. This ensures reliability and performance.
- **Protocol support**: It supports TCP and UDP, making it versatile for applications with varying protocol needs.

When using network load balancing, the application's availability cannot be determined. Routing decisions are made exclusively on the TCP layer and network values without knowing anything about the application. An NLB determines *availability* by using an ICMP ping and seeing whether there is a response or completing a three-way TCP handshake.

The NLB is designed to handle high-throughput, low-latency workloads, such as web applications, gaming, and media streaming services. The NLB can distribute traffic across multiple targets, such as EC2 instances, IP addresses, and containers, using a flow-based load-balancing algorithm that ensures that each flow is consistently routed to the same target. The NLB is highly scalable and provides high availability, with the ability to automatically recover from failed targets and distribute traffic across healthy targets.

NLBs cannot distinguish whether certain traffic belongs to a certain application. The only way this could be possible would be if the applications used different ports. For this reason, if one of the applications crashes and the other doesn't, the NLB will continue sending traffic for both applications. An ALB would be able to make this distinction.

Gateway Load Balancer (GWLBs)

AWS has launched another load balancer called the Gateway Load Balancer. This solution provides scalable and highly available network-level load balancing for virtual network appliances, such as firewalls, intrusion detection and prevention systems, and other security appliances. The NLB is optimized for high-throughput, low-latency workloads, while the GWLB is optimized for virtual network appliances. The NLB is a Layer 4 load balancer that routes traffic based on IP protocol data, while the GWLB is a Layer 3 load balancer that routes traffic based on the content of the IP packet. Key features of the GWLB include the following:

- **Transparent traffic flow**: It acts as a transparent gateway, routing traffic between your **virtual private cloud (VPC)** and your network appliances without modifying the traffic.
- **Scales virtual appliances**: It allows for automatic scaling of virtual appliances, ensuring high availability and consistent performance even during traffic spikes.
- **Packet inspection**: As a Layer 3 load balancer, the GWLB directs traffic based on the IP packet's content, enabling efficient routing and inspection for complex security policies.

- **Elastic and highly available**: Built on the AWS Global Infrastructure, the GWLB ensures robust scalability and fault tolerance, automatically adjusting to traffic demands.
- **Centralized management**: It simplifies the management of network security appliances, consolidating traffic flow and reducing operational complexity.

The following table shows the key differences between GWLBs and NLBs:

Feature	NLB	GWLB
Layer	Layer 4 (transport layer)	Layer 3 (network layer)
Traffic routing	Based on IP protocol and port data	Based on IP packet content
Optimization	Low-latency, high-throughput traffic	Virtual network appliances
Use case	Applications with predictable traffic	Firewalls, IDS/IPS, and NAT gateways

Table 6.8: NLB and GWLB comparison

The GWLB is ideal for organizations needing scalable, cost-effective, centralized network security. Its tight integration with AWS services ensures seamless operation while supporting third-party virtual appliances. It simplifies securing your network infrastructure, enabling agile responses to evolving security needs.

Now that we have learned about the four types of load balancers offered in AWS, let's understand what makes each type different.

AWS load balancers comparison

The ALB is optimized for Layer 7 traffic, such as web applications, microservices, and APIs. In contrast, the NLB is optimized for Layer 4 traffic, such as gaming, media streaming, and other TCP/UDP traffic. The CLB is a legacy load balancer that supports Layer 4 and Layer 7 traffic, but it is less feature-rich than the ALB and NLB. The GWLB is designed for more complex network architectures and provides greater control and visibility.

The following table illustrates the differences between the three types of load balancers. The CLB is retired now, so we are skipping it in the table. This will help in our discussion to decide which load balancer is best for your use cases:

Feature	ALB	NLB	GWLB
Protocols	HTTP HTTPS	TCP UDP	IP
Platforms	VPC	VPC	VPC

Layer	Layer 7	Layer 4	Layer 3
Generation	Newer tech	Newer tech	Newer tech
Performance	High	Highest	High
Health checks	✓	✓	✓
CloudWatch metrics	✓	✓	✓
Logging	✓	✓	✓
AZ failover	✓	✓	✓
Load balancing to multiple ports	✓	✓	✗
IP addresses as targets	✓	✓	✗
Cross-zone load balancing	✓	✓	✗
Sticky sessions	✓	✗	✗
Static and Elastic IPs	✗	✓	✓
Path/host-based routing	✓	✗	✗
Redirects	✓	✗	✗
SSL offloading	✓	✗	✗
Server name indication (SNI)	✓	✗	✗
User authentication	✓	✗	✗
Typical use case	Web apps and microservices that need advanced routing (e.g., path-based)	High-performance or latency-sensitive apps, such as gaming or financial systems	Deploying third-party firewalls or monitoring appliances transparently

Table 6.9: Load balancers comparison

This table highlights the distinctions and use cases for each AWS load balancer, making choosing the right one based on specific requirements easier.

Now that you've explored how to manage ELB and optimize EC2 access, it's a good time to look at how you can reduce infrastructure overhead altogether. Let's dive into serverless computing with AWS Lambda and AWS Fargate, where you can focus more on code and containers, without managing servers.

Serverless computing with AWS Lambda and Fargate

AWS uses the word **serverless** to describe AWS technologies or applications with these characteristics: no server management, automatic scaling, high availability built in, and a pay-as-you-go billing model.

AWS has serverless technologies for compute, integration, and databases, although many users associate serverless with AWS's event-driven compute service, AWS Lambda.

Building serverless applications is one of the primary advantages of moving to the cloud. They reduce the admin overhead of managing infrastructure, thus increasing productivity and further reducing the **total cost of ownership** (**TCO**) in the cloud. A serverless app can be highly performant due to the ease of parallelization and concurrency. Serverless computing is the foundation of serverless apps as it scales automatically, is optimized to reduce latency and cost, and increases throughput. Let's learn about the serverless compute options available in AWS.

AWS Lambda

When it comes to serverless computing, **AWS Lambda** comes to mind first. Lambda is a serverless compute service that allows users to run code in response to events, without provisioning or managing any underlying infrastructure. Lambda is designed to be scalable, highly available, and cost-effective, making it a popular choice for many applications.

With Lambda, users can upload their code as a function and specify the events that should trigger that function. When an event occurs, Lambda automatically runs the code in response, without the user having to worry about managing any underlying infrastructure. This allows users to focus on building and running their applications without having to worry about the details of infrastructure management.

AWS Lambda supports a wide range of programming languages and runtime environments, including Node.js, Python, Java, .NET (C#), Go, and Ruby, and also allows the use of custom runtimes for additional flexibility.

This makes Lambda suitable for diverse applications, from simple web services and microservices to complex distributed systems. Lambda integrates seamlessly with various AWS services, such as Amazon S3, Amazon DynamoDB, and Amazon Kinesis, making it a powerful choice for building scalable and event-driven applications.

In terms of pricing, AWS Lambda offers an economical, pay-as-you-go model. The AWS Free Tier includes 1 million monthly free requests and 400,000 GB-seconds of compute time. Beyond the Free Tier, pricing is based on the number of requests ($0.20 per 1 million requests after the first million) and the function's execution duration. Duration is metered in **millisecond (ms)** increments, with costs depending on memory allocation; for instance, 100 ms with 2 GB of memory costs the same as 200 ms with 1 GB. This flexibility allows developers to optimize costs by adjusting memory settings and execution times to align with application requirements.

AWS Lambda is an excellent fit for serverless architectures, particularly for use cases that involve automated workflows and event-driven processing. One example is building a simple web service that allows users to upload images to Amazon S3, where the images are automatically processed using ML, as shown in the following diagram.

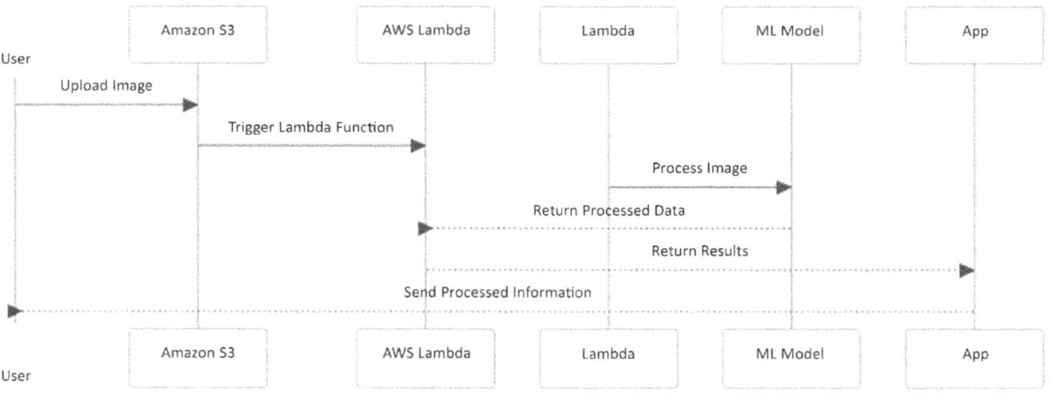

Figure 6.4: AWS Lambda-based serverless app flow

As shown in the preceding diagram, AWS Lambda enables automatic, scalable image processing without requiring users to manage servers or infrastructure. This diagram shows a **serverless image processing workflow** using AWS services. It starts when a user uploads an image to Amazon S3. This upload event automatically triggers an **AWS Lambda function**, which is designed to handle the image processing flow. Lambda then sends the image to an ML model for analysis, such as object detection or facial recognition. Once the ML model processes the image, it returns the results to another Lambda function. That function formats the output and sends the processed results to the application, which the user can then view.

The serverless architecture significantly reduces costs, complexity, and risks associated with infrastructure changes while increasing the speed of application development. This allows users to focus on building features and enhancing functionality, leveraging the seamless scalability, high availability, and event-driven automation of AWS services. The following are some common Lambda use cases:

- **Real-time file processing**: Automatically process images or videos uploaded to Amazon S3
- **API backend**: Build RESTful APIs using Amazon API Gateway and Lambda
- **Event-driven automation**: Trigger workflows in response to database changes, log updates, or custom application events
- **Scheduled tasks**: Run scripts at specific times, such as nightly data cleanup or periodic reporting
- **IoT applications**: Handle data from IoT devices in real time

Lambda acts as a compute service, running the user's code in response to events and providing a highly scalable, highly available, cost-effective execution environment. The user can focus on building and running their application without worrying about managing any underlying infrastructure.

When you need to orchestrate multiple Lambda functions and build a complete workflow, using an orchestration service becomes essential. AWS Step Functions is a serverless orchestration service designed for this purpose. It lets you coordinate multiple AWS services into reliable, scalable workflows without writing complex state management logic. Whether you're building data processing pipelines, automating ML model training, or managing business workflows, Step Functions allows you to define your process as a series of steps using a visual interface or JSON/YAML-based state machines. Each step can trigger Lambda functions, start ECS tasks, run AWS Glue jobs, or interact with services such as SageMaker, which you will learn about in *Part 4, AWS Data Services*. It's especially useful in AI/ML workloads to automate preprocessing, training, and deployment stages. With support for **Standard Workflows** (long-running tasks) and **Express Workflows** (high-throughput, short-duration tasks), Step Functions fits well in both serverless and event-driven application architectures.

This section aimed to introduce you to the concept of AWS Lambda. To understand it better, you need to understand how Lambda can help to achieve different architecture patterns, which you will learn about in *Chapter 13, Building Microservices and Event-Driven Architecture in AWS.*

Containers are becoming famous for building microservice architectures and deploying complex code. AWS has provided the option to deploy serverless containers using Fargate. Let's learn about it in more detail.

AWS Fargate

Adopting containers requires a steep learning curve for deployment, cluster management, security, and monitoring customers. AWS serverless containers can help you focus time and resources on building applications, not managing infrastructure. Amazon ECS provides a simple managed control plane for containers, and **AWS Fargate** provides serverless container hosting. For Kubernetes, you can use Amazon EKS with Fargate to host containers.

Amazon ECS and AWS Fargate offer a choice for modernizing applications through fully managed, native container orchestration, standardized and compliant deployment paths, and automated server patching and provisioning. AWS Fargate's serverless model eliminates the operational complexity of managing container hosts and AMIs.

The following are the advantages of Fargate:

- **NoOps**: Yes, you read it right. You have heard about DevOps, DevSecOps, MLOps, and so on, but wouldn't life be easier if there were NoOps? AWS Fargate removes the complexity of infrastructure management and shifts primary responsibilities, such as OS hardening and patching, onto AWS. You can reduce the resources spent on these tasks and instead focus on adding value to your customers. AWS Fargate automates container orchestration with compute, networking, storage, container runtime config, auto-scaling, and self-healing, and provides serverless computing without AMIs to patch, upgrade, and secure your OS.
- **Lower TCO**: In Fargate, each task runs on its dedicated host, and the resources can be tailored to the task's needs. This dramatically improves utilization, delivering significant cost savings. With fewer container hosts to manage, fewer people must focus on a container infrastructure, significantly reducing TCO. You only pay for what you provision in Fargate. You are billed for CPU and memory utilization on a per-second billing model at the container task level. You can save further with Spot Instances and a Savings Plan.
- **Seamless integrations**: AWS Fargate integrates all the significant aspects of deployment, networking, monitoring, and security. An extensive set of third-party partners, such as Datadog, Aqua Security, Harness, and HashiCorp, provide solutions for monitoring, logging, and runtime security of workloads deployed in AWS Fargate.
- **Security**: In Fargate, each task runs on its own dedicated host. This security isolation, by design, eliminates multiple security concerns of sensitive containers co-existing on a host. With complete integration for IAM, security groups, key management, and secret management, and encrypted, ephemeral disks, customers can deploy with peace of mind for security.

From a cost-saving perspective, Fargate Spot allows you to leverage savings similar to those of your EC2 Spot. With Fargate Spot, AWS runs Fargate tasks on the same EC2 Spot instance and provides a flat 70% discount rate compared to regular Fargate pricing. Here are some common use cases:

- **Microservices applications**: Deploy and scale services independently using containers
- **Batch processing jobs**: Run large-scale, data-processing tasks on demand
- **ML inference**: Serve ML models in containers without managing infrastructure
- **Containerized APIs**: Host RESTful APIs that require longer runtime or complex dependencies than Lambda allows
- **CI/CD workflows**: Use containers in your DevOps pipeline for building, testing, and deploying code

Again, this section aimed to introduce you to the concept of a serverless container. To understand it better, you need to understand how containers help to build microservice architecture patterns, which you will learn about in *Chapter 13, Building Microservices and Event-Driven Architecture in AWS*.

High-performance computing

HPC is a field of computing that involves using specialized hardware and software to solve complex, compute-intensive problems. HPC systems are typically used for scientific and engineering applications requiring high computational power, such as weather forecasting, molecular modeling, and oil and gas exploration. HPC systems require a high level of performance and scalability. Still, they can help organizations achieve results faster and more efficiently, making them an essential tool for many scientific and engineering applications.

HPC workloads are characterized by multiple technologies, such as storage, compute, networking, AI, ML, scheduling and orchestration, and streaming visualization, combined with specialized third-party applications.

HPC workloads are classified to help identify the AWS services and solutions that can best match your needs. These categories include fluid dynamics, weather modeling, and reservoir simulation, typically called **scale-up** or **tightly coupled** workloads. The other HPC workloads are financial risk modeling, genomics, seismic processing, and drug discovery, typically called **scale-out** or **loosely coupled**. Both workloads require large compute power using EC2 Spot instances, application orchestration using AWS Batch, AWS ParallelCluster, scale-out computing, and high-performance storage such as FSx for Lustre and S3. Tightly coupled workloads also require high network performance using an EFA.

AWS offers several services and tools that can be used to run HPC workloads in the cloud. These include the following:

- **EFA**: EFA is a network interface for Amazon EC2 instances that enables low-latency, high-throughput communication between instances. This is essential for scaling HPC applications to thousands of CPUs and GPUs. It provides a purpose-built, low-jitter channel for inter-instance communications, enhancing the performance of distributed ML applications and HPC.
- **Amazon EC2 P Series instances**: These instances have NVIDIA GPUs, delivering HPC capabilities ideal for ML, deep learning, computational fluid dynamics, and other HPC applications. *P* instances offer petaflops of mixed-precision performance per instance, significantly reducing training times and accelerating computational tasks.
- **Amazon EC2 Hpc7g instances**: Powered by AWS Graviton3E processors, *Hpc7g* instances provide enhanced floating-point performance and energy efficiency, making them suitable for compute-intensive HPC workloads. They offer improved internode latency using an EFA, facilitating efficient scaling for tightly coupled applications.
- **Amazon EC2 Hpc7a instances**: These instances are designed for compute-intensive, latency-sensitive HPC workloads, featuring high-performance processors and memory configurations. Compared to previous generations, *Hpc7a* instances enable efficient scaling on fewer nodes, optimizing performance for applications such as computational fluid dynamics and weather forecasting.
- **AWS ParallelCluster**: AWS ParallelCluster is a fully managed HPC platform that allows users to easily deploy and manage HPC clusters on AWS. It includes various tools and utilities, such as a job scheduler and a resource manager, that can help users run HPC workloads on AWS.
- **AWS Batch**: AWS Batch is a service that allows users to run batch computing workloads on AWS. Batch workloads typically involve many independent tasks that can be run in parallel, making them well-suited for HPC applications. AWS Batch can help users manage and scale their batch workloads on AWS.

Overall, AWS provides various services and tools for running HPC workloads on the cloud. HPC is a vast topic; this section aimed to provide a basic understanding of it. You can learn more by visiting the AWS HPC page: `https://aws.amazon.com/hpc/`.

Hybrid compute

While you want to benefit from the advantages of using the cloud, not all your applications can be migrated to AWS due to latency or the need for local data processing. Latency-sensitive applications such as patient care flow require less than 10 ms responses, and any delays can affect critical processes, so you want your compute to be near your equipment. Similarly, there are instances when you can't afford downtime due to intermittent networking and want local data processing, such as manufacturing execution systems, high-frequency trading, or medical diagnostics.

If you can't move to a Region because of data residency, local processing, or latency requirements, you must build and maintain your facility's on-premises infrastructure. In that case, you must keep an IT infrastructure, which involves a complex procurement and provisioning process from multiple vendors with a months-long lead time. In addition, you will have the overhead to patch and update applications running on-premises and schedule maintenance downtime or arrange for on-site resources, impacting operations.

Developers need to build different APIs and services to accommodate various other infrastructures and build different tools for automation, deployment, and security controls. That leads to separate code bases and processes for on-premises and the cloud, creating friction and operational risk. This leads to business challenges such as delayed access to new technologies and longer deployment timelines from testing to production, affecting the business's ability to deliver new features and adapt to changing dynamics.

AWS hybrid cloud services are tools and services that allow you to connect on-premises infrastructure to the cloud, creating a hybrid cloud environment. This will enable users to take advantage of the benefits of both on-premises and cloud computing, allowing them to run workloads in the most appropriate environment for their needs.

AWS hybrid cloud services include tools and services, such as AWS Direct Connect and AWS Client VPN, to help users connect their on-premises infrastructure to the cloud. These services allow users to securely and reliably connect their on-premises environments to the cloud, allowing them to move data and workloads between on-premises and cloud environments easily.

AWS hybrid cloud services include tools and services, such as AWS **Identity and Access Management (IAM)** and AWS Systems Manager, that can help users manage and operate their hybrid cloud environments. These services can help users control access to resources, monitor and manage their environments, and automate common tasks, making operating and maintaining their hybrid cloud environments easier.

From a compute perspective, let's look at AWS Outposts, which brings the cloud on-premises.

AWS Outposts

Compute and storage racks built with AWS-designed hardware, which are fully managed and scalable, are referred to as **AWS Outposts**. These can be used to extend AWS infrastructure, services, and tools to on-premises locations. With Outposts, users can run a consistent, native AWS experience on-premises, allowing them to use the same APIs, tools, and services that they use in the cloud.

AWS offers AWS Outposts, a fully managed service that extends AWS infrastructure, services, APIs, and tools to virtually any on-premises facility. This enables users to run native AWS services on-premises, providing a consistent hybrid experience for applications that require low latency, local data processing, or data residency.

AWS Outposts is designed for seamless deployment and management, supporting a variety of workloads, including compute-intensive HPC tasks, latency-sensitive applications, and those necessitating access to on-premises data or resources. The hardware comprises servers that are 1–2 rack units high (1.75”–3.5”), fitting into standard EIA-310 19”-width racks. This setup allows users to launch AWS Nitro-based Amazon EC2 instances with instance storage, among other services available locally on Outposts.

As shown in the following diagram, AWS offers a suite of services that enables organizations to build and run applications on-premises using the same AWS APIs, control plane, and tools they are familiar with in the AWS cloud, ensuring operational consistency across environments.

Figure 6.5: AWS Outposts locally available services

As shown in the preceding diagram, using Outposts, you can run VMs with EC2 instances in your on-premises facility. Each instance will have instance storage that can be used for AMI launches and data volumes. You can deploy containerized workloads using Amazon ECS or EKS. You can network with Amazon VPC to introduce a logical separation between workloads and secure communication within a workload that spans the Region and your site. Outposts are a good option for IoT workloads to deploy IoT Greengrass for IoT messaging and SageMaker Neo for inference at the edge.

Outposts can help operate smaller sites (such as retail stores or enterprise branch offices) that run point-of-sale systems, security monitoring, smart displays, and develop next-generation facial or voice recognition to customize the customer experience. Healthcare providers can benefit from running the latest tech to assess patient images and process medical data quickly, but they also benefit from cloud tools and long-term storage.

Outposts can power automation, integrate IoT data, monitor systems, and provide feedback to operators in factories, warehouses, and distribution centers.

AWS Outposts can help users extend AWS's benefits to on-premises locations. This allows them to run a consistent, native AWS experience, and easily move workloads between on-premises and cloud environments.

VMware is very popular for running VMs. AWS launched VMware Cloud on AWS in 2017. However, this service was deprecated recently due to significant changes in VMware due to the Broadcom acquisition, which led AWS to offer a new service called EVS. Let's learn more about it.

Amazon Elastic VMware Service

With the recent changes following Broadcom's acquisition of VMware in November 2023, many VMware customers have faced uncertainty, especially around pricing and support. One major shift was the decision to stop selling VMware Cloud on AWS directly through AWS or its channel partners, customers now must go through Broadcom or authorized resellers. This move raised concerns about potential cost increases and long-term access to VMware services on AWS.

In response, AWS introduced **Amazon Elastic VMware Service** (**EVS**) – a new, native service that allows you to run **VMware Cloud Foundation** (**VCF**) directly inside your own Amazon VPC. With EVS, you can bring your own VCF licenses, which helps avoid additional costs during migration. It also makes deployment easier, with guided workflows that let you spin up an entire VCF environment in just a few hours.

For teams already using VMware on-premises, EVS maintains operational consistency, allowing you to move workloads without changing IPs, retraining staff, or rewriting processes. You can also integrate your VMware environment with native AWS services such as S3, RDS, or Lambda, giving you flexibility to modernize while still using tools you know.

Amazon EVS offers a cloud-first path for VMware users who want more control and flexibility than what Broadcom now offers. It's designed to give you the freedom to scale, innovate, and manage costs while staying in an environment your team is already comfortable with. You can learn more about EVS by referring to this link: `https://aws.amazon.com/evs/`.

As you have learned about various compute options, let's look at how to make the right choice.

Tips for choosing the right compute option in AWS

Selecting the correct compute option in AWS involves understanding your workload requirements, application characteristics, and cost considerations. AWS provides various compute services, including Amazon EC2, AWS Lambda, AWS Fargate, and AWS Outposts, each suited to specific scenarios. Here are some practical tips to help you choose the right compute option:

- **Understand the nature of your workload**: When you're choosing a compute option, begin by evaluating how your application works. Stateless applications, such as web frontends or APIs, are perfect for AWS Lambda or AWS Fargate because these services scale automatically and don't require any server maintenance. On the other hand, if your workload is stateful, such as databases or applications that maintain sessions, Amazon EC2 is a better fit. EC2 gives you complete control over instance configurations and storage, making it suitable for custom setups or legacy applications. For example, Coinbase uses AWS Lambda to automate deployments and scale event-driven tasks without server management, improving efficiency and cost savings.
- **Consider scalability requirements**: Your application's ability to scale with demand is critical. If your traffic fluctuates, Amazon EC2 Auto Scaling groups can adjust capacity automatically, just like Intuit does to manage traffic spikes during tax season. For high-performance tasks such as ML or simulations, GPU-powered instances such as the *P4d* provide the necessary compute, used effectively by Volkswagen Group for model training. Hybrid environments needing on-premises compute for compliance or latency reasons benefit from AWS Outposts, which bring AWS infrastructure closer to where the data is created.

- **Match compute power with application needs**: Matching the right compute instance to your workload saves both time and cost. For general-purpose workloads such as websites or small databases, Graviton-based *T4g* or *M6g* instances offer good performance at a lower cost. Instructure used them to support scalable e-learning platforms efficiently. For compute-heavy tasks such as simulations or video encoding, HPC instances such as *C6g* or *Hpc7g* are ideal; Autodesk used AWS compute for faster hydraulic simulations. When your application needs a lot of memory, such as in-memory analytics or biotech workloads, *R6i* or *X2idn* offer the required RAM. For data-heavy tasks such as log analysis or media processing, Storage Optimized instances such as *I4i* provide fast access and throughput.
- **Account for traffic patterns**: Understanding how your application's traffic behaves helps you choose the right compute. AWS Lambda and Fargate work well for unpredictable or bursty workloads because they scale instantly and charge only for usage. If your workload is consistent and high-volume, such as backend services or data pipelines, EC2 with Auto Scaling or Spot Instances may be more cost-efficient. For example, Pismo, a financial services platform, uses AWS Fargate to deploy and manage containerized services that respond to fluctuating financial transaction volumes efficiently.
- **Address security and compliance requirements**: If your application handles sensitive or regulated data, you need compute options that ensure isolation and data protection. Amazon EC2 with Dedicated Hosts or AWS Outposts supports scenarios where data residency, encryption, or dedicated hardware is required. You can also integrate with AWS **Key Management Service (KMS)** to ensure encryption at rest and in transit. For industries such as healthcare and finance, services aligned with HIPAA, SOC 2, or GDPR provide the necessary compliance guarantees. For example, Capital One uses AWS security tools, including KMS and dedicated networking, to ensure that its banking applications meet strict compliance and data privacy requirements.
- **Optimize costs**: Managing costs is essential when scaling in AWS. For flexible workloads such as batch processing or data science jobs, Spot Instances can reduce costs by up to 90%—the Allen Institute for Brain Science used them for large-scale brain simulations. For always-on services such as APIs or backend applications, RIs can save up to 72%. SmugMug used RIs to save nearly $1 million a year. If your architecture includes a mix of EC2, Lambda, and Fargate, AWS Savings Plans offer cross-service discounts based on committed usage, helping you simplify billing while still saving. You can also use AWS Cost Explorer and Pricing Calculator to model expenses based on your real usage.

- **Leverage HPC**: If your projects involve scientific simulations, 3D rendering, or AI training, AWS offers HPC-friendly options such as *Hpc7g* and *P3* instances. These are designed to handle large-scale processing tasks, as seen at the University of California, Riverside, where researchers ran complex climate models in less time than with traditional infrastructure. When workloads need tight internode communication, EFA ensures low-latency networking, making large cluster jobs run faster and more efficiently. For example, Moderna used AWS HPC services to speed up COVID-19 vaccine development by running molecular simulations and analytics in record time.

By understanding your workload's requirements and leveraging AWS tools such as AWS Compute Optimizer, you can ensure that your compute choice aligns with performance, scalability, and cost-efficiency goals. AWS's diverse range of compute services makes it possible to optimize resources for nearly any application or workload

Knowledge check

The following scenario-based questions require a strong grasp of AWS architecture, hybrid solutions, and cost optimization strategies, reflecting the complexity of the AWS Pro-level certification:

1. Your organization needs to deploy an ML pipeline that processes large volumes of video data in near-real time. The pipeline must scale automatically based on the volume of incoming data, and costs should be minimized during low usage. The solution should use GPU resources efficiently. How would you design the compute solution? (Choose two.)

    a. Use EC2 *P4d* instances in an Auto Scaling group with Amazon SageMaker to train models

    b. Use EC2 Spot Instances with *P3* instances for cost-effective GPU utilization

    c. Use Elastic Inference with General Purpose EC2 instances to attach GPU capacity as needed

    d. Use Lambda functions to preprocess the video data and trigger processing

    e. Use EC2 *M6g* instances with a custom machine learning model optimized for Graviton

    Correct answer: a. and b.

    Explanation:

    a. **Correct.** For a GPU-intensive pipeline such as video processing, EC2 P4d instances with SageMaker provide the required GPU capabilities for training and inference.

   b. **Correct.** Using Spot Instances with P3 instances helps reduce costs during low usage by leveraging excess capacity.
   c. Incorrect. This option is less optimal for real-time video processing due to performance constraints.
   d. Incorrect. Same as above: less optimal for real-time video processing due to performance constraints.
   e. Incorrect. EC2 M6g instances lack GPU support.

2. A global e-commerce company is experiencing inconsistent latency in its customer-facing API during high-traffic periods. The API runs on a fleet of EC2 instances behind an ALB. Analysis shows the issue is tied to instances in one of the AZs. Which steps would you take to ensure consistent performance? (Choose two.)

   a. Use AWS Compute Optimizer to identify underperforming instances and recommend resizing
   b. Enable cross-zone load balancing on the ALB to distribute traffic evenly across all AZs
   c. Switch from an ALB to an NLB for lower latency
   d. Use EFA to improve inter-node communication between instances
   e. Implement Auto Scaling policies that increase instance counts in other AZs during peak loads

   Correct answer: a. and b.

   Explanation:

   a. **Correct.** Using Compute Optimizer can identify and resize instances experiencing bottlenecks.
   b. **Correct.** To address uneven performance in an ALB, enabling cross-zone load balancing ensures traffic is evenly distributed across AZs.
   c. Incorrect. ALB is better for HTTP/HTTPS traffic.
   d. Incorrect. Irrelevant as EFA is suited for HPC, not API traffic.
   e. Incorrect. Auto Scaling policies help scale resources but doesn't directly address the root cause of uneven traffic.

3. A healthcare company is required to run latency-sensitive medical imaging applications on a hybrid architecture. Data must remain on-premises due to compliance regulations, but the company wants to leverage AWS services to improve compute performance and scalability. What solution would best meet these requirements?

    a. Use AWS Outposts to deploy AWS infrastructure on-premises and process imaging workloads locally

    b. Use VMware Cloud on AWS for seamless integration with existing on-premises VMware tools

    c. Use a hybrid architecture with Amazon EC2 *Hpc7g* instances and direct connections to on-premises data storage

    d. Use Amazon FSx for Lustre to process imaging workloads locally and synchronize results with AWS storage

    Correct answer: a.

    Explanation:

    a. **Correct**. AWS Outposts is the optimal solution for latency-sensitive and compliance-bound workloads because it provides native AWS infrastructure and services on-premises.

    b. Incorrect. This option is invalid as VMware Cloud on AWS is no longer directly supported by AWS.

    c. Incorrect. It doesn't meet the on-premises data residency requirement.

    d. Incorrect. Amazon FSx doesn't meet the on-premises data residency requirement.

4. A large financial institution wants to migrate its batch processing system to AWS. The system processes millions of transactions overnight and needs to be completed within a fixed window. The solution should minimize costs but still guarantee enough capacity for peak loads. Which architecture would you recommend?

    a. Use Reserved Instances with EC2 *M6g* instances for cost-efficiency and predictable performance

    b. Use EC2 Spot Instances with Compute Optimizer to scale instances based on utilization

    c. Use EC2 On-Demand Instances with AWS Auto Scaling for peak load handling

    d. Use a combination of Reserved Instances for baseline capacity and Spot Instances for peak loads

Correct answer: d.

Explanation:

a. Incorrect. Reserved Instances alone lack flexibility for peak load handling.
b. Incorrect. Spot Instances alone risk interruptions.
c. Incorrect. On-Demand is costly for fixed window tasks.
d. **Correct.** The best solution for cost efficiency and guaranteed capacity is a combination of Reserved Instances (baseline capacity) and Spot Instances (for peaks).

5. Your application uses AWS Lambda and Amazon API Gateway to serve real-time requests. The traffic volume has recently spiked, causing high latencies and occasional errors due to throttling. What actions would you take to resolve these issues? (Choose two.)

a. Increase the memory allocation for the Lambda function to improve execution speed
b. Configure reserved concurrency limits for the Lambda function to handle more parallel requests
c. Use **DynamoDB Accelerator (DAX)** to cache frequent queries and reduce downstream latency
d. Enable caching in API Gateway to reduce the load on Lambda functions for repeated requests
e. Migrate from Lambda to EC2 to remove throttling limits

Correct answer: b. and d.

Explanation:

a. Incorrect. Increasing memory allocation improves execution speed but doesn't address throttling.
b. **Correct.** Increasing reserved concurrency ensures that more requests are processed in parallel.
c. Incorrect. DAX isn't directly related to the given architecture.
d. **Correct.** To address high traffic, enabling API Gateway caching reduces redundant Lambda invocations for repeated requests.
e. Incorrect. Migrating to EC2 defeats the benefits of serverless architecture.

Summary

In this chapter, you learned about compute services available in AWS, which will help you choose the right compute service for your workload requirement. You learned about why terms changed from *servers* to *compute* recently, due to the broad set of options provided by the cloud.

The most popular compute service is EC2, which is the foundation for the rest of the services provided by AWS. For example, a service such as Amazon SageMaker or Amazon DynamoDB under the hood relies on core services such as EC2. You learned about various EC2 families, pricing models, and advantages.

There are so many EC2 options available, which may need to be clarified when optimizing your cost model. You learned about AWS Compute Optimizer, which can help you choose the right compute option and optimize cost. You also learned about AMI, which lets you select the operating system for your workload and spin up EC2 per your needs. Further, you learned about EC2's best practices.

A load balancer is often needed for distributed computing to distribute the workload across multiple servers and prevent any single server from becoming overloaded. You learned about AWS-provided load balancers, which can be used for distributed computing, including CLBs, ALBs, NLBs, and GWLBs.

Compute is not limited to servers, and serverless compute is becoming more popular because it helps you focus on your business logic and avoid the admin overhead of scaling and patching servers. You learned about the two most popular serverless compute options: AWS Lambda and AWS Fargate. You learned about HPC in AWS, which can help you have your mini-supercomputer solve complex algorithmic problems.

Not every workload can be hosted on the cloud. You learned about hybrid compute and how AWS brings its infrastructure on-premises and provides the same experience as the cloud. In the next chapter, you will get knee-deep into another set of fundamental services in AWS that are the workhorse of many successful start-ups and multinationals. That is the beautiful world of databases.

Join us on Discord

For discussions around the book and to connect with your peers, join us on Discord at `https://discord.gg/kbFRRSB2Qs` or scan the QR code below:

7

Selecting the Right Database Service

Building applications is all about data collection and management. If you design an e-commerce application, you want to show available inventory catalog data to customers and collect purchase data as they make a transaction. Similarly, if you are running an autonomous vehicle application, you want to analyze data on the surrounding traffic and provide the right prediction for cars based on that data. As of now, you have learned about networking, storage, and compute in previous chapters. In this chapter, you will learn about the choices of database services available in AWS to complete the core architecture tech stack.

With so many choices at your disposal, it is easy to get analysis paralysis. So, in this chapter, we will first lay a foundation of how the databases and their use cases can be classified, and then use these classifications to help us pick the right service for our particular use case and our circumstances. You will navigate the variety of options, which will give you confidence that you are using the right tool for the job.

In this chapter, you will learn about the following topics:

- A brief history of databases and data-driven innovation trends
- Database consistency model
- Database usage model
- AWS database services
- Benefits of AWS database services
- Choosing the right database for the job
- Migrating databases to AWS

By the end of this chapter, you will have learned about different AWS database service offerings and how to choose a suitable database for your workload.

A brief history of databases

Relational databases have been around for over 50 years. Edgar F. Codd proposed the relational model for database management in 1970. The main feature of a relational database is that data is arranged in rows and columns, and rows in tables are associated with other rows in other tables by using the column values in each row as relationship keys. Another important feature of relational databases is that they normally use **Structured Query Language** (**SQL**) to access, insert, update, and delete records. Interestingly, SQL has its roots in a language called SEQUEL (Structured English Query Language), developed by IBM researchers Raymond Boyce and Donald Chamberlin in the early 1970s. SEQUEL was later renamed to SQL due to trademark issues, but it retained its powerful capabilities and became the standard query language across relational systems. Relational databases and SQL have served us well for decades.

As the internet's popularity increased in the 1990s, we started hitting scalability limits with relational databases. Additionally, a wider variety of data types started cropping up. **Relational Database Management Systems** (**RDBMSs**) were simply not enough anymore. This led to the development of new designs, and we got the term **NoSQL databases**. As confusing as the term is, it does convey the idea that they can deal with data that is not structured, and deal with it with more flexibility.

The term **NoSQL** is attributed to Carlo Strozzi and was first used in 1998 for a relational database that he developed that didn't use the SQL language. The term was then again used in 2009 by Eric Evans and Johan Oskarsson to describe databases that were not relational.

The main difference between relational and non-relational databases is the way they store data and query it. Let's see an example of making a choice between a relational and non-relational database. Take an example of a banking transaction; it is critical for financial transactions in every customer's bank account to always be consistent and roll back in case of any errors. In such a scenario, you want to use a relational database. For a relational database, if some information is not available, then you are forced to store null or some other value. Now take an example of a social media profile, which may have hundreds of attributes to store the user's name, address, education, jobs, personal choices, preferences, and so on. However, many users do not fill in all the information; some users may add just their name, while others add more details, such as their address and education. In such cases, you want to use a non-relational database and store only the information provided by the user without adding null values where the user doesn't provide details (unlike in relational databases).

It is nothing short of amazing what has occurred since then. Hundreds of new offerings have been developed, each trying to solve a different problem. In this environment, deciding the best service or product to solve your problem becomes complicated. You must consider not only your current requirements and workloads but also take into account that your choice of database needs to be able to cover your future requirements and new demands. With so much data being generated, it is natural that a lot of innovation is driven by data. Let's look in detail at how data drives innovation.

Data-driven innovation trends

Since high-speed internet became available everywhere, more and more data is being generated. Before we proceed, let's discuss three significant trends that influence your perspective on data:

- **The surge of data**: Our current era is witnessing an enormous surge in data generation. Managing the vast amount of data originating from your business applications is essential. However, the exponential growth primarily stems from the data produced by network-connected intelligent devices, amplifying the data's diversity and quantity. These "smart" devices, including but not limited to mobile phones, connected vehicles, smart homes, wearable technologies, household appliances, security systems, industrial equipment, machinery, and electronic gadgets, constantly generate real-time data. Applications generate real-time data, such as purchase data from e-commerce sites, user behavior from mobile apps, and social media posts or tweets. The *IDC Data Age 2025* forecast projects global data generation to reach 181 zettabytes by 2025, up from 64.2 ZB in 2020 – an approximate tripling in just five years, necessitating cloud-based solutions to efficiently manage and exploit vast data. You can find report details here: `https://www.red-gate.com/blog/database-development/whats-the-real-story-behind-the-explosive-growth-of-data`.
- **Microservices change analytics requirements**: The advent of microservices is revolutionizing organizations' data and analytics requirements. Rather than developing monolithic applications, companies are shifting toward a microservices architecture that divides complex problems into independent units. This approach enables developers to operate in smaller groups with minimal coordination, respond more efficiently, and work faster. Microservices enable developers to break down their applications into smaller parts, providing them with the flexibility to use multiple databases for various workloads, each suited for its specific purpose. The importance of analytics cannot be overstated, and it must be incorporated into every aspect of the business, rather than just being an after-the-fact activity. Monitoring the organization's operations in real time is critical to fuel innovation and quick decision-making, whether through human intervention or automated processes. Today's well-run businesses thrive on the swift utilization of data.

- **DevOps driving fast changes:** The fast-paced rate of change, driven by DevOps, is transforming how businesses approach IT. To keep up with the rapid innovation and the velocity of IT changes, organizations are adopting the DevOps model. This approach employs automated development tools to facilitate continuous software development, deployment, and enhancement. DevOps emphasizes effective communication, collaboration, and integration between software developers and IT operations. It also involves a rapid rate of change and change management, enabling businesses to adapt to evolving market needs and stay ahead of the competition.
- **Generative AI-driven data growth:** Generative AI applications process vast datasets to train models and generate outputs that mimic human creativity and intelligence. As businesses increasingly adopt GenAI for tasks such as content creation, customer service, code generation, and personalized user experiences, the volume of data generated by these systems is growing exponentially. This includes personalized product recommendations, AI-generated designs, music, interactive content for creative industries, and customer conversations from AI chatbots, all of which require real-time processing and storage. This rapid surge in data generation necessitates cloud-based solutions capable of handling diverse and unstructured data types, such as images, natural language, and multimedia outputs. Additionally, AI-generated data often demands real-time analysis and processing, driving the need for low-latency, scalable architectures to manage and utilize this data effectively.

Having seen the trends that the industry is adopting, let's learn about some basics of databases and learn about the database consistency model in more detail.

Database consistency model

In the context of databases, ensuring transaction data consistency involves restricting any database transaction's ability to modify data in unauthorized ways. When data is written to the database, it must adhere to a set of predefined rules and constraints. These rules are verified, and all checks must be successfully passed before the data can be accessed by other users. This stringent process ensures that data integrity is maintained and that the information stored in the database is accurate and trustworthy. Currently, there are two popular data consistency models. We'll discuss these models in the following subsections.

ACID data consistency model

When database sizes were measured in megabytes, we could have stringent requirements that enforced strict consistency. Since storage has become exponentially cheaper, databases can be much bigger, often measured in terabytes and even petabytes. For this reason, making databases ACID-compliant for storage reasons is much less prevalent depending on use cases. The ACID model guarantees the following:

- **Atomicity**: For an operation to be considered atomic, it should ensure that transactions within the operation either succeed or fail. If one of the transactions fails, all operations should fail and be rolled back. Could you imagine what would happen if you went to the ATM and the machine gave you money but didn't deduct it from your account?
- **Consistency**: The database is structurally sound and consistent after completing each transaction.
- **Isolation**: Transactions are isolated and don't contend with each other. Access to data from multiple users is moderated to avoid contention. Isolation guarantees that two transactions cannot coincide.
- **Durability**: After a transaction is completed, any changes a transaction makes should be durable and permanent, even in a failure such as a power failure.

The ACID model came before the BASE model, which we will describe next. If performance were not a consideration, using the ACID model would always be the right choice. BASE only came into the picture because the ACID model could not scale in many instances, especially with internet applications that serve a worldwide client base.

BASE data consistency model

ACID was taken as the law of the land for many years, but a new model emerged with the advent of larger-scale projects and implementations. In many instances, the ACID model is more pessimistic than required, and it's *too safe* at the expense of scalability and performance.

In most NoSQL databases, the ACID model is not used. These databases have loosened some ACID requirements, such as data freshness, immediate consistency, and accuracy, to gain other benefits, such as scale, speed, and resilience. Some examples of NoSQL databases that use the ACID model are the NET-based RavenDB database and Amazon DynamoDB within a single AWS account and region.

The acronym **BASE** can be broken down as follows: **Basic availability**, **Soft-state**, and **Eventual consistency**. Let's explore what this means further:

- **Basic availability**: The data is available for the majority of the time (but not necessarily all the time). The BASE model emphasizes availability without guaranteeing the consistency of data replication when writing a record.
- **Soft-state**: The database doesn't have to be write-consistent, and different replicas don't always have to be mutually consistent. Take, for example, a system that reports sales figures in real time to multiple destinations and uses multiple copies of the sales figures to provide fault tolerance. As sales come in and get written into the system, different readers may read a different copy of the sales figures. Some of them may be updated with the new numbers, and others may be a few milliseconds behind and not have the latest updates. In this case, the readers will have different results, but if they rerun the query soon after, they will probably get the new figures. In a system like this, not having the latest and greatest numbers may not end the world and may be good enough. The trade-off between getting the results fast versus being entirely up to date may be acceptable.
- **Eventual consistency**: The stored data exhibits consistency eventually, and maybe not until the data is retrieved at a later point.

The BASE model requirements are looser than the ACID model ones, and a direct one-for-one relationship does not exist between ACID and BASE. The BASE consistency model is used mainly in aggregate databases (including wide-column databases), key-value databases, and document databases.

Let's look at the database usage model, which is a crucial differentiator when storing your data.

Database usage model

Two operations can be performed with a database: first, ingest data (or write data into the database), and second, retrieve data (or read data from the database). These two operations will always be present.

On the ingestion side, the data will be ingested in two different ways. It will either be a data update or brand-new data (such as an insert operation). To retrieve data, you will analyze the **change data capture** (**CDC**) set, which is changes in existing data or accessing brand new data. But what drives your choice of database is not the fact that these two operations are present but rather the following:

- How often will the data be retrieved?
- How fast should it be accessed?
- Will the data be updated often, or will it be primarily new?
- How often will the data be ingested?
- How fast does ingestion need to be?
- Will the ingested data be sent in batches or in real time?
- How many users will be consuming the data?
- How many simultaneous processes will there be for ingestion?

The answers to these questions will determine what database technology to use. Two technologies have been the standards to address these questions for many years: **online transaction processing** (**OLTP**) systems and **online analytics processing** (**OLAP**) systems. The main question that needs to be answered is: *Is it more important for the database to perform during data ingestion or retrieval?* These databases can be divided into two categories depending on the use case; they need to be read-heavy or write-heavy.

Online Transaction Processing (OLTP) versus Online Analytical Processing (OLAP)

OLTP systems are designed to handle a high volume of transactions involving frequent data updates, such as inserts and updates, while maintaining data integrity in a multi-user environment. These systems prioritize fast ingestion and modification of data, making them essential for real-time applications such as e-commerce, banking, and logistics. Data in OLTP databases is typically structured to optimize performance and ensure consistency, minimizing redundancy and data anomalies. For example, in an employee database, rather than duplicating supervisor details for multiple employees, the system would organize data to eliminate unnecessary repetition. OLTP systems measure performance in terms of transactions processed per second, making them highly efficient for operational processes that require rapid and reliable data handling.

In contrast, OLAP systems focus on complex data retrieval and analysis rather than frequent data updates. These systems are optimized for querying and aggregating historical data, often sourced from OLTP systems, to support business intelligence and decision-making processes. Data in OLAP systems is typically stored in multidimensional schemas such as the star schema, which enables efficient querying for analytical purposes. For example, a bank might use an OLTP system to process millions of daily transactions, including deposits and withdrawals.

This transactional data is then copied to an OLAP system to perform complex queries and generate reports, such as daily summaries or trend analyses over extended periods. Unlike OLTP, the performance of OLAP systems is measured by the speed and efficiency of query execution, enabling businesses to extract meaningful insights from their data.

The following table shows a comparison between OLTP and OLAP:

	OLTP	OLAP
Focus	Insertion and modification of data.	Retrieval and analysis of data.
Data	OLTP data is normally the source of truth and original data.	OLAP systems are fed by OLTP systems.
Transaction	OLTP has short transactions. Usually a combination of updates and inserts.	OLAP has long transactions. Usually just inserts.
Time	Low processing time of transactions.	High processing time of transactions.
Queries	Simpler queries.	Complex queries.
Normalization	Usually normalized (3NF).	Usually not normalized.
Integrity	Important. Normally ACID.	Not as important. BASE can be used.

Figure 7.1: Comparison between OLTP systems and OLAP systems

As you have learned about the database consistency model and its uses, you must be wondering which model is suitable when combining these properties; ACID is a must-have for OLTP, and BASE can be applied for OLAP.

Let's go further and learn about the various kinds of database services available in AWS and how they fit to address different workload needs.

AWS database services

AWS offers a broad range of database services that are purpose-built for every major use case. These fully managed services allow you to build applications that scale quickly. All these services are battle-tested and provide deep functionality, so you get the high availability, performance, reliability, and security required by production workloads.

The suite of AWS fully managed database services encompasses relational databases for transactional applications, such as Amazon RDS and Amazon Aurora, non-relational databases such as Amazon DynamoDB for internet-scale applications, an in-memory data store called Amazon MemoryDB for caching and real-time workloads, and a graph database, Amazon Neptune, for developing applications with highly connected data. Migrating your existing databases to AWS is made simple and cost-effective with the AWS Database Migration Service. Each of these database services is so vast that going into details warrants a book for each of these services itself. This section will show you various database services overviews and resources to dive further.

Relational databases

There are many offerings in the database space, but relational databases have served us well for many years without needing any other type of database. A relational database is probably the best, cheapest, and most efficient option for any project that does not store millions of records. The following screenshot shows various relational databases available in AWS:

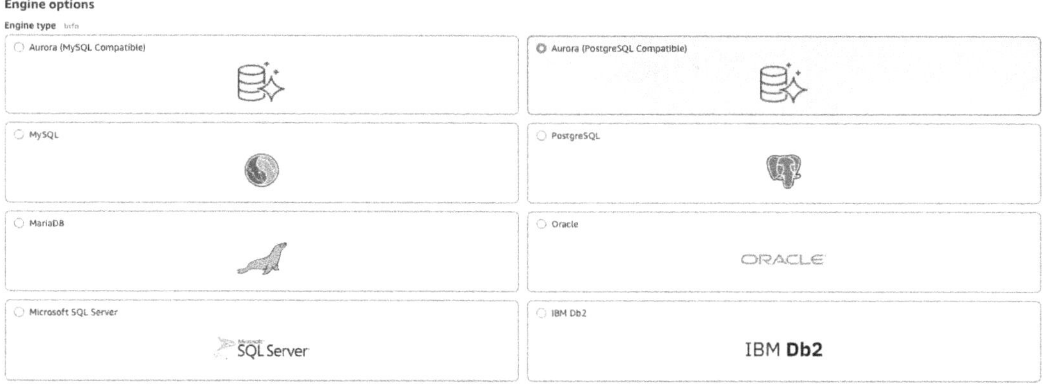

Figure 7.2: Relational Database options in AWS

The preceding screenshot displays the engine selection screen in the AWS RDS console, where you can choose from a variety of popular database engines for deploying managed database instances. The available options include the following:

- **Amazon Aurora (MySQL Compatible and PostgreSQL Compatible):** Fully managed, high-performance versions of MySQL and PostgreSQL
- **MySQL:** Widely used open source relational database
- **PostgreSQL:** Advanced open source database known for reliability and extensibility
- **MariaDB:** MySQL-compatible, community-developed database

- **Oracle**: Enterprise-grade database with robust features
- **Microsoft SQL Server**: Commonly used in enterprise applications
- **IBM Db2**: Enterprise-class RDBMS from IBM, known for scalability

Next, let's analyze the different relational options that AWS offers us.

Amazon Relational Database Service (Amazon RDS)

Given what we said in the previous section, it is not surprising that Amazon has a robust lineup of relational database offerings. They all fall under the umbrella of Amazon RDS. It is certainly possible to install your database in an EC2 instance and manage it yourself. Unless you have an excellent reason to do so, it may be a terrible idea; instead, you should consider using one of the many flavors of Amazon RDS. You may think running your own instance might be cheaper, but if you consider all the costs, including system administration costs, you will most likely be better off and save money using Amazon RDS.

Amazon RDS was designed by AWS to simplify the management of crucial transactional applications. It provides an easy-to-use platform for setting up, operating, and scaling a relational database in the cloud. With RDS, laborious administrative tasks such as hardware provisioning, database configuration, patching, and backups are automated, and a scalable capacity is provided in a cost-efficient manner. RDS is available on various database instance types, optimized for memory, performance, or I/O, and supports six well-known database engines: Amazon Aurora (compatible with MySQL and PostgreSQL), MySQL, PostgreSQL, MariaDB, SQL Server, and Oracle.

If you want more control of your database at the OS level, AWS has now launched **Amazon RDS Custom**. It provisions all AWS resources in your account, enabling full access to the underlying Amazon EC2 resources and database environment.

You can install third-party and packaged applications directly on the database instance as they would be in a self-managed environment, while benefiting from the automation that Amazon RDS traditionally provides.

Amazon RDS's flavors fall into three broad categories:

- **Community** (Postgres, MySQL, and MariaDB): AWS offers RDS with three different open source offerings. This is a good option for development environments, low-usage deployments, defined workloads, and non-critical applications that can afford some downtime.

- **Amazon Aurora** (Postgres and MySQL): As you can see, Postgres and MySQL are here, as they are in the community editions. Is this a typo? No, delivering these applications within the Aurora *wrapper* can add many benefits to a community deployment. Amazon started offering the MySQL service in 2009 and added the Postgres version in 2017. Some of these are as follows:
    a. Automatic allocation of storage space in 10 GB increments up to 128 TBs.
    b. Fivefold performance increases over the vanilla MySQL version and up to three times that of standard PostgreSQL.
    c. Automatic six-way replication across availability zones to improve availability and fault tolerance.
- **Commercial** (Oracle, SQL Server, and Db2): Many organizations still run Oracle workloads, so AWS offers RDS with an Oracle flavor and a Microsoft SQL Server flavor. AWS launched Amazon RDS for Db2 at re:Invent 2023, which allows IBM Db2 deployments in AWS. Here, you will get all the benefits of a fully managed service. However, keep in mind that, bundled with the cost of this service, there will be a licensing cost associated with using commercial databases, which otherwise might not be present if you use a community edition.

Let's look at the key benefits of Amazon RDS.

Amazon RDS benefits

Amazon RDS offers multiple benefits as a managed database service offered by AWS. Let's look at its key attributes to make your database more resilient and performant:

- **Multi-AZ deployments**: Amazon RDS offers Multi-AZ deployments to enhance availability and durability for database instances. In this configuration, RDS synchronously replicates data to a standby instance in a different **Availability Zone (AZ)**. In the event of infrastructure failure, RDS automatically fails over to the standby instance, ensuring minimal disruption. The database endpoint remains consistent during failover, eliminating the need for manual intervention. Recently, AWS introduced Multi-AZ deployments with two readable standbys, providing up to 2x faster transaction commit latency and additional read capacity.

- **Read replicas**: RDS supports the creation of read replicas for MySQL, PostgreSQL, MariaDB, Oracle, and SQL Server engines. These replicas are kept in sync with the primary database and are useful for scaling read-heavy workloads and enhancing disaster recovery strategies. Depending on the database engine, read replicas can be deployed in different regions, providing localized read access and additional failover options. You can create up to five read replicas per primary instance, and they can be promoted to standalone databases if needed.
- **Automated backups**: Amazon RDS offers automated backups that are performed daily during a user-specified window. These backups include the entire instance and transaction logs, allowing point-in-time recovery. The retention period for automated backups can be configured to up to 35 days. In Multi-AZ deployments, backups are taken from the standby instance to avoid I/O suspension on the primary instance, ensuring minimal impact on database performance during backup operations.
- **Database snapshots**: Users can manually create database snapshots, which are stored in Amazon S3 and retained until explicitly deleted. These snapshots can be used to create new instances as needed. Although snapshots function as complete backups, they are charged only for the incremental storage used. This means you pay only for the storage consumed by changes since the last snapshot, making it a cost-effective backup solution.
- **Data storage**: Amazon RDS utilizes Amazon **Elastic Block Store (EBS)** volumes for database and log storage. It offers two SSD-backed storage options: General Purpose (gp2/gp3) for cost-effective storage and Provisioned IOPS (io1/io2) for high-performance OLTP applications. RDS automatically stripes across multiple EBS volumes to enhance performance based on the allocated storage. Storage can be scaled up without downtime, allowing your database to grow with your application needs.
- **Scalability**: RDS allows for the scaling of compute and storage resources, often without downtime. With over 25 instance types available, users can select configurations that best meet their CPU, memory, and pricing requirements. This flexibility enables scaling up during periods of high demand and scaling down during lower usage to optimize costs. Additionally, storage scaling is supported up to 64 TB for most database engines, accommodating significant data growth.
- **Monitoring**: Amazon RDS integrates with Amazon CloudWatch to provide a range of monitoring metrics, including CPU utilization, memory usage, storage capacity, and latency. Enhanced Monitoring offers access to additional metrics with customizable granularity, from one-second to sixty-second intervals. Performance Insights is another tool that provides real-time performance monitoring and recommendations for optimization, helping you identify and resolve performance bottlenecks efficiently.

- **Security**: RDS simplifies network access control by allowing instances to run within an Amazon **Virtual Private Cloud (VPC)**, enabling isolation and secure connectivity. Most RDS engine types support encryption at rest, and all support encryption in transit. RDS also complies with various industry standards, including HIPAA, ensuring robust security for sensitive data. Additionally, RDS supports integration with AWS **Identity and Access Management (IAM)** for fine-grained access control and AWS **Key Management Service (KMS)** for managing encryption keys.
- **Enhanced RDS Recommendations**: AWS improved the RDS Recommendations feature, consolidating configuration best practices, threshold-based performance suggestions, and machine learning-powered performance anomaly detection into a unified interface.
- **Amazon RDS for Oracle Enhancements**: In October 2023, AWS introduced new instance types, data movement capabilities, and multi-tenant support for Amazon RDS for Oracle, enhancing performance and flexibility for Oracle database deployments.
- **Latest version updates**: In November 2024, AWS made PostgreSQL 17.2 available on Amazon RDS, incorporating several fixes and improvements from the PostgreSQL community. In September 2024, AWS released Aurora PostgreSQL 16.4, introducing a fast failover feature to reduce database downtime during planned maintenance.

You can learn more about RDS by visiting the AWS page: `https://aws.amazon.com/rds/`.

As you have learned about RDS, let's dive deeper into AWS cloud-native databases with Amazon Aurora.

Amazon Aurora

Amazon Aurora is a relational database service that blends the availability and rapidity of high-end commercial databases with the simplicity and cost-effectiveness of open source databases. Aurora is built with full compatibility with MySQL and PostgreSQL engines, enabling applications and tools to operate without necessitating modifications. It offers a variety of developer tools to construct serverless and **machine learning (ML)**-driven applications. The service is completely managed and automates time-intensive administration tasks, including hardware provisioning, database setup, patching, and backups. It provides commercial-grade databases' reliability, availability, and security while costing only a fraction of the price.

Amazon Aurora has introduced several key features to enhance its capabilities since its launch in 2014. Here's an updated overview:

- **Serverless configuration**: Amazon Aurora Serverless v2 offers on-demand auto-scaling, allowing your database to automatically start up, shut down, and adjust capacity based on application needs. It scales instantly to accommodate hundreds of thousands of transactions in seconds, fine-tuning capacity in small increments to match your application's requirements. This eliminates the need for manual capacity management, and you pay only for the resources consumed, potentially saving up to 90% compared to provisioning for peak load.
- **Global Database**: Aurora's Global Database feature enables a single Aurora database to span multiple AWS regions, providing fast local reads and rapid disaster recovery. It uses storage-based replication with a typical latency of less than one second. In case of a regional outage, a secondary region can be promoted to full read/write capabilities in less than a minute, ensuring business continuity.
- **Encryption**: Aurora allows you to encrypt your databases using keys managed through AWS KMS. This encryption covers data stored on the underlying storage, automated backups, snapshots, and replicas within the same cluster. Data in transit is secured using SSL with AES-256 encryption.
- **Automatic backups and point-in-time restore**: Aurora provides automatic, continuous, incremental backups, allowing point-in-time recovery for your instance. You can restore your database to any specific second during your retention period, up to the last five minutes. The automatic backup retention period can be configured to up to 35 days. Backups are stored in Amazon S3, designed for 99.999999999% durability, and have no impact on database performance.
- **Multi-AZ deployments with Aurora Replicas**: Aurora supports creating up to 15 read replicas across three AZs. In the event of an instance failure, Aurora automatically fails over to one of these replicas to maintain availability. If no replicas are provisioned, Aurora attempts to create a new DB instance automatically. This multi-AZ deployment enhances fault tolerance and ensures high availability.
- **Compute scaling**: You can scale the compute resources of your Aurora instances up or down using the Amazon RDS APIs or the AWS Management Console. Compute scaling operations typically complete in a few minutes, allowing you to adjust resources to match workload demands efficiently.

- **Storage Auto-Scaling**: Aurora automatically scales your database storage in 10 GB increments, up to a maximum of 128 TB, as your storage needs grow. This eliminates the need to provision excess storage in advance, ensuring cost-effectiveness and flexibility.
- **Fault-tolerant and self-healing storage**: Aurora's storage is designed for high durability and availability. Each 10 GB chunk of your database volume is replicated six times across three AZs. The system can handle the loss of up to two copies without affecting write availability and up to three copies without affecting read availability. Aurora's storage is self-healing, continuously scanning for errors and automatically repairing them.
- **Network isolation**: Aurora operates within an Amazon **Virtual Private Cloud (VPC)**, allowing you to isolate your database in your own virtual network. You can connect to your on-premises IT infrastructure via encrypted IPsec VPNs and manage firewall configurations through Amazon RDS to control network access to your DB instances.
- **Monitoring and metrics**: Aurora integrates with Amazon CloudWatch to provide monitoring of over 20 key operational metrics, including compute, memory, storage, query throughput, cache hit ratio, and active connections. For more detailed insights, Enhanced Monitoring gathers metrics from the operating system instance, and Amazon RDS Performance Insights offers a dashboard for visualizing database load and detecting performance issues.
- **Governance**: AWS CloudTrail records and documents account activity across your AWS infrastructure, providing oversight of storage, analysis, and corrective actions. This helps ensure compliance with regulations such as SOC, PCI, and HIPAA by capturing and unifying user activity and API usage across AWS Regions and accounts in a centralized, controlled environment.
- **Amazon Aurora Machine Learning**: Aurora integrates with AWS machine learning services, allowing you to incorporate ML predictions into your applications using SQL. This provides a straightforward, optimized, and secure integration between Aurora and AWS ML services without the need for custom integrations or data movement.
- **Babelfish for Aurora PostgreSQL**: Babelfish enables seamless migration of applications from Microsoft SQL Server to Amazon Aurora PostgreSQL. It provides compatibility with the T-SQL language, allowing existing SQL Server applications to run on Aurora with minimal changes. This feature simplifies the transition process for businesses looking to leverage the scalability and cost-effectiveness of AWS while retaining their SQL Server-based applications.

- **Aurora PostgreSQL Limitless Database**: In October 2024, Amazon announced the general availability of Aurora PostgreSQL Limitless Database. This feature enables massive horizontal scaling for write throughput and storage by distributing workloads across multiple Aurora instances, all while using standard PostgreSQL queries and syntax.

These features collectively enhance Amazon Aurora's performance, scalability, availability, and ease of use, making it a robust choice for modern relational database needs.

Enterprise use cases for Amazon Aurora span multiple industries. Here are examples of some of the key use cases where Amazon Aurora is an excellent fit, along with specific customer references for each:

- **Revamp corporate applications**: Ensure high availability and performance of enterprise applications, including CRM, ERP, supply chain, and billing applications.
- **Build a Software-as-a-Service (SaaS) application**: Ensure flexible instance and storage scaling to support dependable, high-performing, and multi-tenant SaaS applications. Amazon Aurora is a good choice for building a SaaS application, as it provides the scalability, performance, availability, and security features that are essential for successful SaaS applications. Amazon Aurora automatically creates and maintains multiple replicas of your data, providing high availability and failover capabilities. This ensures that your SaaS application is always available, even in the event of an outage or failure. Amazon Aurora provides several security features, such as encryption at rest and in transit, to help protect your data and ensure compliance with industry standards and regulations.
- **Deploy globally distributed applications**: Achieve multi-region scalability and resilience for internet-scale applications, such as mobile games, social media apps, and online services, with Aurora's flexible instance and storage scaling. To meet high read or write requirements, databases are often split across multiple instances, but this can lead to over-provisioning or under-provisioning, resulting in increased costs or limited scalability. Aurora Serverless solves this problem by automatically scaling the capacity of multiple Aurora instances based on the application's needs, allowing for efficient scaling of databases and enabling the deployment of globally distributed applications. This can provide several benefits, including cost savings, flexibility, and simplicity.
- **Variable and unpredictable workloads**: If you run an infrequently used application where you need to provision for peaks, it will require you to pay for unused resources. A surge in traffic can also be mitigated through the automatic scaling of Aurora Serverless. You will not need to manage or upsize your servers manually. You need to set a min/max capacity unit setting and allow Aurora to scale to meet the load.

As AWS continues updating its Aurora database engine, you can refer to their update page for the latest information: `https://docs.aws.amazon.com/AmazonRDS/latest/AuroraUserGuide/AuroraMySQL.Updates.html`. Recently, AWS launched Amazon Aurora DSQL, the fastest serverless distributed SQL database for always-available applications. Let's learn more details about Aurora DSQL.

Amazon Aurora Distributed SQL (DSQL)

AWS launched Amazon Aurora DSQL in December 2024. DSQL is a serverless distributed SQL database designed for always-available applications. It offers unlimited scale, high availability, and zero infrastructure management. It can handle any workload demand without sharding or instance upgrades. It has an active-active distributed architecture for 99.99% availability in single-Region configurations and 99.999% in multi-Region configurations. Its serverless design eliminates operational burdens. Aurora DSQL is PostgreSQL-compatible, enabling rapid application development. It offers single-region clusters with active-active configuration across three AZs and multi-region clusters for improved availability. It provides strong data consistency, automated failover recovery, and supports ACID transactions. Aurora DSQL scales independently and supports common PostgreSQL drivers and tools. It enhances security with declarative controls, IAM integration, and token-based authentication. It uses optimistic concurrency control for efficient transaction handling.

The following diagram illustrates the architecture of an application using an Aurora DSQL multi-Region cluster.

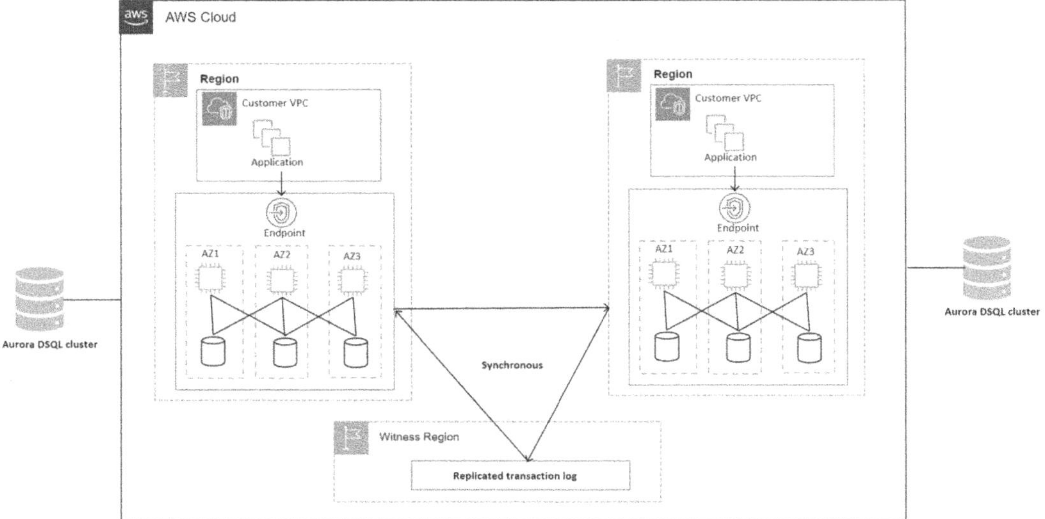

Figure 7.3: Aurora DSQL multi-Region cluster

As shown in the preceding diagram, when you create a multi-Region cluster in Amazon Aurora DSQL, it creates another cluster in a different AWS Region and links them together. This ensures that committed transactions are replicated across the linked Regions, providing strongly consistent reads and writes from any linked cluster. Each linked cluster has its own Regional endpoint.

Aurora DSQL synchronously replicates writes across the linked Regions, ensuring data consistency and availability. A third Region acts as a witness Region, which doesn't have a cluster or an associated endpoint. Instead, it stores a limited window of encrypted transaction logs from the linked clusters.

The witness Region plays a crucial role in providing multi-Region durability and availability for Aurora DSQL. It helps maintain data consistency and enables fast failover in case of a Regional outage or failure. This architecture ensures high availability and data durability for mission-critical applications.

Amazon RDS Proxy works together with Aurora to enhance database efficiency and application scalability by enabling applications to share and pool connections established with the database. Let's learn more details about RDS Proxy.

Amazon RDS Proxy

Amazon RDS Proxy is a service that acts as a database proxy for Amazon RDS. It is fully managed by AWS and helps to increase the scalability and resilience of applications in the face of database failures, while enhancing the security of database traffic. RDS Proxy sits between your application and your database and automatically routes database traffic to the appropriate RDS instances, but it comes with additional costs. However, RDS Proxy provides several benefits, including the following:

- **Improved scalability**: RDS Proxy automatically scales to handle a large number of concurrent connections, making it easier for your application to scale.
- **Better resilience to database failures**: RDS Proxy can automatically fail over to a standby replica if the primary database instance becomes unavailable, reducing downtime and improving availability.
- **Enhanced security**: RDS Proxy can authenticate and authorize incoming connections, helping to prevent unauthorized access to your database. It can also encrypt data in transit, providing an extra security measure for your data.

The following diagram shows an Amazon EC2 web server provisioned with an Aurora database, where database passwords are managed by AWS Secrets Manager. Aurora put across 2 AZs to achieve high availability, where AZ1 hosts Aurora's primary database while AZ2 has the Aurora read replica.

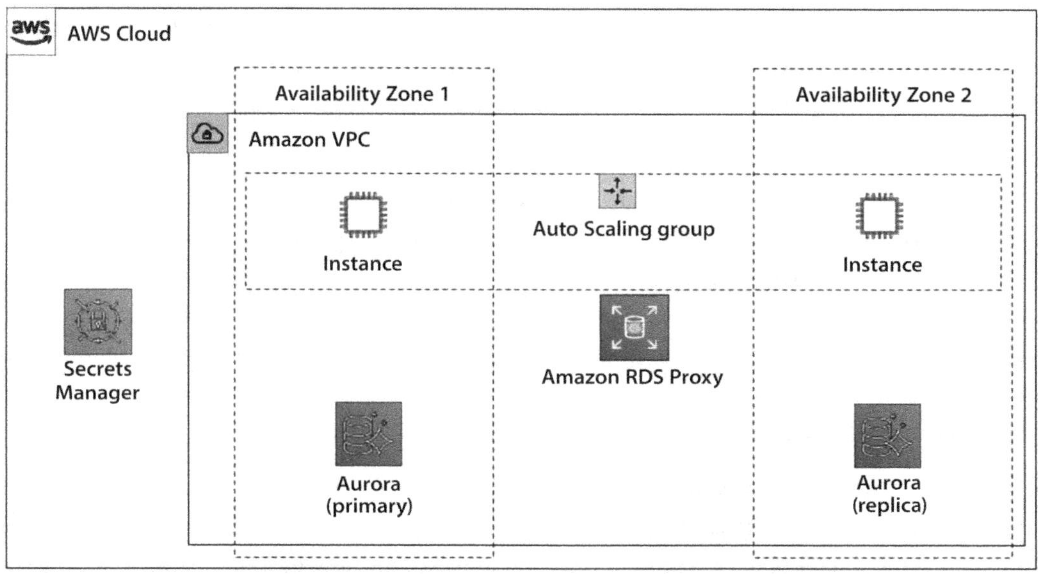

Figure 7.4: Amazon Aurora's high availability with RDS Proxy

With Amazon RDS Proxy, existing application connections are preserved during a failover. Only transactions that are actively processing or transmitting data at the moment of the failover may experience a brief disruption. Meanwhile, the proxy continues to accept new connection requests, queuing them temporarily and automatically forwarding them to the database once it becomes available again.

Amazon RDS Proxy is a useful tool for improving the performance, availability, and security of your database-powered applications. It is fully managed, so you don't have to worry about the underlying infrastructure, and it can help make your applications more scalable, resilient, and secure. You can learn more about RDS Proxy by visiting the AWS page: `https://aws.amazon.com/rds/proxy/`. For high-connection, bursty workloads (e.g., Lambda-heavy or SaaS apps), the savings from avoiding DB over-provisioning usually outweigh the proxy costs.

High availability and performance are a database's most essential and tricky parts. But this problem can be solved in an intelligent way using machine learning. Let's look at Amazon DevOps Guru to help with database performance issues using ML.

Enhancing database performance with Amazon DevOps Guru for RDS

Managing database performance is often complex, especially when you are dealing with high availability, unpredictable workloads, and operational issues. Amazon DevOps Guru for RDS helps simplify this by using ML to continuously monitor your Amazon RDS databases, detect anomalies, and recommend solutions before they become major problems. This proactive tool is designed to enhance database performance while minimizing the need for manual intervention.

With automated anomaly detection, DevOps Guru for RDS identifies unusual behavior in your database such as performance slowdowns, resource bottlenecks, or inefficient SQL queries. Once a problem is detected, it doesn't just alert you, it also provides actionable recommendations so you can fix the issue quickly. For example, if your database is experiencing a spike in read latency due to a sudden query surge, DevOps Guru might suggest tuning indexes or increasing instance capacity. It also offers root cause analysis, helping your team save time by pointing directly to the source of the issue. Since it integrates with RDS performance metrics and logs, it gives you a clear and centralized view of your database health.

By using Amazon DevOps Guru for RDS, you not only improve the reliability and responsiveness of your database but also reduce the operational burden on your engineering teams. It's especially helpful for companies looking to scale, automate operations, and ensure a smooth user experience with minimal downtime or disruption.

Enhancing Amazon RDS with machine learning and generative AI tools

Amazon RDS is evolving beyond traditional database capabilities by integrating ML and GenAI tools, making it smarter, faster, and more automated. These innovations help you build more intelligent applications and simplify complex data operations without moving data across services.

One key advancement is the integration of Amazon Aurora with AWS ML services. This allows you to run ML models directly within your SQL queries, for example, predicting customer churn or detecting fraudulent transactions without exporting data to an external service. You can call services such as Amazon SageMaker or Amazon Comprehend right from the database layer, which means faster, real-time insights with lower complexity.

Another important feature is the `pgvector` extension in Amazon Aurora PostgreSQL-Compatible Edition. This lets you store and index vector embeddings, which is especially useful for GenAI applications such as recommendation systems, similarity matching, or chatbot queries. If you're building an AI-driven search engine or a personalized content app, this extension enables fast and accurate vector searches natively in the database.

Amazon RDS also supports zero-ETL analytics, giving you near real-time access to transactional data for dashboards, ML models, or business reports without needing complex pipelines. This helps teams react quickly to changing data, making your operations more agile and your insights more current.

To simplify database migration, AWS DMS Schema Conversion now uses generative AI to provide intelligent code recommendations. Whether you're moving from Oracle to PostgreSQL or SQL Server to Aurora, this feature speeds up conversions and reduces manual work, helping you modernize databases more easily.

These enhancements position Amazon RDS as more than just a relational database; it's becoming an intelligent data platform, enabling you to innovate with ML, analytics, and GenAI directly within your cloud database environment. Now, let's shift focus and explore how AWS supports NoSQL databases for modern applications.

AWS NoSQL databases

When it comes to NoSQL databases, there are two main categories to understand: key-value and document databases, which can sometimes be confusing:

- Key-value databases are designed for high throughput, low latency, fast reads and writes, and limitless scalability.
- Document databases, on the other hand, store data as documents and allow querying based on any attribute.

These two types are closely related as both rely on keys pointing to values. The key difference is that in document databases, the stored value (document) is transparent and can be indexed for easy retrieval, while in key-value databases, the stored value is opaque, meaning it cannot be scanned, indexed, or accessed without its key. To retrieve a value in a key-value database without a key would require a full table scan.

Key-value databases are straightforward and easy to use, often considered the simplest in the NoSQL world. They support three basic operations:

- Retrieve a value using a key
- Insert or update a value using a key
- Delete a value using a key

Values are typically stored as **Binary Large Objects (BLOBs)**, and the database does not analyze or index the content. Data access is highly performant and scalable since it relies entirely on the key. However, this strength is also a limitation: key-value databases do not support filtering or full table scans effectively. They often use a hash table pattern to store keys, with no column-type relationships, which simplifies implementation.

AWS offers Amazon DynamoDB as its key-value database, providing exceptional scalability, low latency, and simplicity for applications requiring high-speed data access.

However, if you search NoSQL in the AWS console, the following choices will appear:

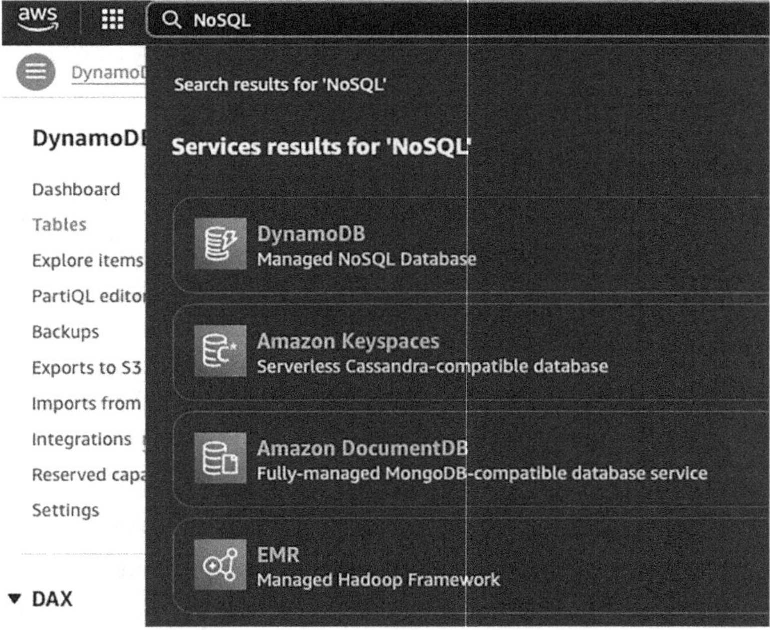

Figure 7.5: NoSQL database choices in AWS

The preceding screenshot shows the **AWS Management Console** search results for the keyword **NoSQL**, highlighting AWS services that support NoSQL database workloads. NoSQL databases are designed to handle large volumes of unstructured or semi-structured data with flexible schema and horizontal scalability that is ideal for modern, high-performance applications.

Here are the services listed:

- **DynamoDB**: A fully managed NoSQL key-value and document database that delivers single-digit millisecond performance at any scale. It's widely used for mobile, gaming, IoT, and real-time web applications. It supports automatic scaling, backup and restore, and in-memory caching (DAX).
- **Amazon DocumentDB (with MongoDB compatibility)**: A fully managed document database service that supports MongoDB workloads. It's ideal for applications that require flexible schema and JSON-like document structures, such as content management systems or catalogs.
- **Amazon Keyspaces (for Apache Cassandra)**: A serverless, scalable, and highly available NoSQL database service compatible with Apache Cassandra. It's great for developers familiar with Cassandra's data model who want a fully managed experience without worrying about infrastructure.
- **Amazon EMR (Elastic MapReduce)**: Though not a NoSQL database itself, EMR is a managed big data platform that supports **Apache Hadoop**, **HBase**, and other NoSQL tools. It enables distributed data processing and can be used for analytical processing over large datasets. You will learn details about EMR in *Chapter 10, Data Engineering and Big Data Analytics in AWS*.

These services offer AWS customers a wide range of NoSQL options depending on the data model and workload type, allowing you to choose the right tool based on performance, scalability, and operational needs. Now, let's explore DynamoDB further.

Amazon DynamoDB

In July 2024, during Amazon's Prime Day event, Amazon DynamoDB played a crucial role in managing the massive influx of customer activity. Over the course of the two-day event, DynamoDB handled tens of trillions of API calls, maintaining high availability and delivering single-digit millisecond response times. At its peak, DynamoDB processed an astonishing 146 million requests per second, underscoring its capacity to scale seamlessly and support significant surges in demand. You can read more details in AWS blogs: `https://aws.amazon.com/blogs/aws/how-aws-powered-prime-day-2024-for-record-breaking-sales/`.

Amazon DynamoDB is a fully managed, serverless NoSQL database service designed to provide consistent single-digit millisecond performance at any scale. It supports both key-value and document data models, offering flexibility in data storage and retrieval. DynamoDB is capable of handling over 10 trillion requests per day and can support exceeding multi-million requests per second, making it ideal for internet-scale applications.

Here are a few key features and benefits:

- **Managed service**: DynamoDB automates tasks such as hardware provisioning, setup, configuration, replication, software patching, and scaling, reducing the operational burden on users.
- **Multi-Region, multi-active replication**: With global tables, DynamoDB provides multi-Region, fully replicated tables for low-latency data access and improved fault tolerance. It offers up to 99.999% availability, ensuring high resilience for critical applications.
- **Flexible data modeling**: DynamoDB supports both key-value and document data structures, allowing for flexible schema designs that can evolve over time without requiring schema migrations.
- **Security**: Integration with AWS IAM enables fine-grained access control, while AWS KMS provides encryption for data at rest. DynamoDB encrypts all data by default, enhancing security for sensitive information.
- **In-memory caching: DynamoDB Accelerator (DAX)** is a fully managed caching service that delivers microsecond response times for read-intensive workloads, offering performance improvements up to 10 times faster than standard DynamoDB queries.
- **Time to Live (TTL)**: This feature allows for automatic deletion of expired items based on a specified timestamp attribute, which is useful for managing temporary data and reducing storage costs.
- **Cost-effective pricing**: DynamoDB offers a pay-per-use pricing model with no minimum fees or setup costs. Users can choose between on-demand and provisioned capacity modes to optimize costs based on their application's traffic patterns.
- **DynamoDB Streams**: This feature captures a time-ordered sequence of item-level modifications in a table, enabling real-time data processing and integration with other AWS services for analytics, archiving, and event-driven architectures.
- **Backup and restore**: DynamoDB provides seamless backup and restore capabilities, including **point-in-time recovery (PITR)**, which safeguards against accidental writes or deletions and allows the restoration of tables to a specified time within the backup retention period.

Amazon DynamoDB introduced several features enhancing its integration with ML and generative AI applications:

- **Zero-ETL integration with Amazon Redshift**: Launched in October 2024, this feature enables seamless data movement from DynamoDB tables to Amazon Redshift without manual **extract, transform, and load (ETL)** processes. Amazon Redshift is a petabyte-scale data warehouse in AWS, which you will learn about in detail later, in *Chapter 10, Data Engineering and Big Data Analytics in AWS*. This feature facilitates efficient, incremental updates, allowing for advanced analytics and ML model training on data replicated from DynamoDB.
- **Zero-ETL integration with Amazon OpenSearch Service**: Launched in November 2023, this integration allows for automatic replication and transformation of DynamoDB data into Amazon OpenSearch Service. It supports advanced search capabilities, including full-text and vector search, which are beneficial for ML applications such as recommendation systems and natural language processing tasks.

DynamoDB's combination of performance, scalability, and comprehensive feature set makes it a compelling choice for developers building modern applications that require reliable and efficient data management.

Defining a DynamoDB table

DynamoDB is a table-based database. When creating a table, you can specify at least three components:

- **Keys**: DynamoDB tables use a primary key to uniquely identify each item. This primary key can be either of the following:
    - **Partition key**: A single attribute used to partition data
    - **Composite key**: Consists of a partition key and a sort key, allowing for more complex data retrieval scenarios
- **Write Capacity Unit (WCU)**: One WCU represents one write per second for an item up to 1 KB in size. For items larger than 1 KB, additional WCUs are required. For example, writing a 2 KB item consumes 2 WCUs.
- **Read Capacity Unit (RCU)**: One RCU represents one strongly consistent read per second for an item up to 4 KB in size, and eventually consistent reads of 0.5 RCU per 4 KB. For items larger than 4 KB, additional RCUs are required. For example, reading an 8 KB item with strong consistency consumes 2 RCUs.

The size of the table automatically increases as you add more items. There is a hard limit for item size of 400 KB. As the size increases, the table is partitioned automatically for you. The size and provisioning capacity of the table are equally distributed for all partitions.

As shown in the following diagram, the data is stored in tables; you can think of a table as the database, and within the table, you have items.

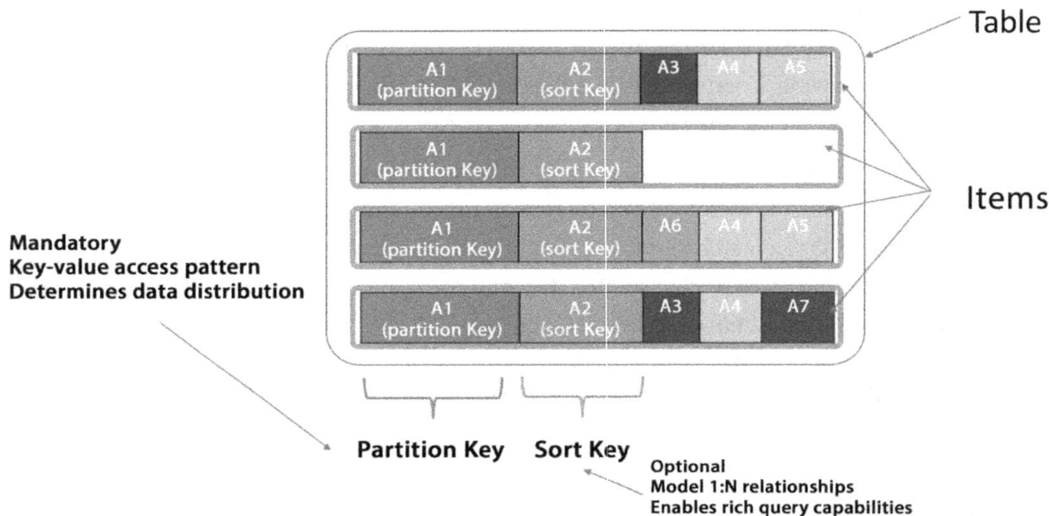

Figure 7.6: DynamoDB table with partition and sort key

As shown in the preceding diagram, the first item has five attributes, and the next item has only two. As more items are added to the table in DynamoDB, it becomes apparent that attributes can differ between items, and each item can have a unique set of attributes. Additionally, the primary key or partition key can be observed, which uniquely identifies each item and determines how the data is partitioned and stored. The partition key is required, while the sort key is optional but useful for establishing one-to-many relationships and facilitating in-range queries.

Sometimes you need to query data using the primary key, and sometimes you need to query by an attribute that is not your primary/secondary key or sort key. To tackle this issue, DynamoDB provides two kinds of indexes:

- **Local Secondary Index (LSI)**: Let's say you want to find out all fulfilled orders. You would have to query for all orders and then look for fulfilled ones in the results, which is not very efficient with large tables. But you have LSIs to help you out. You can create an LSI with the same primary key (`order_ID`) and a different secondary key (`fulfilled`).

Now your query can be based on the key of the LSI. This is fast and efficient. The LSI is located on the same partition as the item in the table, ensuring consistency. Whenever an item is updated, the corresponding LSI is also updated and acknowledged.

The same primary key is used to partition both the LSI and the parent table, even though the parent table can have a different sort key. In the index, you can choose to have just the keys or other attributes projected or include all attributes – depending on what attributes you want to be returned with the query. There is a limit of 10 GB on LSI storage as it uses the partition storage of the original table.

- **Global Secondary Index (GSI)**: A GSI is an extension of the concept of indexes, allowing for more complex queries with various attributes as query criteria. In some cases, using the existing primary/sort key does not suffice. To address this, you can define a GSI as a parallel or secondary table with a partition key that is different from the original table and an alternate sort key. When creating a GSI, you must specify the expected workload for read and write capacity units. Similar to an LSI, you can choose to have just the keys or other attributes projected or include all attributes – depending on what attributes you want to be returned with the query.

The following are the key differences between an LSI and a GSI:

Local Secondary Index (LSI)	Global Secondary Index (GSI)
You have to define an LSI upfront, and it can be created during table creation only.	You can define a GSI at any time, even after table creation.
An LSI shares WCU/RCU with the main table, so you must have enough read/write capacity to accommodate the LSI's needs.	GSI WCU/RCU is independent of the table, so it can scale without impacting the main table.
LSI size is a maximum of 10 GB in sync with the primary table partition, which is limited to 10 GB per partition.	As a GSI is independent of the main table, it has no size limits.
You can create a maximum of 5 LSIs.	You can create up to 20 GSIs.
As LSIs tie up to the main table, they offer "strong consistency," which means current access to the most up-to-date data.	GSIs offer "eventual consistency," which means there may be a slight lag on data updates, which lowers the chances of you getting stable data.

Table 7.1: DynamoDB Index – LSI versus GSI

So, you may ask when to use an LSI versus a GSI. In a nutshell, a GSI is more flexible. An LSI is useful when you want to query data based on an alternate sort key within the same partition key as the base table. It allows you to perform fast, efficient queries with minimal latency, and is best suited for scenarios where you know the specific queries that will be performed on your data. A GSI, on the other hand, allows you to query data based on attributes that are not part of the primary key or sort key of the base table. It's useful when you want to perform ad hoc queries on different attributes of the data or when you need to support multiple access patterns. A GSI can be used to scale read queries beyond the capacity of the base table and can also be used to query data across partitions.

In general, if your data size is small enough, and you only need to query data based on a different sort key within the same partition key, you should use an LSI. If your data size is larger, or you need to query data based on attributes that are not part of the primary key or sort key, you should use a GSI. However, keep in mind that a GSI comes with some additional cost and complexity in terms of provisioned throughput, index maintenance, and eventual consistency.

If an item collection's data size exceeds 10 GB, the only option is to use a GSI, as an LSI limits the data size in a particular partition. If eventual consistency is acceptable for your use case, a GSI can be used as it is suitable for 99% of scenarios.

DynamoDB is very useful in designing serverless event-driven architecture. You can capture an item-level data change – for example, `putItem`, `updateItem`, and `delete` – by using DynamoDB Streams. You can learn more about Amazon DynamoDB by visiting the AWS page: `https://aws.amazon.com/dynamodb/`.

You may want a more sophisticated database when storing JSON documents for indexing and fast search. Let's learn about the AWS document database offering.

Amazon DocumentDB

In this section, let's talk about Amazon DocumentDB, *"a fully managed MongoDB-compatible database service designed from the ground up to be fast, scalable, and highly available"*. DocumentDB is a purpose-built document database engineered for the cloud that provides millions of requests per second with millisecond latency and can scale out to 15 read replicas in minutes. It is compatible with MongoDB 3.6, 4.0, and 5.0 APIs, allowing applications designed for MongoDB to work with DocumentDB with minimal changes. It is fully managed by AWS, eliminating the need for hardware provisioning. It also provides automatic patching, quick setup, and built-in security features.

Recent updates include the general availability of vector search capabilities, enabling efficient storage, indexing, and searching of millions of vectors with millisecond response times. Additionally, Amazon DocumentDB now supports Global Cluster Switchover, allowing seamless changes to your global cluster's primary AWS Region.

If you look at the evolution of document databases, what was the need for document databases in this new world? At some point, JSON became the de facto standard for data interchange and data modeling within applications. Using JSON in an application and then trying to map JSON to relational databases introduced friction and complication.

Object Relational Mappers (ORMs) were created to help with this friction, but there were complications with performance and functionality. A crop of document databases popped up to solve the problem. The need for DocumentDB is primarily driven by the following reasons:

- Data is stored in documents that are in a JSON-like format, and these documents are considered as first-class objects within the database. Unlike traditional databases, where documents are stored as values or data types, in DocumentDB, documents are the key design point of the database.
- Document databases offer flexible schemas, making it easy to represent hierarchical and semi-structured data. Additionally, powerful indexing capabilities make querying such documents much faster.
- Documents naturally map to object-oriented programming, which simplifies the flow of data between your application and the database.
- Document databases come with expressive query languages that are specifically built for handling documents. These query languages enable ad hoc queries and aggregations across documents, making it easier to extract insights from data.

Let's take user profiles as an example. Suppose Jane Doe starts playing a new game called ExplodingSnails. In a document database, you can easily add this new information to her profile without modifying schemas or creating new tables. You simply update the document by adding a new field. Similarly, if Jane earns promotions or achievements, you can store them as an array within the same document. This flexibility allows developers to evolve applications and quickly build new features.

In document databases, records contain structured or semi-structured values, referred to as documents. These documents are typically stored using formats such as **Extensible Markup Language** (**XML**), **JavaScript Object Notation** (**JSON**), or **Binary JavaScript Object Notation** (**BSON**). The document model makes it easier to handle hierarchical and nested data structures, which are common in modern applications. Document databases are well-suited for the following:

- **Content Management Systems (CMSs)**: Managing articles, images, and metadata efficiently
- **E-commerce applications**: Storing product catalogs and customer profiles with dynamic attributes
- **Analytics**: Handling semi-structured logs and event-driven data
- **Blogging platforms**: Managing posts, comments, and user-generated content

While document databases provide flexibility, they may not be ideal for the following:

- **Complex queries or table joins**: If your application requires frequent joins across multiple datasets, relational databases may perform better
- **OLTP applications**: Use relational databases for high-volume transactional workloads that require ACID compliance and strict consistency

Understanding these use cases can help you choose the right database for your application based on performance, flexibility, and scalability needs.

Advantages of Amazon DocumentDB

Amazon DocumentDB offers several advantages over traditional relational databases, making it an excellent choice for modern applications:

- **On-demand instance pricing**: You can pay by the hour without any upfront fees or long-term commitments. This eliminates the complexity of capacity planning and is ideal for short-lived workloads, development, and testing environments.
- **MongoDB compatibility**: Amazon DocumentDB is compatible with MongoDB, allowing you to use existing MongoDB applications and tools with minimal modifications. It supports MongoDB 3.6, 4.0, and 5.0 APIs, ensuring seamless integration and migration from self-managed MongoDB clusters. This lets developers take advantage of DocumentDB's high availability, scalability, and security without rewriting their applications.

- **Migration support**: AWS provides **Database Migration Service (DMS)** to help migrate MongoDB databases from on-premises or Amazon EC2 to DocumentDB with minimal downtime. AWS offers up to six months of free migration per instance when using DMS. Whether migrating from a MongoDB replica set or a sharded cluster, DMS simplifies the process.
- **Flexible schema**: Amazon DocumentDB has a schema-less design, meaning documents can have varying structures. This is useful for storing complex or hierarchical data and for applications where data structures change frequently without requiring schema modifications.
- **High performance**: DocumentDB is optimized for speed, making it well-suited for applications that require fast read and write operations. With millisecond response times, it efficiently handles high-throughput workloads.
- **Scalability**: DocumentDB is horizontally scalable, meaning it can automatically expand to handle large datasets and support thousands of concurrent users. You can scale read capacity by adding up to 15 read replicas, ensuring seamless performance as demand grows.
- **Easy querying**: DocumentDB provides powerful and flexible query languages, making it easy to retrieve and manipulate data. It supports aggregation, filtering, indexing, and full-text search to help developers build intelligent applications efficiently.

With these advantages, Amazon DocumentDB is a powerful, managed document database designed to meet the needs of modern cloud-native applications.

You can learn more about Amazon DocumentDB by visiting the AWS page: `https://aws.amazon.com/documentdb/`.

Amazon DynamoDB versus Amazon DocumentDB

Amazon DynamoDB and DocumentDB are both NoSQL database services provided by AWS, but they serve different use cases. Following is a side-by-side comparison to help you choose the right one for your application.

Feature	Amazon DynamoDB	Amazon DocumentDB
Database Type	Key-value and wide-column store (NoSQL)	Document-oriented database (NoSQL)
Data Model	Table-based with partition key and sort key	JSON-like documents stored in collections

Schema Flexibility	Schema-less but optimized for key-value pairs	Fully flexible schema supporting hierarchical and nested data
Best For	High-performance key-value access, IoT, real-time analytics	Applications needing MongoDB compatibility, content management, catalogs
Query Language	PartiQL (SQL-like queries), API calls	MongoDB Query Language (MQL)
Indexes	Supports primary keys, LSIs, and GSIs	Supports indexes for querying JSON documents
Read/Write Consistency	Offers eventual and strong consistency	Eventual consistency by default, strong consistency optional
Scalability	Fully serverless, auto-scales to handle millions of requests per second	Horizontally scalable with up to 15 read replicas
Performance	Optimized for ultra-low latency, sub-millisecond responses	Designed for millisecond latency, supports large query loads
Use Cases	Real-time transactions, gaming leaderboards, IoT, mobile backends	Content management, product catalogs, user profiles, analytics
Pricing Model	On-demand (pay-per-request) or provisioned mode	Pay-per-instance (similar to RDS)
Replication and Availability	Multi-AZ, global tables for cross-region replication	Multi-AZ, up to 15 read replicas
Backup and Restore	Point-in-time recovery, on-demand backups	Automated backups, manual snapshots

Table 7.2: Amazon DynamoDB and DocumentDB comparison

You should choose DynamoDB if you need a highly scalable key-value store that delivers low latency and automatic scaling, making it ideal for real-time applications and event-driven workloads. On the other hand, if your application requires a document-oriented database that seamlessly integrates with MongoDB, supports complex queries, and allows for a flexible schema, then DocumentDB is the better choice. The decision depends on whether your workload requires high-throughput key-value access or a document-based storage model with advanced querying capabilities.

Wide-column store databases

Wide-column databases can sometimes be referred to as column family databases. A wide-column database is a NoSQL database that can store petabyte-scale amounts of data. Its architecture relies on persistent, sparse matrix, multi-dimensional mapping using a tabular format. Wide-column databases are generally not relational.

When is it a good idea to use wide-column databases?

- Sensor logs and IoT information
- Geolocation data
- User preferences
- Reporting
- Time-series data
- Logging applications
- Many inserts, but not many updates
- Low latency requirements

When are wide-column databases not a good fit? They are good when the use case calls for ad hoc queries:

- Heavy requirements for joins
- High-level aggregations
- Requirements change frequently
- OLTP uses cases

Apache Cassandra is probably the most popular wide-column store implementation today. Its architecture allows deployments without single points of failure. It can be deployed across clusters and data centers.

Amazon Keyspaces (formerly Amazon Managed Apache Cassandra Service, or Amazon MCS) is a fully managed service that allows users to deploy Cassandra workloads. Let's learn more about it.

Amazon Keyspaces (for Apache Cassandra)

Amazon Keyspaces (formerly known as Amazon Cassandra) is a fully managed, scalable, and highly available NoSQL database service. NoSQL databases are a type of database that does not use the traditional table-based relational database model and is well-suited for applications that require fast, scalable access to large amounts of data.

Keyspaces is based on Apache Cassandra, an open source NoSQL database that is widely used for applications that require high performance, scalability, and availability. Keyspaces provides the same functionality as Cassandra, with the added benefits of being fully managed and integrated with other AWS services.

Keyspaces supports both table and **Cassandra Query Language (CQL)** APIs, making it easy to migrate existing Cassandra applications to Keyspaces. It also provides built-in security features, such as encryption at rest and network isolation, using Amazon VPC, and integrates seamlessly with other AWS services, such as Amazon EMR and Amazon SageMaker.

Servers are automatically spun up or brought down, and, as such, users are only charged for the servers Cassandra is using at any one time. Since AWS manages it, users of the service never have to provision, patch, or manage servers, and they don't have to install, configure, or tune software. Cassandra in AWS can be configured to support thousands of user requests per second.

Cassandra is a NoSQL database; as expected, it doesn't support SQL. The query language for Cassandra is CQL. The quickest method to interact with Apache Cassandra is using the CQL shell, which is called **cqlsh**. With cqlsh, you can create tables, insert data into the tables, and access the data via queries, among other operations.

Keyspaces supports the Cassandra CQL API. Because of this, the current code and drivers developed in Cassandra will work without changing the code. Using Amazon Keyspaces instead of just Apache Cassandra is as easy as modifying your database endpoint to point to an Amazon MCS service table.

In addition to Keyspaces being wide-column, the major difference from DynamoDB is that it supports composite partition keys and multiple clustering keys, which are not available in DynamoDB. However, DynamoDB has better connectivity with other AWS services, such as Athena, Kinesis, and Elasticsearch.

Keyspaces provides an SLA for 99.99% availability within an AWS Region. Encryption is enabled by default for tables, and tables are replicated three times in multiple AWS Availability Zones to ensure high availability. You can create continuous backups of tables with hundreds of terabytes of data with no effect on your application's performance, and recover data to any point in time within the last 35 days. You can learn more about Amazon Keyspaces by visiting the AWS page: `https://aws.amazon.com/keyspaces/`.

If you want sub-millisecond performance, you need your data in memory. Let's learn about in-memory databases.

In-memory databases

Studies have shown that if your site is slow, even for just a few seconds, you will lose customers. A slow site results in 90% of your customers leaving the site. 57% of those customers will purchase from a similar retailer, and 25% of them will never return. These statistics are from a report by Business News Daily (`https://www.businessnewsdaily.com/15160-slow-retail-websites-lose-customers.html`). Additionally, you will lose 53% of your mobile users if a page load takes longer than 3 seconds (`https://www.business.com/articles/website-page-speed-affects-behavior/`).

We're no longer in the world of thinking our users are okay with a few seconds of wait time. These are demanding times for services, and to keep up with demand, you need to ensure that users aren't waiting to purchase your service, products, and offerings to continue growing your business and user base. There is a direct link between customers being forced to wait and a loss of revenue.

Applications and databases have changed dramatically not only in the past 50 years but also just in the past 5. Where you might have had a few thousand users who could wait for a few seconds for an application to refresh, now you have microservices and IoT devices sending millions of requests per second across the globe that require immediate responses. These changes have caused the application and database world to rethink how data is stored and accessed. It's essential to use the right tool for the job. In-memory data stores are used when there is a need for maximum performance. This is achieved through extremely low latency per request and incredibly high throughput as you are caching data in memory, which helps to increase the performance by taking less time to read from the original database. Think of this as high-velocity data.

In-memory databases, or **IMDBs** for short, usually store the entire data in the main memory. Contrast this with databases that use a machine's RAM for optimization but do not store all the data simultaneously in primary memory and instead rely on disk storage. IMDBs generally perform better than disk-optimized databases because disk access is slower than direct memory access. In-memory operations are more straightforward and can be performed using fewer CPU cycles. In-memory data access reduces latency when querying, delivering faster and more consistent performance compared to accessing data from long-term storage. To get an idea of the difference in performance, in-memory operations are usually measured in nanoseconds, whereas operations that require disk access are usually measured in milliseconds.

Some use cases of in-memory databases are real-time analytics, chat apps, gaming leaderboards, and caching. AWS provides Amazon ElastiCache to fulfill in-memory data caching needs.

As shown in the following diagram, based on your *data access pattern*, you can use either **lazy caching** or **write-through**. In lazy caching, the cache engine checks whether the data is in the cache and, if not, gets it from the database and keeps it in the cache to serve future requests. Lazy caching is also called the **cache aside pattern.**

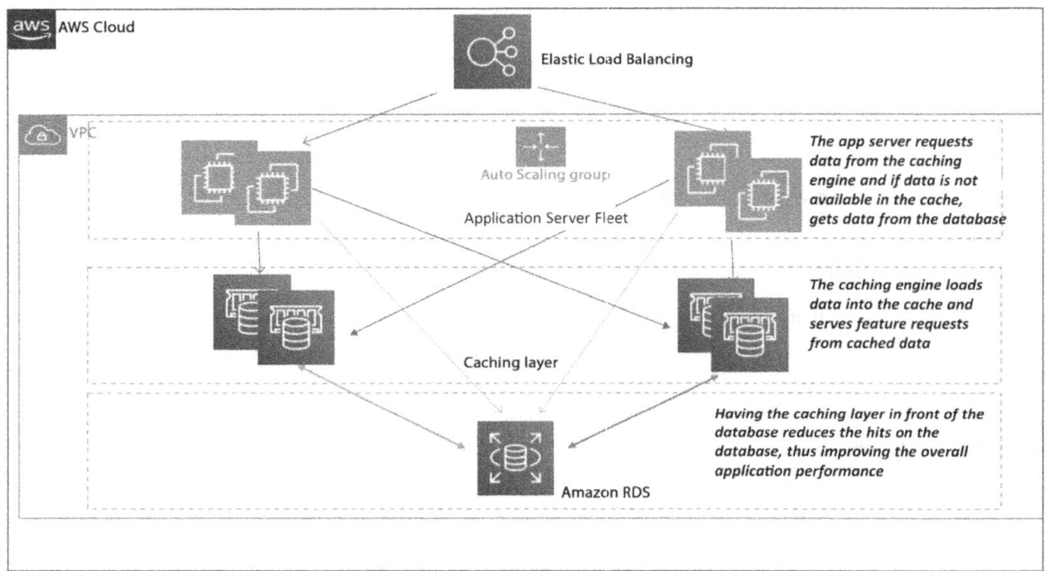

Figure 7.7: Application caching pattern architecture

You can see the caching flow in the preceding diagram, where the first app server sends a data request to the caching engine, which tries to load data from the cache. If data is not available in the cache, then the cache engine goes to the database and loads the required data into the cache.

Lazy caching, also known as cache-aside, works by first checking if the requested data is in the cache. If it's not there (a cache miss), the application fetches the data from the database, stores it in the cache, and returns it to the user. This approach is useful for read-heavy applications because it only loads data into the cache when it's needed. For example, an e-commerce website such as Zalando might use lazy caching to store frequently accessed product information after it's requested for the first time.

Write-through caching, on the other hand, stores data in the cache every time a write operation occurs. This means every time your application updates or inserts data into the database, the cache is also updated immediately. This ensures that the cache always has the most up-to-date data, reducing the chances of stale reads.

Write-through caching is beneficial when you have predictable read patterns and want to minimize cache misses, such as in applications with dashboards or recommendation engines that always show the most current data. For instance, a social media platform could use write-through caching to update user profiles and post feeds in real time to enhance the user experience.

Choosing between these caching strategies depends on your access pattern. If your reads are more frequent and less predictable, lazy caching helps reduce unnecessary cache loads. If consistency and real-time updates are more critical, write-through caching ensures data freshness across your application.

The Amazon MemoryDB and Amazon ElastiCache services are AWS-provided cache databases. But before coming to memory databases, let's learn about the industry's popular memory databases and how AWS supports them.

Redis versus Memcached: choosing the right in-memory database

Redis and Memcached are two of the most widely used in-memory data stores, both designed to provide high-speed caching and data retrieval. While both serve as excellent choices for improving application performance, they cater to different needs based on their capabilities and features. The following table provides a side-by-side comparison of Redis and Memcached to help determine which one best suits your requirements.

Feature	Redis	Memcached
Data Storage Type	Stores data as key-value pairs but supports advanced data types	Stores only simple key-value pairs
Data Structures	Supports strings, lists, sets, sorted sets, hashes, bitmaps, hyperloglogs, and geospatial data	Only string-based key-value pairs
Persistence	Supports Append-Only File (AOF) and Redis Database (RDB) snapshots	No persistence (data is lost on restart)
Performance	Slightly slower for simple caching due to extra features	Faster for simple key-value caching
Memory Efficiency	More memory-efficient for storing complex structures	More memory-efficient for storing large amounts of simple key-value data

Scalability	Supports clustering (horizontal scaling)	Scales only by adding nodes (no built-in clustering)
Replication	Built-in replication (primary-replica mode)	No built-in replication
Transactions	Supports transactions using `MULTI`/`EXEC` commands	No transaction support
Eviction Policies	More than 10 eviction policies for memory management	Supports Least Recently Used (LRU) eviction, but fewer policies than Redis
Pub/Sub Messaging	Supports publish/subscribe (Pub/Sub) messaging	Not supported
Use as Primary Database?	Can be used as a primary in-memory database	Primarily used as a cache only
Common Use Cases	Real-time leaderboards, session storage, message queues, analytics, machine learning feature stores	Web page caching, database query acceleration, session management

Table 7.3: Comparison of Redis and Memcached

When deciding between Redis and Memcached, the choice depends on your specific use case. Redis is the preferred option if you need an in-memory database with advanced data structures, persistence, replication, and clustering. It is well-suited for applications such as real-time leaderboards, message queues, session storage, and machine learning feature stores. On the other hand, Memcached is a better choice if your primary goal is a simple, high-performance caching system that speeds up database queries, web page loads, or API responses without requiring persistence or complex data structures.

Both Redis and Memcached are optimized for speed and scalability, but Redis offers more flexibility and features, making it suitable for a broader range of applications beyond basic caching. AWS provides Amazon MemoryDB and Amazon ElastiCache, two powerful in-memory database solutions designed to enhance application performance. Let's look at them.

Amazon MemoryDB versus Amazon ElastiCache

AWS offers two powerful in-memory database services, Amazon MemoryDB and Amazon ElastiCache, both designed to enhance application performance. These services leverage Redis's data structures and APIs, but they serve different use cases.

AWS introduced Amazon MemoryDB for Redis to address the increasing demand for a durable, high-performance in-memory database. Unlike traditional caching solutions, MemoryDB is designed to be a primary database, offering data durability, ultra-fast access, and full compatibility with Redis 6.2. It is particularly well-suited for modern microservices-based applications that require real-time processing. With MemoryDB, all data is stored in memory, ensuring microsecond read latency and single-digit millisecond write latency. This eliminates the need for a separate cache layer to achieve low-latency performance. If you want to explore more details, visit the AWS MemoryDB page: `https://aws.amazon.com/memorydb/`.

Amazon ElastiCache is an AWS-managed in-memory caching service that supports both Redis and Memcached. It is specifically designed to accelerate data access by caching frequently used data, reducing the need for repeated database queries. ElastiCache can work as a caching layer in front of a primary database or as a temporary data store in scenarios where data loss is acceptable. ElastiCache delivers microsecond latency for both reads and writes, making it ideal for caching application data, speeding up web applications, gaming leaderboards, and session storage. If you are looking for an in-memory cache to optimize your application's performance, visit the AWS ElastiCache page: `https://aws.amazon.com/elasticache/`.

Following is a comparison between Amazon MemoryDB and Amazon ElastiCache.

Feature	Amazon MemoryDB	Amazon ElastiCache
Primary Purpose	Durable in-memory database for microservices and real-time applications	In-memory cache to speed up database performance
Data Persistence	Data is durable across multiple Availability Zones	No built-in durability (data is lost on restart)
Use as Primary Database?	Yes, can serve as a primary database	Primarily used as a cache, not a primary database
Latency	Microsecond read latency, single-digit millisecond write latency	Microsecond read and write latency
Redis Compatibility	Fully compatible with Redis 6.2 APIs	Supports Redis and Memcached
Multi-AZ Support	Multi-AZ replication for high availability	Multi-AZ support available
Best Use Cases	Session stores, real-time analytics, caching with durability	Database caching, gaming leaderboards, session storage

Security & Compliance	Supports encryption, IAM, PCI-DSS, HIPAA, SOC compliance	Supports encryption, IAM, and compliance features
Scaling	Supports horizontal scaling with shards and vertical scaling with node upgrades	Auto-scaling based on demand
Cost Considerations	Higher cost due to durability and high availability	Lower cost since it is used for caching only

Table 7.4: Amazon MemoryDB versus Amazon ElastiCache

If you need an in-memory database that can function as a primary data store and provides durability, high availability, and microsecond latency, MemoryDB is the right choice. It is best suited to microservices, event-driven architectures, and applications needing ultra-low latency with data persistence.

If you are looking for a high-speed caching solution to accelerate database queries and application response times, ElastiCache is a better option. It works well for reducing database load, web application caching, gaming leaderboards, and session management where data loss is acceptable.

Both services provide fast in-memory data access, but MemoryDB is built for primary database durability, while ElastiCache is designed for temporary caching.

Graph databases

Graph databases are data stores that treat relationships between records as first-class citizens. In traditional databases, relationships are often an afterthought. In the case of relational databases, relationships are implicit and manifest themselves as foreign key relationships. In graph databases, relationships are explicit, significant, and optimized using graph database language; these relationships are called edges.

The following visual represents how entities are connected, querying relationships or analyzing behavior patterns in data-intensive applications using a graph database.

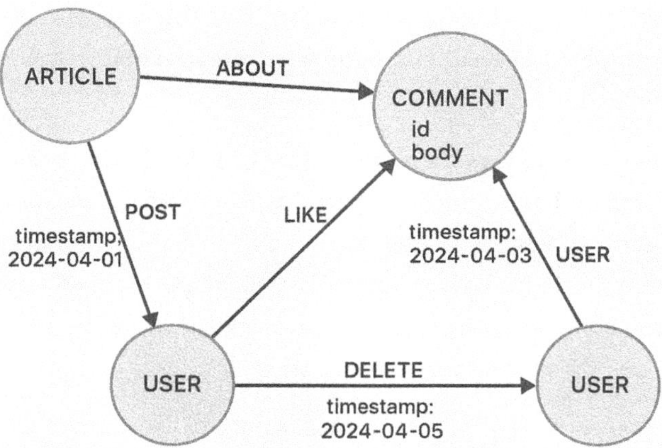

Figure 7.8: Graph database model

This diagram visualizes the relationships between entities such as **ARTICLE**, **COMMENT**, and **USER** using labeled nodes and directed edges. Each arrow (edge) represents a relationship between the nodes, and the timestamps show when each interaction occurred. This model is common in graph databases such as Amazon Neptune or Neo4j, and is often used for social networks, content management systems, or recommendation engines.

Here's what each part represents:

- **ARTICLE → USER (POST)**: A user posted an article on 2024-04-01
- **ARTICLE → COMMENT (ABOUT)**: A comment is associated with or about the article
- **USER → COMMENT (LIKE)**: A user liked the comment on 2024-04-03
- **USER → COMMENT (USER)**: Another user is the author of the comment
- **USER → USER (DELETE)**: One user deleted another user's content or possibly their profile on 2024-04-05

Each edge contains an action such as **POST**, **LIKE**, or **DELETE**, and some are timestamped to track when these interactions occurred. The **COMMENT** node contains data fields such as **id** and **body**, while the **USER** and **ARTICLE** nodes represent actors and content in the system.

In some aspects, graph databases are similar to NoSQL databases. They are also schema-less. For certain use cases, they offer much better data retrieval performance than traditional databases. As you can imagine, graph databases are particularly suited to use cases that place heavy importance on relationships among entities.

Accessing data nodes and edges in a graph database is highly efficient. It usually can occur in constant time. With graph databases, it is not uncommon to be able to traverse millions of edges per second.

Graph databases can handle nodes with many edges regardless of the dataset's number of nodes. You only need a pattern and an initial node to traverse a graph database. Graph databases can easily navigate the adjacent edges and nodes around an initial starting node while caching and aggregating data from the visited nodes and edges. As an example of a pattern and a starting point, you might have a database that contains ancestry information. In this case, the starting point might be you, and the pattern might be a parent.

So, in this case, the query would return the names of both of your parents. The following are the components of a graph database:

- **Nodes**: Nodes are elements or entities in a graph. They contain a series of properties, attributes, or key-value pairs. Nodes can be given tags, which constitute roles in the domain. Node labels can be employed to assign metadata (such as indices or constraints) to the nodes.
- **Edges**: Edges supply directed, named, and semantically significant connections between two nodes. An edge has a direction, a type, a start node, and an end node. Like a node, an edge can also have properties. In some situations, an edge can have quantitative properties, such as weight, cost, and strength. Due to the efficient way an edge is stored, two nodes can share edges regardless of the quantity or type without a performance penalty. Edges have a direction, but edges can be traversed efficiently in both directions.

The following diagram shows the relationship between **Follower** and **Influencer** in a social media application, where the nodes depict the entity type (**Follower** and **Influencer**) and the edge (**Influences**) shows their relationship with their level of influence as the property weight. Here, the level of influence is 100, which means **Follower** just started following **Influencer** and, with time, as they give more likes and views to the influencer's posts, their level could increase to 200, 300, or 400.

Figure 7.9: Example of a relationship

Two primary graph models are widely used. A property graph is a common name for an attributed, multi-relational graph. The leading property graph API is the open standard Apache TinkerPop™ project. It provides an imperative traversal language, called Gremlin, that can be used to write traversals on property graphs, and many open source and vendor implementations support it. You may opt for property graphs to represent relational models, and the Apache TinkerPop Gremlin traversal language could be a favorable option as it offers a method to navigate through property graphs. You might also like openCypher, an open source declarative query language for graphs, as it provides a familiar SQL-like structure to compose queries for graph data.

The second is the **Resource Description Framework** (**RDF**), standardized by the W3C in a set of standards collectively known as the Semantic Web. The SPARQL query language for RDF allows users to express declarative graph queries against RDF graph models. The RDF model is also a labeled, directed multi-graph, but it uses the concept of triples, subject, predicate, and object, to encode the graph. Now let's look at Amazon Neptune, which is Amazon's graph database service.

Amazon Neptune

Amazon Neptune is a fully managed graph database service designed to handle complex relationships between data. Unlike traditional relational databases, which store data in tables with rows and columns, Neptune uses a graph-based model with nodes, edges, and properties to represent relationships. This structure makes it well-suited for applications that require deep data connections, such as social networks, recommendation engines, and fraud detection systems.

Neptune supports two widely used graph models: **Property Graph** and **W3C's RDF Resource Description Framework (RDF)** standards. It integrates with graph query languages such as Gremlin (for property graphs) and SPARQL (for RDF graphs), enabling efficient data traversal and analysis. Gremlin allows users to perform complex graph queries and manipulations with ease, making it powerful for applications that require multi-hop relationships across datasets.

One of Neptune's key advantages is its high scalability and availability. It can handle billions of vertices and edges within a single graph while automatically scaling to meet application demands. Since it is fully managed, AWS takes care of infrastructure provisioning, patching, backup, and recovery, allowing developers to focus on building applications rather than managing the database. Some of the key use cases for Amazon Neptune include the following:

- **Social networks**: Store and analyze user connections, friend-of-friend relationships, and social interactions
- **Recommendation engines**: Model customer behavior and provide personalized product, movie, or content recommendations

- **Fraud detection**: Detect fraudulent transactions by analyzing connections between entities, such as financial transactions, IP addresses, and devices
- **Knowledge graphs**: Organize and retrieve information efficiently using structured relationships, often used in search engines and AI applications
- **Network and IT infrastructure analysis**: Monitor dependencies, detect anomalies, and optimize networks by mapping relationships between systems and services

Amazon Neptune has introduced several notable features and enhancements recently, particularly in the realm of AI and ML:

- **Neptune ML enhancements**: In 2023, Amazon Neptune expanded its machine learning capabilities through Neptune ML. This integration allows users to perform advanced graph machine-learning tasks, such as node classification and link prediction, directly within their graph databases. Notably, Neptune ML introduced support for text feature encoding using FastText and **Sentence BERT (SBERT)**, enabling more effective processing of textual data within graphs.
- **Engine version updates**: Neptune released multiple engine updates for improved performance: v1.2.1.0 in March 2023, v1.3.1.0 in March 2024, and v1.4.0.0 in November 2024. These updates introduced new features and improvements, including changes to parameter group formats and undo log handling. Users upgrading to these versions are advised to review the release notes for detailed information on modifications and potential impacts.
- **Neptune Analytics**: In November 2023, Amazon announced the general availability of Neptune Analytics, a new analytics database engine designed to expedite insights and trend identification in graph data. Neptune Analytics enables data scientists and developers to analyze graph data with tens of billions of connections in seconds, utilizing popular graph analytics algorithms for tasks such as ranking social influencers, detecting fraud groups, and identifying patterns in network activity.

These advancements reflect Amazon Neptune's commitment to integrating AI and ML capabilities, providing users with powerful tools to analyze and derive insights from complex graph data structures. To explore more about Amazon Neptune, visit the AWS Neptune page: `https://aws.amazon.com/neptune/`.

Data with timestamps often requires a specialized approach, especially for trend analysis, forecasting, and real-time monitoring. This is where time-series databases come into play. Let's explore their significance and how AWS provides solutions for storing and analyzing time-series data.

Time-series databases

A **time-series database** (**TSDB**) is a database specifically designed and optimized to store events. What is an event, you ask? It is an action that happens at a specific point in time. With events, it's not only important to track *what* happened but just as important to track *when* it happened. The unit of measure to use for the time depends on the use case. For some applications, it might be enough to know on what day the event happened. But for other applications, it might be required to keep track of the time down to the millisecond. Some examples of projects that might benefit from a TSDB are as follows:

- Performance monitoring
- Networking and infrastructure applications
- Adtech and clickstream processing
- Sensor data from IoT applications
- Event-driven applications
- Financial applications
- Log analysis
- Industrial telemetry data for equipment maintenance
- Other analytics projects

A TSDB is optimized to measure changes over time. Time series values can differ from other data types and require different optimization techniques.

Common operations in a TSDB are as follows:

- Millions of inserts from disparate sources, potentially per second
- Summarization of data for downstream analytics
- Access to individual events

TSDBs are ideally suited for storing and processing IoT data. Time-series data has the following properties (which might not be present with other data types):

- The order in which the events occur may be necessary
- Data is only inserted; it is not updated
- Queries have a time interval component in their filters

RDBMSs can store this data, but they are not optimized to process, store, and analyze this type of data. Amazon Timestream was purpose-built exclusively for this data type and, therefore, is much more efficient.

Do you feel comfortable about when you should use TSDBs? If you need to store events or track logs or trades, or the time and date when something happened to take center stage, then a TSDB is probably an excellent solution to your problem.

Amazon Timestream

Amazon Timestream is a scalable and fully managed TSDB. Amazon Timestream can persist and analyze billions of transactions per minute at about one-tenth of the cost of RDBMS equivalents. IoT devices and smart industrial machines are becoming more popular by the day. These applications generate events that need to be tracked and measured, sometimes with real-time requirements.

Amazon Timestream has an adaptive query processing engine that can make heads or tails of time-series data as it comes in by inferring data location and data format. Amazon Timestream has features that can automate query rollups, retention, tiering, and data compression. Like many other Amazon services, Timestream is serverless, so it can automatically scale up or down depending on how much data is coming into the streams. Also, because it's serverless and fully managed, tasks such as provisioning, operating system patching, configuration, backups, and tiering are not the responsibility of the DevOps team, allowing them to focus on more important tasks.

Timestream enables you to store multiple measures in a single table row with its multi-measure records feature, instead of one measure per table row, making it easier to migrate existing data from relational databases to Timestream with minimal changes. Scheduled computations are also available, allowing you to define a computation or query and its schedule. Timestream will automatically and periodically run the queries and store the results in a separate table. Additionally, Timestream automatically determines whether data should be written to memory or the magnetic store based on the data's timestamp and configured data retention window, thereby reducing costs.

AWS has expanded its time-series database offerings with the introduction of Amazon Timestream for InfluxDB, a managed service for the popular InfluxDB open source time-series database. Additionally, Amazon Timestream has enhanced its cost-effectiveness by updating its metadata metering, no longer charging customers for dimension names and measure names associated with ingesting, storing, and querying data written.

You can learn more about Amazon Timestream by visiting the AWS page: `https://aws.amazon.com/timestream/`.

Benefits of AWS database services

In the new world of cloud-born applications, a one-size-fits-all database model no longer works. Modern organizations will not only use multiple types of databases for multiple applications, but many will use multiple types of databases in a single application. To get more value from data, you can choose the following three options available in AWS based on your workload.

Moving to fully managed database services

Managing and scaling databases in a legacy infrastructure, whether on-premises or self-managed in the cloud (on EC2), can be a tedious, time-consuming, and costly process. You have to worry about operational efficiency issues such as the following:

- The process of installing hardware and software, configuring settings, patching, and creating backups can be time-consuming and laborious
- Performance and availability issues
- Scalability issues, such as capacity planning and scaling clusters for compute and storage
- Security and compliance issues, such as network isolation, encryption, and compliance programs, including PCI, HIPAA, FedRAMP, ISO, and SOC

Instead of dealing with the challenges mentioned, you would rather spend your time innovating and creating new applications instead of managing infrastructure. With AWS-managed databases, you can avoid the need to over- or under-provision infrastructure to accommodate application growth, spikes, and performance requirements, as well as the associated fixed capital costs such as software licensing, hardware refresh, and maintenance resources. AWS manages everything for you, so you can focus on innovation and application development, rather than infrastructure management. You won't need to worry about administrative tasks such as server provisioning, patching, setup, configuration, backups, or recovery. AWS continuously monitors your clusters to ensure your workloads are running with self-healing storage and automated scaling, allowing you to focus on higher-value tasks such as schema design and query optimization.

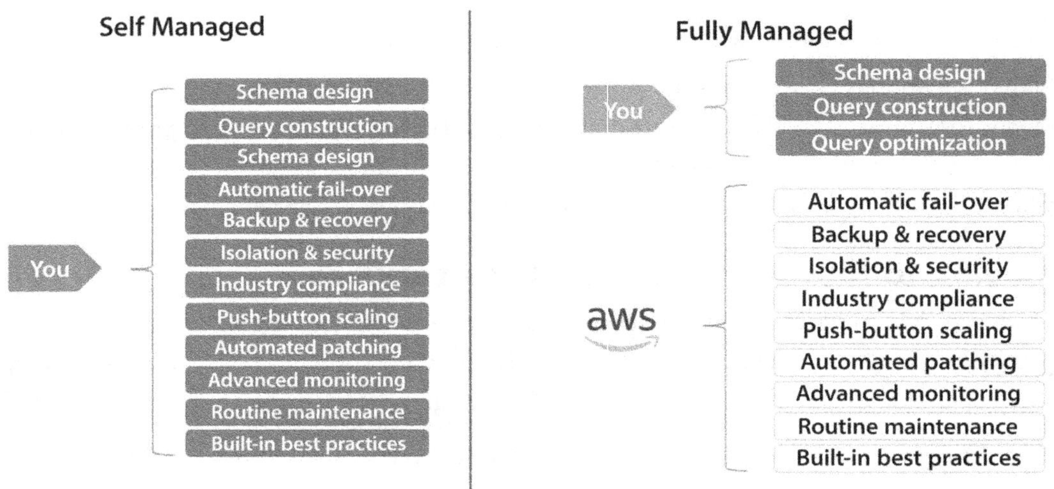

Figure 7.10: Fully managed database services on AWS

Let's look at the next benefit of using a purpose-built database. With purpose-built databases, your application doesn't need a one-size-fits-all architecture, and it doesn't have to be molded to accommodate a decade-old relational database. Purpose-built databases help you to achieve maximum output and performance as per the nature of your application.

Building modern applications with purpose-built databases

In the 60s and 70s, mainframes were the primary means of building applications, but by the 80s, client-server architecture was introduced and significantly changed application development. Applications became more distributed, but the underlying data model remained mostly structured, and the database often functioned as a monolith. With the advent of the internet in the 90s, three-tier application architecture emerged. Although client and application code became more distributed, the underlying data model continued to be mainly structured, and the database remained a monolith. For nearly three decades, developers typically built applications against a single database. That is an interesting data point because if you have been in the industry for a while, you often bump into folks whose mental model is, *"Hey, I've been building apps for a long time, and it's always against this one database."*

But what has changed? Fast forward to today, and microservice architectures are how applications are built in the cloud. Microservices have now extended to databases, providing developers with the ability to break down larger applications into smaller, specialized services that cater to specific tasks.

This allows developers to choose the best tool for the job instead of relying on a single, overworked database with a single storage and compute engine that struggles to handle every access pattern.

Today's developers and end users have different expectations compared to the past. They require lower latency and the ability to handle millions of transactions per second with many concurrent users. As a result, data management systems have evolved to include specialized storage and compute layers optimized for specific use cases and workloads. This allows developers to avoid trade-offs between functionality, performance, and scale.

Plus, what we've seen over the last few years is that more and more companies are hiring technical talent in-house to take advantage of the enormous wave of technological innovation that the cloud provides. These developers are building not in the monolithic ways of the past but with microservices, where they compose the different elements together using the right tool for the right job. This has led to the highly distributed, loosely coupled application architectures we see powering the most demanding workloads in the cloud.

Many factors contribute to the performance, scale, and availability requirements of modern apps:

- **Users**: User growth is a common KPI for businesses, and the cloud's global reach enables businesses to touch millions of new customers.
- **Data volume**: Businesses are capturing more data about their customers to either increase the value of their existing products or sell them new products. This results in terabyte- or even petabyte-scale data.
- **Locality**: Businesses often expand their presence into new markets to reach new users, which complicates the architecture of their solutions/products.
- **Performance**: Businesses don't want to dilute the user experience to reach new markets or grow their customer base. If customers find a better alternative, they'll use it.
- **Request rate**: As businesses use the cloud's global reach to develop more interactive user experiences in more markets, they need their apps and databases to handle unprecedented levels of throughput.
- **Access/scale**: As businesses embark on their digital transformations, these scale measures are compounded by the number of devices that access their applications. There are billions of smartphones worldwide, and businesses connect smartphones, cars, manufacturing plants, devices in our homes, and more to the cloud. This means many, many billions of devices are connected to the cloud.

- **Economics**: Businesses can't invest millions of dollars in hardware and licenses up front and hope they'll succeed; that model is unrealistic in 2023. Instead, they have to hedge their success by only paying for what they use, without capping how much they can grow. These dynamics combined have changed how businesses build applications. These modern applications have wildly different database requirements, which are more advanced and nuanced than simply running everything in a relational database.

The traditional approach of using a relational database as the sole data store for an application is no longer sufficient. To address this, developers are leveraging their expertise in breaking down complex applications into smaller components and choosing the most appropriate tool for each task. This results in well-architected applications that can scale effectively. The optimal tool for a given task often varies by use case, leading developers to build highly distributed applications using multiple specialized databases.

Now you have learned about the different types of AWS databases, let's go into more detail about moving on from legacy databases.

Moving on from legacy databases

Numerous legacy applications have been developed on conventional databases, and consumers have had to grapple with database providers that are expensive, proprietary, and impose punishing licensing terms and frequent audits. Oracle, for instance, announced that it would double licensing fees if its software was run on AWS or Microsoft. As a result, customers are attempting to switch as soon as possible to open source databases such as MySQL, PostgreSQL, and MariaDB.

Customers who are migrating to open source databases are seeking to strike a balance between the pricing, freedom, and flexibility of open source databases and the performance of commercial-grade databases. Achieving the same level of performance on open source databases as on commercial-grade databases can be challenging and necessitates a lot of fine-tuning.

AWS introduced Amazon Aurora, a cloud-native relational database that is compatible with MySQL and PostgreSQL to address this need. Aurora aims to provide a balance between the performance and availability of high-end commercial databases and the simplicity and cost-effectiveness of open source databases. It boasts five times better performance than standard MySQL and 3 times better performance than standard PostgreSQL, while maintaining the security, availability, and reliability of commercial-grade databases, all at a fraction of the cost. Additionally, customers can migrate their workloads to other AWS services, such as DynamoDB, to achieve application scalability.

In this section, you learned about the benefits of AWS database services. Now, there are so many database services that you have learned about, so let's put them together and learn how to choose the right database.

Choosing the right database for the job

In the previous sections, you learned how to classify databases and the different database services that AWS provides. In a nutshell, you learned about the following database services under different categories:

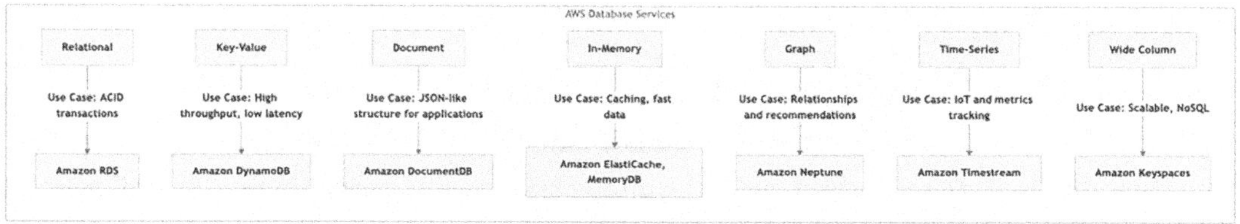

Figure 7.11: AWS database services in a nutshell

Quick tip: Need to see a high-resolution version of this image? Open this book in the next-gen Packt Reader or view it in the PDF/ePub copy.

The next-gen Packt Reader is included for free with the purchase of this book. Scan the QR code OR go to `packtpub.com/unlock`, then use the search bar to find this book by name. Double-check the edition shown to make sure you get the right one.

When you think about the collection of databases shown in the preceding diagram, you may think, "Oh, no. You don't need that many databases. I have a relational database, and it can take care of all this for you." Swiss Army knives are hardly the best solution for anything other than the most straightforward task. If you want the right tool for the right job that gives you the expected performance, productivity, and customer experience, you want a unified purpose-built database. So no one tool rules the world, and you should have the right tool for the right job to make you spend less money, be more productive, and change the customer experience.

Consider focusing on common database categories to choose the right database instead of browsing through hundreds of different databases. One such category is "relational," which many people are familiar with. Suppose you have a workload where strong consistency is crucial, where you will collaborate with the team to define schemas, and you need to figure out every single query that will be asked of the data and require consistent answers. In that case, a relational database is a good fit.

Popular options for this category include Amazon Aurora, Amazon RDS, open source engines such as PostgreSQL, MySQL, and MariaDB, as well as RDS commercial engines such as SQL Server, IBM Db2, and Oracle Database.

AWS has developed several purpose-built non-relational databases to facilitate the evolution of application development. For instance, in the key-value category, Amazon DynamoDB is a database that provides optimal performance for running key-value pairs at a single-digit millisecond latency and at a large scale. On the other hand, if you require a flexible method for storing and querying data in the same document model used in your application code, then Amazon DocumentDB is a suitable choice. This document database is designed to handle JSON documents in their natural format efficiently and can be scaled effortlessly.

Do you recall the era of XML? XML 1.0 was established in 1998. Commercial systems then added an XML data type to become an XML database. However, this approach had limitations, as many database operators needed help working with that data type. Today, document databases have replaced XML databases. Amazon DocumentDB, launched in January 2019, is an excellent example of such a database.

If your application requires faster response times than single-digit millisecond latency, consider an in-memory database and cache that can access data in microseconds. Amazon ElastiCache offers management for Redis and Memcached, making it possible to retrieve data rapidly for real-time processing use cases such as messaging, and real-time geospatial data such as drive distance.

Suppose you have large datasets with many connections between them. For instance, a sports company should link its athletes with its followers and provide personalized recommendations based on the interests of millions of users. Managing all these connections and providing fast queries can be challenging with traditional relational databases. In this case, you can use Amazon Neptune, a graph database designed to efficiently handle complex queries with interconnected data.

Time-series data is not just a timestamp or a data type that you might use in a relational database. Instead, a time-series database's core feature is that the primary axis of the data model is time. This allows for the optimization of data storage, scaling, and retrieval. Amazon Timestream is an example of a purpose-built time-series database that provides fast and scalable querying of time-series data.

A wide-column database is an excellent choice for applications that require fast data processing with low latency, such as industrial equipment maintenance, trade monitoring, fleet management, and route optimization. Amazon Keyspaces for Apache Cassandra provides a wide-column database option that allows you to develop applications that can handle thousands of requests per second with practically unlimited throughput and storage.

You should spend a significant amount of time clearly articulating the business problem you are trying to solve. Some of the questions the requirements should answer are as follows:

- How many users are expected?
- How many transactions per day will occur?
- How many records need to be stored?
- Will there be more writes or reads?
- How will the data need to be accessed (only by primary key, by filtering, or some other way)?

Why are these questions important? SQL has served us well for several decades now, as it is pervasive and has a lot of mindshare. So, why would we use anything else? The answer is performance. In instances where there is a lot of data and it needs to be accessed quickly, NoSQL databases might be a better solution. SQL vendors realize this and are constantly trying to improve their offerings to better compete with NoSQL, including adopting techniques from the NoSQL world. For example, Aurora is a SQL service, and it now offers Aurora Serverless, taking a page out of the NoSQL playbook.

As services get better, the line between NoSQL and SQL databases keeps on blurring, making the decision about what service to use more and more difficult. Depending on your project, you might want to draw up a proof of concept using a couple of options to determine which option performs better and fits your needs better.

Another reason to choose SQL or NoSQL might be the feature offered by NoSQL to create schema-less databases. Creating databases without a schema allows for fast prototyping and flexibility. However, tread carefully. Not having a schema might come at a high price.

Allowing users to enter records without the benefit of a schema may lead to inconsistent data, which becomes too variable and creates more problems than it solves. Just because we can create databases without a schema in a NoSQL environment, we should not forgo validation checks before creating a record. If possible, a validation scheme should be implemented, even when using a NoSQL option.

It is true that going schema-less increases implementation agility during the data ingestion phase. However, it increases complexity during the data access phase. So, make your choice by making a required trade-off between data context versus data performance.

Migrating databases to AWS

If you find it challenging to maintain your relational databases as they scale, consider switching to a managed database service such as Amazon RDS or Amazon Aurora. With these services, you can migrate your workloads and applications without the need to redesign your application, and you can continue to utilize your current database skills.

Consider moving to a managed relational database if the following apply:

- Your database is currently hosted on-premises or in EC2
- You want to reduce the burden of database administration and allocate DBA resources to application-centric work
- You prefer not to rearchitect your application and wish to use the same skill sets in the cloud
- You need a straightforward path to a managed service in the cloud for database workloads
- You require improved performance, availability, scalability, and security

Self-managed databases such as Oracle, SQL Server, MySQL, PostgreSQL, and MariaDB can be migrated to Amazon RDS using the lift and shift approach. For better performance and availability, MySQL and PostgreSQL databases can be moved to Amazon Aurora, which offers 3-5 times better throughput. Non-relational databases such as MongoDB and Redis are popularly used for document and in-memory databases in use cases such as content management, personalization, mobile apps, catalogs, and real-time use cases such as caching, gaming leaderboards, and session stores. To maintain non-relational databases at scale, organizations can move to a managed database service such as Amazon DocumentDB for self-managed MongoDB databases or Amazon ElastiCache for self-managed in-memory databases such as Redis. These services provide a straightforward solution to manage the databases without rearchitecting the application and enable the same DB skill sets to be leveraged while migrating workloads and applications.

As you understand the different choices of databases, the question comes of how to migrate your database to the cloud; there are five types of database migration paths available in AWS:

- **Self-service**: For many migrations, the self-service path using the DMS and **Schema Conversion Tool (SCT)** offers the tools necessary to execute. With over half a million migrations completed through DMS, customers have successfully migrated their instances to AWS. Using the **Database Migration Service (DMS)**, you can make homogeneous migrations from your legacy database service to a managed service on AWS, such as from Oracle to RDS Oracle. Alternatively, by leveraging DMS and the SCT, heterogeneous conversions are possible, such as converting from SQL Server to Amazon Aurora. The SCT assesses the source compatibility and recommends the best target engine.
- **Commercially licensed to AWS databases**: This type of migration is best for customers looking to move away from the licensing costs of commercial database vendors and avoid vendor lock-in. Most of these migrations have been from Oracle, Db2, and SQL Server to open source databases and Aurora, but there are use cases for migrating to NoSQL databases as well. For example, an online store may have started on a commercial or open source database, but now is growing so fast that it would need a NoSQL database such as DynamoDB to scale to millions of transactions per minute. Refactoring, however, typically requires application changes and takes more time to migrate than the other migration methods. AWS provides the Database Freedom program to assist with such migration. You can learn more about the AWS Database Freedom program by visiting the AWS page: `https://aws.amazon.com/solutions/databasemigrations/database-freedom/`.
- **MySQL database migrations**: Standard MySQL import and export tools can be used for MySQL database migrations to Amazon Aurora. Additionally, you can create a new Amazon Aurora database from an Amazon RDS for MySQL database snapshot with ease. Migration operations based on DB snapshots typically take less than an hour, although the duration may vary depending on the amount and format of data being migrated.
- **PostgreSQL database migrations**: For PostgreSQL database migrations, standard PostgreSQL import and export tools such as `pg_dump` and `pg_restore` can be used with Amazon Aurora. Amazon Aurora also supports snapshot imports from Amazon RDS for PostgreSQL and replication with AWS DMS.

In addition to the preceding, AWS has an extensive Partner Network of consulting and software vendor partners who can provide expertise and tools to migrate your data to AWS.

AWS database management and operations

When managing databases on AWS, your goal is to keep them highly available, secure, and optimized while reducing the manual effort required for day-to-day operations. AWS offers fully managed database services such as Amazon RDS, Aurora, DynamoDB, and DocumentDB, which simplify many operational tasks such as patching, monitoring, and database engine upgrades. Managing databases on AWS becomes more efficient and reliable when you leverage its built-in tools for backup, scaling, monitoring, and high availability. These services are designed to help you focus on developing your applications while AWS handles the heavy lifting of database operations. Let's look at some key areas to focus on for effective database management in AWS:

- **Database backup and recovery**: AWS offers automated backup solutions for services such as Amazon RDS and Aurora. These backups are stored in Amazon S3 and support point-in-time recovery, allowing you to restore your database to any specific moment within the backup retention period. For example, Amazon RDS creates daily snapshots and transaction logs, enabling you to recover your database to any second within the retention window. Additionally, AWS Backup provides centralized backup management across AWS services, simplifying compliance and data protection strategies.
- **Scaling and performance tuning**: As your application grows, AWS allows you to scale your databases vertically by upgrading to larger instance types or horizontally by adding read replicas. For instance, Amazon Aurora supports up to 15 read replicas, distributing read traffic and improving performance. Tools such as Amazon RDS Performance Insights help you identify slow queries and optimize them, ensuring efficient database operations. DynamoDB Auto Scaling adjusts throughput based on demand. Tools such as Amazon CloudWatch help you identify slow queries, CPU spikes, or memory bottlenecks so you can optimize indexes, queries, and instance sizes accordingly. Proper tuning ensures better performance and user experience without overprovisioning resources.
- **Monitoring and alerting**: Monitoring is critical for understanding database health. AWS provides built-in monitoring with Amazon CloudWatch, which tracks metrics such as CPU, memory, disk I/O, and connection count. You can set custom alarms to get notified when something goes wrong – such as high CPU usage or storage running low. Services such as DevOps Guru for RDS go a step further by using machine learning to detect anomalies and suggest performance improvements automatically.

- **Automated maintenance and patching**: With AWS managed databases, you can schedule automatic minor version upgrades to keep your systems secure and stable. RDS and Aurora handle patching of the underlying OS and database engine during defined maintenance windows, minimizing disruption. This reduces your operational burden and ensures compliance with security best practices, without requiring manual intervention. You can schedule maintenance windows to apply updates during off-peak hours, minimizing disruptions.
- **High availability and disaster recovery**: AWS offers built-in high-availability options. Amazon Aurora and RDS Multi-AZ deployments replicate your data across multiple Availability Zones, enabling automatic failover during outages. For disaster recovery, you can use cross-region replication and automate failover routing with Amazon Route 53. DynamoDB global tables enable active-active replication across regions, ensuring low-latency access and resilience.

  For mission-critical applications, AWS provides high availability through Multi-AZ deployments. In this setup, AWS automatically replicates your database to a standby instance in a different Availability Zone. In case of a failure, AWS handles failover to the standby, ensuring minimal downtime.

Knowledge check

The following are some sample questions that align with the difficulty and scope typically found in the *AWS Certified Solutions Architect - Professional* exam.

1. A global e-commerce company is migrating its database to AWS and has chosen Amazon Aurora as its primary relational database service due to its high performance and compatibility with MySQL. The company wants to ensure high availability and disaster recovery for its database. Which of the following configurations would provide the *best* solution for cross-region disaster recovery while maintaining high availability within a region?

    a. Deploy an Amazon Aurora MySQL database with multiple Aurora Replicas within a single AWS region.

    b. Deploy an Amazon Aurora MySQL database with multiple Aurora Replicas in one region and use AWS **Database Migration Service** (**DMS**) to replicate data to another region.

    c. Deploy Amazon Aurora Global Database with a primary cluster in one region and Aurora Replicas in another region.

   d. Deploy two separate Amazon Aurora MySQL databases in two different regions and use AWS Lambda to synchronize data between them.

Answer: c.

Explanation:

   a. Incorrect. While this ensures high availability within a single region through Aurora Replicas, it does not provide cross-region disaster recovery.
   b. Incorrect. Using AWS DMS for cross-region replication can be complex and may introduce latency. It is not as seamless or performant as Aurora Global Database for read scalability and disaster recovery.
   c. **Correct**. Amazon Aurora Global Database is designed specifically for global, high-availability deployments. It allows you to have a primary cluster in one region and read replicas in other regions, providing both high availability and disaster recovery across regions.
   d. Incorrect. Using AWS Lambda for data synchronization is not an efficient or reliable method for ensuring high availability and disaster recovery compared to Aurora Global Database.

2. You have a DynamoDB table with a partition key and a sort key. The table stores data for multiple customers, and each customer can have multiple orders. You need to design a solution that allows you to efficiently retrieve all the orders for a specific customer within a given date range. Which of the following approaches would you use? (Choose two.)

   a. Create a **global secondary index (GSI)** with the partition key as `customer_id` and the sort key as `order_date`.
   b. Create a **local secondary index (LSI)** with the sort key as `order_date`.
   c. Create a **global secondary index (GSI)** with the partition key as a composite key of `customer_id` and `order_date`.
   d. Use a DynamoDB stream to capture changes and store the data in a separate data store optimized for date range queries.
   e. Use **DynamoDB Accelerator (DAX)** to cache frequently accessed data and improve query performance.

Answer: a. and c.

Explanation:

a. **Correct**. Creating a **global secondary index (GSI)** with the partition key as `customer_id` and the sort key as `order_date` allows you to efficiently query for all orders of a specific customer within a date range. The GSI essentially creates a new view of the data with the desired key structure, making it easier to perform the required queries.

b. Incorrect. A **local secondary index (LSI)** is not suitable for this scenario because it inherits the partition key from the base table. To query orders within a date range, you need a different partition key, which can only be achieved with a global secondary index.

c. **Correct**. Creating a **global secondary index (GSI)** with a composite partition key of `customer_id` and `order_date` is another valid approach. This design allows you to efficiently query for orders within a date range for a specific customer by using the composite key as the partition key in the GSI.

d. Incorrect. While DynamoDB Streams can capture changes to the table, streams are not designed for efficient date range queries. DynamoDB streams are primarily used for capturing changes and replicating data to other data stores or triggering downstream processing.

e. Incorrect. **DynamoDB Accelerator (DAX)** is an in-memory cache that improves read performance by caching frequently accessed data. While DAX can improve query performance in general, it does not directly address the specific requirement of efficiently retrieving orders within a date range for a specific customer. The underlying data model and indexing strategy are still necessary to support the desired query pattern.

3. You are designing a solution for a social media platform that requires efficient querying of complex graph data to recommend friends and display relationship networks. Which two features of Amazon Neptune would you leverage to optimize performance and scalability for this use case? (Choose two.)

    a. Neptune's support for the Gremlin graph traversal language
    b. Neptune's built-in support for Apache TinkerPop
    c. Neptune's integration with Amazon SageMaker for machine learning
    d. Neptune's auto-scaling capabilities to handle varying loads
    e. Neptune's support for the RDF query language SPARQL

Answer: a. and d.

Explanation:

a. **Correct.** Gremlin is a graph traversal language that allows for complex queries and traversals within graph databases. For a social media platform, Gremlin would be essential for efficiently querying and traversing the relationship networks to recommend friends and display connections.

b. Incorrect. Social media platforms experience fluctuating traffic patterns. Neptune's auto-scaling capabilities ensure that the database can handle varying loads efficiently, maintaining performance during peak times and scaling down during off-peak times to optimize costs.

c. Incorrect. While Neptune does support Apache TinkerPop, which includes Gremlin, this option is less specific than option A, which directly mentions Gremlin.

d. **Correct.** Neptune does not have direct integration with SageMaker. While machine learning can be beneficial, this is not a native feature of Neptune.

e. Incorrect. SPARQL is useful for RDF data, which is less relevant for typical social media graph traversals compared to Gremlin.

4. You are tasked with migrating a large, monolithic MySQL database from an on-premises data center to Amazon RDS. The database is approximately 10 TB in size and has a high number of read and write operations. Which two methods would you recommend to ensure minimal downtime during the migration process? (Choose two.)

   a. Use AWS **Database Migration Service (DMS)** to perform an ongoing replication from the source database to the target RDS instance.

   b. Perform a manual export of the database using `mysqldump` and import it into the RDS instance using the `mysql` command.

   c. Utilize AWS Snowball to transfer the database files physically and then restore them on the RDS instance.

   d. Employ AWS **Schema Conversion Tool (SCT)** to convert the database schema and then use AWS DMS for data migration.

   e. Use AWS Data Pipeline to schedule and automate the data transfer from the on-premises database to the RDS instance.

Answer: a. and d.

Explanation:

a. **Correct.** AWS **Database Migration Service (DMS)** is designed to minimize downtime during migration by allowing you to perform ongoing replication. Initially, it performs a full load of the data and then applies any changes that occur during the migration process, ensuring that the RDS instance is up to date with minimal downtime.

b. Incorrect. Using `mysqldump` and `mysql` for a 10 TB database would be time-consuming and not practical for minimal downtime.

c. Incorrect. AWS Snowball is useful for physical data transfer but does not directly support restoring data into RDS; it's more suited for initial data transfer rather than ongoing replication.

d. **Correct.** AWS **Schema Conversion Tool (SCT)** helps in converting the database schema from the source database to a format compatible with Amazon RDS. After the schema is converted, AWS DMS can be used to migrate the data, ensuring that both schema and data are accurately transferred with minimal disruption.

e. Incorrect. AWS Data Pipeline is more suited for ETL processes and scheduled data transfers.

5. A company is running multiple Amazon RDS MySQL databases for different applications. The security team requires that all database connections must be encrypted, and all sensitive data stored in the databases must be encrypted. Additionally, they need to rotate encryption keys periodically according to their compliance requirements. Which combination of actions should be taken to meet these security requirements? (Choose two.)

   a. Enable SSL/TLS encryption for database connections and force all clients to use the `require_secure_transport=1` parameter in the DB parameter group.

   b. Create a custom KMS key with automatic rotation enabled, use it to enable encryption at rest for the RDS instances, and configure SSL certificates for data in transit.

   c. Enable default RDS encryption using the AWS-managed KMS key and configure IAM authentication for database connections.

   d. Deploy SSL certificates on application servers and configure the RDS instance endpoint to use the HTTPS protocol.

   e. Enable encryption at rest using an AWS KMS custom key, manually rotate the key every 90 days, and force SSL connections using the `rds.force_ssl` parameter.

Answer: a. and b.

Explanation:

a. **Correct.** Enabling SSL/TLS encryption for all database connections and the `require_secure_transport=1` parameter ensures that all clients must use encrypted connections. This addresses the requirement for encrypted database connections.

b. **Correct.** RDS MySQL uses a custom KMS key with automatic rotation, which satisfies the periodic key rotation requirement. It enables encryption at rest for the RDS instances, protecting stored data, and includes SSL certificate configuration for data in transit.

c. Incorrect. AWS-managed KMS keys cannot be rotated manually or automatically. IAM authentication is about access control, not encryption.

d. Incorrect. HTTPS protocol is not used for RDS connections, and this approach doesn't address encryption at rest. RDS uses SSL/TLS certificates, not HTTPS.

e. Incorrect. Manual rotation of KMS keys is unnecessary and prone to human error when automatic rotation is available. It creates operational overhead and potential security risks during manual rotation.

Summary

In this chapter, you learned how to choose the right AWS database service for your application by first exploring the evolution of databases; from traditional relational databases (RDBMS) to more flexible non-relational (NoSQL) databases. You saw that relational databases are ideal for structured and consistent data, such as that used in financial systems. In contrast, NoSQL databases are better suited for handling unstructured or semi-structured data, such as user profiles on social media platforms.

The chapter guided you through various AWS-managed database services, including Amazon RDS for relational workloads and Amazon DynamoDB for NoSQL use cases. It explained how these services offer key benefits, such as scalability, high availability, automated backups, and reduced operational overhead, allowing you to focus more on application development than on infrastructure management.

You also explored database consistency models, best practices for matching the right database to different workload types, and how to plan for both current and future scalability needs. Finally, the chapter introduced AWS **Database Migration Service** (**DMS**) as a helpful tool for moving existing databases to AWS, reinforcing that selecting the right database architecture requires a thoughtful balance between performance, flexibility, and long-term maintainability.

Part 3

AWS Cloud Security and Monitoring

This part helps you strengthen the security of your AWS environments. You'll learn how to manage identity with IAM, enforce policies using AWS Organizations, and detect threats using services such as GuardDuty and Macie. You'll also explore strategies for encrypting data and staying compliant with regulations. In *Chapter 9*, you'll dive into operational efficiency with DevOps and automation tools, learning how to monitor and manage infrastructure using CloudWatch, CloudFormation, and other AWS-native tools.

This part of the book includes the following chapters:

- *Chapter 8, Application Security, Identity, and Compliance*
- *Chapter 9, Driving Efficiency with Cloud Operation Automation and DevOps in AWS*

8

Best Practices for Application Security, Identity, and Compliance

In the early 2010s, when cloud started to pick up, a common refrain from companies was that they were hesitant to move to the cloud because they believed the cloud was not secure. A big part of this pushback was that companies didn't understand the cloud or its capabilities. It is possible to have security vulnerabilities even if you use cloud infrastructure. However, as we will see in this chapter, AWS provides a comprehensive catalog of services enabling you to create highly secure sites and applications.

When creating applications and implementing workflows, it is imperative to consider security from the start of your design and not as an afterthought. First, you will understand why security is essential in any system, not just in the cloud. Next, you will learn how AWS, in general, and **identity and access management** (**IAM**), in particular, can help us design and build robust and secure cloud applications. Also, as you will see in this chapter, AWS provides a comprehensive set of security services.

In this chapter, we will cover the following topics:

- Understanding the importance of security, identity, and compliance in AWS
- AWS's Shared Responsibility Model
- Getting familiar with IAM
- Managing resources, permissions, and identities using IAM
- Applying security controls and infrastructure protection in AWS
- Building data protection

- Adhering to compliance
- Learning about other AWS security services
- AWS security best practices

By the end of this chapter, you will have learned how to secure your AWS cloud environment and about the AWS services available to make your environment secure. AWS offers a plethora of security services to assist with these requirements. In this chapter, we will review these services in detail.

Understanding the importance of security, identity, and compliance in AWS

Many organizations face challenges in maintaining and managing the security of their on-premises infrastructure. In an on-premises environment, it can be challenging to know what resources and data are out there at any given time, where they are moving, and who is utilizing/accessing them. Accurate, real-time asset inventory requires expensive and complex tooling, making it inaccessible for most organizations. This lack of visibility in their on-premises environment hinders their ability to ensure adequate security and compliance of infrastructure and data. With AWS, you can see all your infrastructure and application resources in one place and maintain servers, storage, and database inventory records and access patterns.

AWS enhances your capacity to adhere to key security and compliance standards, such as data locality, protection, and confidentiality, through its extensive services and features. AWS has one of the largest networks of security partners, and its capabilities can be further extended through familiar security technology and consulting providers. AWS is compliant with major security standards and certifications, such as PCI-DSS, HIPAA/HITECH, FedRAMP, SEC Rule 17a-4, the EU Data Protection Directive, and FISMA, thereby enabling organizations to meet compliance requirements globally.

Another common problem is the reliance on manual processes for remediation. This may involve the manual copying of access information from one tool to another or the manual application of security patches. Automating key security tasks has been challenging due to the lack of interoperability between third-party and custom-made tools. These manual processes result in inconsistent execution and longer wait times to address all systems, and often negatively impact the customer experience. Automation aims to solve these issues by programmatically managing security tasks, such as checking whether access to an application server is exposed to the internet or ensuring that an S3 bucket is not left public unintentionally.

As with any computer system, ensuring that it's secure and that only authorized users access the system is paramount. Security should be incorporated at the beginning of your application design and not as an afterthought. AWS provides a broad set of security offerings that assist in keeping your applications secure and your data protected. Notice that we used the word *assist*. Just because you are using AWS does not mean that your applications will be instantly secure.

Here is a quick example of how easy it is to expose your data: There is nothing barring you from creating a bucket in AWS that is both unencrypted and public. You may get some warnings asking you whether you are certain that you want to proceed, but AWS won't disallow it. You could then put a client file in that bucket that may contain emails, passwords, names, addresses, and so on. This combination would immediately make this data accessible to anyone in the world with an internet connection (including any threat actors). However, S3 public access is blocked by default from AWS.

Even though you may not have published the URL for the bucket, please don't assume it is secure. Threat actors know these mistakes happen sometimes. They constantly send requests to random Amazon S3 buckets, trying to guess whether they were created unsecured and exposed. And occasionally, they get lucky and hit pay dirt.

In the following section, we will learn more about what security AWS provides without involving the user and what services and tools AWS provides to its users to keep their systems secure.

Understanding the Shared Responsibility Model

AWS uses the **Shared Responsibility Model**, which means that AWS and its users are responsible for keeping applications secure. However, the lines of responsibility are pretty clear. AWS is solely responsible for some aspects (for example, physical data center security), and users are solely responsible for other aspects (for example, making sure that Amazon S3 buckets that will contain sensitive information are private, accessible to only authorized users, and encrypted).

This model enables AWS to reduce the burden of securing some components needed to create applications while enabling users to customize the applications to suit their clients' needs and budgets.

Depending on the service chosen, some responsibilities may fall on AWS or the user. For example, if you use Amazon RDS to stand up an instance of MySQL, the patching of the database and the underlying operating system would be performed by AWS.

Suppose you instead decide to install MySQL directly into an Amazon EC2 instance. In that case, you will still be able to use the MySQL functionality. But in this case, the responsibility to patch the operating system and the database would fall on you.

One common refrain heard to distinguish which components are the responsibility of AWS and which are the responsibility of the customer is as follows:

- AWS is responsible for the security *of* the cloud
- The AWS customer is responsible for security *in* the cloud

The following diagram illustrates the separation of duties:

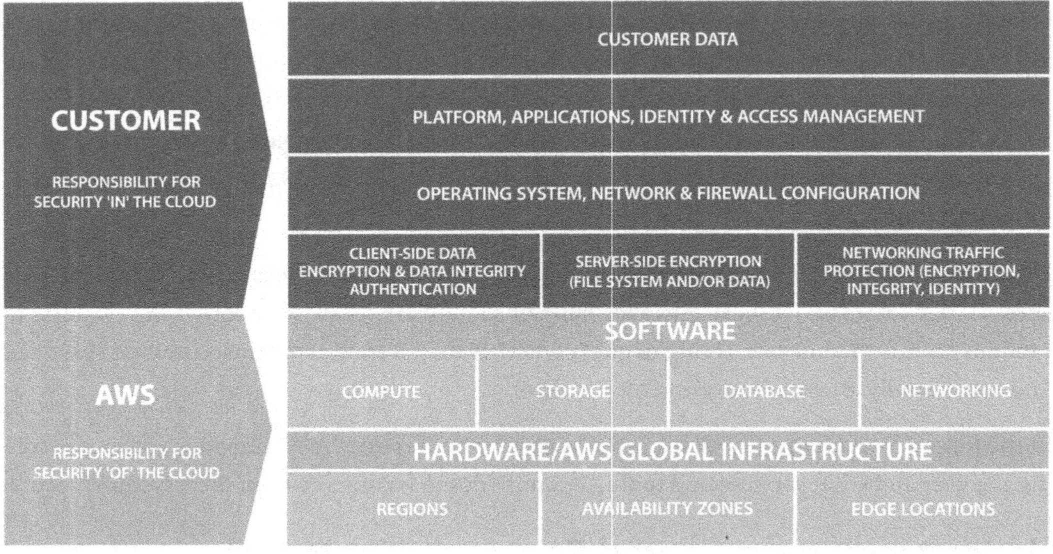

Figure 8.1: Shared Responsibility Model (source: https://docs.aws.amazon.com/whitepapers/latest/aws-risk-and-compliance/shared-responsibility-model.html)

The preceding figure shows in broad strokes how the responsibilities are broken down. For example, it clearly shows that the responsibility of AWS is for infrastructure elements such as regions, edge locations, and **Availability Zones (AZs)**. This includes the physical security of the data centers. You may have passed an AWS data center and not noticed; AWS data centers are always unmarked buildings. On the other hand, customer data is the customer's responsibility. When it comes to customer data, the encryption of the data is also the customer's responsibility.

These areas of responsibility can be fuzzy depending on how a certain functionality is implemented. We see in the chart that databases fall under the purview of AWS, but as we saw previously, the customer can install a database, in which case they would be responsible for its management. Similarly, the chart in *Figure 8.2* shows the customer's responsibility for operating systems, the network, and firewall configuration. But the Shared Responsibility Model varies depending on the services provided to you by AWS.

The following diagram shows various levels of security responsibilities shared by AWS:

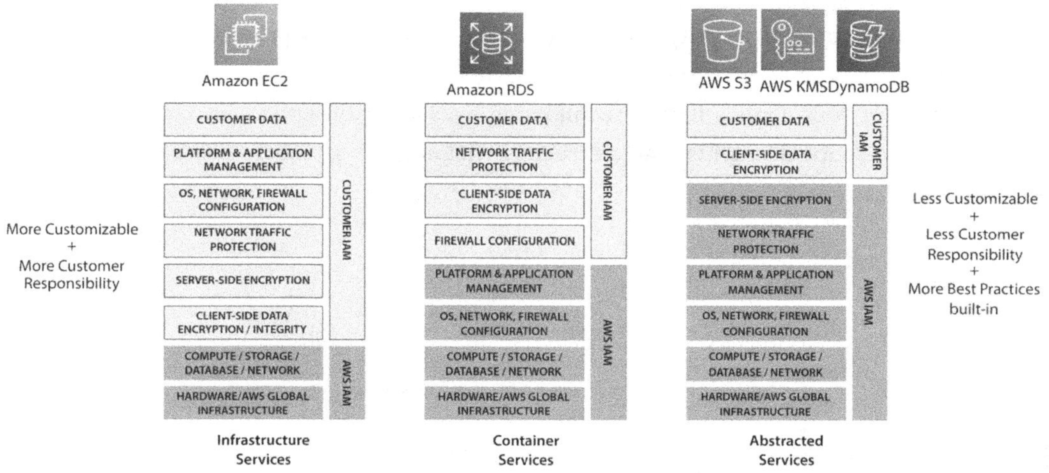

Figure 8.2: Shared Responsibility Model for different AWS service categories

As shown in the preceding diagram, in some cases (for example, when using Amazon S3), the management of most items is the responsibility of AWS. For EC2, AWS only handles infrastructure security, while RDS security is managed at the platform level. For DynamoDB, you just need to manage data and its access, while everything else in the layer, up until network traffic and server encryption, is managed by AWS.

Another way to understand how security in AWS works is by using the analogy of locks and doors. AWS provides you with the doors and the locks to secure your applications and data, but you can still leave the door open and not secure the lock, leaving the contents of your home exposed to the world.

For example, Amazon RDS is a managed service. AWS does much of the heavy lifting to make a database secure. However, you can still publish the credentials to access your Amazon RDS instance on GitHub and let anyone who views these credentials access your database.

Overall, with AWS, you own your data and applications, and under the Shared Responsibility Model, it becomes your responsibility to secure them by using various security services provided by AWS, from access management to encryption.

AWS security, identity, and compliance solutions

AWS has a broad range of security services available to fulfill every protection need of its customers. AWS is built to support the creation of secure, high-performing, resilient, and efficient infrastructure for your applications. The following AWS security services and solutions are designed to provide critical benefits that are crucial in helping you attain the best security posture for your organization:

Identity and access management	Detective controls	Infrastructure protection	Data protection	Incident response	Compliance
AWS Identity and Access Management (IAM)	AWS Security Hub	AWS Firewall Manager	Amazon Macie	Amazon Detective	AWS Artifact
AWS IAM Identity Center (successor to AWS SSO)	Amazon GuardDuty	AWS Network Firewall	AWS Key Management Service (KMS)	Amazon EventBridge	AWS Audit Manager
AWS Organizations	Amazon Inspector	AWS Shield	AWS CloudHSM	AWS Backup	
AWS Directory Service	Amazon CloudWatch	AWS WAF	AWS Certificate Manager	AWS Security Hub	
Amazon Cognito	AWS Config	Amazon VPC	AWS Secrets Manager	AWS Elastic Disaster Recovery	
AWS Resource Access Manager	AWS CloudTrail	AWS PrivateLink	AWS VPN		
	VPC Flow Logs	AWS Systems Manager	Server-Side Encryption		
	AWS IoT Device Defender				

Figure 8.3: AWS security services

As shown in the preceding table, AWS divides security services into the following pillars:

- **Identity and access management**: Establish, enforce, and monitor user access to AWS services, actions, and resources.
- **Detective controls**: Obtain the necessary visibility to identify potential issues before they affect your business, enhance your security posture, and minimize the risk to your environment.
- **Infrastructure protection**: Minimize the surface area to manage and enhance the privacy, control, and security of your overall infrastructure on AWS.
- **Data protection**: A collection of services that automate and simplify various data protection and security tasks, such as key management and storage, and credential management.
- **Incident response**: During a security incident, containing the event and restoring to a secure state are critical steps in a response plan. AWS offers tools to automate parts of this best practice.
- **Compliance**: Provide audit traces and artifacts in order to meet compliance requirements.

Let's look into individual services belonging to these security pillars.

Getting familiar with IAM

IAM is the most fundamental security posture for any organization, and AWS provides the following services in this category:

- **AWS IAM**: Securely manage access to AWS services and resources
- **AWS Organizations**: Policy-based management for multiple AWS accounts
- **AWS Directory Service**: Managed Microsoft **Active Directory** (**AD**), Simple AD, and AD Connector in AWS
- **AWS IAM Identity Center** (successor to AWS SSO): Centrally manage **single sign-on** (**SSO**) access to multiple AWS accounts and business apps
- **AWS Resource Access Manager**: A simple, secure service for sharing AWS resources
- **Amazon Cognito**: Add user sign-up, sign-in, and access control to your web and mobile apps

Let's look into each of the preceding services in detail.

AWS IAM

Perhaps the most fundamental and important service in AWS is IAM, which can be used in conjunction with the software services offered by AWS. AWS IAM offers precise access control across all AWS services. This level of control allows you to define who can access specific services and resources and under what conditions. By creating IAM policies, you can manage access permissions for your users or applications to ensure minimal privilege access. IAM is a complementary service provided by AWS at no extra cost. More specifically, AWS IAM can be used to do the following:

- Grant others shared access to your AWS account without sharing passwords or access keys
- Provide granular permissions for different people and resources
- Securely access AWS resources using IAM credentials for applications running on EC2 instances and other resources
- Enhance security with **multi-factor authentication** (**MFA**)
- Facilitate identity federation for temporary access to your AWS account with external passwords

Due to eventual consistency, make sure IAM changes are replicated globally. However, it is recommended not to include IAM changes in high-availability code paths and to verify that changes have propagated before usage.

Here are a few use cases for AWS IAM:

- **Access control for AWS services:** IAM can be used to control who has access to various AWS services, such as EC2, S3, and DynamoDB, as well as what actions they can perform on those services
- **MFA:** IAM supports MFA, which can be used to add an extra layer of security to an AWS account
- **Secure application credentials:** IAM can be used to securely provide credentials for applications running on EC2 instances and other resources so that those applications can access other AWS resources
- **Identity federation:** IAM can be used to grant temporary access to AWS resources for users with existing passwords, for example, in a corporate network or with an internet identity provider
- **Billing and cost allocation:** IAM can be used to manage access to billing and cost allocation information for an AWS account

Suppose you have a company that uses AWS to host its applications. You can use IAM to create a group for your developers, granting them access to EC2 instances, S3 buckets, and DynamoDB tables, while only allowing them read-only access to your billing information. You can also use IAM to set up MFA for the root account and individual IAM users to add an extra layer of security.

Managing resources, permissions, and identities using IAM

To understand AWS IAM, we must first understand how authentication and identity management work. Users, groups, roles, permissions, and policies are fundamental concepts that need to be fully understood to grasp how resources are secured using AWS IAM. The purpose of using IAM is to regulate the authentication and authorization of individuals who wish to utilize resources. This is achieved by establishing precise permissions through IAM, thereby determining who has access to what. IAM consistently implements these permissions for every request made. By default, all requests are denied (except for the root user, which is allowed by default) unless an explicit "allow" is specified. An explicit "deny" overrides any allows.

In the following sections, you will learn about AWS IAM terms.

IAM users

An **IAM user** is an IAM principal you create in AWS to represent the person or application that uses it to interact with AWS. An **IAM principal** is a user, group, or service that is authenticated and authorized to access resources in an AWS account. An IAM principal can be an AWS account root user, an IAM user, an IAM role, or a federated user.

An AWS user comprises a username and associated credentials. Take, for instance, a user named John. Upon creating an IAM user account for John, you'll need to establish a password for that user. You have the option to assign IAM user-specific permissions, such as the ability to start a particular Amazon EC2 instance.

An IAM user is an individual who needs to access, interact with, and potentially modify data and AWS resources. Users can interact in one of three ways:

- The AWS Management Console
- The AWS **Command-Line Interface** (**CLI**)
- The AWS API

Other than the root user, no implicit permissions or credentials are given when a new user is set up. That new user cannot access any resources until permission is explicitly assigned.

The IAM service in AWS enables you to securely control access to AWS resources and the actions that can be performed on those resources. You can use IAM to create and manage IAM principals, as well as to assign permissions to these principals to allow or deny access to AWS resources. For example, you can use IAM to create an IAM user for a person in your organization, and then grant that user permissions to access specific AWS resources or perform certain actions. Overall, using IAM helps you securely and effectively manage access to your AWS resources, and helps you enforce the principle of least privilege by granting only the necessary permissions to IAM principals.

IAM user groups

An **IAM user group** is an assembly of IAM users. By organizing IAM users into groups, you can efficiently manage their permissions as a collective. As an illustration, consider a user group named `Dev`, to which you have assigned the typical permissions required for developers. Any IAM user belonging to this group will automatically inherit the permissions assigned to the `Dev` user group.

When a new member joins your organization and requires developer privileges, you can grant the necessary permissions by adding them to the relevant user group.

On the other hand, if an individual changes their role within your organization, you can simply transfer them from their current user group to the appropriate new user group, rather than modifying their individual permissions. The following diagram shows IAM users assigned to different user groups:

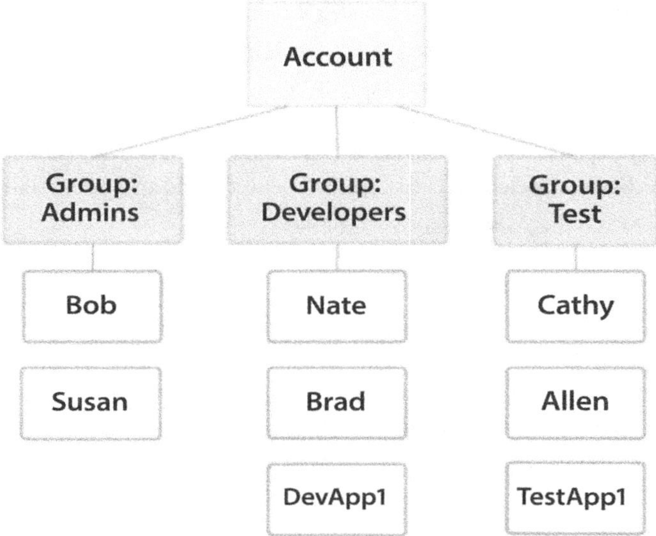

Figure 8.4: AWS IAM user groups and IAM user

The preceding diagram shows three user groups, **Admins**, **Developers**, and **Test**, and IAM users assigned to those groups with the same credentials set. Putting users into groups facilitates permission management and gives system administrators a more efficient way to administer permissions. Users who have similar profiles are grouped. They could be grouped based on similar characteristics and on having similar needs, such as the following:

- Job function or role
- Department
- Persona

Then, permissions for users that belong to one group can be managed all at once through the group. It is recommended to put all users in one group who need the same access level. Often, organizations use AD to group employees, and in that case, you can map IAM groups to your AD groups. If you have been around technology for a while, the idea of users and groups should not be new. However, IAM roles may require a little more explanation. Let's continue discussing them in the next section.

IAM roles

An **IAM role** is a way to grant permission to access AWS resources to users or processes that do not have their own AWS credentials. The major difference is that, unlike users, IAM roles provide temporary security credentials rather than long-term access keys or passwords.

As shown in the following diagram, you can use an IAM role to allow a user to access an S3 bucket. For that, first, you need to create an IAM role that has the necessary permissions to access the S3 bucket. This can be done through the AWS Management Console or using the AWS CLI. For example, you might create a role that has the `AmazonS3FullAccess` policy attached to it. Next, create a user and associate the IAM role with the user. The user can then access the S3 bucket using the AWS Management Console or the AWS SDKs by assuming the IAM role. This will allow the user to use the permissions of the IAM role to access the S3 bucket, without the need for the user to have their own AWS credentials.

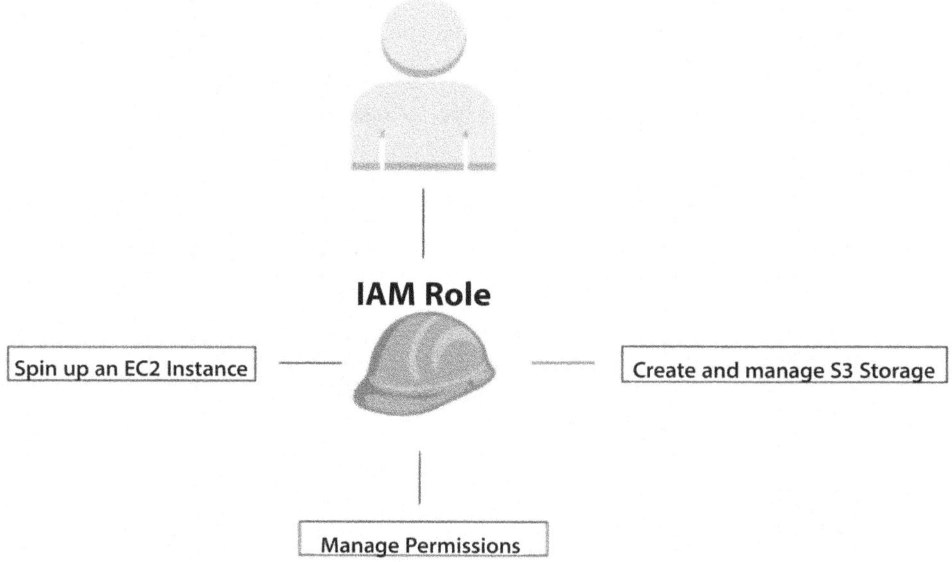

Figure 8.5: AWS IAM role

In IAM, a role is an object definition that configures a set of permissions assigned to that role. The role can be assigned to other entities, such as a user. A role is not directly connected to a person or a service. Instead, the role can be assumed by an entity that is given the role. Role credentials are always only temporary and rotated on a schedule defined by the AWS **Security Token Service (STS)**. It is best practice to use roles whenever possible instead of granting permissions directly to a user or group.

STS allows you to request short-lived, restricted credentials for both AWS IAM users and federated users. This service is frequently utilized to grant temporary access to resources for trusted users, such as by granting them an IAM role that has a more limited set of permissions compared to their standard IAM user or federated user permissions.

STS enables you to grant trusted users temporary permissions to resources without having to share long-term AWS access keys. For example, you can use STS to grant temporary access to an IAM role that allows users to perform specific tasks in your AWS account, such as creating and managing Amazon EC2 instances or uploading objects to Amazon S3. STS can also be used to provide federated users with temporary credentials to access resources in the AWS cloud.

You can use STS to grant temporary credentials in several ways:

- `AssumeRole`: This operation enables you to grant a trusted user temporary access to an IAM role
- `GetFederationToken`: This operation enables you to grant a trusted user temporary access to AWS resources that you specify in the permissions policy associated with the token
- `GetSessionToken`: This operation enables you to obtain temporary credentials for an IAM user or for a federated user

Using STS helps you secure your AWS resources and provides flexibility for granting temporary access to your resources. In Python, the user can use the `boto3` library to assume the IAM role and then access the S3 bucket like this:

```
import boto3
# Assume the IAM role
sts_client = boto3.client('sts')
assumed_role_object = sts_client.assume_role(
    RoleArn='arn:aws:iam::123456789012:role/my-iam-role',
    RoleSessionName='my_session'
)
# Use the temporary credentials provided by the assume_role method to
access S3
s3_client = boto3.client('s3', aws_access_key_id=assumed_role_
object['Credentials']['AccessKeyId',aws_secret_access_key=assumed_role_
object['Credentials']['SecretAccessKey'],
aws_session_token=assumed_role_object['Credentials']['SessionToken'])
# List the objects in the S3 bucket
objects = s3_client.list_objects(Bucket='my-s3-bucket')
print(objects)
```

Furthermore, roles enable you to grant multi-account access to users, services, and applications. Assigning a role to users not part of your organization is possible. Obviously, this has to be done judiciously and with flexibility as required.

IAM roles carry out a fundamental task in the security access landscape. By assigning permissions to a role instead of directly to a user or group, roles facilitate and simplify system administration and allow these permissions to only be given temporarily.

Policies and permissions

Access control in AWS is achieved through the creation and attachment of policies to IAM identities (such as users, groups, or roles) or AWS resources. These policies, which are objects in AWS, define the permissions of the associated identity or resource when they are attached. When an IAM principal, such as a user or role, makes a request, AWS evaluates the relevant policies to determine whether the request should be granted or denied. The majority of these policies are stored in AWS in the form of JSON documents.

A policy is a named document with a set of rules that specify what actions can be performed. Each policy laid out in the document gives a set of permissions. These policies can then be assigned to the IAM principals covered previously: users, groups, and roles. The syntax for AWS policy documents comes in two flavors:

- JSON
- YAML

The following is the syntax for defining a policy and permissions:

```
Version: 2012-10-17
Statement:
  - Effect: Allow
    Action:
      - ec2:DescribeInstances
    Resource: "*"
```

Quick tip: Enhance your coding experience with the **AI Code Explainer** and **Quick Copy** features. Open this book in the next-gen Packt Reader. Click the **Copy** button

(1) to quickly copy code into your coding environment, or click the **Explain** button

(2) to get the AI assistant to explain a block of code to you.

```
function calculate(a, b) {
  return {sum: a + b};
};
```

Copy (1) Explain (2)

The next-gen Packt Reader is included for free with the purchase of this book. Scan the QR code OR visit `packtpub.com/unlock`, then use the search bar to find this book by name. Double-check the edition shown to make sure you get the right one.

The preceding policy allows the `ec2:DescribeInstances` action to be performed on all resources. The `Version` field specifies the version of the policy language being used. The `Statement` field is a list of individual statements that together make up the policy.

Each statement consists of an `Effect` field (either `Allow` or `Deny`), an `Action` field that lists the actions that are allowed or denied by the `Effect` field, and a `Resource` field that specifies the resources that the actions apply to. IAM policies can be attached to IAM users, groups, and roles to grant permissions to perform various actions on AWS resources.

Policies can be defined in the following two ways:

- **Managed policies**: When policies are defined as managed policies, they are created as standalone policies, and therefore, they can be attached to multiple entities. Out of the box, AWS provides a set of predefined managed policies that can be used in many use cases. Managed policies can be combined to deliver additional access to roles, users, or groups. Finally, AWS users can define and customize their own managed policies.

- **Inline policies:** Inline policies are created within the definition of an IAM entity and can only be assigned to the entity to which they are attached. They do not have their own **Amazon Resource Name (ARN)**. Since inline policies are related to a specific entity, they are not reusable. An ARN is an identifier used to uniquely identify AWS resources. It is a string that consists of several different parts, including the service, region, and resource identifier. Here is an example of an AWS ARN: `arn:aws:s3:::my_bucket/example.jpg`. In this example, `arn:aws:s3` indicates that the resource is an S3 bucket, `my_bucket` is the name of the bucket, and `example.jpg` is the name of a file stored in the bucket.

It is best practice to use managed policies whenever possible and use inline policies only when there is a good reason to do so.

Permissions are lists of actions that can be taken on AWS resources. When a user or group is created, initially, they have no permissions. One or more policies can be attached to the new user or group to enable access to resources.

When creating policies, it is a good idea to abide by the principle of least privilege. In simple terms, this means that entities should be given a high enough level of access to perform assigned tasks, but nothing more. For example, suppose an Amazon EC2 instance is created, and we know that only five users with five different IPs will access it. In that case, we should use `allowlist` for those IPs and only give them access instead of opening the Amazon EC2 instance to the whole world.

Here is an example IAM policy that allows an EC2 instance to perform certain actions on S3 and EC2 resources, but only from a specific IP address range:

```
{
"Version": "2012-10-17",
"Statement": [
{
"Effect": "Allow",
"Action": [
"s3:ListBucket",
"s3:GetObject"
],
"Resource": [
"arn:aws:s3:::my-s3-bucket"
],
"Condition": {
"IpAddress": {
```

```
"aws:SourceIp": "10.0.0.0/16"
}
}
},
{
"Effect": "Allow",
"Action": [
"ec2:StartInstances",
"ec2:StopInstances"
],
"Resource": "*",
"Condition": {
"IpAddress": {
"aws:SourceIp": "10.0.1.1/16"
}
        }
    }
  ]
}
```

This policy allows the EC2 instance to list the contents of the `my-s3-bucket` S3 bucket and retrieve objects from it, as well as to start and stop other EC2 instances, but only if the request originates from an IP address in the range `10.0.1.1/16`. You can attach this policy to an IAM role and then associate the role with an EC2 instance to apply the permissions to the instance.

This is just one example of how IAM policies can be used to `allowlist` EC2 IP addresses. There are many other ways to write IAM policies, and you should carefully consider the specific needs of your use case when writing your own policies. AWS provides a policy simulator. This policy simulator can test new policies you may create and ensure they have the correct syntax. You can learn more here: `https://docs.aws.amazon.com/IAM/latest/UserGuide/access_policies_testing-policies.html`.

Permissions can be assigned to AWS users, groups, and roles via policies. These permissions can be given with policies in one of two ways:

- **Identity-based policies:** In this case, the policies are attached to users, groups, or roles
- **Resource-based policies:** In this case, the policies are attached to AWS resources such as Amazon S3 buckets, Amazon EC2 instances, and AWS Lambda functions

Identity-based policies are attached to an AWS identity and grant permissions to the identity. AWS identities include IAM users, IAM roles, and AWS service accounts. Identity-based policies can be used to grant permissions to IAM users or roles in your AWS account or to grant permissions to other AWS accounts.

Resource-based policies are attached to a resource, such as an Amazon S3 bucket or an Amazon SNS topic, and grant permissions for the resource. These permissions can be used by any AWS identity that has access to the resource.

Both types of policies use the same syntax and structure, and you can use them together to fine-tune access to your resources. It is important to choose the right type of policy for your use case and to design your policies carefully to ensure that they provide the right level of access to your resources. Now, let's learn how to manage multiple AWS accounts using AWS Organizations.

AWS Organizations

AWS Organizations is a service that can be used to manage multiple AWS accounts in a consolidated manner. It provides a centralized location where you can see all your organization's bills and manage all your AWS accounts from one place. This central location makes it much easier to establish, manage, and enforce your organization's security policies. This central control ensures that security administrators and auditors can perform their jobs more efficiently and confidently.

These are the most important and relevant concepts when working with the AWS Organizations service:

- **Organization:** The overarching owner that will control all AWS accounts.
- **Root account:** The owner account for all other AWS accounts. Only one root account can exist across the organization. The root account needs to be created when the organization is created.
- **Organizational unit (OU):** A grouping of underlying AWS accounts and/or other OUs. An OU can be the parent of other OUs. This enables the potential creation of a hierarchy of OUs that resembles a family tree. See the following diagram for more clarity.

- **AWS account**: A traditional AWS account that manages AWS resources and services. AWS accounts reside under an organizational unit or the root account.
- **Service control policy (SCP)**: An SCP specifies the services and permissions for users and roles. An SCP can be associated with an AWS account or OU. SCP restricts permissions for IAM users/roles in the account, including the root of the account.

The following figure illustrates how these components interact with each other:

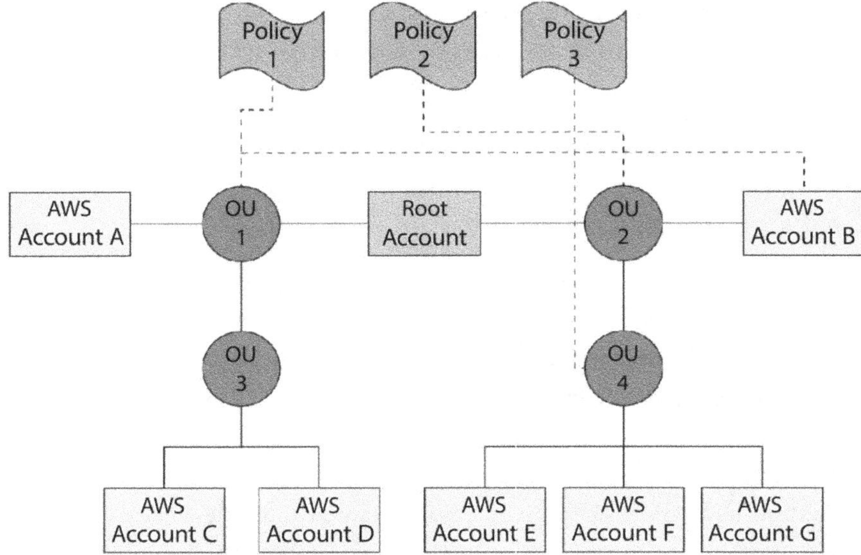

Figure 8.6: Sample OU hierarchy

As you can see in the preceding diagram, **Policy 1** is associated with **OU 1** and with **AWS Account B**. **Policy 1** is also applied to all children of **OU 1** (**OU 3, AWS Account A, C**, and **AWS Account D**).

Since **Policy 1** is associated with **AWS Account B** directly, it overrides **Policy 2**, which is associated with **OU 2** and all its children except for **AWS Account B**. **Policy 3** is associated with **OU 4** and all its children (**AWS Accounts E, F**, and **G**). However, note that SCPs do not override the policies. They are combined and evaluated together. Deny always takes precedence.

The following diagram shows an AWS organizational structure created in the AWS console:

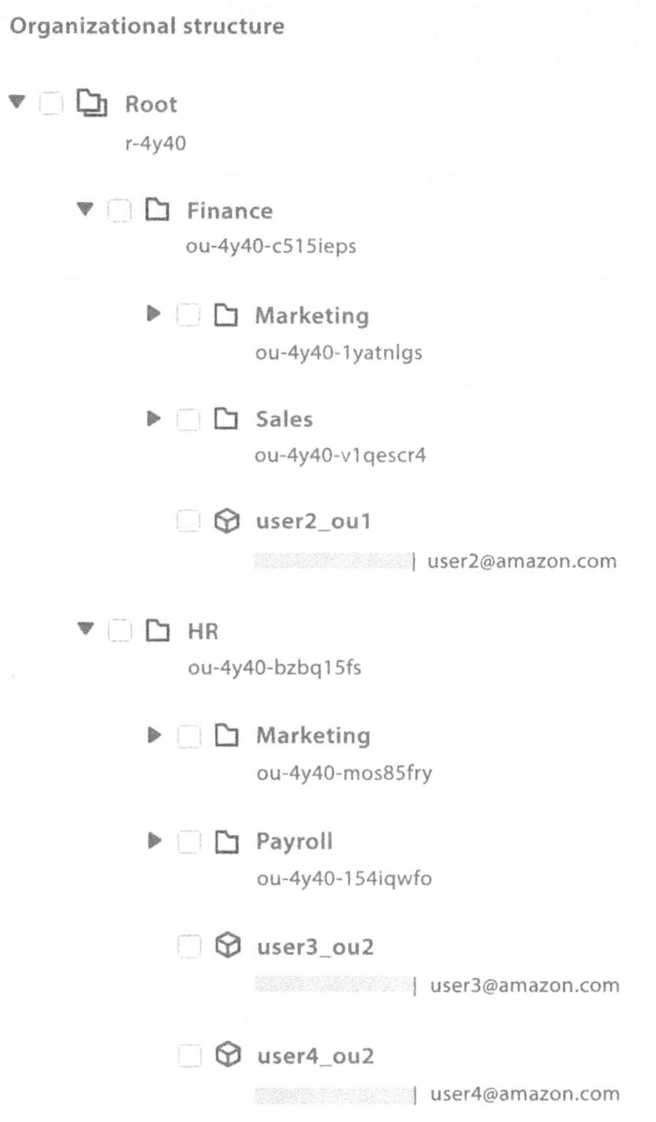

Organizational structure

Root
r-4y40

Finance
ou-4y40-c515ieps

Marketing
ou-4y40-1yatnlgs

Sales
ou-4y40-v1qescr4

user2_ou1
| user2@amazon.com

HR
ou-4y40-bzbq15fs

Marketing
ou-4y40-mos85fry

Payroll
ou-4y40-154iqwfo

user3_ou2
| user3@amazon.com

user4_ou2
| user4@amazon.com

Figure 8.7: AWS OU hierarchy in an AWS account

As you can see in the preceding diagram, two OUs are under the root account, and each unit has its own sub-unit and AWS accounts.

The following are the key benefits of AWS Organizations:

- It provides tools to centrally govern and manage your cloud environment. You can quickly scale by creating accounts and allocating resources, and provision common resources and permissions to new and existing accounts using AWS CloudFormation StackSets.
- You can customize your environment by applying governance policies and can simplify access management for users by providing cross-application permissions with your identity source and AWS's SSO service.
- You can secure and audit your environment by logging all events in AWS CloudTrail.
- You can apply scheduled backups with AWS Backup for all accounts in the organization.
- You can manage costs and identify cost-saving measures and consolidate billing charges for your organization, and take advantage of volume discounts for qualifying services.

Without AWS Organizations' SCP, all these policies would have to be repeated individually for each account. Every time there was a change to a policy, it would have to be changed individually in each account. This old approach had a high likelihood of policies that were supposed to be identical getting out of sync. You can learn more about AWS Organizations by visiting the AWS page here: `https://aws.amazon.com/organizations/`.

Managing multiple accounts could be complicated. If you'd like to start your AWS environment using a simple UI and built-in best practices, it's better to use AWS Control Tower.

When you assign permission to a user or resource, you want to see the policy evaluation and how it will work. You can refer to details on IAM policy evaluation here: `https://docs.aws.amazon.com/IAM/latest/UserGuide/reference_policies_evaluation-logic.html`.

Hopefully, the concepts of users, groups, roles, permissions, and policies are clearer now. IAM is far from the only security service that AWS offers. AWS IAM is a vast topic that warrants a book in itself. You can find more details about AWS IAM here: `https://aws.amazon.com/iam/`. Let's learn about the next service in the IAM category: AWS Directory Service.

AWS Managed Microsoft AD Service

Microsoft AD has been a popular choice for user and role management for decades, which, in computer years, is a long time. Given this popularity, AWS offers a fully managed implementation of Microsoft AD. AWS Directory Service for Microsoft AD, also known as **AWS Managed Microsoft AD**, allows AWS services that require directory services to integrate with Microsoft AD.

AWS Managed Microsoft AD uses the actual Microsoft AD. It does not need to stay in sync because it does not copy the contents of existing ADs to the cloud. For this reason, the standard Microsoft AD administration tools can be used, and you can leverage the built-in AD capabilities, such as group policies and SSO. Using AWS Managed Microsoft AD, you can integrate Amazon EC2 and Amazon RDS for SQL Server instances with Microsoft AD.

In addition, AWS offers Simple AD and AD Connector to help you integrate your on-premises AD with AWS resources, especially when managing user access securely and collaboratively. Simple AD is a standalone, managed directory powered by Samba 4. It is ideal for small to medium-sized businesses that need basic AD features such as user authentication, group management, and joining Amazon EC2 instances to a domain without the overhead of managing a full Microsoft AD. It's cost-effective and easy to set up, but doesn't support complex AD features. On the other hand, AD Connector acts as a proxy that connects your AWS environment to your existing on-premises Microsoft AD. This lets you use your on-premises AD credentials to log in to AWS applications and services such as Amazon WorkSpaces, QuickSight, or AWS Management Console, without replicating your AD data to the cloud. It's a great choice for organizations that want to maintain a single source of truth for identity and credentials on-premises while enabling cloud integration.

You can learn more about AWS Directory Service here: `https://aws.amazon.com/directoryservice/`. Let's learn about how AWS offers support for SSO.

AWS IAM Identity Center (successor to AWS SSO)

Being able to sign on to multiple enterprise applications using a user's network login ID has been a pervasive way to manage application access for a while now.

AWS IAM Identity Center has replaced AWS SSO and offers a secure way to establish and link workforce identities, as well as to centrally manage their access across AWS accounts and applications. With AWS IAM Identity Center, SSO can be implemented without too much effort, and it can also be centrally managed, even in a multi-account AWS environment. It can be used to manage user access and permissions for multiple AWS accounts in one central place by leveraging AWS Organizations. IAM Identity Center can be used to configure and maintain all account permissions automatically. It does not need additional configuration for each account. User permissions can be assigned using roles. The following are the benefits of IAM Identity Center:

- Manage users and groups where you want; connect to AWS once.
- Centrally assign and manage access to AWS accounts, AWS SSO-integrated, and cloud-based business applications.
- Provide an SSO user portal to assigned AWS accounts, AWS, and business applications.

- It works with existing processes for joiners, leavers, and movers.
- Increase developer productivity with the AWS CLI v2.
- External IdP connections sync through **System for Cross-domain Identity Management (SCIM)**. SCIM is a standardized protocol used to automate the exchange of user identity information between identity providers and cloud applications.

You can use the following simple steps to set up application access through SSO:

1. Choose an identity resource, which could be an IAM user, group, or resource.
2. Define permission sets for each role.
3. Assign groups/users to permission sets in selected accounts.
4. Connect cloud apps with SAML.
5. Assign groups/users to apps.

To manage user identities, IAM Identity Center provides an identity store or can connect with an existing identity store. Some of the supported identity stores are the following:

- Microsoft AD
- Microsoft Entra ID
- Okta Universal Directory

Any activity that occurs when using IAM Identity Center will be recorded using AWS CloudTrail. You can find more details about configuring SSO using AWS IAM Identity Center here: `https://aws.amazon.com/iam/identity-center/`. You have now learned how to manage access for multiple users.

AWS Control Tower

AWS first brought the concept of a **landing zone** as an AWS account vending mechanism. A landing zone in AWS refers to a well-architected, secure, and scalable environment that acts as a starting point for setting up and governing a multi-account AWS environment. Think of it as a blueprint or foundation that helps you quickly set up AWS accounts with security baselines, logging, compliance, and centralized identity in place from the beginning. When you build applications or workloads across different AWS accounts, a landing zone ensures that all these accounts follow consistent security and operational standards.

Setting up a landing zone manually can be complex. It involves creating multiple accounts (such as dev, test, and prod), configuring AWS Organizations, applying SCPs, setting up centralized logging, configuring identity providers, and more. This is where the AWS Control Tower simplifies the process.

If you have a simple AWS setup with a few servers and only one AWS account, then you don't need AWS Control Tower. But if you are part of an environment with hundreds or thousands of resources and multiple AWS accounts and teams, then you will want to learn about and leverage AWS Control Tower. **AWS Control Tower** simplifies the administration, governance, and security setup of a multi-account environment.

Control Tower helps you quickly set up and govern multi-account environments securely. It automatically applies management features from existing AWS services, such as Organizations, AWS Config, AWS Cloud Trail, and IAM Identity Center, and implements default account structure and governance policies based on AWS best practices from thousands of customers.

You can continue to use native features from AWS Organizations, such as tags or backup policies, and integrated AWS services. AWS Control Tower enables you to set up company-wide policies using the out-of-the-box preventive, detective, and proactive controls across multiple AWS accounts. Without AWS Control Tower, you would have to apply the individual policies to each account, opening up the possibility of having inconsistencies in your accounts. You can learn more about AWS Control Tower by visiting the AWS page here: `https://aws.amazon.com/controltower/`. Now, let's learn how to manage multiple resources across OUs using AWS Resource Access Manager.

AWS Resource Access Manager

The AWS **Resource Access Manager** (**RAM**) service allows you to share AWS resources with other AWS accounts or within your own organization. AWS RAM allows you to share resources such as Amazon EC2 instances, Amazon RDS database instances, and **Amazon Virtual Private Cloud** (**Amazon VPC**) with other AWS accounts or within your organization.

You can use AWS RAM to manage resource sharing by creating resource shares, which are collections of resources that you want to share with specific AWS accounts or within your organization. You can specify the accounts or OUs that you want to share the resources with, and set permissions to control how the resources can be accessed.

AWS RAM is useful for scenarios where you want to share resources with other teams or organizations, or when you want to centralize the management of resource sharing within your organization. It helps you simplify resource sharing, reduce the complexity of resource management, and maintain control over the resources that you share. Here are the steps you can follow to use AWS RAM:

1. Sign in to the AWS Management Console and open the AWS RAM console at `https://console.aws.amazon.com/ram/`.
2. In the left navigation pane, choose **Resource Shares**.

3. Choose **Create resource share**.
4. On the **Create resource share** page, enter a name and optional description for your resource share.
5. Select the resources that you want to share and specify the accounts or OUs that you want to share the resources with.
6. Choose **Create resource share**.
7. To view the status of the resource share, choose the resource share in the list and then choose the **Status** tab.
8. To modify the resource share, choose the resource share in the list and then choose the **Modify** tab.

Note that you can only share resources that support sharing, and some resources have additional sharing requirements. For example, you can't share an EC2 instance unless it's in a VPC. You can learn more about AWS RAM by visiting the AWS page here: `https://aws.amazon.com/ram/`.

As of now, you have learned that managing users' security is the responsibility of your organization, but what if you are developing a web or mobile app open to the world? In those scenarios, you must manage millions of users, secure their credentials, and provide the required access. Amazon Cognito fulfills these needs. Let's learn more about it.

Amazon Cognito

Amazon Cognito enables developers to add user sign-in, sign-up, and access control to their web and mobile apps. It provides granular APIs and SDKs to manage end user authentication and authorization workflows that can be customized using out-of-the-box integration with AWS Lambda.

Cognito is fully managed with a built-in hosted UI and provides out-of-the-box support for open standards authentication protocols such as OAuth 2.

You can easily integrate your app to authenticate users using federation with Facebook or log in with Amazon, Google, and custom OpenID Connect or SAML providers. It provides a serverless, fully managed directory to store and securely manage user information using MFA through SMS and email. Amazon Cognito offers authentication, authorization, and user management services for web and mobile applications. Here are some of the security features of Amazon Cognito:

- **MFA**: Amazon Cognito supports MFA to help protect against unauthorized access to user accounts. MFA can be configured to require a one-time code sent to the user's phone or email, or a hardware token.

- **Password policies**: It allows you to set password policies to ensure that users choose strong passwords.
- **Encryption**: It stores user data and passwords in an encrypted format, using AES-256 encryption.
- **Access control**: It provides fine-grained access control to resources using IAM policies.
- **Activity tracking**: It tracks user sign-in and sign-out activity, as well as changes to user attributes. This information can be used to monitor for suspicious activity and alert administrators.
- **Security tokens**: It issues **JSON Web Tokens (JWTs)** to authenticated users, which can be used to access authorized resources. JWTs have a limited lifespan and can be easily invalidated if a user's security is compromised.
- **Account recovery**: It provides options for users to recover their accounts if they forget their passwords or lose access to their MFA devices.

You can learn more about Amazon Cognito by visiting the AWS page here: `https://aws.amazon.com/cognito/`.

In this section about the security services in AWS's IAM pillar, you learned about managing user security in AWS. As AWS security is a vast topic that would require multiple books to cover in detail, in the upcoming section, you will learn a bit about each AWS service belonging to different security pillars, with resources to learn more. Let's learn about the next security pillar, which helps you detect and control security threats.

Applying security controls

Security is more about preventive gestures than reactive, as any security incident can cause significant damage to organizations, so it's better to detect and fix incidents before a security leak can cause damage. AWS provides an array of services to help you monitor, detect, and mitigate security threats. The following are common security audit services:

- **AWS Config**: AWS Config enables you to assess, track, and evaluate the configurations of your AWS resources. With AWS Config, you can monitor the changes to your resources and assess their compliance with internal policies and regulatory standards. Additionally, you can use AWS Config to conduct security analysis and improve the visibility of your resource configurations, making it easier to identify potential security risks and respond to any incidents. Overall, AWS Config provides a centralized and automated way to manage the configuration of your AWS resources, ensuring that they remain compliant and secure over time. You can learn more about Config by visiting the AWS page here: `https://aws.amazon.com/config/`.

- **AWS CloudTrail**: AWS CloudTrail provides a record of all API calls made to your AWS account. This service enables you to monitor and audit your AWS resource activity, including changes to your resources and the actions of your users and applications. With AWS CloudTrail, you can gain greater visibility of your resource usage and security posture, as well as quickly identify and respond to any suspicious or unauthorized activity. AWS CloudTrail supports multiple platforms, including the AWS Management Console, AWS CLI, and AWS SDKs, making it easy to track and manage your AWS resource activity from a variety of sources. You can learn more about CloudTrail by visiting the AWS page here: `https://aws.amazon.com/cloudtrail/`.
- **Amazon VPC Flow Logs**: The VPC Flow Logs service enables you to capture information about the IP traffic going to and from network interfaces in your VPC. This service allows you to track the traffic flow and troubleshoot network connectivity issues, as well as improve the security of your network by identifying any potential network threats or unauthorized access. You can learn more about Flow Logs by visiting the AWS page here: `https://docs.aws.amazon.com/vpc/latest/userguide/flow-logs.html`.
- **Amazon CloudWatch**: CloudWatch is a monitoring service that enables you to monitor your AWS resources and applications in real time. With CloudWatch, you can monitor metrics, logs, and events generated by your resources and applications, and set alarms to be notified of any issues. This service provides a centralized and automated way to monitor your environment, making it easier to detect and resolve issues, improve the performance of your resources, and ensure the availability of your applications. CloudWatch supports a variety of resources and services, including Amazon EC2 instances, Amazon RDS databases, AWS Lambda functions, and many more. You can also use CloudWatch to monitor custom metrics, such as the number of requests made to an application, the response time of a database, or the disk usage of an EC2 instance. You can learn more about CloudWatch by visiting the AWS page here: `https://aws.amazon.com/cloudwatch/`.

Let's learn about security control services in detail.

Amazon GuardDuty

Amazon GuardDuty is an AWS service that can detect unauthorized actors' threats, malicious behavior, and activity. It protects all other AWS resources and your enterprise's data. Getting more traffic in the application is usually good news because it typically means more business, but additional traffic requires more work to track and monitor additional logs and activity. The following screenshot shows services being monitored by GuardDuty:

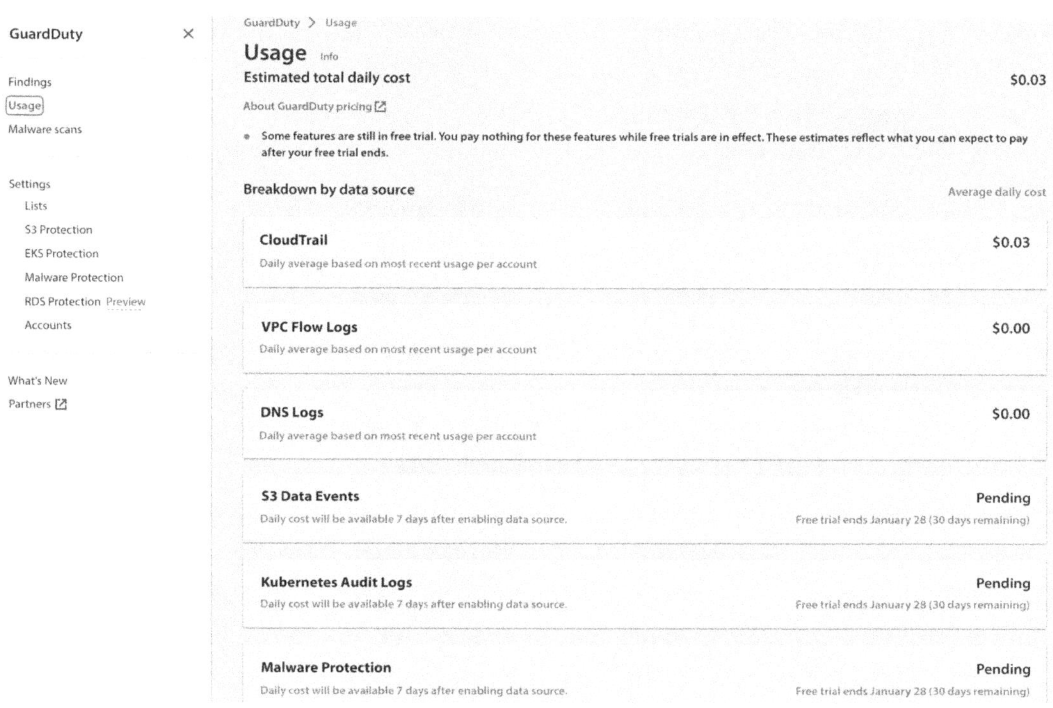

Figure 8.8: Amazon GuardDuty data source list

Amazon GuardDuty enables and simplifies the monitoring of this activity. It leverages machine learning and advanced anomaly detection to compile, process, and prioritize potential malicious activity. GuardDuty can analyze billions of real-time events across various AWS real-time and near-real-time streams such as AWS CloudTrail logs, Amazon VPC Flow Logs, and DNS logs.

However, keep in mind that Amazon GuardDuty doesn't do anything with the analysis. It is an intrusion detection system, not an intrusion prevention system. If you need enforcement for malicious IPs, you will need a third-party solution such as Aviatrix GuardDuty Enforcement. You can learn more about GuardDuty by visiting the AWS page here: `https://aws.amazon.com/guardduty/`.

Amazon Inspector

Amazon Inspector is a service that automatically checks application compliance against certain predefined policies and is used to increase compliance. Amazon Inspector can identify vulnerabilities, exposures, and deviations from predefined best practices. Once the assessment has been completed, the service generates a comprehensive report of security flaws and issues sorted by severity level. These findings can then be used to close these security gaps.

Amazon Inspector security assessments enable users to look for unauthorized network access to Amazon EC2 instances. It can find vulnerabilities in EC2 instances and containers. Amazon Inspector assessments are available as predefined rule components that can map to security best practices and vulnerability definitions. Some samples of predefined rules are as follows:

- Someone trying to access EC2 instances from outside your network
- Someone turning on the remote root login
- Identifying software and operating system versions that are due for patching

These rules are constantly monitored and enhanced by the AWS security team. You can learn more about Amazon Inspector by visiting the AWS page here: `https://aws.amazon.com/inspector/`.

Building infrastructure protection

Infrastructure protection is the first line of defense when it comes to security. AWS secures physical infrastructure with multi-layered security in its data centers. However, securing the logical infrastructure boundary and network traffic becomes your responsibility, as AWS provides you with more control to manage boundaries for your logical cloud infrastructure. AWS provides the following services to protect your cloud infrastructure:

- **AWS Web Application Firewall (WAF)**: WAF is a firewall that allows you to monitor HTTP and HTTPS requests made to your applications and block, allow, or count requests based on conditions that you define, such as IP addresses, headers, and content.
- **AWS Firewall Manager**: Firewall Manager is a security service that makes it easier to manage the firewall rules for your Amazon VPC security groups.
- **AWS Shield**: Shield is a managed **distributed denial of service** (**DDoS**) protection service for AWS customers.

Let's learn about AWS infrastructure security services in detail.

AWS WAF

AWS WAF, as the name implies, is a firewall for your web applications. It can create a layer of protection around your web applications and RESTful APIs. It guards against the most well-known web exploits. AWS WAF can be used to control network traffic. This traffic is controlled by creating rules. These rules can target well-known exploits such as SQL injections or XSS attacks. With WAF, you can define rules to allow, block, or monitor requests based on IP addresses, HTTP headers, query strings, URI paths, and more. To simplify management, you can group multiple rules into rule groups, which can be reused across various web ACLs, making policy enforcement more efficient and scalable.

Additionally, AWS WAF supports rate-based rules, which automatically block IP addresses sending requests at rates exceeding a specified threshold, helping to mitigate DoS attempts or abusive bot behavior. By combining custom rules, rule groups, managed rule sets, and rate-based protections, AWS WAF offers a flexible and powerful layer of security for your web-facing resources.

Furthermore, these rules can be customized to filter transactions that meet user-defined patterns. AWS WAF has AWS Managed Rules, which simplifies management. AWS can manage these rules, and AWS Marketplace sellers also offer preconfigured rules. AWS and Marketplace rules are constantly modified as new threats are identified. AWS WAF also provides an API to assist in developing, deploying, and maintaining these security rules.

AWS WAF can be deployed on the following:

- Amazon CloudFront
- Application Load Balancer
- Origin servers running on EC2
- Amazon API Gateway
- AWS AppSync

AWS WAF pricing depends on the number of rules deployed and the number of requests that applications receive. You can learn more about WAF by visiting the AWS page here: `https://aws.amazon.com/waf/`.

AWS Firewall Manager

AWS Firewall Manager makes setting up firewalls simple. It enables users to administer firewall rules in a central dashboard. This can be achieved even across multiple AWS accounts and applications.

Cloud environments are dynamic. This can create maintenance headaches as new applications come online. AWS Firewall Manager simplifies the process of provisioning new applications and ensuring they comply with an enterprise's security policies by enabling users to manage firewall settings from one location.

If new security rules need to be created or if existing rules need to be modified, they can also be changed only once. Some of the services in AWS that can benefit from AWS Firewall Manager are the following:

- Application Load Balancer
- API Gateway
- Amazon CloudFront distributions
- Amazon EC2

AWS Firewall Manager allows adding AWS WAF rules, AWS Shield Advanced protection, security groups, and AWS Network Firewall rules to VPCs across accounts and resources using a centralized dashboard. You can learn more about Firewall Manager by visiting the AWS page here: `https://aws.amazon.com/firewall-manager/`.

AWS Shield

AWS Shield is an AWS-managed DDoS protection service used to protect systems and data. AWS Shield delivers automatic attack detection and resolution that can keep your application running, or at least reduce the amount of downtime. Since AWS Shield Standard comes with all AWS accounts, you normally have to contact AWS support to assist you if you suffer a DDoS attack. AWS Shield comes in two flavors:

- **AWS Shield Standard**: Provided at no additional charge to all AWS customers
- **AWS Shield Advanced**: Provides a higher level of protection but at an additional cost

AWS Shield Standard can protect against and handle the more common types of attacks. The more common DDoS attacks happen at the network and transport layers. AWS Shield Standard can help you protect Amazon CloudFront and Amazon Route 53 against Layer 3 and Layer 4 attacks.

AWS Shield Advanced provides higher protection for more services. It can be used to defend against attacks targeting the following:

- Amazon EC2 instances
- Elastic Load Balancing
- Amazon CloudFront
- AWS Global Accelerator
- Amazon Route 53

To get this level of protection, you will need to subscribe to AWS Shield Advanced and pay an additional fee. AWS Shield Advanced not only protects against network and transport layer attacks but also delivers additional monitoring and resolution, protecting against large and sophisticated DDoS attacks and providing real-time reporting when attacks occur. It integrates with AWS WAF. AWS Shield Advanced provides 24-hour support from AWS's DDoS response team as an additional feature. Finally, with AWS Shield Advanced, AWS will cover any charges your account incurs for certain services that can be attributed to an attack. You can learn more about AWS Shield by visiting the AWS page here: `https://aws.amazon.com/shield/`.

Data is the essential thing that any organization wants to protect. Let's learn about AWS services available for data protection.

Building data protection

Data is key for any application or organization. Most hacking attempts are made to steal data, and the leakage of your customer data can be very harmful to your organization in terms of customer trust and financial damage. You need to have multi-layer security to protect your customer data. As you are the owner of the data, most of the time, the responsibility for data protection lies with you. AWS provides a number of services to protect data:

- **Amazon Macie**: Amazon Macie is a security service that uses machine learning to automatically discover, classify, and protect sensitive data in AWS.
- **AWS Key Management Service (KMS)**: KMS is a managed service that makes it easy for you to create and control the encryption keys used to encrypt your data.
- **AWS CloudHSM**: CloudHSM is a **hardware security module (HSM)** service that provides secure key storage for cryptographic operations within the AWS cloud.
- **AWS Certificate Manager (ACM)**: ACM is a service that makes it easy for you to manage SSL/TLS certificates for your AWS-hosted websites and applications.
- **AWS Secrets Manager**: Secrets Manager is a secure and scalable service that enables you to store, manage, and rotate your secrets, such as database credentials, API keys, and SSH keys.
- **Server-side encryption (SSE)**: SSE is a security feature for encrypting data stored in AWS storage services, such as Amazon S3 and Amazon EBS. You learned about SSE in *Chapter 5, Storage in AWS: Choosing the Right Tool for the Job*. You can explore more about SSE by visiting the SSE page here: `https://docs.aws.amazon.com/AmazonS3/latest/userguide/serv-side-encryption.html`.

Let's learn about some of these services in more detail.

Amazon Macie

Amazon Macie is another fully managed security service. It can be used to protect your data and its privacy. It leverages artificial intelligence and machine learning to find and protect sensitive data in AWS environments.

In today's enterprises, data comes in at an ever-increasing speed. Handling those growing volumes of data creates scalability issues with more data and complexity, making expenses increase. Amazon Macie enables the automation of sensitive data discovery.

Since it leverages machine learning, it can scale and handle petabyte-sized datasets. Macie creates a list of Amazon S3 buckets in a user's account. It can flag which ones are unencrypted, which ones can be accessed publicly, and buckets that are being shared with other AWS accounts that are not defined in AWS Organizations.

Amazon Macie uses machine learning and pattern matching on these buckets. Amazon Macie can be configured to identify sensitive data, such as personally identifiable information, and deliver alerts to a predefined user base. Once these alerts and issues are generated, they can be quickly sorted and filtered in the AWS Management Console. It can then be integrated with other AWS services such as Security Hub, EventBridge, Organizations, and CloudWatch using workflow or event management systems. It can also be used together with other AWS services.

An example is AWS Step Functions. AWS Step Functions can leverage automated remediation actions. This can assist with compliance with rules and regulations, such as the **Health Insurance Portability and Accountability Act** (**HIPAA**) and the **General Data Protection Regulation** (**GDPR**). You can learn more about Macie by visiting the AWS page here: `https://aws.amazon.com/macie/`.

AWS KMS

AWS KMS is a service offered by AWS that simplifies the process of creating and managing encryption keys. It provides a central, secure location for storing and managing your encryption keys, and it integrates with other AWS services to help you easily encrypt and decrypt data in the cloud. It is a secure and fault-tolerant service. AWS KMS can be used to assist in the management of the encryption of data at rest. It provides the ability to create and manage cryptographic keys. It can also be used to manage which users, services, and applications have access to them.

Behind the scenes, AWS KMS uses HSMs to protect your encryption keys, ensuring that they are kept secure even if an attacker gains access to your systems. It also provides auditing and logging capabilities to help you track the use of your keys and meet compliance requirements.

You can use AWS KMS to encrypt data in a number of different ways, including the following:

- Encrypting data at rest, such as data stored in Amazon S3 or Amazon EBS.
- Encrypting data in transit, such as data transmitted over the network or data transmitted between AWS regions.
- Encrypting data in use, such as data stored in memory or data being processed by an application.
- **Customer master keys** (**CMKs**) are the primary resources in AWS KMS. You can create and manage these keys in your account, define usage policies, enable key rotation, and audit key usage. CMKs are best when you need full control over your encryption keys and their lifecycle.

- **AWS managed keys** are keys automatically created and managed by AWS for specific AWS services such as Amazon S3, EBS, or RDS. You can use them for encryption without handling the keys yourself, but they are visible in your AWS KMS console with limited configuration options.
- **AWS owned keys** are encryption keys fully managed by AWS and not visible in your account. They're used by AWS services to encrypt your data without any user-level visibility or control. They are best for scenarios where encryption is needed but key management by the user is not required.

The HSMs that AWS KMS uses comply with **Federal Information Processing Standard (FIPS)** 140-2. AWS KMS integrates with AWS CloudTrail so that it is simple to see who has used the keys and when. You can learn more about KMS by visiting the AWS page here: `https://aws.amazon.com/kms/`.

AWS CloudHSM

AWS makes encrypting data at rest quite simple if you use encryption keys provided by AWS through KMS. However, KMS works under the shared tenancy model, which means that behind the scenes, a single HSM may be storing keys from different customers. In some instances, such as in the finance industry, you cannot use shared storage to store encryption keys in order to comply with regulations, which state you have to have your own dedicated HSM for key storage.

For that, AWS provides a service called **AWS CloudHSM**.

AWS CloudHSM is an HSM that empowers users to generate their own encryption keys. CloudHSM provides the ability to create encryption keys using FIPS 140-2 Level 3 validated HSMs. AWS CloudHSM can be integrated with other AWS services via well-defined industry-standard APIs. Some of the APIs supported are as follows:

- PKCS#11
- Microsoft **CryptoNG (CNG)** libraries
- **Java Cryptography Extensions (JCEs)**

AWS CloudHSM complies with many security standards. It is also possible to export the generated keys to various third-party HSMs. Like many of the other security services we have learned about in this section, AWS CloudHSM is fully managed by AWS, enabling you to focus on your applications and not the administration of your key management service. Some of the tasks that AWS handles when using this service are as follows:

- Provisioning the required hardware to run the service
- Applying software patching

- Making sure the service is highly available
- Performing backups

Like other cloud services, you can use CloudHSM with an on-demand, pay-as-you-go model. You can learn more about CloudHSM by visiting the AWS page here: `https://aws.amazon.com/cloudhsm/`.

AWS Certificate Manager

AWS Certificate Manager is another security service. It can create, maintain, and deploy public and private SSL/TLS certificates that can be added to other AWS services and applications. SSL/TLS certificates can secure network communications by enabling encryption. They can also be used to authenticate a website's identity in public and private networks. AWS Certificate Manager streamlines and automates the certificate management process.

AWS Certificate Manager can be used to provision and renew a certificate and install it on another AWS service, such as Elastic Load Balancing, Amazon CloudFront, and APIs on API Gateway. It can also be used to create private certificates for internal applications. These certificates can then be centrally managed.

There is no charge when you provision public and private certificates using AWS Certificate Manager. The cost is bundled with spinning up the underlying resources (such as an EC2 instance). When you use **AWS Private Certificate Authority** (**AWS Private CA**), there is a monthly charge for the use of Private CA and for the private certificates that are issued. You can learn more about Certificate Manager by visiting the AWS page here: `https://aws.amazon.com/certificate-manager/`.

AWS Secrets Manager

AWS Secrets Manager is a security service that can be used to protect secrets. These secrets may be strings such as passwords that can be used to access services, applications, and IT resources. AWS Secrets Manager facilitates the rotation, management, and retrieval of API keys, database credentials, passwords, and other secrets. These secrets can be retrieved using the Secrets Manager APIs. The need to store passwords clearly in plain text files is obviated by using AWS Secrets Manager. Some of the services that can integrate with AWS Secrets Manager are as follows:

- Amazon RDS
- Amazon Redshift
- Amazon DynamoDB
- Amazon Neptune

- Amazon DocumentDB

AWS Secrets Manager can be customized to support additional types of secrets. Some examples of use cases are the following:

- API keys
- OAuth authentication tokens

Another feature of AWS Secrets Manager is that it allows secrets to be rotated periodically without impacting applications that use them for password management and other uses.

You can learn more about Secrets Manager by visiting the AWS page here: `https://aws.amazon.com/secrets-manager/`.

There are so many AWS services that collect data, and security needs to look across all the logs and data collected. However, collecting data across services such as VPC Flow Logs, AWS CloudTrail logs, audit logs, GuardDuty, and so on could be very tedious. You need a unified view of logs to understand any security issues. AWS provides a way to quickly analyze the issue through a service called Amazon Detective. Let's learn about Amazon Detective in more detail.

Amazon Detective

Amazon Detective is a security solution that employs machine learning, statistical analysis, and graph theory to help customers identify and investigate security issues in their AWS accounts. This service provides a powerful tool for analyzing and understanding security-related activity in your AWS environment, making it easier for you to quickly identify the root cause of any suspicious activity or security incidents. It can be used to identify unusual activity or suspicious behavior in your account, such as resource provisioning or access patterns that deviate from normal behavior.

To use Amazon Detective, you first need to enable the service in your AWS account and then connect your AWS resources, such as Amazon EC2 instances and Amazon RDS databases, to it. Amazon Detective then analyzes log data from your AWS resources, creates a linked set of data that provides you with a comprehensive view of your security posture, and builds a graph of the interactions and relationships between them. It uses machine learning algorithms to identify patterns and anomalies in the data that may indicate security issues or suspicious activity.

Once Amazon Detective has identified a potential issue, it provides a detailed investigation summary that includes a timeline of events, relevant log data, and recommended actions for further investigation or remediation. You can use this summary to quickly understand the issue and take the appropriate action to resolve it. Detective automatically processes data from GuardDuty findings, VPC Flow Logs, CloudTrail logs, Amazon EKS audit logs, AWS Security Hub findings, and so on.

With Amazon Detective, you can use advanced algorithms to analyze security-related activity in your AWS environment and gain insights into potential security risks. The service also provides visualizations and summaries that help you triage security findings and prioritize your investigations, making it easier for you to focus on the most critical issues.

By automating the collection and analysis of security data, Amazon Detective helps you streamline your security investigations and resolve security incidents more quickly. This helps you reduce the risk of security breaches and ensure that your AWS environment remains secure and compliant. You can learn more about Amazon Detective by visiting the AWS page here: `https://aws.amazon.com/detective/`.

AWS Security Hub

AWS Security Hub is a security management service that provides a central place to manage security alerts and findings from multiple AWS services, as well as from other **AWS Partner Network (APN)** security solutions. It provides a comprehensive view of your security posture across your AWS accounts, making it easier to identify and prioritize security issues.

Security Hub integrates with a number of AWS services, including Amazon GuardDuty, Amazon Inspector, and Amazon Macie, as well as third-party security solutions from APN partners. It also provides APIs that enable you to automate the process of responding to security findings. With Security Hub, you can do the following:

- Consolidate security alerts and findings from multiple sources into a single view
- Prioritize and triage security issues based on their severity and the likelihood of impact
- Automate the process of responding to security findings, using AWS Config rules and AWS Lambda functions
- Collaborate with your team to investigate and resolve security issues

Security Hub helps you improve your organization's security posture by providing a central place to manage security alerts and findings, and by enabling you to automate the process of responding to security issues. You can learn more about Security Hub by visiting the AWS page here: `https://aws.amazon.com/security-hub/`.

While security is essential, to operationalize it, it's important to configure all access; that's where IAM Access Analyzer comes into the picture. Let's learn more about it.

AWS IAM Access Analyzer

AWS IAM Access Analyzer helps organizations maintain secure and compliant access to their AWS resources. Its primary function is to analyze the resource policies attached to AWS resources, such as Amazon S3 buckets and AWS IAM roles, and identify any potential security risks or unintended access.

One of the key features of AWS IAM Access Analyzer is its ability to generate findings. These findings highlight situations where resource policies grant broader access than intended, either to external entities or to other AWS accounts within the same organization. Another notable feature of AWS IAM Access Analyzer is its support for zone of trust analysis. This analysis helps organizations understand the flow of access within their AWS environment, allowing them to identify and mitigate any potential risks associated with cross-account access or access from external sources.

You can learn more about IAM Access Analyzer by visiting the AWS page here: `https://aws.amazon.com/iam/access-analyzer/`.

Amazon S3 Access Points

Amazon S3 Access Points is a feature introduced by AWS to simplify data access and management in Amazon S3. It allows customers to create unique access control policies for each access point, enabling granular control over shared datasets. This feature is particularly useful for organizations that store shared data in S3, such as data lakes, media archives, and user-generated content, where different applications, teams, and individuals require varying levels of access.

With S3 Access Points, customers can create individualized access points with customized names and permissions tailored to each application's requirements. This eliminates the need for a single, complex bucket policy that controls access for multiple applications, making it easier to manage and audit access permissions. Additionally, S3 Access Points can be restricted to a VPC, effectively firewalling S3 data access within a customer's private network, enhancing security and compliance. AWS SCPS can be used to ensure that all access points are VPC-restricted, further strengthening data protection measures.

Amazon S3 Multi-Region Access Points

Amazon S3 Multi-Region Access Points give you a single global endpoint to route your S3 data request traffic across multiple AWS Regions. This means you don't need to deal with complex networking setups or manage separate endpoints in each Region. Whether your traffic comes from an Amazon VPC, your on-premises data center through AWS PrivateLink, or even the public internet, you can keep it simple and consistent.

Setting up an AWS PrivateLink connection to an S3 Multi-Region Access Point lets you route S3 requests privately into AWS or across Regions and accounts without needing VPC peering. It helps you streamline your network architecture while keeping data transfers secure and fast.

Moreover, you get full control with S3 Multi-Region Access Points' built-in failover features. You can route all your S3 requests through this one global endpoint and shift traffic between AWS Regions anytime you want. If there's a planned event or an unexpected outage in one Region, you can fail over to another bucket in a different Region or account within minutes, keeping your applications highly available and your users happy.

Adhering to compliance

AWS offers a variety of services and tools to help organizations comply with a wide range of regulations and standards, such as the GDPR, HIPAA, and the **Payment Card Industry Data Security Standard** (**PCI DSS**).

AWS provides broad support for security standards and compliance certifications, including HITECH, FedRAMP, GDPR, FIPS 140-2, and NIST 800-171, to help meet the compliance requirements of regulatory agencies around the world. This extensive coverage makes it easier for organizations to achieve and maintain compliance with a wide range of security standards and regulations, regardless of their location or the specific regulatory requirements they must adhere to.

By supporting these security standards and certifications, AWS helps organizations ensure that their data and applications are protected by rigorous security controls and processes, reducing the risk of data breaches and security incidents. This helps organizations meet their regulatory obligations and maintain the trust of their customers, employees, and stakeholders.

The following are the services provided by AWS to audit your compliance needs:

- **AWS Artifact**: No-cost, self-service portal for on-demand access to AWS compliance reports.

- **AWS Audit Manager**: AWS Audit Manager is a security and compliance auditing service that makes it easy for customers to automate the process of auditing their AWS accounts. With Audit Manager, customers can assess their compliance with AWS security best practices, industry standards and regulations, and internal policies. You can learn more about AWS Audit Manager by visiting the AWS page here: `https://aws.amazon.com/audit-manager/`.
- **AWS IAM**: AWS IAM allows you to set up and manage users and their permissions within your AWS account. This can help you ensure that only authorized users have access to sensitive resources and data.
- **AWS Config**: AWS Config provides visibility of resource configurations and changes in your AWS environment. It can help you track changes to resources, ensure that resources are compliant with your internal policies, and audit resource configurations for compliance with external regulations.
- **AWS Encryption SDK**: The AWS Encryption SDK is a set of libraries that you can use to build encryption into your applications. It helps you protect data in transit and at rest, and can be used to meet compliance requirements for data encryption. The AWS Encryption SDK is specifically a client-side encryption library that implements envelope encryption and provides additional security features such as algorithm suites and data key caching.
- **AWS PrivateLink**: AWS PrivateLink is a network interface that you can use to connect your on-premises data centers to AWS services, without the data traversing the public internet. This can help you comply with regulations that require the use of private networks for certain types of data.

There are many other AWS services and features that can help with compliance, depending on your specific needs. If you have specific questions about how AWS can help with compliance in your organization, you can contact AWS Support or consult with a security and compliance specialist.

Let's learn about AWS Artifact in detail.

AWS Artifact reports

Compliance is a non-negotiable requirement for any application, especially when expanding into specific regions or countries. Each geography has its own regulatory frameworks that must be followed, such as FedRAMP in the United States for government workloads and GDPR in the EU region for data privacy. Additionally, when building applications for specific industries, it is essential to align with industry-specific compliance standards. For example, the **banking, financial services, and insurance (BFSI)** sector typically requires PCI-DSS compliance for handling payment data. At the same time, the healthcare industry must adhere to HIPAA regulations to protect patient health information.

AWS Artifact is a portal that provides on-demand access to AWS's security and compliance documents. It includes AWS compliance reports, **Service Organization Controls** (**SOC**) reports, and other documents that can be used to demonstrate compliance with various regulations and standards.

The **AWS Artifact Reports** service delivers a centralized repository to store, manage, and access a variety of compliance reports from third-party auditors who have audited and certified that a given standard or regulation is met by the AWS infrastructure or by a given service. These rules, standards, and regulations may be global, regional, or industry-specific. As these rules and regulations change, AWS is constantly engaging third parties to ensure that compliance is up to date.

The **AWS Artifact Agreements** service provides the ability to access, approve, terminate, and manage agreements with AWS. It can be used to manage one AWS account or leverage AWS Organizations to manage multiple AWS accounts.

Some of the types of reports that can be managed with AWS Artifact are as follows:

- SOC reports
- **Payment Card Industry** (**PCI**) reports
- Certifications from accreditation agencies around the world
- Industry-specific compliance reports
- Compliance reports about AWS security controls
- **Business Associate Addendum** (**BAA**) agreements
- Non-disclosure agreements

You can learn more about AWS Artifact by visiting the AWS page here: `https://aws.amazon.com/artifact/`.

In this section, you have learned about AWS security and compliance services. Let's look at the *best of the best* tips for security in the AWS cloud.

Best practices for AWS security

While AWS provides a number of security services, it's essential to understand how to apply them to secure your application. AWS offers a wide range of security features and services, but customers are responsible for properly configuring and managing these features to meet their specific security requirements. Here are some best practices for AWS security:

- **Implement a strong IAM policy**:
    - Use MFA for privileged users

    - Grant the least privilege, meaning only provide access to the resources and actions that users need to do their jobs
    - Regularly rotate AWS access keys and passwords to reduce the risk of compromise
- **Encrypt data at rest and in transit**:
    - Encrypt sensitive data, such as databases and backups, using AWS KMS or SSE
    - Use SSL or TLS to encrypt data in transit
- **Monitor and log activity**:
    - Use Amazon CloudWatch Logs to monitor and store log data from EC2 instances, ELB, and other AWS services
    - Use AWS CloudTrail to track API activity and changes to your AWS resources
    - Enable VPC Flow Logs to monitor network traffic in your VPC
- **Implement security groups and network access control lists (NACLs)**:
    - Use security groups to control inbound and outbound network traffic to your EC2 instances
    - Use NACLs to control traffic to and from subnets within your VPC
- **Use Amazon VPC to segment your network**:
    - Use a VPC to create isolated networks and control access to your AWS resources
    - Use Amazon VPC peering to connect multiple VPCs for communication between resources
- **Use AWS Shield for DDoS protection**:
    - AWS Shield provides protection against DDoS attacks
    - Consider using AWS WAF to protect against web-based attacks
- **Implement Amazon Macie for data protection**:
    - Use Macie to discover, classify, and protect sensitive data in AWS
    - Use Macie to monitor access to your data and detect any unauthorized access or data leaks
- **Use AWS Config to track resource configurations**:
    - Use AWS Config to monitor changes to your resources and ensure that configurations remain compliant with your policies

In conclusion, security is a top priority for AWS, and there are many best practices that customers can follow to secure their AWS environments. By implementing these best practices, customers can ensure that their AWS resources are secure and protected against a variety of security threats.

Overall, more automation improves security outcomes. You should minimize human intervention and always make smaller changes, and do these more often to stay on top of vulnerabilities as quickly as they are discovered.

Building a security-aware architecture

The **AWS Security Reference Architecture** (**AWS SRA**) gives you a solid starting point from day one to build security into your cloud setup. Since every organization's cloud journey is different, you must first define your ideal security state, assess where you currently stand, and then take an agile, step-by-step approach to bridge gaps.

In this section, you'll walk through the common stages of a typical cloud journey using a structured framework. These phases closely follow the security principles outlined in the AWS Well-Architected Framework, helping you ensure that your cloud design stays secure and aligned with best practices as you grow.

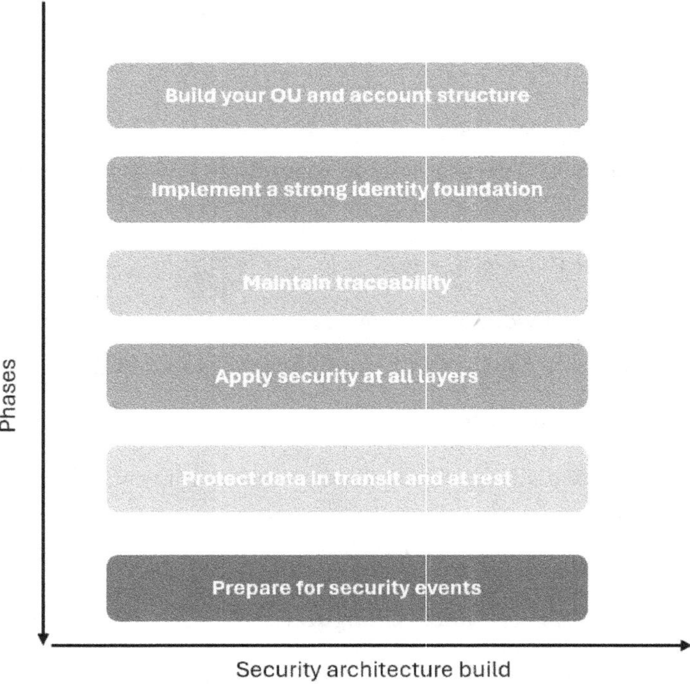

Figure 8.9: AWS SRA

As shown in the previous diagram, let's walk through each phase of building a security-aware architecture, starting with the foundation:

- **Phase 1 – Build your OU and account structure**: When you're setting up your AWS environment, designing your OUs and account structure the right way is key to building a strong security foundation. A well-structured setup helps you isolate different workloads and business units, making it easier to scale securely. With AWS Organizations, you can manage multiple AWS accounts centrally and use features such as trusted access and delegated administrators. AWS Control Tower can automate this setup by launching a preconfigured landing zone, making it easier to manage your environment as you grow. Even if you're just starting out, maybe prototyping or in the ideation phase, it's smart to adopt a multi-account strategy early. Whether you're a start-up, a mid-size company, or an enterprise, setting up multiple accounts for production workloads immediately helps you manage risk, cost, and permissions more effectively. As you finalize your OU and account structure, plan for security policies across the organization using SCPs to enforce guardrails.

Design tip

Don't base your OU structure on your company's organizational chart. Instead, group accounts based on workload types and shared security requirements. Start small by defining your foundational OUs, and expand gradually as your workload grows. You can move accounts between OUs during early design stages to explore what works best. Just keep in mind that doing so may require extra effort in managing IAM permissions and SCP rules, depending on how your OUs and account paths are structured.

- **Phase 2 – Implement a strong identity foundation**: Once you've set up multiple AWS accounts, the next step is to give your teams access to resources in those accounts securely. This starts with implementing a solid workforce IAM strategy. Instead of using IAM users, which can be hard to manage securely at scale, you should rely on IAM roles. This aligns with AWS SRA best practices. The recommended approach is to use AWS IAM Identity Center to centrally manage SSO across your *Org Management* and *Shared Services* accounts. If you're unable to use IAM Identity Center due to specific limitations, you can set up IAM federation with your existing identity provider. To strengthen your identity setup, tools such as IAM Access Analyzer and IAM Access Advisor help you track permissions and ensure you're granting only the truly needed access.

Design tip

Practicing least privilege access is one of the most effective ways to secure your AWS environment. This means giving every user or service the minimum permissions they need to do their job, and nothing more. Over time, as you learn more about how roles and services interact, you should continue to refine and reduce these permissions. This responsibility should be shared between your central security and application teams, making it scalable across your organization. Take advantage of tools such as resource-based policies, permission boundaries, **attribute-based access control** (**ABAC**), and session policies for precise access control. These help you define tight and accurate access rules, putting the right level of control in the hands of your app owners.

- **Phase 3 – Maintain traceability**: As your teams begin using AWS and launching applications, it becomes essential to track who is doing what, when, and from where. This visibility helps you quickly detect unexpected behavior, spot potential security issues, and respond to threats. By understanding these activities, you can better prioritize your security actions. To get this visibility, start by enabling an organization-wide trail with AWS CloudTrail, which logs all API calls across your AWS accounts. Ensure that these logs are sent to a central *Log Archive* account, giving you a secure and auditable activity history. For detecting and responding to security events, you can rely on tools such as AWS Security Hub for centralized insights, Amazon GuardDuty for threat detection, AWS Config for configuration tracking, and Amazon Security Lake for aggregating and analyzing security-related logs across services.

Design tip

As you begin using more AWS services, turn on service-specific logging wherever available, such as VPC Flow Logs, S3 access logs, or Lambda execution logs. Ensure that all these logs are directed to your central logging setup. This not only helps with real-time monitoring but also builds a reliable audit trail to support investigations and compliance needs.

- **Phase 4 – Apply security at all layers**: By this point, you should already have key security foundations in place – your AWS account and OU structure are defined, you've implemented preventive controls with SCPs, and you've built least privilege IAM roles to manage access securely.

You should also log activity with AWS CloudTrail, detect security threats with Amazon GuardDuty, AWS Security Hub, and AWS Config, and run advanced security analytics using Amazon Security Lake. Now, it's time to go deeper and apply security across every layer of your AWS environment. At the network level, use services such as AWS WAF, AWS Shield, AWS Firewall Manager, AWS Network Firewall, ACM, Amazon Route 53, Amazon CloudFront, and Amazon VPC to protect your traffic and control how data moves. Then, as you go deeper into the application layer, apply targeted security controls using tools such as Amazon Inspector for vulnerability scanning, AWS Systems Manager for patch management, AWS Secrets Manager for handling credentials securely, and Amazon Cognito for user identity and access.

Design tip

Security is a shared responsibility, especially at scale. Your central security team can't know the ins and outs of every application across your organization. So, empower your application teams to take ownership of their own security. Give them the right tools, frameworks, and guidance so they can design security controls that fit their workloads. This decentralized model ensures that security is built into every layer while staying scalable and efficient.

To understand the scaling mechanisms that AWS uses to adopt a more shift-left approach to security, refer to the following blog post: *How AWS built the Security Guardians program, a mechanism to distribute security ownership.*

- **Phase 5 – Protect data in transit and at rest**: Your business and customer data are among your most valuable assets, and protecting them is non-negotiable. AWS provides you with a wide range of services and features to keep this data safe, both while it's being transmitted and when it's stored. To secure data in transit over the internet, use Amazon CloudFront with ACM to encrypt and distribute traffic globally. Combine an Application Load Balancer with AWS Private CA for internal network communications to secure data flow. When it comes to protecting data at rest, AWS offers AWS KMS and AWS CloudHSM to help you securely manage and control access to encryption keys. Don't forget compliance. Whether you're dealing with GDPR, HIPAA, or PCI-DSS, use tools such as AWS Artifact to access compliance reports and AWS CloudTrail for full visibility into who accessed what data and when. Also, continuous security monitoring should be set up using Amazon CloudWatch Logs, AWS Security Hub, and Amazon GuardDuty to detect unusual access patterns or threats. Lastly, enforce least privilege access by defining strict IAM roles and policies to ensure only the right people can access sensitive data and keys.

Design tip

Your goal should be to ensure end-to-end encryption – use TLS 1.2 or higher for data in transit and AES-256 encryption for data at rest. While encryption can sometimes introduce performance overhead, services such as CloudFront can optimize delivery by caching encrypted content close to your users. Instead of manually managing SSL/TLS certificates, let ACM handle the automation, which reduces human error and saves time. For key management, AWS KMS helps you centrally store, rotate, and audit encryption keys, making sure only authorized users can access them.

- **Phase 6 – Prepare for security events:** As you manage your AWS environment, you'll inevitably face security events; unexpected activities or changes that may signal a policy breach or a breakdown in your security controls. Detecting, analyzing, and responding quickly is crucial to minimizing the impact. The AWS SRA recommends setting up a central *Log Archive* account to securely collect and store all your operational and security logs across accounts. To investigate and analyze these logs, you can use CloudWatch Logs Insights for logs in CloudWatch, or Amazon Athena and Amazon OpenSearch Service for logs stored in S3. Amazon Security Lake further streamlines this process by consolidating security data from AWS, SaaS tools, on-premises systems, and even other cloud providers; all into a central repository. Following SRA guidance, you can then assign subscribers in a dedicated *Security Tooling* account to query and monitor this data for threats.

Design tip

Don't wait until something goes wrong, prepare from day one. Start by classifying your AWS resources based on the criticality of the data and business function they support. This way, if a security event occurs, you'll know exactly where to focus your triage efforts and how to prioritize responses. It helps you make the most of your security team's time and tools, especially when incidents hit multiple areas at once. Early preparation ensures faster recovery and better protection for your most valuable assets.

Refer to the following link to know more about the concept: `https://docs.aws.amazon.com/prescriptive-guidance/latest/security-reference-architecture/phases.html`.

Knowledge check

The following are some sample questions that align with the difficulty and scope typically found in the *AWS Certified Solutions Architect - Professional* exam:

1. Your company has a requirement to grant temporary access to a third-party vendor for a specific AWS service in your account. The vendor should have the least privileged access required to perform their tasks, and the access should be automatically revoked after a specified duration. Which AWS service or feature would you use to fulfill this requirement?

    a. AWS **Identity and Access Management** (**IAM**) roles with a session policy

    b. AWS IAM user with a custom policy

    c. AWS **Security Token Service** (**STS**) with `AssumeRole` and temporary credentials

    d. AWS IAM groups with a managed policy

    Answer: c.

    Explanation:

    a. Incorrect. It does not provide a mechanism for automatically revoking access after a specified duration.

    b. Incorrect. It creates a long-term access credential that does not automatically expire or revoke access.

    c. **Correct**. AWS STS allows you to grant limited and temporary access to AWS resources. The third-party vendor can assume an IAM role using the `AssumeRole` operation, which generates temporary security credentials with a specified duration. These temporary credentials have the permissions defined by the IAM role's policies and can be configured to automatically expire after the specified duration, revoking access without manual intervention.

    d. Incorrect. It does not provide a mechanism for automatically revoking access after a specified duration, and it does not align with the principle of least privilege for temporary access.

2. You are designing a secure solution for an application that needs to access sensitive credentials, such as database passwords and API keys, across multiple AWS accounts and regions. The solution should allow centralized management and rotation of these secrets while ensuring high availability and durability. Which AWS service would you choose to meet these requirements?

    a. AWS Systems Manager Parameter Store

    b. AWS Secrets Manager

    c. AWS **Key Management Service** (**KMS**)

    d. AWS Config

    Answer: b.

    Explanation:

    a. Incorrect. While AWS Systems Manager Parameter Store can also store sensitive data, it is primarily designed for configuration data and does not provide automatic rotation capabilities.

    b. **Correct**. AWS Secrets Manager is the most appropriate choice for the given requirements, as it provides centralized management, secure storage, automatic rotation, and access control for sensitive credentials across multiple AWS accounts and regions.

    c. Incorrect. AWS KMS is a key management service used for encrypting data, but it does not provide centralized storage and management of secrets.

    d. Incorrect. AWS Config is a service for recording and evaluating resource configurations, but it is not designed for storing and managing secrets.

3. You are an AWS Certified solutions architect working for a large e-commerce company that frequently experiences **distributed denial-of-service** (**DDoS**) attacks targeting its application load balancers. You have been tasked with designing a solution to mitigate these attacks and protect your application's availability. Which of the following AWS services would you recommend using?

    a. AWS Shield Advanced

    b. AWS **Web Application Firewall** (**WAF**)

    c. Amazon CloudFront with AWS Shield Standard

    d. AWS Network Firewall

    Answer: a.

Explanation:

a. **Correct**. AWS Shield Advanced is a paid service that provides advanced DDoS mitigation capabilities, including enhanced detection and automatic application of mitigation techniques against sophisticated DDoS attacks. It is designed to protect against volumetric and state-exhaustion attacks targeting web applications running on **Elastic Load Balancing** (**ELB**), Amazon CloudFront, Amazon Route 53, and AWS Global Accelerator.

b. Incorrect. AWS WAF is designed to protect web applications from common web exploits and can help mitigate web application layer attacks, but it is not primarily focused on mitigating DDoS attacks.

c. Incorrect. Amazon CloudFront with AWS Shield Standard can provide basic DDoS protection for content delivered through CloudFront, but for advanced DDoS mitigation, AWS Shield Advanced is recommended.

d. Incorrect. AWS Network Firewall is a managed service that allows you to deploy essential network protection across your Amazon **virtual private clouds** (**VPCs**) to protect against common network-level threats, but it is not specifically designed for DDoS mitigation.

4. A company is using AWS Control Tower to manage its multi-account AWS environment. The company's security team wants to ensure that all AWS accounts within the organization comply with specific security standards and best practices. Which two solutions should they consider? (Choose two.)

   a. Deploy an AWS Config conformance pack using AWS CloudFormation StackSets from the AWS Control Tower management account

   b. Enable AWS Security Hub for the organization and designate one AWS account as the delegated administrator

   c. Use AWS Lambda functions to periodically check the security configurations of all AWS accounts

   d. Create custom AWS CloudTrail rules to monitor and log security-related events across all AWS accounts

   e. Implement AWS Config rules and AWS Config remediation actions to automatically remediate non-compliant resources

Answer: a. and e.

Explanation:

a. **Correct.** Deploying an AWS Config conformance pack using AWS CloudFormation StackSets from the AWS Control Tower management account allows you to consistently apply security configurations and best practices across all AWS accounts within the organization.

b. Incorrect. While enabling AWS Security Hub and designating a delegated administrator account is a valid approach, it is not specifically mentioned in the question's requirements.

c. Incorrect. Using AWS Lambda functions to periodically check security configurations can be a valid approach, but it is not the most efficient or scalable solution compared to using AWS Config and remediation actions.

d. Incorrect. Creating custom AWS CloudTrail rules can be useful for monitoring security-related events, but it does not directly address the requirement of ensuring compliance with security standards and best practices.

e. **Correct.** Implementing AWS Config rules and AWS Config remediation actions allows you to automatically detect and remediate non-compliant resources, ensuring that all AWS accounts within the organization comply with the specified security standards and best practices.

5. Your company has a mission-critical web application running on Amazon EC2 instances in an Auto Scaling group across multiple Availability Zones. The application handles sensitive customer data and must comply with stringent security regulations. You want to ensure that your EC2 instances are continuously assessed for vulnerabilities and potential security risks. Which combination of AWS services and features should you use to achieve this objective while minimizing operational overhead and maximizing cost-effectiveness?

   a. Use AWS Inspector to perform periodic vulnerability assessments on your EC2 instances. Configure Amazon CloudWatch Events to trigger AWS Inspector assessments on a scheduled basis, and use AWS Systems Manager Run Command to automatically install and uninstall the AWS Inspector agent on your instances as needed.

   b. Deploy AWS Lambda functions to periodically scan your EC2 instances for vulnerabilities using third-party security scanning tools. Use Amazon EventBridge to schedule the Lambda functions and Amazon SNS to receive notifications about potential security risks.

c. Use AWS Config rules to continuously monitor the configuration of your EC2 instances for security best practices and compliance. Configure AWS Config to record configuration changes and send notifications to an Amazon SNS topic when non-compliant resources are detected.
d. Deploy an Amazon EKS cluster and use AWS Distro for OpenTelemetry to collect security telemetry data from your EC2 instances.
e. Use Amazon Managed Service for Prometheus and Amazon Managed Grafana to visualize and analyze the security metrics, and configure Amazon CloudWatch anomaly detection to detect potential security anomalies.

Answer: a.

Explanation:

a. **Correct.** AWS Inspector is a vulnerability management service that helps you automatically assess the security state of your AWS resources, including EC2 instances. By using AWS Inspector, you can continuously scan your instances for potential security vulnerabilities and unintended network exposure.
b. Incorrect. This approach is not optimal because it involves deploying and maintaining third-party security scanning tools, which can increase operational complexity and costs. Additionally, using AWS Lambda for periodic scanning may not be as efficient as using a dedicated vulnerability management service such as AWS Inspector, which is specifically designed for this purpose.
c. Incorrect. AWS Config rules can help you monitor and evaluate the configuration of your AWS resources, including EC2 instances, against predefined rules. However, this approach focuses more on configuration compliance and does not provide the same level of vulnerability assessment capabilities as AWS Inspector. AWS Config rules can complement AWS Inspector, but should not be used as a complete replacement for vulnerability management.
d. Incorrect. This approach involves deploying and managing an Amazon EKS cluster, which is overkill for the given scenario.
e. Incorrect. While AWS Distro for OpenTelemetry, Amazon Managed Service for Prometheus, Amazon Managed Grafana, and Amazon CloudWatch anomaly detection can be useful for collecting and analyzing security telemetry data, they do not directly address the requirement for continuous vulnerability assessments on EC2 instances. This solution would introduce unnecessary complexity and operational overhead.

Summary

In this chapter, you learned how to build a security-first AWS environment using a phased approach based on the AWS Security Reference Architecture. You began by understanding the importance of designing your organizational units and account structure properly, setting the stage for strong isolation and policy enforcement. You then focused on establishing a secure identity foundation using IAM roles, AWS IAM Identity Center, and tools such as IAM Access Analyzer to enforce least privilege.

As your AWS usage grows, the chapter guided you through best practices for monitoring activities, using AWS CloudTrail for logging and AWS Security Hub, Amazon GuardDuty, and AWS Config for real-time detection and security insights. You also explored how to apply security at every layer—from network and application-level protections to advanced tools such as AWS WAF, Amazon Inspector, and AWS Secrets Manager.

A key part of your learning was how to protect data in transit and at rest using AWS KMS, CloudHSM, and Certificate Manager, while ensuring compliance and audit readiness with tools such as AWS Artifact and CloudTrail. Lastly, the chapter emphasized being ready for security events by setting up log aggregation with Amazon Security Lake and preparing for efficient detection and response strategies. By following this structured approach, you now have the foundational knowledge to architect secure, scalable, and compliant cloud environments using AWS services.

After completing this chapter, you should now feel more confident about using AWS to write world-class applications that offer the highest levels of security. In the next chapter, you will further explore some more elements of cloud automation.

Join us on Discord

For discussions around the book and to connect with your peers, join us on Discord at `https://discord.gg/kbFRRSB2Qs` or scan the QR code below:

Driving Efficiency with Cloud Operation Automation and DevOps in AWS

Organizations migrating to the cloud need management and governance to ensure best practices in their cloud IT operations. Whether you manage modern applications built using microservices-based architectures, containers, serverless stacks, or legacy applications that have been re-hosted or re-architected for the cloud, you will realize that traditional application development and operations processes could be more effective.

Automation has always been vital for managing cloud operations, increasing efficiency, and avoiding human error disruption. However, you will still observe many manual tasks in most organizations, especially IT workload management. With the rise of the cloud, automation has become more critical due to its pay-as-you-go model. Automation helps you improve productivity, resulting in substantial cost savings in human effort and IT resource expenditure. Automation has become key to reducing daily operational costs, and cloud organizations spend more on operations than upfront capital investment.

Automation is crucial for cost and other aspects, such as enduring application security and reliability. Automation goes hand in hand with monitoring and alerts. Automation will only work if you have proper monitoring, alerting your automation script when to take a certain action, for example, if you want to run your production app server without compromising the user experience due to a capacity crunch. It's always recommended to monitor server capacity, such as if the server has exhausted memory capacity to 80% or CPU capacity to 70%, and send an alert to autoscaling for server scaling as needed.

AWS provides several services and tools to fully automate your cloud infrastructure and application with CloudOps, or if you want to automate security, using DevSecOps. In this chapter, you will learn about the following topics in detail to understand the need for cloud automation, monitoring, and alerts:

- What is CloudOps?
- AWS CloudOps pillars
- DevOps and DevSecOps in AWS
- AWS cloud management tools for automation
- Cloud automation best practice

By the end of this chapter, you will understand various automation strategies to manage cloud operations. You will learn about multiple AWS services available for cloud automation, monitoring, and alerts and how to use them in your workload.

What is the cloud operation (CloudOps) model, and what role does automation play?

CloudOps, or the cloud operational model, encompasses a collection of guidelines and safeguards that are established, tracked, and adjusted as needed to manage expenses and operational resilience, boost productivity, and mitigate potential security risks. It can help guide your people, processes, and the technology associated with your cloud infrastructure, security, and operations. An operational model also enables you to develop and implement controls to manage security, budget, and compliance across your cloud workloads.

Implementing cloud automation empowers organizations to construct streamlined cloud operational models through the automated creation, modification, and removal of cloud resources. Although cloud computing initially promised the ability to utilize services as required, many organizations still rely on manual processes to provision resources, conduct testing, recognize resource redundancy, and decommission resources. This approach can result in substantial labor, error-proneness, and expense.

Businesses migrating to the cloud need management and governance to ensure best practices in their cloud IT operations. AWS management and governance services provide faster innovation and firm control over cost, compliance, and security.

The following are the key benefits of the cloud operation model:

- Organizations can unlock the speed and agility of the cloud and accelerate their cloud adoption and application modernization efforts as part of their digital transformation journey.
- You can use the power of automation for routine tasks to reduce manual errors and interventions.
- You can continue to scale your businesses with the certainty that cloud governance spans all different environments uniformly and at scale.
- You can use your skilled personnel effectively to deliver business outcomes.
- Organizations can avoid unexpected cost overruns.

While implementing cloud automation can initially demand significant effort, the potential rewards are considerable. Once the initial hurdles are overcome, the ability to perform intricate tasks through code transforms an organization's operations. In addition to minimizing manual labor, cloud automation offers several other advantages, including the following:

- **Improved security and resilience**: Automation helps you improve security, as there are always chances of security lapses due to human error or changes that can be left out, which is outside of individual knowledge for setting up security credentials for a newly added dev environment. Also, automation helps to improve resiliency by automating recovery of the environment; for example, if your server goes over capacity, you can take proactive action by adding more CPU or memory to avoid downtime.
- **Improved backup processes**: Automated backup is essential for continuing business processes. Protecting data helps minimize business loss by winning customer trust and rebuilding your environment quickly in case of a disaster recovery event. Automated backup enables you to ensure all backups are secure and not rely on one individual who may forget to take one.
- **Improved governance**: Automation helps improve governance by ensuring that all activity is captured across the environment. For example, an automated governance model can help you determine what servers and database inventories are running across your company's IT workload and who is accessing those environments.

AWS provides a set of services and third-party tools for modern enterprises as they adopt the cloud operation model. It can help you drive more innovation, faster cloud adoption, improved application performance, and quicker response times to customer feedback while maintaining governance and compliance.

Let's look at the CloudOps pillars and the services provided to fulfill the requirements of each pillar.

CloudOps pillars

While planning your CloudOps model, you need to take a 360-degree look. You want to provision and operate your environment for business agility and governance control. Establishing a CloudOps model, regardless of your cloud migration journey, helps you attain consistent governance and efficient operations across different infrastructure environments. This helps free up critical resources to deliver business outcomes and time-to-market faster while improving safety, ease, efficiency, and cost control. The following diagram shows the key pillars of cloud operation for complete coverage of your IT workload automation.

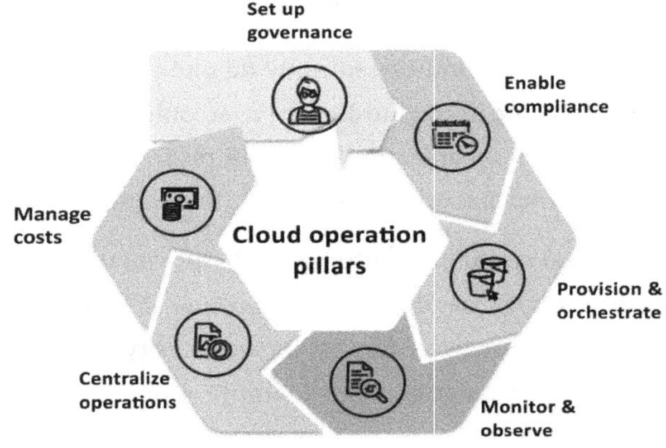

Figure 9.1: The pillars of CloudOps

Quick tip: Need to see a high-resolution version of this image? Open this book in the next-gen Packt Reader or view it in the PDF/ePub copy.

The next-gen Packt Reader is included for free with the purchase of this book. Scan the QR code OR go to `packtpub.com/unlock`, then use the search bar to find this book by name. Double-check the edition shown to make sure you get the right one.

As shown in the preceding diagram, the following are the key pillars of CloudOps:

1. **Set up governance**: Set up a well-architected, multi-account AWS environment with guardrails to build the foundation for governance.
2. **Enable compliance**: Continuously monitor compliance and configurations for your resources, remediate failures automatically, and gather evidence for audits.
3. **Provision & orchestrate**: Speed up application and resource provisioning with infrastructure-as-code (IaC) while maintaining consistency and compliance.
4. **Monitor & observe**: Measure and manage your applications and resources to identify and resolve issues quickly.
5. **Centralize operations**: Take seamless and automated operational actions across your entire application portfolio.
6. **Manage costs**: It helps manage costs through transparency, control, regular forecasting, and optimization.

Let's look at what each of these pillars helps you to achieve in your efforts to enable governance in cloud environments. You will also learn about the AWS services that predominantly fulfill the requirements of each pillar.

First pillar – Set up governance

The first and best place to start is by laying a very strong foundation for your governance. The AWS environment begins by setting up a well-architected, multi-account AWS environment and setting up guardrails in each account. You learned about the Well-Architected Framework in *Chapter 2, Understanding the AWS Well-Architected Framework and Getting Certified*, where you saw that AWS has a comprehensive checklist to make sure your environment is set up properly to monitor cost, security, performance, reliability, and high availability. You can refer to AWS's Well-Architected labs at `https://www.wellarchitectedlabs.com/`, which provide a comprehensive, practical, hands-on guide to enable those guardrails against each Well-Architected pillar. The environment you build must be secure and extensible so that you don't halt experimentation and innovation as you grow your footprint on AWS. You need it to scale with your usage.

Your business needs to evolve continuously, so you should keep yourself from a single mode of architecting and operating in AWS. Most customers' environments don't remain static. They tend to grow with their business. You want to ensure your landing zone grows with your business without encumbrance while adhering to organizational policies. AWS Landing Zone is an offering that assists clients in swiftly configuring a secure and multi-account AWS environment built around AWS's industry-leading practices.

The solution delivers a preconfigured and secure infrastructure encompassing key services, standardized AWS account architecture, and robust security controls. The goal of Landing Zone is to provide a secure, well-architected multi-account environment that serves as a starting point for new AWS accounts. It helps customers get started with AWS faster by providing a set of reusable blueprints for common patterns and practices, such as account VPCs, security controls, and identity and access management.

You need a well-defined AWS environment to accommodate the following needs:

- **Many teams:** Multiple teams could be in the same account, overstepping one another.
- **Isolation:** Each team may have different security needs and want to isolate themselves from one another by using a different security profile.
- **Security controls:** Different applications might have different controls around them to address security and compliance. For example, talking to an auditor is far easier than pointing to a single account hosting the PCI solution. However, even within an organization, security controls can isolate certain things based on security isolation needs.
- **Business process:** Different **business units** (**BUs**) or products exist. For example, the Sales BU differs from the HR BU because it has a different business process.
- **Billing:** An account is the primary way to divide items at a billing level. Each AWS account is billed separately and has its resources and associated charges. This means that if an organization has multiple accounts, each account will have its own billing and cost allocation data.

To enable account control, AWS provides **AWS Organizations** that help you establish a multi-account structure for centralized governance. You can use it to develop granular control over your AWS accounts, manage across accounts easily, and apply policies as broadly or as narrowly as you need. In the previous chapter, *Chapter 8, Best Practices for Application Security, Identity, and Compliance*, you learned about AWS Organizations and AWS Control Tower.

For automated setup, AWS provides **AWS Control Tower**, a self-service solution to set up and govern a secure, compliant multi-account AWS environment. It abstracts multiple AWS services under the covers, so you can use it to set up your environment based on best practices without needing a lot of AWS knowledge. AWS Control Tower provides the following benefits:

- Automate the setup of your landing zone based on best-practice blueprints
- Apply guardrails for ongoing governance over your AWS workloads
- Automate your account provisioning workflow with an account factory
- Get dashboard visibility into your organizational units, accounts, and guardrails

AWS professional services provide the AWS **Landing Zone Accelerator** (**LZA**), a set of tools and resources designed to help customers accelerate the deployment of a secure, multi-account AWS environment.

LZA builds on the AWS Landing Zone service, which provides a pre-built, opinionated framework for setting up a secure, multi-account environment.

LZA provides a modular set of landing zone components that can be customized to meet specific requirements. It leverages automation to speed up the deployment process. LZA also allows access to AWS experts who can provide guidance and best practices to help ensure a successful deployment. You can learn more about LZA using the AWS user guide here: `https://aws.amazon.com/solutions/implementations/landing-zone-accelerator-on-aws/`.

LZA is designed to accelerate the process of setting up a landing zone for workloads migrating to AWS. This makes LZA a good fit for customers who need to set up a landing zone quickly and want more control over the individual components of their environment.

On the other hand, **Control Tower** (**CT**) is designed to help customers set up and govern a multi-account AWS environment. Control Tower provides a pre-built set of rules and policies to enforce governance and security best practices across multiple AWS accounts. CT also provides a central dashboard for managing and monitoring multiple accounts, making it easier for customers to maintain governance and compliance across their environment while enabling best practices for account vending. This makes CT a good fit for customers who need to manage multiple AWS accounts and want a pre-built set of governance policies to enforce best practices.

Having the correct foundation when starting your cloud journey is extremely important. AWS services such as Control Tower, in combination with the Well-Architected Framework, help you with an automated way to establish the right environment. The teams building this out are not a bottleneck and enable you to be flexible in your approach and know that you might need new accounts, processes, or isolation solutions. That flexibility is what allows us to succeed in the long term. After setting up governance, you must ensure your applications meet compliance requirements. Let's learn more about automating compliance.

Second pillar – Managing configuration, compliance, and audit

As you migrate workloads to the cloud, you must know that you can maintain cloud compliance and get assurance for your workloads. Once compliance mechanisms and processes are in place, you can empower your development teams to build and innovate while having peace of mind that they are staying compliant.

A resource inventory helps you maintain environment configurations, track change history, ensure resources depend on one another, and ensure they are correctly configured. Once you establish proper configurations, you want to be able to audit, manage, and remediate them quickly.

How many hours would you spend today collecting evidence in response to an audit? Whether internal or external? Wouldn't it be easier if you could keep a running log of all auditable events and remediation actions? That's where AWS configuration, compliance, and auditing tools come in. You must continuously monitor configuration and compliance changes within your AWS environment and keep a running audit log to get visibility into your organization's resource configurations.

Many customers follow the **Institute of Internal Auditors (IIA)** guidance for the three lines of defense:

- **First line**: *How to automate compliance management and manage risk* – Implementing AWS CloudTrail, AWS Config, AWS Control Tower, and AWS License Manager can aid in automating compliance management such as HIPAA for healthcare, PCI-DSS for the finance industry, GDPR for the European market, and risk mitigation within an AWS environment.
- **Second line**: *How to implement continuous oversight and oversee risk* – Utilizing Amazon CloudWatch for environmental monitoring and AWS Security Hub for centralized security monitoring helps to understand AWS accounts' operational health and security status.
- **Third Line**: *How to assess and independently gather risk management assurance* – AWS Audit Manager helps companies evaluate their security, change management, and software licensing controls.

You learned about AWS Security Hub and Control Tower in the previous chapter. Let's learn about the other services for managing cloud audits and compliance. You can use the combination of these services your IT workload needs to automate configuration, compliance, and audit.

AWS CloudTrail

AWS API calls handle all interactions with AWS services and resources, which are monitored and logged by AWS CloudTrail. AWS CloudTrail records all API calls made in your AWS account and provides a complete history of user activity and API usage. This information can be used for security analysis, compliance auditing, and troubleshooting.

If configured for long-term log retention, CloudTrail stores all generated log files in an Amazon S3 bucket you define. These log files are encrypted using **Amazon S3 server-side encryption (SSE)**, which provides an additional layer of security for your logs.

You can also use **Customer Managed Keys (CMKs)** as per your organization's standard. It's also worth noting that CloudTrail logs all API calls, regardless of whether they come directly from a user or on behalf of a user by an AWS service. Also, AWS maintains these logs integrally, which means that if any modification, update, or deletion of the logs is made, it can be tracked and audited.

This lets you understand all API activity in your AWS environment, which can be crucial for security and compliance. You can learn more about it by referring to the link here: `https://docs.aws.amazon.com/awscloudtrail/latest/userguide/cloudtrail-log-file-validation-intro.html`.

AWS CloudTrail is a service that enables governance, compliance, operations, and risk auditing for AWS accounts by logging and monitoring account activity related to actions across the AWS infrastructure in conjunction with other services such as CloudWatch and AWS Config. Using CloudTrail, you can continuously monitor and retain logs of all account activity, providing a complete history of your AWS account's event history. This event history includes actions taken through the AWS Management Console, AWS SDKs, command-line tools, and other AWS services.

These logs can aid governance, compliance, and risk management by providing a clear activity record across your AWS infrastructure. With CloudTrail, you can create custom alerts and notifications to help you identify and respond to potential security issues and compliance risks in real time.

Once enabled, CloudTrail will automatically track all management events at no charge. CloudTrail is enabled by default and provides visibility into management events for 90 days on all AWS accounts. Depending on your application and compliance needs, you can opt into several data event sources, including network activity events for VPC endpoints. This event history is another source of observability data, simplifying security analysis, resource change tracking, and troubleshooting. You can learn more about AWS CloudTrail by visiting the AWS page here: `https://aws.amazon.com/cloudtrail/`.

AWS Config

You learned about AWS Config in *Chapter 5, Storage in AWS: Choosing the Right Tool for the Job*, in the context of S3. AWS Config records and evaluates your AWS resource configuration. AWS Config performs the following activities for AWS resources: record, evaluate, and visualize. Let's learn about these in more detail in the context of CloudOps:

Record

- **Configuration history of AWS resources**: AWS Config records the details of changes made to your AWS resources, providing you with a configuration history timeline. This enables you to track any changes made to a resource's configuration at any time in the past.

- **Resource relationship tracking:** AWS Config can discover, map, and track relationships between AWS resources in your account. For example, if a new **Amazon Elastic Compute Cloud (Amazon EC2)** security group is associated with an Amazon EC2 instance, AWS Config will record the updated configurations of both the Amazon EC2 security group and the Amazon EC2 instance.
- **Configuration history of software:** AWS Config can also record software configuration changes within your Amazon EC2 instances and servers running on-premises or with other cloud providers. It provides a history of both OS and system-level configuration changes and infrastructure configuration changes recorded for Amazon EC2 instances.

Evaluate

- **Configurable and customizable rules:** Assess your resource configurations and resource changes for compliance against built-in AWS managed rules or custom rules and automate the remediation of non-compliant resources. You can customize pre-built rules provided by AWS Config or create your own custom rules with AWS Lambda to define your internal guidelines and best practices for resource configurations.
- **Conformance packs:** These simplify organization-wide deployment and compliance reporting. A pack of config rules and remediation actions is deployed to your AWS Organization.
- **Automatic remediation:** This enables you to remediate non-compliant resources using Systems Manager Automation documents.

Visualize

- **Cloud governance dashboard:** This feature provides a visual dashboard that lets you easily identify non-compliant resources and take corrective action. You can customize the dashboard to monitor resources based on cost and security.
- **Multi-account, multi-region data aggregation:** AWS Config allows you to aggregate data from multiple AWS accounts and regions, providing you with a centralized view of your resources and their compliance status with AWS Config rules. This feature is particularly useful for enterprise-scale organizations.
- **Configuration snapshots:** AWS Config can take snapshots of your resource configurations at specific points in time. This allows you to quickly identify changes to your resources and compare their configurations over time.

Here is an example AWS Config rule that checks whether Amazon EC2 instances have an associated security group with inbound rules that allow traffic on port 22 (SSH):

```
{
  "Name": "ec2-security-group-has-inbound-rules-on-port-22",
  "Description": "Checks whether the security group associated with an EC2 
instance has inbound rules that allow traffic on port 22."
  "Scope": {
    "ComplianceResourceTypes": [
      "AWS::EC2::Instance"
    ]
  },
  "Source": {
    "Owner": "AWS",
    "SourceIdentifier": "EC2_INSTANCE_HAS_SECURITY_GROUP_WITH_INBOUND_
RULES_ON_PORT_22"
  },
  "InputParameters": "{\"allowedProtocols\":\"tcp\",\"portNumber\":22}"
}
```

This rule checks whether the security group associated with each Amazon EC2 instance has inbound rules that allow traffic on port 22. If any instances do not have such a security group, they will be flagged as non-compliant.

AWS Config helps keep AWS resources compliant. You can learn more about it by visiting the AWS page: `https://aws.amazon.com/config/`. Let's look at the next service for tracking and auditing licenses.

AWS License Manager

AWS License Manager is a one-stop solution for managing licenses from various software vendors across hybrid environments. This helps you to stay compliant within your organizational structure and processes. There are no additional charges for using AWS License Manager.

AWS License Manager targets IT administrators who manage licenses and software assets. This includes license administrators, procurement administrators, or asset managers responsible for managing license true-ups and vendor audits. In contrast, users spin up instances and use the licensed software on those instances. With AWS License Manager, administrators can now easily manage licenses. Organizational users are not required to do additional work to manage licenses and can focus on business as usual.

You can complete your licensing true-ups and audits using AWS License Manager. Administrators start by creating rules based on their enterprise agreements. They can do this using the AWS Management Console, CLI, or API. Furthermore, administrators can enforce licensing rules by attaching them to instance launches. Once rules are enforced, the service automatically keeps track of instances as users spin them up and down.

The organization stays compliant with its license terms, and administrators can discover users' software after spinning up instances. Finally, they can keep track of usage through AWS License Manager's built-in dashboard.

AWS License Manager automatically tracks instance launches, and the built-in dashboard is populated. Administrators can view usage limit alerts and take actions such as procuring more licenses as needed. Administrators no longer have to determine which instances use which licenses when there is an upcoming license true-up or audit. With the built-in dashboard, figuring out how many licenses they use and which resources are using them is no longer a challenge. You can learn more about AWS License Manager by visiting the AWS page here: `https://aws.amazon.com/license-manager/`.

Amazon CloudWatch

CloudWatch is an essential service for running your cloud operation. It allows you to monitor your AWS workload and take action based on alerts. In addition, CloudWatch provides observability for your AWS resources on a single platform across applications and infrastructure.

Amazon CloudWatch is a powerful monitoring service designed to help you optimize your AWS resources and applications. It offers a wide range of capabilities, including the following:

- **Data and operational insights**: CloudWatch provides valuable insights into the performance and health of your AWS resources and applications. It allows you to collect and track metrics, monitor log files, and set alarms.
- **Resource monitoring**: CloudWatch can monitor various AWS resources, including Amazon EC2 instances, Amazon S3 buckets, and Amazon RDS instances. This allows you to identify and troubleshoot any issues that arise quickly.
- **Custom metrics**: CloudWatch allows you to create custom metrics based on the data generated by your applications. This provides you with greater flexibility and control over the monitoring process.
- **Log monitoring**: CloudWatch can also monitor the log files generated by your applications. This enables you to quickly identify and troubleshoot any issues related to your application code.

Amazon CloudWatch is an essential tool for anyone running applications on the AWS cloud platform. Its powerful monitoring capabilities can help you optimize your resources, improve application performance, and maintain the operational health of your systems.

CloudWatch alarms

CloudWatch alarms are a powerful feature that enables you to receive notifications or automate actions based on your defined rules. With CloudWatch alarms, you can monitor a wide range of metrics and set up alerts that notify you when certain conditions are met.

For example, you can send an email alert to the admin whenever the average network latency of an Amazon RDS database exceeds 10 seconds or when the CPU usage of an Amazon EC2 instance falls below 10%. You can also create more complex alarms that automatically trigger actions, such as launching additional instances to handle increased traffic or scaling down resources during periods of low demand.

CloudWatch alarms provide a flexible and customizable way to monitor your AWS resources and take automated actions based on your needs. Whether you need to monitor resource utilization, application performance, or other key metrics, CloudWatch alarms can help you manage your cloud infrastructure and ensure it is always running at peak performance.

In addition, CloudWatch provides data for the past two weeks so that you can access historical data to analyze past events. It also integrates with other AWS services, such as Amazon EC2 Auto Scaling, Amazon SNS, and AWS Lambda, enabling you to use CloudWatch to react to changes in your resources and applications.

Some key features of CloudWatch include the following:

- **Metrics**: CloudWatch allows you to collect metrics for your resources and applications, such as CPU usage, network traffic, and disk reads/writes. You can view these metrics in the CloudWatch console or use the CloudWatch API to retrieve them programmatically.
- **Alarms**: You can set alarms in CloudWatch to be notified when certain thresholds are breached. For example, you can schedule an alarm to send an email or SMS message to you if the CPU usage on one of your Amazon EC2 instances exceeds a certain threshold.
- **Logs**: CloudWatch allows you to store and access your log files in a centralized location. You can use CloudWatch Logs Insights to search and analyze your log data or use CloudWatch Logs to export your log data to third-party tools for further analysis.
- **Dashboards**: CloudWatch dashboards allow you to create custom views of your metrics and log data, giving you a quick overview of your system's health and performance.

Amazon CloudWatch is a powerful and flexible monitoring service that can help you ensure the availability, performance, and efficiency of your AWS resources and applications.

Amazon EventBridge

Amazon EventBridge was formerly called Amazon CloudWatch Events. EventBridge is a fully managed, serverless event bus service that simplifies connecting your applications, integrated SaaS applications, and AWS services. By creating event-driven architectures, EventBridge allows various applications and services to communicate with each other in a flexible and scalable manner.

The following screenshot shows an EventBridge rule set up to send information to Elasticsearch using Lambda for an instance start failure during autoscaling. This Lambda function sends information to Elasticsearch, allowing you to analyze and troubleshoot the failure.

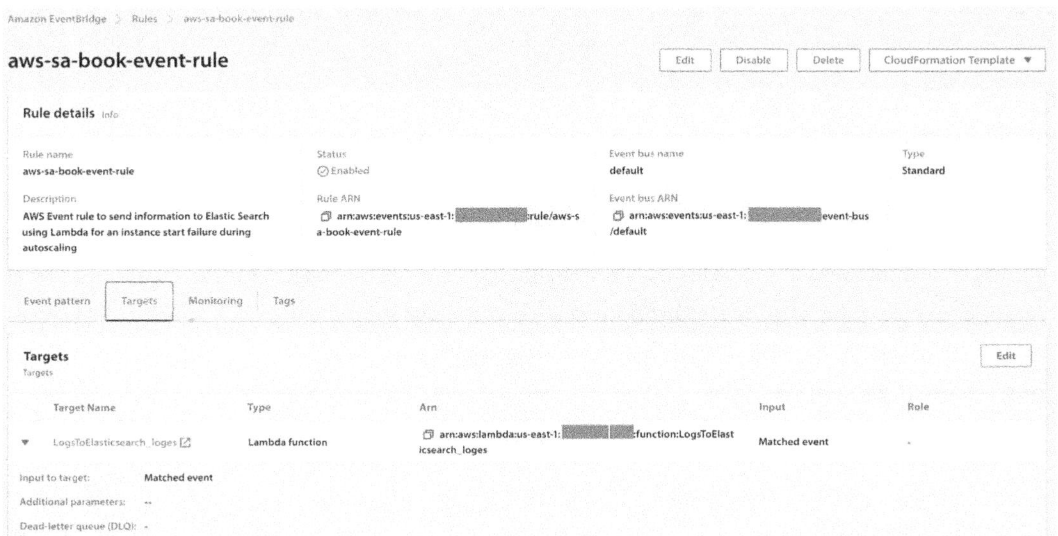

Figure 9.2: An AWS EventBridge rule for an autoscaling failure

EventBridge simplifies the setup and management of rules that dictate event routing and processing, enabling you to create complex and resilient architectures for your applications. With EventBridge, you can easily build event-driven applications and receive notifications about events from AWS DevOps services and automation application deployment pipelines. You can explore more about EventBridge by visiting the AWS page here: `https://aws.amazon.com/eventbridge/`.

AWS Audit Manager

AWS Audit Manager continuously accesses risk and compliance controls and provides the following benefits:

- Easily map your AWS usage to controls. Use pre-built compliance frameworks such as PCI, HIPAA, GDPR, and so on, or build custom frameworks to collect evidence for compliance controls.
- Save time by collecting evidence automatically across accounts. Review the relevant evidence to ensure your controls work as intended.
- Be continually prepared to produce audit-ready reports. Audit Manager continuously collects and organizes evidence so you can effortlessly search, filter, and review it to ensure controls are working as intended.
- Ensure assessment report and evidence integrity. When an audit is due, build assessment reports with evidence that has been continuously collected, securely stored, and remains unaltered.

Here, you can find a screenshot of AWS Audit Manager:

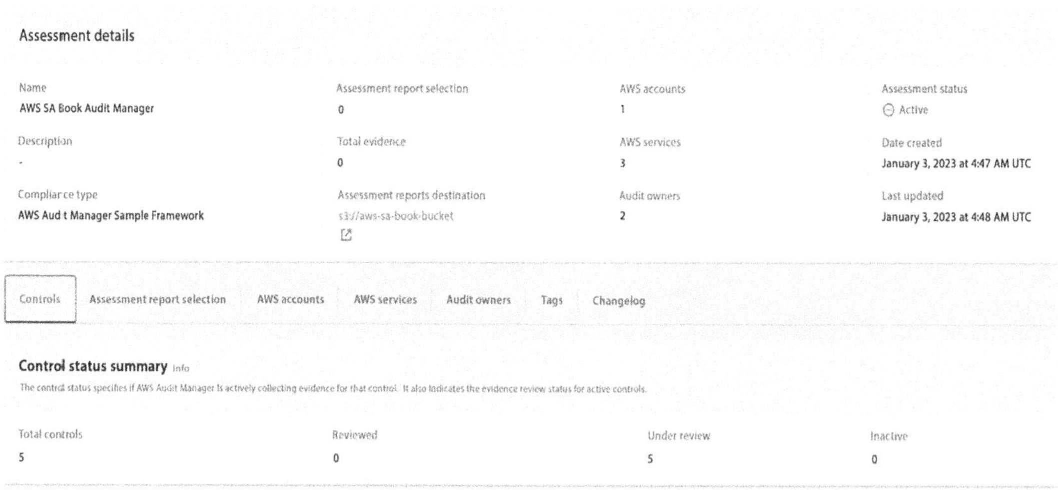

Figure 9.3: AWS Audit Manager

You can learn more about AWS Audit Manager by visiting the AWS page here: `https://aws.amazon.com/audit-manager/`.

AWS Systems Manager

AWS Systems Manager is a management service that allows you to act on your AWS resources as necessary. It provides you with a quick view of operational data for groups of resources, making it easy to detect any issues that could impact applications that rely on those resources. You can group resources by various criteria, such as applications, application layers, or production versus development environments. Systems Manager displays operational data for your resource groups on a single dashboard, eliminating the need to switch between different AWS consoles. For example, you can create a resource group for an application that uses Amazon EC2, Amazon S3, and Amazon RDS. Systems Manager can check for software changes installed on your Amazon EC2 instances, changes in your S3 objects, or stopped database instances.

The following screenshot shows a configuration deployment status for servers in a given AWS account:

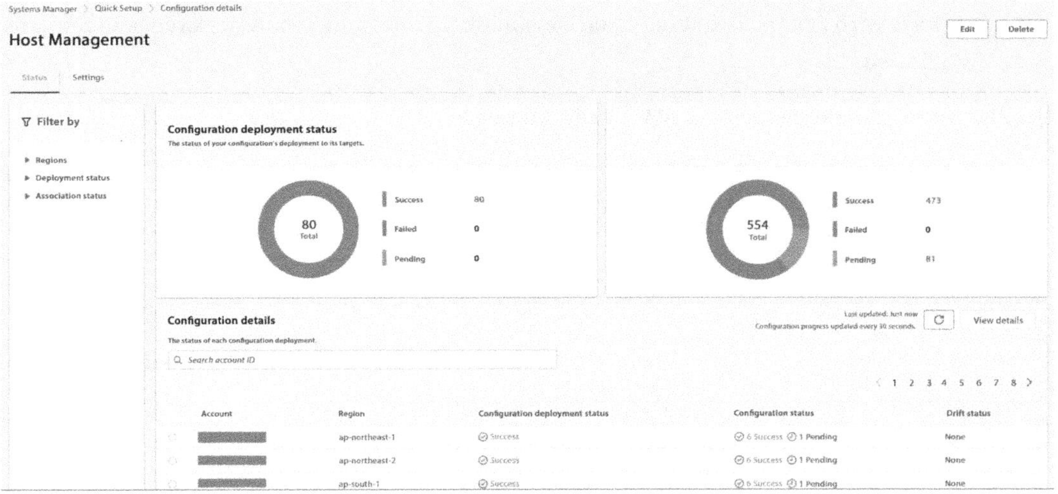

Figure 9.4: AWS Systems Manager host management

AWS Systems Manager provides detailed insights into the current state of your resource groups, allowing you to understand and control them quickly. The **Systems Manager Explorer** and **Inventory** dashboards offer various tools for viewing system configurations, such as operating system patch levels, software installations, and application configurations. Moreover, they are integrated with AWS Config, allowing you to track changes across your resources over time.

AWS Systems Manager offers several features to help maintain security and compliance in your environment. It can scan your instances against your patch, configuration, and custom policies, helping you identify and address potential security issues. With Systems Manager, you can define patch baselines, ensure that your anti-virus definitions are up to date, and enforce firewall policies, among other things. Systems Manager also enables you to manage your servers at scale remotely without manually logging in to each server. This feature can be especially helpful in large-scale environments, where managing resources individually can be time-consuming and error-prone.

In addition, **AWS Systems Manager (SSM)** acts as a central hub for secure and at-scale management of your infrastructure and operations. One of its key features is **Parameter Store**, which lets you store configuration data and secrets such as database connection strings, passwords, and license codes separately from your application code. This not only improves security by avoiding hardcoded credentials but also simplifies your development and deployment pipelines. Beyond configuration and secrets management, Systems Manager offers several other powerful capabilities:

- **Automation Runbooks**: These are predefined workflows that help you automate common operational tasks such as patching, instance provisioning, and remediation steps. You can create custom runbooks using AWS Systems Manager Automation documents (SSM documents) to streamline tasks across AWS environments.
- **Session Manager**: This allows you to securely connect to your EC2 instances without the need for SSH access or bastion hosts. It uses IAM policies and AWS logging tools to provide secure, auditable browser-based or CLI sessions, making it ideal for regulated or sensitive environments.
- **Fleet Manager**: A unified operations dashboard that helps you view and manage your entire server fleet from a single location. This includes both AWS and on-premises servers, offering insights such as instance health, OS details, and more without needing direct logins.
- **OpsCenter and Incident Manager**: These tools integrate with CloudWatch, CloudTrail, and AWS Config to alert you of operational issues, offer root cause insights, and guide you through remediation workflows.

Calling out these capabilities is important because Systems Manager plays a critical role in day-to-day operations, helping you manage infrastructure more efficiently, enforce security best practices, and reduce manual intervention through automation.

You can use Systems Manager to achieve all components of the second pillar, as it provides a one-stop shop, as shown in the left-hand navigation bar in the following screenshot:

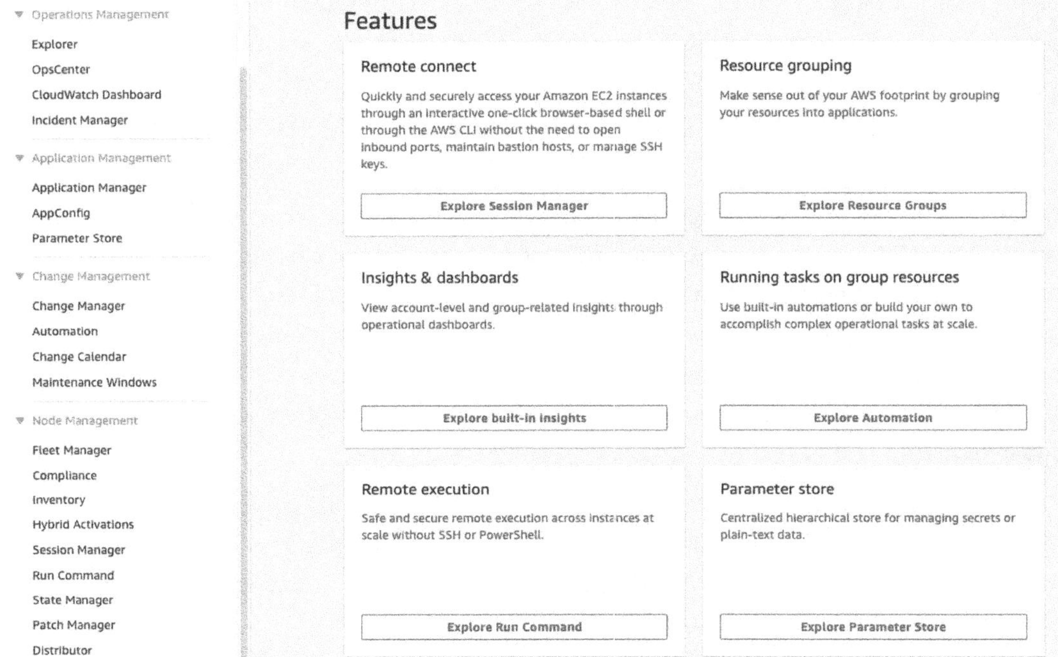

Figure 9.5: AWS Systems Manager for CloudOps monitoring and audit

AWS Systems Manager is the hub of your operation for managing all your AWS applications, resources, and on-premise environments. It keeps everything in one place for easy monitoring and auditing. AWS has done a great job explaining how Systems Manager works, which you can learn about at this link: `https://docs.aws.amazon.com/systems-manager/latest/userguide/what-is-systems-manager.html`.

In this section, you learned about managing cloud configuration and compliance, along with various AWS services that can help to achieve that. Now, let's learn about the following steps: provisioning and orchestration.

Third pillar – Provision & orchestrate

Once you have set up the environment, you need to speed up the provisioning and orchestration of your applications and any associated resources in a repeatable and immutable fashion.

Let's look at history; in the old days, infrastructure deployment started with manual deployments, where you used wikis and playbooks, which were sometimes outdated. Most of us can relate to a project where we had to use them. They were occasionally obsolete, with details often outdated or missing, and you encountered provisioning scenarios that should have been included in the manual. The best way to solve the problem was to ask the person who did it the last few times in the past, and hope that person was not on vacation and was still working at the company!

The next step was scripting everything in Bash. This worked well until the complexity became too great. Bash was not designed to build complex deployment frameworks, so it was hard to maintain. The best advice was: It worked the last time; don't touch it!

As digital transformation increasingly occurs within an organization, more applications either move to or are built on the cloud. These applications themselves solve complex problems and require complex infrastructure. Teams need more tools to manage this complexity, be productive, and innovate. You need highly specialized tools to manage the applications and to be able to choose from a varied set of tools based on their use cases. Managing infrastructure is a big part of managing cloud complexity, and one of the ways to manage infrastructure is by treating infrastructure as code.

Infrastructure-as-code (**IaC**) templates help you to model and provision resources, whether AWS-native, third-party, or open source, and applications on AWS and on-premises. So, you can speed up application and resource provisioning while improving consistency and compliance. For example, a developer wants to provision an S3 bucket that meets their company's security requirements. They will no longer have to dig through documentation to determine what bucket resource properties to set or how to set them. Instead, they can reuse a pre-built Secure S3 bucket module to provision a bucket quickly while automatically aligning with their company's requirements.

A cloud application typically consists of many components: networking (i.e., traffic gateways), compute (Amazon EC2, containers), databases, streams, security groups, users, roles, and so on. All these servers and resources are the infrastructure components of your cloud application. Managing cloud applications involves managing the life cycle of their resources: create, update, or delete. By codifying your infrastructure, you can manage your infrastructure code similarly to your application code. You can use a code editor to create it, store it in a version control system, and collaborate with your team members before deploying it to production. The advantages of using IaC are numerous, including the following:

- A single source of truth for deploying the entire stack
- The ability to replicate, redeploy, and repurpose your infrastructure

- The ability to version control both your infrastructure and your application code
- Automatic rollback to the previous working state in case of failures
- The ability to build and test your infrastructure as part of your CI/CD pipeline

AWS offers multiple services to help customers manage their infrastructure. The provisioning engine, AWS CloudFormation, speeds up cloud provisioning with IaC.

AWS Service Catalog allows organizations to create and maintain a list of IT services authorized on the AWS platform. These lists can include everything from VM images, servers, software, and databases to complete multi-tier application architectures. Users can then browse and launch these pre-approved IT services through a self-service portal, which helps ensure they use approved resources that meet compliance and security requirements. Additionally, administrators can set up workflows to automatically provision resources and control access and permissions to specific resources within the catalog.

You can choose to combine these services as per your workload needs. Let's learn about these services in more detail.

AWS CloudFormation

CloudFormation is a tool that supports the implementation of IaC. With CloudFormation, you can write your IaC using the CloudFormation template language, which is available in YAML and JSON formats. You can start from scratch or leverage pre-existing sample templates to create your infrastructure. You can use the CloudFormation service through a web-based console, command-line tools, or APIs to create a stack based on your template code. Once you have defined your stack and resources in the template, CloudFormation provisions will be configured accordingly.

CloudFormation helps you model, provision, and manage AWS resources. It allows you to use a template to create and delete multiple related AWS resources predictably and consistently. Here is a simple example of a CloudFormation template written in YAML syntax:

```yaml
---
AWSTemplateFormatVersion: '2010-09-09'
Resources:
  MyEC2Instance:
    Type: AWS::EC2::Instance
    Properties:
      ImageId: ami-101013
      InstanceType: m4.xlarge
      KeyName: gen-key-pair
```

```
      SecurityGroups:
        - !Ref ServerSecurityGroup
  ServerSecurityGroup:
    Type: AWS::EC2::SecurityGroup
    Properties:
      GroupDescription: Allow ssh access
      SecurityGroupIngress:
        - IpProtocol: tcp
          FromPort: '22'
          ToPort: '22'
          CidrIp: 10.1.1.16/0
```

This template creates an Amazon EC2 instance with a security group that allows incoming SSH connections. The security group is created first and then referenced when creating the Amazon EC2 instance.

To use this template, save it to a file (e.g., `servertemplate.yml`) and then use the AWS CLI to create a stack:

```
aws cloudformation create-stack --stack-name sa-book-stack --template-body
file://servertemplate.yml
```

One powerful feature you should be aware of, especially when working in multi-account or multi-region environments, is **AWS CloudFormation StackSets**. StackSets lets you deploy a single CloudFormation template across multiple AWS accounts and regions with just a few clicks or commands. This is extremely useful for organizations that must apply consistent infrastructure, compliance rules, or security controls across many environments. For example, you can use StackSets to enforce guardrails, deploy logging configurations, or set up shared VPCs across all your accounts in AWS Organizations. Using StackSets saves time, reduces errors, and ensures governance and uniformity across your global AWS footprint.

You can then use the AWS Management Console, the AWS CLI, or the CloudFormation API to monitor the progress of stack creation. Once the stack is created, you will have an Amazon EC2 instance running in your AWS account. You can change the stack by updating the template and using the `update-stack` command. You can learn more about AWS CloudFormation by visiting the AWS page here: `https://aws.amazon.com/cloudformation/`.

AWS Service Catalog

AWS Service Catalog provides a centralized platform for managing IT service catalogs, ensuring adherence to corporate standards and compliance. Organizations can easily control IT service availability, configurations, and access permissions by individual, group, department, or cost center. The platform also simplifies finding and deploying approved IT services for employees. Organizations can define their catalog of AWS services and AWS Marketplace software and make them available for their employees through a self-service portal.

AWS Service Management Connectors allow **IT service management** (**ITSM**) administrators to enhance the governance of provisioned AWS and third-party products.

For instance, by integrating with AWS Service Catalog, ServiceNow, and Jira's service desk, they can request, provision, and manage AWS and third-party services and resources for their users, streamlining the ITSM process.

AWS Service Catalog AppRegistry is a centralized repository that enables organizations to manage and govern their application resources on AWS. It provides a single place for collecting and managing application metadata, including the name, owner, purpose, and associated resources. This information can improve application visibility and governance and enable better collaboration between teams that work on different parts of the application stack. With AppRegistry, you can track and manage all your applications' resources, including AWS resources, third-party software, and external resources such as domain names or IP addresses. The following screenshot shows an app registry in System Catalog:

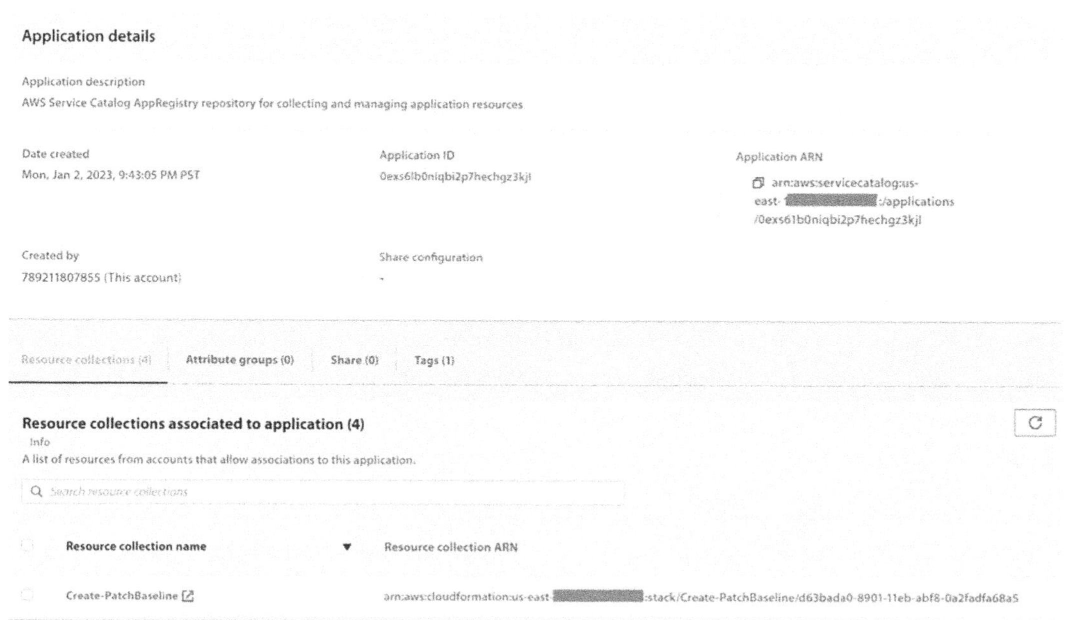

Figure 9.6: AWS System Catalog app registry

With AppRegistry, you can define your application metadata, such as ownership, data sensitivity, and cost centers, and include a reference to your application within the infrastructure code. This helps business stakeholders have up-to-date information about the application's contents and metadata. In addition, AppRegistry provides a central place to track and manage changes to your application resources, helping you maintain a comprehensive view of your applications and their dependencies.

AWS provides the **Getting Started Library** in AWS Service Catalog to make your job easier. This library offers a curated set of pre-built, well-architected templates for common use cases, such as setting up VPCs, deploying web apps, or launching secure workloads. These templates follow AWS best practices and are ready to use or customize, saving time and helping you onboard teams faster.

You can learn more about AWS Service Catalog by visiting the AWS page here: `https://aws.amazon.com/servicecatalog/`.

AWS Proton

AWS Proton is a managed application deployment service that allows developers to quickly and easily deploy and manage container and serverless applications on AWS. It provides a fully managed, opinionated environment for defining, deploying, and managing applications. With Proton, developers can focus on writing code and building applications while the service handles the underlying infrastructure and deployment workflows. This helps to accelerate the development process, reduce the risk of errors, and improve overall application quality.

AWS provides sample Proton templates that help you start building your application's infrastructure. You can fork those samples using the AWS samples code link (`https://github.com/aws-samples/aws-proton-cloudformation-sample-templates`) and refer to them while building the Proton environment.

AWS Proton can help you update out-of-date applications with a single click when you adopt a new feature or best practice. This helps ensure that your applications remain up to date and compliant with industry standards. Additionally, by providing a consistent architecture across your organization, Proton helps improve collaboration and reduces the risk of errors or misconfigurations. You can learn more about AWS Proton by visiting the AWS page here: `https://aws.amazon.com/proton/`.

AWS Cloud Development Kit (CDK)

The AWS CDK is an open source software development framework that enables developers to define cloud infrastructure and resources using familiar programming languages such as TypeScript, JavaScript, Python, Java, and C#. It provisions and deploys the infrastructure using AWS CloudFormation, providing the benefits of IaC.

You will work much faster with CDK because you use your familiar language, concepts, classes, and methods without a context switch. You also have all the tool support from the programming language, such as autocomplete, inline documentation, tests, and a debugger. The most important part is that you can build your abstractions and components of the infrastructure and application. AWS provides many default values, so there is no need to read much documentation; you can start quickly.

AWS CDK consists of three main components: the core framework, the AWS Construct library, and the CLI. The core framework enables you to define and organize your AWS infrastructure using high-level programming languages. You can create and structure apps that consist of one or multiple stacks. Stacks are the fundamental deployment unit in AWS CDK.

They are a logical grouping of AWS resources that are provisioned and managed as a single unit. Each stack is mapped one to one to a CloudFormation stack and can be independently deployed, updated, or deleted.

It is good practice to divide resources into stacks with different life cycles. You would create one stack for network infrastructure, such as a VPC, another stack would have an Elastic Container Service cluster, and yet another stack would be the application that is running in this cluster.

The AWS Construct library in CDK is a collection of pre-built components designed by AWS to create resources for specific services. This allows for decoupling libraries and using only the necessary dependencies in your project. The library is developed with best practices and security considerations in mind to provide an excellent developer experience, ease of use, and fast iteration cycles. The CDK CLI interacts with the core framework, helping to initialize project structure, inspect deployment differences, and deploy your project quickly to AWS. Here is an example of creating an Amazon S3 bucket using CDK in TypeScript:

```
import * as cdk from 'aws-cdk-lib';
import * as s3 from 'aws-cdk-lib/aws-s3';
class MyBookStack extends cdk.Stack {
  constructor(scope: CDK.App, id: string, props?: CDK.StackProps) {
    super(scope, id, props);
    new s3.Bucket(this, 'BookBucket', {
      bucketName: 'aws-sa-book-bucket',
      publicReadAccess: true
    });
  }
}
const app = new cdk.App();
new MyBookStack(app, 'MyBookStack');
app.synth();
```

This code defines a CDK stack with a single Amazon S3 bucket and synthesizes a CloudFormation template. Then, you can use the `cdk deploy` command to deploy the stack to your AWS account.

A key concept in CDK is the use of **constructs**, which are reusable building blocks for AWS resources. Constructs are organized into three levels:

- **Level 1 (L1) constructs**: These are low-level constructs that directly map to AWS CloudFormation resources (such as `CfnBucket`, `CfnInstance`). They give you fine-grained control but require more configuration and understanding of the raw AWS APIs.

- **Level 2 (L2) constructs**: These are higher-level, opinionated constructs that abstract away some of the complexity. For example, instead of manually defining an S3 bucket policy, you can use the Bucket construct and configure access settings directly in code. L2 constructs strike a balance between flexibility and simplicity.
- **Level 3 (L3) constructs or patterns**: These are even higher-level abstractions that represent complete architectures or patterns, such as a full static website setup or a Lambda-backed API gateway. They bundle multiple resources together with best practices, making it easy to deploy complex stacks with minimal effort.

Understanding these construct levels helps you choose the right level of abstraction for your use case – whether you're looking for granular control or quick, standardized deployments.

AWS CDK provides a paradigm shift in how you provision multiple environments. With CloudFormation, you can use one template with parameters for multiple environments – for example, dev and test. But with CDK, you have a shift where multiple templates are generated for each environment, ending in different stacks. This decoupling helps us to contain and maintain differences between environments by having fewer expensive resources in the dev environment. You can learn more about AWS CDK by visiting the AWS page here: `https://aws.amazon.com/cdk/`.

AWS Amplify

AWS Amplify is a suite of specialized tools designed to help developers quickly build feature-rich, full-stack web and mobile applications on AWS. It allows developers to utilize a wide range of AWS services as their use cases evolve. With Amplify, developers can configure a backend for their web or mobile app, visually create a web frontend UI, connect the two, and manage app content without needing to access the AWS console. At a high level, AWS Amplify provides the following features, tools, and services:

- **Amplify libraries**: Frontend developers can use purpose-built Amplify libraries to interact with AWS services. The case-centric Amplify libraries connect frontend iOS, Android, web, and React Native apps to an AWS backend and UI components for auth data and storage. Customers can use Amplify libraries to build a new app backend or connect an existing backend.
- **Amplify Hosting**: Amplify Hosting is a fully managed CI/CD service for modern web apps. It offers hundreds of global points of presence for fast and reliable hosting of static and server-side rendered apps that scale with your business needs. With Amplify Hosting, you can deploy updates to your web app on every code commit to the Git repository. The app is then deployed and hosted globally using CloudFront. Amplify Hosting supports modern web frameworks such as React, Angular, Vue, Next.js, Gatsby, Hugo, Jekyll, and more.

- **Amplify Studio**: Amplify Studio is a visual development environment that provides an abstraction layer on top of the Amplify CLI. It allows you to create full-stack apps on AWS by building an app backend, creating custom UI components, and connecting a UI to the app backend with minimal coding. With Amplify Studio, you can select from dozens of popular React components, such as buttons, forms, and marketing templates, and customize them to fit your style guide. You can also import UX designs from the popular design prototyping tool, Figma, as clean React code for seamless collaboration. Amplify Studio exports all UI and infrastructure artifacts as code so you can maintain complete control over your app design and behavior.
- **The Amplify CLI**: The Amplify CLI provides flexibility and integration with existing CI/CD tools through the new Amplify extensibility features. It allows frontend developers to easily set up backend resources in the cloud. It's designed to work with the Amplify JavaScript library and the AWS Mobile SDKs for iOS and Android. The Amplify CLI provisions and manages the mobile or web backend with guided workflows for common app use cases such as authentication, data, and storage on AWS. You can reconfigure Amplify-generated backend resources to optimize for specific use cases, leveraging the entire feature set of AWS, or modify Amplify deployment operations to comply with your enterprise DevOps guidelines.

Here's a code example of how to use AWS Amplify in a web application to store and retrieve data from a cloud database:

```
import { API, graphqlOperation } from 'aws-amplify'
// Add a new item to the cloud database
async function addItem(item) {
  const AddItemMutation = `mutation AddItem($item: ItemInput!) {
    addItem(item: $item) {
      id
      name
      description
    }
  }`
  const result = await API.graphql(graphqlOperation(AddItemMutation, {
item }))
  console.log(result)
}
// Retrieve a list of items from the cloud database
```

```
async function listItems() {
  const ListItemsQuery = `query ListItems {
    listItems {
      items {
        id
        name
        description
      }
    }
  }`
  const result = await API.graphql(graphqlOperation(ListItemsQuery))
  console.log(result)
}
```

The `API` object provided by Amplify enables you to call GraphQL operations to interact with the cloud database. The `addItem` function uses the `addItem` mutation to create a new item in the database, while the `listItems` function uses the `listItems` query to retrieve a list of items.

AWS Amplify ties into a broader array of tools and services provided by AWS. You can customize your Amplify toolkit and leverage AWS services' breadth and depth to service your modern application development needs. You can choose the services that suit your application and business requirements and scale confidently on AWS. You can learn more about AWS Amplify by visiting the AWS page here: `https://aws.amazon.com/amplify/`.

In this section, you were introduced to AWS CDK, which is a provisioning and orchestration solution that facilitates the consistent and repeatable provisioning of resources. By utilizing AWS CDK, you can scale your organization's infrastructure and applications on AWS in a sustainable manner. Additionally, AWS CDK allows you to create your infrastructure as code using programming languages. You can simplify and accelerate the governance and distribution of IaC templates using AWS Service Catalog to create repeatable infrastructure and application patterns with best practices. Now let's learn about the next step to set up monitoring and observations from your applications.

AWS Lightsail

If you're looking for a simple and low-cost way to run cloud applications, Amazon Lightsail is a great place to start. Lightsail is designed for developers, small businesses, and students who want to launch virtual servers, databases, websites, and more without needing deep AWS experience.

With Lightsail, you can launch a **virtual private server (VPS)** in just a few clicks. It provides pre-configured options for popular applications such as WordPress, Magento, Joomla, and even development stacks such as LAMP or Node.js. You don't need to worry about configuring the networking, storage, or operating system from scratch; AWS does most of the setup for you.

What makes Lightsail popular is its predictable, flat-rate pricing. Plans start at just $3.50 per month (which includes 512 MB memory, 1 vCPU, 20 GB SSD storage, and 1 TB data transfer), includes compute, storage, and data transfer. This is helpful if you're running a personal blog, a portfolio website, or even a small e-commerce platform and want to keep costs under control. Lightsail's pricing is transparent and easy to understand. Higher-tier plans offer more resources, such as the $5 per month plan with 1 GB memory and 40 GB SSD storage. This predictable pricing model helps you manage your budget effectively without unexpected costs.

Let's say you're a freelance developer building websites for clients. With Lightsail, you can quickly spin up a WordPress instance, apply security settings, and send your client a working website without having to manually install Apache, MySQL, and PHP.

In addition to virtual machines, Lightsail supports managed databases, block storage, load balancers, and even containers, so you can scale your apps easily as your needs grow. It also integrates with other AWS services when you're ready to move to a more advanced setup.

Amazon Lightsail provides a simplified, cost-effective solution for hosting applications and websites. Its ease of use, predictable pricing, and integration with AWS services make it an excellent starting point for developers and small businesses venturing into the cloud.

Fourth pillar – Monitor & observe

As the saying goes, you manage what you measure, so after you've provisioned your application, you have to be able to start measuring its health and performance. Monitoring and observability tools help to collect metrics, logs, traces, and event data. You can quickly identify and resolve application issues for serverless, containerized, or other applications built using microservices-based architectures.

AWS provides native monitoring, logging, alarming, and dashboards with CloudWatch and tracing through X-Ray. When deployed together, they provide the three pillars of an observability solution: metrics, logs, and traces. X-Ray (tracing) is fundamental to observability and is therefore included in the motions alongside CloudWatch. Furthermore, AWS provides open source observability for Prometheus and Grafana and support for OpenTelemetry. A well-defined monitoring and observability strategy implemented with CloudWatch and X-Ray provides insights and data to monitor and respond to your application's performance issues by providing a consolidated view of the operation.

The following are the key AWS services for observability and monitoring, which you can choose to use as per your workload needs or combine them:

- **AWS CloudWatch** helps you collect, view, and analyze metrics and set alarms to get notified when certain thresholds are breached. Here, you can see a screenshot of the billing metrics dashboard in CloudWatch:

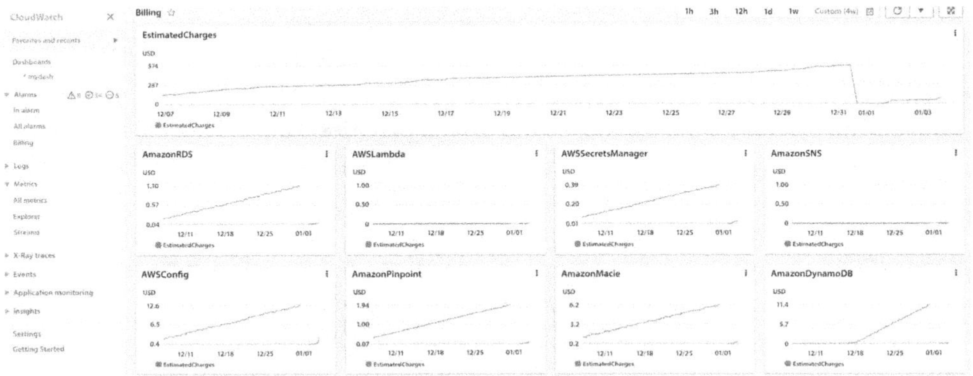

Figure 9.7: AWS CloudWatch billing metrics dashboard

You can also use CloudWatch to track log files from Amazon EC2 instances, Amazon RDS DB instances, and other resources and troubleshoot issues with your applications. You learned about AWS CloudWatch earlier in this chapter.

However, as observability needs grow, AWS has introduced new capabilities to help you monitor complex, distributed applications more effectively. One such feature is Application Signals, which automatically instruments and monitors critical performance metrics such as latency, error rates, and throughput across your application stack without requiring manual setup. It simplifies application observability and gives you near-real-time insights into your services' performance. CloudWatch also offers native support for **OpenTelemetry (OTEL)**, an open source observability framework. You can use OTEL to collect traces and metrics from your applications, whether in AWS or on-premises, and send that data directly to CloudWatch for centralized visibility. This support makes adopting standardized, vendor-neutral monitoring easier across your entire environment.

- **AWS X-Ray** is a distributed tracing service that allows developers to analyze and debug their applications, especially those built using a microservices architecture. It helps identify performance bottlenecks and errors, allowing developers to optimize application performance and enhance the end-user experience.

  It allows you to trace requests as they flow through your application and see the performance of each component of your application:

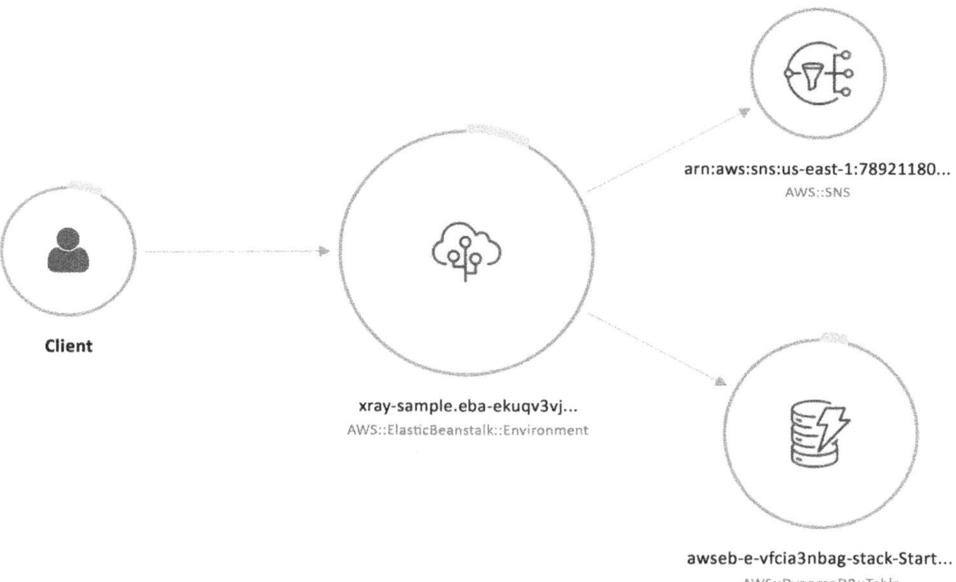

Figure 9.8: AWS X-Ray service map graph

In the AWS X-Ray console, you can view a trace of a request as it flows through your application and see the performance of each trace segment. You can also use the console to search for traces and analyze performance data for your application. To use AWS X-Ray, you first need to instrument your application code to send data to the X-Ray service. This can be done using one of the AWS SDKs or the X-Ray daemon. You can then view and analyze the data using the X-Ray console or the X-Ray API. You can learn more about AWS X-Ray by visiting the AWS page here: `https://aws.amazon.com/xray/`.

- **Amazon Managed Service for Prometheus (AMSP)** is a fully managed service that makes it easy to run and scale Prometheus, an open source monitoring and alerting system, in the cloud. AMSP automatically handles tasks such as scaling and maintenance, allowing you to focus on monitoring your applications. It also includes integration with other AWS services, such as Amazon CloudWatch and Amazon SNS, which allows you to view and analyze your monitoring data and set up alerts and notifications. The following are the benefits of using AMSP:
  - **Fully managed**: AMSP takes care of the underlying infrastructure and maintenance tasks, so you can focus on monitoring your applications.
  - **Scalability**: AMSP automatically scales to handle changes in workload, so you don't have to worry about capacity planning.
  - **Integration with other AWS services**: AMSP integrates with other AWS services, such as CloudWatch and SNS, which allows you to view and analyze your monitoring data and set up alerts and notifications.
  - **Security**: AMSP includes built-in security measures, such as encryption at rest and network isolation, to help protect your monitoring data.
  - **Cost-effective**: AMSP is a pay-as-you-go service, which means you only pay for the resources you use. This can be more cost-effective than running and maintaining your own Prometheus infrastructure.

  You can learn more about AMSP by visiting the AWS page here: `https://aws.amazon.com/prometheus/`.
- **Amazon Managed Service for Grafana (AMG)** is a fully managed service that simplifies the visualization and analysis of operational data at scale. It leverages the popular open source analytics platform Grafana to query, visualize, and alert on metrics stored across AWS, third-party ISVs, databases, and other IT resources. AMG removes the need for server provisioning, software configuration, and security and scaling concerns, enabling you to analyze your metrics, logs, and traces without the heavy lifting in production. You can learn more about AMG by visiting the AWS page here: `https://aws.amazon.com/grafana/`.

In this section, you learned that an observable environment reduces risk, increases agility, and improves user experience. Observability provides insights and context about the environment you monitor. AWS enables you to transform from monitoring to observability so that you can have full-service visibility from metrics, logs, and traces by combining AWS CloudWatch and X-Ray. Let's learn about the next step in building centralized operations.

Fifth pillar – Centralize operations

IT teams need to take operational actions across hundreds, sometimes thousands, of applications while maintaining safety, security, and compliance simultaneously. To help make ops management as easy and efficient as possible, you must safely manage and operate your IT infrastructure at scale. To achieve that, you should have a central location and interface to view operational data from multiple AWS services. You can then automate operational tasks on applications and resources, especially common operational changes, such as rotating certificates, increasing service limits, taking backups, and resizing instances. You laid all the foundations without compromising any safety, security, or compliance guardrails in the foundation stage.

To help enable cloud operations, you can use **AWS Systems Manager**. Systems Manager is a fully managed service that helps customers safely manage and operate their IT infrastructure at scale. It provides a central location and interfaces to view operational data from multiple AWS services. Customers can then use it to automate operational tasks on their applications and resources, especially common operational changes, such as rotating certificates, increasing service limits, taking backups, and resizing instances.

You learned about AWS Systems Manager earlier in this chapter. Here, you will learn about Systems Manager's ability to view, manage, operate, and report on cloud operations. There are **four** stages of implementing CloudOps using AWS Systems Manager:

1. **Build a foundation for cloud operations**: To build a foundation for cloud operations, Systems Manager helps you set up the management of service configurations, IT assets, infrastructure, and platforms. Systems Manager integrates with AWS Config to collect and maintain an inventory of infrastructure resources and application and OS data, starting with your environment and account structure. Simple, automated setup processes allow you to quickly enable operational best practices, such as continuous vulnerability scanning and collecting insights into improving an application's performance and availability. It also helps you to automate operational best practices by codifying operations runbooks and defining execution parameters, such as freeze periods and permissions. AWS Config rules enable continuous compliance by enforcing security, risk, and compliance policies.
2. **Enable visibility into applications and infrastructure**: The second stage is to enable visibility into applications and infrastructure by continuously tracking key technical and business measures, providing visibility, and triggering automation and actions if needed.

Systems Manager provides operational visibility and actionable insights to customers through a widget-based, customizable dashboard that can be tailored for users such as IT operators, DevOps engineers, IT leaders, and executives. Operational teams can set up operational event management and reporting for their infrastructure and resources at scale using pre-defined configuration bundles that reflect operational best practices to filter out and capture specific operational events that require an operator's attention for diagnosis and action/remediation. The dashboard provides a holistic view of relevant data across multiple AWS accounts and AWS Regions, such as inventory and CMDB, patch, resource configuration and compliance, support tickets, insights from EC2 Compute Optimizer, Trusted Advisor, Personal Health Dashboard, Amazon CloudWatch, and trends on outstanding operational issues.

3. **Automate operations at scale**: To proactively automate operations at scale, Systems Manager gives teams the ability to automate patch management to keep resources secure. Systems Manager provides change management capabilities with built-in approval workflows and secures automated or manual change execution when making application and environment changes. Only approved changes can be deployed to the environment by authorized resources, and these come with detailed reporting. You can automate server administration, providing central IT teams with a consistent, integrated console to perform common administrative tasks. Additionally, you can manage and troubleshoot resources on AWS and on-premises. Operators can manage their VM fleet when manual actions are required by connecting directly from the console. You can also operationalize risk management by creating rules. Here is an example AWS Systems Manager runbook that operationalizes risk management by checking for security vulnerabilities in installed software packages on Amazon EC2 instances:

```
{
  "Name": "ec2-check-for-security-vulnerabilities",
  "Description": "Scans installed software packages on EC2 instances
for security vulnerabilities",
  "ResourceId": "*",
  "ResourceType": "AWS::EC2::Instance",
  "ComplianceType": "NON_COMPLIANT",
  "RulePriority": 1,
  "Operator": "EQUALS",
```

```
    "Parameters": {
      "ExecutionFrequency": "OneTime",
      "OutputS3BucketName": "sa-book-s3-bucket",
      "OutputS3KeyPrefix": "ec2-security-scans/"
    },
    "Actions": [
      {
        "Type": "RunCommand",
        "Properties": {
          "Comment": "Scan installed software packages for security
vulnerabilities",
          "OutputS3BucketName": "sa-book-s3-bucket",
          "OutputS3KeyPrefix": "ec2-security-scans/",
          "DocumentName": "AWS-RunShellScript",
          "Parameters": {
            "commands": [
              "apt update",
              "apt-get install -y unattended-upgrades",
              "apt-get install -y --only-upgrade bash glibc libstdc++6
libgcc1 libc6 libc-bin libpam-modules libpam-runtime libpam0g
login passwd libssl1.0.0 openssl dpkg apt libapt-pkg4.12 apt-utils
libdb5.3 bzip2 libbz2-1.0 liblzma5 libtinfo5 libreadline7"
            ]
          }
        }
      }
    ]
}
```

By running analyses to proactively detect and remediate risks across applications and infrastructure, such as expiring certificates, a lack of database backup, and the use of blocked software, identified risks are assigned to owners and can be remediated using automation runbooks with automated reporting.

4. **Remediate issues and incidents**: Finally, when unexpected issues arise, you must be able to remediate issues and incidents quickly. With the incident, event, and risk management capabilities within Systems Manager, you can employ various AWS services to trigger relevant issues or incidents. It integrates with Amazon GuardDuty for threat detection and AWS Inspector for security assessments, keeps a running check on vulnerabilities in the environment, and allows automated remediation. It provides a consolidated view of incidents, changes, operational risks and failures, operational alarms, compliance, and vulnerability management reports. It allows operations teams to take manual or automated action to resolve issues. Systems Manager speeds up issue resolution by automating common, repeatable remediation actions, such as failover to a backup system and capturing failed state for root cause analysis.

For a hybrid workload, **SSM Agent** plays a crucial role in AWS Systems Manager by enabling features such as Session Manager, Run Command, and Patch Manager. It's installed on EC2 instances by default but can also be manually installed on **non-AWS resources**, such as on-prem servers or VMs running in other clouds. This makes it a powerful tool for managing a hybrid infrastructure securely and centrally, without needing open SSH ports or bastion hosts.

Systems Manager's incident management capability automates a response plan for application issues by notifying the appropriate people to respond, providing them with relevant troubleshooting data, and enabling chat-based collaboration. You can easily access and analyze operational data from multiple AWS services and track updates related to incidents, such as changes in alarm status and response plans. Operators can resolve incidents manually by logging into the instance or executing automation runbooks. Systems Manager integrates with AWS Chatbot to invoke commands in the appropriate channel for an incident so central IT teams can resolve issues quickly. Let's learn about the final and most important step in the cloud operation model: managing cost.

Sixth pillar – Manage your cloud's finances

Cloud adoption has enabled technology teams to innovate faster by reducing approval, procurement, and infrastructure deployment cycles. It also helps finance organizations eliminate failure costs, as cloud resources can be terminated with just a few clicks or API calls. As a result, technology teams are no longer just builders but also operate and own their products.

They are responsible for most activities that were traditionally associated with finance and operations teams, such as procurement and deployment.

Cloud Financial Management (**CFM**) enables finance, product, technology, and business organizations to manage, optimize, and plan costs as they grow their usage and scale on AWS. The primary goal of CFM is to enable customers to achieve their business outcomes cost-efficiently and accelerate economic and business value creation while balancing agility and control. CFM has the following four dimensions to manage and save costs:

Plan and evaluate

When planning for future cloud spending, you should first define a goal for the monthly cost of the individual project. The project team needs to make sure cloud resources related to a project are correctly tagged with cost allocation tags and/or cost categories. This way, they can calculate and track the monthly cost of the project with the cost and usage data available in AWS Cost Explorer and AWS Cost and Usage Reports. These reports provide the data you need to understand how your AWS costs are incurred and optimize your AWS usage and cost management. These reports can be customized to include only the needed data and can be delivered to an Amazon S3 bucket or an Amazon SNS topic. You can also use the data in these reports to create custom cost and usage reports, set up cost and usage alarms, and create budgets.

You can decide on a project's budget based on the growth trend of the project as well as the available funds set aside for the project. Then, you can set the budget thresholds using AWS Budgets for cost or resource usage. You can also use AWS Budgets to set coverage and utilization targets for the project team's Reserved Instances and Savings Plans. These are two options that allow you to save money on your AWS usage costs. They both enable you to purchase a discounted rate for your AWS usage, in exchange for committing to a certain usage level over a specific period. **Reserved Instances** are a type of pricing model that allows you to save up to 75% on your Amazon EC2 and RDS usage costs by committing to a one- or three-year term. With Reserved Instances, you pay a discounted hourly rate for the usage of a specific instance type in a specific region, and you can choose between Standard and Convertible Reserved Instances.

AWS Savings Plans is a new pricing model that allows you to save up to 72% on your AWS usage costs by committing to a one-year or three-year term. With Savings Plans, you pay a discounted hourly rate for your AWS usage, and you can choose between Compute Savings Plans and Amazon EC2 Instance Savings Plans. Compute Savings Plans offer a discount on a wide range of AWS services, including Amazon EC2, Fargate, and Lambda, while Amazon EC2 Instance Savings Plans only offer a discount on Amazon EC2 usage.

The AWS Budgets Reports dashboard allows you to monitor the progress of your budget portfolio by comparing actual costs with the budgeted costs and forecasted costs with the budgeted costs. You can set up notification alerts to receive updates when the cost and usage are expected to exceed the threshold limit. These alerts can be sent via email or Amazon **Simple Notification Service** (**SNS**). You can learn more about AWS Budgets by visiting the AWS page here: `https://aws.amazon.com/aws-cost-management/aws-budgets/`. After planning your budget, let's learn about managing it.

Manage and Control

As businesses grow and scale on AWS, you need to give your team the freedom to experiment and innovate in the cloud while maintaining control over cost, governance, and security. And while fostering innovation and speed is essential, you also want to avoid getting surprised by the bill.

You can achieve this by establishing centralized ownership through a center of excellence. Cost management elements are shared responsibilities across the entire organization. A centralized team is essential to design policies and governance mechanisms, implement and monitor the effort, and help drive company-wide best practices.

You can utilize services such as **Identity and Access Management** (**IAM**) to ensure secure access control to AWS resources. IAM allows you to create and manage user identities, groups, and roles and grants permissions for IAM users to access specific AWS resources. This way, you can control and restrict individual and group access to AWS resources, ensuring the security of your infrastructure and data.

Use **AWS Organizations** to enable automatic policy-based account creation, management, and billing at scale. Finally, using the **AWS Billing Console**, you can easily track overall spending and view cost breakdown by service and account by accessing the billing dashboard. You can view the overall monthly spending from last month, the current month, and the current forecasted month.

The following screenshot is a sample billing dashboard:

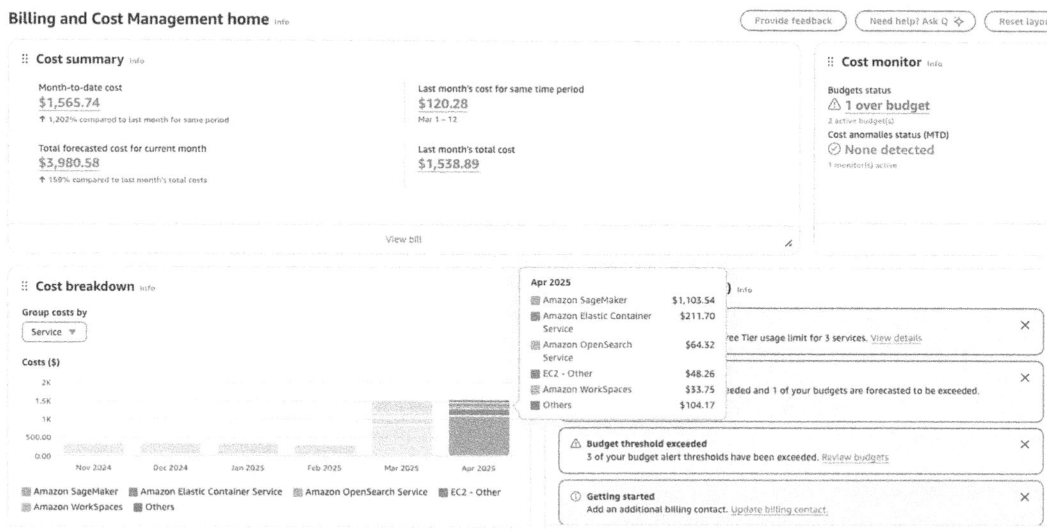

Figure 9.9: AWS billing dashboard

The preceding billing dashboard shows six months' spend by service and cost trend. Using the Billing Console, you can receive a unified view of spend in a single bill and establish rules for organizing costs, sharing discount benefits associated with Reserved Instances and Savings Plans, and many other controls. You can learn more about the AWS Billing Console by visiting the AWS page here: `https://aws.amazon.com/aws-cost-management/aws-billing/`.

AWS Purchase Order Management enables you to use **purchase orders (POs)** to procure AWS services and approve invoices for payment. With this service, you can configure multiple POs, map them to your invoices, and access the invoices generated against those POs. Additionally, you can manage the status of your POs, track their balance and expiration, and set up email notifications for contacts to receive alerts when POs are running low on balance or close to their expiration date. You can learn more about AWS Purchase Order Management by visiting the AWS page here: `https://aws.amazon.com/aws-cost-management/aws-purchase-order-management/`.

AWS Cost Anomaly Detection is a machine learning service that automates cost anomaly alerts and root cause analysis. It can save time investigating spending anomalies by providing automated root cause analysis and identifying potential cost drivers, such as specific AWS services, usage types (e.g., data transfer cost), regions, and member accounts. You can learn more about AWS Cost Anomaly Detection by visiting the AWS page here: `https://aws.amazon.com/aws-cost-management/aws-cost-anomaly-detection/`. As you manage your cost, let's learn how to track it.

Track and allocate

You need to ask three questions to understand your billing uses. The **first** is, *What is causing our bill to increase?* AWS provides **AWS Cost Explorer** to help answer this question. Cost Explorer provides a quick visualization of cost and utilization with default reports and creates specific views with filters and grouping, as shown in the following figure. This tool can help show which AWS services are leading to increased spending:

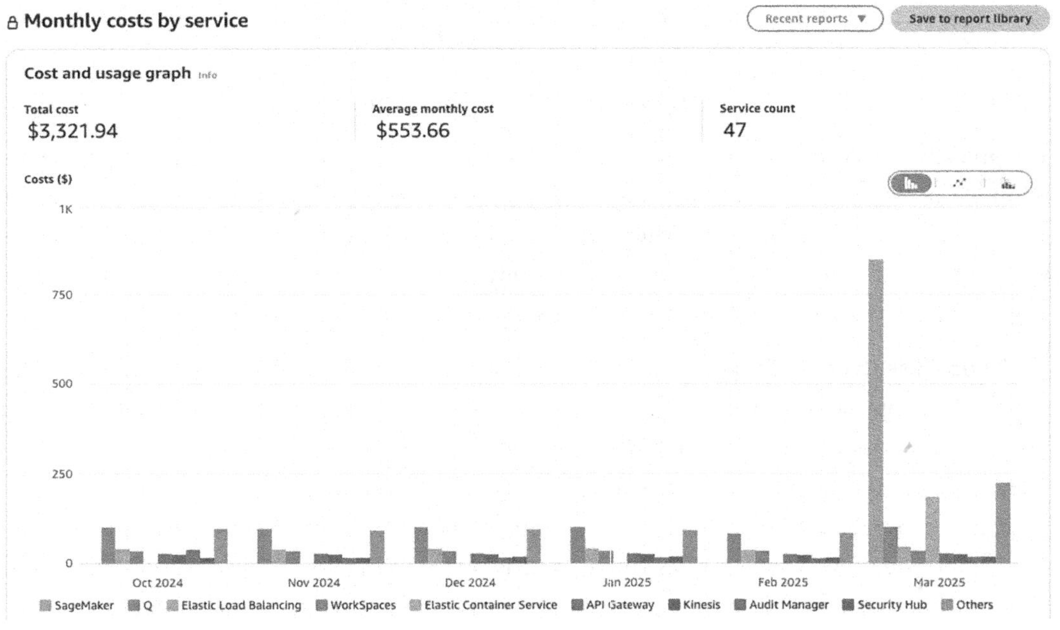

Figure 9.10: AWS Cost Explorer

In the preceding Cost Explorer dashboard, you can see service expense grouping in the costs chart, showing SageMaker has the highest cost, followed by ECS and other services. It also provides the ability to download CSV files for detailed analysis. You can learn more about AWS Cost Explorer by visiting the AWS page here: `https://aws.amazon.com/aws-cost-management/aws-cost-explorer/`.

The **second** question is a common follow-up: *Which of my lines of business, teams, or organizations drove increased spending and usage?* AWS Cost Explorer's data becomes even more valuable when paired with cost allocation tags. These features allow customers to categorize their resources and spending to fit their organization's needs. Categorizing spending by specific teams, sometimes referred to as showback, allows for better analysis and easier identification of savings opportunities. You can also use the AWS **Cost and Usage Report** (**CUR**) to bring cost and usage data, including tags, into your analysis tool of choice. This approach also allows for combining the data with other business-specific data. You can learn more about CUR by visiting the AWS page here: `https://aws.amazon.com/aws-cost-management/aws-cost-and-usage-reporting/`.

Finally, the **third** question is, *How do I understand the cost impact of Reserved Instances?* AWS Cost Explorer provides multiple ways to view and dive deep into this data, such as tagging service with meaningful info (e.g., owner, project, application), or you can define cost categories by group accounts, tags, services, and charge types with custom rules. You can use CUR to deliver cost data to the S3 bucket, which can be integrated with Amazon Athena and/or ingested into your ERP system.

Furthermore, **AWS Billing Conductor** is a billing and cost management tool that helps you monitor and optimize your AWS costs and usage and provides insights into how you are using your resources. AWS Billing Conductor provides recommendations for ways to optimize your costs, such as by identifying idle or underutilized resources that can be turned off or scaled down. You can learn more about AWS Billing Conductor by visiting the AWS page here: `https://aws.amazon.com/aws-cost-management/aws-billing-conductor/`.

AWS Application Cost Profiler is a service that allows you to collect and correlate usage data from your multi-tenant applications with your AWS billing information. This enables you to generate detailed, tenant-specific cost reports with hourly granularity delivered daily or monthly. This can be useful for understanding the cost breakdown of your multi-tenant application and allocating costs to individual tenants or customers. You can learn more about AWS Application Cost Profiler by visiting the AWS page here: `https://aws.amazon.com/aws-cost-management/aws-application-cost-profiler/`.

Having a well-defined **tagging strategy** is essential when managing your cloud finances in AWS. Tags are key-value pairs that you can assign to most AWS resources, and they play a critical role in tracking, allocating, and optimizing your costs. A strong tagging strategy helps you organize resources by projects, teams, environments (such as dev, test, prod), or cost centers, making it easier to break down your AWS bill and identify which parts of your organization are driving usage.

Defining mandatory tags such as Owner, Project, Environment, and CostCenter, you can enforce these using tag policies in AWS Organizations to ensure consistency. AWS services such as AWS Cost Explorer, AWS Budgets, and AWS **Cost and Usage Reports** (**CUR**) rely heavily on these tags for granular visibility. You can also use AWS Resource Groups to manage resources based on tags, making both operational and financial management more efficient.

A tagging strategy not only improves cost transparency but also supports governance, automation, and compliance tracking – critical for long-term cloud financial management.

Now let's learn about the final step to optimize costs and increase savings.

Optimize and save

Cost optimization is about making sure you pay only for what you need. AWS offers tools and services that make it easier for you to build cost-efficient workloads, which help you to continue saving as you scale on AWS. While there are hundreds of ways you can minimize spending, the following are two of the most impactful levers you can pull to optimize spending.

Using the right pricing models

AWS offers services through multiple pricing models – on-demand, pay-as-you-go, commitment-based Reserved Instances, and Spot instances for up to 90% discount compared to on-demand pricing. Amazon EC2 Spot Instances are a type of AWS computing resource that is available at a reduced price and can be used to run your applications. These instances are spare capacities in the AWS cloud that can be interrupted at any time, based on the resource demand. Spot Instances are suitable for applications with flexible start and end times that can handle interruptions without causing significant issues.

Suppose you have predictable, steady workloads on Amazon EC2, Amazon ECS, and Amazon RDS. If you use Reserved Instances, you can save up to 72% over on-demand capacity. Reserved Instances are a pricing option in AWS that allows you to pay up front for a commitment to use a certain amount of resources over a specific period in exchange for a discounted price. There are three options for purchasing Reserved Instances:

- **All up-front (AURI)**: This option requires you to pay for the entire term of the Reserved Instance up front and provides the most significant discount.
- **Partial up-front (PURI)**: This option requires a partial payment up front and provides a smaller discount than the AURI option.
- **No upfront payments (NURI)**: This option does not require any up front payment and provides the smallest discount.

By choosing the AURI option, you can receive the largest discount on your Reserved Instances. The PURI and NURI options offer lower discounts but allow you to pay less up front or avoid upfront payments altogether.

AWS offers Reserved Instances and Savings Plans purchase recommendations via Cost Explorer based on your past usage. Cost Explorer identifies and recommends the estimated value resulting in the largest savings. It allows you to generate a recommendation specific to your purchase preference. From there, you can track your investment using Cost Explorer. Any usage above the commitment level will be charged at on-demand rates. You can revisit commitment levels, make incremental purchases, and track coverage and utilization using pre-built reports in Cost Explorer.

With AWS purchase option recommendations, you can receive tailored Reserved Instances or Savings Plans purchase recommendations based on your historical usage. You can select parameters for recommendations, such as the type of plan, term commitment, and payment option, that make sense for your business.

Identify and eliminate idle or over-provisioned resources

AWS Cost Explorer resources can be used for top-level **key performance indicators** (**KPIs**), rightsizing, and instance selection. Cost Explorer will estimate monthly savings, which is the sum of the projected monthly savings associated with each recommendation.

Cost Explorer rightsizing recommendations generate recommendations by identifying idle and underutilized instances and searching for smaller instance sizes in the same instance family. Idle instances are defined as CPU utilization of <1%, while underutilized instances are defined as those with CPU utilization between 1% and 40%.

In this section, you learned about various ways to manage your costs and make the cloud more profitable to run your workload and business.

Knowledge check

As you have learned about CloudOps throughout this chapter, let's do a knowledge check:

1. Your organization manages sensitive healthcare data on AWS, requiring strict compliance with HIPAA regulations. A recent audit revealed that several Amazon S3 buckets were publicly accessible and lacked server-side encryption. To address this, you need an automated solution that does the following:

    - Continuously monitors AWS resources for compliance violations

- Automatically remediates non-compliant resources without manual intervention
- Provides a centralized dashboard for compliance status across all AWS accounts

Which of the following AWS services and configurations would best meet these requirements? (Choose two.)

a. Implement AWS Config rules to evaluate the compliance of AWS resources and associate them with AWS Systems Manager Automation documents for automatic remediation of non-compliant resources.
b. Use AWS CloudTrail to monitor API calls and manually identify non-compliant resources for remediation.
c. Deploy AWS Trusted Advisor to receive real-time notifications about non-compliant resources and automatically remediate them.
d. Set up Amazon GuardDuty to detect non-compliant configurations and trigger AWS Lambda functions for remediation.

Answer: a. and d.

Explanation:

a. **Correct.** AWS Config allows you to define rules that evaluate the compliance of AWS resources. By associating these rules with AWS Systems Manager Automation documents, you can automatically remediate non-compliant resources. This setup provides continuous compliance monitoring and remediation.
b. Incorrect. While AWS CloudTrail logs API calls, it does not provide automated compliance checks or remediation capabilities. Manual analysis of logs is required to identify non-compliant resources.
c. Incorrect. AWS Trusted Advisor offers recommendations for AWS best practices but does not provide real-time notifications or automated remediation for compliance violations.
d. **Correct.** Amazon GuardDuty is a threat detection service that continuously monitors for malicious activity and unauthorized behavior. By integrating GuardDuty findings with AWS Lambda, you can automate the remediation of certain non-compliant configurations.

2. Your company operates an e-commerce site on AWS that experiences heavy traffic spikes during promotions. Recently, the system crashed when EC2 instances hit 100% CPU. Unused instances also remained running for days after the sale, causing high AWS charges. You are asked to build an automated CloudOps solution to do the following:

    - Monitor system load in real time
    - Scale infrastructure dynamically based on usage
    - Stop idle instances to reduce cost
    - Alert engineers before resources become critical

    Which options best meet these requirements?

    a. Use a fixed EC2 Instance Scheduler to stop instances every night at a specific time, regardless of actual usage trends or demand.
    b. Use AWS Trusted Advisor to identify unused resources and schedule manual reviews to remove them monthly.
    c. Set CloudWatch alarms to trigger Auto Scaling when CPU or memory exceeds thresholds, and use Lambda functions to shut down idle EC2 instances.
    d. Manually monitor CloudWatch metrics and adjust instance sizes during peak usage to reduce performance bottlenecks.

    Answer: c.

    Explanation:

    a. Incorrect. Fixed shutdowns don't consider live traffic or user demand and can cause outages.
    b. Incorrect. Trusted Advisor offers suggestions but doesn't take automated action.
    c. **Correct.** This combination of CloudWatch and Lambda provides a real-time, automated solution that dynamically scales resources up or down. It improves performance and reduces cost without manual intervention.
    d. Incorrect. Manual monitoring defeats the purpose of CloudOps automation and is not scalable.

3. A financial services company operates multiple AWS accounts across different departments. Each department manages its own Amazon EC2 instances, Amazon RDS databases, and Amazon EFS file systems. The company faces challenges in ensuring consistent backup policies, monitoring backup statuses, and maintaining compliance across all accounts. To address these issues, the company seeks a centralized solution that does the following:

   - Automates backup scheduling for EC2, RDS, and EFS resources
   - Applies consistent backup policies across multiple AWS accounts
   - Provides centralized monitoring and reporting of backup activities
   - Ensures compliance with data retention and encryption standards

   Which of the following approaches would best fulfill these requirements? (Choose two.)

   a. Implement AWS Backup to create centralized backup plans that define schedules, retention policies, and encryption settings, and apply them across AWS accounts using AWS Organizations.
   b. Configure AWS Backup to tag resources automatically and apply backup plans based on these tags, ensuring consistent backup policies across resources.
   c. Use individual AWS Lambda functions in each account to schedule backups and send status reports to a central monitoring system.
   d. Rely on each department to manually configure backups for their resources and submit monthly compliance reports to the central IT team.

   Answer: a. and b.

   Explanation:

   a. **Correct.** AWS Backup allows the creation of centralized backup plans that can define backup schedules, retention policies, and encryption settings. By integrating with AWS Organizations, these plans can be applied across multiple AWS accounts, ensuring consistency and compliance.
   b. **Correct.** AWS Backup supports resource tagging, enabling automatic application of backup plans to tagged resources. This ensures that backup policies are consistently applied across various AWS services and resources.
   c. Incorrect. While AWS Lambda can automate tasks, managing individual functions across multiple accounts increases complexity and may lead to inconsistent backup policies and monitoring challenges.

   d. Incorrect. Manual backup configurations and reporting are prone to human error and do not provide the centralized control and automation required for compliance and efficiency.

4. Your company has grown and now operates five AWS accounts—one per department. Each team manages its resources independently. Recently, Finance launched untagged EC2 instances in a high-cost region. The CIO asks you to implement a central governance model that does the following:

   - Provides cross-account visibility
   - Enforces policies (such as tagging and encryption)
   - Captures API activity for audit
   - Maintains flexibility for each department

   Which solution best addresses the CIO's goals using AWS-native CloudOps tools?

   a. Restrict all developers to one shared AWS account and enforce compliance through IAM roles and security groups.
   b. Use AWS Organizations with **Service Control Policies** (**SCPs**), and enable Config and CloudTrail across accounts for real-time governance.
   c. Ask department leads to email weekly usage reports to IT and manually validate them for tagging and cost.
   d. Install browser extensions for all developers that monitor their usage and submit it to a shared Slack channel.

   Answer: b.

   Explanation:

   a. Incorrect. A shared account creates complexity, security issues, and friction.
   b. **Correct.** This approach enables centralized control using AWS-native services, supports cross-account policy enforcement, and maintains developer autonomy with visibility.
   c. Incorrect. Manual reports are not scalable or enforceable.
   d. Incorrect. Browser tools don't integrate with AWS infrastructure and aren't suitable for enterprise governance.

5. A vehicle tracking system hosted on AWS faced a major outage last week due to a backend EC2 server reaching high memory usage. There was no Auto Scaling or proactive monitoring in place. Your CTO has asked you to implement a resilient, self-healing CloudOps solution that can do the following:

    - Automatically detect memory and CPU bottlenecks
    - Trigger infrastructure scaling during peak demand
    - Alert the engineering team before system failure
    - Minimize reliance on manual intervention

    Which of the following solutions would be most appropriate?

    a. Use Auto Scaling based only on CPU metrics with default thresholds and allow engineers to manually review performance metrics weekly.
    b. Set up CloudWatch alarms to detect memory and CPU thresholds, and use Lambda to provision new resources dynamically before failure.
    c. Use a cron job inside the EC2 instance to monitor memory and send logs to a text file every 5 minutes.
    d. Reboot all servers every morning using AWS Systems Manager to flush system memory and reduce long-term memory usage.

    Answer: b.

    Explanation:

    a. Incorrect. CPU-only metrics miss memory issues and reviewing weekly adds unacceptable delays.
    b. **Correct.** Combining CloudWatch + Lambda provides a real-time response to resource pressure, scaling up automatically and maintaining resilience.
    c. Incorrect. Cron jobs and local logging are not scalable or responsive enough for real-time cloud environments.
    d. Incorrect. Scheduled reboots don't fix runtime memory issues during high traffic and can interrupt users.

Summary

Working in a cloud environment is different from on-premises. The out-of-the-box tools and services available in AWS can make a huge difference when operating your workload in the cloud. To realize the full value of the cloud, it's important to understand cloud operations and how to apply automation everywhere. In this chapter, you learned about the cloud operation model and the six pillars of CloudOps to ensure secure and efficient cloud management. Monitoring and observability provide real-time visibility using tools such as CloudWatch and X-Ray. Incident management helps detect and respond to issues quickly with automated alerts and workflows. Security and compliance protect your environment through IAM, Config, and GuardDuty. Automation and IaC streamline operations using CloudFormation and CDK. Cost optimization uses budgets and tagging for better spending control, while backup and disaster recovery ensure data protection and continuity with AWS backup and elastic disaster recovery.

Under the CloudOps pillars, you learned about building cloud governance, infrastructure provisioning, monitoring, centralized operation management, and cost optimization. You learned about various AWS services that can help you build end-to-end cloud operation pillars. These services include AWS CloudTrail, AWS Config, AWS CloudWatch, AWS Systems Manager, AWS CloudFormation, AWS Service Catalog, and AWS Cost Explorer.

Data is one of the important drivers of moving to the cloud. In the next chapter, you will learn about the AWS services available for extracting, transforming, and loading large volumes of data in AWS.

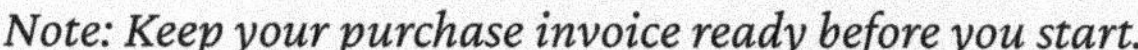

Part 4

AWS Advance Analytics, ML, and GenAI Service Offerings

This section focuses on building data-first architectures in AWS. You'll start by learning how to process and analyze both batch and streaming data using tools such as Glue, EMR, Kinesis, and MSK. Then you'll move into machine learning, where you'll use SageMaker to build, train, and deploy models. A dedicated part of this chapter introduces you to Generative AI with Amazon Bedrock and Jumpstart, enabling you to create intelligent applications powered by foundational models.

This part of the book includes the following chapters:

- *Chapter 10, Data Engineering and Big Data Analytics in AWS*
- *Chapter 11, Machine Learning and Generative AI in AWS*

10

Data Engineering and Big Data Analytics in AWS

Traditionally, a business's most important resources are its human and financial capital. However, in the last few decades, more businesses have realized that another resource may be just as vital, if not more so: their data capital.

Data has taken a special place at the center of some of today's most successful enterprises. For this reason, business leaders have concluded that to survive in today's business climate, they must collect, process, transform, distill, and safeguard their data like their other traditional business capital.

Reducing cloud storage costs made it more feasible for businesses to store more data. Additionally, with pay-as-you-go and on-demand storage and compute options, analyzing data to gain insights is now more accessible. Businesses can store all relevant data points, even as they grow to massive volumes, and analyze the data in various ways to extract insights. This can drive innovation within an organization and result in a competitive advantage.

In *Chapter 5, Storage in AWS: Choosing the Right Tool for the Job*, you learned about the files and object storage services offered by AWS. You learned about various AWS database services in *Chapter 7, Selecting the Right Database Service*. Now, the question is how to query and analyze the data available in different storage and databases.

In this chapter, you will dive deep into AWS's analytics services. First, you will learn about Amazon **Elastic MapReduce** (**EMR**), which is Hadoop in the cloud, and about AWS's data cataloging offering, AWS Glue. Finally, you will look at how to handle streaming data using AWS. In this chapter, you will learn about the following topics:

- Why use the cloud for big data analytics?
- Amazon EMR
- Introduction to AWS Glue
- Choosing between AWS Glue and Amazon EMR
- Handling streaming data in AWS
- Choosing between Amazon Kinesis and Amazon MSK
- Data warehouses in AWS with Amazon Redshift
- Data query with Amazon Athena
- Business intelligence in AWS with Amazon QuickSight
- Share, search, and discover data at scale across organizational boundaries with Amazon DataZone

By the end of this chapter, you will know about the various AWS services available to build an analytics pipeline and perform **Extract, Transform, and Load** (**ETL**) operations on your significant data workload. Let's roll up our sleeves and get to it.

Why use the cloud for data engineering and big data analytics?

In today's world, you're likely dealing with massive amounts of data – from clickstream logs and voice recordings to social media feeds and customer transactions. With data coming in various forms (structured, semi-structured, and unstructured), managing and analyzing it on-premises can quickly become a headache. It's not just about having enough storage, but also about scaling compute, managing security, ensuring compliance, and providing the right tools to your teams. This is where the cloud, especially AWS, becomes a game-changer for data engineering and big data analytics.

The cloud gives you scalable, flexible, and cost-efficient infrastructure. With services such as Amazon S3, Redshift, EMR, and Glue (which you will learn about in this chapter), you can store and process petabytes of data without worrying about capacity planning or hardware failures. For instance, you can use Amazon EMR to run on-demand open source tools such as Apache Spark or Hadoop rather than buying expensive servers upfront. This lets your team process large datasets quickly without setting up or managing the underlying infrastructure. Companies such as Netflix and Airbnb use AWS to manage and analyze massive datasets daily, helping them personalize user experiences and drive better business decisions in real time. Using cloud services to analyze customer behavior, track product performance, or forecast demand, you can do the same.

In addition to scale and speed, the cloud also offers robust data governance tools. With AWS services such as IAM, KMS, and a combination of CloudTrail, Config, and Audit Manager, you can control who accesses what data, encrypt it at rest and in transit, and audit every action for compliance. This is especially important if you're working in a regulated industry such as finance or healthcare.

Finally, using the cloud helps separate storage from compute, so you only pay for what you use. If you need to store a large amount of data but only process parts of it occasionally, AWS lets you scale storage independently of processing power. This flexibility helps you reduce costs and avoid overprovisioning.

Moving your data engineering and big data analytics to the cloud saves time, money, and resources while unlocking new insights and innovations that would be difficult to achieve with traditional on-premises systems.

Data engineering components

As a solutions architect, you often face the challenge of helping your teams manage and process large volumes of data efficiently. Data engineering on AWS simplifies this task by offering a set of reliable services that handle everything from data collection to analysis. Whether you're building real-time dashboards or running **machine learning** (**ML**) models, understanding the core components of data engineering is key to success. The following diagram shows the high-level flow of data engineering:

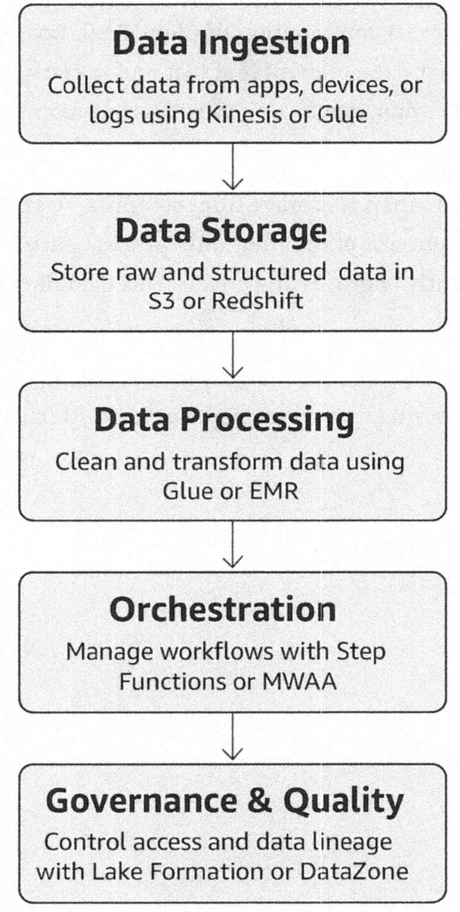
AWS Data Engineering Flow
Data Ingestion
Collect data from apps, devices, or logs using Kinesis or Glue
Data Storage
Store raw and structured data in S3 or Redshift
Data Processing
Clean and transform data using Glue or EMR
Orchestration
Manage workflows with Step Functions or MWAA
Governance & Quality
Control access and data lineage with Lake Formation or DataZone

Figure 10.1: Data engineering components and their flow

As shown in the preceding diagram, data ingestion is the first step in handling data in the cloud. This involves bringing data from different sources, such as web apps, sensors, or logs, into the cloud. On AWS, tools such as Amazon Kinesis let you collect streaming data in real time, while AWS Glue supports batch ingestion from databases or files. For example, Netflix uses Amazon Kinesis to monitor real-time user activity, helping it improve user recommendations instantly.

After collecting data, you store it using services such as Amazon S3 or Amazon Redshift. S3 works well for raw data, while Redshift is used for structured data and fast querying. **Expedia Group**, for example, stores clickstream data in S3 and uses Redshift to analyze travel trends and customer behavior.

Next, you move on to data transformation, where raw data is cleaned and prepared. AWS Glue helps automate these ETL tasks. For example, a healthcare company might use AWS Glue to clean medical records and mask sensitive data before sharing it for research.

Once your data is processed, you need to schedule and manage your workflows. Services such as Step Functions and Amazon **Managed Workflows for Apache Airflow** (**MWAA**) help you create and control complex data pipelines. A media company might schedule daily workflows to load video metadata into analytics dashboards, giving insights into what content performs best.

Maintaining data quality and governance is also critical. With AWS Lake Formation and DataZone, you can control who sees what data and track data usage. This is especially useful for financial or healthcare companies where compliance is mandatory. For instance, FINRA uses AWS to process billions of market events daily while meeting strict security and audit requirements. You can explore these case studies here: `https://aws.amazon.com/solutions/case-studies/`.

Finally, your data needs to be easy to access. Tools such as Amazon Athena allow analysts to query S3 directly using SQL, and Amazon QuickSight creates dashboards for business users. You can build a strong and scalable data engineering platform by using these AWS tools for ingestion, storage, processing, governance, and access.

Now, throughout this chapter, you will learn about various AWS services that allow you to deliver business insights faster, support better decisions, and reduce manual overhead – all while staying secure and compliant.

Ingesting batch data in AWS

As a solutions architect, you know how important it is to efficiently move data into your cloud systems. When files arrive in chunks, such as daily sales reports, weekly logs, or monthly backups, you're working with batch data ingestion. This approach is helpful when the data doesn't need to be processed immediately but still needs to be collected regularly, stored securely, and ready for analytics.

In AWS, batch ingestion usually starts with landing data into Amazon S3, which offers scalable storage at a low cost. You can upload files manually, schedule transfers, or automate everything with tools such as AWS DataSync. DataSync is especially useful if you migrate large volumes of data from your on-premises systems to AWS. For example, the Australian Electoral Commission used DataSync to transfer voter records securely to AWS ahead of its elections, helping it modernize operations without overloading IT staff.

Another common method is AWS Transfer Family, which supports secure file transfers over SFTP, FTPS, and FTP. This is great when your partners or vendors regularly need to upload files to your system. Fox Sports, for instance, uses Transfer Family to receive and manage sports footage from multiple content partners, then stores it in Amazon S3 for editing and distribution.

If your batch data is stored in databases, AWS Glue can help you move it. Glue crawlers scan your source data and automatically build ETL jobs. You will learn more about Glue later in this chapter.

Batch data ingestion is not just about moving files; it's about ensuring data gets to the right place, on time, and in a format your team can work with. Using AWS services such as S3, Glue, DataSync, and Transfer Family, you can create a reliable pipeline that supports your business needs without constant manual effort. You save time, reduce errors, and make your data available faster for analytics, ML, or customer reporting.

Ingesting and handling streaming data in AWS

In today's world, businesses aim to gain a competitive edge by providing timely, tailored experiences to consumers. Consumers expect personalized experiences that meet their needs and reject those that don't, such as when applying for a loan, investing, shopping online, tracking health alerts, or monitoring home security systems. As a result, speed has become a critical characteristic that businesses strive to achieve. Insights from data are perishable and can lose value quickly. Streaming data processing allows analytical insights to be gathered and acted upon instantly to deliver the desired customer experience.

Batch processing data doesn't allow for real-time risk mitigation or customer authentication. If action isn't taken in real time, the customer experience can be ruined, and it is hard to recover. Acting on real-time data can help prevent fraud and increase customer loyalty. Untimely data, on the other hand, can inhibit your firm's ability to grow.

To enable real-time analytics, you need to ingest, process, and analyze large volumes of high-velocity data from various sources in real time. Devices and/or applications produce real-time data at high velocity. In the case of IoT devices, tens of thousands of data sources need to be collected and ingested in real time. After that, you store data in the order it was received for a set duration and allow it to be replayed indefinitely during this time. You must enable real-time analytics or streaming ETL and store the final data in a data lake or warehouse.

AWS provides a streaming data processing ability through its serverless offering, Amazon Kinesis, and Kafka offers it through Amazon **Managed Streaming for Apache Kafka** (**MSK**). Let's begin by learning about MSK in more detail.

Amazon Managed Streaming for Apache Kafka (MSK)

Apache Kafka is one of the most popular open source platforms for building real-time streaming data pipelines and applications. Managing Apache Kafka clusters in production can be difficult, requiring careful planning and ongoing maintenance. Setting up and configuring Apache Kafka requires provisioning servers and performing manual tasks. Additionally, you must continuously monitor and maintain the servers to ensure their reliability, security, and performance. Tasks involved in managing a cluster encompass several activities such as replacing failed servers, orchestrating patches and upgrades, designing the cluster for high availability, storing data durably, setting up monitoring and alarms, and planning scaling events to support changing workloads. Overall, managing Apache Kafka clusters in production can be a complex and time-consuming process.

Amazon MSK is a fully managed service provided by AWS that allows users to build and run production applications on Apache Kafka without requiring in-house Apache Kafka infrastructure management expertise. With Amazon MSK, AWS handles infrastructure management tasks such as server replacement, patching, upgrades, and high-availability design. This enables users to focus on building their applications and leveraging the features of Apache Kafka, such as its ability to handle real-time, high-throughput, fault-tolerant data streaming. MSK allows you to launch clusters across multiple **Availability Zones** (**AZs**) with customizable configurations to achieve high-performance and high-availability environments. You can scale out compute by adding brokers to existing clusters, and scale up storage without downtime.

Let's look into Amazon MSK cluster architecture in detail.

Amazon MSK cluster architecture

With MSK, you can focus on your applications and use cases rather than worrying about the underlying infrastructure and operational tasks. MSK handles the provisioning and maintenance of the Kafka clusters and provides features such as automatic scaling, self-healing, and monitoring to ensure high availability and performance. The complete list of operations is available in the Amazon MSK API reference guide: `https://docs.aws.amazon.com/msk/1.0/apireference/resources.html`.

The following diagram provides insight into an Amazon MSK cluster. Amazon MSK can create clusters that utilize Apache Kafka versions up to 3.8. AWS keeps adding new versions as they become available, allowing users to take advantage of Apache Kafka's latest features and improvements without worrying about infrastructure management. Please refer to the Amazon MSK developer guide for the latest information on the Amazon MSK-supported version of Kafka (`https://docs.aws.amazon.com/msk/latest/developerguide/supported-kafka-versions.html`):

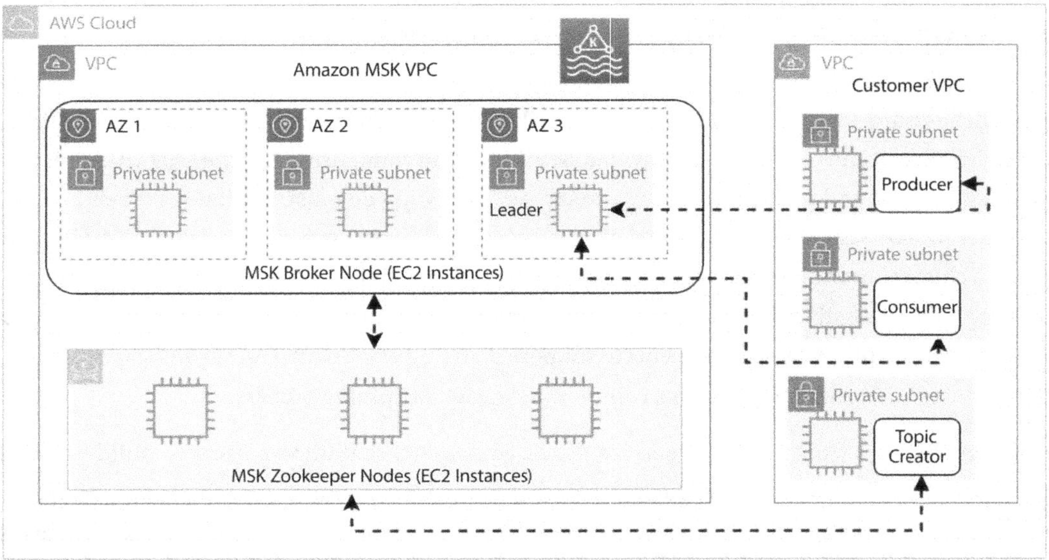

Figure 10.2: Amazon MSK architecture

The architecture of Amazon MSK consists of the following components:

- **Kafka clusters**: An MSK cluster is a group of Amazon **Elastic Compute Cloud (EC2)** instances that run the Apache Kafka software. An MSK cluster can have one or more Kafka brokers and can be scaled up or down to support your applications' processing and storage requirements.
- **ZooKeeper**: Apache Kafka uses Apache ZooKeeper to store metadata and coordinate the Kafka brokers. In an MSK cluster, ZooKeeper is automatically deployed and configured as part of the cluster.
- **Producers and consumers**: Producers are applications or systems that produce data and send it to a Kafka cluster, while consumers are applications or systems that receive and process data from a Kafka cluster. In an MSK cluster, you can use the Apache Kafka producer and consumer APIs to produce and consume data, or use higher-level libraries and tools such as Kafka Connect or **Kinesis Data Analytics (KDA)** to simplify the process.
- **Data storage**: Apache Kafka stores data in topics, which are partitioned and replicated across the cluster's Kafka brokers. Depending on your chosen storage type, data is stored in an MSK cluster in Amazon EBS volumes or Amazon S3 buckets.
- **Networking**: Amazon MSK uses Amazon VPC to provide a secure and isolated network environment for your Kafka clusters. You can specify the VPC, subnets, and security groups to use when you create an MSK cluster.

You need to provide an existing VPC and specify two or more subnets across different AZs for the MSK cluster. MSK then configures the security groups to allow traffic between the Kafka brokers, producers, and consumers. However, you can also choose to use an existing VPC and subnets, or create a custom VPC and subnets using AWS CloudFormation templates. Once the MSK cluster has been created, the Kafka brokers and the ZooKeeper nodes are launched in the specified subnets and are automatically registered with the security groups. The Kafka brokers and the ZooKeeper nodes communicate with each other and with the producers and consumers using private IP addresses within the VPC.

You can also use VPC peering or a VPN to connect your MSK cluster to other VPCs or on-premises networks and enable communication between the Kafka brokers, producers, and consumers using public or private IP addresses. Overall, the networking configuration of an MSK cluster determines how the Kafka brokers, the ZooKeeper nodes, and the producers and consumers communicate with each other and with the rest of your network. It is important to carefully plan and configure the networking for your MSK cluster to ensure the high availability and performance of your Kafka-based applications.

Amazon MSK provides various tools and features to help you monitor and manage your Kafka clusters and applications. This includes integration with Amazon CloudWatch for monitoring, Amazon CloudFormation for infrastructure as code, and the AWS Management Console for visual management.

AWS also offers MSK Serverless, which helps you to run Apache Kafka clusters easily without needing to adjust the size of the cluster capacity or worry about overprovisioning. With Amazon MSK Serverless, you can instantly scale **input and output** (**I/O**) without manually managing capacity or partition reassignments. This service is designed to provide a simplified and cost-effective way to stream and retain data with pricing based on throughput. Additionally, you only pay for the data volume you stream and retain, making it a cost-efficient option for managing streaming data workloads. If you are planning to migrate your existing Apache Kafka workload to MSK, AWS has published an MSK migration guide to help you, which you can find by visiting the link here: `https://docs.aws.amazon.com/whitepapers/latest/amazon-msk-migration-guide`.

Handling data cataloging for streaming data can be complicated. Let's learn about AWS's new streaming data cataloging offering.

Amazon Kinesis

Amazon Kinesis is a powerful, real-time data streaming service enabling businesses to collect, process, and analyze diverse data types, such as video, audio, logs, clickstreams, and IoT telemetry. It facilitates real-time analytics, ML, and other applications, empowering organizations to respond quickly to data-driven insights. Let's look at the list of Kinesis services:

- **Amazon Kinesis Data Streams (KDS)**: KDS is designed for real-time data capture and analysis, enabling businesses to process and analyze streaming data as it arrives. It utilizes data shards, each capable of ingesting up to 1 MB of data per second and supporting 2 MB per second reads. KDS offers flexible data retention, storing data for 24 hours to 1 year, and supports replaying and debugging during this retention window. **Enhanced fan-out (EFO)** ensures ultra-low latency, as low as 70 ms for advanced applications requiring immediate data access, delivering efficient and rapid data processing.
- **Amazon Kinesis Data Firehose (KDF)**: KDF is a serverless service designed to transform and deliver streaming data to storage destinations such as Amazon S3, Redshift, Elasticsearch, and other endpoints. It supports real-time data format conversions, enabling flexibility in handling data streams. KDF also facilitates direct delivery to HTTP endpoints, making it ideal for use cases such as e-commerce clickstream analysis and IoT telemetry monitoring. With seamless integration into AWS services and compatibility with external tools such as Datadog and MongoDB, KDF provides an efficient solution for near-real-time analytics and data-driven decision-making. At re:Invent 2024, Amazon launched a new capability in Amazon KDF that captures changes made in databases such as PostgreSQL and MySQL and replicates the updates to Apache Iceberg tables on Amazon S3.
- **Amazon KDA:** KDA enables real-time processing of data streams using Apache Flink applications. It offers sub-second latency for filtering, aggregation, and data transformation tasks, ensuring swift and effective analytics. KDA includes interactive tools such as KDA Studio, allowing users to build, test, and debug analytics pipelines easily. Leveraging Apache Flink, KDA supports advanced stateful processing and high throughput, making it a robust solution for analyzing and responding to streaming data in real time.

Amazon Kinesis offers an integrated ecosystem for businesses to process streaming data efficiently, making it a cornerstone for modern, data-driven enterprises.

Choosing between Amazon Kinesis and Amazon MSK

AWS launched Kinesis in 2013, and it was the only streaming data offering until 2018, when AWS launched MSK, in response to the high demand from their customers for managed Apache Kafka clusters. Now, both are similar offerings, so you must be wondering when to choose one versus the other. If you already have an existing Kafka workload on-premises or are running Kafka in EC2, it's better to migrate to MSK, as you don't need to make any changes to the code. You can use the existing **MirrorMaker** tool to migrate. The following diagrams show key architectural differences between MSK and Kinesis:

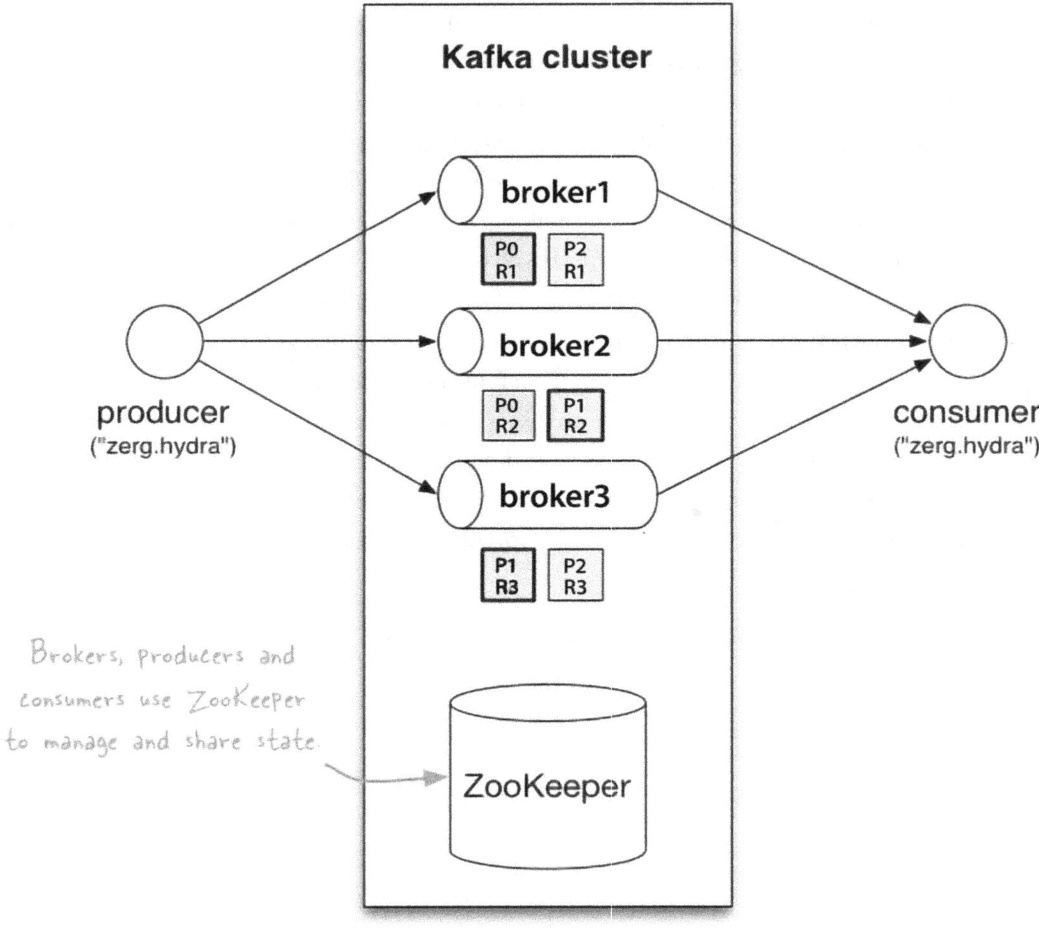

Figure 10.3: Amazon MSK architecture

The preceding diagram shows MSK's architecture; you can compare it with Kinesis's architecture as shown in the following diagram:

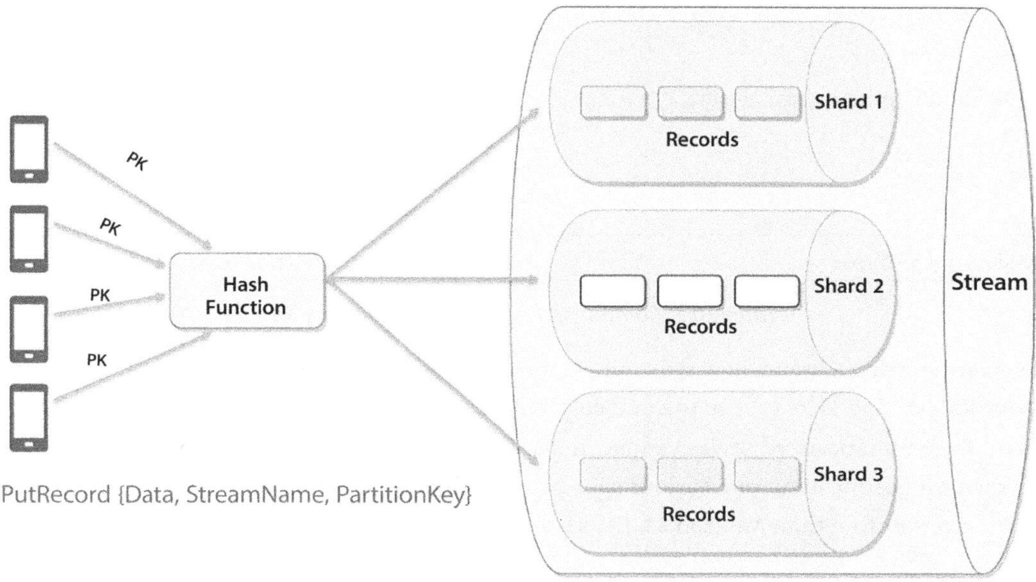

Figure 10.4: Amazon Kinesis architecture

As shown in the preceding diagrams, there are similarities between the MSK and Kinesis architectures. In the MSK cluster, you have brokers to store and ingest data, while in Kinesis, you have shards. In MSK, you need ZooKeeper to manage configuration, while AWS takes care of this admin overhead in Kinesis. The following table shows some more differentiating attributes:

Amazon MSK	Amazon Kinesis
You need to decide on the number of clusters, brokers per cluster, topics per broker, and portions per topic to operate the MSK cluster.	You need to decide on the number of data streams and shards per stream to operate the Kinesis data stream.
MSK operates under the cluster provision model, which has a higher cost than Kinesis.	Kinesis needs a throughput provision model, which has a lower cost as you only pay for the data you use.
You can only increase the number of partitions; decreasing partitions is not possible.	You can increase or decrease the number of shards.
MSK integrates with a few AWS services, such as KDA for Apache Flink.	Kinesis fully integrates with many AWS services, such as Lambda, KDA, etc.

Amazon MSK	Amazon Kinesis
MSK has no limit on throughput.	There is no upper limit. Maximum throughput depends on the number of shards provisioned for the stream. Each shard can support up to 1 MB/second or 1,000 records/second write throughput, or up to 2 MB/second or 2,000 records/second read throughput.
MSK is open source.	Kinesis is an AWS native service.

Table 10.1: Comparison between MSK and Kinesis

If you are starting a brand-new streaming data ingestion and processing pipeline, it's better to go for Kinesis due to its ease of use and cost. Often, organizations use Kafka as an event bus to establish communication between applications, and in that case, you should continue with Kafka. As you are ingesting data from various sources, it needs to be stored in a scalable storage system, which is none other than Amazon S3. Let's learn more about how to organize the storage layer.

Building a storage layer with Amazon S3

When you are designing a data architecture on AWS, a clean, well-structured storage layer is key to making your data easy to manage and secure, and it is cost-effective. Amazon S3 is an ideal service for this, and one of the best practices is to structure your storage into logical layers: raw, processed, and curated. Here's how you can build that step by step:

1. **Set up the raw data layer (landing zone)**: You drop data exactly as it arrives, whether it's logs, files from external systems, or sensor readings. Think of it as your "intake bin." Create an S3 bucket (e.g., `my-org-raw-data`) and enable versioning to keep track of every file version, which helps in auditing or recovering from accidental overwrites. Organize data using folder prefixes by source or date (`/store1/2025/06/14/`), and apply simple access policies to limit who can write or read.
2. **Configure the processed data layer**: Once the data is cleaned or transformed (using tools such as AWS Glue or Lambda functions), move it to a separate S3 bucket or a different prefix under the same bucket—for example, `my-org-processed-data/2025/06/14/`. This separation makes it easier to control access, monitor usage, and apply life cycle rules (e.g., delete after 30 days). You might also add object tags to track file types or processing stages.

3. **Build the curated data layer**: This is your "ready-to-use" layer – data that's been transformed, filtered, and structured for analytics or reporting. Set up an S3 bucket such as `my-org-curated-data`, and consider partitioning it by Region, business unit, or data type. This layer integrates easily with services such as Amazon Athena or Redshift Spectrum, allowing users to run SQL queries directly on this data.
4. **Add access controls and life cycle policies**: Now that your layers are set, tighten your security and cost management. Use bucket policies, IAM roles, and S3 Access Points to control who can access what. Then set life cycle rules to automatically archive older files to S3 Glacier or delete them when they're no longer needed.

By following the above structure, you're not just dumping data into buckets, you're creating a scalable system that supports governance, cost efficiency, and analytics. Whether you're a startup or managing petabytes of data, this layered approach keeps your storage clean, controlled, and future-ready.

Now, let's learn about various AWS data cataloging and processing services to implement this storage.

Data cataloging and processing

As a solutions architect, organizing and processing your data is key to building scalable and insightful data platforms. On AWS, powerful tools for data cataloging and processing make this easy. These tools help you ensure that your data is easy to find, secure, and ready for analysis across teams and use cases.

To start, data cataloging is like building a searchable directory of your data. When you store files in Amazon S3 or databases, they don't automatically include useful metadata. That's where the AWS Glue Data Catalog comes in. In addition to Glue, AWS offers Amazon EMR, which is AWS's managed big data platform for open source frameworks such as Hadoop, Spark, Hive, and Presto. EMR is a Hadoop solution for the cloud, meaning you don't need to reskill your workforce to move on to the cloud. Let's learn more about Glue and EMR in the following sections.

Introduction to AWS Glue

Data-driven businesses can increase profitability and efficiency, reduce costs, deliver new products and services, better serve their customers, comply with regulatory requirements, and ultimately thrive. Unfortunately, as we have seen many examples in recent years, companies that don't make this transition will not survive. An important part of a data-driven enterprise is the ability to ingest, process, transform, and analyze this data.

AWS Glue is a foundational service at the heart of the AWS offering.

With the introduction of Apache Spark, enterprises can process petabytes' worth of data daily. Processing this amount of data opens the door to making data an enterprise's most valuable asset. Processing this data at this scale allows enterprises to create new industries and markets. Some examples of business activities that have significantly benefited from this massive data processing are as follows:

- Personalized marketing
- Drug discovery
- Anomaly detection (such as fraud detection)
- Real-time log and clickstream processing

AWS has created a service that leverages Apache Spark and takes it to the next level. The name of that service is AWS Glue.

What is AWS Glue? AWS Glue is a fully managed service used to extract data from data sources, ingest the data into other AWS services, such as Amazon S3, and transform this data to be used by consuming services or users. While AWS Glue is optimized for larger workloads, it may not be cost-effective for small batches and files. Under the hood, AWS Glue runs Apache Spark in a serverless environment.

Another important feature of AWS Glue is that it can handle disparate sources, such as SQL and NoSQL databases and Amazon S3 files.

Let's look at a simple but powerful example. The traditional way to set up Apache Spark is to create a cluster of powerful machines. Spark clusters with dozens or even hundreds of nodes are not uncommon, depending on how much data will be ingested and how many transformations need to be performed. As you can imagine, a dedicated infrastructure setup like this can be costly.

Using AWS Glue, you can create a similarly powerful cluster of machines that is spun up when demand requires it. Importantly, the cluster can also be spun down when demand wanes.

If no work is processed, the cluster can be completely shut down, and the compute costs go down to zero. By making costs variable and not having to pay for idle machines, the number of use cases that AWS Glue can handle compared to a traditional Apache Spark cluster increases exponentially. Projects that would have been prohibitively expensive before now have become economically feasible.

Here is a list of common use cases that leverage AWS Glue:

- The population of data lakes, data warehouses, and lake houses
- Event-driven ETL pipelines
- The creation and cleansing of datasets for ML

AWS Glue has a series of components that help achieve its intended purpose as an ETL service. These are as follows:

- The AWS Glue console
- The AWS Glue Data Catalog
- AWS Glue classifiers
- AWS Glue crawlers
- AWS Glue code generators

Let's look at how various components of AWS Glue go together.

Operating the AWS Glue console

The AWS Glue console creates, configures, orchestrates, and develops ingestion workflows. The AWS Glue console interacts with other components in AWS Glue by calling APIs to update the AWS Glue Data Catalog and to run AWS Glue jobs. These jobs can be run to accomplish the following kinds of actions:

- **Definition of AWS Glue objects such as connections, jobs, crawlers, and tables**: The console can create various AWS Glue objects. We will learn more about crawlers in an upcoming section. A table in AWS Glue is simply a file after it is processed. Once processed, the file can act as an SQL table, and SQL commands can be run against it. As with any SQL database, we need to create a connection to the table. All these objects can be created in the AWS Glue console.
- **Crawler scheduling**: AWS Glue crawlers, which we will learn about shortly, must be scheduled. This scheduling is another action that can be performed in the AWS console.
- **Job trigger scheduling**: AWS Glue can also implement the scheduling of job triggers that execute ETL code.

- **Filtering of AWS Glue objects**: In the simplest AWS Glue implementations, it may be easy to locate different objects by simply browsing through the objects listed. Once things start getting a little complicated, we will need to have the ability to filter these objects by name, date created, and so on. This filtering can be performed in the AWS Glue console.
- **Transformation script editing**: Lastly, the creation and maintenance of ETL scripts is one more task that can be accomplished in the AWS Glue console.

AWS also launched AWS Glue visual ETL, a graphical interface that creates ETL jobs in AWS Glue. With visual ETL, you can visually create and edit ETL jobs by connecting data sources, transformations, and destinations in a flowchart-like diagram. This makes it easy to build and modify ETL jobs, even if you don't have experience with Python or other programming languages. Not everyone is an expert in writing Python code to improve data quality. For that, AWS provides Glue DataBrew.

AWS Glue DataBrew

As a solutions architect, you often work with teams that include data analysts, business users, or non-developers who still need to work with data but may not be comfortable writing Python or SQL. That's exactly where AWS Glue DataBrew makes a difference. It's a visual, no-code tool that helps your team clean, prepare, and transform data quickly, without writing a single line of code.

AWS Glue DataBrew provides a user-friendly interface where anyone can explore and manipulate data stored in AWS data sources such as Amazon S3, Redshift, and RDS. It's fully integrated with AWS Glue, which means the data you prepare visually can easily become part of your larger data pipeline. As of 2025, using DataBrew, you can apply over 250 pre-built transformations, such as filtering rows, changing column types, removing duplicates, or pivoting tables – all through a few clicks.

For example, your marketing team needs to clean customer survey data collected from various sources. Instead of waiting on a developer to write Python scripts, they can use DataBrew to filter responses by Region, correct inconsistent date formats, and summarize customer satisfaction scores, all on their own. This enables faster analysis and decision-making.

One of DataBrew's best features is its data profiling and visualization. You can easily view column statistics, detect missing values, and preview how your transformations affect the dataset in real time. Once you're happy with the changes, you can schedule the recipes to run at regular intervals or trigger them as part of your workflow. If you need more control, you can export the entire recipe as a Glue ETL job or Python code for automated pipelines.

A real-world example of DataBrew in action is Ventia, an infrastructure services company in Australia. They use AWS Glue DataBrew to standardize and prepare operational data from various business systems, helping them automate and improve their data quality without needing to write complex code. You can learn more about this by watching this video featured on the AWS YouTube channel: `https://youtu.be/L9NW7RhkLK0`.

So, when you support users who want to prepare data themselves or speed up repetitive data-cleaning tasks, DataBrew is an excellent tool to include in your AWS architecture. It bridges the gap between raw data and business-ready insights while reducing the workload on your data engineering team.

So far, in this section, we have learned about the basics of AWS Glue. You also learned about the components that make up AWS Glue and make it a juggernaut. In the next section, we will explain how the various elements work together to provide a powerful combination and deliver one of the most popular services in the AWS ecosystem.

Putting AWS Glue components together

Now that we have learned about all the major components in AWS Glue, let's look at how all the pieces fit together. The following diagram illustrates this:

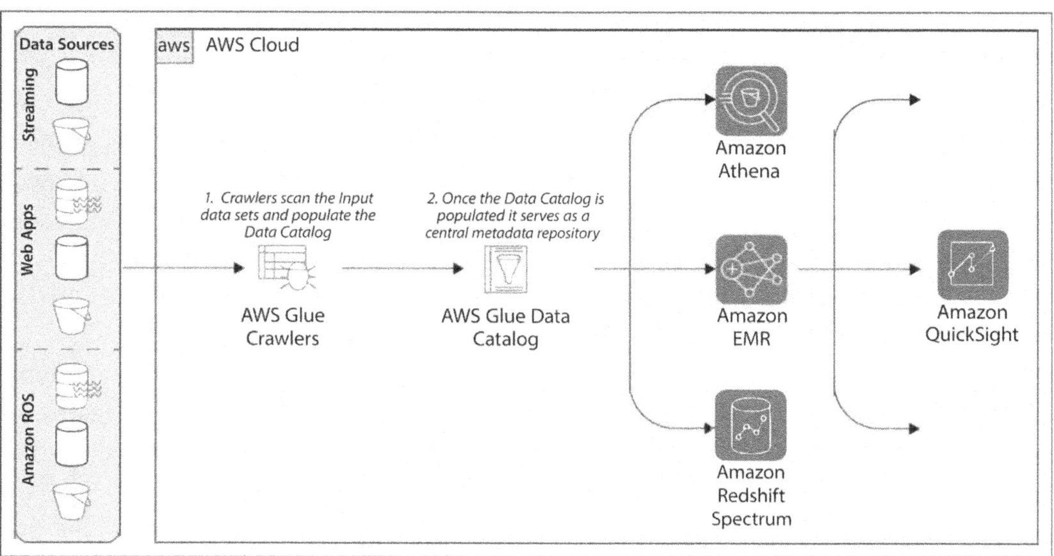

Figure 10.5: AWS Glue typical workflow steps

The preceding diagram shows the various steps that can take place when AWS Glue runs. The steps are explained in the following points:

1. The first step is for the crawlers to scan sources and extract metadata from them.
2. This metadata can then be used to seed the AWS Glue Data Catalog.
3. Other AWS services, such as Amazon Athena, an AWS-provided query service, Redshift Spectrum, an AWS-provided cloud data warehouse service, and Amazon EMR, can use this metadata. These services can then write queries against the ingested data, using the metadata from the AWS Glue Data Catalog to build these queries.
4. Finally, the results of these queries can be used for visualizations in other AWS services, including Amazon QuickSight (an AWS-provided **business intelligence** (**BI**) service).

You will learn about Amazon Redshift, Athena, and QuickSight in later sections of this chapter.

AWS Glue can ingest various data sources, such as Amazon S3 objects, Amazon RDS records, or web application data via APIs.

Hopefully, the discussion in these sections has given you a good taste of the basics of AWS Glue and its importance in the AWS ecosystem. We will now spend some time learning the best ways to implement AWS Glue in your environment.

AWS Glue best practices

As we have done with many of the other services covered in the book, we will now provide some recommendations on how to best architect the configuration of your AWS Glue jobs. As you have learned, under the hood, AWS Glue runs its ETL jobs using Apache Spark. Knowing the underlying technologies used by these AWS services will enable you to leverage and optimize your use of AWS Glue better. Let's look at some best practices.

Choosing the right worker type

When running AWS Glue jobs, choosing the right worker type, also called a **data processing unit** (**DPU**), is a key decision that affects cost and performance. AWS Glue supports three main categories of workers: Standard, G.025X, and G-series (G.1X to G.8X). Each has different capabilities, so selecting the right one depends on the size and complexity of your workload.

The Standard worker is a good default option. It provides 16 GB of memory, four vCPUs, and 50 GB of EBS storage and runs two Spark executors. This makes it more compute efficient for tasks that can benefit from multiple parallel executors on the same node. This type works well for general-purpose jobs that aren't too memory-intensive but still need decent processing speed.

The G-series worker types offer more granular control and are well suited for jobs that need more memory or compute power per executor. It's ideal for lightweight or development jobs, starting with G.025X, which provides 4 GB of memory, two vCPUs, and 64 GB of EBS storage. Moving up, G.1X has 16 GB of memory and four vCPUs, just like Standard, but only includes one Spark executor. This makes it better for jobs that need more memory per executor rather than more executors. G.2X, G.4X, and G.8X further scale these specs with 32, 64, and 128 GB of memory, respectively, along with proportional increases in CPU and EBS storage. These higher-tier workers are the best choice for memory-intensive jobs, such as large joins, heavy aggregations, or handling skewed data.

Glue's serverless architecture uses Apache Spark under the hood and supports horizontal scaling, meaning your job can run across many worker nodes in parallel. This helps reduce the runtime regardless of which worker type you use. However, for jobs requiring vertical scaling; for example, if a single transformation step needs more memory, you'll want to use G.1X or higher.

For example, if you're running a job that transforms large datasets from a retail data lake and experiences memory errors during aggregation, switching from a Standard or G.1X worker to a G.4X or G.8X can improve stability and speed. On the other hand, if you ingest and clean small log files daily, the G.025X is often the most cost-effective choice.

By understanding the differences between worker types and aligning them with your job's specific needs, you can ensure smooth performance and optimized cost-efficiency for your Glue ETL workflows.

Optimizing file splitting

As a solutions architect, optimizing how your files are split during processing can significantly improve the performance and cost-efficiency of your AWS Glue jobs. AWS Glue automatically supports file splitting for common formats such as CSV, JSON, Avro, and Parquet using the `DynamicFrame` class. A file split refers to a chunk of a file that an AWS Glue worker can handle independently, enabling Spark jobs to run in parallel across multiple workers. This horizontal scaling is especially useful when you're working with file sizes in the hundreds of megabytes to a few gigabytes range.

For example, if you are processing large clickstream data logs stored in Parquet format in Amazon S3, Glue can split these files and run transformations in parallel across different workers, drastically reducing processing time. However, some compression formats, such as gzip, bzip2, and Zstandard, don't support splitting. AWS recommends using multiple medium-sized files instead of a single large file in those cases. This allows Glue to distribute the load more evenly, even if each file is processed in full by a separate worker.

Once files are split and read into AWS Glue, they are stored in DynamicFrames, which are flexible containers for partitioned data. These partitions allow Spark to apply filters, aggregations, and transformations without simultaneously loading all data into memory. Glue uses lazy evaluation, which means data is only transformed when needed. This prevents memory overload and keeps your job stable. But if a job explicitly caches large partitions or spills data onto disk, it can cause **out-of-memory (OOM)** or disk errors. To handle this, you can use higher-memory worker types, such as G.2X or G.4X, to scale your job and prevent failures vertically.

A good real-world example is a telecom company that uses Glue to process **call detail records (CDRs)**. The company stores data in Parquet format, which supports efficient splitting. This allows it to run large jobs quickly, even when data volumes spike. When switching to Gzip for archiving, it splits the data into smaller files to maintain performance during decompression.

So, when designing data pipelines with AWS Glue, remember how file formats and sizes affect processing. Choosing splittable formats and appropriate file sizes can help you scale efficiently, reduce costs, and keep your Glue jobs running smoothly. For more on how to use partitioned data effectively with AWS Glue, you can explore the official AWS blog on working with partitioned data: `https://aws.amazon.com/blogs/big-data/work-with-partitioned-data-in-aws-glue/`.

Exceeding YARN's memory overhead allocation

As a solutions architect working with AWS Glue and Apache Spark, understanding resource management is essential for building stable, scalable jobs, especially when dealing with large datasets or memory-heavy operations. Behind the scenes, Apache **YARN** (which stands for **Yet Another Resource Negotiator**) manages resource allocation for Spark applications, including AWS Glue jobs. YARN handles memory and CPU distribution across Spark executors and reserves additional memory for the **Java Virtual Machine (JVM)** overhead, including metadata and other system-level operations.

By default, YARN sets aside about 10% of executor memory for this overhead. This means if your Spark job uses large joins or aggregations, or is processing data with skewed distributions, it may exceed this limit and trigger an OOM error. If you anticipate a memory-intensive workload, increasing the overhead allocation up front is a good idea to prevent unexpected failures.

Another practical way to reduce memory-related errors is to use AWS Glue's vertical scaling. By selecting worker types such as G.1X, G.2X, or G.4X, which come with more memory and compute power, you give your Spark executors extra room to handle large partitions or uneven data splits. For example, if your ETL job transforms millions of records with wide tables or nested JSON, choosing a higher-memory worker type will help avoid memory crashes and ensure smoother performance.

AWS Glue also provides a job metrics **dashboard** that shows how much memory and disk space your job uses. Reviewing these metrics after each run can help identify performance bottlenecks and adjust resource settings accordingly. This is especially helpful when debugging OOM errors or optimizing large-scale data pipelines.

For a deeper understanding and troubleshooting guidance, AWS offers detailed documentation on debugging memory issues in Glue at `https://docs.aws.amazon.com/glue/latest/dg/monitor-profile-debug-oom-abnormalities.html`. This resource is valuable if you regularly manage jobs with high memory demands.

Leveraging the Apache Spark UI

Another helpful tool in the Spark arsenal is the Apache Spark UI. This interface gives you deep visibility into how your Glue job is running by showing detailed metrics and visual representations of its execution flow.

The Spark UI displays **directed acyclic graphs** (**DAGs**), which help you understand the sequence and dependencies of the different stages in your job. It also highlights shuffle operations, often the most performance-intensive parts of a Spark job, and lets you inspect query execution plans. Analyzing this information enables you to quickly pinpoint performance bottlenecks such as long-running stages, skewed data distributions, or large memory spills.

For example, if you're running a job that joins multiple datasets and notice a delay during the shuffle stage, the Spark UI might reveal that one partition is much larger than the others. With that insight, you can redesign your data processing logic by repartitioning or optimizing data formats to balance the load and improve performance.

AWS Glue automatically captures the Spark UI data for completed jobs and keeps it accessible for a limited time through the Glue console. To learn how to access and interpret this data, you can check out the official AWS Glue documentation on the Spark UI: `https://docs.aws.amazon.com/glue/latest/dg/monitor-spark-ui.html`.

Using the Spark UI effectively helps you make informed decisions to fine-tune your Glue jobs and ensure they run efficiently at scale.

Processing many small files

When working with large-scale data pipelines in AWS Glue, it's common to encounter jobs that process thousands or even millions of small files. This is especially true in use cases involving Amazon KDF or event-driven data ingestion from applications and IoT devices. However, processing too many small files at once can overwhelm the Apache Spark driver, causing memory issues or even job failures.

By default, Apache Spark 2.2 in AWS Glue can handle up to 600,000 files using standard worker types. But you may start seeing OOM errors once you go beyond that. AWS Glue provides two practical solutions to prevent this: using more capable workers and enabling file grouping.

One option is switching to a G1.X worker type, which offers more memory per executor than the standard type. This helps Spark handle more files in memory without crashing. A more flexible solution, however, is to use AWS Glue's file grouping feature by setting the `groupFiles` and `groupSize` parameters when creating a DynamicFrame. Take the following example:

```
dyf = glueContext.create_dynamic_frame_from_options("s3",
    {'paths': ["s3://path-to-files/"],
    'recurse':True,
    'groupFiles': 'inPartition',
    'groupSize': '2084236'},
    format="json")
```

This code snippet groups multiple small files into batches for more efficient processing. The `groupFiles` parameter can be set to group files either within an S3 partition or across partitions. Most of the time, grouping within each partition is sufficient to reduce the number of Spark tasks and memory usage.

In real-world testing by AWS, using file grouping on ETL jobs handling over 300,000 files across 100 S3 partitions showed up to a 7x performance boost compared to not using grouping. This is because Spark spends a lot of time and memory building in-memory indices and scheduling many short-lived tasks when dealing with numerous small files. Grouping reduces overhead by batching files, letting fewer tasks process more data each, and making better use of cluster resources.

AWS Glue will automatically turn on grouping when more than 50,000 files are detected, and it will even calculate a suitable `groupSize` to avoid excessive parallelism. Still, fine-tuning this value based on your dataset's structure can lead to better resource utilization and performance.

So, if you're dealing with high file counts in your Glue jobs, especially in formats such as JSON or CSV, use file grouping and consider G-series workers to keep your jobs efficient, stable, and scalable.

Data partitioning and predicate pushdown

Partitioning files is an important technique that allows splitting datasets to be carried out quickly and efficiently. Picking an excellent key to split files is critical to achieving these efficiencies. For example, a dataset may be divided into folders using the ingestion date as the key. In this case, you may have a series of subfolders organized by year, month, and day.

Here is an example of what a directory using this naming scheme could look like:

```
s3://employees/year=2020/month=01/day=01/
```

You can use the `INSERT INTO` statement in HiveQL (Hive's SQL-like query language) with `HiveOutputFormat` and the appropriate file format. For example, you can use the following HiveQL statement to write the results of a `SELECT` query to the specified S3 location as ORC files:

```
INSERT INTO TABLE employees
    PARTITION (year=2020, month=01, day=01)
    SELECT * FROM source_table
    WHERE year=2020 AND month=01 AND day=01;
```

Partitioning the data in such a way enables predicate pushdown. Predicate pushdown is a fancy way of saying that by partitioning the data, we don't need to read all the directories and files to get the results we need when we have a query with a filter.

Predicate pushdown uses filter criteria and partition columns. With a predicate pushdown, the data is not first read into memory and then filtered. Instead, because the data is pre-sorted, we know which files meet the criteria being sought, and only those files are brought into memory, while the rest are skipped.

For example, imagine you have a query like this:

```
Select * from employees where year = 2019
```

Here, `year` is the partition and `2019` is the filter criterion. In this case, the file we had as an example previously would be skipped.

Using pruning can deliver massive performance boosts and greatly reduce response times. Performance can be improved by providing even more filters in the selection criteria, eliminating additional partitions.

Partitioning data while writing to Amazon S3

The last task during processing is to persist the transformed output in Amazon S3. Once this is done, other services, such as Amazon Athena, can be used for their retrieval. By default, when a DynamicFrame is persisted, it is not partitioned. The results are persisted in a single output path. Until recently, it was only possible to partition a DynamicFrame by converting it into a Spark SQL DataFrame before it persisted. However, native partitioning using a key sequence can be used to write out a DynamicFrame.

This can be accomplished by setting the `partitionKeys` parameter during sink creation. As an example, the following code can be used to output a dataset:

```
%spark
glueContext.getSinkWithFormat(
    connectionType = "s3",
    options = JsonOptions(Map("path" -> "$output_path", "partitionKeys" ->
Seq("process_year"))),
    format = "parquet").writeDynamicFrame(employees)
```

This method creates a data sink that persists data to an output destination. For example, the destination can be a repository on Amazon S3 or Amazon RDS.

This method allows you to set the data format to be used when persisting the data.

In this case, `$output_path` is the output directory in Amazon S3. The `partitionKeys` parameter specifies the column used as a partition when writing the data to Amazon S3.

When data is written out, the `process_year` column is removed from the dataset and used instead to help form the directory structure. Here is how the directory might look if we listed it out:

```
PRE year=2020
PRE year=2019
PRE year=2018
PRE year=2017
PRE year=2016
```

So, what are some good columns to use when selecting partition keys? There are two criteria that should drive this selection:

- Use columns that have a low (but not extremely low) cardinality. For example, a person's name, phone number, or email address would not be a good candidate. Conversely, a column with only one or two values is also not a good candidate.
- Use columns that are expected to be used often and will be used as filters.

For example, if your dataset contains log data, using dates and partitioning them by year, month, and day is often a good strategy. The cardinality should be just right. We should have plenty of results for each day of the logs, and using predicate pushdown would result in only retrieving files for individual days.

There is another benefit to partitioning files correctly, in addition to improving query performance. A proper partition minimizes costly Apache Spark shuffle transformations for downstream ETL jobs.

Repartitioning a dataset by frequently calling the `repartition()` or `coalesce()` function leads workers to shuffle data. This can hurt the time it takes to run ETL jobs and will most likely require more memory. By contrast, writing data into Amazon S3 from the start using Apache Hive partitions does not require the data to be shuffled, and it can be sorted locally within a worker node. In Apache Hive, a partition is a way to divide a table into smaller and more manageable pieces, based on the values of certain columns. For example, you can partition a table by date, so that each partition corresponds to a specific day, month, or year. Partitions can improve query performance by enabling the Hive query optimizer to skip over irrelevant partitions and by allowing data to be stored more efficiently.

They can also facilitate managing and organizing large datasets by allowing users to delete or exchange individual partitions as needed.

This list is by no means exhaustive and only scratches the surface. Deploying AWS Glue at scale is not trivial, and architects can build a career by mastering this powerful and fundamental service. Now, let's examine the details of the other alternative, EMR.

Amazon Elastic MapReduce (EMR)

In 2009, AWS introduced EMR, a tool that can handle large amounts of data (terabytes and petabytes) using the latest open source big data tools such as Spark, Hive, Presto, HBase, Flink, and Hudi in the cloud. Amazon EMR is a managed cluster platform that makes it easier to run big data tools, such as Apache Hadoop and Apache Spark, on the AWS cloud for processing and analyzing massive datasets. It is a wrapper around distributed open source computing frameworks. This wrapper abstracts the effort required to set up infrastructure, security, network communication, disaster recovery, and scalability. Additionally, EMR offers 100% compliance with open source APIs. So, there is no need to change your application code when you move to EMR from the on-premises Hadoop system.

EMR runs directly against the data stored in your S3 data lake, so you don't need to move or transform it. You can store data in the data lake in its raw and processed forms and formats, including log files and images. S3 data lakes are popular because they are scalable, secure, and cost-effective. You will learn more about AWS data lakes in *Chapter 12, Data Lake Patterns: Integrating Your Data Across the Enterprise*.

EMR makes it simple to produce clusters and set up one, hundreds, or thousands of computing units to manage data of any magnitude. EMR also automatically scales cluster sizes based on usage, and you only pay for the resources you consume.

Because you're running against S3, multiple clusters can operate on the same data. Using Amazon S3 for storage also provides strong business continuity. Rather than depending on one cluster that will go down in the case of a DC failure, EMR clusters in multiple AZs have equal access to Amazon S3. In the event of a failure, you can quickly switch traffic to the other cluster or spin up a new cluster in another AZ.

EMR decouples compute and storage to optimize costs, allowing you to scale each independently. For storage, you can take advantage of the tiered storage of Amazon S3, and for computing, you can take advantage of EC2 Spot Instances to save up to 80% off the cost of using On-Demand Instances. EMR also enables data analysts and scientists to carry out interactive analytics by integrating with other AWS ML services. Let's dive deeper into learning about EMR clusters.

Understanding EMR clusters and nodes

Amazon EMR is a service centered around clusters, which are groups of Amazon EC2 instances. These instances, known as nodes, each have a specific function within the cluster and are equipped with different software tools depending on their role. Each node serves a unique purpose in an Amazon EMR cluster. As you can see in the following diagrams, the node groups are leader nodes, core nodes, and task nodes.

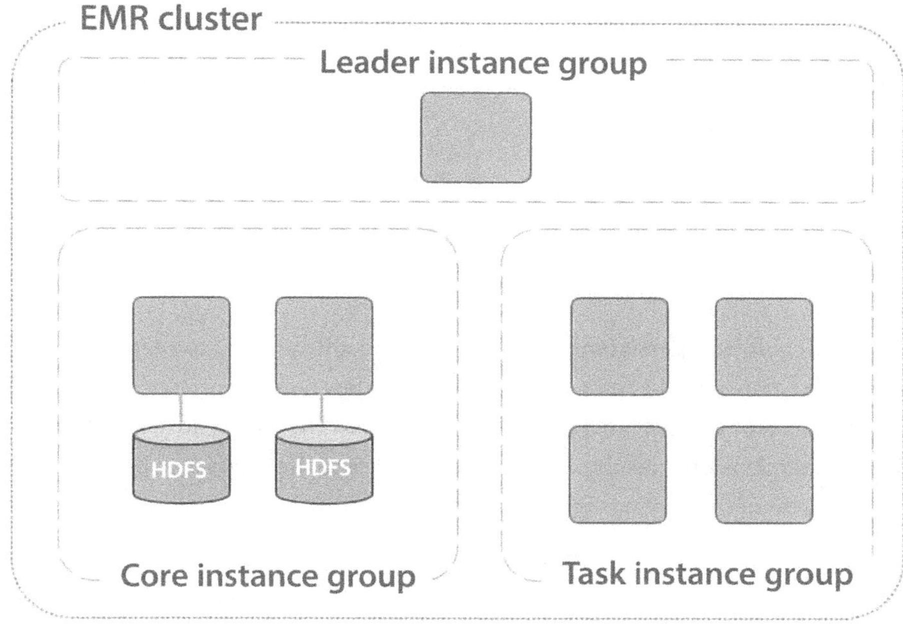

Figure 10.6: Amazon EMR node types

As shown in the preceding diagram, the following is the role of each node type:

- **Leader node**: The primary node is the central control point for the cluster. It manages the job flow and coordinates the work of the other nodes.
- **Core nodes**: Core nodes are worker nodes that store data and process tasks. They run tasks as the primary node directs and stores intermediate data in memory or on a local disk.
- **Task nodes**: Task nodes are similar to core nodes, but they are used only to run tasks and do not store data. They are typically used when a large number of compute resources are needed for a short period.

In addition, there are other nodes to support EMR jobs. For example, there are gateway nodes, which connect to external data sources and stage data in and out of the cluster. Client nodes submit jobs to the cluster and view their status. They do not store data or run tasks, but can access the cluster's data and resources.

An Amazon EMR cluster can be configured with three leader nodes to provide high availability. If the primary leader node fails, Amazon EMR automatically switches to a standby leader node to ensure the cluster remains operational. If a leader node fails, Amazon EMR will also automatically replace it with a new leader node configured in the same way and with the same bootstrap actions as the failed node. This helps to ensure that the cluster remains available and can continue to process data even in the event of a failure.

EMR provides a wide variety of EC2 instances to choose from. It allows you to select the instance families suitable for your workload. The processing ability of your core nodes and the size of your data determine how much information you can manage. While processing, the input, intermediate, and output datasets are stored on the cluster.

The cluster type could be a **persistent cluster**, where you always want to keep it on to run interactive queries, or a transient cluster, which you need for a few hours to process batch jobs for data processing. A **transient cluster** can have the same lifetime as its workload. Once the application or workload is completed, the results are stored inside S3, and the cluster can be terminated. This provides the benefit of cost savings while running EMR.

Amazon EMR offers a feature called **EMR Managed Scaling**, which allows you to automatically adjust the size of your cluster based on your workload. This can help you optimize the cost and speed of your cluster by scaling it up or down as needed to meet the demands of your workload. EMR Managed Scaling continuously monitors cluster metrics to make decisions about scaling and ensures that your cluster is always sized appropriately to meet your needs. AWS manages all the configuration, with no policies for you to define except for the minimum and maximum number of instances.

AWS also provides the ability to deploy **Amazon EMR on EKS**. This new deployment mode allows you to run EMR on EKS-managed Kubernetes clusters. EMR on EKS brings the power of both EMR and EKS services into a consolidated offering so you can run Spark applications on Kubernetes easily and securely. With EMR on EKS, there are no more clusters to build specifically for your analytics workload. AWS containerizes the Spark runtime so applications can quickly run on an existing EKS cluster. You'll also be able to consolidate resources into a single cluster and improve their overall utilization, which drives cost savings. This allows you to run multiple versions of Spark on the same cluster and build a job-centric security model.

AWS also launched **Amazon EMR Serverless** at re:Invent 2021. EMR Serverless automatically determines and provisions the compute and memory resources needed to run the application and scales them up and down based on changing requirements.

For example, Amazon EMR Serverless automatically provisions and adjusts the resources required to run Spark applications as the data volumes being processed change. You can check the status of running jobs in **EMR Studio** or the AWS console, review job history, and use familiar open source tools to debug jobs. EMR Studio is a fully managed, web-based notebook environment that you can use to interactively explore, visualize, and analyze data using Apache Spark and other popular open source libraries. It is integrated with Amazon EMR, so you can easily run and debug your code on a live cluster, and it includes collaboration features such as version control and the ability to share notebooks with other users.

In this section, you've learned about computing in EMR. Now, let's examine storage in EMR with the supported filesystem.

Understanding the EMR File System (EMFRS)

To run a large data workload, you need scalable storage and a filesystem to support that storage. One major differentiation for EMR is its support for S3, for which AWS built a proprietary file system called EMRFS, which continues to support other traditional filesystems. Let's look into the filesystems supported by EMR:

- **Hadoop Distributed File System (HDFS)**: HDFS is a filesystem designed to operate on low-cost, commodity hardware in a distributed computing environment. EMR mainly utilizes HDFS as its primary storage system, and it is well suited for storing large amounts of data that need to be processed by `MapReduce` jobs.
- **Elastic MapReduce File System (EMRFS)**: EMRFS is a Hadoop-compliant file system designed to work seamlessly with Amazon S3. It allows you to store data in S3 and access it through the HDFS interface. EMRFS provides consistent, low-latency data access while maintaining S3's durability and cost-effectiveness.
- **The local filesystem**: EMR can also use the local filesystem of the cluster instances as the filesystem. This can be useful for storing intermediate data generated by MapReduce jobs or small amounts of data used by the jobs.

Using EMRFS and utilizing the power of S3 until you need sub-millisecond latency helps you reduce costs by decoupling compute and storage.

You don't want to limit your data pipeline to just seeing historical data. The actual value for data comes when you can predict the future using ML and play with your data using a developed, friendly interface. AWS has launched EMR Studio, offering to make your data analysis future-looking. Let's look into more details.

Securing data in Amazon EMR

Amazon EMR allows you to specify security configurations to ensure data encryption at rest, in transit, or both. You can use these configurations to encrypt data stored in Amazon S3 or on the local disks of your cluster instances. The security configurations are stored separately from the cluster configuration, so they can easily be reused whenever you create a new cluster. In addition, in-transit encryption can be enabled to secure data as it is transmitted between various cluster components.

There are several ways to secure data in Amazon EMR:

- **Encrypting data at rest**: Data at rest refers to data stored on disk, such as in Amazon S3 or on the local disks of your EMR cluster instances. To safeguard data at rest in EMR, you can create a security configuration that establishes the necessary parameters for encrypting data stored in Amazon S3 or on the local disks of your cluster instances. This helps ensure that your data is secure and unreadable by unauthorized users.
- **Encrypting data in transit**: Data in transit refers to data transmitted between components of your EMR cluster, such as data transmitted between Amazon EC2 instances or between Amazon EC2 instances and Amazon S3. To encrypt data in transit in EMR, you can use **Secure Sockets Layer (SSL)**/TLS to secure data transmitted over the network.
- **Using secure access to Amazon S3**: When accessing data stored in Amazon S3 from your EMR cluster, you can use SSL to encrypt the data transmitted over the network. You can also use AWS **Identity and Access Management (IAM)** to control access to your data in Amazon S3 and ensure that only authorized users and applications have access to your data.
- **Using security groups**: You can manage the flow of incoming and outgoing traffic to and from your EMR cluster instances. This helps to limit access to only authorized users and resources and enhances the overall security of your cluster. This also allows you to restrict access to your cluster instances and to specify which IP addresses and protocols are allowed to access your cluster.

- **Using network isolation**: You can use Amazon **Virtual Private Cloud (VPC)** to create a virtual network isolated from the rest of the internet and launch your EMR cluster in this virtual network. This allows you to further secure your cluster by creating a private network that is isolated from the public internet.

For authentication, you can use IAM and Kerberos. You can also use AWS SSO through the corporate Active Directory to verify the user's validity. Furthermore, EMR allows you to perform audits through logs and AWS CloudTrail.

Here is an example of using EMR to process data stored in Amazon S3 using a `MapReduce` job written in Python:

1. First, you will need to create an Amazon S3 bucket to store your input data and output data.
2. Next, you will need to upload your input data to Amazon S3. This can be done using the AWS Management Console, the AWS CLI, or the Amazon S3 API.
3. Then, you will need to create an EMR cluster using the AWS Management Console, the AWS CLI, or the Amazon EMR API. When creating the cluster, you will need to specify the number of instances you want in the cluster, the instance type, and the EC2 key pair that you want to use to access the cluster instances.
4. Once the cluster is up and running, you can submit a `MapReduce` job to the cluster using the AWS Management Console, the AWS CLI, or the Amazon EMR API. The `MapReduce` job should specify the location of the input data in Amazon S3 and the location where you want the output data to be stored.
5. The `MapReduce` job will then be executed on the EMR cluster, and the output data will be stored in the specified location in Amazon S3.

Here is an example of the AWS CLI command to submit a `MapReduce` job to an EMR cluster:

```
aws emr add-steps --cluster-id j-123456789EXAMPLE --steps Type=CUSTOM_
JAR,Name=SABookCustomJar,ActionOnFailure=CONTINUE,Jar=s3://sa-book-bucket/
book-jar.jar,Args=["s3://sa-book-bucket/input-data","s3://sa-book-bucket/
output-data"]
```

This command will submit a `MapReduce` job that runs the `book-jar.jar` JAR file on the input data located in `s3://sa-book-bucket/input-data` and stores the output data in `s3://sa-book-bucket/output-data`.

EMR is a vast topic that warrants its own book. You can learn more about it by visiting the AWS page at `https://aws.amazon.com/emr/`.

As you have learned about both Glue and EMR, let's now see how to choose between them.

Choosing between AWS Glue and Amazon EMR

Having learned about Glue and EMR, you must be wondering whether these offerings, to some extent, do a similar job in data processing and when to choose one over the other. Yes, AWS has two similar offerings, which can be unclear sometimes, but both have a specific purpose. Amazon always works backward from the customer, so all these offerings are available because customers have asked for them. The following table shows a clear difference between these two services, which will help you to make the right decision:

Feature/Use Case	AWS Glue	Amazon EMR
Primary purpose	Serverless ETL and data preparation	Big data processing using Hadoop, Spark, Hive, Presto, etc.
Serverless support	Yes (fully serverless by default)	Yes (available via EMR Serverless)
Framework support	Apache Spark only	Multiple frameworks: Spark, Hive, Presto, Hadoop, HBase, Flink, etc.
Ease of use	Easy to set up; no infrastructure management	Requires more setup unless using EMR Serverless
Infrastructure control	Limited (fully managed)	Full control (instance type, OS-level configuration, bootstrap actions)
Cost model	Pay per DPU and runtime	Pay per instance/hour or via EMR Serverless pricing
Job orchestration	Built-in with Glue workflows	Needs external orchestration (e.g., Step Functions, Airflow) unless using EMR Studio
Use case fit: ETL pipelines	Excellent (especially with DynamicFrames and crawlers)	Possible, but requires more setup
Use case fit: ML model training	Basic (mainly data prep for ML)	Strong (supports full ML pipelines using Spark MLlib, TensorFlow, etc.)
Data cataloging	Native AWS Glue Data Catalog	Can integrate with the Glue Data Catalog
Startup time	Faster (serverless provisioning)	Slower for cluster-based unless using EMR Serverless
Ad hoc analysis and notebooks	Limited (preview data only)	Excellent (supports Zeppelin, Jupyter, RStudio on EMR notebooks)

Data volume handling	Best for small to medium-sized data jobs	Best for large-scale distributed data workloads
Migration fit (e.g., Hadoop)	Not ideal for direct migrations	Ideal—supports existing Hadoop/Spark code with minimal changes
Real-time stream processing	Limited (with Glue streaming jobs)	Strong (with Spark Streaming, Flink, or Kafka integrations)

Table 10.2: Glue and EMR comparisons

In short, choose AWS Glue if you need a simple, managed, serverless ETL solution, especially for Spark jobs, and if your team is less infrastructure-focused. Choose Amazon EMR if you need control, flexibility, or support for multiple big data tools or are migrating existing Hadoop-based jobs. Both tools are powerful; you just need to match the right one to your workload.

As you learned about data processing and cataloging, the next important step is to store this refined data where it can be queried easily and quickly. For many years, businesses have relied on data warehouses to support reporting and BI needs. AWS offers Amazon Redshift, a fully managed, petabyte-scale data warehouse service to meet this need at scale. Now, let's learn about it.

Data warehouses in AWS with Amazon Redshift

Data is a strategic asset for organizations, not just new businesses and gaming companies. In recent times, the cost and difficulty of storing data have significantly reduced, making it an essential aspect of many companies' business models. Organizations are leveraging data to make informed decisions, such as launching new product offerings, introducing revenue streams, automating processes, and earning customer trust. These data-driven decisions can propel innovation and steer businesses toward success.

You want to leverage your data to gain business insights, but this data is distributed into silos. For example, structured data resides in relational databases, semi-structured data is stored in object stores, and clickstream data streaming from the internet is stored in streaming storage. In addition, you also need to address emerging use cases such as ML. Business users in your organization want to access and analyze live data for instant insights, making performance increasingly important from querying and ETL ingestion perspectives. In fact, slower query performance can lead to missing these service-level agreements and a bad end user experience. Finally, given all these challenges, you still need to solve this cost-efficiently and comply with security and compliance rules.

For a long time, organizations have used data warehouses to store and analyze large amounts of data. A data warehouse is designed to allow fast data querying and analysis and is typically used in BI. Data warehouses are often used to store historical data that is used for reporting and analysis, as well as to support decision-making processes. They are typically designed to store data from multiple sources and support complex queries and analysis across them. Data warehouses are expensive to maintain, and they used to hold only the data necessary for gaining business insights, while the majority of data was discarded and sat in an archive. As the cloud provided cheaper options for storing data, this gave birth to the concept of a **data lake**. A data lake is different from a traditional data warehouse in that it is designed to handle a much wider variety of data types and can scale to store and process much larger volumes of data. Data warehouses typically store structured data that has been transformed and cleaned, while data lakes are designed to store both structured and unstructured data in its raw form. This makes data lakes more flexible than data warehouses, as they can store data in its original format and allow you to apply different processing and analysis techniques as needed.

Transforming data and moving it into your data warehouse can be complex. However, including data from your data lake in reports and dashboards makes it much easier to analyze all your data and deliver the insights your business needs. AWS provides a petabyte-scale data warehouse service called **Amazon Redshift** to address these challenges.

Redshift is a data warehouse system that automatically adjusts to optimize performance for your workloads without manual tuning. It can handle large volumes of data, from gigabytes to petabytes, and can support many users concurrently. Its Concurrency Scaling feature ensures that sufficient resources are available to manage increased workloads as the number of users grows. Let's learn more about Redshift's architecture and understand how Redshift achieves scale and performance.

Amazon Redshift's architecture

On-premises data warehouses are installed and run on hardware owned and operated by the organization using them. This means the organization is responsible for managing and maintaining the hardware, software, and infrastructure on which the data warehouse runs. Amazon Redshift is a fully managed data warehouse service that runs on AWS. This means that Amazon is responsible for managing and maintaining the hardware, software, and infrastructure on which Redshift runs.

There are a few key differences between on-premises data warehouses and Amazon Redshift:

- **Cost**: On-premises data warehouses require upfront capital expenditure on hardware and infrastructure, as well as ongoing expenses for maintenance and operation. Amazon Redshift is a pay-as-you-go service, so you only pay for the resources you use.
- **Scalability**: Scaling up on-premises data warehouses may require the purchase of additional hardware and infrastructure, which can be time-consuming and costly. Amazon Redshift is fully managed and can scale up and down automatically and elastically without purchasing additional hardware.
- **Maintenance**: With an on-premises data warehouse, you manage and maintain the hardware and software, including patching and upgrading. With Amazon Redshift, however, Amazon handles these tasks, so you don't have to worry about them.
- **Location**: With an on-premises data warehouse, the data and hardware are located within your organization's physical location. With Amazon Redshift, the data and hardware are located in Amazon's data centers. This can be a consideration for organizations with data sovereignty or compliance requirements.

Amazon Redshift is a managed data warehouse that does not require security patches, software upgrades, node deployment or configuration, node monitoring, or recovery. It offers security features, including encryption and compliance with certifications such as SOC 1/2/3, HIPAA, and FedRAMP.

Amazon Redshift started as a Postgres fork, but AWS rewrote the storage engine to be columnar and added analytics functions to make it an OLAP relational data store. Redshift is still compatible with Postgres; you can use a Postgres driver to connect to it. Still, it is important to note that Redshift is an OLAP relational database, not an OLTP relational database like Postgres.

Redshift is well integrated with other AWS services, such as VPC, KMS, and IAM for security, S3 for data lake integration and backups, and CloudWatch for monitoring. Its massively parallel columnar architecture helps achieve high performance. Let's take a closer look at the Redshift architecture.

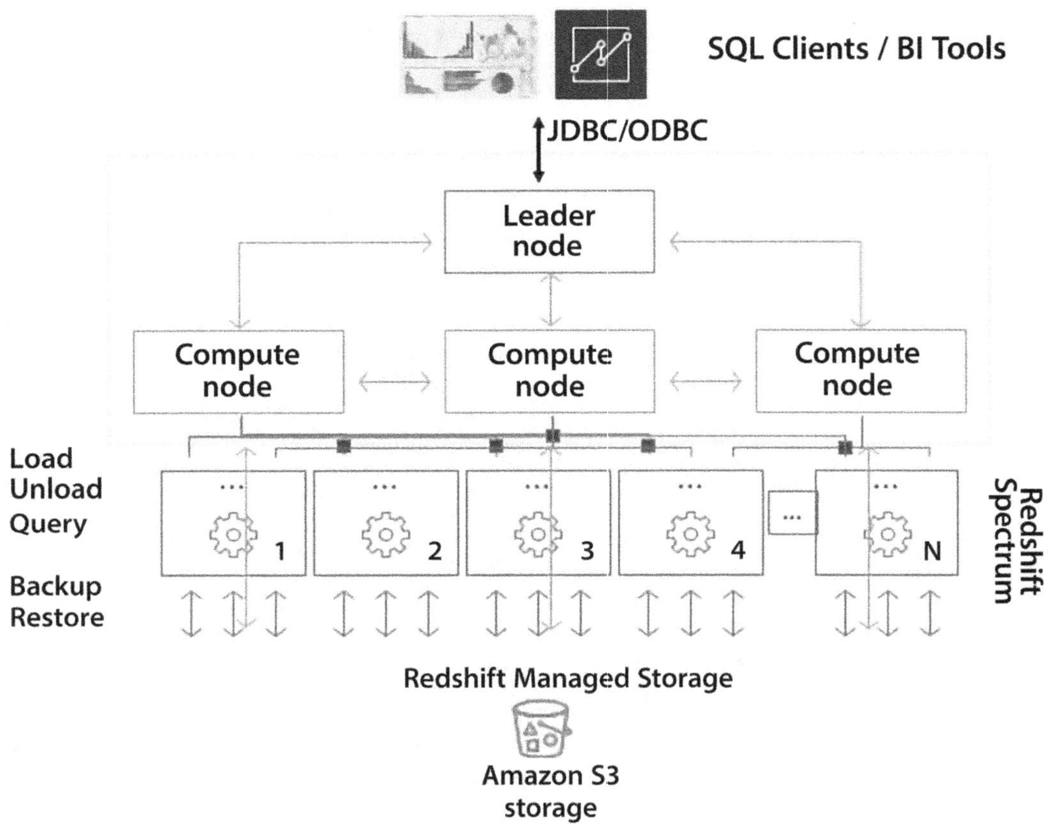

Figure 10.7: Redshift cluster architecture

The preceding diagram shows that Redshift has one leader node and multiple compute nodes. The leader node is required and automatically provisioned in every Redshift cluster, but customers are not charged for the leader node. The leader is responsible for being the user's JDBC/ODBC entry point to the cluster, storing metadata, compiling queries, and coordinating parallel SQL processing.

When the leader node receives your query, it converts it into C++ code, which is compiled and sent down to all the compute nodes by the leader node. Behind the leader node are the compute nodes responsible for query execution and data manipulation. Compute nodes operate in parallel.

Redshift clusters can be as small as one node that houses both the leader node and the compute node, or as large as 128 compute nodes.

Next, these compute nodes also talk to other AWS services, primarily S3. You ingest data from S3 and unload data to S3. AWS continuously backs up your cluster to S3, all happening in the background and in parallel. Compute nodes also interact with Spectrum nodes, a Redshift feature that allows a Redshift cluster to query external data like that in an S3 data lake.

In Amazon Redshift, each component plays a specific role in making the service powerful and efficient for analytics at scale. Here's a simple explanation of the key elements and their responsibilities:

- The leader node is the brain of your Redshift cluster. It acts as the SQL endpoint where all your queries are submitted. This node stores metadata about your data (such as table definitions and user access) and coordinates SQL query planning and execution across the compute nodes. It doesn't store user data or run queries, but ensures all the compute nodes work together. A nice benefit is that there's no cost for the leader node when you launch a Redshift cluster.
- The compute nodes are where your data lives and your queries are executed. Each compute node uses local, columnar storage, which is great for performance because it reads only the columns needed for a query. These nodes work in parallel, which means they can quickly process large amounts of data. Compute nodes are also responsible for data loading and unloading from Amazon S3 and backup and restore operations.
- Redshift Spectrum nodes extend your analytics power by allowing you to run queries directly on data stored in Amazon S3, without needing to load it into your Redshift tables. This is especially useful when you're dealing with huge amounts of data stored in formats such as Parquet or ORC. Spectrum gives you the flexibility to separate storage and compute while still using the familiar SQL interface of Redshift.

These components make Amazon Redshift a flexible, high-performance solution for modern analytics. It allows you to run complex queries on petabytes of structured and semi-structured data.

In Redshift, compute nodes are divided into smaller units called "slices," which act like virtual compute nodes. Each slice is allocated a certain amount of memory and disk space from the physical compute node. The leader node is responsible for processing a portion of the workload assigned to the compute node and distributing data to the slices. It also assigns tasks related to queries and other database operations to the slices.

The slices work in parallel and only operate on their assigned data, but they can request data from other slices if needed to complete their tasks. The number of slices per node varies depending on the instance type, with small instance types having two slices per node and large instance types having 16 slices per node.

Data sharing in Redshift enables you to share data with other Amazon Redshift clusters and databases, as well as with Athena and Amazon QuickSight. This is useful if you have multiple Amazon Redshift clusters needing access to the same data or want to use Athena or QuickSight to analyze data stored in an Amazon Redshift cluster.

You can share data in Amazon Redshift by creating a read-only external schema that points to the data, and then grant access to that schema to other Amazon Redshift clusters or databases. This allows the other clusters or databases to query the data as if it were stored locally.

Redshift supports **materialized views (MVs)**. MVs are pre-computed results of a `SELECT` query stored in a table. MVs can be used to speed up query performance by storing the results of a `SELECT` query in a table so that the `SELECT` query can be run faster the next time it is needed. MVs are especially useful when the data used in the `SELECT` query does not change frequently because the results of the `SELECT` query can be refreshed periodically to ensure that the data in the MV is up to date. Let's learn about the Redshift instance types.

Redshift instance types

Amazon Redshift offers a variety of node types to support different workloads and performance requirements:

- **RA3 node types**: These are the latest generation of Amazon Redshift node types, and they offer the ability to scale compute and storage independently. RA3 node types are suitable for workloads requiring high-performance computing and high-capacity storage. They are available in both single-node and multi-node configurations. The RA3 node is a technology that allows independent computing and storage scaling. It utilizes **Redshift Managed Storage (RMS)** as its resilient storage layer, providing virtually limitless storage capacity where data is committed back to Amazon S3. This allows for new functionalities, such as data sharing, where RMS can be shared storage across numerous clusters.
- **Dense compute (DC) node types**: These node types are designed for high-performance computing and are suitable for workloads that require fast query performance, such as data warehousing and BI. DC node types offer a balance of CPU, memory, and storage, and are available in both single-node and multi-node configurations.

Redshift launched with **dense storage (DS)** nodes on the path to deprecation. DS nodes are optimized for high-capacity storage and are suitable for workloads requiring large amounts of data, such as data lakes and big data analytics.

A Redshift cluster can have up to 128 ra3.16xlarge nodes, which is 16 petabytes of managed storage. When a data warehouse stores such a massive amount of data, it is important to ensure it can scale and provide query performance.

Redshift's key features

The following are some key Redshift features:

- **Redshift Concurrency Scaling**: This feature automatically adjusts cluster capacity to handle unexpected spikes in user demand, allowing thousands of users to work simultaneously without any degradation in performance.
- **Advanced Query Accelerator (AQUA)**: A hardware-level cache that takes performance to the next level, accelerating query speed up to 10x.
- **Redshift federated queries**: Allow you to combine data from multiple sources and query it as if it were all stored in a single Amazon Redshift database. This is useful if you have data stored in different data stores, such as Amazon S3, Amazon RDS, or even other Amazon Redshift clusters, and you want to analyze it using Amazon Redshift.
- **Automatic workload management (WLM)**: Provides fine-grained control, such as query monitoring rules, to promote or demote query priorities at execution time based on certain runtime metrics, such as queue wait, execution time, and CPU usage.
- **Elastic resize**: Enables the in-place addition or removal of nodes to/from existing clusters within a few minutes.
- **Auto-vacuum**: Monitors changes to your workload and automatically reclaims disk space occupied by rows affected by `UPDATE` and `DELETE` operations.
- **Redshift Advisor**: Continuously monitors and automatically provides optimization recommendations.
- **Redshift Query Editor**: Web-based query interface to run single SQL statement queries in an Amazon Redshift cluster directly from the AWS Management Console.
- **Redshift ML**: Amazon Redshift ML is a feature of Amazon Redshift that allows you to use SQL to build and train ML models on data stored in an Amazon Redshift cluster. With Redshift ML, you can use standard SQL statements to create and train ML models without learning a new programming language or using specialized ML libraries.

As you expand analytics throughout organizations, you need to make data easily and rapidly accessible to line-of-business users with little or no knowledge about data warehouse management. You do not want to consider selecting instances, sizing, scaling, and tuning the data warehouse. Instead, you want a simplified, self-service, automated data warehouse experience that allows them to focus on rapidly building business applications. AWS launched **Amazon Redshift Serverless** to address these challenges at re:Invent 2021. You can go to the Amazon Redshift console and enable a serverless endpoint for your AWS account. You can start with queries from the query editor tool with Amazon Redshift or connect from your favorite tool via JDBC/ODBC or data API. You don't need to select node types to specify the node or do another manual configuration, such as workload management or scaling configurations.

Amazon Redshift and Amazon Redshift Serverless are both fully managed data warehousing solutions. However, there are some key differences between the two offerings that you should consider when deciding which one is right for your use case:

- One of the main differences between Redshift and Redshift Serverless is the way they are priced. Amazon Redshift is priced based on the number and type of nodes in your cluster, as well as the amount of data you store and the amount of data you query. You pay a fixed hourly rate for each node in your cluster, and you can scale the number of nodes up or down as needed to meet changing workload demands.

  In contrast, Redshift Serverless is priced based on the data you store and the number of queries you run. You don't need to provision any nodes or worry about scaling the number of nodes up or down. Instead, Amazon Redshift Serverless automatically scales the compute resources required to run your queries based on the workload demand. You only pay for the resources you use, and you can pause and resume your cluster as needed to save costs.

- Another key difference between the two offerings is how they handle concurrency and workload management. Amazon Redshift uses a leader node to manage the workload and distribute tasks to compute nodes, which can be scaled up or down as needed. On the other hand, Amazon Redshift Serverless uses a shared pool of resources to run queries and automatically allocates more resources as required to handle increased concurrency and workload demands.

In general, Amazon Redshift is a good choice if you have a high-concurrency workload that requires fast query performance and you want to be able to scale the number of compute resources up or down as needed. Amazon Redshift Serverless is a good choice if you have a lower-concurrency workload that varies over time, and you want a more cost-effective solution that automatically scales compute resources as needed. Let's look at some tips and tricks to optimize a Redshift workload.

Optimizing Redshift workloads

There are several strategies you can use to optimize the performance of your Amazon Redshift workload:

- **Use the right node type**: Based on your queries' performance and storage requirements, choose the right node type for your workload. Amazon Redshift offers various node types, including DC, DS, memory-optimized, and RA3, which are optimized for different workloads.
- **Use columnar storage**: Amazon Redshift stores data using a columnar storage layout optimized for data warehousing workloads. To get the best performance from Amazon Redshift, design your tables using a columnar layout and use data types optimized for columnar storage.
- **Use sort and distribution keys**: Sort and distribution keys optimize data storage and querying in Amazon Redshift. Sort keys order the data in each block stored on a node, and distribution keys distribute data evenly across nodes. This can improve query performance by reducing the amount of data that needs to be read and processed.
- **Use MVs**: MVs are pre-computed results of a `SELECT` query stored in a table. They can speed up query performance by storing the results in a table so that the `SELECT` query can be run faster the next time it is needed.
- **Use query optimization techniques**: There are several techniques you can use to optimize the performance of your queries in Amazon Redshift, including using the `EXPLAIN` command to understand query execution plans, using the right join type, and minimizing the use of functions and expressions in your queries.
- **Use Redshift Spectrum**: Redshift Spectrum is an Amazon Redshift feature that enables you to query data stored in Amazon S3 using SQL without loading the data into an Amazon Redshift cluster. This can be a cost-effective way to query large amounts of data and can also help improve query performance by offloading data processing to Amazon S3's scale-out architecture.

In this section, you learned about the high-level architecture and key features of Redshift, which gave you a pointer to start your learning. Redshift is a very vast topic that warrants an entire book in itself. Refer to *Amazon Redshift Cookbook* to dive deeper into Redshift: `https://www.amazon.com/dp/1800569688/`.

While Redshift is a relational engine and operates on structured data, you might be curious about getting insight from other semi-structured data coming in at a high velocity and volume. To help mine this data without hassle, AWS provides Amazon Athena. This allows you to query data directly from S3.

Querying your data lake in AWS with Amazon Athena

Water, water everywhere, and not a drop to drink... This may be the feeling you get in today's enterprise environments. We are producing data at an exponential rate, but it is sometimes difficult to find a way to analyze this data and gain insights from it. Some of the data that we are generating at a prodigious rate is of the following types:

- Application logging
- Clickstream data
- Surveillance video
- Smart and IoT devices
- Commercial transactions

Often, this data is captured without analysis or is at least not analyzed to the fullest extent.

Previously, one stumbling block to analyzing this data was that much of this information resided in flat files. To analyze them, we had to ingest these files into a database to be able to perform analytics. Amazon Athena allows you to analyze these files without going through an ETL process.

Amazon Athena treats any file like a database table, allowing you to run `SELECT` queries. Amazon Athena also now supports insert and update statements. The ACID transactions in Athena enable various operations, such as writing, deleting, and updating, to be performed on Athena's SQL **data manipulation language** (**DML**).

You can greatly increase processing speeds and lower costs by running queries directly on a file without first performing ETL on it or loading it into a database. Amazon Athena enables you to run standard SQL queries to analyze and explore Amazon S3 objects. Amazon Athena is serverless. In other words, there are no servers to manage.

Amazon Athena is extremely simple to use. All you need to do is this:

1. Identify the object you want to query in Amazon S3.
2. Define the schema for the object.
3. Query the object with standard SQL.

Depending on the size and format of the file, query results can take a few seconds. As we will see later, a few optimizations can reduce query time as files get bigger.

Amazon Athena can be integrated with the AWS Glue Data Catalog, creating a unified metadata repository across services.

Let's get even deeper into the power and features of Amazon Athena and how it integrates with other AWS services.

Learning about Amazon Athena workgroups

Another feature of Amazon Athena is the concept of workgroups. Workgroups enable administrators to give different groups of users different access to databases, tables, and other Athena resources. They also limit how much data a query or a whole workgroup can access, enabling you to track costs. Since workgroups act like any other resource in AWS, resource-level identity-based policies can be set up to control access to individual workgroups.

Workgroups can also be integrated with SNS and CloudWatch. If query metrics are turned on, they can be published to CloudWatch. Additionally, alarms can be created for certain workgroup users if their usage exceeds a pre-established threshold.

By default, Amazon Athena queries run in the default primary workgroup. AWS administrators can add new workgroups and then run separate workloads in each workgroup. A common use case is to use workgroups to separate audiences, such as users who will run ad hoc queries and users who will run pre-canned reports. Each workgroup can then be associated with a specific location. Any queries associated with an individual workgroup will have their results stored in the assigned area. Following this paradigm ensures that only users who should be able to access certain data can access that data.

Another way to restrict access is by applying different encryption keys to the output files depending on the workgroup.

Workgroups greatly simplify the onboarding of new users. You can override the client-side settings and apply a predefined configuration for all the queries executed in a workgroup. Users within a workgroup do not have to configure where their queries will be stored or specify encryption keys for the S3 buckets. Instead, the values defined at the workgroup level will be used as a default.

Also, each workgroup keeps a separate history of all executed queries and any saved queries, making troubleshooting easier.

Optimizing Amazon Athena

As with any SQL operation, you can take steps to optimize the performance of your queries and inserts. However, as with traditional databases, optimizing data access performance usually comes at the expense of data ingestion, and vice versa.

Let's look at some tips that you can use to increase and optimize performance.

Optimization of data partitions

One way to improve performance is to break up files into smaller files, called partitions. A common partition scheme breaks up a file using a divider that occurs with some regularity in the data. Some examples follow:

- Country
- Region
- Date
- Product

Partitions operate as virtual columns and reduce the amount of data that needs to be read for each query. They are normally defined when a table or file is created.

Amazon Athena can use Apache Hive partitions. Hive partitions use this name convention:

```
s3://BucketName/TablePath/<PARTITION_COLUMN_NAME>=<VALUE>/<PARTITION_
COLUMN_NAME>=<VALUE>/
```

When this format is used, the `MSCK REPAIR` command can automatically add additional partitions.

Partitions are not restricted to a single column. Multiple columns can be used to partition data. Alternatively, you can divide a single field to create a hierarchy of partitions. For example, it is not uncommon to divide a date into three pieces and partition the data using the year, the month, and the day.

An example of partitions using this scheme may look like this:

```
s3://a-simple-examples/data/parquet/year=2000/month=1/day=1/
s3://a-simple-examples/data/parquet/year=2000/month=2/day=1/
s3://a-simple-examples/data/parquet/year=2000/month=3/day=1/
s3://a-simple-examples/data/parquet/year=2000/month=4/day=1/
```

So, which column would be the best for partitioning files, and are there any best practices for partitioning? Consider the following:

- Any column normally used to filter data is a good partition candidate.
- Don't over-partition. Suppose the number of partitions is too high; the retrieval overhead increases. If the partitions are too small, this prevents any benefit derived from partitioning the data.

It is also important to partition smartly and try to choose an evenly distributed value as your partition key. For example, if your data involves election ballots, you may want to use them to partition the candidates in the election. But what if one or two candidates take most of the votes? Your partitions will be heavily skewed toward those candidates, and your performance will suffer.

Data bucketing

Another scheme to partition data is to use buckets within a single partition. When using bucketing, a column or multiple columns are used to group rows together and "bucket" or categorize them. The best columns to use for bucketing are columns that will often be used to filter the data. So, when queries use these columns as filters, not as much data will need to be scanned and read when performing these queries.

High cardinality is another characteristic that makes a column a good candidate for bucketing. In other words, you want to use columns that have a large number of unique values. So, primary key columns are ideal bucketing columns.

Amazon Athena offers the `CLUSTERED BY` clause to simplify which columns will be bucketed during table creation. An example of a table creation statement using this clause follows:

```
CREATE EXTERNAL TABLE employee (
id string,
name string,
salary double,
address string,
timestamp bigint)
```

```
PARTITIONED BY (
timestamp string,
department string)
CLUSTERED BY (
id,
timestamp)
INTO 50 BUCKETS
```

You can learn more about data partitioning in Athena by visiting the AWS documentation here: `https://docs.aws.amazon.com/athena/latest/ug/partitions.html`.

File compression

Intuitively, queries can be sped up by using compression. When files are compressed, not as much data needs to be read, and the decompression overhead is not high enough to negate its benefits. Also, when going across the wire, a smaller file will take less time to get through the network than a bigger file. Finally, faster reads and transmission over the network will result in less spending, which will result in real savings over time when you multiply these by hundreds and thousands of queries.

Compression offers the highest benefits when files are of a certain size. The optimal file size is around 200 megabytes to 1 gigabyte. You can learn about these best practices in detail by referring to the AWS Analytics Lens page here: `https://docs.aws.amazon.com/wellarchitected/latest/analytics-lens/design-principle-10.html`. Smaller files translate into multiple files that can be processed simultaneously, taking advantage of the parallelism available with Amazon Athena. If there is only one file, only one reader can be used on the file while the other readers sit idle.

One simple way to achieve compression is to utilize Apache Parquet or Apache ORC format. Files in these formats can be easily split, and these formats are compressed by default. Two compression formats are often combined with Parquet and ORC to improve performance further. These compression formats are gzip and bzip2. The following chart shows how these compression formats compare with other popular compression algorithms:

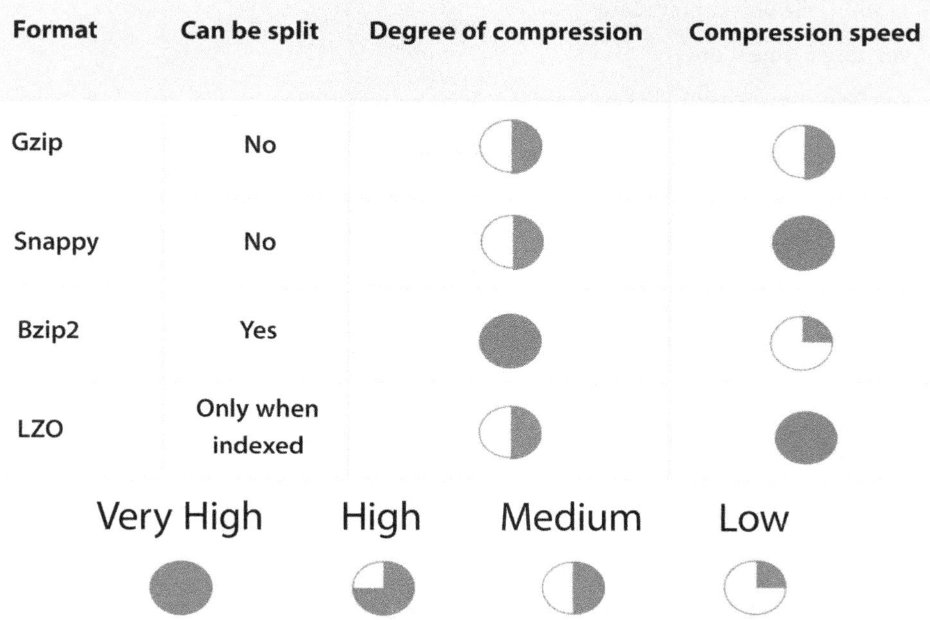

Format
Can be split
Degree of compression
Compression speed
Gzip
No
Snappy
No
Bzip2
Yes
LZO
Only when indexed
Very High
High
Medium
Low

Figure 10.8: Compression formats

Each format offers different advantages. The figure shows that **gzip** and **Snappy** files cannot be split. **bzip2** can be split, but only in special cases. bzip2 provides the highest compression level, and LZO and Snappy provide the fastest compression speeds.

Let's continue learning about other ways to optimize Amazon Athena. Another thing to do is to ensure the optimal file size.

File size optimization

As we have seen in quite a few examples in this book, one of the game-changing characteristics of the cloud is its elasticity. This elasticity enables us to run queries in parallel easily and efficiently. File formats that allow file splitting assist in this parallelization process. If files are too big or are not split, too many readers will be idle, and parallelization will not occur. On the flip side, files that are too small (generally in the range of 128 megabytes or less) will incur additional overhead with the following operations, to name a few:

- Opening files
- Listing directories

- Reading file object metadata
- Reading file headers
- Reading compression dictionaries

So, just as it's a good idea to split bigger files to increase parallelism, consolidating smaller files is recommended. Amazon EMR has a utility called `S3DistCP` that can merge smaller files into larger ones. `S3DistCP` can also efficiently transfer large files from HDFS to Amazon S3 and vice versa, as well as from one S3 bucket to another. Here is an example of how to use `S3DistCP` to copy data from an S3 bucket to an EMR cluster:

```
aws s3-dist-cp --src s3://sa-book-source-bucket/path/to/data/ \
              --dest hdfs:///path/to/destination/sa-book/ \
              --s3-client-region us-east-2 \
              --s3-client-endpoint s3.us-east-2.amazonaws.com \
              --src-pattern '*.csv' \
              --group-by '.*(part|PARTS)\..*'
```

The preceding example copies all `.csv` files from the `sa-book-source-bucket` S3 bucket to the `/path/to/destination/sa-book/` directory on the EMR cluster. The `--src-pattern` option specifies a regular expression to match the files that should be copied, and the `--group-by` option specifies a regular expression to group the files into larger blocks for more efficient transfer.

The `--s3-client-region` and `--s3-client-endpoint` options specify the Region and endpoint of the S3 bucket.

`S3DistCP` has many other options that you can use to customize the data transfer process, such as options to specify the number of mappers to use, the maximum number of retries, and the maximum number of concurrent connections. You can find more information about these options in the `S3DistCP` documentation: `https://aws.amazon.com/fr/blogs/big-data/seven-tips-for-using-s3distcp-on-amazon-emr-to-move-data-efficiently-between-hdfs-and-amazon-s3/`.

Columnar data store generation optimization

As mentioned earlier, Apache Parquet and Apache ORC are popular columnar data store formats. The formats efficiently compress data by leveraging the following:

- Columnar-wise compression scheme
- Datatype-based compression
- Predicate pushdown
- File splitting

To further optimize compression, fine-tune the file's block or stripe size. Bigger block and stripe sizes enable us to store more rows per block. The default Apache Parquet block size is 128 megabytes, and the default Apache ORC stripe size is 64 megabytes. A larger block size is recommended for tables with a large number of columns. This ensures that each column is reasonable in size and enables efficient sequential I/O.

When datasets are 10 gigabytes or less, the default compression algorithm with Parquet and ORC is enough to achieve decent performance. However, using other compression algorithms, such as gzip, with Parquet and ORC is not a bad idea for datasets bigger than that.

Yet another parameter that can be customized is the compression algorithm used on the storage data blocks. The Parquet format, by default, uses Snappy, but it also supports these other formats:

- gzip
- LZO
- No compression

The ORC format uses zlib compression by default, but it also supports the following:

- Snappy
- No compression

The recommended way to choose a compression algorithm is to use the default algorithm. No further optimization is needed if the performance is good enough for your use case. If not, try the other supported formats to see whether they deliver better results.

Column selection

An obvious way to reduce network traffic is to ensure that only the required columns are included in each query. Therefore, it is not recommended to use the following syntax unless your application requires that every single column in a table be used. Even if that's true today, it may not be true tomorrow. If additional columns are later added to the table schema, they may not be required for existing queries. Take this, for instance:

```
Select * from the table
```

Instead of that, use this:

```
select column1, column2, column3 from table
```

By explicitly naming columns, instead of using the star operator, we reduce the number of columns that get passed back and lower the number of bytes that need to be pushed across the wire.

Let's now learn about yet another way to optimize our use of Amazon Athena and explore the concept of predicate pushdown.

Predicate pushdown

The core concept behind predicate pushdown (also referred to as predicate filtering) is that specific sections of an SQL query (a predicate) can be "pushed down" to the location where the data exists. Performing this optimization can help reduce (often drastically) the time it takes a query to respond by filtering out results earlier in the process. Sometimes, predicate pushdown is achieved by filtering data in situ before transferring it over the network or loading it into memory.

The ORC and Parquet formats support predicate pushdown. These formats have data blocks representing column values. In each block, statistics are stored for the data held in the block. Two examples of the statistics stored are the minimum and maximum values. When a query is run, these statistics are read before the rest of the block and, depending on the statistics, it is determined whether the complete block should be read.

To maximize the use of predicate pushdown, it is recommended to identify the column that will be used most when executing queries before writing to disk and sort by that column. Let's look at a quick example to illustrate this point.

File 1

Stats: Min=1; Max 3
Value
1
2
3

File 2

Stats: Min=4; Max 6
Value
4
5
6

File 3

Stats: Min=7; Max 9
Value
7
8
9

Figure 10.9: Example

In the preceding example, there are three files. As you can tell, the data is already sorted using the value stored in the column labeled **Value**. Let's say we want to run the following query:

```
select * from Table where Value = 5
```

As mentioned before, we can look at the statistics first and observe that the first file's maximum value is `3`, so we can skip that file. In the second file, we see that our key (`Value = 5`) falls within the range of values in the file. We would then read this file. Since the maximum value of the second file is greater than the value of our key, we don't need to read any more files after reading the second file.

Predicate pushdown reduces the amount of data that needs to be scanned when executing a query in Amazon Athena. Predicate pushdown works by pushing down filtering conditions (predicates) to the data sources being queried, so that the data sources can filter the data before returning it to Athena. This can significantly reduce the amount of data that needs to be scanned and processed by Athena, which can improve query performance and reduce costs. You should use it whenever you have a query with predicates that can be applied to the data sources being queried.

ORDER BY clause optimization

Due to how sorting works, when we invoke a query containing an `ORDER BY` clause, it needs to be handled by a single worker thread. This can cause query slowdown and even failure. There are several strategies you can use to optimize the performance of the `ORDER BY` clause in Athena:

- **Use a sort key**: If you have a large table that you frequently need to sort, you can improve query performance by using a sort key. A sort key is a column or set of columns used to order the data in the table. When you use a sort key, Athena stores the data in the table in a sorted order, which can significantly reduce the time it takes to sort the data when you run a query.
- **Use a LIMIT clause**: If you only need the top *N* rows of a query, you can use the `LIMIT` clause to limit the number of rows returned. This can reduce the amount of data that needs to be sorted and returned, improving query performance.
- **Use a computed column**: If you frequently need to sort a table based on a derived value, you can create a computed column containing the derived value and use it in the `ORDER BY` clause.

Join optimization

Table joins can be expensive operations, so they should be avoided whenever possible. However, sometimes, it makes sense to "pre-join" tables and merge two tables into a single one to improve performance when queries are executed later.

That is not always possible or efficient. Another way to optimize joins is to ensure that larger tables are always on the left side of the join and smaller tables are on the right. When Amazon Athena runs a query with a `join` clause, the right-hand-side tables are delegated to worker nodes, bringing them into memory. The table on the left is then streamed to perform the join. This approach uses less memory, and the query performs better.

Now, let's explore another optimization with `GROUP BY` clauses.

GROUP BY clause optimization

When a `GROUP BY` clause is present, arranging the columns according to the highest cardinality is best practice. For example, if you have a dataset that contains data on ZIP codes and gender, it is recommended to write the query like this:

```
SELECT zip_code, gender, COUNT(*)FROM dataset GROUP BY zip_code, gender
```

This way is not recommended:

```
Select zip code, gender, count(*) from the dataset group by gender
```

This is because it is more likely that the ZIP code will have a higher cardinality (there will be more unique values) in that column.

This is not always possible, but it is recommended that the number of columns in the `SELECT` clause be minimized when a `GROUP BY` clause is present.

Approximate function use

Amazon Athena has a series of approximation functions. For example, there is an approximation function for the `DISTINCT()` function. If you don't need an exact count, you can instead use `APPROX_DISTINCT()`, which may not return the same number of distinct values for a column in a given table but will provide a good approximation for many use cases.

For example, to get an approximation, you should *not* use this query:

```
Select DISTINCT(last_name) from employee
```

Instead, you should use this query:

```
Select APPROX_DISTINCT(last_name) from employee
```

This may be suitable for a given use case if an exact count is not required.

This concludes the optimization section for Amazon Athena. It is by no means a comprehensive list, but rather it is a list of the most common and practical optimization techniques that can be used to gain efficiency and increase query performance quickly.

You have now learned about Amazon Redshift and Amazon Athena. Let's look at some examples of when to use Athena and Redshift Spectrum to query data.

Using Amazon Athena versus Redshift Spectrum

Amazon Athena and Redshift Spectrum are two data querying services offered by AWS that allow users to analyze data stored in Amazon S3 using standard SQL.

Amazon Athena is a serverless interactive query service that quickly analyzes data in Amazon S3 using standard SQL. It allows users to analyze data directly from Amazon S3 without creating or managing infrastructure. Athena is best suited for ad hoc querying and interactive analysis of large amounts of unstructured data stored in Amazon S3.

For example, imagine a marketing team needs to analyze customer behavior data stored in Amazon S3 to make informed decisions about their marketing campaigns. They can use Athena to query the data in S3, extract insights, and make informed decisions about improving their campaigns.

On the other hand, Amazon Redshift Spectrum (an extension of Amazon Redshift) allows users to analyze data stored in Amazon S3 with the same SQL interface used to analyze data in their Redshift cluster. It extends Redshift's querying capabilities beyond the data stored in its nodes to include data stored in S3.

Redshift Spectrum allows users to store data in S3 and query it as if it were in their Redshift cluster without loading or transforming it. Redshift Spectrum is best suited for users who want to query large amounts of structured data stored in S3 and join it with data already stored in their Redshift cluster.

For example, a retail company might store its transactional data in Redshift and its historical data in S3. The company can use Redshift Spectrum to join its Redshift transactional data with its historical data in S3 to gain deeper insights into customer behavior.

In summary, Amazon Athena and Amazon Redshift Spectrum are powerful data querying services that allow users to analyze data stored in Amazon S3 using standard SQL. The choice between the two largely depends on the type of data being analyzed and the specific use case. Athena is best suited for ad hoc querying and interactive analysis of large amounts of unstructured data. In contrast, Redshift Spectrum is best suited for querying large amounts of structured data stored in S3 and joining it with data already stored in a Redshift cluster.

As is said, a picture is worth a thousand words, so it is always preferable to present data insights in a visual format using a BI tool. AWS provides a cloud-based tool called Amazon QuickSight, which visualizes data and provides ML-based insights. Let's learn more details about BI in AWS.

Visualizing data with Amazon QuickSight

Data is an organizational asset that should be easily and securely accessible to anyone who needs access. It is no longer solely the property of analysts and scientists. Presenting data simply and visually enables teams to make better, more informed decisions, improve efficiency, uncover new opportunities, and drive innovation.

Most traditional on-premises BI solutions have a client-server architecture and minimum licensing requirements. To use BI tools, you must sign up for annual commitments around users or servers, which requires upfront investments. To keep your systems in compliance, you will need to build extensive monitoring and management, infrastructure growth, software patches, and periodic data backups. In addition, delivering data and insights to your customers and other third parties usually requires separate systems and tools for each audience.

Amazon QuickSight is an AWS-provided cloud-native BI SaaS solution, which means no servers or software to manage, and it can scale from single users to thousands of users under a pay-as-you-go model. With Amazon QuickSight, you can address several use cases to deliver insights for internal or external users. You can equip different lines of business with interactive dashboards, visualization, and the ability to do ad hoc analysis. QuickSight allows you to email highly formatted static reports to internal and external audiences. Further, you can enhance your end-user-facing products by embedding QuickSight visuals and dashboards into a website or application. There are several ways you can use QuickSight to analyze your data:

- **Visualize and explore data:** QuickSight allows you to create interactive visualizations and dashboards using your data. You can explore and visualize your data using various chart types, including line graphs, bar charts, scatter plots, and heat maps. You can also use QuickSight's built-in filters and drill-down capabilities to examine specific data points and gain more detailed insights.

- **Perform ad hoc analysis**: QuickSight includes a powerful SQL-based analysis tool, **Super-fast, Parallel, In-memory Calculation Engine (SPICE)**, that allows you to perform ad hoc analysis on your data. You can use SPICE to write custom SQL queries, perform calculations on your data, and then visualize the results using QuickSight's visualization tools. SPICE provides consistently fast performance for concurrent users automatically. As of 2025, you can import quite a bit of data into your SPICE datasets – up to 1 billion rows or 1 TB each – and have as many SPICE datasets as you need. You can refresh each SPICE dataset every 15 minutes using incremental refresh without affecting performance or downtime. You can explore more about its limits using the AWS docs: `https://docs.aws.amazon.com/en_us/quicksight/latest/user/data-source-limits.html`.
- **Use ML**: QuickSight includes built-in ML capabilities that allow you to use predictive analytics to forecast future trends and patterns in your data. You can use QuickSight's ML algorithms to create predictive models, generate forecasts, and then visualize the results using QuickSight's visualization tools. QuickSight leverages ML to help users extract more value from their data with less effort. For instance, QuickSight Q is a **natural language query (NLQ)** engine that empowers users to ask questions about their data in plain English. QuickSight also generates insights using **natural language processing (NLP)** to make it easy for any user, no matter their data savviness, to understand the key highlights hidden in their data. QuickSight also provides one-click forecasting and anomaly detection using an ML model.

The following is an example of a QuickSight dashboard that provides an analysis of home prices in the US:

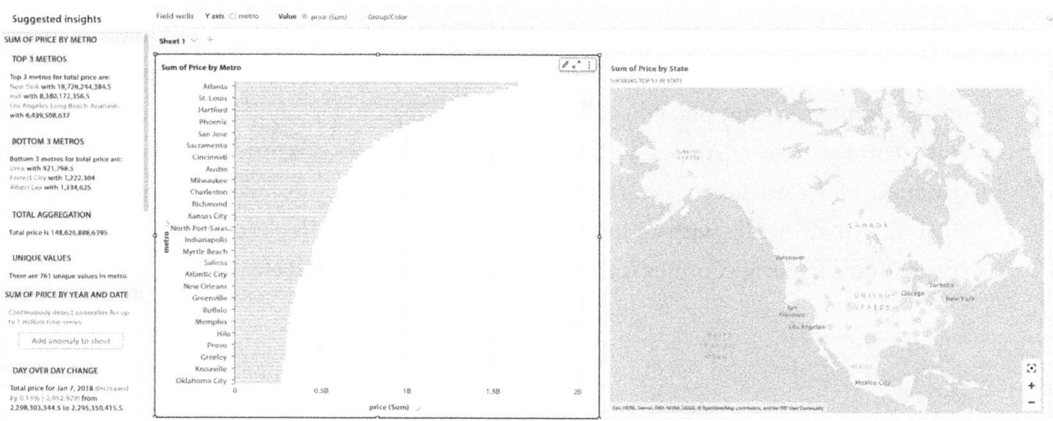

Figure 10.10: QuickSight geospatial and bar chart

In the preceding dashboard, QuickSight shows a bar chart for median home prices in the US by city in the first chart and a geolocation graph with bubbles in the second chart. On the left-hand side, you can see ML-based insights, which make the graph easy to understand in simple language.

Amazon Q is a work-oriented, AI-driven assistant that can be customized for your business. It performs tasks, provides answers to queries, creates content, and assists in problem-solving. At re:Invent 2023, it was announced that Amazon Q in QuickSight had been expanded with generative BI capabilities in QuickSight Enterprise Edition. Let's look at some of the highlights of this launch:

- **Build dashboards fast using natural language**: Amazon QuickSight allows Author Pro users to create visuals, perform calculations, and refine visuals by simply describing their desired outcome in natural language. This reduces the time and effort required for applying filters, aggregations, and formatting and defining complex scenarios.
- **Get contextual answers with multi-visual Q&A**: Amazon QuickSight's enhanced Q&A experience revolutionizes data interaction by providing contextual answers through multiple related visualizations, addressing the limitations of traditional single-answer NLQ systems. The platform now intelligently suggests AI-generated questions and offers data previews, helping users understand how to effectively phrase their queries and explore available data within specific topics. When users pose questions, even vague ones such as "What are the best products?" the system responds with comprehensive, multi-visual answers that provide deeper context and build confidence in the data interpretation. This innovative approach not only accommodates imprecise queries but also enriches the response with related data points and alternative suggestions, ensuring users receive complete, meaningful insights regardless of their query specificity.
- **Use generative BI to create compelling stories**: Amazon QuickSight's generative BI capabilities empower users to transform raw data into engaging narratives through simple natural language prompts, where Amazon Q intelligently analyzes selected visuals and crafts comprehensive stories with actionable insights. This innovative feature not only streamlines the process of creating data-driven presentations but also enables users to customize their stories with additional elements and refine the content using AI-powered suggestions, making complex data storytelling accessible and efficient.

- **Get instant insights with executive summaries:** Executive summaries in Amazon QuickSight empower users to generate comprehensive data insights instantly. With a single click, they transform complex dashboard information into clear, actionable narratives highlighting key trends and business performance metrics.

Putting AWS analytics services together

Let's combine our learning on how to build a data processing pipeline. The following diagram shows a data processing and analytics architecture in AWS that applies various analytics services to create an end-to-end solution:

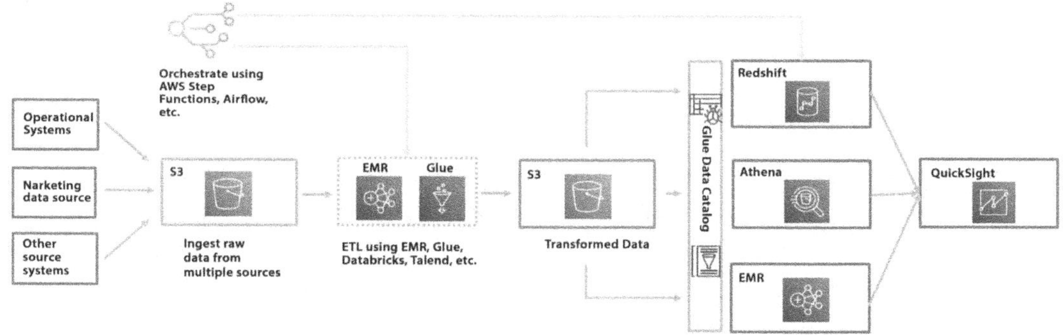

Figure 10.11: Data analytics architecture in AWS

As shown in the preceding diagram, data is ingested from various sources, such as operational systems and marketing, in S3. You want to ingest data fast without losing it, so this data is collected in a raw format first. You can clean, process, and transform this data using an ETL platform such as EMR or Glue. Using the Apache Spark framework and writing data processing code from scratch is recommended when using Glue; otherwise, you can use EMR if you have Hadoop skill sets in your team. Transformed data is stored in another S3 bucket, which is further consumed by the data warehouse system in Redshift, the data processing system in EMR, and direct queries with Athena. To visualize this data, you can connect QuickSight to any consumer.

The preceding is just one way to build a data pipeline. However, multiple ways exist to create data analytics architectures, such as data lakes, lake houses, and data meshes. You will learn about these architectures in *Chapter 12, Data Lake Patterns: Integrating Your Data Across the Enterprise.*

Amazon DataZone

As a developer or data professional, you often face challenges in managing data across multiple teams, AWS accounts, and departments. Amazon DataZone helps solve this by giving you one place to discover, organize, and safely share data across your organization. It's like a data catalog, sharing tool, and governance dashboard all in one, designed to make it easier for you and your team to find trusted data and use it responsibly.

With Amazon DataZone, your company can create a central data catalog that stores metadata about all your datasets – from Amazon S3 buckets, data lakes, and databases. You can browse this catalog to find what's available, see what each dataset contains, and even preview data before using it. For example, a marketing team could quickly search for "customer behavior" data and see which tables or files exist, who owns them, and how to access them, without needing to ask the data engineering team.

Sharing data across AWS accounts is often complex, especially when you need to enforce security and compliance. Amazon DataZone makes this easier by enabling secure, cross-account data sharing. You can set rules to control who can see or access the data, and all data access is logged so that you can comply with internal and external policies. For instance, a retail company using separate AWS accounts for Regions can now let analysts from the US view sales data from the EU without violating GDPR or internal policies.

Governance is built into the platform. With policy management, you can define rules around data classification, access, quality, and lineage. This is essential if you work in a regulated industry such as finance or healthcare. You can also run audits and generate compliance reports, helping your organization prove that it handles data responsibly.

Another big plus is integration with popular AWS services. Amazon DataZone works with Amazon S3, AWS Glue, Amazon Redshift, Lake Formation, and more, so you can automate data pipelines, manage transformations, and push clean, governed data into your analytics tools. Imagine a pipeline that ingests raw data from S3, cleans it with Glue, catalogs it in DataZone, and makes it searchable by teams in minutes.

Amazon DataZone brings structure and control to your data ecosystem. It helps you use data more confidently, reduces the time spent searching for datasets, and ensures you stay compliant while encouraging innovation through secure data sharing. Whether you're a data engineer, analyst, or architect, it's a powerful tool for building a smarter, more connected data strategy on AWS.

Here are some simple and practical use cases that show how different organizations can benefit from using Amazon DataZone to manage and share their data securely:

- **Cross-organizational data collaboration**: If you work in a large company with many departments or Regions, it can be hard to collaborate on data-driven projects. For example, a multinational corporation running operations in Asia, Europe, and North America might want to run a global sales analysis. With Amazon DataZone, you can build a shared data catalog that connects data across all accounts and Regions. Only the right people get access, and sensitive data is protected with fine-grained access controls. This makes global data projects easier without compromising on security.
- **Data governance and compliance**: If your company handles sensitive data, such as in financial services, you need to comply with regulations such as GDPR or CCPA. Amazon DataZone helps by letting you classify data, track how it flows, and check its quality. It also keeps detailed audit logs, so when regulators come knocking, you're ready with compliance reports. For instance, a bank could use DataZone to track customer data access and ensure it only goes where it's allowed.
- **Unified analytics environment**: Let's say you're part of a retail company with sales, marketing, and customer data spread across different platforms. Your analysts and data scientists need all this data in one place. Amazon DataZone creates a central catalog, helping your team quickly search, filter, and preview datasets. You can connect it directly with tools such as Amazon Redshift and Amazon QuickSight, so your teams, from data engineers to business users, can work together using one analytics platform. This helps speed up decisions and reduces confusion.
- **Data monetization**: Some businesses have valuable data they want to share or sell to partners or customers. For example, a market research firm might want to offer insights to retailers. Amazon DataZone makes this safe and easy by allowing the organization to publish datasets securely, control who accesses them, and even apply pricing models for different access levels. This means you can profit from your data while keeping it secure and governed.

By using Amazon DataZone, you're not just organizing your data better, you're enabling secure sharing, faster analytics, stronger compliance, and even new revenue opportunities. It's a powerful way to get more value from your data while staying in control.

Knowledge check

The following are sample questions that align with the difficulty and scope of the *AWS Certified Solutions Architect – Professional* exam:

1. You are designing an ETL pipeline for a large-scale data analytics project using AWS Glue. The pipeline needs to handle semi-structured data stored in Amazon S3, transform it, and load it into an Amazon Redshift data warehouse. Additionally, the pipeline must support incremental loads to handle new data arriving daily. Which two AWS Glue features should you use to achieve this efficiently? (Select two.)

    a. AWS Glue Data Catalog

    b. AWS Glue Studio

    c. AWS Glue triggers

    d. AWS Glue job bookmarks

    e. AWS Glue development endpoints

    Answers: a. and d.

    Explanation:

    a. **Correct**. The AWS Glue Data Catalog is a persistent metadata store. It plays a crucial role in the ETL process by providing a central repository for all data metadata. This allows the ETL jobs to easily locate and understand the schema and structure of the data stored in Amazon S3, facilitating the transformation process.

    b. Incorrect. While AWS Glue Studio is a visual interface that simplifies the creation and running of ETL jobs, it is not a feature that directly contributes to handling incremental loads or tracking processed data. It is more about the ease of use and visual job authoring.

    c. Incorrect. AWS Glue triggers are used to start jobs based on a schedule or in response to an event, such as the arrival of new data in an S3 bucket. Although they are useful for automating the ETL process, they do not inherently support the mechanism for tracking processed data or handling incremental loads.

    d. **Correct**. AWS Glue job bookmarks are essential for handling incremental data loads. They track already-processed data, allowing the ETL job to pick up only new or updated data during subsequent runs. This feature is critical for maintaining efficiency and avoiding redundant data processing already loaded into the data warehouse.

e. Incorrect. AWS Glue development endpoints provide an environment to author and test **extract, transform, and load** (**ETL**) scripts. While they are useful for development and testing purposes, they do not directly contribute to the functionality of handling incremental data loads or tracking processed data in production ETL pipelines.

2. A company runs a large-scale data analytics application on Amazon EMR. The application processes sensitive healthcare data and needs to meet strict compliance requirements. The solution architect needs to design a solution that provides the following:

   - Encryption of data at rest and in transit
   - Ability to use custom AMIs for EMR nodes
   - Integration with on-premises Active Directory for authentication
   - Ability to run multiple processing frameworks (Spark, Hive, and Presto)
   - Cost optimization for both storage and compute

   Which combination of configurations would meet these requirements in the most secure and cost-effective way? (Select two.)

   a. Launch the EMR cluster in a private subnet with a NAT gateway. Use EMRFS with SSE-KMS for S3 encryption. Configure the security configuration with TLS certificates. Enable Kerberos authentication with an external KDC. Use an instance fleet with Spot Instances for task nodes.
   b. Launch the EMR cluster in a public subnet, enable cluster encryption using AWS KMS, and use EC2 security groups for network isolation. Configure LDAP authentication. Use uniform instance groups with On-Demand Instances.
   c. Launch the EMR cluster in a private subnet with VPC endpoints. Enable cluster encryption using AWS KMS. Encrypt EBS volumes using LUKS. Configure IAM roles for service access. Use Reserved Instances for core nodes.
   d. Launch the EMR cluster in a public subnet with an internet gateway. Enable client-side encryption for S3 data. Enable security groups with broad access. Use password authentication. Use On-Demand Instances for all node types.
   e. Launch an EMR cluster in a private subnet with VPC endpoints. Enable cluster encryption with AWS KMS. Configure TLS certificates for in-transit encryption. Enable Kerberos authentication with cross-realm trust. Use an instance fleet with a mix of Spot and Reserved Instances.

   Answers: a. and e.

Explanation:

a. **Correct**. A NAT gateway provides the necessary outbound internet access while maintaining security. EMRFS with SSE-KMS is the recommended approach for S3 encryption. An external KDC setup allows for integration with the existing Active Directory.

b. Incorrect. Public subnet deployment is less secure. LDAP authentication alone isn't as secure as Kerberos. Uniform instance groups with only On-Demand Instances are not cost-effective.

c. Incorrect. LUKS encryption adds unnecessary complexity. It relies solely on Reserved Instances and lacks cost optimization opportunities with Spot Instances. It lacks specific authentication integration with Active Directory.

d. Incorrect. A public subnet with an internet gateway poses security risks. Client-side encryption alone is insufficient. Broad security group access is not secure. Using only On-Demand Instances is not cost-effective.

e. **Correct**. VPC endpoints provide secure access to AWS services without internet exposure. Cross-realm trust enables seamless integration with on-premises Active Directory. A mix of Spot and Reserved Instances provides optimal cost management.

3. A global retail company uses Amazon Kinesis to implement a real-time analytics solution. The application needs to process millions of events per second from IoT devices in their stores worldwide. The events must be processed for each device, and the solution must be able to handle replay of the data in case of processing failures. The company also wants to minimize the operational overhead and ensure optimal cost efficiency. Which combination of the following options would best meet these requirements? (Select two.)

   a. Use Kinesis Data Streams with enhanced fan-out consumers and configure the stream with 1,000 shards. Use DynamoDB for checkpointing and Lambda for processing.

   b. Use Kinesis Data Streams with shared throughput consumers and implement a custom message ordering solution using SQS FIFO queues.

   c. Use Kinesis Data Streams with enhanced fan-out consumers and configure the stream with dynamic scaling. For message replay capabilities, use Amazon MSK.

   d. Use Kinesis Data Streams with enhanced fan-out consumers, configure the stream with appropriate sharding, and use **Kinesis Client Library** (**KCL**) with DynamoDB for checkpointing.

e. Use Kinesis Data Firehose with direct PUT and configure Lambda to transform and process the data before loading it into Amazon S3.

Answers: a. and d.

Explanation:

a. **Correct**. The solution uses **enhanced fan-out** (**EFO**) consumers, which provide dedicated throughput of 2 MB/second per consumer, reduce latency (70 ms versus 200 ms for shared throughput), and scale better for multiple consumers. The solution uses DynamoDB for checkpointing, which maintains processing state, enables replay capabilities, and ensures exactly once processing. The solution ensures order processing data within a shard is in the correct order and partition keys can be used to ensure device-level ordering.

b. Incorrect. Shared throughput consumers would limit scalability, and using SQS FIFO queues would add unnecessary complexity and potential bottlenecks.

c. Incorrect. Amazon MSK is unnecessary overhead when Kinesis already provides replay capabilities through shard iterators and sequence numbers.

d. **Correct**. Same as A.

e. Incorrect. Kinesis Data Firehose doesn't guarantee ordering and is primarily for data delivery to destinations, not real-time processing. It also doesn't support replay capabilities natively.

4. A large e-commerce company stores customer transaction data in Amazon S3 as JSON files. The data science team needs to perform complex analytical queries on this data using Amazon Athena. The dataset grows by approximately 500 GB daily, and query performance has become a significant concern. The team needs to optimize query performance while minimizing costs. Which combination of approaches would provide the most effective solution for this scenario? (Select two.)

   a. Using AWS Glue jobs, convert the JSON files to Apache Parquet format and partition the data by date. Use Athena workgroups with per-query data usage limits and implement result caching.

   b. Implement columnar compression on the JSON files using gzip and create materialized views in Athena for frequently accessed query patterns.

   c. Use AWS Lambda to convert JSON files to CSV format and implement Athena federation to query multiple data sources simultaneously.

d. Create an Amazon RDS instance to store the processed data and use Athena federated queries to access it.

e. Convert data to Apache ORC format using AWS Glue, implement partitioning by date and customer Region, and use Athena query result reuse through workgroups.

Answers: a. and e.

Explanation:

a. **Correct**. Converting to Parquet format provides significant performance benefits through columnar storage. Partitioning by date helps Athena scan less data. Workgroups with data usage limits help control costs, and result caching improves performance for repeated queries.

b. Incorrect. GZIP compression on JSON files doesn't provide the same performance benefits as columnar formats. Materialized views in Athena have limitations and don't persist between query executions.

c. Incorrect. CSV format doesn't provide the performance benefits of columnar formats. The Athena federation isn't necessary for this scenario and adds unnecessary complexity.

d. Incorrect. Moving data to RDS introduces unnecessary complexity and costs. This approach doesn't leverage Athena's core strengths with S3 data lake architecture.

e. **Correct**. Apache ORC, like Parquet, is a columnar format that significantly improves query performance. Multi-level partitioning (date and Region) provides better query optimization. Query result reuse reduces repeated processing of the same data.

5. A global retail company uses Amazon QuickSight for BI and reporting. Its datasets are stored in Amazon S3, Amazon RDS, and on-premises SQL Server databases. The company wants to implement **row-level security (RLS)** to ensure regional managers can only view data from their assigned geographical Regions. Additionally, it needs to refresh its datasets multiple times daily while optimizing costs. Which combination of actions should the solutions architect recommend?

    a. Create direct queries for the data sources and implement RLS using custom rules in QuickSight datasets. Schedule SPICE refreshes every four hours.

    b. Use SPICE to import all data sources, implement RLS using IAM roles, and schedule automatic AWS Lambda refreshes.

c. Create a QuickSight dataset using SPICE, implement RLS using user-based rules with dynamic mapping, and use QuickSight's scheduled refresh with incremental refresh enabled.

d. Set up direct query access to all data sources, implement RLS using database-level permissions, and use AWS Glue to manage data refresh schedules.

Answer: c.

Explanation:

a. Incorrect. Direct queries would be more expensive and slower for frequent access.

b. Incorrect. Implementing RLS through IAM roles wouldn't provide the granular control needed for regional access, and using Lambda for refreshes would be unnecessarily complex.

c. **Correct**. SPICE is QuickSight's in-memory engine optimized for fast analytics. SPICE is more cost-effective than direct queries when data needs to be accessed frequently throughout the day, as it reduces the number of queries to the source databases. SPICE also supports incremental refreshes, which means only changed data needs to be updated, significantly reducing processing time and costs compared to full refreshes. RLS in QuickSight is best implemented using user-based rules with dynamic mapping, as this allows for flexible and granular control over data access. This approach enables you to create rules based on user attributes (such as Region assignments) and dynamically map them to the corresponding data rows.

d. Incorrect. Direct queries would be costly, and database-level permissions would be more difficult to manage across multiple data sources and require maintaining permissions in various places.

Summary

This chapter explored the benefits of using the cloud for big data analytics, focusing on key AWS services. It began with Amazon EMR, AWS's Hadoop-based offering, including its serverless variant. You learned about EMR clusters, filesystems, and security features. Next, the chapter introduced AWS Glue, covering its components such as the Glue console, Data Catalog, crawlers, and code generators, along with best practices and when to choose Glue over EMR.

The importance of real-time data processing was highlighted with Amazon Kinesis. The chapter also covered Amazon MSK, AWS's managed Kafka offering, explaining its architecture and comparing it with Kinesis for different use cases.

We then explored querying and visualizing data with Amazon Redshift, AWS's cloud data warehouse, and its architecture. Amazon Athena was introduced as a tool to query file contents using SQL, with governance features such as workgroups to enhance security. Scenarios where Athena excels or alternatives such as Amazon RDS might be better were also discussed.

Lastly, you learned about Amazon QuickSight, AWS's cloud-native BI tool, its SPICE engine for performance optimization, and its generative BI capability. The chapter concluded with an example of a complete data processing pipeline combining various AWS analytics and DataZone services. The next chapter will explore advanced use cases, including ML and generative AI.

Join us on Discord

For discussions around the book and to connect with your peers, join us on Discord at `https://discord.gg/kbFRRSB2Qs` or scan the QR code below:

11

Machine Learning and Generative AI in AWS

Monetization of emerging technology, such as **Machine Learning** (**ML**) and **Artificial Intelligence** (**AI**), started as experiments by a handful of technology companies. Over the years, major technology companies, including Amazon, Google, Meta, and Apple, have driven exponential growth by utilizing the latest emerging technology and staying ahead of the competition.

Generative AI is currently the most influential emerging technology, transforming how people interact with machines and consume information. Tools such as ChatGPT are used by millions of people every day for tasks ranging from content creation and coding assistance to education and customer support. Similarly, platforms such as `Perplexity.ai` are challenging traditional search engines by combining AI-generated answers with real-time web data, marking a shift in how users discover and verify information.

This shift is often referred to as a "search revolution." While Google still dominates the market, new AI-native search engines are providing more conversational, context-aware, and personalized responses. These platforms don't just provide links; they synthesize answers and help users understand complex topics more quickly.

This technological gold rush is similar to the early days of the cloud when AWS led the transformation. As GenAI matures, companies leveraging cloud-based AI tools will likely lead the next wave of digital innovation.

With the cloud, emerging technologies have become accessible to everyone. That is another reason why organizations are rushing to adopt the cloud, as it opens the door for innovation with tested technology by industry leaders such as Amazon, Microsoft, and Google through their cloud platforms.

AWS offers a comprehensive technology stack for building, training, and deploying ML and GenAI applications, ranging from custom silicon chips to powerful AI services accessible via simple APIs. In this chapter, you will learn about the following emerging technology platforms available in AWS:

- ML in AWS with Amazon SageMaker
- Generative AI in AWS with Amazon Bedrock
- Amazon Q

Let's start diving deep and learn about these innovative technologies in detail.

What is AI/ML?

While Generative AI is grabbing headlines, having a solid foundation in ML is essential first. Think of ML as the backbone, and GenAI as a specific, powerful branch of it – best used when it's truly the right fit.

Let's put this into simple terms.

You wouldn't use a sword when a needle could do the job, right? Similarly, not every business or technical problem needs GenAI. Sometimes, traditional ML models – such as those used for forecasting, classification, or clustering – are more accurate, easier to implement, and cost-effective.

Take **Thomson Reuters**, for example. They utilized classical **Machine Learning (ML)** with Amazon SageMaker to classify documents and extract data. After mastering this, they added NLP and GenAI features to summarize and enhance user queries.

It's like learning to drive a basic car before jumping into a Formula 1 race car. If you don't understand the controls, speed alone won't get you to the finish line – it could cause a crash.

So, before you chase buzzwords such as "foundation models" and "zero-shot learning," spend some time getting hands-on with ML. Tools such as Amazon SageMaker are perfect for this because they guide you from the basics to advanced modeling at your own pace.

ML enables your application to automatically improve performance by learning from data without being explicitly programmed. It is a way of teaching applications to recognize patterns and make predictions based on examples. There are several types of ML, each with its unique characteristics and use cases. The main types of ML are as follows:

- **Supervised learning**: Supervised learning is the most widely used form of machine learning, involving training a model on a labeled dataset to predict the output for new, unseen data. Linear regression, logistic regression, and decision trees are some examples of supervised learning algorithms.
- **Unsupervised learning**: Unsupervised learning, on the other hand, does not use labeled data; instead, it discovers patterns and structures within the input data. Examples of unsupervised learning algorithms include clustering, dimensionality reduction, and anomaly detection.
- **Semi-supervised learning**: This type of ML is a combination of supervised and unsupervised learning, where the model is given some labeled data and some unlabeled data and must find patterns and structure in the input data while also making predictions.
- **Reinforcement learning**: Reinforcement learning is used in decision-making and control systems, where an agent interacts with an environment and learns to perform actions that maximize a reward signal.
- **Deep learning**: Deep learning is a subset of ML that utilizes deep neural networks with multiple layers to learn from data and make predictions or informed decisions. This method is particularly useful for tasks such as image and speech recognition, **Natural Language Processing (NLP)**, and decision-making.
- **Transfer learning**: This is an ML method you use when your current task or data differs from what the model was originally trained on. Instead of starting from scratch, you take a pre-trained model and apply its existing knowledge to improve the performance of your new model, saving time and often boosting accuracy.

When discussing model training in machine learning, it's important to understand whether the model is overfitting or underfitting. A model is said to be overfitting when it learns the training data too well, including its noise and outliers, which makes it perform poorly on new, unseen data. This usually happens when the model is too complex for the amount of data or not regularized properly. On the other hand, underfitting occurs when the model is too simple to capture the underlying patterns in the data, leading to poor performance on training and test data. A good model balances learning enough to generalize well, but not so much that it memorizes the training data.

AI, on the other hand, is a more comprehensive term that encompasses ML and other technologies that empower machines to undertake activities that conventionally require human intelligence, including comprehending natural language, identifying objects, and making decisions. In basic terms, AI is a means for computers to accomplish tasks that ordinarily demand human intelligence, such as understanding spoken language, recognizing facial features, and playing strategic games such as chess. AI can be implemented in various ways, ranging from simple rule-based systems to more advanced techniques such as ML and deep learning, which enable computers to learn from data and make predictions or informed decisions. There are several types of AI, each with its own characteristics and use cases. The main types of AI are as follows:

- **Reactive machines**: These types of AI can only react to their environment; they can't form memories or learn from past experiences. Reactive machines are commonly employed in applications such as autonomous vehicles and artificial intelligence in video games.
- **Limited memory**: These types of AI can take into account past experiences and use that information to make decisions. Examples of limited memory AI include robots that can navigate a room or a self-driving car that can change its driving behavior based on recent experiences.
- **Narrow AI**: These are AI systems designed to perform a specific task, such as image recognition or speech recognition. These systems are not general-purpose and can only perform the task for which they were designed.
- **Theory of mind**: This type of AI is designed to comprehend mental states, including beliefs, intentions, and desires. This type of AI is still in the research phase and has not been fully implemented.
- **Self-aware**: This is the most advanced type of AI, where the AI is aware of its own existence and consciousness. This type of AI is still in the realm of science fiction and has not yet been achieved.
- **General AI**: These are AI systems that can perform any intellectual task that a human can, also known as artificial general intelligence. These systems do not yet exist but are the ultimate goal of AI research.

In this section, you saw a quick overview of AI/ML. This is a broad topic, and numerous books explain these concepts in detail. Within the context of this book, let's focus on AI/ML in AWS.

AI/ML in AWS

In recent years, ML has rapidly transitioned from a cutting-edge technology to a mainstream one; however, it is now embedded everywhere in our lives. In the past, ML was primarily accessible to a select group of large tech companies and academic researchers. However, with the advent of cloud computing, the resources required for working with ML, such as computing power and data, have become more widely available, enabling a broader range of organizations to utilize and benefit from ML technology.

ML has become an essential technology for many industries, and AWS is at the forefront of providing ML services to its customers. Some of the key trends in ML using AWS include the following:

- **Serverless ML**: AWS is making it easier to build, train, and deploy ML models without the need to manage servers. With services such as Amazon SageMaker, customers can build and train models using a managed Jupyter notebook and then deploy them to a serverless endpoint with just a few clicks.
- **Automated ML**: Automating the model-building process is becoming increasingly popular, allowing customers to achieve good results with minimal expertise. AWS offers services such as Amazon SageMaker Autopilot, which automatically builds and tunes ML models and selects the best algorithm with hyperparameters for a given dataset.
- **Transfer learning**: With the amount of data available today, it is becoming increasingly difficult to train models from scratch. Transfer learning allows customers to use a pre-trained model as a starting point and fine-tune it for their specific use case.
- **Reinforcement learning**: Reinforcement learning is a type of ML that is well-suited for problems where the feedback is delayed or non-deterministic. AWS offers services such as Amazon SageMaker RL, which allows customers to easily build, train, and deploy reinforcement learning models.
- **Federated learning**: Federated learning is a distributed ML technique that allows customers to train models on multiple devices while keeping the data private.

AWS provides a wide range of services that make it easy for you to build, train, and deploy ML models. With the growing adoption of ML, AWS is well-positioned to continue to lead the way in providing ML services to its customers. The following figure represents the services stack for AI/ML in AWS, divided into three parts: **AI services, ML services**, and **ML frameworks and infrastructure**.

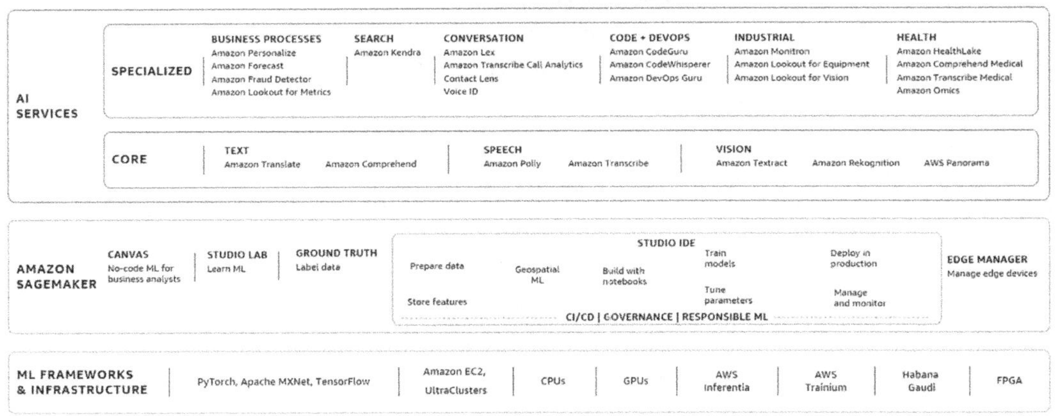

Figure 11.1: AWS ML services stack

Quick tip: Need to see a high-resolution version of this image? Open this book in the next-gen Packt Reader or view it in the PDF/ePub copy.

The next-gen Packt Reader is included for free with the purchase of this book. Scan the QR code OR go to packtpub.com/unlock, then use the search bar to find this book by name. Double-check the edition shown to make sure you get the right one.

The diagram illustrates a stack of options for working with ML. Starting with the lowest level, ML frameworks and infrastructures require detailed programming and are best suited for field data scientists. This option offers the most flexibility and control, enabling you to develop an ML model from scratch using open source libraries and languages.

At the top, purpose-built AI services are pre-built and ready to be invoked, such as Amazon Rekognition, which can perform facial analysis on an image without requiring any ML code to be written.

In the middle is Amazon SageMaker, the most feature-rich option, which offers a complete suite of subservices for preparing data, working on notebooks, performing experiments, monitoring performance, and more, including no-code visual ML.

Let's examine each layer of the preceding service stack in detail, starting with ML frameworks and infrastructure and progressing upward.

AWS ML frameworks and infrastructure

AWS provides a variety of infrastructure services for building and deploying ML models. Some of the key services include the following:

- **Amazon EC2 for ML workloads**: AWS offers a range of EC2 instance types suitable for ML workloads. Depending on the workload's needs, these instances can be configured with different amounts of CPU, memory, and GPU resources. For example, the P3 and G5 instances are designed explicitly for ML workloads and provide high-performance GPU resources.
- **AWS Inferentia**: AWS offers a custom-built chip called Inferentia, designed to perform low-latency, high-throughput inferences on deep learning workloads. It is designed to provide high performance at a low cost and can be used with Amazon SageMaker.
- **AWS Trainium**: AWS Trainium is a chip designed specifically to address the budget constraints development teams face while training their deep learning models and applications. AWS Trainium-based EC2 Trn1 and Trn2 instances provide a solution to this challenge by delivering faster training times and cost savings of up to 50% compared to similar GPU-based instances, allowing teams to train their models more frequently and at a lower cost.

AWS provides a variety of frameworks and libraries for ML development, allowing customers to easily build, train, and deploy ML models. Some of the main ML frameworks and libraries available on AWS include the following:

- **TensorFlow**: TensorFlow is an open source ML framework developed by Google, which can be used for a wide variety of tasks, such as NLP, image classification, and time series analysis.
- **Apache MXNet**: MXNet is an open source ML framework developed by Amazon, which can be used for tasks such as image classification, object detection, and time series analysis.

- **PyTorch**: PyTorch is an open source ML framework developed by Facebook, which can be used for tasks such as image classification, NLP, and time series analysis.
- **Keras**: Keras is a high-level open source ML library that can be used as a wrapper for other ML frameworks such as TensorFlow and MXNet, making it easier to build, train, and deploy ML models.

In this section, you learned about the ML frameworks and infrastructure provided by AWS. Let's learn about the middle layer of the service stack, Amazon SageMaker, which is the key ML service and the backbone of AWS ML. We will also see how to use this infrastructure to train, build, and deploy an ML model.

Amazon SageMaker

Amazon SageMaker is a fully managed service for building, deploying, and managing ML models on the AWS platform. It offers a range of tools and features for data preparation, model training, and deployment, along with pre-built algorithms and models. One of the primary features of SageMaker is its capability to train ML models in a distributed manner, utilizing multiple machines in parallel, enabling customers to train large models quickly and at scale. SageMaker also provides a variety of pre-built algorithms and models, such as image classification, object detection, and NLP, which can be easily integrated into a customer's application.

You can use SageMaker to train a model to predict product prices based on historical sales data. A retail company can use SageMaker to train a model on a dataset containing information about past sales, including the date, product, and price. The model could then be deployed and integrated into the company's e-commerce platform, enabling it to predict prices for new products and adjust prices in real time based on demand. If you want to improve the accuracy of detecting and classifying objects in images, you can use SageMaker to train object detection models using a dataset of labeled images.

Amazon SageMaker offers SageMaker Studio, an integrated development environment accessible through a web browser, for creating, training, and deploying ML models on AWS. The studio provides a single, web-based interface that streamlines the process of building, training, deploying, and monitoring ML models.

The end-to-end ML pipeline is a process that takes a business use case and turns it into a working ML model. The pipeline typically consists of several stages, including data engineering, data preparation, model training, model evaluation, and deployment. AWS SageMaker enables this process by providing a suite of services that support each stage of the ML pipeline. The ML pipeline typically includes the following stages:

1. **Business use case**: Identifying a business problem that can be solved using ML.
2. **Data engineering**: Collecting and integrating the required data, which is often stored in Amazon S3 due to its ability to store large amounts of data with durability and reliability. Other AWS services, such as AWS Data Migration Service, AWS DataSync, and Amazon Kinesis, can also help with data integration.
3. **Data preparation**: Cleansing, transforming, and pre-processing the data to prepare it for model training.
4. **Model training**: Training the ML model using an assortment of algorithms, such as supervised and unsupervised learning, on the prepared data.
5. **Model evaluation**: Evaluating the performance of the trained model using metrics such as accuracy, precision, and recall.
6. **Model deployment**: Deploying the trained model to a production environment, where it can be used to make predictions or decisions.

As shown in the following diagram, SageMaker offers a suite of services for each stage in the ML pipeline. SageMaker provides a Jupyter-based notebook environment that enables data scientists and developers to interactively work on their ML models and quickly iterate on their experiments. SageMaker offers various monitoring and debugging tools, including real-time metrics and logging, which enable customers to easily monitor and troubleshoot their models. SageMaker also provides a variety of pre-built algorithms and models, such as image classification, object detection, and NLP, which can be easily integrated into a customer's application.

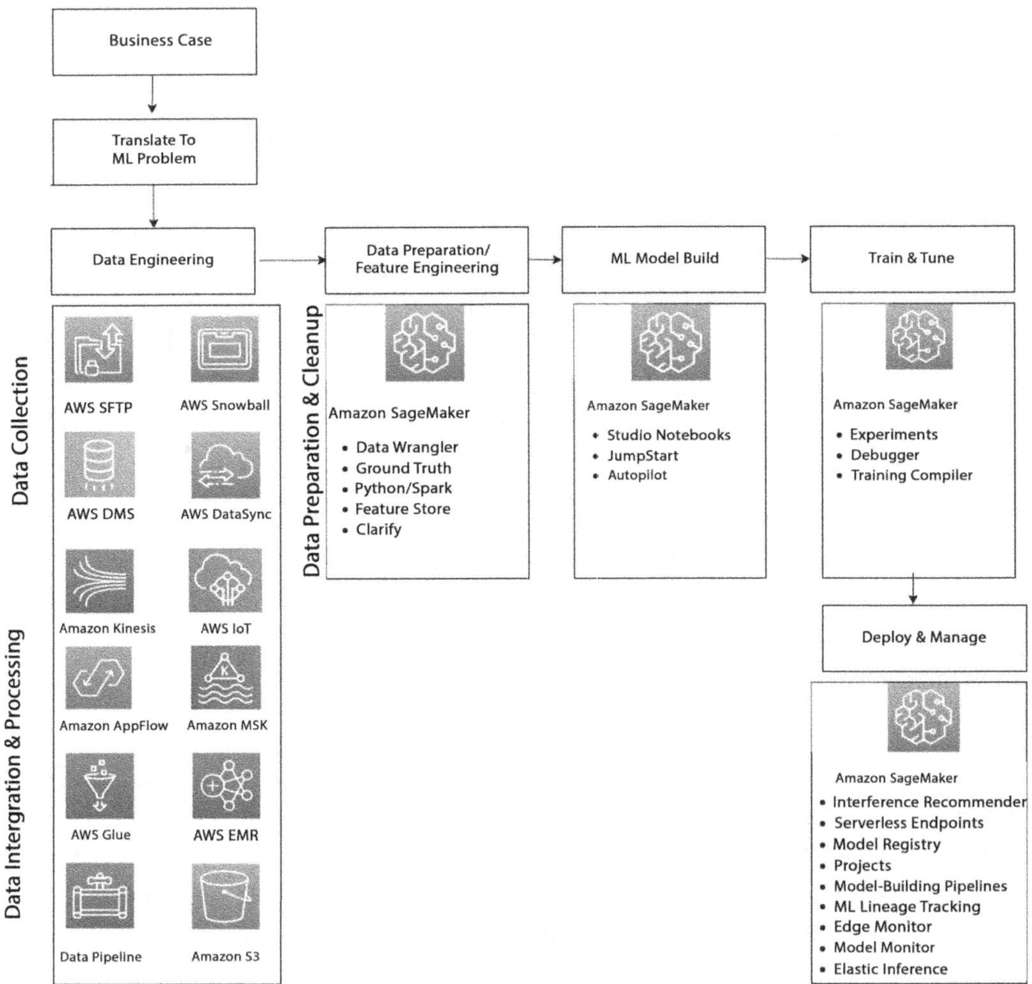

Figure 11.2: AI/ML pipeline and Amazon SageMaker

As shown in the preceding diagram, Amazon SageMaker's capabilities can be understood by examining four main categories: data preparation, model building, training and tuning, and deployment and management.

ML data preparation

Data preparation, also known as data preprocessing or feature engineering, is a crucial step in the ML pipeline. It involves cleaning, transforming, and preparing the data for model training and deployment. It is essential to understand the data first and figure out what kind of preparation is needed.

One common feature engineering case is dealing with missing data. Ignoring missing data can introduce bias into the model or compromise its quality. Several techniques can be employed to handle missing data, including imputing the missing values with the mean or median of the data, or utilizing ML algorithms that can effectively handle missing data. Another important case is when dealing with imbalanced data, where one class has significantly more samples than the others. This can impact the model's performance and can be addressed by oversampling the small dataset, undersampling the large dataset, or using techniques such as cost-sensitive learning or synthetic data generation.

Outliers can also negatively impact the model's performance and can be addressed through techniques such as data transformation, outlier removal, or the use of robust models. Text-based data can also be transformed into numerical columns through methods such as one-hot encoding or word embedding.

Data preparation is a crucial step in the ML pipeline, and feature engineering techniques can be employed to enhance the quality and effectiveness of the model. SageMaker provides a Jupyter-based notebook environment and data preparation tools, such as Data Wrangler, to simplify data preparation for machine learning.

Data Wrangler is a tool within SageMaker Studio that enables data scientists and developers to visually and interactively prepare and preprocess their data for machine learning. With Data Wrangler, you can import, analyze, organize, and add features to your data with no or minimal coding. Data Wrangler provides a simple and intuitive user interface that allows you to perform common data preparation tasks such as filtering, renaming, and pivoting columns, as well as more advanced tasks such as feature engineering, data visualization, and data transformations. Data Wrangler also integrates with other AWS services, such as Amazon S3 and Amazon Redshift, making it easy to import and export data from various data sources. Additionally, Data Wrangler enables you to add custom scripts and data transformations, providing flexibility and extensibility to meet your data preparation needs. After data preparation, the next step is to build the model.

ML model building

Amazon SageMaker Studio notebooks are a popular service within SageMaker that allows data scientists and ML engineers to build ML models without worrying about managing the underlying infrastructure. With Studio notebooks, data scientists and developers can effectively collaborate on their ML models and promptly refine their experiments using a Jupyter-based notebook environment that facilitates interactive work.

One of the key features of Studio notebooks is single-click sharing, which makes collaboration between builders very easy. Studio notebooks also support a variety of popular ML frameworks, such as PyTorch, TensorFlow, and MXNet, and allow users to install additional libraries and frameworks as needed. In addition to Studio notebooks, SageMaker also provides other "no-code" or "low-code" options for building models. **SageMaker JumpStart**, for example, offers pre-built solutions, example notebooks, and pre-trained models for common use cases, making it easy for customers to get started with ML.

SageMaker Autopilot is another offering that enables customers to automatically create ML models for building classification and regression models quickly. It automatically pre-processes the data, selects the best algorithm, and tunes the model, making it easy for customers to get started with ML, even if they have no prior experience. These tools make it easy for customers to quickly build, train, and deploy ML models on the AWS platform. Amazon SageMaker provides a variety of built-in algorithms that can be used for various ML tasks such as classification, regression, and clustering. Some of the popular built-in algorithms provided by SageMaker are as follows:

- **Linear Learner**: A supervised learning algorithm that can be used for classification and regression tasks
- **XGBoost**: A gradient-boosting algorithm that can be used for classification and regression tasks
- **Random Cut Forest**: An unsupervised learning algorithm that can be used for anomaly detection
- **K-Means**: A clustering algorithm that can be used to group similar data points
- **Factorization Machines**: A supervised learning algorithm that can be used for classification and regression tasks
- **Neural Topic Model**: An unsupervised learning algorithm that can be used for topic modeling

The preceding algorithms are designed to work well with large datasets and can handle sparse and dense data. These built-in algorithms can quickly train and deploy models on SageMaker and can be easily integrated into a customer's application. Additionally, SageMaker enables customers to utilize custom algorithms or import their pre-trained models.

After building the model, the next step is to train and tune it.

ML model training and tuning

After building an ML model, it needs to be trained by feeding it with training data as input. This process may involve multiple iterations of training and tuning the model until the desired model quality is achieved. Let's explore how AWS services can assist you in this journey.

- **Automating ML workflows with Amazon SageMaker Pipelines**: After developing an ML model, the next step involves training it with data, tuning its parameters, and deploying it for use. This process can be complex and time-consuming. With Amazon SageMaker Pipelines, you can automate the entire workflow for building models, from data preparation and feature engineering to model training, tuning, and validation. You can schedule SageMaker Pipelines to run automatically, triggered by specific events or on a predetermined schedule. Additionally, you can launch them manually when required. Amazon SageMaker Pipelines is ideal for teams looking to automate and orchestrate the entire ML lifecycle, ensuring end-to-end workflow management and CI/CD integration.
- **Experiment tracking with Amazon SageMaker MLflow**: Managing multiple ML experiments can be challenging. SageMaker MLflow is a fully managed capability that integrates the popular open source MLflow platform with Amazon SageMaker. Announced at AWS re:Invent 2023, this service enables data scientists and machine learning engineers to track experiments, package code into reproducible runs, and share and deploy models without managing the underlying infrastructure. SageMaker MLflow provides a central repository for tracking experiment metrics, parameters, artifacts, and models across teams, allowing for streamlined collaboration and enhanced model governance. It maintains full compatibility with open source MLflow APIs while adding AWS security features, identity management, and scalability. Users can track experiments locally on their computers, with results automatically synced to a centralized SageMaker MLflow tracking server. The service also offers seamless deployment of models through MLflow APIs and integrates with SageMaker's model registry and deployment, supporting both traditional ML and generative AI workloads. Amazon SageMaker MLflow is Ideal for data scientists and ML engineers who need to track experiments, manage models, and ensure reproducibility.

- **Hyperparameter optimization with SageMaker automatic model tuning**: Finding the optimal set of hyperparameters is crucial for achieving the best model performance. SageMaker automatic model tuning automates this process by testing thousands of parameter combinations to identify the most precise predictions. This not only saves time but also enhances model accuracy. It utilizes thousands of algorithm parameter combinations that are automatically tested to achieve the most accurate predictions, ultimately saving weeks of time and effort.
- **Managing experiments with Amazon SageMaker Experiments**: Keeping track of different model versions and their performance metrics is essential. SageMaker Experiments helps capture, organize, and compare every step of the experiment, making it easier to manage and track the model training process's progress. For example, a project involving customer clustering utilized SageMaker Experiments extensively to test various clustering algorithms and feature combinations.
- **Debugging and profiling with Amazon SageMaker Debugger**: During model training, it's essential to detect and diagnose issues such as overfitting or underfitting. **SageMaker Debugger** is another service that helps to debug and profile the training data throughout the training process. It enables data scientists and developers to detect and diagnose issues during training, such as overfitting or underfitting, by providing real-time metrics and alerts on commonly occurring error scenarios, including excessively large or small parameter values. SageMaker Experiments and SageMaker Debugger work together to provide an end-to-end solution for managing and tracking the ML pipeline. You can learn more about model training using SageMaker by visiting the AWS user docs here: `https://aws.amazon.com/sagemaker/train/?`.
- **Ensuring fairness with Amazon SageMaker Clarify**: Building trustworthy AI systems requires detecting potential biases and understanding model predictions. SageMaker Clarify helps improve your machine learning models by detecting potential bias and helping explain how these models make predictions. It provides tools to identify bias across the machine learning workflow – during data preparation, after model training, and in deployed models. SageMaker Clarify generates feature importance values to explain which attributes in the training data contribute most to a model prediction. The capability integrates seamlessly with Amazon SageMaker Studio to provide visual dashboards that help customers understand and explain model predictions. By providing these capabilities, SageMaker Clarify enables organizations to build greater trust in their AI systems and meet their fairness and compliance goals.

Now that your ML model is ready, it's time to deploy it in production.

ML model deployment and monitoring

Once you are satisfied with the quality of the ML model that you have built, it is time to deploy it in a production environment to realize its business benefits. Amazon SageMaker provides several options for deploying models, including the following:

- **SageMaker Endpoints**: It offers flexible options for deploying machine learning models based on your workload needs. You can choose real-time endpoints backed by dedicated instances, where you define the instance type and count to support consistent, high-throughput inference. For workloads with intermittent or unpredictable traffic, **SageMaker Serverless Inference** is available – it automatically provisions and scales compute capacity as needed, without requiring you to manage the infrastructure. This makes it easier to optimize costs while still delivering responsive inference for your models.
- **SageMaker Projects**: This is a service that helps to create end-to-end ML solutions with **continuous integration and continuous deployment** (CI/CD) capabilities. This allows for easy collaboration and version control of the models and code.
- **SageMaker Model Monitor**: This is a service that allows you to maintain the accuracy of deployed models by monitoring the model quality, data quality, and bias in production. It also allows you to detect and diagnose issues with the deployed model, such as drift or bias, and take corrective actions.

Amazon SageMaker offers a comprehensive and user-friendly platform for deploying ML models in production, featuring built-in support for serverless hosting, CI/CD, and monitoring and debugging capabilities to ensure the accuracy of deployed models over time.

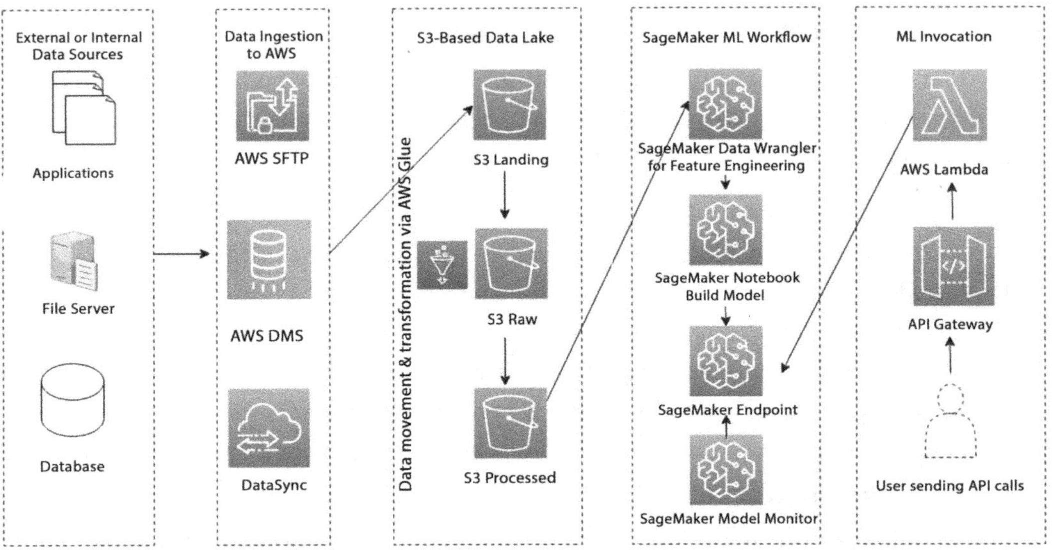

Figure 11.3: End-to-end ML pipeline in AWS

This reference architecture is an example of how an end-to-end ML pipeline can be implemented using AWS SageMaker services:

1. **Data ingestion**: Various types of data are ingested into an Amazon S3-based data lake. This source data can originate internally in an organization or come from external source systems. The data is typically stored in three S3 buckets, and AWS Glue is used to integrate and transform the data in the lake.
2. **Data preparation**: Amazon SageMaker then feature-engineers the data in the lake using Data Wrangler. This step involves cleaning and pre-processing the data and adding any necessary features to the dataset.
3. **Model building**: Using SageMaker notebooks, data scientists and ML engineers can create and train models using the prepared data. This step involves selecting an appropriate algorithm and instances, adjusting parameters to optimize performance, and training the model.
4. **Model deployment**: Once the model is trained, it is deployed as an endpoint in production using SageMaker Endpoints. The endpoint is then ready to be invoked in real time.

5. **Real-time invocation**: To invoke the SageMaker endpoint, an API layer is created using AWS API Gateway and AWS Lambda functions. This enables the endpoint to be accessed by various applications and systems in real time. You can also use Amazon SageMaker Batch Transform to perform batch inference on large datasets. With Batch Transform, you can easily process large volumes of data and get inference results in a timely and cost-effective manner.

This reference architecture demonstrates how AWS SageMaker services can be used to create an end-to-end ML pipeline, from data ingestion and preparation to model building, deployment, and real-time invocation.

You've now learned about various AWS AI/ML stacks and their use cases. It is essential to launch your model in production seamlessly and take action when any model drift occurs. Let's learn about **Machine Learning Operations** (**MLOps**) to understand how to put an ML model in production using AWS offerings.

Building ML best practices with MLOps

MLOps refers to the practices and tools used to manage the entire lifecycle of ML models, from development to deployment and maintenance. The goal of MLOps is to make deploying ML models to production as seamless and efficient as possible.

Managing an ML application in production requires a robust MLOps pipeline to ensure that the model is continuously updated and relevant as new data becomes available. MLOps helps automate the development, testing, and deployment of machine learning models. It manages the data and resources used to train and evaluate models, applying mechanisms to monitor and maintain deployed models to detect and address drift, data quality issues, and bias. It also enables communication and collaboration between data scientists, engineers, and other stakeholders.

The first step in implementing MLOps in AWS is to clearly define the ML workflow, including data ingestion, pre-processing, model training, and deployment stages. The following are the key MLOps steps for managing an ML application in production using AWS:

1. **Set up a data pipeline**: AWS offers a wide range of services for data pipeline management, including AWS Glue, Amazon Kinesis, and Amazon S3, which can be utilized to automate data ingestion, preprocessing, and storage. Use Amazon SageMaker Data Wrangler for data engineering.
2. **Use SageMaker for model training and deployment**: Utilize SageMaker for training and deploying machine learning models. As you learned, it provides a variety of built-in algorithms and tools for feature engineering, model training, and hyperparameter tuning. Use Amazon SageMaker Pipelines to build a training pipeline.
3. **Automate model testing and validation**: Use SageMaker Debugger and SageMaker Experiments to automate the testing and verification of your models.
4. **Implement CI/CD**: Utilize AWS CodePipeline and CodeBuild to automate the continuous integration and deployment of your ML models, enabling you to quickly and easily update your models as new data becomes available. Utilize source control management tools, such as Git, to store and manage your ML code and maintain version control.
5. **Monitor and maintain your models**: Use Amazon CloudWatch and Amazon SageMaker Model Monitor to track the performance of your models in production and take action when model drift occurs.
6. **Deploy models in real time**: Use Amazon SageMaker endpoints to deploy your models and make real-time predictions.
7. **Use auto-scaling**: Utilize auto-scaling to adjust the number of instances based on traffic levels dynamically.
8. **Security and Compliance**: Utilize SageMaker's built-in security features to safeguard your data and models, ensuring compliance with relevant industry and regulatory standards.

By following the preceding best practices, you can ensure that your ML models are built, trained, and deployed as efficiently and effectively as possible and perform well in production. You can learn more about how to build MLOps using Amazon SageMaker by referring to the AWS page here: `https://aws.amazon.com/sagemaker/mlops/`.

As you learned about AI/ML in this section, let's now explore the next technology trend: Generative AI, which is becoming mainstream and driving the modern industrial revolution.

Introduction to Generative AI

With the launch of ChatGPT, Generative AI has become a topic of widespread discussion. It has opened endless possibilities for revolutionizing the way we work today. This revolution is comparable to the innovation brought about by computers, and how the world moved from typewriters to shiny new computers, which made things more efficient. ChatGPT is just one dimension that shows the world the art of possibility and brings much-needed innovation that the world has been waiting for for a long time. Over the last two decades, you might have wondered who can challenge the position of Google in the AI market, especially Google Search. But, as you know, there is always a disruptor; if you don't innovate fast enough, someone else will do it. ChatGPT has brought that innovation into the hands of everyone.

Let's first understand what generative AI is.

Generative AI utilizes AI algorithms to generate new content that resembles existing content within a specific domain. This type of AI differs from other types of AI, which are designed to recognize patterns or make predictions based on existing data. Generative AI focuses on creating new data that did not previously exist. Generative AI can be used in various applications, from creating realistic images and videos to generating text and audio. For example, generative AI can be used to create realistic images of people, animals, or landscapes and develop new pieces of music or poetry that are similar to existing works. One of the advantages of generative AI is its ability to create personalized and unique content. With generative AI, it is possible to create custom content tailored to a specific audience or user based on their preferences or other data.

Generative AI uses **Large Language Models (LLMs)** to generate new text that is similar in style and content to an existing text. These models are trained on large amounts of text data and can generate coherent, natural-sounding text in various contexts. It has numerous applications, ranging from creating chatbots and virtual assistants to understanding and responding to natural language queries, generating text for marketing campaigns, and other content creation tasks. With generative AI that utilizes LLMs, it is possible to create personalized, engaging content that resonates with users and drives meaningful engagement.

Generative AI vocabulary

As you delve deeper into Generative AI, understanding the essential vocabulary is crucial for making informed decisions and effectively utilizing these technologies in real-world projects. You don't need to be a data scientist to grasp these terms, but as a solutions architect, knowing them will help you better plan solutions, communicate with technical teams, and guide clients on what's possible.

Start with **Artificial General Intelligence (AGI)**. While it may sound futuristic, AGI refers to AI that exhibits human-like thinking capabilities. It's not here yet, but it's the direction many researchers are working toward. What we use today are forms of narrow AI, such as LLMs. LLMs, such as GPT-4o and BERT, are excellent at understanding and generating text. You'll often use these models for chatbots, report generation, or summarization tasks. If you need similar functionality on a device with limited resources, such as a mobile app or an IoT device, you can consider **Small Language Models (SLMs)** such as DistilBERT or Phi2.

You'll also hear the term **Foundation Models (FMs)**. These are broader than LLMs – they work not just with text but also with images, audio, and video. Amazon Titan, for example, is AWS's foundation model that supports multimodal applications. FMs are what you use when you want to build something such as a virtual assistant that can read documents, analyze graphs, and talk back, all in one workflow.

When working with these models, remember that they operate on tokens, not just words. A context window is the limit of how many tokens a model can handle in one go. Bigger context windows are more beneficial for complex tasks, such as processing lengthy legal documents or analyzing historical chat logs.

One key risk is hallucination; this occurs when the model provides incorrect or fabricated answers that appear genuine. It's especially important to watch out for this in regulated industries, such as healthcare or banking. One of the best ways to reduce hallucinations is by using **Retrieval Augmented Generation (RAG)**. This technique pulls in real-time, factual data from trusted sources (such as an internal database or PDF) to provide the model with more accurate answers.

Ultimately, to achieve the best results with GenAI, you require effective prompts. Writing these prompts, known as prompt engineering, is part art and part science. Whether you're building a chatbot for customer service or a content generation tool for marketing, crafting your prompts well will help the AI deliver high-quality results.

Next, let's see where GenAI fits in the overall AI landscape.

Generative AI use case

The applications of generative AI span an exceptionally broad range of domains. The following are some of the most significant use cases:

- **Content creation:** Generative AI excels at creating new content, including text, images, audio, and video. For instance, Adore Beauty, an Australian online retailer, utilizes AWS's generative AI services to automatically generate product descriptions. This automation allows their catalog team to scale efficiently while keeping site content fresh, enhancing customer satisfaction. Here are some popular use cases of GenAI for content creation:
    - **Text generation**: Modern language models can write articles, stories, marketing copy, and technical documentation with increasing fluency. They excel at adapting to different tones, styles, and formats while maintaining coherence across long outputs.
    - **Image generation**: Text-to-image models, such as Midjourney, DALL-E, and Stable Diffusion, can create detailed visual content from textual descriptions, revolutionizing illustration, concept art, and design processes.
    - **Audio generation**: Models can generate music compositions, realistic speech, and sound effects, and even clone voices.
    - **Video generation**: Emerging text-to-video models can create short animated sequences and videos from textual prompts, though this remains less mature than other modalities.
    - **Code generation**: AI assistants can write functional code across multiple programming languages, complete functions based on comments or partial implementations, and even build simple applications.
- **Creative augmentation:** Generative AI can aid in ideation and brainstorming by generating diverse ideas and perspectives. Amazon Bedrock provides access to foundation models, such as Claude from Anthropic, which can develop creative content and assist in drafting marketing materials, enabling teams to overcome creative blocks and explore new directions. Let's look at some use cases:
    - **Ideation and brainstorming**: Generative AI excels at generating diverse ideas and perspectives, helping humans overcome creative blocks and explore new directions.
    - **Draft generation and iteration**: By producing initial drafts that can be refined, generative AI accelerates creative workflows for writers, designers, programmers, and other creators.

    - **Style transfer and adaptation:** AI can adapt existing content to new styles, tones, or formats, translating casual emails into formal business communications, converting prose to poetry, or reimagining images in different artistic styles.

- **Communication and interaction:** In customer service, generative AI enhances communication through chatbots and virtual assistants, facilitating seamless interaction. Rocket Mortgage utilizes AWS AI tools to optimize call center operations, resulting in significant time savings and enhanced customer service through automated responses to common queries. Here are some popular use cases:
    - **Conversational agents:** AI assistants can maintain increasingly natural, contextually aware conversations across a wide range of diverse topics.
    - **Personalized communication:** Generative AI can tailor messages to specific audiences or individuals, enhancing engagement in marketing, education, and customer service.
    - **Translation and localization:** Neural machine translation models can adapt content across languages while preserving tone, intent, and cultural nuances.
- **Data generation and augmentation:** Generative AI facilitates the creation of synthetic data for training machine learning models, particularly when working with limited or sensitive datasets. In the manufacturing sector, DXC Technology collaborated with AWS to generate synthetic image datasets, improving computer vision models for defect detection in manufacturing processes. Some examples are as follows:
    - **Synthetic data generation:** Creating realistic but artificial datasets for training other AI systems, particularly valuable in domains with privacy concerns or limited data availability.
    - **Data augmentation:** Generating variations of existing training data to improve the robustness of machine learning models.
    - **Simulation:** Creating realistic environments for testing systems, training agents, or modeling scenarios that are too costly or dangerous to reproduce in reality.
- **Software development:** Generative AI streamlines software development by automating code generation and documentation. Amazon Q Developer and AWS Transform are AI-powered assistants that help developers by generating real-time code suggestions, automating documentation, and identifying potential bugs, thereby accelerating the development process:

- **Code generation**: Producing functional code from specifications or natural language descriptions
- **Test generation**: Creating comprehensive test cases to validate software functionality
- **Documentation**: Automatically generating technical documentation from code bases
- **Debugging assistance**: Identifying potential bugs and suggesting fixes based on code patterns and best practices

Generative AI is truly revolutionizing multiple industries by automating tasks, improving customer experiences, and accelerating innovation. In the **banking, financial services, and insurance (BFSI)** sector, it helps automate customer support, generate reports, and enhance fraud detection through smarter analysis of transaction patterns. In retail, companies utilize GenAI to create personalized product recommendations, automatically generate marketing content, and optimize their supply chains. In the automotive industry, manufacturers are using it to simulate vehicle designs, create virtual assistants for in-car systems, and accelerate testing with synthetic data. **Healthcare and life sciences (HCLS)** organizations utilize GenAI to draft clinical documentation, assist in medical imaging analysis, and generate synthetic patient data for research purposes, all while ensuring patient privacy. Whether you're a financial analyst, a product designer, or a healthcare researcher, GenAI enables faster decisions, reduces costs, and unlocks new levels of productivity across every domain.

While in this section you've explored the basics of Generative AI, it's important to recognize that this is just the beginning. Generative AI is a vast and rapidly evolving field; understanding foundation models, training workflows, inference strategies, and safety mechanisms could easily fill an entire book.

The good news? You don't have to start from scratch.

If you're serious about building your GenAI knowledge, especially with hands-on skills in AWS and open source tools, check out the book *Generative AI for Software Developers*. It's tailored for solutions architects and builders like you who want practical guidance, covering the entire GenAI lifecycle from model selection to deployment and cost optimization. You can get your copy here: *Generative AI for Software Developers on Amazon:* `https://www.amazon.com/gp/product/B0DYZV9X9N/`.

This book will help you go beyond concepts and start building real-world applications confidently, whether you're working on chatbots, virtual assistants, recommendation engines, or creative content tools.

Generative AI in AWS

In recent years, everyone has jumped onto the bandwagon of generative AI: whether it is Google with its LLM called **Bidirectional Encoder Representations from Transformers** (**BERT**), or Microsoft putting its weight behind OpenAI's ChatGPT and embedding it in its Office 365 products and Bing search engine. While big tech companies are rolling out their offerings and launching hundreds of AI tools every day, Amazon has not been left behind. As shown in the following diagram, Amazon launched its offering in this space, with **Amazon Bedrock** providing a model marketplace, Amazon Nova as a foundation model, and Amazon Q offerings for business knowledge assistance and software development.

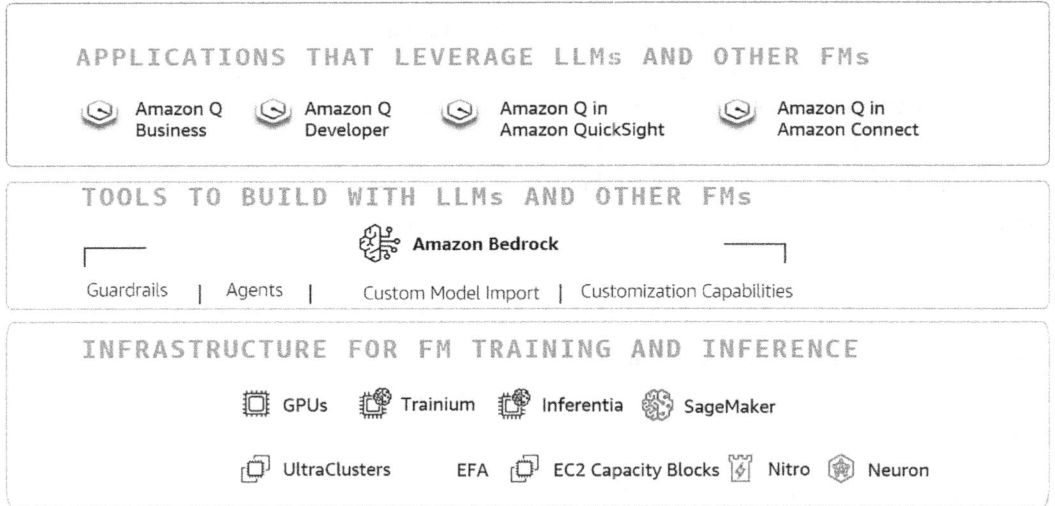

Figure 11.4: Generative AI tech stack in AWS

As shown in the preceding diagram, let's examine each layer of the service stack in detail, starting with the infrastructure for FM training and inference, and moving upward.

Infrastructure for FM training and inference

The foundation model revolution has fundamentally transformed the AI landscape, with models such as GPT, Llama, and BERT demonstrating unprecedented capabilities across language understanding, image generation, and multimodal tasks. However, these breakthroughs come with significant computational demands. Training foundation models requires massive computing resources, specialized accelerators, and optimized infrastructure. Similarly, deploying these models for inference at scale presents unique challenges in balancing performance, cost, and latency.

AWS has built a comprehensive ecosystem of hardware, software, and services specifically designed to address the demands of foundation model development and deployment.

Before diving into specific AWS offerings, let's understand the distinct phases of foundation model development and their unique infrastructure demands:

1. **Pre-training phase**: Creating foundation models from scratch with massive datasets, requiring extraordinary compute power and specialized hardware for weeks or months of continuous training.
2. **Fine-tuning phase**: Adapting pre-trained models for specific use cases, requiring significant but more targeted compute resources.
3. **Inference phase**: Deploying models to serve predictions, requiring optimized hardware for cost-effective, low-latency responses at scale.
4. **Management and optimization phase**: Continuous monitoring, iteration, and optimization of models throughout their lifecycle.

Let's explore how AWS's purpose-built infrastructure supports each of these phases.

At the heart of AWS's AI infrastructure strategy are custom-designed chips that address the unique requirements of foundation models.

AWS Trainium

AWS Trainium is a specialized chip designed by AWS to accelerate deep learning model training and make it more cost-effective. If you're working with large-scale AI models, especially foundation models such as GPT or BERT, Trainium gives you an edge by offering significant performance improvements over traditional GPUs. The latest version, Trainium 2, delivers up to 4 times the performance of the earlier model and can reduce training costs by as much as 65%, while also training models up to 2 times faster compared to equivalent GPU-based EC2 instances.

This makes a significant difference when training transformer-based architectures, which serve as the backbone of modern language models and generative AI applications. Whether you're doing pre-training (from scratch) or fine-tuning (adapting existing models to your specific industry), Trainium handles the heavy lifting efficiently. It's particularly powerful in managing dense and sparse matrix operations, which are common in deep learning workloads.

For example, a healthcare research company training a medical language model can use Trainium to reduce its compute costs and time-to-market. By using AWS Trainium-powered instances, such as Trn2, you can build and scale your GenAI solutions confidently, with the added benefit of AWS infrastructure reliability.

AWS Inferentia

AWS Inferentia is AWS's custom-built chip designed to run machine learning models, particularly LLMs, more efficiently during the inference phase, when the model makes predictions or generates outputs. This phase is critical when transitioning from training your model to deploying it in production, such as powering chatbots, virtual assistants, recommendation engines, or real-time analytics.

The latest version, Inferentia 2, offers up to 4 times the throughput and 10 times lower latency than the first generation. That means your GenAI applications can respond more quickly and handle a higher volume of user requests without slowing down. It's designed to work exceptionally well with transformer models, which are widely used in nearly all current generative AI applications.

Inferentia 2 is designed with features such as dynamic batching, sequence length flexibility, and KV caching, which are crucial for efficient LLM serving. These optimizations help reduce overhead and make sure that even large, complex prompts are processed quickly and cost-effectively.

In terms of pricing, AWS reports up to 50% lower costs when using Inferentia 2 compared to similar GPU-based instances for inference workloads. For example, a fintech company using LLMs to automate customer support could deploy their model on Inf2 instances and serve thousands of requests with better speed and reduced compute expenses.

So, if you're deploying a GenAI application at scale, especially something such as a real-time Q&A assistant or a personalization engine, AWS Inferentia gives you high performance and cost efficiency, making it easier to maintain great user experiences without breaking your budget.

NVIDIA GPU

In addition to its custom chips, such as Trainium and Inferentia, AWS also provides full support for NVIDIA GPUs, offering flexibility to choose the best hardware for your specific AI and ML workloads. Suppose you or your team already have experience with NVIDIA's ecosystem, or you need support for certain deep learning libraries and frameworks. In that case, AWS's NVIDIA-powered instances offer a reliable and powerful option.

At the top end, you have P5 instances, which are powered by NVIDIA H100 Tensor Core GPUs – currently NVIDIA's most advanced GPU for training huge foundation models. These are ideal when you're working with billion-parameter models such as GPT-4-sized systems, and you want the best performance available on the market.

Next, P4d instances use NVIDIA A100 GPUs, which are excellent for both training and inference. Many enterprises building LLMs, computer vision, or recommendation engines rely on P4d to handle large-scale training runs with high throughput and energy efficiency.

For more balanced workloads that may include training, inference, and even graphics tasks such as rendering or visualization, G5 instances are a strong choice. These are powered by NVIDIA A10G GPUs, which are cost-effective for use cases such as real-time personalization, digital twin modeling, or content generation.

Whether you're training a new AI model from scratch or deploying it across production environments, AWS's partnership with NVIDIA ensures that you have access to the latest GPU infrastructure to scale your projects with confidence and performance.

UltraCluster

If you're working on training extremely large FMs, those with hundreds of billions or even trillions of parameters, AWS UltraCluster is the infrastructure built for that scale. Think of it as a supercomputer purpose-built for deep learning, combining thousands of accelerators such as AWS Trainium or NVIDIA GPUs into a single, interconnected high-performance cluster.

What makes UltraCluster special is its **Elastic Fabric Adapter (EFA)**, which delivers near-line-rate, low-latency networking. This means massive models can be trained faster with minimal delays in data movement across compute nodes. It also scales horizontally, allowing you to run training jobs using thousands of accelerators while maintaining synchronization efficiency, critical for model convergence.

UltraClusters also offer automated management, including fault tolerance and recovery, so your training runs are not only fast but also resilient. This is especially useful during the pre-training phase, where training a large foundation model can take days or weeks.

For example, Amazon itself has used UltraClusters to train its Nova foundation models, which are now available through Amazon Bedrock. If you're building enterprise-grade GenAI products and need supercomputer-level power with cloud flexibility, UltraCluster is your go-to platform.

Amazon SageMaker HyperPod

Amazon SageMaker HyperPod is AWS's specialized infrastructure designed for training foundation models with maximum reliability and speed. When you're running large-scale model training, especially for LLMs or multimodal AI, you can't afford downtime or failures that force you to start over. That's exactly the problem HyperPod solves.

It provides a persistent, distributed training cluster with built-in checkpointing and automatic recovery, so even if a few nodes fail during a multi-day training job, your model continues training from the last saved point, without requiring a restart of the entire process. This setup can reduce training interruptions by up to 80%, helping you avoid days of lost effort and compute costs.

HyperPod supports both AWS Trainium and NVIDIA GPU-based accelerators, and is pre-configured with optimized ML libraries, including DeepSpeed, Hugging Face Transformers, and PyTorch Lightning. It seamlessly integrates into the Amazon SageMaker ecosystem, providing integration with experiment tracking, model versioning, and deployment tools.

This makes SageMaker HyperPod ideal for organizations that train large models in-house; whether you're pre-training a custom language model or fine-tuning an existing one for your specific domain, such as healthcare, law, or finance.

End-to-end infrastructure for the FM lifecycle

The following table provides a structured overview of how AWS services map to each phase of the foundation model lifecycle. From pre-training massive language models to deploying them at scale, each phase requires a combination of specialized compute, storage, and supporting tools. AWS offers a comprehensive set of services, ranging from custom silicon, such as Trainium and Inferentia, to managed infrastructure solutions, such as SageMaker HyperPod, that help you manage every step of the machine learning pipeline efficiently.

Phase Number	Phase Name	Compute Options	Storage	Supporting Services	Phase Description
Phase 1	Pre-training from Scratch	Trn1 or P5 instances	Amazon FSx for Lustre	AWS Glue, Amazon S3, SageMaker Data Wrangler	Training foundation models from scratch using massive datasets and high-performance compute.
Phase 2	Fine-tuning and Adaptation	Trn1, P5, or P4d instances	Amazon EBS or FSx	SageMaker Experiments, Processing, CloudWatch	Adapting pre-trained models to specific tasks or domains such as healthcare, finance, or legal.
Phase 3	Inference and Deployment	Inf2, G5, or P4d instances	N/A	SageMaker Model Monitor, AWS Auto Scaling, API Gateway	Deploying trained models for real-time inference and integrating them into applications.
Phase 4	Management and Optimization	N/A	N/A	SageMaker Feature Store, Step Functions, CloudWatch, IAM	Managing model versions, monitoring performance, and automating ML workflows for long-term scalability.

Table 11.1: AWS service for FM lifecycle

The preceding table mapping helps you, as a solutions architect, design, build, and manage scalable generative AI systems tailored to your business or domain-specific needs. By aligning the right AWS services with each phase of model development, you can reduce costs, enhance performance, and expedite deployment timelines while ensuring reliability and security.

Cost-optimization strategies for FM infrastructure

Optimizing costs is essential when working with FMs, as these workloads often involve high compute and storage demands. AWS provides a range of strategies to help you manage expenses while still maintaining performance and scalability.

First, by choosing AWS custom silicon such as Trainium and Inferentia, you can cut costs significantly – up to 65% for training and 40% for inference compared to traditional GPU-based instances. This is especially useful when you're running large-scale training jobs or deploying models in production for continuous inference.

Next, for fault-tolerant workloads, using EC2 Spot Instances through SageMaker managed spot training can reduce costs by up to 90%. This is ideal for batch jobs or long-running training tasks that can be interrupted and resumed without loss of data.

You should also focus on right-sizing your deployments. AWS SageMaker offers multi-model endpoints, serverless inference, and autoscaling, allowing you to match compute resources to real-time traffic. This ensures you're not overpaying during idle times.

To prevent unnecessary spending on unused resources, automated lifecycle management is crucial. With SageMaker Studio and related tools, you can set policies to shut down development environments automatically when not in use.

Finally, for inference, apply optimization techniques such as knowledge distillation, quantization, and model pruning. These approaches reduce the model's computational needs while keeping performance close to the original. This helps especially when deploying to edge devices or cost-sensitive cloud environments.

Let's bring the cost-optimization strategy to life with a real-world example. A global financial services firm wanted to deploy a generative AI chatbot to handle thousands of daily customer queries across multiple languages. They initially trained an LLM using GPU-based EC2 instances, but soon realized that training and inference costs were climbing fast. To reduce expenses and scale effectively, they adopted several AWS cost-optimization strategies.

They transitioned their training to Amazon SageMaker using Trainium-based Trn1 instances, resulting in a nearly 60% reduction in training costs compared to their previous setup. For inference, they deployed their model using Inf2 instances (Inferentia 2), which reduced the inference cost per request by over 40%.

To handle unpredictable traffic, the team implemented SageMaker Serverless Inference and Auto Scaling, ensuring that compute resources were only used when needed. During development, they set up automated policies in SageMaker Studio to shut down idle notebooks and training jobs, cutting dev environment costs by nearly 30%.

They also applied knowledge distillation, creating a smaller, faster version of the model that retained over 90% accuracy. This reduced compute requirements and allowed more concurrent users to access the chatbot without latency issues.

By combining AWS's custom silicon, spot pricing, right-sizing tools, and model optimization techniques, the firm achieved a 70% overall cost reduction while maintaining high performance and availability.

This example shows how you can leverage AWS's ecosystem to make your GenAI projects both powerful and cost-efficient. Now, let's move forward and look at Amazon Bedrock, the middle layer that simplifies working with foundation models through an API-based approach.

Amazon Bedrock

Amazon Bedrock is made for businesses seeking to develop generative AI applications without the complexity of training or managing models and infrastructure. As shown in the following diagram, Bedrock is a fully managed AWS service that provides easy access to a variety of high-performing FMs from leading AI providers, including Anthropic (Claude), Cohere, AI21 Labs, Meta (Llama), and Amazon Nova. You can experiment with multiple models using a unified API, making it easier to test and choose the best fit for your use case.

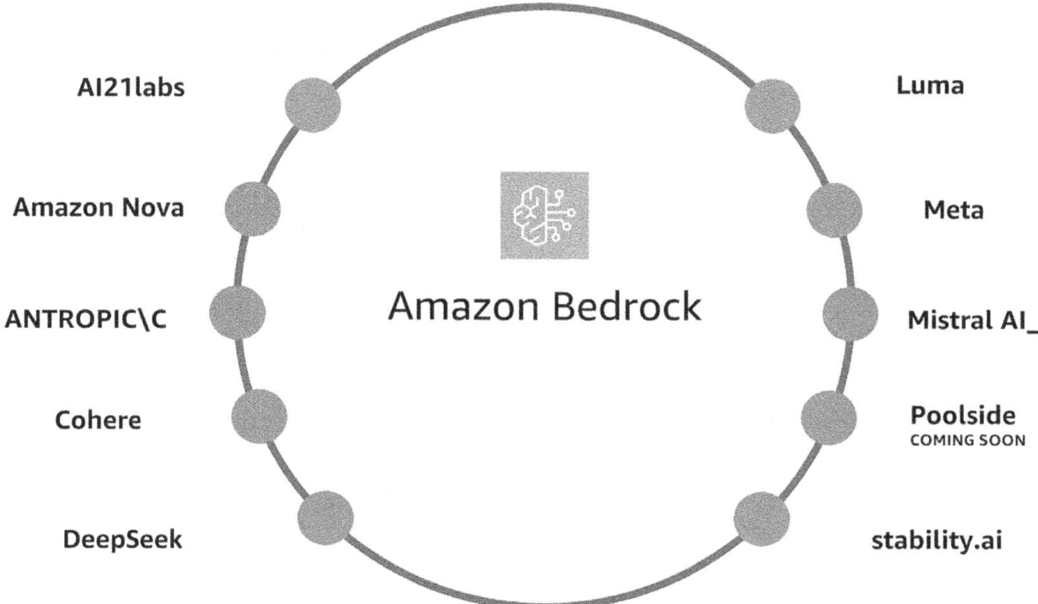

Figure 11.5: Amazon Bedrock FMs ecosystems

What sets Amazon Bedrock apart is its enterprise-ready capabilities. You can securely run your applications using VPC endpoints, apply encryption for data at rest and in transit, and manage access with IAM roles. This ensures that your generative AI solutions are private, compliant, and secure, essential for those operating in regulated industries such as finance or healthcare.

Amazon Bedrock also supports fine-tuning, so you can customize foundation models to reflect your domain-specific language or customer preferences without retraining from scratch. It includes tools for model evaluation, letting you compare performance across models in real business scenarios. For example, Thomson Reuters uses Amazon Bedrock to integrate generative AI into its legal and financial content platforms. This enables them to deliver summarized insights and draft documents efficiently, thereby improving customer productivity.

You can learn more about Amazon Bedrock by referring to the AWS page here: `https://aws.amazon.com/bedrock/`.

Benefits

Here are some of the key benefits of using Amazon Bedrock:

- **Unified access to pre-trained models**: Amazon Bedrock offers a vast repository of pre-trained models across various domains, including natural language processing, computer vision, and more. This extensive collection enables developers to leverage state-of-the-art models without the need for extensive training or data preparation, thereby significantly reducing the time-to-market for AI applications.
- **Scalability and performance**: Built on the robust AWS infrastructure, Amazon Bedrock ensures high scalability and performance. It can handle large volumes of requests with minimal latency, making it suitable for both small-scale prototypes and large-scale production deployments.
- **Cost-effectiveness**: By abstracting the complexities of model deployment and management, Amazon Bedrock enables cost savings. Customers pay only for the resources they use, avoiding the expenses associated with maintaining their own AI infrastructure.
- **Security and compliance**: AWS is renowned for its strong security practices, and Amazon Bedrock is no exception. It adheres to stringent security standards and compliance requirements, ensuring that customer data and applications are protected.

Features

AWS has provided a broader feature set for Amazon Bedrock, like Amazon SageMaker. Let's start learning about them:

Amazon Bedrock Guardrails

Bedrock Guardrails is one of the most powerful features designed to help you deploy generative AI responsibly and securely across your organization. As you scale AI-powered applications, ensuring consistent safety, compliance, and content quality becomes critical, especially when working across multiple foundation models from different providers. That's where Guardrails comes in.

With Bedrock Guardrails, you can define and enforce content filtering rules that apply uniformly across all supported models – whether you're using Claude from Anthropic, Titan and Nova from Amazon, or Llama from Meta. This model-agnostic architecture means you only need to set policies once, and they'll work regardless of which foundation model your app uses.

Here are some real-world examples of how this helps:

- A **healthcare chatbot** can utilize guardrails to block unauthorized medical advice or personal health queries that should only be addressed by certified professionals.
- An **e-commerce assistant** can maintain brand tone and prevent AI from suggesting competitor products or making inaccurate promises.

Guardrails actively scans both user prompts and model responses to prevent unsafe outputs. This not only protects against harmful content, bias, or misinformation but also defends against prompt injection attacks, where users try to manipulate the AI to bypass rules.

So, if your business operates in regulated industries such as finance, legal, or healthcare, or if maintaining your brand's integrity is vital, Amazon Bedrock Guardrails gives you the tools to go live with confidence while ensuring responsible and safe use of AI.

Amazon Bedrock multi-agent collaboration

Bedrock multi-agent collaboration is a powerful feature that brings human-like teamwork to generative AI systems. Instead of relying on a single AI model to solve complex business tasks, you can now build multi-agent systems, where each AI agent has a specialized role, just like members of a human team. This is particularly helpful when one task requires different skills, such as data lookup, reasoning, calculations, or content generation.

With this setup, you define individual agents for specific functions, such as a knowledge agent for retrieving documents, a calculator agent for performing financial computations, or a writer agent for generating content. You then build a collaborative workflow, with an orchestrator agent acting as the central coordinator. The orchestrator breaks down the task, assigns subtasks to the relevant agents, and compiles the results into one coherent response.

For example, in customer service, a complex support ticket might require accessing product manuals, performing a warranty check, and calculating a refund amount. With multi-agent collaboration, the orchestrator agent routes each task to the right sub-agent, collects their responses, and delivers a complete answer to the customer. This improves resolution accuracy and response time.

Even more impressively, you can combine different FMs from Bedrock in the same solution; using Claude for reasoning, Titan for summarization, and Cohere for search, all working together through this framework. This not only maximizes each model's strength but also gives you full control over problem-solving pipelines without custom ML engineering.

Multi-agent collaboration in Bedrock allows you to scale intelligent task automation across departments, from legal and finance to operations and marketing, enabling your business to handle complex workflows with AI-powered precision and efficiency.

Intelligent Prompt Routing and caching

When you're deploying generative AI applications at an enterprise scale, cost and latency become major concerns, especially when usage volumes grow rapidly. Amazon Bedrock addresses these challenges with two powerful features: Intelligent Prompt Routing and prompt caching, both designed to help you maintain performance without overspending.

With Intelligent Prompt Routing, Bedrock can automatically direct each prompt to the FM that best fits the task. For example, on a customer service platform, simple FAQs, such as "What is my order status?", can be handled by a smaller, faster, and more cost-effective model, while complex billing or policy questions can be routed to a more advanced model, such as Claude or Nova, for more accurate reasoning. This smart distribution helps you balance response quality with cost efficiency, making sure you don't overuse high-end models for simple tasks.

In parallel, prompt caching enables you to store responses to frequently asked prompts. When a user sends a similar query again, Bedrock can deliver the answer instantly from the cache, without re-running the model. This significantly reduces response times and also cuts down inference costs, especially in high-traffic apps such as chatbots, support portals, or internal knowledge bases.

Together, these features enable your organization to scale generative AI applications cost-effectively, without compromising user experience or encountering performance bottlenecks. They're especially valuable when you're deploying in production environments where every millisecond and dollar counts.

Model fine-tuning and customization

While FMs offer strong general-purpose capabilities, most enterprise applications need more than just "out-of-the-box" performance. To unlock true business value, you often need a model that understands your specific industry terminology, internal processes, or customer interaction patterns. That's where fine-tuning becomes essential, and Amazon Bedrock makes it easier than ever.

With Bedrock's fine-tuning features, you can tailor foundation models such as Claude, Cohere, or Titan to your unique business context. This process significantly improves the model's accuracy on specialized tasks, ensures it produces consistent outputs that match your brand's voice, and enables it to grasp internal jargon and workflows that generic models might overlook.

For example, if you work in healthcare, you can fine-tune a model to understand complex medical terms and generate clinical summaries. If you're in finance, the model can be trained to handle compliance-specific language or generate precise investment summaries. The best part? Bedrock abstracts the complexity. You provide examples of prompts and desired responses, and Bedrock takes care of adapting the model; no need to write training pipelines or manage infrastructure.

This approach empowers business teams and subject matter experts to drive AI customization, instead of relying entirely on ML engineers. It reduces the technical barrier, making it faster and easier for organizations to build high-performing, domain-specific AI tools that perfectly fit their needs.

Continued pre-training

For organizations with deep customization needs, Amazon Bedrock also supports a more advanced technique known as continued pre-training. Unlike fine-tuning, which focuses on teaching the model specific input-output behavior, continued pre-training allows you to further train an FM on a large corpus of your domain-specific text, such as industry reports, internal documentation, support tickets, and more.

This method enables the model to internalize your field's unique linguistic patterns, technical terms, and document structures, resulting in a more context-aware and knowledgeable AI system. It's especially useful when working in complex domains, such as law, medicine, manufacturing, or finance, where general-purpose models may lack the depth of understanding required to be truly effective.

For example, a legal firm can utilize continued pre-training to familiarize the model with case law citations and contract language. A biotech company might train the model on scientific papers and lab protocols to support research automation. By doing so, the model doesn't just "respond better" – it thinks more like your business, resulting in richer, more accurate responses across a wide range of tasks.

Amazon Bedrock handles the infrastructure and training orchestration, allowing you to focus on providing the data, while AWS takes care of scaling and efficiency. Continued pre-training empowers your team to build expert-level AI assistants that are aligned with your organization's knowledge and mission.

Model distillation

When you're building generative AI solutions for environments with tight resource constraints or low-latency requirements, using large FMs isn't always practical. That's where Amazon Bedrock's model distillation capabilities come into play. This approach enables you to create a smaller, faster version of an FM – ideal for use cases such as mobile apps, IoT devices, or real-time systems where speed and efficiency are crucial.

Here's how it works: A large, powerful model acts as the "teacher," and a compact "student" model is trained to mimic its behavior. The student learns how to produce similar outputs for a given set of inputs, capturing the most relevant knowledge while trimming down size and complexity. This means you get a model that is highly optimized for specific tasks, without needing the full compute power or infrastructure that larger models require.

The results are powerful:

- **Lower costs**: Smaller models use fewer resources, making them cost-effective for **high-volume applications**, such as chat support or content personalization.
- **Reduced latency**: They respond faster, making them ideal for **real-time applications** such as virtual assistants or recommendation engines.
- **Edge deployment**: These distilled models are lightweight enough to run on **edge devices**, enabling smart assistants in retail kiosks, manufacturing floors, or wearable tech.
- **Smarter resource usage**: You maximize efficiency while still delivering high-quality AI experiences.

This capability is especially valuable for industries such as retail, automotive, manufacturing, or healthcare, where deploying AI on edge or mobile platforms can unlock new levels of customer engagement, automation, and operational insight.

With this, Amazon Bedrock doesn't just offer powerful models; it provides a comprehensive framework for building scalable, cost-efficient, and tailored generative AI systems that meet real business needs.

Now that you've explored the infrastructure and middle layers, let's move on to the top layer of the generative AI stack, where applications come to life and transform how you deliver value to users.

Amazon Q

Amazon Q is AWS's generative AI-powered assistant, designed to help businesses improve productivity, decision-making, and customer service across multiple departments. It's built to make working with AWS services, software development, data analysis, and enterprise operations faster, smarter, and more efficient, regardless of your organization's size or industry. What makes Amazon Q powerful is that it offers various tools tailored to different roles within your business. Let's have a look at each product in detail.

Amazon Q CLI

Recently launched at re:invent 2024, Amazon Q CLI is a powerful command-line interface that brings the capabilities of Amazon Q directly to your terminal, helping you interact with AWS services faster and more efficiently. Designed for developers, DevOps engineers, and cloud architects, this tool makes it easier to get answers, troubleshoot issues, and generate code without switching away from your current development environment.

One of the key features of Amazon Q CLI is its ability to understand natural language queries about AWS. You can ask questions about specific services, deployment steps, best practices, or even error messages, and Q will respond with accurate, actionable guidance. It's like having an AWS expert available right in your terminal. Another major advantage is its context awareness. Amazon Q CLI can analyze your local project files, such as CloudFormation templates, Terraform scripts, or CDK stacks, and provide explanations or troubleshooting advice based on what it finds. This makes it especially useful for debugging infrastructure code or reviewing policy documents.

Additionally, Q CLI supports code generation and step-by-step guidance for tasks such as setting up new AWS resources, configuring IAM roles, or writing Lambda functions. It helps you reduce time spent searching documentation or writing boilerplate code. You can learn more about QCLI by referring to the AWS doc link here: `https://docs.aws.amazon.com/amazonq/latest/qdeveloper-ug/command-line.html`.

Amazon Q Business

Q Business is a game-changing AI-powered assistant tailored to help your organization access and use information more efficiently. Built with advanced ML and NLP, it connects seamlessly with your company's internal data, whether it's stored in SharePoint, Salesforce, Confluence, email systems, or file servers through connectors. For a complete list, refer to `https://docs.aws.amazon.com/amazonq/latest/qbusiness-ug/connectors-list.html`.

Instead of digging through thousands of documents, employees can ask Amazon Q Business questions in plain language, such as, "What's our onboarding policy?" or "Summarize last quarter's financial report." The assistant understands the context, retrieves relevant data, and provides clear and concise responses. This enables teams to make faster, data-driven decisions without needing technical skills.

It also supports content generation and task automation, which enhances productivity across various departments, including HR, sales, marketing, and legal. For example, a sales rep can use it to instantly generate customer summaries, while HR can automate policy responses.

Security is built in – Amazon Q Business respects existing access controls and ensures that sensitive information is only shared with authorized users, helping to maintain compliance and data privacy standards. This makes it ideal for industries with strict governance, such as finance, healthcare, and government.

In short, Amazon Q Business transforms your enterprise knowledge into a smart, accessible resource, enabling your employees to accomplish more with less time and effort, while keeping your data secure.

Amazon Q Developer and AWS Transform

Amazon Q Developer is designed to assist developers by streamlining the development process and making it more efficient. It utilizes smart AI technology to provide code suggestions, fix errors, and integrate with various AWS services, enabling developers to save time and focus on creating innovative solutions.

AWS Transform, a capability built on Amazon Q Developer, is revolutionizing how organizations modernize their critical enterprise applications. This AI-powered solution dramatically accelerates the modernization journey for legacy systems built on .NET, Java, Mainframe, and VMware technologies:

- For **Mainframe environments**, AWS Transform facilitates the complex migration from COBOL applications to cloud-native architectures, preserving decades of business logic while enabling cloud scalability.

- **Java applications** benefit from automated refactoring to contemporary frameworks and dependency updates.
- **Migrations from .NET** to .NET Core or .NET 6+ become streamlined processes, reducing the need for costly rewrites and refactoring.
- **VMware workloads** can be optimized and transformed for AWS cloud environments with unprecedented efficiency.

What distinguishes AWS Transform is its ability to deliver these complex transformations with detailed explanations of changes, support for incremental modernization approaches, and maintenance of application functionality throughout the process. By reducing what would typically be months or years of manual effort into manageable, automated workflows, AWS Transform empowers enterprises to overcome technical debt and leverage modern cloud capabilities, without sacrificing the institutional knowledge embedded in their legacy systems.

Amazon Q in QuickSight

Amazon Q in QuickSight is a powerful generative AI assistant that changes how you and your team interact with data. Traditionally, working with business intelligence tools required writing complex queries or relying on analysts. With Amazon Q, that's no longer the case. You can now ask questions in plain English, such as "What were the sales last quarter by region?", and Amazon Q will translate that into an accurate query and deliver the results instantly.

This democratizes data access across your organization, empowering non-technical users, such as sales representatives, marketers, or HR professionals, to explore data and make informed decisions without requiring SQL skills or technical support. It dramatically reduces the time to insight and makes analytics part of everyone's workflow.

Beyond just answering questions, Amazon Q in QuickSight also provides intelligent summaries, identifies trends, and spots anomalies in your data. For example, it might highlight a sudden dip in customer satisfaction scores or an unexpected spike in expenses, before you even have a chance to ask.

By making data more accessible, intuitive, and interactive, Amazon Q in QuickSight helps businesses become truly data-driven. It not only boosts productivity but also ensures that decision-making is based on real-time insights rather than outdated reports or guesswork. Whether you're tracking KPIs, analyzing performance, or exploring new opportunities, Amazon Q in QuickSight makes analytics simple, fast, and actionable for everyone.

Amazon Q in Amazon Connect

Q in Amazon Connect brings generative AI directly into your contact center, transforming the way customer service is delivered. With this integration, agents are equipped with a real-time AI assistant that helps them respond faster, more accurately, and with greater context. Instead of manually searching knowledge bases or switching between multiple screens, agents can now ask Amazon Q for help and instantly get the information they need, whether it's a policy detail, an order status, or a product recommendation.

This dramatically boosts agent productivity by automating routine tasks, such as summarizing calls, suggesting next-best actions, or drafting follow-up emails. The assistant also understands the flow of conversation and adjusts its responses accordingly, ensuring consistency and quality across customer interactions.

Even better, Amazon Q can analyze customer sentiment in real time and predict needs before they're explicitly stated. For example, if a customer sounds frustrated, Q can alert the agent and suggest more empathetic messaging or offer a proactive solution, turning a potential complaint into a positive experience.

By integrating with Amazon Connect, businesses can reduce response times, improve first-call resolution, and increase customer satisfaction – all while lowering operational overhead. It's a smarter, faster, and more scalable way to deliver exceptional service in today's digital-first world.

Knowledge check

The following are some sample questions that align with the difficulty and scope typically found in the *AWS Certified Solutions Architect – Professional* exam:

1. A multinational company is deploying an ML solution using Amazon SageMaker to predict customer churn. The solution involves multiple stages, including data preparation, model training, and deployment. The company is particularly concerned about fairness and bias in their ML models, as they operate in various regions with diverse customer demographics. The company wants to implement a robust bias detection mechanism that can be triggered periodically to ensure that the deployed models do not exhibit significant bias over time. The training data is stored in Amazon S3, and the models are deployed using SageMaker endpoints. Additionally, the solution must ensure that the data used for bias detection is securely isolated and adheres to the company's data governance policies.

Which combination of actions will effectively meet these requirements?

a. Configure the application to use Amazon SageMaker Clarify for bias detection by setting up an AWS Lambda function that triggers a SageMaker Clarify processing job on a schedule. Ensure that the IAM roles used by SageMaker and Lambda have the necessary permissions to access the data in S3 and perform the Clarify processing job.
b. Use AWS Step Functions to create a workflow that pulls the `sagemaker-model-monitor-analyzer` built-in SageMaker image, runs it in a SageMaker processing job, and stores the results in Amazon S3. Configure AWS Glue to periodically trigger this workflow.
c. Implement AWS Glue Data Quality to perform bias detection by scheduling periodic jobs that analyze the model predictions and compare them against a baseline. Use Amazon S3 to store the results and set up Amazon CloudWatch alarms to notify the team of any significant bias detected.
d. Use SageMaker notebooks to manually run bias detection scripts that compare the model predictions against historical data. Schedule these notebooks to run periodically using Amazon EventBridge (CloudWatch Events).

Answer: a.

Explanation:

a. **Correct**. Amazon SageMaker Clarify is specifically designed to help detect bias in an ML model. It provides tools to detect pre-training and post-training bias, making it an ideal choice for this scenario. AWS Lambda can be used to automate the triggering of SageMaker Clarify processing jobs on a schedule. This ensures that bias detection is performed periodically without manual intervention. IAM roles are crucial for ensuring that both SageMaker and Lambda have the necessary permissions to access the data in Amazon S3 and execute the Clarify processing job. This aligns with the requirement for secure and isolated use of training data.
b. Incorrect. While AWS Step Functions and the `sagemaker-model-monitor-analyzer` image can be used for model monitoring, they are not specifically tailored for bias detection like SageMaker Clarify. Additionally, this option does not explicitly mention the use of IAM roles for secure data access.

c. Incorrect. AWS Glue Data Quality is more suited for data quality checks rather than bias detection in ML models. It does not provide the specialized tools that SageMaker Clarify offers for bias and fairness.

d. Incorrect. Using SageMaker notebooks for manual bias detection scripts lacks automation and scalability. It also does not provide the robust framework that SageMaker Clarify offers for bias detection.

2. A data scientist has developed a neural network for text classification. The model achieves a training accuracy of 98% but a validation accuracy of 70%. The model employs three dense layers with 512 neurons each, each followed by ReLU activation. Which combination of techniques should be implemented to address this performance gap?

   a. Add more dense layers and increase the number of neurons to make the model more complex.

   b. Implement dropout layers between dense layers and reduce the number of neurons to prevent co-adaptation.

   c. Increase the learning rate and add more training epochs to reach better convergence.

   d. Remove one dense layer and reduce the learning rate to simplify the model.

   Answer: b.

   Explanation:

   a. Incorrect. Adding more layers or neurons would increase model complexity, likely exacerbating overfitting.

   b. **Correct**. Dropout layers randomly "turn off" a proportion of neurons during training, which prevents neurons from co-adapting excessively, forces the network to learn more robust features, and acts as a form of model ensemble. Reducing neurons: Having too many neurons can lead to the model memorizing training data. Reducing them will decrease model complexity, improve generalization, and reduce the risk of overfitting.

   c. Increasing the learning rate and epochs does not address overfitting and may even exacerbate it by allowing the model to memorize the training data more effectively.

   d. While simplifying the model might help, just removing a layer and reducing the learning rate doesn't directly address the co-adaptation issue that dropout helps solve.

3. A data science team is using Amazon SageMaker to train a deep learning model for image classification. The team needs to monitor the model's training progress and wants to be alerted when the validation loss starts increasing while the training loss continues to decrease. Additionally, the security team requires all API calls to be logged for compliance purposes. Which combination of services should be implemented to meet these requirements with minimal effort?

    a. Enable AWS CloudWatch to monitor training metrics, create a Lambda function to track API calls, and use Amazon SNS for notifications.

    b. Use AWS CloudTrail for API logging, configure CloudWatch metrics for model training, and set up CloudWatch alarms with SNS notifications.

    c. Implement custom logging using Amazon S3, create a Lambda function to monitor metrics, and use Amazon SES for email notifications.

    d. Set up Amazon EventBridge to monitor API calls, use Amazon Kinesis for metric streaming, and configure SNS topics for alerts.

    Answer: b.

    Explanation:

    a. Incorrect. Using Lambda to track API calls is unnecessary when CloudTrail provides this functionality natively.

    b. **Correct.** It provides the most efficient and comprehensive solution with minimal effort. AWS CloudTrail automatically logs all API calls made to Amazon SageMaker. It provides audit trails for compliance requirements. No custom code is required for implementation. Amazon SageMaker automatically publishes training metrics to CloudWatch and can track both training and validation loss metrics. It has built-in integration that requires no additional setup. CloudWatch alarms with SNS can create alarms based on metric conditions. It can also set up mathematical expressions to compare training and validation loss. It is easy to integrate with **social networking services** (**SNS**) for notifications.

    c. Incorrect. Custom logging with S3 requires more effort and code compared to using built-in services. Amazon SES would require additional setup compared to SNS.

    d. Incorrect. EventBridge is unnecessary for this use case, and Kinesis would be overengineering the solution when CloudWatch metrics are already available.

4. An AI engineer is developing a complex application that requires real-time code assistance to increase productivity. The team has already deployed several AWS services and seeks to implement a solution that provides contextual code suggestions, answers technical questions about AWS services, and aids in troubleshooting issues. Which AWS service would be most appropriate for this use case?

    a. Amazon SageMaker Studio
    b. Amazon Q Developer
    c. Amazon Comprehend
    d. AWS DeepRacer

    Answer: b.

    Explanation:

    a. Incorrect. Amazon SageMaker Studio is primarily an ML development environment for building, training, and deploying ML models, not a general-purpose coding assistant.
    b. **Correct.** Amazon Q Developer is the correct answer because it's AWS's AI-powered developer tool specifically designed to provide real-time assistance for coding tasks within AWS environments. Amazon Q Developer offers contextual code completion and generation based on your code base and comments, as well as answers to technical questions about AWS services and best practices, and troubleshooting assistance for AWS service errors and issues.
    c. Incorrect. Amazon Comprehend is incorrect because it's a natural language processing service for extracting insights from text, not a developer assistance tool.
    d. Incorrect. AWS DeepRacer is incorrect because it's a reinforcement learning service focused on autonomous racing, completely unrelated to developer assistance.

5. A company wants to deploy a generative AI application that allows their marketing team to create product descriptions with specific brand voice guidelines. They need the solution to be fully managed with minimal operational overhead, support prompt engineering capabilities, and provide fine-tuning options for model customization. Which AWS service best meets these requirements?

    a. Amazon SageMaker JumpStart
    b. Amazon Bedrock
    c. Amazon Comprehend
    d. AWS Lambda with custom ML code

Answer: b.

Explanation:

a. Incorrect. While SageMaker JumpStart does provide pre-trained models, it requires more technical expertise and operational management compared to Bedrock. It doesn't offer the same streamlined access to foundation models specifically tailored for generative AI tasks.

b. **Correct**. Amazon Bedrock is a fully managed service that provides access to FMs from leading AI companies through a unified API, eliminating the need for operational overhead in managing the infrastructure. It offers built-in prompt engineering capabilities through features such as prompt flows and prompt management, which enable the marketing team to create consistent product descriptions that adhere to brand voice guidelines. Amazon Bedrock supports model customization through fine-tuning, allowing the company to adapt FMs to better align with their specific brand voice and product terminology. Bedrock provides access to various models from providers such as Anthropic (Claude), AI21 Labs (Jurassic), Amazon's own Titan models, and others, allowing the company to select the most suitable model for its use case.

c. Incorrect. Amazon Comprehend is primarily an NLP service for extracting insights and relationships from text, rather than generating new content, such as product descriptions.

d. Incorrect. This approach would require significant development effort, model hosting, and management overhead, which contradicts the requirement for a fully managed solution with minimal operational overhead.

Summary

To remain competitive, organizations must leverage emerging technologies to foster innovation and maintain agility. Cloud providers such as AWS make these advanced technologies readily accessible for experimentation and integration into various use cases.

In this chapter, we explored the fundamentals of **machine learning (ML)** and **artificial intelligence (AI)**, highlighting how AWS services facilitate the creation of a comprehensive ML pipeline. This pipeline guides an ML workload from its initial concept to full-scale production. We examined the three tiers of AWS AI/ML services, beginning with the foundational ML infrastructure that AWS offers for training models.

We then delved into Amazon SageMaker, a pivotal component of AWS's ML technology stack, which supports the building, training, deployment, tuning, and monitoring of ML models. Following this, we discussed the top layer of AWS AI services, which includes pre-trained models accessible via simple API calls, eliminating the need for in-depth ML expertise. These services cater to a wide range of applications, including vision, speech recognition, chatbots, forecasting, and personalized recommendations. Additionally, you learned the importance of applying ML best practices through MLOps to manage ML workloads effectively in production.

The chapter also provided an in-depth look at generative AI and how AWS supports the development of generative AI applications using Amazon Bedrock and Amazon Q. We explored key use cases for generative AI and dissected the various layers and offerings of the Amazon generative AI stack.

Finally, we reviewed the essential features of Amazon Bedrock, such as its multi-agent capabilities, guardrails, model fine-tuning, and model distillation. We also explored Amazon Q and its diverse product offerings, including Amazon Q Business, Amazon Q Developer, as well as AWS Transform, Amazon Q for QuickSight, and Amazon Q for Connect.

Part 5

Applying Architectural Patterns and Reference Architectures

Here, you'll apply your AWS knowledge to design real-world architectures. You'll start by learning how to build data lakes and adopt data mesh or lakehouse patterns using tools such as Lake Formation and S3. Then, you'll shift focus to modern application architectures, where you'll design microservices and event-driven systems with tools such as API Gateway, Lambda, and Amazon EventBridge. This part will help you connect the dots across services and build scalable, modular, and resilient systems.

This part of the book includes the following chapters:

- *Chapter 12, Data Lake Patterns: Integrating Your Data Across the Enterprise*
- *Chapter 13, Building Microservices and Event-Driven Architectures in AWS*

12

Data Lake Patterns: Integrating Your Data Across the Enterprise

Today, technology companies such as Amazon, Google, Netflix, and Facebook drive immense success by gaining insight from their data and understanding what customers want. They personalize the experience in front of you, for example, movie suggestions from Netflix, shopping suggestions from Amazon, and search selections from Google. All of their success is attributed to their ability to analyze data and utilize it for customer engagement. That's why data is now considered the new gold.

Picture this: you are getting ready to watch television, excited to see your favorite show. You sit down and try to change the channel, only to find that the remote control is not working. You try to find batteries. You know you have some in the house, but you can't remember where you put them. Panic sets in, and you finally give up searching, heading to the store to buy more batteries.

A similar pattern repeats over and over in today's enterprises. Many companies possess the data they need to survive and thrive. Still, they often require assistance in accessing the data effectively, transforming it into actionable and valuable information, and distributing that information to the right people in a timely manner.

The data lake pattern is particularly useful in today's enterprises to overcome this challenge. In this chapter, you will learn about data lakes through the following main topics:

- The definition of a data lake
- The purpose of a data lake
- Data lake components

- AWS Lake Formation
- Data lake best practices
- Key metrics of a data lake
- Lakehouse and data mesh architecture
- Choosing between a data lake, lakehouse, and data mesh architecture
- Building a data lake for generative AI

Let's delve into the world of data and explore ways to gain meaningful insights from data.

Definition of a data lake

Data is everywhere today. It was always there, but it was too expensive to keep. With the massive drop in storage costs, enterprises are retaining much of what they previously discarded. And this is the problem. Many enterprises collect, ingest, and purchase vast amounts of data, but they often need help gaining meaningful insights from it. Many Fortune 500 companies are generating data faster than they can process it. The maxim that *data is the new gold* has a lot of truth, but just like gold, data needs to be mined, refined, and presented effectively.

The data that companies generate is richer than ever before, and the amount they produce is growing at an exponential rate. Fortunately, the processing power required to harness this data deluge is increasing and becoming more affordable. Cloud technologies, such as AWS, allow us to process data almost instantaneously and on a massive scale.

A **data lake** is an architectural approach that enables the management of multiple data types from a wide variety of structured and unstructured sources through a unified set of tools. A data lake is a centralized repository for storing structured, semi-structured, and unstructured data at any scale. Data can be stored in its raw form without any transformations, or some preprocessing can be done before it is consumed. From this repository, data can be extracted and utilized to populate dashboards, perform analytics, and drive machine learning pipelines, thereby deriving insights and enhancing decision-making. Hence, the data stored in a data lake is readily available for categorization, processing, analysis, and consumption by diverse organizational groups.

Data lakes enable you to break down data silos and consolidate data into a single, central repository, such as Amazon **Simple Storage Service (S3)**. You can store various data formats at any scale and at a low cost. Data lakes provide you with a single source of truth and allow you to access the same data using a variety of analytics and machine learning tools.

The following diagram shows the key components of modern data architecture:

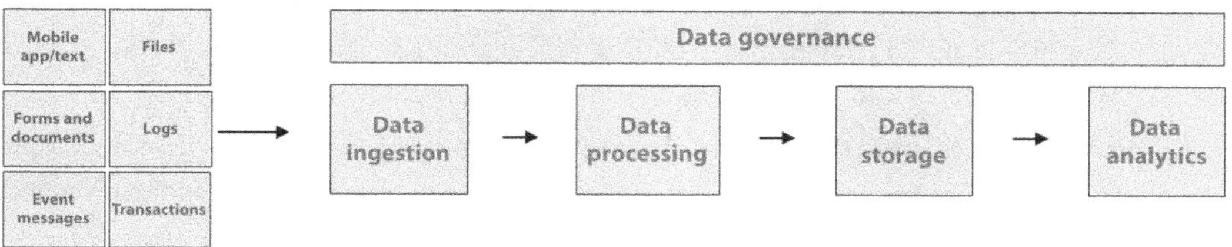

Figure 12.1: Key components of a modern data lake

The preceding diagram illustrates modern data architecture, where data is ingested in various formats, including logs, files, messages, and documents. After that, this data is processed according to business needs, and the processed data is stored and utilized by various businesses for data analytics.

The key considerations of modern data lakes include the ability to handle the increasing volume, velocity, and variety of data, where each component, such as data storage and processing, should be independently scalable, and data should be easily accessible by various stakeholders.

The purpose of a data lake

You might not need a data lake if your company is a bootstrap start-up with a small client base. However, even the smaller entities that adopt the data lake pattern in their data ingestion and consumption will be nimbler than their competitors. Adopting a data lake will come at a high cost, especially if you already have other systems in place. The benefits must outweigh these costs, but this might be the difference between outperforming your competitors and being relegated to the ranks of failed companies in the long run.

The purpose of a data lake is to provide a single store for all data types, structures, and volumes, to support multiple use cases such as big data analytics, data warehousing, machine learning, and more. It enables organizations to store data in its raw form and perform transformations as needed, making it easier to extract value from data. When you are building a data lake, consider the following five Vs of big data:

- **Volume**: This refers to the sheer amount of data generated and stored by various sources, such as social media, **Internet of Things** (IoT) devices, and transactional systems. For example, a large retailer may generate and store petabytes of data from online and in-store sales transactions, customer behavior data, and product information.

- **Velocity**: This refers to the speed at which data is generated and processed. Data can be generated in real time, such as stock market prices or weather readings from IoT devices. For example, a financial firm may need to process high-frequency stock market data in real time to make informed trading decisions.
- **Variety**: This refers to the different types of data generated by various sources, including structured data (e.g., relational databases), semi-structured data (e.g., XML and JSON), and unstructured data (e.g., text, images, and audio). For example, a healthcare organization may need to process and analyze a variety of data types, including electronic medical records, imaging data, and patient feedback.
- **Veracity**: This refers to the uncertainty, ambiguity, and incompleteness of data. Big data often comes from sources that cannot be controlled, such as social media, and may contain errors, inconsistencies, and biases. For example, a political campaign may utilize social media data to gain insights into public opinion, but must also be aware of the potential for false or misleading information.
- **Value**: This refers to the potential of data to provide insights and drive business decisions. The value of big data lies in its ability to reveal patterns, trends, and relationships that can inform strategy and decision-making. For example, a retail company may use big data analytics to identify purchasing patterns and make personalized product recommendations to customers.

Some of the benefits of having a data lake are as follows:

- **Increasing operational efficiency**: Finding and deriving insights from your data becomes more accessible with a data lake.
- **Making data more accessible across organizations and breaking down silos**: Having a centralized location will enable everyone in the organization to access the same data if they are authorized to do so.
- **Lowering transactional costs**: Having the correct data at the right time and with minimal effort will invariably result in lower costs.
- **Removing load from operational systems, such as mainframes and data warehouses**: This is crucial. Having a dedicated data lake enables you to optimize it for analytical processing, allowing you to optimize your operational systems to focus on their primary mission of supporting day-to-day transactions and operations.

C-suite executives are no longer asking "*Do we need a data lake?*" but are instead asking "*How do we implement a data lake?*". They realize that many of their competitors are doing the same, and studies have shown that organizations derive real value from data lakes. A survey by Aberdeen found that enterprises that deploy a data lake within their organization can outperform competitors by 9% in incremental revenue growth. You can find more information on the Aberdeen survey here: `https://tinyurl.com/r26c2lg`.

Components of a data lake

The concept of a data lake can have varying meanings for different individuals. As previously mentioned, a data lake can comprise various components, including both structured and unstructured data, raw and processed data, and a combination of different data types and sources. As a result, there is no one-size-fits-all approach to creating a data lake. The process of constructing a clean and secure data lake can be time-consuming and may take several months to complete, as there are numerous steps involved in the process. Let's take a look at the components that need to be used when building a data lake:

- **Data ingestion**: The process of collecting and importing data into the data lake from various sources such as databases, logs, APIs, and IoT devices. For example, a data lake may ingest data from a relational database, log files from web servers, and real-time data from IoT devices.
- **Data storage**: The component that stores the raw data in its original format without any transformations or schema enforcement. Typically, data is stored in a distributed filesystem such as Hadoop HDFS or Amazon S3. For example, a data lake may store petabytes of data in its raw form, including structured, semi-structured, and unstructured data.
- **Data catalog**: A metadata management system that keeps track of the data stored in the data lake, including data lineage, definitions, and relationships between data elements. For example, a data catalog may provide information about the structure of data in the data lake, including who created it, when it was created, and how it can be utilized.
- **Data processing**: The component that performs transformations on the data to prepare it for analysis. This can include data cleansing, enrichment, and aggregation. For example, a data processing layer may perform data cleansing to remove errors and inconsistencies from the data or perform data enrichment to add additional information to the data.

- **Data analytics**: The component that provides tools and technologies for data analysis and visualization. This can include SQL engines, machine learning libraries, and visualization tools. For example, a data analytics layer may provide an SQL engine for running ad-hoc queries or a machine learning library for building predictive models.
- **Data access**: The component that provides access to the data in the data lake, including data APIs, data virtualization, and data integration. For example, a data access layer may provide APIs for accessing data in the data lake or through data virtualization, providing a unified view of data from multiple sources.

It is common to divide a data lake into different zones based on data access patterns, privacy and security requirements, and data retention policies. Let's look at various data lake zones.

Data lake zones

Creating a data lake can be a lengthy and demanding undertaking that requires substantial effort to establish workflows for data access and transformation, configure security and policy settings, and deploy various tools and services for data movement, storage, cataloging, security, analytics, and machine learning. In general, many data lakes are implemented using the following logical zones:

- **Raw zone**: This is the initial storage area for incoming data in its original format without any modification or transformation. The data is stored as-is, allowing for easy access and preservation of its original state. An example use case for this zone could be storing social media data as raw JSON files for later analysis.
- **Landing zone**: This is a temporary storage area for incoming data that undergoes basic validation, quality checks, and initial processing. Data is moved from the raw zone to the landing zone before being transferred to the next stage. An example use case for the landing zone is performing data quality checks, such as duplicate removal and data type validation, on incoming sales data before it is moved to the next stage.
- **Staging zone**: This is where data is transformed and integrated with other data sources before being stored in the final storage area. The data is processed in this zone to prepare it for analysis and to help ensure consistency and accuracy. An example use case for the staging zone is transforming incoming sales data into a common format and integrating it with other data sources to create a unified view of the data.
- **Analytics zone**: This is optimized for data analysis and exploration. Data stored in this zone is made available to data scientists, business analysts, and other users for reporting and analysis. An example use case for this zone could be storing sales data in a columnar format for faster querying and analysis.

- **Data mart zone:** This is used to create isolated and curated data subsets for specific business or operational use cases. This zone is optimized for specific business requirements and can be used to support reporting, analysis, and decision-making. An example use case for the data mart zone could be creating a data subset of sales data for a specific product line for analysis.
- **Archive zone:** This is the final storage area for data that is no longer needed for active use but must be retained for compliance or historical purposes. Data stored in this zone is typically rarely accessed and is optimized for long-term storage. An example use case for this zone could be storing customer data that is no longer needed for active use but must be retained for compliance purposes.

Each zone in a data lake has specific security and access controls, data retention policies, and data management processes tailored to the particular use case and data requirements.

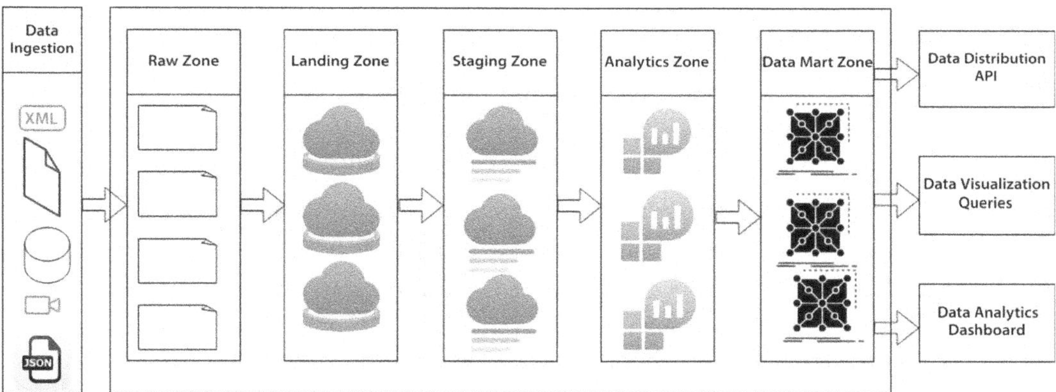

Figure 12.2: The different zones of a data lake

As shown in the preceding diagram, the flow of data among the different zones in a data lake is a key aspect of the architecture. It typically follows these steps:

1. Raw data is collected and stored in the raw zone in its original format.
2. The data is then transferred to the landing zone, where it undergoes initial processing, including basic validation, quality checks, and duplicate removal.
3. After the initial processing, the data is moved to the staging zone, where it undergoes transformation and integration with other data sources to prepare it for analysis.
4. The processed data is then moved to the analytics zone, where it is optimized for analysis and made available to data scientists, business analysts, and other users for exploration and reporting.

5. Based on specific business or operational requirements, subsets of the data may be created and stored in the data mart zone for specific analysis and reporting needs.

This flow ensures that the data is processed and stored to support its intended use, meeting the required security, privacy, and compliance requirements. The flow also helps ensure data consistency and accuracy as the data moves through the different processing stages. If data is no longer needed for active use but needs to be retained for compliance or historical purposes, you can also create an archive zone for long-term storage.

These zones and their names should not be taken as dogma. Many folks use other labels for these zones and might use more or fewer zones. But these zones capture the general idea of what is required for a well-architected data lake.

An analogy that can help understand how the various zones in a data lake work is the process of gold mining, distribution, and sale. Gold is a scarce resource and is often found in small quantities combined with many other materials that have no value to the people mining it.

When it's mined in industrial quantities, excavators dump dirt into a truck or a conveyor belt (this is the ingestion step in the landing zone and raw zone). This dirt goes through a cleansing process (analogous to the data quality step in the curated or staging zone). The gold is set aside, turned into ingots or bars, and transported for further processing, such as curation in the analytics zone. Finally, these gold bars can be melted down and transformed into jewelry or industrial parts, allowing individuals to utilize them for various purposes, which aligns with the data mart zone.

Data lakes in AWS with Lake Formation

Lake Formation is a fully managed data lake service provided by AWS, enabling data engineers and analysts to build a secure data lake. Lake Formation provides an orchestration layer that combines AWS services, such as S3, **Relational Database Service** (**RDS**), EMR, and Glue, to ingest and clean data while offering centralized, fine-grained data security management.

Lake Formation enables you to establish your data lake on Amazon S3 and start incorporating readily accessible data. As you incorporate additional data sources, Lake Formation will scan those sources and transfer the data into your Amazon S3 data lake. Utilizing machine learning, Lake Formation will automatically structure the data into Amazon S3 partitions, convert it into more efficient formats for analytics, such as Apache Parquet and ORC, and eliminate duplicates to identify matching records, thereby enhancing the quality of your data.

It enables you to establish all necessary permissions for your data lake, which will be enforced across all services that access the data, such as Amazon Redshift, Amazon Athena, and Amazon EMR. This eliminates the need to reapply policies across multiple services, ensuring consistent enforcement and adherence to those policies, thereby streamlining compliance.

Lake Formation relies on AWS Glue behind the scenes, where Glue crawlers and connections facilitate the connection to and identification of the raw data that requires ingestion. Glue jobs then generate the necessary code to transfer the data into the data lake. The Glue Data Catalog organizes the metadata, and Glue workflows link together crawlers and jobs, enabling the monitoring of individual work processes. The following diagram shows a comprehensive view of the AWS data lake:

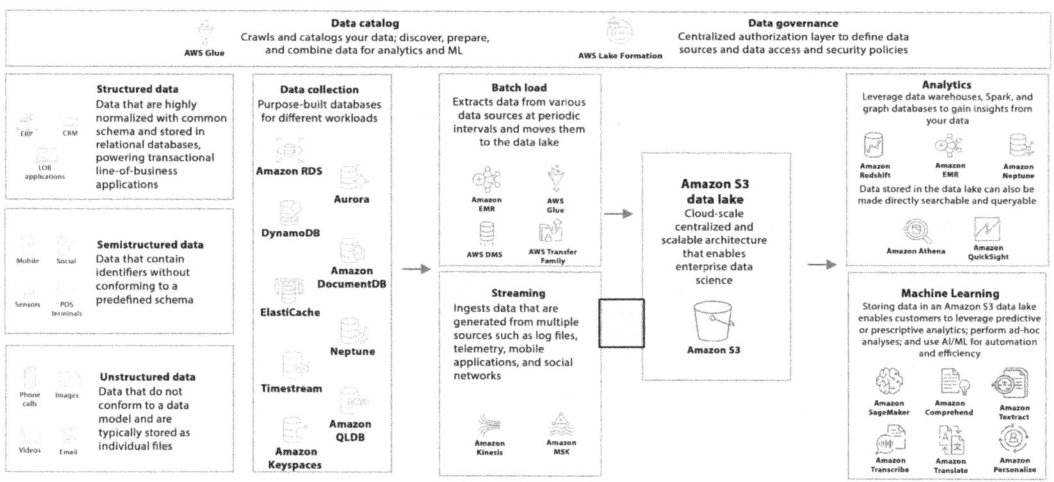

Figure 12.3: AWS data lake components

As shown in the preceding diagram, here are the steps to create a data lake in AWS using Lake Formation:

1. Set up an AWS account and create an **Identity and Access Management** (**IAM**) role with the necessary permissions to access Lake Formation and other AWS services.
2. Launch the Lake Formation console and create a new data lake.
3. Ingest data into the data lake from a variety of sources such as Amazon S3, Amazon Redshift, Amazon RDS, and others.
4. Define the data catalog by creating tables, columns, and partitions, and then register them with the Lake Formation data catalog.

5. Set up data access and security policies using IAM and Lake Formation to control who can access the data and what actions they can perform.
6. Perform transformations on the data in the data lake using AWS Glue or other tools.
7. Analyze the data using Amazon QuickSight, Amazon Athena, or other analytics tools.

Let's say you want to create a data lake to store customer data from an e-commerce website. For this, you need to ingest customer data from your e-commerce website's database, which is stored in Amazon RDS, into the data lake. Then, you can define the data catalog by creating tables for customer information, purchase history, and product information, and registering them with the Lake Formation data catalog. You can perform transformations on the customer data in the data lake using AWS Glue to convert the data into a common format, remove duplicates, and perform data validation. Finally, you can analyze the customer data using Amazon QuickSight or Amazon Athena to create visualizations and reports on customer behavior and purchase patterns.

The steps and tools used may vary depending on the requirements and data sources. These steps are provided as a general guide and may need to be adapted based on the specific needs of your use case. You can refer to the AWS Lake Formation guide for more details: `https://docs.aws.amazon.com/lake-formation/latest/dg/getting-started.html`.

From a data security perspective, the Lake Formation admin sets up permissions on the database, table, and column, and grants granular row and column-level permissions to data lake users for data access. Lake Formation integrates with AWS IAM to establish security controls. Lake Formation enhances the search functionality by enabling text-based and faceted search across all metadata. It also adds attributes, such as data owners and stewards, as table properties, along with column properties and definitions, including data sensitivity levels. Additionally, it offers audit logs for data lake auditing during data ingestion and cataloging, while notifications are published to Amazon CloudWatch events and the console.

BMW adopted AWS Lake Formation to build fine-grained access controls, enabling table-, column-, and row-level data visibility. This allowed different teams to access just the subsets of data they needed, eliminating excessive data duplication. As a result, BMW achieved up to 25% savings in compute and storage costs, while improving governance and reducing compliance overhead. You can learn about how BMW built its **Cloud Data Hub** (**CDH**) on Amazon S3, which manages over 10 PB of data, 1,500 data assets, and serves 9,000 users across more than 1,000 use cases. Initially, the CDH supported only coarse-grained access to entire datasets, and this led to inefficiencies and data duplication. You can read the full case study in the AWS *Big Data* blog: `https://aws.amazon.com/blogs/big-data/how-bmw-streamlined-data-access-using-aws-lake-formation-fine-grained-access-control/`.

Now, let's look at some of the best practices to build your data lake in AWS.

Data lake best practices

In this section, you will learn about the best practices to improve the usability of your data lake implementation that will empower users to get their work done more efficiently and allow them to find what they need more quickly.

Centralized data management

Depending on your company culture, and regardless of how robust your technology stack is, you may encounter a mindset roadblock among your ranks, where departments within the enterprise still maintain a tribal mentality and resist sharing information outside of their domain.

For this reason, when implementing your data lake, it is critical to ensure that this mentality does not persist in the new environment. Establishing a well-architected enterprise data lake can significantly reduce the impact of these silos.

Centralized data management refers to the practice of storing all data in a single, centralized repository rather than in disparate locations or silos. This makes managing, accessing, and analyzing data easier, eliminating the risk of data duplication and inconsistency.

A use case for centralized data management could be a large e-commerce company that stores customer data in multiple systems, such as an online store, a call center database, and a mobile app. The company could centralize this data in a data lake to improve data accuracy, ensure consistency, and provide a single source of truth for customer data.

In this scenario, the process of centralized data management would involve extracting data from various systems, cleaning and transforming it to ensure consistency, and then storing it in a data lake. This centralized repository can be accessed by multiple departments within the company, including marketing, sales, and customer service, to support their decision-making and enhance the customer experience.

By centralizing data, the company can improve data governance, minimize the risk of data duplication and inconsistency, and reduce the time and effort required to access and analyze the data. This ultimately leads to improved business outcomes and competitive advantage.

Data governance

One of the biggest challenges when implementing a data lake is the ability to fully trust the current data's integrity, source, and lineage.

For the data in a lake to provide value, more is needed than just dumping the data into the lake. Raw data will not be valuable if it lacks structure and a connection to the business, and if it is not cleansed and deduplicated. If data governance were built for the lake, users would be able to trust the data in the lake. Ungoverned data that lacks data lineage is significantly less valuable and trustworthy than data with these qualities. **Data lineage** refers to the complete history of a data element, including its origin, transformations, movements, and dependencies. Ungoverned data increases regulatory and compliance risks related to privacy.

To fully trust and track the data in the lake, we need to provide context to the data by instituting policy-driven processes to enable the classification and identification of the ingested data. You need to establish a data governance program for the data lake and leverage any existing data governance frameworks. Wherever possible, we should use existing data governance frameworks and councils to govern the data lake.

The enormous volume and variability of data in today's organizations complicate the tagging and enrichment of data with information about its origin, format, lineage, organization, classification, and ownership. Most data is fluid and dynamic, and performing exploratory data analysis to understand it is often essential to determine its quality and significance. Data governance provides a systematic structure to gain an understanding of and confidence in your data assets. To set a foundation, let's agree on a definition of data governance.

Data governance refers to the set of policies, processes, and roles that organizations establish to ensure the quality, security, and availability of their data. Data governance aims to enhance data management and decision-making by ensuring that data is accurate, consistent, secure, and accessible to those who need it.

A use case for data governance could be a healthcare organization that collects patient data from various sources, including electronic medical records, clinical trials, and wearable devices. The organization must ensure that this data is protected and used in a manner that complies with relevant privacy regulations and patient consent requirements.

The process of implementing data governance in this scenario would involve defining policies and processes for data collection, storage, use, and protection. This could include methods for data classification, data access controls, data quality control, and data auditing. The organization would also establish clear roles and responsibilities for data governance, including data stewards, administrators, and security personnel.

If the data's integrity can be trusted, it can inform decisions and provide valuable insights. Data governance is imperative, yet many enterprises need to place a higher value on it. The only thing worse than data that you know is inaccurate is data that you think is accurate, even though it's incorrect.

Here are a few business benefits of data lake governance:

- Data governance enables the identification of data ownership, which aids in understanding who has the answers if you have questions about the data. For example, were these numbers produced by the CFO or an external agency? Did the CFO approve them?
- Data governance facilitates the adoption of data definitions and standards that help relate technical metadata to business terms, thereby enhancing the understanding of data. For example, we may have the technical metadata terms `f_name`, `first_name`, and `fn`, but they all refer to the standardized business term *First Name*. They have been associated via a data governance process.
- Data governance facilitates the remediation processes required for data by providing workflows and escalation procedures to report data inaccuracies. For example, a data governance tool with workflows, such as Informatica MDM, Talend Data Stewardship, or Collibra, may be implemented to provide this escalation process. Has this quarter's inventory been performed, validated, and approved by the appropriate parties?
- Data governance enables us to assess the usability of data for a specific business domain, thereby minimizing the likelihood of errors and inconsistencies when creating reports and deriving insights. For example, how clean is the list of email addresses we received? If the quality is low, we can still use them, knowing we will get many bounce-backs. You can use tools such as ZeroBounce or NeverBounce to validate emails.
- Data governance enables the lockdown of sensitive data and helps you implement controls on the authorized users of the data. This minimizes the possibility of data theft and the theft of trade secrets. For example, for any sensitive data, we should consistently implement a "need-to-know" policy and restrict access as much as possible. A "need-to-know" policy is a principle that prohibits access to information to only those individuals who require it to perform their job responsibilities effectively.

By implementing data governance, healthcare organizations can ensure that patient data is protected and used responsibly, improve the quality and consistency of their data, and reduce the risk of data breaches and regulatory violations. This ultimately leads to enhanced patient trust and better decision-making based on accurate and secure data.

Data cataloging

Data cataloging refers to the process of organizing, documenting, and storing metadata about data assets within an organization. The purpose of data cataloging is to provide a central repository of information about data assets, making it easier for organizations to discover, understand, and manage their data. For example, a company maintains a customer information database that includes customer names, addresses, phone numbers, and order histories. The data catalog for this database may include metadata about the database itself, such as its purpose, data sources, update frequency, data owners and stewards, and any known data quality issues. It would also include information about each data element, such as its definition, data type, and any transformations or calculations that have been performed.

It would be beneficial to utilize metadata and data catalogs to enhance discovery and facilitate reuse. Let's list some of the metadata that is tracked by many successful implementations and that we might want to track in our implementation:

- **Access control list (ACL)**: An access list for the resource (allow or, in rare cases, deny). For example, Joe, Mary, and Bill can access the inventory data. Bill can also modify the data. No one else has access.
- **Owner**: The responsible party for this resource. For example, Bill is the owner of the inventory data.
- **Date created**: The date the resource was created. For example, the inventory data was last updated on December 20, 2024.
- **Data source and lineage**: The origin and lineage path for the resource. In most cases, the lineage metadata should be included as part of the ingestion process in an automated manner. In rare instances where metadata is not included during ingestion, the lineage metadata information can be added manually. An example of this is when files are imported into the data lake outside of the normal ingestion process. Users should be able to quickly determine the origin of data and how it arrived at its current state. The provenance of a certain data point should be recorded to track its lineage.
- **Job name**: The name of the job that ingested and/or transformed the file.
- **Data quality**: For some of the data in the lake, data quality metrics will be applied to the data after it is loaded, and the resulting data quality score will be recorded in the metadata. The data in the lake is only sometimes perfectly clean, but there should be a mechanism to determine the data quality. This context will add transparency and confidence to the data in the lake. Users will confidently derive insights and create reports from the data lake with the assurance that the underlying data is trustworthy. For example, the metadata may be that a list of emails had a 7% bounce rate the last time it was used.

- **Format type**: With some file formats, it is not immediately apparent what the file format is. Having this information in the metadata can be helpful in some instances. For example, types may include JSON, XML, Parquet, Avro, and so on.
- **File structure**: For formats such as JSON, XML, and similar semi-structured formats, referencing a metadata definition can be helpful.
- **Approval and certification**: Once either automated or manual processes have validated a file, the associated metadata indicating this approval and accreditation will be appended to the metadata. Has the data been approved and/or certified by the appropriate parties? Datasets should only be moved to the trusted data zone once this certification has been achieved. For example, inventory numbers may be approved by the finance department.
- **Business term mappings**: Any technical metadata items, such as tables and columns, always have a corresponding business term. For example, a table cryptically called `SFDC_ACCTS` could have an associated corresponding business term, such as `Authorized Accounts`. This business term data doesn't necessarily have to be embedded in the metadata. We could reference the location of the definition for the business term in the enterprise business glossary.
- **Personally identifiable information (PII), General Data Protection Regulation (GDPR), confidential, restricted, and other flags and labels**: Sometimes, we can determine whether data contains PII based on its location; however, to further enhance compliance, data should be tagged with the appropriate sensitivity labels.
- **Physical structure, redundancy checks, and job validation**: Data associated with data validation. For example, this could be the number of columns, rows, and so on.
- **Business purpose and reason**: A requirement to add data to a lake is that the data should be at least potentially useful. Minimum requirements should be established to ingest data into the lake, and the purpose of the data or a reference to its purpose can be included in the metadata.
- **Data domain and meaning**: It is only sometimes apparent what business terms and domains are associated with data. It is helpful to have this available.

There are various ways to track data governance metadata. The recommended approaches are as follows:

- **S3 Metadata**: Amazon S3 automatically stores system-defined metadata (such as file size, creation date, and content type), and you can also add custom user-defined metadata. This information helps track the origin, purpose, or owner of a data object, which is useful for audits, traceability, and lifecycle decisions.

- **S3 tags**: Tags are key-value pairs that can be assigned to S3 objects. They enable you to categorize data based on business units, sensitivity levels, or compliance requirements. Tags also integrate with AWS services such as IAM and AWS Billing to enforce security policies or allocate costs more accurately, making them highly valuable for governance and chargeback.
- **AWS Glue Data Catalog**: AWS Glue provides a central metadata repository where you can register your datasets along with schema information, data classifications, and table-level descriptions. This enhanced catalog enables searchability, lineage tracking, and access control integration with Lake Formation. It helps users discover the right data for analytics while ensuring governance teams maintain oversight over how data is structured and used.

Data cataloging plays a crucial role in modern data management, enabling organizations to better understand their data assets, improve data quality, and support data-driven decision-making.

Data quality control

You need to validate and clean the data before storing it in the data lake to ensure data accuracy and completeness. Data quality control refers to the set of processes, techniques, and tools used to ensure that data is accurate, complete, consistent, and reliable. Data quality control seeks to enhance the quality of data used in decision-making, thereby reducing the risk of errors and fostering greater trust in the data.

For example, a retail company wants to ensure that the data it collects about its customers is accurate and up to date. The company may implement data quality control processes, such as data profiling, data cleansing, and data standardization, to achieve this goal. **Data profiling** involves analyzing data to identify patterns and anomalies, while **data cleansing** consists of correcting or removing inaccuracies and duplicates. **Data standardization** involves ensuring that data is consistently formatted and entered in a standardized manner. The following are some use cases for data quality control:

- **Decision-making**: By ensuring that data is accurate, complete, and consistent, data quality control enables organizations to make informed decisions based on reliable data.
- **Data integration**: Data quality control is crucial for successful data integration, as it ensures that data from various sources can be combined seamlessly without errors.
- **Customer relationship management**: High-quality data is crucial for effective customer relationship management, as it enables enterprises to gain a deeper understanding of their customers and deliver personalized experiences.

- **Fraud detection**: Data quality control helps organizations detect and prevent fraud by identifying and correcting errors and inconsistencies in data.
- **Compliance**: By ensuring that data is accurate and consistent, data quality control helps organizations meet regulatory compliance requirements and avoid penalties.

Data quality control is a crucial aspect of modern data management, helping organizations ensure their data is reliable and supporting informed decision-making.

Data quality metrics

The other key aspect to track is data quality metrics, which are essential for ensuring the reliability and usability of your data assets. These metrics typically include the following:

- **Completeness**: Whether all required data is present
- **Accuracy**: Whether the data correctly represents real-world values
- **Consistency**: Whether data is uniform across sources
- **Timeliness**: How up-to-date the data is
- **Uniqueness**: Ensuring no duplicate entries

AWS tools, such as AWS Glue DataBrew and Deequ, help you measure and monitor these metrics by profiling datasets and applying validation rules. Tracking data quality metrics allows your teams to identify issues early, improve trust in analytics outputs, and maintain compliance with data governance standards. Now, let's look at a key aspect of data: security.

Data security

You should implement security measures to ensure the confidentiality, integrity, and availability of your data. Data security best practices for data lakes can be divided into several categories, including the following:

- **Access control**: Control access to the data lake and its contents through **role-based access management** (**RBAC**) and **multi-factor authentication** (**MFA**). Use access control policies that specify who can access specific data and what actions they are authorized to perform. For example, an online retailer can use access control to restrict access to its customer data to only those employees who need it to perform their job functions.
- **Data encryption**: Encrypt sensitive data at rest, in transit, and during processing. The data lake can use encryption keys managed by **Key Management Service** (**KMS**) to encrypt data. For example, a healthcare organization can utilize data encryption to safeguard patient health information stored in its data lake.

- **Data masking**: Mask sensitive data elements within the data lake to prevent unauthorized access to sensitive data. Masking can be applied to columns, rows, or entire tables. For example, a financial organization can utilize data masking to safeguard sensitive customer information, such as account numbers and personal details, within its data lake.
- **Data auditing**: Monitor and log all access to data in the data lake, including the identity of the user, the time of access, and the actions performed. This helps to detect and respond to security incidents. For example, an energy company can utilize data auditing to monitor and log access to its data in the data lake, thereby helping to detect and respond to security incidents.

Security is always a critical consideration when implementing search projects across the enterprise. AWS realized this early on. Like many other services in the AWS stack, many AWS offerings in the search space integrate seamlessly and easily with the AWS IAM service. Having this integration does not mean we can simply push a button and guarantee the security of our search solution. Similar to other integrations with IAM, we must ensure that our IAM policies align with our business security policies. We have robust security measures in place to ensure that authorized users can only access sensitive data and that our company's system administrators have the necessary permissions to modify these security settings.

As mentioned earlier in this chapter, AWS Lake Formation is a service that simplifies the process of building, securing, and managing data lakes. It also provides several security features to ensure that the data stored in the data lake is secure:

- **Access control**: Lake Formation provides fine-grained access control to data in the lake using AWS IAM policies. You can grant or revoke permissions to access the data lake and its contents (for example, data tables and columns) based on user identities, such as AWS accounts or **AWS IAM Identity Center** identities.
- **Data encryption**: Lake Formation integrates with AWS KMS to provide encryption of data at rest and in transit. You can encrypt data in the lake using encryption keys managed by KMS to secure sensitive data.
- **VPC protection**: Lake Formation integrates with Amazon VPC to provide network-level security for data in the lake. You can secure access to the data lake by limiting access to specific **virtual private clouds (VPCs)** or IP addresses.
- **Audit logging**: Lake Formation provides audit logging for data access, modification, and deletion. You can use audit logs to monitor and track activities performed on the data lake and its contents.

- **Data masking**: Lake Formation offers data masking to safeguard sensitive data within the lake. You can mask sensitive data elements within the data lake to prevent unauthorized access, including columns, rows, or entire tables.
- **Data governance**: Lake Formation provides data governance features to manage and enforce data usage and protection policies. This includes classifying data based on its sensitivity, implementing retention policies, and enforcing data retention schedules.

These security features in Lake Formation help you secure data in the data lake and meet regulatory requirements for protecting sensitive data. They allow you to control access to the data lake and its contents, encrypt sensitive data, and monitor and log all activities performed on the data lake.

Data ingestion

As you learned in *Chapter 10, Data Engineering and Big Data Analytics in AWS*, you should automate data ingestion from multiple sources to ensure timely, consistent, and reliable data loading into your data lake or warehouse. Manual ingestion processes are not only time-consuming but also prone to errors and delays. With automation, you can regularly extract data from diverse sources, including on-premises databases, SaaS platforms, IoT devices, and third-party APIs, without requiring human intervention.

For example, using AWS Glue jobs, AWS DataSync, or Amazon AppFlow, you can set up scheduled or event-driven pipelines that automatically **extract, transform, and load** (**ETL**) data into Amazon S3 or Redshift. This automation helps you maintain a steady flow of fresh data for downstream analytics and reporting, reduces operational overhead, and improves data accuracy.

To ensure efficient, secure, and high-quality data ingestion, it's important to follow best practices, including the following:

- **Data validation**: Validate the data before ingestion to ensure that it is complete, accurate, and consistent. This includes checking for missing values, incorrect data types, and values that are out of range. For example, an e-commerce company can use data validation to ensure that customer data is complete, accurate, and consistent before storing it in the data lake.
- **Data transformation**: Transform the data into a consistent format suitable for storage in the data lake. This includes standardizing data types, converting data into a common format, and removing duplicates. For example, a telecommunications company can use data transformation to convert customer call records into a common format suitable for storage in the data lake.

- **Data normalization**: Normalize the data to ensure that it's structured in a way that makes it easier to analyze. This includes defining common data definitions, data relationships, and data hierarchies. For example, a financial organization can utilize data normalization to ensure that financial data is structured in a manner that facilitates easier analysis.
- **Data indexing**: Index the data to facilitate easier search and retrieval. This includes creating metadata indices, full-text indices, and columnar indices. For example, an online retailer can utilize data indexing to facilitate easier search and retrieval of customer data stored in the data lake.
- **Data compression**: Compress the data to reduce its size and improve ingestion performance. This includes using compression algorithms such as Gzip, Snappy, and LZ4. For example, a media company can use data compression to reduce the size of video files stored in the data lake, improving ingestion performance.
- **Data partitioning**: Partitioning of the data to enhance performance and scalability. This includes partitioning the data by date, time, location, or other relevant criteria. For example, a logistics company can use data partitioning to improve the performance and scalability of delivery data stored in the data lake, partitioning the data by delivery location.

Your data lake may store terabytes to petabytes of data. Let's see data lake scalability best practices.

Data lake scalability

You should design your data lake to be scalable, accommodating future growth in data volume, velocity, and variety. Data lake scalability refers to the ability of a data lake to handle increasing amounts of data and processing requirements over time. The scalability of a data lake is critical to ensure that it can support growing business needs and meet evolving data processing requirements. Here are a few best practices:

- Data partitioning divides data into smaller chunks, allowing for parallel processing and reducing the amount of data that needs to be processed at any given time, thereby improving scalability.
- You can utilize distributed storage to store data across multiple nodes in a distributed manner, thereby increasing storage capacity and enhancing processing power, thus improving scalability.
- Compressing data can reduce its size, improve scalability by reducing the storage required, and enhance processing time.

- From an AWS perspective, you can utilize Amazon S3 as your storage, which enables a serverless computing model for data processing and allows for the automatic scaling of resources based on demand, thereby improving scalability. You can use EMR and Glue to process data from S3 and store it back whenever needed.

In this way, you will decouple storage and compute, which will help achieve scalability and reduce costs. Let's look at best practices to reduce costs.

Data lake cost optimization

To optimize costs in your data lake, utilize cost-effective AWS features, such as Amazon S3 storage tiering. This approach involves keeping frequently accessed data in S3 Standard and moving older data to lower-cost options, such as S3 Intelligent-Tiering or Glacier. Implement lifecycle policies to automatically archive or delete stale data and use object tags for better cost tracking and allocation. Avoid duplicate datasets by managing access securely with AWS Glue Data Catalog and Lake Formation, ensuring that teams use shared, trusted data. For querying, services such as Amazon Athena let you run SQL directly on S3 data, and using partitioning helps minimize scanned data costs. Tools such as AWS Cost Explorer and Budgets provide visibility and alerts, helping you monitor and manage your data lake expenses effectively.

By utilizing these cost-effective solutions and optimizing data processing tasks, you can minimize storage and processing costs. Data lake costs can quickly escalate, particularly as the amount of data stored in the lake increases over time. To reduce and optimize the price of a data lake, it's important to follow best practices such as the following:

- Compressing data to reduce its size, thus reducing storage costs and improving processing time
- Partitioning data into smaller chunks to allow for parallel processing
- Reducing the amount of data that needs to be processed at any given time, thus improving processing performance and reducing costs

Furthermore, you can optimize the use of compute and storage resources, reduce costs by minimizing resource waste, and maximize resource utilization and cost-effective storage options, such as Amazon S3 object storage or tiered storage, which can lower storage costs while maintaining adequate storage capacity. For example, implementing a serverless computing model with AWS Glue for data processing can reduce costs by allowing for the automatic scaling of resources based on demand, reducing the need for expensive dedicated resources.

Data lake performance optimization

To ensure your data lake runs efficiently, it's essential to monitor and optimize its performance continuously:

1. Start by tracking query execution times and data scan volumes using tools such as Amazon Athena, AWS Glue, and Amazon Redshift Spectrum.
2. Identify queries that scan large amounts of unnecessary data and optimize them by properly partitioning and compressing your datasets in Amazon S3.
3. Use columnar formats, such as Parquet or ORC, to reduce I/O and speed up data retrieval.
4. Additionally, utilize Amazon CloudWatch to establish custom metrics and alerts for job performance, resource utilization, and potential bottlenecks.

These practices help ensure that the data lake functions optimally and that any performance issues are promptly identified and resolved.

Continuously monitoring the performance of the data lake, including storage and compute utilization, can help identify and resolve performance issues before they become critical. You should define and track performance metrics, such as query response time and data processing time, which can help identify performance bottlenecks and inform optimization efforts.

Furthermore, analyzing log data can provide valuable insights into the performance of the data lake and help identify potential performance issues. Regularly loading and testing the data lake can help identify performance bottlenecks and inform optimization efforts. Automatically scaling resources, such as compute and storage, based on usage patterns can improve performance and prevent performance issues. The following are the best practices for resource scaling based on data volume:

- **Enable auto scaling for compute services**: Use services such as AWS Glue or Amazon EMR with auto scaling to automatically adjust the number of workers based on the workload size, ensuring optimal processing time without manual intervention.
- **Use S3 Intelligent-Tiering for storage**: This storage class automatically moves data between *frequent* and *infrequent* access tiers based on usage, ensuring fast access to active data while reducing latency for analytics.
- **Leverage Amazon Redshift RA3 or Spectrum**: With Redshift's managed storage or Spectrum's serverless query model, storage and compute scale independently based on query demand, helping maintain high performance during peak usage times.

Flexible data processing in the data lake

You should choose a data processing solution, as mentioned in this list, that can handle batch, real-time, and streaming data processing to accommodate a variety of use cases:

- **Batch processing**: Batch processing is ideal for handling large volumes of data at scheduled intervals. You can use services such as AWS Glue or Amazon EMR to run automated ETL jobs. These jobs can process historical data on a daily or hourly basis to support reporting and business intelligence. The transformed data can then be stored in Amazon S3 using optimized file formats such as Parquet or ORC for faster querying and analytics.
- **Real-time processing**: For time-sensitive use cases, real-time processing ensures that data is acted on as it arrives. Amazon Kinesis Data Analytics enables you to analyze streaming data in near-real time, making it ideal for dashboards and alert systems. Event-driven architectures using AWS Lambda can react instantly to changes, such as new files in S3 or updates in DynamoDB. With Kinesis Firehose, you can continuously stream data to storage or analytics destinations, such as Amazon S3 and Redshift.
- **Streaming data**: When dealing with continuous, high-throughput data, streaming architectures offer robust and scalable solutions. Amazon **Managed Streaming for Apache Kafka (MSK)** enables you to collect and process large volumes of streaming data with low latency. You can perform real-time transformations using Apache Flink or Kinesis Data Streams. This setup is ideal for ingesting data from IoT devices, application logs, or clickstreams, enabling use cases such as real-time monitoring, anomaly detection, and personalized user experiences.

Flexible data processing is a crucial aspect of data lake design, enabling the processing of diverse data types using various tools and techniques. A data lake should support a variety of data formats, including structured, semi-structured, and unstructured data, to enable flexible data processing and the use of open source tools such as Apache Spark and Apache Hive, which can facilitate efficient data processing and minimize the cost of proprietary tools.

A data lake should support multiple processing engines, including batch processing, stream processing, and real-time processing, to enable flexible data processing. A data lake with a decoupled architecture, where the data lake is separated from the processing layer, can allow for flexible data processing and minimize the impact of changes to the processing layer on the data lake.

The data lake should be integrated with data analytics tools, such as business intelligence and machine learning tools, to allow for flexible data processing and analysis.

Now that we have gone over some of the best practices to implement a data lake, let's review some ways to measure the success of your data lake implementation.

Key metrics in a data lake

Now more than ever, digital transformation projects have tight deadlines and are compelled to achieve more with fewer resources. It is vital to demonstrate added value and results quickly.

Ensuring the success and longevity of a data lake implementation is crucial for a corporation, and effectively communicating its value is essential. However, determining whether the implementation is adding value or not is often not a binary metric and requires a more granular analysis than a simple "green" or "red" project status.

The following list of metrics is provided as a starting point to help gauge the success of your data lake implementation. It is not intended to be an exhaustive list but rather a guide to generate metrics that are relevant to your specific implementation:

- **Size**: It's important to monitor two metrics when evaluating a lake – the overall size of the lake and the size of its trusted zone. While the total size of the lake alone may not be significant or informative, the contents of the lake can range from valuable data to meaningless information. Regardless, this volume has a substantial impact on your billing expenses. Implementing an archival or purging policy is an effective method for controlling the volume and minimizing costs. Your documents can be transferred to a long-term storage location, such as Amazon S3 Glacier, or eliminated. Amazon S3 provides an easy approach to deleting files using lifecycle policies. A larger size of the trusted zone indicates a better scenario. It represents the extent of clean data within the lake. Although you can store massive amounts of data in the raw data zone, it only serves its purpose when it undergoes transformation, cleaning, and governance.
- **Governability**: Measuring governability can be challenging, but it is crucial for effective governance. It's essential to identify the critical data that requires governance and add a governance layer accordingly, as not all data requires governance. There are many opportunities to track governability. The criticality of data is key to establishing an efficient data governance program. Data on the annual financial report for the company is more critical than data on the times the ping-pong club meets every week. Data deemed critical to track is dubbed a **critical data element** (**CDE**).

To ensure efficient governability, you can assign CDEs and associate them with the lake's data at the dataset level. Then, you can monitor the proportion of CDEs matched and resolved at the column level. Another approach is to keep track of the number of authorized CDEs in relation to the total number of CDEs. Lastly, you can track the count of CDE modifications made after they are approved.

- **Quality**: Data quality is not always perfect, but it should meet the standards for its intended domain. For instance, when using a dataset to generate financial reports for the current quarter, the accuracy of the numbers used is crucial. On the other hand, if the use case is to determine recipients for marketing emails, the data still needs to be reasonably clean. Still, a few invalid emails may not significantly impact the results.
- **Usage**: Usage tracking is crucial for maintaining an effective data lake. It is essential to monitor the data ingestion rate, processing rate, error and failure rates, as well as the individual components of the lake. These metrics can provide valuable insights into where to focus your efforts. If a particular section of the data lake needs more traffic, consider phasing it out. AWS offers an easy way to track usage metrics through SQL queries against AWS CloudTrail using Amazon Athena.
- **Variety**: It is essential to assess the variety aspect of the data lake and evaluate the system's capability to handle various types of data sources. It should be able to accommodate multiple input types, including relational database management systems, NoSQL databases such as DynamoDB, CRM application data, JSON, XML, emails, logs, and other data formats. While the data ingested into the lake can be of diverse types, it is recommended to standardize the data format and storage type as much as possible. For example, you can standardize on the Apache Parquet format or ORC format for all data stored in your Amazon S3 buckets. This allows users of the data lake to access it in a standard manner. Achieving complete uniformity in the data lake might not always be practical or necessary. It is essential to consider the context and purpose of the data before determining the level of homogenization required. For instance, it may not make sense to convert unstructured data into Parquet. Therefore, it is best to use this metric as a general guideline rather than a rigid rule.
- **Speed**: When it comes to speed, two measurements are valuable. Firstly, track the time it takes to update the trusted data zone from the start of the ingestion process. Secondly, track the time it takes for users to access the data. It's not necessary to squeeze every millisecond out of the process, but it should be good enough. For example, if the nightly window to populate the data lake is four hours, and the process takes two hours, it might be acceptable. However, if you expect the input data to double, you may need to find ways to speed up the process to avoid hitting the limit.

Similarly, if user queries take a few seconds to populate reports, the performance might be acceptable, and optimizing the queries further might not be a priority.

- **Customer satisfaction**: Continuous tracking of customer satisfaction is crucial, as it is one of the most important metrics, second only to security. The success of your data lake initiative depends on your users' satisfaction, and a lack of users or unhappy users can lead to its failure. There are several ways to measure customer satisfaction, ranging from informal to formal approaches. The informal method involves periodically seeking feedback from the project sponsor. However, a formal survey of the data lake users is recommended to obtain a more accurate metric. You can multiply the opinions of each survey participant by their usage level. For instance, if the lake receives low ratings from a few sporadic users but excellent ratings from hardcore users, it could imply that your data lake implementation has a steep learning curve. Still, users can become hyper-productive once they become familiar with it.
- **Security**: Security is a crucial aspect of data lake management, and compromising it is not an option. It is vital to ensure that the data lake is secure and that users have access only to their data, thereby preventing unauthorized access and data breaches. Even a single breach can result in a significant loss of critical data, which competitors or other malicious entities can exploit. Another essential factor related to security is the storage of sensitive and PII. Mishandling PII data can result in severe penalties, including damage to reputation, fines, and lost business opportunities. To mitigate this risk, AWS provides Amazon Macie, which can automatically scan your data lake and identify any PII data in your repositories, allowing you to take necessary actions to safeguard it. However, even with security metrics, there may be instances where "good enough" is acceptable. For example, banks and credit card issuers have a certain level of credit card fraud that they find acceptable. Eliminating credit card fraud might be a laudable goal, but it might not be achievable.

Now that you have learned about the various components of a data lake and some best practices for managing and assessing data lakes, let's examine other evolved modern data architecture patterns.

Lakehouse in AWS

A **lakehouse** architecture is a modern data architecture that merges the scalability of a data lake with the structured data management features of a data warehouse. While a traditional data lake stores all types of raw, unstructured, and structured data in one central location, it lacks built-in tools for organizing and querying data efficiently for analytics. To perform reporting or advanced analytics, you typically need to clean and transform this raw data before loading it into a warehouse.

In contrast, a lakehouse integrates these two systems, offering a single platform that stores raw data like a data lake but also supports ACID transactions, schema enforcement, and structured queries like a warehouse. This gives you a unified view of data that is both flexible for storage and efficient for analytics, reducing the need to move data between platforms and streamlining data management workflows.

Let's take an example to understand the difference between a data lake and a lakehouse. A media company stores all of its raw video and audio content in a data lake. The data lake serves as a central repository for content, but the media company must perform additional processing and preparation to make the content usable for analysis and reporting. The same media company implements a lakehouse architecture in addition to the data lake. The data warehouse offers a structured view of video and audio content, facilitating easier analysis and reporting on the content. The company can utilize this structured data to gain valuable insights into audience engagement and enhance the quality of its content. The following diagram shows how you can use AWS Glue to build a lakehouse architecture:

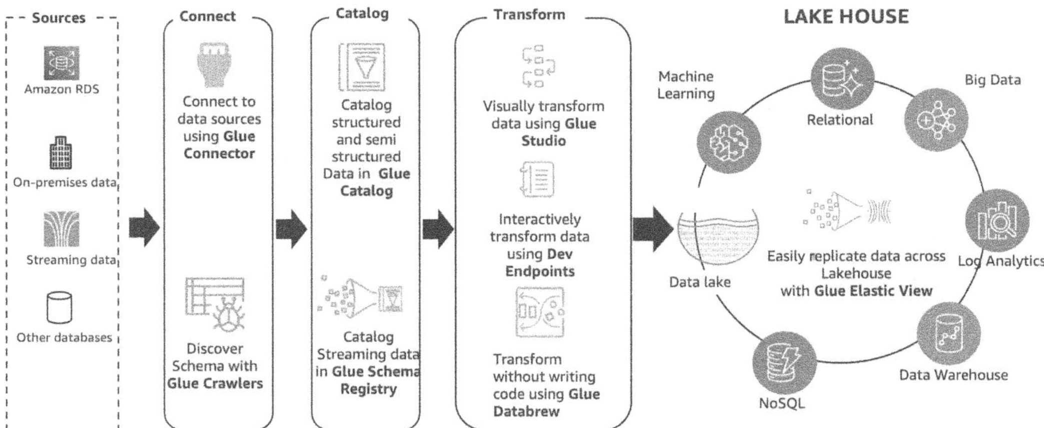

Figure 12.4: Lakehouse architecture using AWS Glue (source: https://aws.amazon.com/blogs/architecture/how-to-accelerate-building-a-lake-house-architecture-with-aws-glue/)

As shown in the preceding diagram, in an AWS lakehouse architecture, data flows through its key stages: source, connect, catalog, transform, and lakehouse access. Data originates from various sources, including Amazon RDS, on-premises databases, streaming platforms, and other databases. Using AWS Glue connectors, this data is connected and made accessible. Next, Glue crawlers and the Glue Schema Registry help discover, catalog, and manage structured and semi-structured data within the AWS Glue Data Catalog.

Once cataloged, the data is transformed using tools such as AWS Glue Studio for visual ETL, dev endpoints for interactive development, and DataBrew for no-code transformations. Finally, this prepared data becomes accessible across the lakehouse environment, enabling use cases in machine learning, big data, relational queries, NoSQL, log analytics, and data warehousing. Through AWS Glue Elastic Views, data can be easily replicated across services, giving you a unified and scalable platform to analyze and process data efficiently. Here are the steps to implement a lakehouse architecture in AWS:

1. **Set up a data lake**: Begin by establishing a data lake using Amazon S3 as the storage layer. This will provide a central repository for all types of data, including structured, semi-structured, and unstructured data.
2. **Define data ingestion pipelines**: Utilize tools such as Amazon Kinesis, Amazon Glue, or AWS Data Pipeline to establish data ingestion pipelines for your data sources. This will allow you to automatically collect and store data in the data lake as it becomes available.
3. **Create a data warehouse**: Use Amazon Redshift as your data storage solution. Amazon Redshift provides fast, managed data warehousing that can handle large amounts of data.
4. **Load data into the data warehouse**: Use Amazon Glue or AWS Data Pipeline to load the data from the data lake into the data warehouse. This will provide a structured view of the data for analysis and reporting.
5. **Perform data transformations**: Use Amazon Glue or AWS Data Pipeline to perform data transformations on the data in the data lake, if necessary. This will ensure that the data is clean, consistent, and ready for analysis.
6. **Analyze data**: Utilize Amazon Redshift to perform data analysis and generate reports. Amazon Redshift offers fast and flexible data analysis capabilities, enabling easy and efficient complex data analysis. You can use Redshift Spectrum to join data residing in a data lake with Redshift data in a single query and get the desired result. You don't need to load all the data into the data warehouse for a query.
7. **Monitor and manage the lakehouse architecture**: Use Amazon CloudWatch and AWS Glue metrics to monitor and manage your lakehouse architecture. This will help ensure that the architecture performs optimally and that any issues are quickly identified and resolved.

These are the general steps to implement a lakehouse architecture in AWS. The exact implementation details will vary depending on the specific requirements of your organization and the data sources you are using.

Data mesh in AWS

While data lakes are a popular concept, they have their issues. While consolidating data in one place creates a single source of truth, it also makes a single point of failure, violating standard architecture principles that aim to build high availability.

Another problem is that the data lake is maintained by a centralized team of data engineers who may require more domain-specific knowledge to clean the data effectively. This results in back-and-forth communication with business users. Over time, your data lake can become a data swamp.

The ultimate target of collecting data is to get business insight and retain the business domain context while processing that data. What is the solution? That's where a **data mesh** comes into the picture. With a data mesh, you can treat data as a product, where the business team owns the data and exposes it as a product that can be consumed by various other teams that need it in their accounts. It addresses the challenge of maintaining domain knowledge while ensuring the necessary isolation and scalability for business operations. As data is accessed across accounts, you need centralized security governance.

Data mesh is an architectural pattern for managing data that emphasizes data ownership, consistency, and accessibility. The goal of a data mesh is to provide a scalable and flexible data architecture that supports multiple domains, organizations, and products. In a data mesh architecture, data is treated as a first-class citizen and managed independently from applications and services. Data products are created to manage and govern data, providing a single source of truth for the data and its metadata. This makes it easier to manage data, reduces data silos, and promotes the reuse of data.

Data mesh also emphasizes the importance of data governance, providing clear ownership of data and clear processes for data management. This makes managing and maintaining data quality, security, and privacy easier. Organizations typically use a combination of data products, pipelines, APIs, and catalogs to implement a data mesh architecture. These tools and services are used to collect, store, and manage data, making it easier to access and use data across the organization. For example, an e-commerce company can use a data mesh to manage customer, product, and sales data. This can include creating data products for customer profiles, product catalogs, and sales data, making it easier to manage and use this data across the organization.

The following diagram shows the data mesh architecture in AWS for a banking customer:

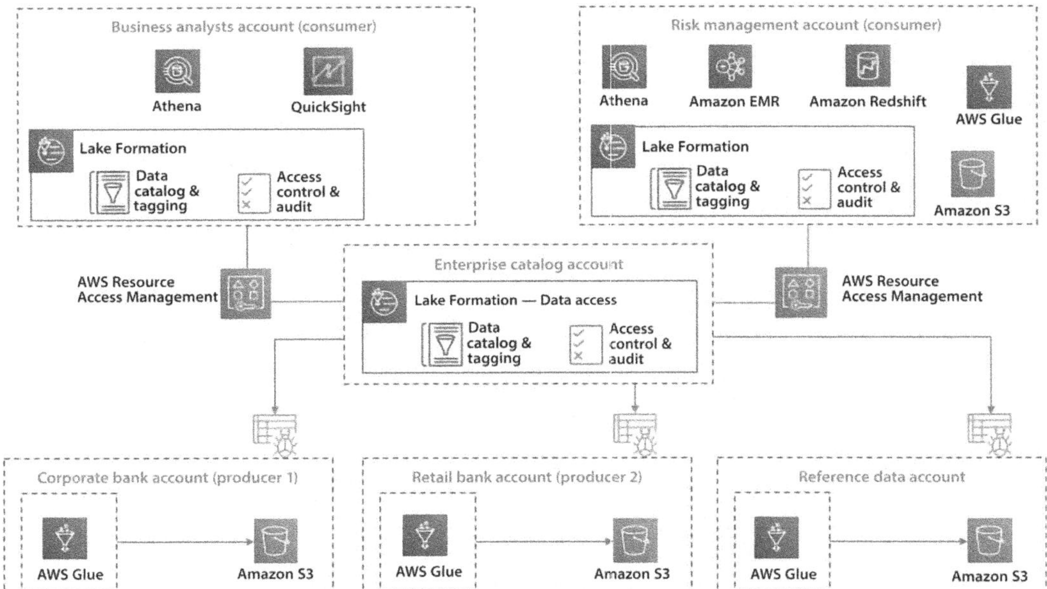

Figure 12.5: Data mesh architecture in AWS

As shown in the preceding diagram, the consumer account and consumer risk departments manage their data and expose it as a product consumed by the corporate account and retail account departments. Each of these departments operates within its own account, and cross-account access is managed through a centralized enterprise account. The centralized account also manages the data catalog and tagging, as well as resource access management, which facilitates communication between data producers and consumers, allowing them to access data as needed.

Here are the steps to implement a data mesh in AWS:

1. **Define data domains**: The first step in implementing a data mesh is to define the data domains in your organization. This involves identifying the various areas of the business that produce and utilize data, as well as determining the relationships between these data domains.
2. **Create data products**: Once you have defined your data domains, the next step is to create data products. A data product is a self-contained unit of data that can be managed and governed independently from the rest of the organization. In AWS, you can create data products using AWS Glue, Amazon S3, and Amazon Redshift.

3. **Implement data pipelines:** To ensure data consistency and accuracy, establish and maintain data pipelines. A data pipeline is a series of steps that are used to extract, transform, and load data from various sources into a data lake or data warehouse. In AWS, you can implement data pipelines using AWS Glue, Amazon S3, and Amazon Redshift.
4. **Use data catalogs:** To make it easier to manage and access data, you need to use data catalogs. A data catalog is a metadata repository that provides a centralized location for storing and managing metadata about your data products. In AWS, you can use AWS Glue or Amazon Athena as your data catalog.
5. **Implement data APIs:** To facilitate easier access to data, implement data APIs. A data API is a set of APIs that provides a programmatic interface for accessing data products. In AWS, you can implement data APIs using AWS Lambda and Amazon API Gateway.
6. **Ensure data security:** Implement effective data security measures to ensure data security. In AWS, you can use Amazon S3 bucket policies, IAM policies, and encryption to secure your data.

To implement a data mesh in AWS, you need to define data domains, create data products, implement data pipelines, utilize data catalogs, establish data APIs, and ensure data security. These steps can help you build a scalable and flexible data architecture that can support multiple domains, organizations, and products.

Choosing between a data lake, lakehouse, and data mesh architecture

In brief, data lake, lakehouse, and data mesh architectures are three distinct approaches to organizing and managing data within an organization:

- A data lake is a centralized repository that enables the storage of all structured and unstructured data at any scale. A data lake provides the raw data and is often used for data warehousing, big data processing, and analytics.
- A lakehouse is a modern data architecture that combines the scale and flexibility of a data lake with the governance and security of a traditional data warehouse. A lakehouse provides raw and curated data, making it easier for data warehousing and analytics.
- A data mesh organizes and manages data, prioritizing decentralized data ownership and fostering cross-functional collaboration. In a data mesh architecture, each business unit is responsible for its own data and shares data with others as needed, creating a network of data products.

Here are some factors to consider when deciding between a data lake, data mesh, and lakehouse architecture:

Criteria	Data lake	Lakehouse	Data mesh
Definition	Centralized repository for structured and unstructured data at scale	Combines features of a data lake and a data warehouse in one architecture	Decentralized architecture promoting domain-oriented data ownership
Data governance	Challenging to manage; governance is minimal unless additional tools are used	Strong governance and centralized management with built-in security features	High focus on governance, with data treated as a product by individual domains
Data processing	Ideal for big data processing, including batch and real-time workloads	Supports unified storage and processing, enabling both structured queries and big data processing	Enables flexible, domain-specific processing using APIs and pipelines
Data access	Can be difficult to access for non-technical users	Provides easier access through unified query interfaces	Improves accessibility through domain-managed data products
Cost	Cost-effective, especially for large datasets due to low storage costs	Can be costlier than data lakes but cheaper than full data warehouse setups	Higher cost due to added layers of management and governance
Best use case	Best when you need to store and analyze large volumes of raw data	Ideal when you need both analytics and ML on raw and curated data	Best for large organizations needing cross-functional data sharing and ownership

Table 12.1: Comparison between various data architectures

Consider using a data lake if you need to store large amounts of raw data and process it using big data technologies. Consider using a data mesh if you need to manage and govern data across the organization. Consider using a lakehouse if you need a centralized repository for storing and managing data with a focus on data governance and performance.

Amazon SageMaker Lakehouse: a data lake for machine learning

Amazon SageMaker Lakehouse is a solution designed to unify data lakes and data warehouses, providing a seamless environment for data processing, analytics, and machine learning. Amazon SageMaker Lakehouse helps you bridge the gap between your raw data and actionable machine learning insights. It combines the scalable storage of a data lake with the fast query and structure capabilities of a data warehouse – all deeply integrated with Amazon SageMaker's machine learning features. This makes it easier for you to prepare, explore, and utilize your data for advanced machine learning applications without switching tools or systems.

As shown in the following diagram, Amazon SageMaker Lakehouse combines the best features of data lakes and data warehouses, providing a unified platform for data storage, analytics, and machine learning.

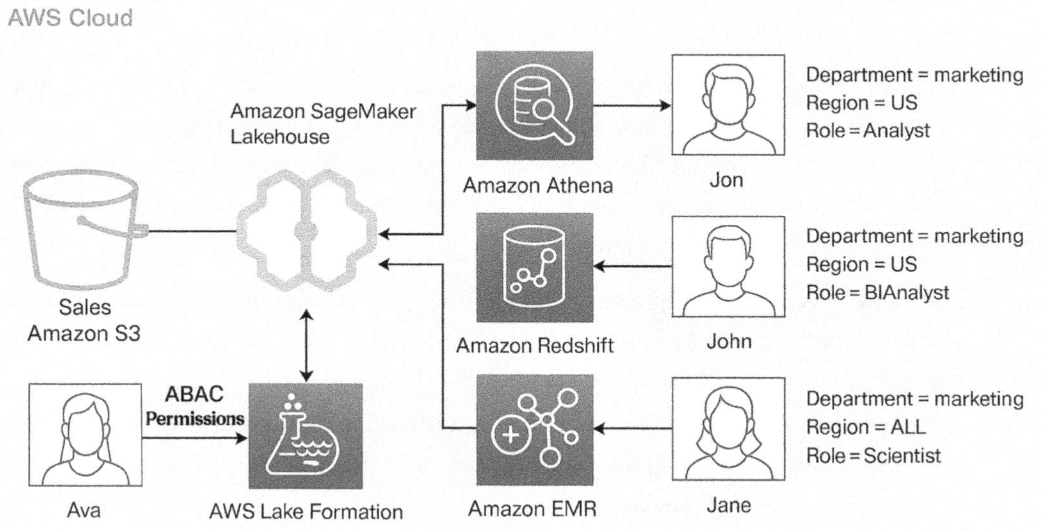

Figure 12.6: Amazon SageMaker Lakehouse architecture

As shown in the preceding diagram, Amazon SageMaker Lakehouse integrates with other AWS services to provide a secure, unified data platform that supports diverse analytics and machine learning workloads across different user roles, all governed by AWS Lake Formation.

At the center of the architecture is Amazon S3, which stores raw and processed sales data. This data is made accessible through the SageMaker Lakehouse, which acts as a bridge between the data stored in S3 and the analytics and ML services used downstream. AWS Lake Formation applies **attribute-based access control (ABAC)** to enforce fine-grained permissions based on user attributes such as department, region, and role. Ava manages these access permissions centrally through Lake Formation.

The SageMaker Lakehouse enables different types of users to work with the same governed dataset using tools that suit their roles:

- **Jon**, a marketing analyst in the US, uses Amazon Athena to run SQL queries for ad hoc insights.
- **John**, a BI analyst in the same department and region, works with Amazon Redshift for structured analytics and dashboarding.
- **Jane**, a data scientist with broader access across all regions, leverages Amazon EMR for large-scale data processing and training machine learning models.

Through this architecture, Amazon SageMaker Lakehouse ensures that all users, from analysts to data scientists, can collaborate on a unified dataset without compromising security or data governance. It simplifies access, reduces duplication, and accelerates analytics and ML development within a secure, scalable framework. The architecture of SageMaker Lakehouse can be broken down into several key components:

- **Data lake**: A centralized repository that allows for the storage of vast amounts of structured and unstructured data. SageMaker Lakehouse leverages Amazon S3 for its data lake capabilities, enabling scalable and cost-effective storage.
- **Data warehouse**: A structured repository optimized for complex queries and analytics. SageMaker Lakehouse integrates with Amazon Redshift, providing high-performance querying and analytics capabilities.
- **Transactional storage**: Ensures data consistency and reliability. SageMaker Lakehouse utilizes transactional storage to handle updates, deletes, and inserts efficiently.
- **Data processing**: Tools and frameworks for data transformation and preparation. SageMaker Lakehouse supports a variety of data processing tools, including Amazon SageMaker Data Wrangler and AWS Glue.
- **Machine learning**: Integration with Amazon SageMaker for building, training, and deploying machine learning models. SageMaker Lakehouse provides a seamless pipeline for end-to-end machine learning workflows.

Features

Amazon SageMaker Lakehouse offers a range of features designed to enhance data management and machine learning capabilities:

- **Unified data access**: You get a single platform to access both raw data from your Amazon S3 data lake and processed, structured data from Amazon Redshift. This means you don't have to move data around or duplicate it. For example, a financial services company analyzing both raw trading logs and cleaned transactional data can query them simultaneously from a single location.
- **Scalable storage**: Utilizing Amazon S3 as the storage layer enables you to scale to petabytes of data without worrying about infrastructure. With S3's tiered storage options, such as Intelligent-Tiering or Glacier, you can also reduce costs based on how often the data is accessed. For example, Netflix uses Amazon S3 to store massive volumes of video logs and customer behavior data, which feeds their recommendation models.
- **High-performance querying**: By integrating with Amazon Redshift and Redshift Spectrum, SageMaker Lakehouse enables you to run fast queries directly on S3 data, eliminating the need to load it into the warehouse. For example, a retail chain can run a quick analysis on sales logs from S3 during flash sales, without waiting for full data load into Redshift.
- **ACID-compliant transactional storage**: You can update, insert, or delete records safely thanks to transactional storage support. This ensures consistency across your datasets during analytics or machine learning processes. In e-commerce, inventory data updates every second. With transaction support, your model always trains on the most accurate data.
- **Integrated data processing tools**: SageMaker Data Wrangler provides an easy-to-use interface for data transformation, eliminating the need for coding. AWS Glue automates data ingestion, cataloging, and ETL pipelines. For example, a media company can quickly clean up subtitles and video metadata using Glue and Data Wrangler before training a recommendation engine.
- **Amazon S3 Tables for structured access**: With S3 Tables, you can treat raw files in S3 as if they were structured tables, improving query speed and simplicity. For example, you can query customer feedback stored in JSON or Parquet format without needing to convert or copy the data.
- **End-to-end machine learning**: Amazon SageMaker integration enables you to train, tune, and deploy your models directly where your data resides. This removes delays in moving data between systems. For example, healthcare providers analyzing patient records can directly build models to predict hospital readmission rates using SageMaker pipelines.

- **Security and compliance**: SageMaker Lakehouse supports encryption, fine-grained access control with AWS Lake Formation, and integration with AWS IAM, ensuring your data and models are secure. For example, a bank implementing fraud detection can restrict model access only to compliance-approved analysts.

Benefits

Now, let's learn about the benefits of Amazon SageMaker Lakehouse, written in a practical and relatable way for you as a solutions architect:

- **Simplified data management**: With SageMaker Lakehouse, you don't need to worry about managing multiple platforms for raw and structured data. It brings Amazon S3 (data lake) and Amazon Redshift (data warehouse) together into one integrated system. You can connect to and query various types of data from a single interface without building complex ETL pipelines. A media company managing video files in S3 and user profiles in Redshift can now analyze both in the same ML workflow without extra data transfers.
- **Cost efficiency**: Because the Lakehouse uses Amazon S3 for storing large volumes of data, you benefit from its lower cost compared to traditional data warehouses. You also have tiered storage options, such as S3 Glacier, for archiving rarely accessed data. You spend less on storage while still keeping data accessible when needed. Expedia stores petabytes of travel logs on S3 and uses them to feed analytics and ML pipelines, saving significant costs compared to maintaining an on-premises solution.
- **High performance**: By integrating with Amazon Redshift and Redshift Spectrum, Lakehouse enables you to run fast queries directly on your S3 data. You don't have to move everything into Redshift first. You gain fast insights, especially when making real-time business decisions. A retail chain running seasonal campaigns can quickly analyze customer behavior and adjust pricing on the fly using Athena and Redshift.
- **Data reliability**: Thanks to ACID-compliant transactional storage, you don't have to worry about data integrity issues when your pipelines are updating, inserting, or deleting records. You can confidently use your data for training without fear of corruption or inconsistency. Financial institutions that utilize transactional updates on stock market data benefit from clean, consistent training data for their machine learning models.
- **Comprehensive machine learning**: Lakehouse tightly integrates with Amazon SageMaker, providing a full pipeline, data preparation, training, tuning, and deployment, all in one place. You can experiment faster, iterate more often, and deploy ML models without switching tools or platforms. GE Healthcare uses SageMaker to train models on imaging data stored in S3 and validate results across multiple hospital systems, accelerating AI-driven diagnostics.

The integration of Amazon S3 Tables with Amazon SageMaker Lakehouse significantly enhances data processing and ML workflows for businesses and data scientists. Amazon S3 Tables simplifies managing and querying data stored in Amazon S3 by presenting it in a structured, table-like format, eliminating the need to deal with underlying file formats or partitioning schemes. Amazon SageMaker Lakehouse, an extension of AWS's SageMaker service, combines data lake capabilities with data warehouse performance, optimizing the environment for ML tasks. This integration allows data scientists and ML engineers to access and query S3 data directly from SageMaker notebooks, streamlining the transition from data preparation to model training.

Amazon SageMaker Lakehouse can be applied to a variety of use cases across different industries:

- **Customer analytics**: Organizations can utilize SageMaker Lakehouse to analyze customer data stored in data lakes and data warehouses, thereby gaining valuable insights into customer behavior and preferences.
- **Predictive maintenance**: Manufacturing companies can leverage SageMaker Lakehouse to analyze sensor data from machinery, predicting maintenance needs and preventing downtime.
- **Fraud detection**: Financial institutions can utilize SageMaker Lakehouse to identify and detect fraudulent activities by analyzing transaction data stored in data lakes and data warehouses.
- **Healthcare analytics**: Healthcare providers can analyze patient data to identify trends, predict outcomes, and improve patient care.
- **Supply chain optimization**: Retailers and manufacturers can use SageMaker Lakehouse to analyze supply chain data, optimizing inventory management and logistics.

As generative AI is the most sought-after technology now, let's see how a data lake can support it.

AWS data lake and generative AI

As generative AI becomes a key part of business innovation, your AWS data lake becomes more critical than ever. A well-architected data lake in Amazon S3 serves as the foundation for generative AI applications by storing massive amounts of training data, including structured, semi-structured, and unstructured formats. With services such as Amazon SageMaker, you can train foundation models directly on data stored in your lake. AWS Lake Formation ensures that this data is secure, well-governed, and easily discoverable.

For example, healthcare providers can develop generative AI models that summarize patient records or suggest clinical decisions by securely accessing and processing patient data stored in a data lake. Similarly, retailers use data lakes to train recommendation engines that power personalized shopping experiences.

In addition to SageMaker, Amazon Bedrock plays a crucial role in making generative AI accessible. Bedrock enables you to utilize foundation models from leading AI providers through a simple API, eliminating the need to manage infrastructure. It integrates with data stored in your AWS environment, including S3, enabling quick prototyping and deployment of generative AI applications. For instance, you can use Bedrock to build a chatbot that leverages customer feedback data from your data lake or create marketing content tailored to user preferences stored in structured data formats.

By combining AWS's scalable storage, analytics tools, SageMaker for model training, and Bedrock for managed model deployment, you can harness the full potential of your data lake to fuel generative AI, enabling faster innovation, greater cost efficiency, and a competitive advantage.

Building a data lake for generative AI

To build a high-performance data lake tailored for generative AI workloads, it is essential to design with scalability, governance, and support for diverse data modalities in mind. Generative AI models require massive and varied datasets, including structured records, text, images, audio, and videos, to perform accurately and produce meaningful results. The following diagram shows a data lake used for generative AI using Amazon Bedrock.

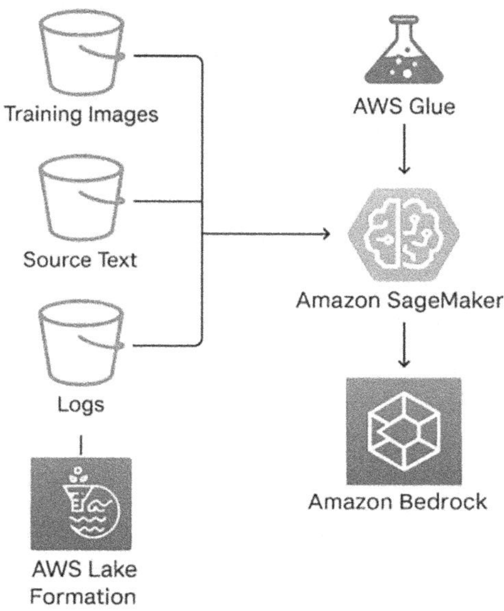

Figure 12.7: Data lake for generative AI

As shown in the preceding diagram, let's look at the setup of a generative AI-focused data lake:

1. Start by storing these datasets in Amazon S3, which provides a durable, scalable, and cost-effective foundation for your data. It's important to organize your S3 buckets by data type and sensitivity level. For example, keep training images, source text, and logs in separate buckets, and use lifecycle rules to move older, infrequently accessed files to lower-cost storage, such as Amazon S3 Glacier.
2. Next, use AWS Glue to crawl these S3 datasets and build a centralized data catalog. This enables consistent data discovery and metadata management. Glue supports schema detection for semi-structured data, such as JSON or Parquet, and integrates with AWS Lake Formation for fine-grained access control. Tag data assets by use case (e.g., marketing copy or product images) to make them easier to locate during model training or evaluation.

3. Once your data is cataloged, integrate Amazon SageMaker to develop and deploy generative models. For preprocessing and feature engineering, SageMaker Data Wrangler enables you to visually clean, transform, and join datasets. When you're ready to train, use SageMaker Pipelines to automate the machine learning lifecycle – from preprocessing to model evaluation – ensuring consistency and repeatability. You can store models in SageMaker Model Registry and manage deployment with SageMaker endpoints.

   For teams looking to avoid the complexities of model training, Amazon Bedrock offers an easier alternative. You can connect Bedrock with your curated datasets in S3 to fine-tune or augment foundation models via a simple API. This is especially helpful for tasks such as Q&A bots, content summarization, or personalized marketing, where using a pretrained model with minimal customization is more cost-effective than building one from scratch.

4. Security and governance are crucial when handling enterprise data. Use AWS Lake Formation to manage data access at the row and column level and enable audit logging. Define data zones (raw, staging, curated, etc.) in your S3 structure to implement data quality workflows. Encrypt sensitive data using AWS KMS and enforce policies using IAM and Lake Formation permissions.

For example, a retail company wants to develop a product description generator that utilizes customer reviews, product specifications, and marketing data. They ingest customer reviews and product metadata into S3, use Glue to extract and catalog this information, then use SageMaker to fine-tune a foundation model to generate unique product descriptions. Alternatively, they can use Bedrock to access foundation models such as Amazon Nova, Meta Llama, or Claude. They deploy the model via SageMaker endpoints, integrating it with their e-commerce backend to automatically generate and A/B test new content.

Similarly, a media company building a text-to-image generative AI application can store historical text descriptions and image data in S3, label and organize them using Glue, and then utilize SageMaker to train models such as Stable Diffusion. Using this setup, they can fine-tune models for specific artistic styles or customer preferences.

Some benefits of this architecture are as follows:

- Independent scaling of storage and compute, reducing bottlenecks
- Cost savings from spot instances, serverless analytics (Athena), and S3 tiering
- Full traceability and compliance with integrated logging and access controls
- Flexibility to adapt to different teams and use cases across departments

By investing in a robust data lake architecture utilizing AWS tools such as S3, Glue, SageMaker, Lake Formation, and Bedrock, you equip your organization to harness the power of generative AI efficiently and responsibly.

This architecture allows you to scale storage and compute independently, optimize costs with lifecycle policies, and maintain data quality. It also provides the flexibility to support future generative AI innovations across departments and various use cases.

Knowledge check

The following are some sample questions that align with the difficulty and scope typically found in the *AWS Certified Solutions Architect* exam:

1. You are designing a data lake architecture using Amazon SageMaker Lakehouse. Which of the following storage options is primarily used for storing and managing data lakes cost-effectively, while also providing seamless integration with SageMaker Lakehouse for machine learning tasks?

    a. Amazon RDS

    b. Amazon Redshift

    c. Amazon DynamoDB

    d. Amazon S3

    Answer: d.

    Explanation:

    a. Incorrect. While RDS is excellent for structured data and relational databases, it is not designed for the scale and flexibility required for data lakes.

    b. Incorrect. Redshift is a data warehousing solution optimized for large-scale data analytics. While it can handle large datasets, it is more suited for structured data and complex queries rather than the diverse and often unstructured data found in data lakes.

    c. Incorrect. DynamoDB is a NoSQL database service that offers high performance and scalability for key-value and document data models. However, it is not designed for the vast and varied data types typically stored in data lakes.

   d. **Correct.** Amazon S3 is the primary storage option used for storing and managing data lakes cost-effectively. It is designed to store large amounts of data with high durability, availability, and scalability. Amazon S3 provides seamless integration with Amazon SageMaker Lakehouse, allowing data scientists and machine learning engineers to easily access and manipulate the data stored in S3 for their machine learning tasks.

2. You are designing a data lake architecture for a large-scale machine learning project on AWS. Your goal is to enable seamless data integration, transformation, and analysis for machine learning workflows. Which AWS service would best support this architecture by providing a unified view of data across different formats and sources, enabling efficient data management and querying for machine learning tasks?

   a. Amazon Redshift
   b. Amazon S3
   c. Amazon SageMaker Lakehouse
   d. AWS Glue

   Answer: c.

   Explanation:

   a. Incorrect. While Amazon Redshift is a powerful data warehousing solution, it primarily focuses on structured data and SQL-based analytics, which may not be as flexible for the diverse data formats and sources required in machine learning projects.
   b. Incorrect. Amazon S3 is a scalable object storage service commonly used for data lakes, but it does not provide the unified data management and querying capabilities that SageMaker Lakehouse offers.
   c. **Correct.** Amazon SageMaker Lakehouse is specifically designed to provide a unified view of data across different formats and sources, making it an ideal choice for large-scale machine learning projects. It integrates seamlessly with Amazon SageMaker, enabling efficient data management, transformation, and querying for machine learning tasks. SageMaker Lakehouse allows data scientists and machine learning engineers to access and process data stored in data lakes directly, without the need for complex ETL processes. This enhances the efficiency and agility of machine learning workflows, making it a superior choice for this scenario.

   d. Incorrect. AWS Glue is a fully managed ETL service that can be used to catalog and prepare data for analytics; however, it does not provide the integrated data management and querying features specifically designed for machine learning tasks, which SageMaker Lakehouse offers.

3. You are designing an Amazon data lake to support a variety of big data analytical workloads. Your organization needs to ensure that data is easily accessible, secure, and cost-effective. Which of the following AWS services would be the best choice to store and catalog the data in your data lake?

   a. Amazon RDS
   b. Amazon S3 and AWS Glue
   c. Amazon Redshift
   d. Amazon DynamoDB

   Answer: b.

   Explanation:

   a. Incorrect. Amazon RDS is a managed relational database service, not designed for large-scale, unstructured data storage, which is typical of a data lake.
   b. **Correct**. Amazon S3 is an object storage service that offers scalability, data availability, security, and performance. It is ideally suited for storing large volumes of data, making it a perfect fit for a data lake. Amazon S3 offers cost-effective storage options, including S3 Standard, S3 Intelligent-Tiering, and S3 Glacier, to optimize costs based on access patterns. AWS Glue is a fully managed ETL service that makes it easy to move data between your data stores and data lakes. It also provides a data catalog to store metadata, making it simpler to discover and manage data in your data lake. AWS Glue can automatically crawl your data sources to identify data formats and schemas, thus creating a unified metadata repository. Combining Amazon S3 for storage and AWS Glue for cataloging and ETL processes ensures that your data lake is easily accessible, secure, and cost-effective. This combination allows for efficient data querying, transformation, and integration with various analytical tools and services.
   c. Incorrect. Amazon Redshift is a data warehousing service designed for large-scale data storage and complex query processing. Still, it is more suited for structured data and does not offer the same level of cost-effectiveness and flexibility as Amazon S3 for a data lake.

d. Incorrect. Amazon DynamoDB is a NoSQL database service that provides fast and predictable performance with seamless scalability; however, it is not designed for the broad range of data types and storage requirements typical of a data lake.

4. You are the lead architect for a large e-commerce company that is building a data lake on AWS. Your data lake currently stores 5 PB of data and is expected to grow by 1 PB per year. You need to optimize the storage costs while ensuring high availability and durability. Which of the following strategies would you recommend to reduce the overall storage costs of your data lake?

   a. Use Amazon S3 Glacier for all data storage needs
   b. Store all data in Amazon S3 Standard storage class and use lifecycle policies to transition older data to S3 Glacier Deep Archive
   c. Use Amazon S3 Intelligent-Tiering for all data storage needs
   d. Store frequently accessed data in Amazon S3 Standard and infrequently accessed data in Amazon S3 Standard-IA, using lifecycle policies to transition older data to S3 Glacier

Answer: d.

Explanation:

a. Incorrect. Using Amazon S3 Glacier for all data storage needs would be too restrictive and not suitable for frequently accessed data due to its retrieval times and higher retrieval costs.

b. Incorrect. Storing all data in Amazon S3 Standard and transitioning to S3 Glacier Deep Archive would be cost-prohibitive for frequently accessed data, as it would not effectively optimize costs.

c. Incorrect. Utilizing Amazon S3 Intelligent-Tiering for all data storage needs can be a cost-effective approach. Still, it might not be the most cost-optimized solution compared to manually managing the data lifecycle based on known access patterns.

d. **Correct.** For a data lake with 5 PB of data and an expected annual growth of 1 PB, it's crucial to balance cost, availability, and durability. Here's why option D is the optimal choice:

   - **Amazon S3 Standard**: This storage class is ideal for frequently accessed data. It offers low latency and high throughput performance. By storing frequently accessed data in S3 Standard, you ensure that the most critical and often-used data is readily available.

- **Amazon S3 Standard-IA**: This storage class is suitable for infrequently accessed data. It offers lower storage costs compared to S3 Standard, but with a slightly higher retrieval cost. Storing infrequently accessed data here helps in reducing costs without sacrificing availability.
- **Lifecycle policies**: Utilizing lifecycle policies to transition older data to S3 Glacier ensures that data that is rarely accessed but still needs to be retained for compliance or long-term storage is moved to a more cost-effective storage class. S3 Glacier is ideal for archival purposes and has even lower storage costs.

5. You are designing a data lake for a highly regulated financial services company using AWS Lake Formation. The company requires that data access be tightly controlled based on user roles and the sensitivity of the data. Which of the following approaches will best meet these security requirements?

    a. Use AWS IAM policies to manage access to the data lake
    b. Implement AWS Lake Formation with fine-grained access control using data location and data attributes
    c. Utilize AWS KMS to encrypt the data and manage encryption keys manually
    d. Rely on S3 bucket policies to control access to different data sets within the data lake

    Answer: b.

    Explanation:

    a. Incorrect. Using AWS IAM policies alone would not provide the granularity needed to control access to specific datasets or columns within the data lake. IAM policies are more suited for broad access control.
    b. **Correct**. AWS Lake Formation provides a comprehensive set of tools to build, secure, and manage a data lake. For highly regulated environments, such as financial services, fine-grained access control is essential. Lake Formation allows you to define and enforce permissions at a granular level based on data location (such as S3 buckets or folders) and data attributes (such as column-level access in databases).
    c. Incorrect. While AWS KMS is essential for encrypting data at rest and managing encryption keys, it does not address the need for fine-grained access control. Encryption is important for data security, but it does not handle user access permissions.

d. Incorrect. S3 bucket policies can control access at the bucket or object level. Still, they do not provide the level of granularity needed for column-level access control or complex role-based access management within a data lake.

Summary

In this chapter, you gained a comprehensive understanding of data lakes and their significance for large-scale organizations. You learned about the different zones within a data lake, as well as the key components and features that contribute to its success.

You also learned how to build a data lake using AWS Lake Formation and explored the concept of data mesh architecture, which enables multiple data lakes across different accounts to collaborate. Additionally, you explored ways to optimize the structure of a data lake and the various metrics that can be tracked to manage it effectively.

You learned about lakehouse architecture and how to decide between data lake, lakehouse, and data mesh setups. You also got an overview of Amazon SageMaker Lakehouse, its key features, and some real-world applications. Finally, you learned about how a data lake can support a generative AI architecture.

In this chapter, you learned about various ways to handle data. Now, let's understand how to put our AWS services learning to use and build a microservice and event-driven focused application in the next chapter.

Join us on Discord

For discussions around the book and to connect with your peers, join us on Discord at `https://discord.gg/kbFRRSB2Qs` or scan the QR code below:

13

Building Microservices and Event-Driven Architecture in AWS

Until now, you have learned about various AWS technologies and how each plays a role in building modern cloud solutions. You also explored how to choose the right service for the right workload, depending on your application's needs. In this chapter, you will combine these LEGO blocks to build real-world enterprise applications using some of the most popular and proven design patterns.

You will learn why microservices, **event-driven architecture** (**EDA**), and **domain-driven design** (**DDD**) are not just buzzwords but critical building blocks for modern application development on AWS. As you have already seen in earlier chapters, moving to the cloud and using serverless and containers allows you to scale and innovate faster. However, when you combine those technologies with smart architectural patterns such as microservices and EDA, you take it to the next level. These patterns help you build applications that are more resilient, flexible, and easier to manage as they grow.

Microservices break down your applications into small, independent services focused on specific business capabilities. EDA allows these services to communicate in real time and react quickly to changes and new information. DDD ensures that your microservices are deeply aligned with your business needs, making your architecture logical and easier to evolve.

In this chapter, you will dive deep into how you can use AWS services such as Lambda, ECS, EventBridge, DynamoDB, and others to design and build powerful microservice architectures. You will explore why leading companies such as Netflix, Amazon, and Uber have adopted these patterns and how they use them to stay ahead of the competition. With real AWS examples, you will also learn about the best practices, benefits, and real-world challenges of microservices and event-driven systems.

In this chapter, you will dive deeply into the ins and outs of microservice patterns. Specifically, you will learn about the following topics:

- Understanding microservices
- Microservice architecture patterns
- Building a layered architecture
- Benefits of EDA
- Disadvantages of EDA
- Reviewing microservices best practices
- Implementing DDD

By the end of this chapter, you will be confident in designing microservice-based architectures, know when to use EDA, and understand how DDD fits perfectly into your AWS cloud strategy.

Let's get started!

Understanding microservices

Like many popular technology ideas, it is difficult to pinpoint an exact definition of microservices. Different groups co-opt the term and provide their unique twists on it, but the popularity of microservices is hard to ignore. It is one of the most common patterns used in new software development today. However, the definition has not stayed static and has evolved.

Given these caveats, let's try to define what a microservice is.

A **microservice** is a software application that follows an architectural style that structures the application as a loosely coupled service, easily deployable, testable, and organized in a well-defined business domain. A **loosely coupled system** is one where components have little or no knowledge about other components and have few or no dependencies between these components.

In addition, a certain consensus has been reached around the concept of microservices. Some of the defining features that are commonly associated with microservices are the following:

- In the context of a microservice architecture, services communicate with each other over a network to accomplish a goal using a technology-agnostic protocol (most often, HTTP).
- Services can be deployed independently. In theory, deploying a new version of one service should not impact any associated services.
- Services are assembled and built around business domains and capabilities.
- Services should be developed using different operating systems, programming languages, data stores, and hardware infrastructure, and they should still be able to communicate with each other because of their common protocol and agreed-upon **application programming interfaces (APIs)**.
- Services are modular, small, message-based, context-bound, independently assembled, deployed, and decentralized.
- Services are built and released using an automated process, often a **continuous integration (CI)** and **continuous delivery (CD)** methodology.
- Services have a well-defined interface and operations. Both consumers and service producers know exactly what the interfaces are.
- Service interfaces normally remain the same or have background compatibility when code changes. Therefore, clients of these services do not need to make changes when the code changes.
- Services are maintainable and testable. Often, these tests can be fully automated via a CI/CD process.
- Services allow for the fast, continuous, and reliable delivery and deployment of large and complex projects. They also help organizations evolve their technology stack.

Microservices are one of the answers to monolithic architectures that were common in mainframe development. Applications that follow a monolithic architecture are hard to maintain, tightly coupled, and difficult to understand. Also, microservices aren't simply a layer in a modularized application, as was common in early web applications that leveraged the **model/view/controller (MVC)** pattern. Instead, they are self-contained, fully independent components with business functionality and delineated interfaces. This doesn't mean a microservice might not leverage other architectural patterns and have its own internal components.

Doug McIlroy is credited with describing the philosophy surrounding Unix; microservices implement the Unix philosophy of "*Do one thing and do it well.*"

Martin Fowler describes microservices as those services that possess the following features:

- Software that can leverage a CI/CD development process. A small modification in one part of the application does not require the wholesale rebuild and deployment of the system; it only requires rebuilding, deploying, and distributing a few components or services.
- Software that follows certain development principles, such as fine-grained interfaces.

Microservices fit hand in glove with the cloud and serverless computing. They are ideally suited to be deployed using container and serverless technology. In a monolithic deployment, if you need to scale up to handle more traffic, you must scale the full application. Only the services receiving additional calls need to be scaled when using a microservice architecture. Depending on how the services are deployed and assuming they are deployed effectively, you will only need to scale up or scale out the services to handle additional traffic. You can leave the servers with services that are not in demand untouched.

Microservices have grown in popularity in recent years as organizations are becoming nimbler. In parallel, more and more organizations have moved to adopt a DevOps and CI/CD culture. Microservices are well suited for this. Microservice architectures are the answer to monolithic applications. A high-level comparison between the two is shown in the following diagram:

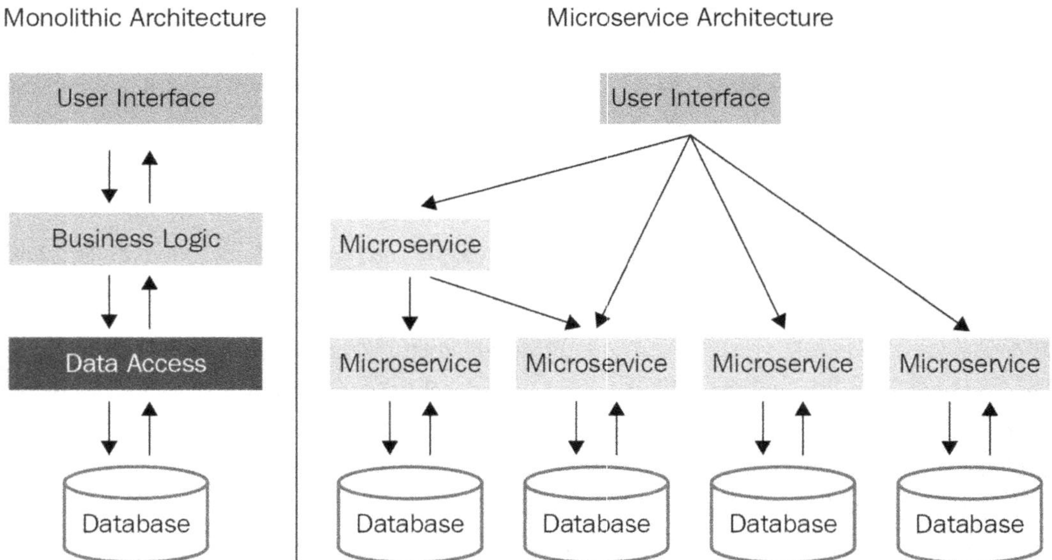

Figure 13.1: Monolithic versus microservice architectures

In a monolithic architecture, communication occurs across the whole application, independent of business boundaries. Initially, and for simple applications, this architecture may be appropriate, but complexity increases quickly as the number of business domains that the application handles increases.

In a microservice architecture, each service is typically responsible for a specific business capability and is built and deployed independently of other services. As part of this separation, each service normally has its own database and API. Having a separate database for each service allows for better scalability, as each service's data storage and retrieval needs can be optimized independently. It also allows for more flexibility regarding the technology choices for each service, as different services can use other types of databases, depending on their needs.

A separate API for each service separates concerns and promotes loose coupling between services. It also facilitates their evolution, as changes to one service's API do not affect other services.

This can also facilitate the service's versioning. However, it's important to note that this approach has some trade-offs. One of the main trade-offs is the increased complexity of managing and integrating multiple services.

The following diagram shows a high-level microservice architecture in AWS. In this architecture, a request goes through the API gateway. It is routed to a different microservice based on the container manager, Amazon ECS, and the serverless microservices built on AWS Lambda. All microservices have their own Amazon Aurora database instances.

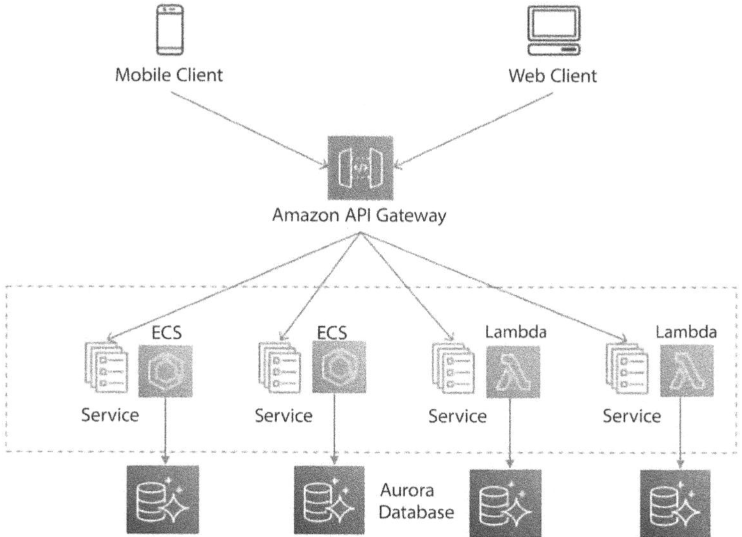

Figure 13.2: Microservice architectures in AWS

With this architecture, requests to the microservices would go through API Gateway, which would then route the requests to the appropriate microservice running in a container on ECS. The microservice would then interact with its own Aurora database to retrieve or store data:

- **API Gateway**: This service can create and manage microservices' APIs. It allows for creating RESTful and WebSocket APIs and can handle authentication, authorization, traffic management, and caching.
- **ECS**: This service deploys and manages the containers that run the microservices. It allows you to scale and update the services easily, and it also provides service discovery and load balancing.
- **Aurora**: This service can manage a relational database for microservices. It can create, configure, and manage such databases. Aurora also provides automatic backups, software patching, and replication for high availability. To further reduce operational overhead, you can use Aurora Serverless.

This is just one example of how to build a microservice architecture using AWS services. Depending on the application's specific requirements, many other services and configurations can be used.

Other components go into microservice architecture, such as security, networking, caching, and so on, which are not mentioned in the diagram to keep it simple. However, you will learn about these in more detail in the upcoming sections. In a microservice architecture, the boundaries between services are well defined according to business domains. This enables applications to scale more smoothly and increases maintainability. Let's see a head-to-head comparison between monolithic and microservice architecture in the following table:

Aspect	Monolithic architecture	Microservices architecture
Code base	Single large code base for all functions	Independent code bases for each service
Deployment	Deployed as a single unit (all or nothing)	Deployed independently per service
Scalability	Scale the entire app, even if only one part needs it	Scale individual services based on their specific demand
Failure impact	One bug can crash the entire system	Failure is isolated to the affected service only
Technology choices	Typically, one technology stack	Freedom to use different technology stacks for different services

Database	One shared database for all components	Each service often has its own dedicated database
Resource Utilization	Higher, even for small changes	Optimized, pay only for what each service needs
Maintenance	Becomes difficult as the application grows	Easier to maintain, update, and scale independently
Development teams	Usually, one big team working on the same code base	Smaller, independent teams responsible for individual services
AWS deployment example	Monolithic app hosted on Amazon EC2 or Elastic Beanstalk	Microservices deployed using Amazon ECS, AWS Lambda, API Gateway, and EventBridge
Scaling in AWS	Auto-scaling the full EC2 instance or environment	Auto-scaling individual services (Lambda functions and ECS services)
Monitoring in AWS	Single-point monitoring (EC2/ Elastic Beanstalk metrics)	Distributed monitoring (CloudWatch Logs, AWS X-Ray per service)
Examples	Early enterprise apps, legacy systems, and CRM apps	Netflix, Amazon, Uber, PayPal, and Spotify

Table 13.1: Monolithic vs. microservices architecture comparison

If you are building a small prototype or a **minimum viable product (MVP)**, starting with a monolithic approach, such as hosting your application on Amazon EC2 or using AWS Elastic Beanstalk, may allow you to move faster and simplify early development. However, if you are targeting enterprise-scale, highly scalable, and agile applications, adopting a microservices architecture from the beginning is a better long-term strategy. You can achieve this on AWS using services such as Amazon ECS, Amazon EKS, AWS Lambda, API Gateway, and EventBridge, which are purpose-built to support flexible, decoupled, and scalable microservices environments.

In this section, you saw the fundamentals of microservices. Next, we will learn about popular architecture patterns often used to create microservices. The most popular pattern is layered architecture, so let's start with it.

Layered architecture

This pattern is quite common in software development. As the name indicates, the code is implemented in layers in this pattern. Having this layering enables the implementation of the **separation of concerns**. This is a fancy way of saying that each layer focuses on doing a few things well and nothing else, which makes it easier to understand, develop, and maintain the software.

The topmost layer communicates with users or other systems. The middle layer handles the business logic and routing of requests, and the bottom layer's responsibility is to ensure that data is permanently stored, usually in a database.

Having this separation of concerns or these individual duties for each layer allows us to focus on the most important properties for each layer. For example, in the presentation layer, accessibility and usability will be important considerations, whereas in the persistence layer, data integrity, performance, and privacy may be more important. Some factors will be important regardless of the layer. An example of a ubiquitous concern is security. But, having these concerns separate enables teams not to require personnel who are experts in too many technologies. With this pattern, we can hire UI experts for the presentation layer and database administrators for the persistence layer. It also provides a clear delineation of responsibilities. If something breaks, it can often be isolated to a layer, and once it is, you can reach out to the owner of the layer.

From a security standpoint, a layered architecture offers advantages over monolithic architectures. In a layered architecture, you normally place only the presentation layer load balancer in a public subnet and the rest of the layers in a private subnet. This ensures that only the presentation layer is exposed to the internet, minimizing the attack surface. As a best practice, you should only put the load balancer in the public domain with web application firewall protection.

If a hacker wanted to use the database unauthorizedly, they would have to find a way to penetrate through the presentation layer and the business logic layer to access the persistence layer. This by no means implies that your system is impenetrable. You still want to use all security best practices and maybe even hire a white hat group to attempt to penetrate your system. An example of an attack that could still happen in this architecture is a SQL injection attack. That said, the layered architecture will limit the attack surface to the presentation layer only, so this architecture is still more secure than a monolithic architecture.

Another advantage of having a layered architecture is the ability to swap out a layer without modifying any other layers. For example, you may decide that AngularJS is no longer a good option for the presentation layer, and instead, you want to start using React. You can also start using Amazon Aurora PostgreSQL instead of Oracle. If your layers were truly independent and decoupled, you could convert the layers to the new technology without modifying the other layers.

In a microservice-based architecture, the layers are typically broken down as follows:

- **Presentation layer**: This layer handles the user interface and presents the data to the user. It can be further divided into client-side and server-side parts.
- **Business layer**: This layer implements the system's business logic. It communicates with the presentation layer to receive requests and the data access layer to retrieve and update data.
- **Data access layer**: This layer communicates with the database and other data storage systems. It provides an abstraction layer between the business layer and the data storage, allowing the business layer to focus on the logic and not worry about data access details.

You can keep an additional layer that hosts security, logging, monitoring, and service discovery services. Each layer is a separate microservice that can be developed, deployed, and scaled independently. This promotes the system's flexibility, scalability, and maintainability. In microservice architectures, adding more layers between them, such as a security layer, API Gateway layer, service discovery layer, and so on, is possible.

The following diagram shows a three-layer architecture in AWS, where the user experience frontend is deployed in the presentation layer, the business layer handles all business logic, and data is stored in the data access layer:

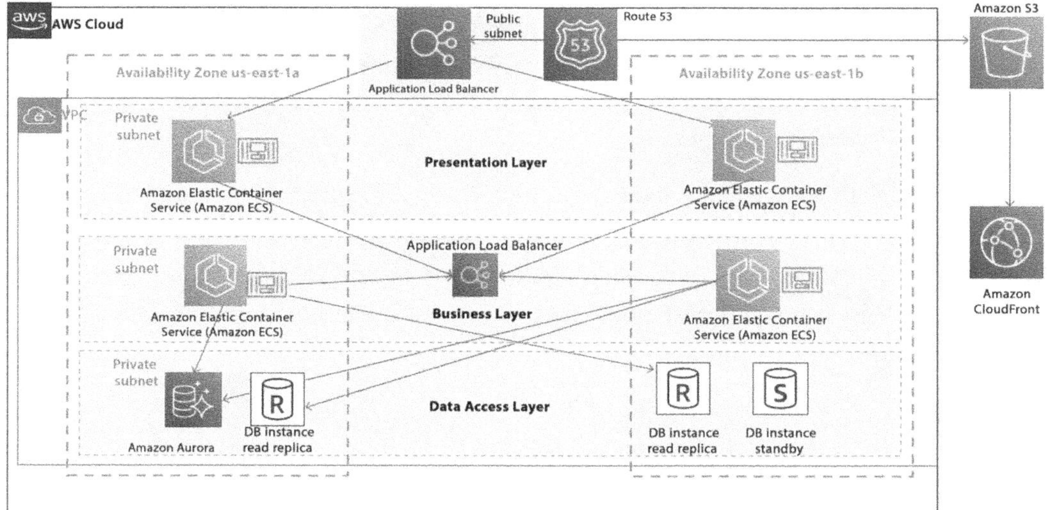

Figure 13.3: Three-layer microservice architecture in AWS

As shown in the preceding diagram, all web and application servers are deployed in containers managed by Amazon ECS, where requests are routed through an elastic load balancer, and a VPC protects the entire environment. You can also choose Lambda or Fargate for a completely serverless implementation and Aurora Serverless for your database.

Just because you are using a layered approach, it does not mean that your application will be bug-free or easy to maintain. It is not uncommon to create interdependencies among the layers. When something goes wrong in a layered architecture, the first step in troubleshooting the issue is to identify which layer the problem occurs in, which is where services such as AWS X-Ray can be very useful. Each layer has a specific role and responsibility, and the problem will typically be related to that layer's functionality. Once the layer has been identified, you can focus on the specific components within that layer that are causing the problem.

Here are some examples of how troubleshooting might proceed for different layers:

- **Presentation layer**: If the problem is related to the user interface, you might investigate issues with the client-side code, such as JavaScript errors or browser compatibility issues. On the server side, you might investigate issues with the routing, rendering, or handling of user input.
- **Business layer**: If the problem is related to business logic, you might investigate issues with the logic's implementation, such as incorrect calculations or validation rules. You might also examine issues with communication between the business layer and other layers, such as the presentation layer or data access layer.
- **Data access layer**: If the problem is related to data access, you might investigate issues with the database connections, queries, or transactions. You might also investigate issues with the mapping between the data model and the database schema, such as incorrect column names or data types.

  Finally, if the problem is related to the underlying infrastructure, you might investigate issues with the network connections, security configurations, or service discovery mechanisms. Once you have identified the specific component causing the problem, you can use various debugging and monitoring tools to gather more information and diagnose the issue.

It's worth noting that a clear and well-defined layered architecture can make troubleshooting more straightforward and efficient. It allows you to focus on a specific layer and its related components instead of considering the entire system.

Common patterns in microservices architecture

As you build microservices-based applications, a few common patterns help you manage complexity, improve reliability, and scale efficiently. In this section, you will learn about three important patterns: API gateway, circuit breaker, and service registry. Each plays a crucial role in ensuring your distributed systems work seamlessly at scale.

API gateway pattern

When you are building applications using microservices, you often deal with many different services, each handling a specific function such as payments, orders, or customer profiles. Managing how clients (such as mobile apps, websites, or third-party systems) communicate with all these services can get complicated quickly. This is where the API gateway pattern becomes extremely important.

An **API gateway** acts as a single entry point for all client requests. Instead of calling multiple microservices directly, the client sends one request to the API gateway. The API gateway then forwards the request to the appropriate backend service, collects the response, and sends it back to the client. This simplifies communication and helps you control traffic, manage security, and monitor API usage more easily.

A real-world example is Netflix, which uses an API gateway called Zuul2 to route and manage millions of requests every second to its backend microservices. This design helped Netflix build a highly scalable, secure, and resilient system that powers its video streaming worldwide. You can learn more about the Netflix case study here: `https://netflixtechblog.com/zuul-2-the-netflix-journey-to-asynchronous-non-blocking-systems-45947377fb5c`.

In AWS, you can implement this pattern using Amazon API Gateway. This fully managed service allows you to create REST, HTTP, and WebSocket APIs at any scale. Amazon API Gateway also supports features such as request validation, throttling (rate limiting), authentication (using AWS Cognito, IAM, or OAuth), monitoring with CloudWatch, and integration with AWS Lambda, ECS, or backend services hosted on EC2. The following diagram depicts a typical API Gateway architecture on AWS:

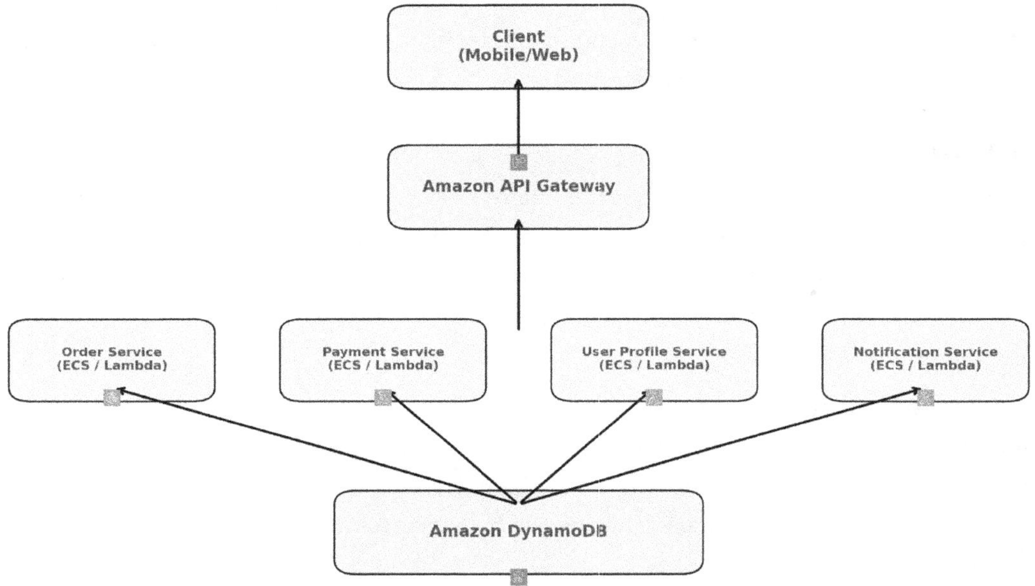

Figure 13.4: API Gateway architecture

As shown in the preceding diagram, the key elements in this architecture are as follows:

- **Client**: A user accesses your system through a mobile app, web application, or third-party system.
- **Amazon API Gateway**: Acts as the central gateway, handling all requests and routing them to appropriate microservices.

- **Microservices layer:** Each service is built independently. You can run these services on Amazon ECS, AWS Fargate, or even as AWS Lambda functions if you prefer serverless computing.
- **Database layer:** Each microservice can interact with its database, such as Amazon DynamoDB for NoSQL or Amazon RDS for relational data storage.

When you look at real-world examples, you will see that some of the biggest companies rely heavily on API Gateway and Lambda on AWS. For instance, Amazon uses API Gateway and Lambda internally to dynamically scale its backend operations, especially for systems requiring low latency and high throughput. This combination allows them to handle sudden spikes in demand without performance bottlenecks. Similarly, Airbnb uses Amazon API Gateway and AWS Lambda to build scalable APIs, helping their services interact seamlessly without worrying about server provisioning or scaling limitations.

AWS has published several case studies in which companies that use API Gateway combined with AWS Lambda have reported up to 75% reductions in operational overhead and 60% faster API deployment times than traditional, server-hosted API systems. You can learn more about them here: `https://aws.amazon.com/lambda/resources/customer-case-studies/`. These improvements not only save costs but also allow businesses to innovate and deliver features to market much faster.

Circuit breaker pattern

When you are building applications with microservices, you will often notice that different services depend on each other to complete tasks. However, if one of these services fails – say, due to a high number of requests, a coding bug, or a backend issue – it can start causing a chain reaction that brings down other services too. This type of cascading failure can seriously hurt your application's reliability and user experience.

To protect your system from this type of failure, you can use the **circuit breaker** pattern. Think of it like an electric circuit breaker in your home; when there's a power surge or fault, the breaker automatically stops the flow of electricity to prevent further damage. Similarly, the circuit breaker monitors service interactions in software and temporarily halts requests to a failing service. This gives the service time to recover while the rest of the system remains operational and responsive. The following diagram depicts how the circuit breaker pattern is implemented in AWS:

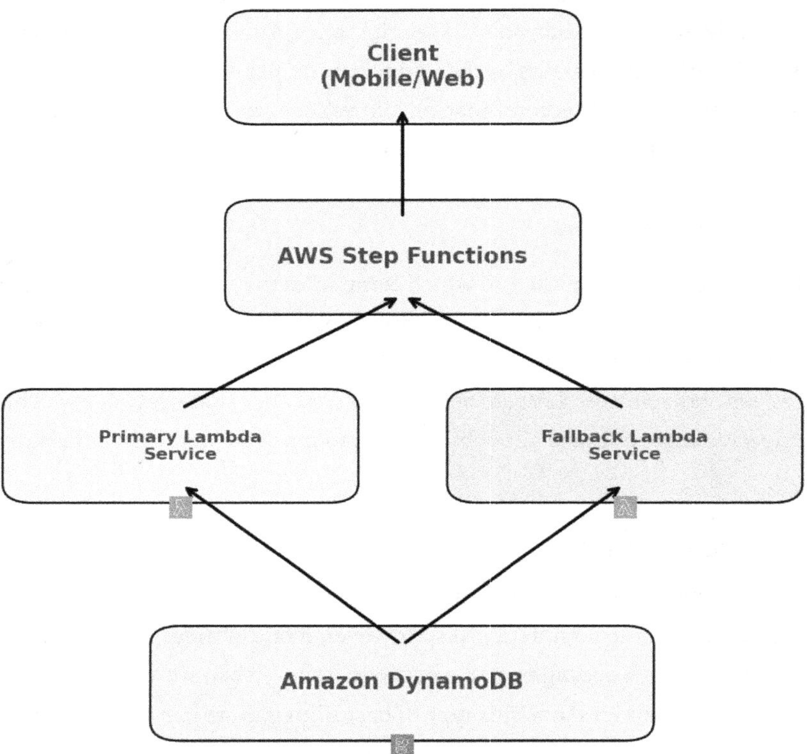

Figure 13.5: Circuit breaker pattern in AWS

As shown in the preceding diagram, in AWS, several services help you build this pattern efficiently. For example, you can use AWS Step Functions to orchestrate your service calls. Step Functions lets you easily add built-in error handling, retries, and fallback logic. If a service starts failing, Step Functions can automatically trip the circuit, stop sending requests, and either retry later or trigger an alternative workflow. You can also store service status information in Amazon DynamoDB or use AWS Lambda to write custom logic to monitor and manage failures in real-time.

A good real-world use case is seen in large e-commerce platforms such as `Amazon.com`. During high-traffic seasons such as Prime Day, multiple backend services handle everything from user authentication to payment processing and order management. If the payment service goes down, the circuit breaker ensures that other services such as browsing, cart management, and wishlisting continue functioning normally instead of crashing the entire system.

AWS has a great blog post that provides a deeper technical explanation of building this architecture: `https://aws.amazon.com/blogs/compute/using-the-circuit-breaker-pattern-with-aws-step-functions-and-amazon-dynamodb/`.

Service registry pattern

When you are working with microservices, especially in a large application, it can become challenging for one service to find and talk to another service. Microservices are dynamic – they can scale up, scale down, or even restart on different servers. This constant change makes it difficult to hardcode service addresses. That's where the service registry pattern becomes essential.

A **service registry** acts like a directory or phonebook that keeps track of where all your services are located. When a service wants to talk to another service, it first checks the service registry to find the latest address. This ensures that communication remains smooth even when services change their network locations dynamically.

Netflix's Eureka is a well-known example of a service registry, enabling services to dynamically register themselves and discover others. F5 explains service discovery in detail, which you can learn from here: `https://www.f5.com/de_de/company/blog/nginx/service-discovery-in-a-microservices-architecture?utm_source=chatgpt.com`.

As shown in the following diagram, you can implement this pattern on AWS using AWS Cloud Map or Amazon ECS service discovery. These tools facilitate seamless service registration and discovery within your applications.

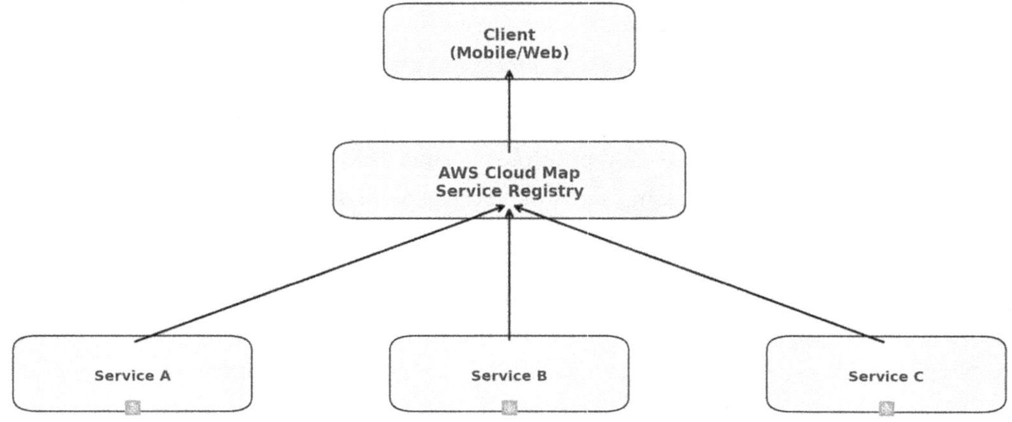

Figure 13.6: Service registry pattern in AWS

In this architecture, the client first queries AWS Cloud Map, which acts as the service registry, to find the latest locations of available services. AWS Cloud Map returns the updated endpoints for all registered services, ensuring the client always has the correct address, even if services have scaled or moved. Based on the information received, the client dynamically connects to Service A, Service B, or Service C, allowing seamless communication and service discovery within the microservices environment.

You can build resilient, scalable, and manageable microservices architectures on AWS by incorporating these patterns: API gateway, circuit breaker, and service registry.

Event-driven architecture

EDA is another pattern commonly used when implementing microservices. In this pattern, creating, messaging, processing, and storing events are critical functions of the service. Contrast this with the layered pattern we just examined, which is more of a request/response model and where the user interface takes a more prominent role.

Another difference is that layered architecture applications are normally synchronous, whereas an EDA relies on the asynchronous nature of queues and events.

More and more applications are being designed using EDA from the ground up. EDA applications can be developed using a variety of development stacks and languages. EDA is a programming philosophy, not a technology or language. It facilitates code decoupling, making applications more robust and flexible. At the center of EDA is the concept of events. Let's spend some time understanding them.

Understanding events

To better understand the event-driven pattern, let's first define an event. **Events** are messages or notifications generated by one system component and consumed by other elements. These events represent something significant that has occurred within the system and that other components need to know about to take appropriate action. Essentially, an event is a change in state in a system. Examples of changes that could be events are the following:

- A database is modified
- An application has a runtime error
- A request is submitted by a user
- An EC2 instance fails
- A threshold is exceeded
- A code change that has been checked into a CI/CD pipeline
- A new customer is registered in the system
- A payment is processed
- A stock price changes
- A sensor reports a temperature reading
- A user interacts with a mobile app

Not all system changes or actions are considered events in an EDA. For example, a change to a configuration setting or a log message might not be considered an event because it does not represent something significant that other system components need to know about.

It's also worth noting that the distinction between an event and a non-event can be context-dependent and may vary depending on the specific implementation of the EDA.

Certain changes or actions that would not typically be considered events might be treated as such if they are deemed important or relevant to certain components or use cases within the system.

In the next section, you will learn about two other critical elements in EDA: producers and consumers.

Producers and consumers

Events by themselves are useless. If a tree falls in the forest and no one is around to hear or see it, did it really fall? The same question is appropriate for events. Events are worthless if no one is consuming them, and to have events, producers of the events are needed as well. These two actors are essential components of EDA. Let's explore them at a deeper level:

- **Producers**: An event producer first detects a change of state. If an important change is being monitored, it generates an event and sends a message to notify others.
- **Consumers**: Once an event has been detected, the message is transmitted to a queue. Importantly, once the event has been placed in the queue and the producer forgets about the message, consumers fetch messages from the queue in an asynchronous manner. Once a consumer fetches a message, they may or may not perform an action based on that message. Examples of these actions are as follows:
    - Triggering an alarm
    - Sending out an email
    - Updating a database record
    - Opening a door
    - Performing a calculation

    In essence, almost any process can be a consumer action.

As you can imagine, EDA is highly scalable and efficient due to its asynchronous nature.

EDA is a loosely coupled architecture. Event producers are unaware of who will consume their output, and event consumers are unaware of who generated the events. Let's now learn about two popular types of models designed around EDA.

EDA models

There are a couple of ways to design an event-driven model. One of the main design decisions that needs to be made is whether events need to be processed by only one or multiple consumers. The first instance is known as the event streaming pattern. The second pattern is most commonly known as the publish and subscribe pattern. EDA can be implemented using either of these two main patterns. Depending on the use case, one pattern may better fit the other. Let's learn more about these two models.

Event streaming (a message queuing model)

In the **event streaming** model, events are *popped off* the queue as soon as one of the consumers processes the message. In this model, the queue receives a message from the producer, and the system ensures that the message is processed by one and only one consumer.

Event streaming is well suited for workloads that need to be highly scalable and can be highly variable. Adding capacity is simply a matter of adding more consumers to the queue, and we can reduce capacity just as easily by removing some of the consumers (and reducing our bill). In this architecture, it is extremely important that only one consumer processes messages. Once a message is allotted to a consumer, it is removed from the queue to be processed. The only time that it will be placed back in the queue is if the consumer of the message fails to process the message, and it needs to be reprocessed.

Once a message is delivered to a consumer from a queue, it becomes temporarily invisible to other consumers for a specific duration known as the visibility timeout. This allows the consumer time to process the message without risk of duplication. If the message is successfully processed, it's deleted from the queue. However, the message becomes visible again if the consumer fails to process it within the visibility timeout, due to an error or timeout. It is returned to the queue for reprocessing by another consumer. You can configure a **dead-letter queue (DLQ)** to avoid repeatedly processing faulty messages. This is a separate queue where messages are sent after a defined number of failed processing attempts. DLQs help isolate and inspect problematic messages, ensuring that they don't block the successful processing of others and giving you a reliable mechanism for error handling and debugging in your message-driven architecture.

Use cases that are well suited for this model require that each message be processed only once, but the order in which the messages are processed is not necessarily important.

Let's look at a diagram of how an event streaming architecture would be implemented:

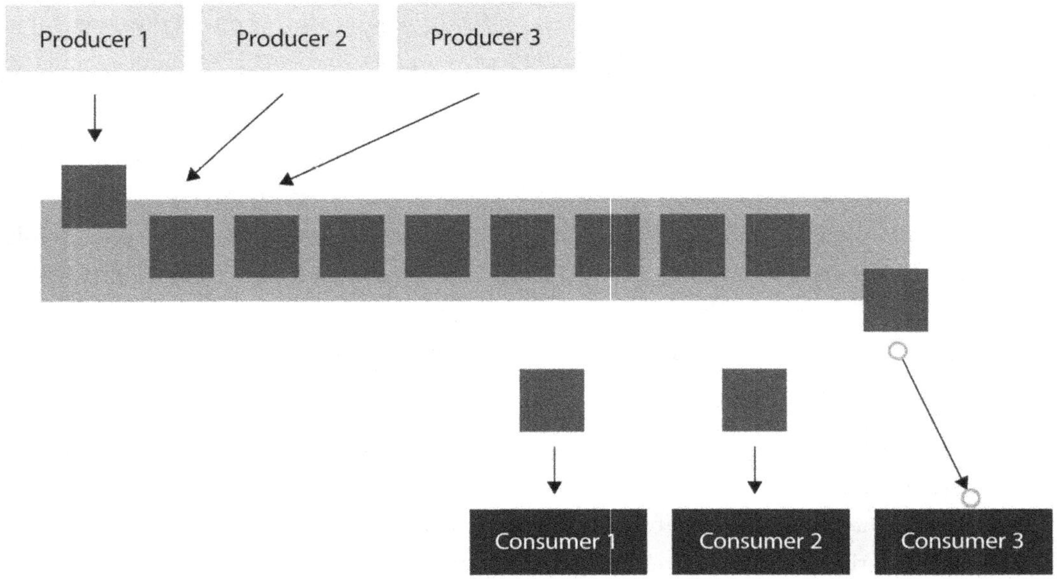

Figure 13.7: Event streaming model

In the preceding diagram, multiple producers generate events and place them into a single queue (on the left-hand side). We also have multiple consumers consuming events off the queue (on the right-hand side). Once a consumer takes an event from the queue, it gets removed, and no other consumer can consume it. The only exception is if there is an error and the consumer cannot complete the event consumption. In this case, we should put some logic in our process to put the unconsumed event back in the queue so that another consumer can process the event.

Let's make this more concrete with a real-life example.

Example scenario

To visualize this model, think of the queues common in banks, where a single queue feeds into all the tellers. When a teller becomes available, the first person in the queue goes to that teller for processing. The customer needs to visit only one teller to handle their transaction. As tellers go on a break or new tellers come in to handle the increased demand, the model can gracefully and transparently handle these changes. In this case, the bank customers are the producers – they are generating events (for example, making a check deposit), and the bank tellers are the consumers – they are processing the events that the customers are creating.

The following diagram shows how to implement a queue model using Amazon **Simple Queue Service (SQS)**.

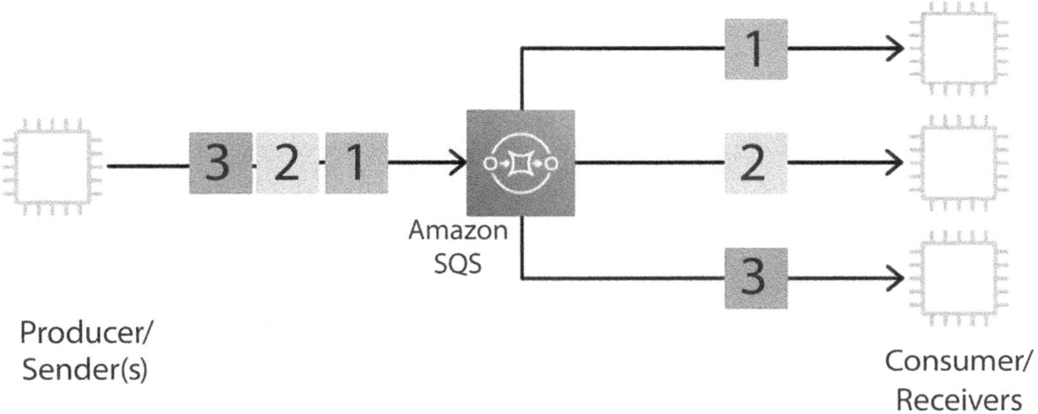

Figure 13.8: Event-driven message queuing model in AWS

As shown in the preceding diagram, messages come from the producer and go into Amazon SQS. Amazon SQS is a serverless, scalable queue service that allows consumers to take messages from the queue and process them according to their needs. If your application uses an industry-standard queue service such as JMS or RabbitMQ, you can use Amazon MQ, which provides managed support for RabbitMQ and Apache ActiveMQ.

Now, let's move on and learn about another type of event-driven model: the pub/sub model.

Publish and subscribe model

As with event streaming, the **publish and subscribe** model (also known as the **pub/sub** model) assists in communicating events from producers to consumers. However, unlike event streaming, this model allows several consumers to process the same message. Furthermore, the pub/sub model may guarantee the order in which the messages are received.

As the *publish* part of the name indicates, message producers broadcast messages to anyone interested in them. You express interest in the message by subscribing to a topic.

The pub/sub messaging model suits cases where more than one consumer needs to receive messages. In this model, many publishers push events into a **pub/sub cache** (or queue). The events can be classified by topic. As shown in the following diagram, subscribers listen to the queue and check for events being placed in it. Whenever events make it to the queue, the consumers notice them and process them accordingly. Unlike the model in the previous section, when a subscriber sees a new event in the queue, it does not pop it off the queue; it leaves it there, and other subscribers can also consume it, and perhaps take a completely different action for the same event.

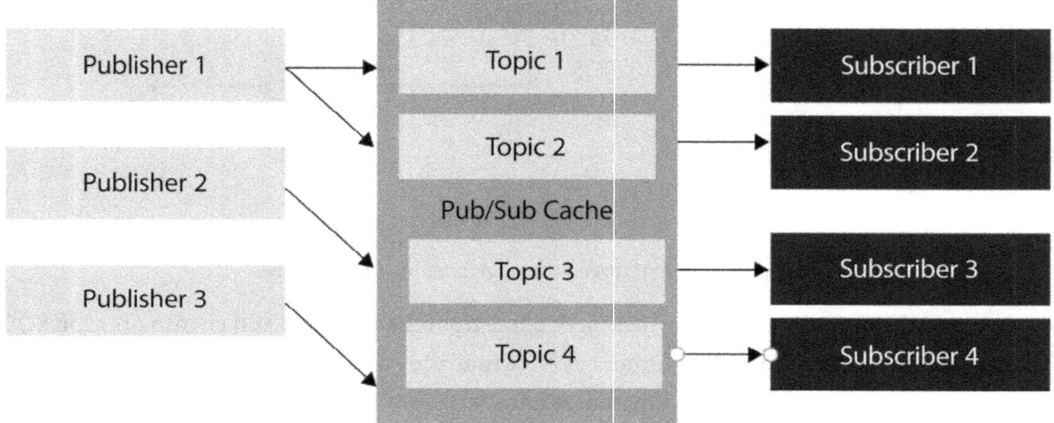

Figure 13.9: The pub/sub model

Optionally, the events in the cache can be classified by topic, and subscribers can subscribe only to the issues they are interested in and ignore the rest. The following diagram shows the pub/sub model that Amazon **Simple Notification Service** (**SNS**) achieved.

A managed service that AWS provides for a pub/sub model is **EventBridge**. Amazon EventBridge is a serverless event bus service that allows you to connect different applications and services using a pub/sub model. With EventBridge, you can create rules that automatically trigger specific actions in response to events from various sources, such as changes in an S3 bucket or the creation of a new item in a DynamoDB table. This lets you easily integrate different application parts and automate tasks without writing custom code. EventBridge supports both custom events and events from AWS services, making it a powerful tool for building event-driven architectures.

Example scenario

An example of this is a stock price service. In this case, many market participants are typically interested in receiving prices in real time on a topic of their choosing (in this case, the topics are the individual tickers). Here, the order in which the order tickers are received is incredibly important. If two traders put in a purchase to buy stock for the same price, the system must process the order that was received first. If it doesn't, the market maker might get in trouble with accusations of front-running trades.

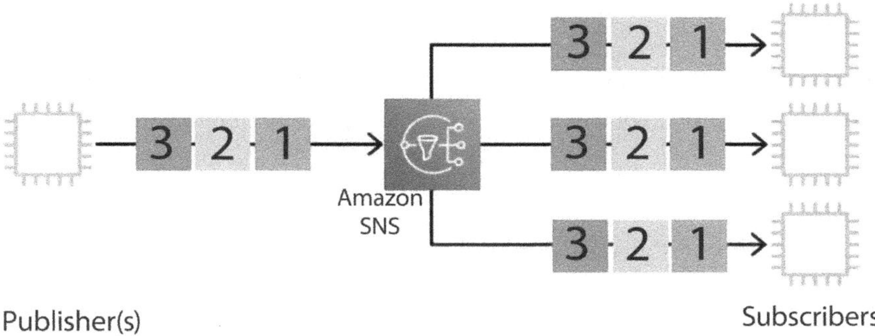

Figure 13.10: Event-driven pub/sub model in AWS

> **Quick tip**: Need to see a high-resolution version of this image? Open this book in the next-gen Packt Reader or view it in the PDF/ePub copy.
>
> **The next-gen Packt Reader** is included for free with the purchase of this book. Scan the QR code OR go to `packtpub.com/unlock`, then use the search bar to find this book by name. Double-check the edition shown to make sure you get the right one.

As shown in the preceding diagram, messages from different publishers go to SNS, where multiple consumers are subscribed to receive them. SNS then sends messages to all the subscribers for further processing, per the application's requirements.

The pub/sub model is frequently used with stateful applications. In a stateful application, the order in which the messages are received is important, as the order can impact the application state.

Point-to-point model

In an event-driven system, the **point-to-point** model is one of the most common ways to deliver events. In this model, when a producer service generates an event, it sends it into a queue. Exactly one consumer service processes that event; no other service picks up the same event. This ensures that each event is processed only once, preventing duplicate work and maintaining system integrity.

The following diagram shows how to easily implement the Point-to-Point model on AWS using Amazon SQS. When a service places a message in SQS, one available consumer retrieves and processes it.

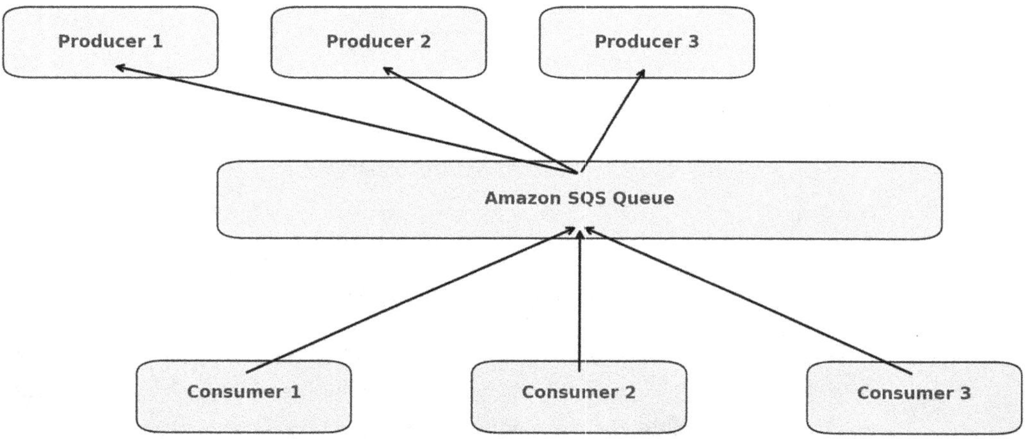

Figure 13.11: Point-to-point EDA model using Amazon SQS

If the consumer fails to process the event properly, the message can be returned to the queue for another attempt or moved to a DLQ for further inspection.

A real-world example is Capital One, a leading financial services company. It uses Amazon SQS to handle millions of customer transactions in its backend systems. Each transaction event is placed into a queue, and a specific processing service picks it up to update accounts, send notifications, or trigger fraud detection workflows without overwhelming its systems or losing data.

Benefits of EDA

EDA can help an organization gain an advantage over its competitors. This edge stems from the benefits that the pub/sub model can provide. The following subsections explain some of these benefits.

No more polling

The pub/sub model delivers the benefit of real-time events through a *push* delivery mechanism. It eliminates the need to fetch sources to see whether data has changed constantly. If you use a polling mechanism, you will either waste resources by checking for changes when no changes have occurred or delay actions if changes happen when you haven't polled.

Using a push mechanism minimizes message delivery latency. Depending on your application, message delivery delays could cost millions of dollars.

For example, let's say you have a trading application. You want to buy stock only when a certain price is reached. If you were using polling, you would have to constantly ping every so often to see whether the price had changed. This has two problems:

- Computing resources will have to be used with every ping. This is wasteful.
- If the price changes between pings and then changes again, the trade may not be executed even though the target price has been reached.

With events, the ping will be generated only once when the target price is reached, greatly increasing the likelihood that the trade will happen.

Dynamic targeting

EDA effortlessly and naturally simplifies service discovery, minimizing potential errors. In EDA, data consumers are not tracked; instead, interested parties subscribe to the topics they are interested in. If parties are interested in the messages, they all consume them. In the pub/sub model, if there are no interested consumers, the message is broadcast without anyone taking action.

Continuing with our trading application example, let's assume each stock represents a topic. Having application users select what topic/stock interests them will greatly reduce the number of events generated and minimize resource consumption.

Communication simplicity

EDA minimizes code complexity by eliminating direct point-to-point communication between producers and consumers. The number of connections is greatly reduced by having a central queue where producers place their messages and consumers collect messages.

Suppose our trading application has 10 stock shares and 10 users. If we didn't have an intermediate queue to hold the events, every stock share would have to be connected to every user for 100 connections. However, having a queue in the middle would mean that we only have 10 connections from the stock to the queue and 10 connections from the users to the queue, giving us 20 connections, greatly simplifying the system.

Decoupling and scalability

The pub/sub model increases software flexibility. There is no explicit coupling between publishers and subscribers. They are all decoupled and work independently of each other. Having this decoupling promotes the individual development of services, which, in turn, allows us to deploy and scale these services independently. Functionality changes in one part of the application should not affect the rest so long as design patterns are followed and the code is truly modularized. So long as the agreed-upon APIs stay stable, changing the publisher code should not affect the consumer code.

In our trading application example, users don't need a new connection to the new stock if a new stock ticker is added. You create a connection from the new stock to the queue, and now anybody can listen for events in that new topic. Something similar happens when new users are added. The user just needs to specify which stocks they are interested in. The system needs to change nothing else, making the overall architecture quite scalable.

Improved performance and responsiveness

One of the biggest advantages of using an EDA is that it greatly improves the performance and responsiveness of your applications. In traditional systems, services often wait for each other to complete tasks before moving on. This can cause delays, create bottlenecks, and waste valuable resources. However, in an event-driven system, once an event occurs, it is immediately pushed into a queue or topic without waiting for an immediate response. This allows your services to continue running and handle other tasks in parallel.

In AWS, you can easily build this pattern using services such as Amazon EventBridge, Amazon SNS, and Amazon SQS. For example, Airbnb uses event-driven systems to handle real-time updates such as reservation confirmations, host notifications, and payment processing. Events flow asynchronously, which means Airbnb can instantly react to millions of changes every second without slowing down its platform.

Because events are processed asynchronously, your application can scale horizontally by adding more consumers only when needed. This also helps handle sudden traffic spikes, such as during a big sale or flash event, without crashing the system.

Disadvantages of EDA

As with other technologies, EDA has drawbacks. The following subsections explain some of these.

EDA is not a silver bullet

It is worth noting that, like any other technology, the EDA pattern should not be viewed as a solution that can solve all problems. A problem may not require the added complexity of setting up a message queue. We might only need a "point-to-point" communication channel because we don't foresee having additional producers or consumers. The EDA pattern is quite popular with new IoT applications, but it is not suitable for other use cases. If your application is synchronous and only requires accessing and updating a database, using EDA may not be necessary and might be overcomplicated. It is important to determine how much interactivity and inter-process communication will be required in our application before recommending EDA as a pattern for a given problem. EDA applications require some effort to maintain and troubleshoot when issues arise (by having to check consumers, producers, and queues), and an individual problem might not warrant their use.

For example, what if our trading application focused only on one stock share? In that particular example, we might want to avoid the complexity of creating queues, topics, and so on, and keep it simple without using a queue.

When things go wrong

Like any other technology that depends on an underlying infrastructure, messages can get lost in an EDA implementation for various reasons, including the failure of hardware components. Dealing with such shortcomings can be difficult to troubleshoot and even more difficult to find a solution to recover from. These issues stem from the asynchronous nature of the architecture. This property makes the resulting applications massively scalable, but with the downside of potentially losing messages. Overcoming this shortcoming can be challenging.

Troubleshooting EDA applications is not easy due to their asynchronous nature. For example, a hard failure might cause us to lose a message in our trading application. We obviously want to minimize or even eliminate these occurrences. However, replicating the behavior to debug it may be difficult, if not impossible. You can use managed, serverless, AWS-native services such as EventBridge to reduce the risk.

Microservices best practices

As with any technology, the devil is in the details. It is certainly possible to create bad microservices. Let's delve into how some common pitfalls can be avoided and some recommended best practices.

Best practice #1 – Decide whether microservices are the right tool

The world's leading technology companies, such as eBay, Facebook/Meta, Amazon, Microsoft, X/Twitter, and PayPal, are heavy users of microservice architecture and rely on it for much of their development. However, it's not a panacea. As technologists, everything looks like a nail once we get a hammer. Make sure that your particular use case is best suited for this architecture. If breaking down your application into functional domains is hard, a microservice architecture might not be the best choice.

Best practice #2 – Clearly define the requirements and design of the microservice

Like other software projects, creating microservices requires preparation and focus. A sure way for a software project to fail is to start coding without a clear goal for the software's function.

Requirements should be detailed and approved by all stakeholders. Once the requirements are completed, a design should be created using language and artifacts understood by all parties involved, including domain experts.

A clear distinction should be made between business requirements and functions, the services provided, and the microservices implemented to deliver those services. Without this delineation, the microservices will likely be too big and not fragmented enough, and no benefit will be delivered from using a microservice architecture. On the other hand, it is also possible for your design to have too many microservices and for you to over-engineer the solution. Too many microservices will make the solution difficult to maintain, understand, and troubleshoot.

Best practice #3 – Leverage DDD to create microservices

Later in this chapter, we will learn about the DDD methodology. DDD is ideally suited for developing microservices. It is a set of design principles that allows us to define an object-oriented model using concepts and nomenclature that all stakeholders can understand using a unified model language. This allows all participants in the software definition process to understand the relevant business domains and deliver better microservices fully because you can get buy-in and understanding from everyone more quickly.

Best practice #4 – Ensure buy-in from all stakeholders

Software development involves many parties in an organization: developers, architects, testers, domain experts, managers, and decision-makers, among others. To ensure your project's success, you need to get buy-ins from all of them. It is highly recommended that you get approval from all stakeholders at every major milestone, particularly during the business requirement and design phase. In today's Agile culture, the initial requirements and design can often change, and in those instances, it is also important to keep stakeholders updated and in agreement.

Deploying a microservice entails much more than just technology. The key is gaining approval and mindshare from the status quo. This cultural transformation can be arduous and expensive. Depending on the team's exposure to this new paradigm, it might require a significant effort, especially if they are accustomed to building their applications in a monolithic manner.

Once you start delivering results and business value, you establish a cadence and harmonious state with all team members. Therefore, it is important to start delivering value as soon as possible. A common approach is to deliver an MVP that provides the core functionality to derive value. Once the MVP is deployed to production and used, you can continue building and enhancing the service.

Best practice #5 – Leverage logging and tracing tools

One of the disadvantages of using a microservice architecture is the added burden of logging and tracing many components. In a monolithic application, there is one software component to monitor. Each microservice generates its own logging and error messages in a microservice architecture. With a microservice architecture, software development is simplified, but operations become a little more complicated. For this reason, it is important that your services leverage AWS's logging and tracing services, such as Amazon CloudWatch, AWS X-Ray, and AWS CloudTrail, where the logging and error messages generated are as uniform as possible. Ideally, all the microservice teams will agree on the logging libraries and standards to increase uniformity. Two products that are quite popular for implementing logging are the **ELK** stack (consisting of **Elasticsearch, Logstash, and Kibana**) and Splunk.

Best practice #6 – Think microservices first

Software development can be a fine art more than a hard science. There are always conflicting forces at play. You want to deliver functionality in production as quickly as possible, but at the same time, you want to ensure that your solution endures for many years and is easily maintainable and expandable. For this reason, some developers like using a monolithic architecture at the beginning of projects and then try to convert it to a microservice architecture.

If possible, it is best to fight this temptation. The tight coupling that will exist because of the architecture choice will be difficult to untangle once embedded. Additionally, expectations rise once your application is in production because any changes you make must be thoroughly tested. You want to ensure that any new changes don't break existing functionality. You might think that code refactoring to ease maintenance is a valid reason to change code in production. However, explaining to your boss why the production code broke when you were introducing a change that did not add any new functionality will not be an easy conversation. You may be able to deliver the initial functionality faster using a monolithic architecture, but it will be cumbersome to convert it into a more modular architecture later.

You should spend some time correctly designing your microservices' boundaries from the start. If you use an Agile methodology, there will undoubtedly be some refactoring of microservices as your architecture evolves, and that's okay. But do your best to design your boundaries properly at the beginning.

Best practice #7 – Minimize the number of languages and technologies

One advantage of the microservice architecture is the ability to create different services using different technology stacks. For example, you could create *Service A* using Java, the Spring MVC framework, and MariaDB, and *Service B* using Python with a Postgres backend. This is doable because when *Service A* communicates with *Service B*, they will communicate through the HTTP protocol and the RESTful API without either one caring about the details of the other's implementation.

Just because you can do something doesn't mean you should do it. It still behooves you to minimize the number of languages used to create microservices. Having a small number of languages, or even using just one, will enable you to switch people from one group to another, act more nimbly, and be more flexible.

There is a case to be made that one stack might be superior to the other and better suited to implementing a particular service. However, you should ensure a compelling business case to increase your technological footprint whenever you have to deviate from your company's standard stack.

Best practice #8 – Leverage RESTful APIs

A key feature of the microservice pattern is its functionality, which is delivered via a RESTful API. **RESTful APIs** are powerful for various reasons, including that no client code needs to be deployed to start using them and that, if implemented properly, they can be self-documenting.

Best practice #9 – Implement microservice communication asynchronously

Communication between microservices should be asynchronous whenever possible. One of the tricky parts of designing microservices is deciding the boundaries between the services. Do you offer granular microservices or only a few services? If you provide many services that perform a few tasks well, there will undoubtedly be more inter-service communication.

To perform a task, it may be necessary for *Service A* to call *Service B*, which, in turn, needs to call *Service C*. If the services are called synchronously, this interdependency can make the application brittle. For example, what happens if *Service C* is down? *Service A* won't work and will hopefully return an error. The alternative is for the services to communicate asynchronously. In this case, if *Service C* is down, *Service A* will put a request in a queue, and *Service C* will handle it when it returns online. Implementing asynchronous communication between services creates more overhead. It is more difficult than synchronous communication, but the upfront development cost will be offset by increasing the reliability and scalability of the final solution.

Best practice #10 – Implement a clear separation between microservice frontends and backends

Even today, many backend developers have an outdated perspective about developing UIs and tend to oversimplify the complexities involved in constructing user-friendly frontends. The UI can often be neglected in design sessions. A microservice architecture with fine-grained backend services that has a monolithic frontend can run into trouble in the long run. There are great options out there that can help create sharp-looking frontends. Some of the most popular frontend web development frameworks currently are the following:

- Vue
- React
- Angular

However, picking the hottest SPA tool to develop your frontend is not enough. Having a clear separation between backend and frontend development is imperative. The interaction and dependencies between the two should be minimal, if they are not completely independent.

As new UIs become more popular or easier to use, we should be able to swap out the frontend with minimal interruptions and changes to the backend.

Another reason for this independence is when multiple UIs are required. For example, our application may need a web UI, an Android application, and an iOS application.

Best practice #11 – Organize your team around microservices

On a related note to the previous best practice, there might be different teams for individual microservices, and it's important to assign ownership of each of these services to individuals in your team. However, your team will be as cross-functional as possible, and team members can jump from one microservice to another if needed. In general, there should be a good reason to pull one team member from developing one service to another, but when this happens, hopefully, they can make the leap and fill the gap.

In addition, the team should understand the project's overall objectives and the project plan for all services. A narrow view of only one service could prove fatal to the business's success if the team doesn't fully understand the business impact that a change in that service could have on other services.

Best practice #12 – Provision individual data stores for each microservice

Separating your garbage into recyclables and non-recyclables and watching the garbage collector co-mingle them can be frustrating. The same is true of microservices that have well-defined and architected boundaries and share the same database. Using the same database creates strong coupling between the microservices, which we want to avoid whenever possible. Having a common database will require constant synchronization between the various microservice developers. Transactions will also become more complicated if there is a common database.

Having a separate data store makes services more modular and reusable. However, having one database per microservice requires that any data that needs to be shared between services be passed along with the RESTful calls. Still, this drawback is insufficient to prevent separating service databases whenever possible.

Ideally, every microservice will have an individual allocation for its data store and be responsible for its persistence. Data can be reused across services, but should only be stored once and shared via APIs. However, data sharing across microservices should be avoided whenever possible, as it leads to service coupling. This coupling negates some of the advantages of a microservice architecture's separation of concerns, so it should be avoided as much as possible.

Best practice #13 – Self-documentation and full documentation

A well-designed RESTful API should be intuitive if you correctly choose your domain and operation names.

Take special care when using labels for your APIs that closely match your business domains. If you do this, you won't need to create endless documents to support your application. However, your documentation should be able to fill the gaps and take over where the intuitiveness of your API ends. One of the most popular tools for creating this documentation is **Swagger**. You can learn more about the Swagger tool here: `https://swagger.io/`.

Best practice #14 – Use a DevOps toolset

Another methodology that goes hand in hand with microservice development (in addition to DDD) is the popular **DevOps paradigm**. A robust DevOps program and a mature CI/CD pipeline will allow you to develop, test, and maintain your microservices quickly and effortlessly.

A popular combination is to use Jenkins for deployment and Docker as a container service with GitHub. AWS CodePipeline can be used to automate an end-to-end DevOps pipeline.

Best practice #15 – Invest in monitoring

As we learned in the preceding section regarding the disadvantages of microservices, they can be more difficult to monitor and troubleshoot than legacy monolithic architectures. This increased complexity must be accounted for, and new monitoring tools that can be adapted to the latest microservice architecture must be used.

Ideally, the monitoring solution offers a central repository for messages and logs regardless of what component of the architecture generated the event.

The monitoring tools should be able to be used for each microservice, and the monitoring system should facilitate root cause analysis. Fortunately, AWS offers a nice selection of monitoring services, including the following:

- Amazon CloudWatch
- AWS CloudTrail
- AWS X-Ray

To learn more about these and other monitoring services in AWS, you can visit `https://docs.aws.amazon.com/AWSEC2/latest/UserGuide/monitoring_ec2.html`.

Best practice #16 – Use least privilege IAM policies per service for security

In a microservices architecture, it's crucial to apply the principle of least privilege by assigning each service its own IAM role with only the specific permissions it requires to function. Avoid using overly permissive policies or sharing IAM roles across services, as this increases the blast radius in case of a security breach. For example, suppose your application includes payment processing and reporting services. In that case, the payment service should not be granted access to the S3 bucket storing analytics data used solely by the reporting service. By scoping IAM roles tightly, you ensure that a vulnerability in one service cannot be exploited to access other parts of your application.

A real-world example of this is with Amazon ECS or EKS, where you can assign IAM roles to specific ECS tasks or Kubernetes service accounts using IAM roles for tasks or **IAM roles for service accounts** (**IRSA**). This approach ensures fine-grained control and better access auditing. Additionally, you can use AWS IAM Access Analyzer to review which resources a role has access to and further minimize unnecessary permissions.

Best practice #17 – Use serverless where appropriate for cost optimization

Cost efficiency is a key advantage of cloud-native microservices, and using serverless technologies can significantly reduce overhead, especially for workloads with inconsistent or unpredictable traffic. Services such as AWS Lambda and AWS Fargate are ideal for microservices without continuous uptime or variable demand. These platforms automatically scale based on request volume and charge only for actual compute time used, helping you avoid costs from idle instances.

For instance, a user sign-up service that only triggers during user registration events is a great candidate for Lambda. At the same time, a data processing job that runs every few hours might be well suited for Fargate. For higher-volume microservices, you can use EC2 Auto Scaling groups or EKS with Cluster Autoscaler to scale in and out based on traffic patterns. To maintain financial visibility, leverage AWS Cost Explorer, AWS Budgets, and resource tags to monitor and optimize cost per service.

Best practice #18 – Two pizzas should be enough to feed your team

This is a rule popularized by Jeff Bezos. He famously only invites enough people to meetings so that two large pizzas can feed the attendees. Bezos popularized the *two-pizza* rule for meetings and project teams to encourage a decentralized, creative working environment and to keep the start-up spirit alive and well.

This rule aims to avoid **groupthink**, a phenomenon that occurs when large groups of people start following the consensus instead of feeling comfortable challenging what they think are bad ideas. In some ways, it is human nature to be more hesitant to disagree in large groups.

It is not uncommon for members of the group who are lower in the corporate hierarchy to be intimidated by authority figures such as their boss and people with bigger titles. Keeping groups small and encouraging dialogue can overcome some of this hesitancy, and better ideas may be generated.

Bezos's idea to keep meetings and teams small to foster collaboration and productivity is supported by science. After 50 years of studying and researching teams, J. Richard Hackman concluded that 4 to 6 is the optimal number of team members for many projects and that teams should never be larger than 10.

According to Hackman, communication issues "*grow exponentially as team size increases.*" Perhaps counterintuitively, the larger a team is, the more time will be spent communicating, reducing the time that can be used productively to achieve goals.

In the context of microservice development, the two-pizza rule is also applicable. You don't want your microservice development and deployment teams to be much bigger than a dozen people or so. If you need more staff, you are better off splitting the microservice domains so that you can have two teams creating two microservices rather than one huge team creating an incredibly big and complex microservice.

Obviously, there is no hard rule about exactly how many people are too many, but at some point, the number becomes too big and unmanageable. For example, a 100-person monolithic team with no hierarchy or natural division would likely be too unmanageable.

Best practice #19 – Twelve-factor design

A popular methodology for enhancing microservice development is the **twelve-factor design**. This methodology accelerates and simplifies software development by making suggestions, such as ensuring that you use a version control tool to keep track of your code.

The twelve-factor design is a methodology for building **software-as-a-service** (**SaaS**) applications that are easy to scale and maintain. Adam Wiggins, co-founder of Heroku, a cloud platform for creating and deploying web applications, first introduced it in a 2011 article.

The 12 factors are as follows:

1. **Code base**: One code base is tracked in revision control for many deployments.
2. **Dependencies**: Explicitly declare and isolate dependencies.
3. **Config**: Store config in the environment.
4. **Backing services**: Treat backing services as attached resources.
5. **Build, release, run**: Strictly separate build and run stages.
6. **Processes**: Execute the app as one or more stateless processes.
7. **Port binding**: Export services via port binding.
8. **Concurrency**: Scale out via the process model.
9. **Disposability**: Maximize robustness with fast startup and graceful shutdown.
10. **Dev/prod parity**: Keep development, staging, and production as similar as possible.
11. **Logs**: Treat logs as event streams.
12. **Admin processes**: Run admin/management tasks as one-off processes.

The twelve-factor methodology aims to simplify scaling and maintaining SaaS applications by breaking them down into small, loosely coupled services that can be run in different environments and deployed on cloud-based platforms. You can learn more about this methodology at `https://12factor.net/`.

Many of the best practices mentioned in this section apply not only to microservice development but also to software development in general. Following these practices from the beginning of your project will greatly increase the chances of a successful implementation on time and budget, as well as ensure that these microservices are useful, adaptable, flexible, and easily maintainable.

In today's world, software is used to solve many complicated problems. From meeting worldwide demand for your e-commerce site to enabling a real-time stock trading platform, many companies, big and small, are leveraging DDD to bring their products and services to market on time. Let's take a look at the DDD pattern.

Domain-driven design

DDD might fall into the shiny new object category, as many people see it as the latest trendy pattern. However, DDD builds upon decades of evolutionary software design and engineering wisdom. To better understand it, let's briefly look at how the ideas behind DDD came about with a brief overview of **object-oriented programming** (OOP).

DDD has its roots in the OOP concepts pioneered by Alan Kay and Ivan Sutherland. Kay coined the term *OOP* around 1966 or 1967 while in grad school. OOP is a powerful programming paradigm that allows for the creation of well-structured, maintainable, and reusable code and is widely used in the development of modern software applications.

OOP is a programming approach based on the concept of objects. Objects can be thought of as instances of a class and are used to represent and manipulate real-world entities. OOP uses objects and their interactions to design and write programs. It's like building a house: You use different blocks (objects) to make other rooms (programs), and you can use the same blocks (objects) in various ways to build different rooms (programs).

Imagine you're making a video game where you control a character, such as Mario in Super Mario Bros. In OOP, you would create an "object" representing Mario, and give it properties such as its position on the screen, how fast it can move, and how many lives it has. You would also give it "methods" that tell it what to do, such as moving left or right, jumping, and so on. The whole game would comprise many objects, each with its own properties and methods. For example, there would be objects for the Goombas (enemies), pipes, coins, and so on. All these objects would interact with each other in a way that makes sense for the game.

OOP also includes other concepts, such as inheritance, polymorphism, encapsulation, and abstraction, which help organize and maintain code.

OOP languages such as Java, C++, Python, C#, and others are widely used in the industry. These languages provide features such as classes, objects, inheritance, polymorphism, encapsulation, and so on to build OOP-based applications.

Ivan Sutherland created an application called **Sketchpad**, an early inspiration for OOP. Sutherland started working on this application in 1963. In this early OOP application, objects were primitive data structures displayed as images on the screen. They started using the concept of inheritance even in those early days. Sketchpad has some similarities with JavaScript's prototypal inheritance.

OOP arose because developers and designers were increasingly ambitious about tackling more complex problems, and procedural languages were insufficient. Another seminal development was the creation of a language called **Simula**. Simula is considered the first fully OOP language. Two Norwegian computer scientists, Ole-Johan Dahl and Kristen Nygaard, developed it.

A lot of development and many projects relied heavily on OOP for a long time. Building upon the advances of OOP, Eric Evans wrote the book *Domain-Driven Design: Tackling Complexity in the Heart of Software* in 2003. In his book, Evans introduced us to DDD and posited that DDD represents a new, better, and more mature way to develop software, building on the evolution of **object-oriented analysis and design (OOAD)**.

DDD builds upon OOP by providing a set of principles and practices for designing software that models complex business domains. While OOP focuses on the implementation of objects and their interactions, DDD focuses on modeling the business domain and creating a rich, domain-specific language that accurately captures its complexities. DDD uses this language to drive the design and implementation of the software. DDD and OOP have a lot of similarities, and many of the concepts of OOP are present in DDD. Some of the key OOP concepts that are present in DDD include the following:

- **Encapsulation**: DDD encourages using encapsulation to hide the internal details of domain objects and expose their behavior through a public interface. This allows domain objects to be treated as black boxes that can be interacted with through a set of predefined methods without the need to understand their internal workings.
- **Inheritance**: DDD uses inheritance to model "is-a" relationships between domain objects. For example, a specific product type might inherit from a more general product class.
- **Polymorphism**: DDD uses polymorphism to model "like" relationships between domain objects. For example, different products might share some common behavior but have unique behaviors specific to their type.
- **Abstraction**: DDD encourages using abstraction to break down complex problems into smaller, more manageable parts.

In addition to the preceding OOP concepts, DDD introduces several other concepts, such as bounded contexts, aggregates, domain services, value objects, entities, repositories, and so on, which help to model the business domain more accurately and efficiently.

Definition of a domain

Now that we have taken a drive down memory lane regarding the history of DDD, let's first nail down what a domain is before we delve into the definition of DDD. According to the Oxford English Dictionary, one of the definitions of a domain is *"a sphere of knowledge or activity."*

Applying this definition to the software realm, a domain refers to the subject or topic area in which an application will operate. In application development terms, the domain is the *sphere of knowledge and activity used during application development*, and the activity is specific to a particular business or application. It includes the concepts, rules, and relationships that make up the problem space that the application tries to solve. The domain is the core of the application and is where the business logic resides.

For example, if you build an e-commerce application, the domain would include products, customers, orders, and payments. It would also include rules and relationships such as how products are categorized, how customers can place orders, and how payments are processed. The domain is the starting point for DDD and the source of the domain-specific language used throughout the development process. By creating a rich, domain-specific language, the development team can communicate more effectively and create a more accurate and efficient design. The domain model represents the domain in the software application; it is the core of the application and contains the business logic, rules, and relationships. The model should be created from the domain experts' knowledge; it should be accurate and able to capture the complexity of the domain.

Another common way this word is used is to refer to the domain layer or domain logic. Many developers also refer to this as the business layer or business logic. In software development, the business layer refers to the application layer that contains the business logic and implements the application's business rules. Business logic is the rules and processes governing how an application behaves and interacts with the domain. Business objects represent the business entities and implement the business logic.

A business rule is a specific rule or constraint that governs the behavior of business objects and the application as a whole. These rules can be specific to a business or industry and dictate how the company operates and interacts with the outside world.

For example, in an e-commerce application, a business rule might be that customers must be at least 18 years old to purchase items. This rule would be implemented in the business logic and enforced by the application when a customer attempts to buy. The business layer also contains the business object, representing a business entity, such as a customer, product, or order. These objects encapsulate the data and behavior of the corresponding business entity, providing a way for the application to interact with the domain. The business objects are responsible for implementing the business logic, including enforcing the rules.

Suppose a bank account holder tries to retrieve a certain amount of money from their bank, and their account does not have enough balance to honor the request. In that case, the bank should not allow the account holder to retrieve any funds (and charge them an *insufficient funds fee*).

Can you spot the potential business objects in this example? Pause for a second before we give you the answer to see whether you can figure it out. Two candidates are these:

- Bank account holder
- Bank account

Depending on the application, you might not want to model the holder as a separate object and rely on the account. This will depend on the operations that must be performed on the objects. Merging the account with the holder might generate data duplication (for example, you might store the same address twice when a holder has two accounts and only one address). However, this might not be an issue at all during your implementation.

Principles of DDD

As we mentioned earlier, Eric Evans coined the term *DDD*, so who better to ask for a definition than Evans? As it turns out, even for him, the definition has been a moving target, and the definition he initially gave in his book is no longer his preferred definition. Moreover, defining DDD is not a simple exercise, and Evans defines DDD in multiple ways. This is not necessarily a bad thing; by having multiple definitions, we can cover the term using different lenses.

DDD focuses on understanding and modeling the complex business domains that software systems support. DDD aims to align software systems with the underlying business domains they support, resulting in flexible, scalable, and maintainable systems. Here are the core principles of DDD in detail:

- **Ubiquitous language**: This principle states that domain experts and software developers should establish a common language. This language should be used consistently throughout development, including modeling, coding, testing, and documentation. This helps to ensure that everyone involved in the development process has a shared understanding of the domain and reduces the risk of misunderstandings and miscommunication. For example, a financial institution's domain experts and software developers establish a common language to describe financial instruments such as bonds, stocks, and mutual funds. They use this language consistently throughout the development process, which helps ensure that everyone involved has a shared understanding of these concepts and reduces the risk of misunderstandings and miscommunication.
- **Bounded contexts**: This principle states that different parts of a complex business domain should be divided into separate contexts. Each context should have a clear boundary and its own ubiquitous language. This helps ensure that each context can be understood, modeled, and developed in isolation, reducing complexity and improving maintainability. For example, a retail company's business domain is divided into separate contexts for customer management, order management, inventory management, and shipping management.
- **Strategic design**: This principle states that the overall architecture and design of the software system should align with the long-term goals and vision of the business domain. This helps ensure that the system is flexible and scalable, and can support the changing needs of the business over time. For example, a manufacturing company's software system is designed strategically to support the company's long-term goals and vision. The system is designed to be flexible and scalable, and to support the company's changing needs over time, such as changes to the product line or manufacturing processes.

By following the preceding principles, DDD helps to ensure that software systems are aligned with the core business domains they are intended to support. Let's look into the components of DDD.

Components of DDD

While you have learned about the principles of DDD, to build your architecture, it is important to understand the various components of it. The following are the key components that make up DDD:

- **Context mapping**: Context mapping is a technique for defining and organizing the different contexts within a business domain. Each context represents a distinct part of the business and has its own rules and processes. The goal of context mapping is to identify each context's boundaries and define a common language used within each context. For example, a retail company may have a context for its online store, a context for its brick-and-mortar store, and a context for its fulfillment center. Each of these contexts would have a different set of business rules and processes, and a common language used within each context would help ensure clear communication between the different parts of the business.
- **Domain model**: The domain model is the heart of DDD and represents the business domain as entities, value objects, services, and aggregates. It provides a way to understand and describe the business domain and align the software system with it.

  For example, in a retail company, the domain model might include entities for products, customers, and orders, and value objects for prices and addresses.
- **Entity**: An entity is an object that represents a core business concept and has an identity that distinguishes it from other objects. An entity should encapsulate business logic and represent a meaningful, persistent part of the business domain. For example, in a retail company, the customer entity might include information about the customer, such as their name, address, and order history, as well as methods for performing actions, such as placing an order or updating their information.
- **Value object**: A value object is an object that represents a value or attribute and lacks an identity of its own. A value object should be freely used and shared, and should not change once created. For example, in a retail company, the price value object might represent the cost of a product, while the address value object might represent the shipping address for an order.

- **Aggregate**: An aggregate is a cluster of objects that should be treated as a single unit when data changes. It should have a root object and a clear boundary that defines what objects belong to it. The goal of aggregates is to ensure consistency and maintain data integrity when making changes to the data. For example, in a retail company, the order aggregate might include the order, customer, and product entities.
- **Service**: A service is an object that encapsulates business logic that doesn't fit neatly into entities or value objects. A service should represent a business capability or process. For example, in a retail company, the order service might handle creating and submitting an order, including checking inventory levels and calculating shipping costs.
- **Repository**: A repository is a pattern that defines a data access layer that abstracts the persistence of entities and aggregates. Its goal is to provide a way to retrieve and store data in persistent storage, such as a database, while abstracting the underlying storage mechanism. For example, the order repository might provide a way to retrieve an order by its order number or store a new order in the database.
- **Factory**: A factory is a pattern that defines a way to create objects, typically entities or aggregates, in a consistent and maintainable way. The goal of a factory is to provide a way to create objects in a standardized way, with any necessary dependencies, without having to write repetitive code. For example, the order factory might provide a way to create a new order object, complete with the customer and product entities that are part of the order.
- **Modules**: Modules are a way of organizing the code and defining boundaries within a system. A module is a collection of related entities, value objects, services, and repositories that work together to provide a specific business capability. Modules are used to separate the system's concerns and reduce complexity. Modules should be autonomous and self-contained, and maintain their integrity and consistency. An example of a module could be a module for handling customer orders in an e-commerce system. This module could include entities such as `Order`, `OrderItem`, `Customer`, and `Payment`, and services such as `OrderService`, `PaymentService`, and `ShippingService`.

Now that you have learned about the principles and components of DDD, let's examine how you can implement it on the AWS platform.

Implementing DDD in AWS

Every application you build is associated with solving a specific business problem, especially when solving real-life problems in an industry domain. An industry use case can be very complex, as seen in the previous section, where we used a retail industry use case to help understand various components of DDD. Now, let's learn how to design this complex architecture using the services provided by AWS. Implementing an `Amazon.com`-like e-commerce application using DDD in AWS would be a complex and multi-step process, but the following diagram shows a general outline of the steps involved:

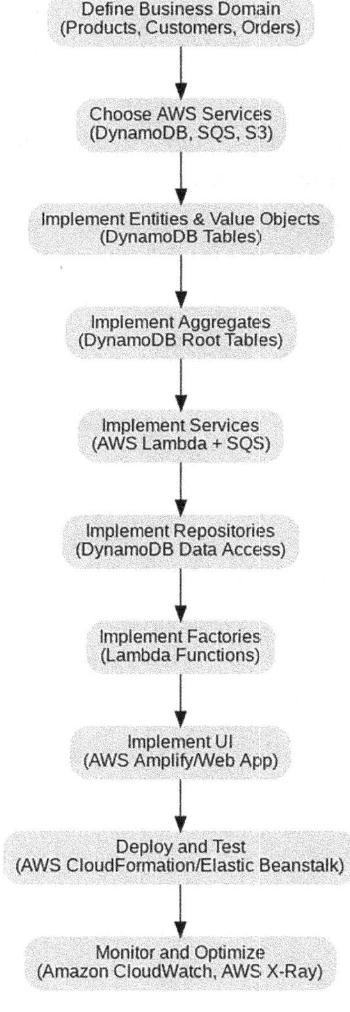

Figure 13.12: Implementation of DDD in AWS

As shown in the preceding diagram, the following are the steps to create a domain-driven design in AWS:

1. **Define the business domain**: Start by defining the different contexts within the business domain, such as the shopping context, the product context, and the fulfillment context. Create a domain model that represents the core business concepts, such as products, customers, and orders, and define their relationships with each other.
2. **Choose the right AWS services**: Based on the domain model, choose the right AWS services to implement the different components of DDD. For example, Amazon DynamoDB can store entities and aggregate roots, Amazon SQS can implement services, and Amazon S3 can store files.
3. **Implement the entities and value objects**: Implement the entities and value objects as DynamoDB tables, each with its own set of attributes and methods. Ensure that the data model is consistent with the domain model and that the entities and value objects are properly encapsulated.
4. **Implement the aggregates**: Implement the aggregates as a set of DynamoDB tables, with the root aggregate as the main table. Ensure that the aggregate boundaries are well defined and that the data is consistent within the aggregate. Implement the aggregates as classes representing a set of related entities that enforce consistency within the aggregate.
5. **Implement the services**: Implement the services as classes using AWS Lambda functions, which use SQS to handle messages. Ensure that the services are aligned with the business processes and that they have access to the necessary data and entities.
6. **Implement the repositories**: Implement the repositories as DynamoDB Data Access Objects, which provide a way to store and retrieve data in persistent storage. Ensure that the repositories align with the domain model and provide a consistent way to access data.
7. **Implement the factories**: Implement the factories as AWS Lambda functions, which store and retrieve data using DynamoDB tables. Ensure that the factories are aligned with the domain model and provide a consistent way to create objects.
8. **Implement the user interface**: Implement the user interface as a web application hosted in AWS that communicates with the backend services and repositories. Ensure the user interface is aligned with the domain model and provides customers with a consistent and intuitive experience.
9. **Deploy and test the system**: Deploy the system in AWS using the appropriate AWS services and tools, such as AWS CloudFormation or AWS Elastic Beanstalk. Test the system to ensure it is working as expected and the data is consistent and accurate.

10. **Monitor and optimize**: Monitor the system using Amazon CloudWatch and other AWS tools to ensure that it runs efficiently and that any issues are quickly addressed. Optimize the system as needed to improve performance and reduce costs.

You can choose an OOP language such as Java or Python to implement the entities, value objects, aggregates, services, repositories, and factories. In this case, objects and classes represent the core business concepts and their attributes and behaviors. Here is an example of how objects and classes might be used in an e-commerce website:

- **Product**: A product is a core business concept in an e-commerce website and represents a physical or digital item that can be sold. A product object might have a name, description, price, and image attributes. A product class might have methods such as `addToCart()`, `removeFromCart()`, and `getDetails()`.
- **Customer**: A customer is another core business concept in an e-commerce website and represents a person who can purchase products. A customer object might have attributes such as name, address, email, and phone number. A customer class might have methods such as `signUp()`, `login()`, and `updateProfile()`.
- **Order**: An order is a key business concept in an e-commerce website and represents a request by a customer to purchase one or more products. An order object might have attributes such as order number, customer, products, and total cost. An order class might have methods such as `placeOrder()`, `cancelOrder()`, and `getOrderHistory()`.
- **Cart**: A cart is a useful business concept in an e-commerce website and represents temporary storage for products that a customer has selected for purchase. A cart object might have attributes such as products and total cost. A cart class might have methods such as `addProduct()`, `removeProduct()`, and `checkout()`.

These objects and classes can be combined to implement the business processes and workflows of an e-commerce website, such as adding products to a cart, placing an order, and updating the customer's profile. By using OOP techniques such as inheritance, encapsulation, and polymorphism, it is possible to build a scalable, maintainable, and reusable system that meets the needs of the business.

The preceding steps are just a general outline, and the implementation details will vary depending on the specific requirements of your e-commerce business use case. However, by following the principles of DDD and using the right AWS services, you can build a scalable, reliable, and efficient system that meets your business's needs.

Reasons to use DDD

In this section, we will learn about the most compelling benefits of DDD and what makes it so powerful. These benefits are described in the following list:

- **Better alignment with business goals**: DDD emphasizes the importance of a deep understanding of the business domain and its needs, leading to better alignment between the software system and the business goals.
- **Increased developer productivity**: By using clear and ubiquitous language and concepts, DDD helps reduce misunderstandings and improve communication between developers, stakeholders, and domain experts. This leads to faster development and fewer mistakes.
- **Improved maintainability**: DDD encourages using a rich and expressive domain model, which can help make the software system more understandable and maintainable over time.
- **Improved scalability**: DDD promotes using modular, scalable, and flexible architecture patterns, which can help ensure that the software system can easily adapt to changing business needs.
- **Improved domain knowledge**: By working closely with domain experts, developers can better understand the business domain. This understanding can inform future development efforts and lead to better software solutions.
- **Better testing and validation**: DDD encourages **test-driven development** (**TDD**) and **behavior-driven development** (**BDD**) techniques, which can help ensure that the software system meets the business's needs and can be easily validated and tested.

DDD can lead to improved software development outcomes and better alignment with business goals, resulting in increased productivity; improved maintainability, scalability, and domain knowledge; and better testing and validation.

Challenges with DDD

As is the case with any technology and any design philosophy, DDD is not a magic bullet. Now, we will examine the challenges that you might encounter when implementing the DDD methodology in your projects in your organization:

- **Domain expertise**: Your project might have experienced developers and architects who are well versed in the tools used. However, the project will fail if at least some of your team members don't have domain expertise in the domain being modeled. If you don't have this domain expertise, it's best not to use DDD and start your project until someone on your team acquires this skill set, regardless of the methodology used.

- **Iterative development**: Agile development has become a popular methodology. A well-implemented Agile program allows companies to deliver value quickly and at less cost. DDD heavily relies on iterative practices such as Agile. One of the key benefits of combining DDD and Agile is the ability to quickly and iteratively refine the software system as the needs of the business change over time. This can help ensure that the software system remains aligned with business goals and can adapt to changing business requirements. However, enterprises often struggle to transition from the traditional and less flexible waterfall models to the new methodologies.
- **Technical projects**: There is no magic hammer in software development, and DDD is no exception. DDD shines with projects that have a great deal of domain complexity. The more complicated the business logic of your application, the more relevant DDD is. DDD is not well suited for applications with low domain complexity but a lot of technical complexity.

An example of low domain complexity with high technical complexity could be a system for tracking weather data. The domain is relatively simple, with a few concepts such as temperature, humidity, and wind speed. However, the technical complexity of the system could be high, due to the need to process large amounts of data in real time, handle multiple data sources, and display the data in a user-friendly way. An example of high domain complexity with low technical complexity could be a banking system. The domain is complex, with many concepts, such as accounts, transactions, loans, and investments. However, the technical complexity of the system may be low, as the implementation could be based on established and well-understood banking software systems. DDD is well-suited for projects with high domain and low technical complexity, where a deep understanding of the business domain is essential to the project's success. This is because DDD focuses on building a rich and expressive domain model, which is used as the foundation for the software system, and to ensure that the software system accurately reflects the business domain.

Although these disadvantages exist, using DDD for microservice architectures can still improve software development outcomes in many scenarios.

Knowledge check

As you have now learned about various architectures, it's time to do a knowledge check.

1. Your company is building an e-commerce platform using a microservices architecture deployed on AWS. Each microservice has its own database, and you use API Gateway to manage client access. Recently, your team noticed that during peak traffic hours, some backend microservices fail, causing cascading failures that impact the user shopping experience. You have been tasked with designing a robust solution that ensures that if one microservice fails, the others remain operational, and users continue interacting with the system seamlessly without downtime. Considering best practices, what AWS design pattern would you primarily implement to meet these requirements?

    a. Use the service registry pattern with AWS Cloud Map so that clients always connect to healthy instances and avoid failed services entirely.

    b. Use the circuit breaker pattern with AWS Step Functions and DynamoDB to detect failures early, stop routing traffic to failing services, and prevent cascading failures across the system.

    c. Use API Gateway throttling to reject excess traffic to backend services during peak hours, ensuring no service is overwhelmed.

    d. Use the SNS pub/sub model to replicate data between microservices so that another can take over automatically if one fails.

    Answer: b.

    Explanation:

    a. Incorrect. Service registry helps services discover each other, but it doesn't stop cascading failures when one service starts failing.

    b. **Correct**. The circuit breaker pattern is designed to halt communication with a failing service, allow recovery time, and protect the rest of the system.

    c. Incorrect. Throttling protects against traffic overload but doesn't solve the problem if the service fails internally.

    d. Incorrect. SNS helps with event broadcasting but doesn't isolate failures between services.

2. You are designing a new EDA system on AWS where multiple internal applications must receive real-time inventory updates whenever stock levels change. You need to ensure that multiple systems receive the same event notification simultaneously, and each system processes the event independently. According to *Chapter 13* best practices, which AWS services and architecture patterns should you choose to implement this? (Choose two.)

    a. Implement Amazon SQS with FIFO queues so that only one consumer processes each inventory event sequentially.
    b. Implement Amazon SNS as a pub/sub service, simultaneously broadcasting inventory updates to multiple subscribers.
    c. Use Amazon EventBridge to fan out events to multiple targets such as Lambda, SQS, or Step Functions with minimal custom code.
    d. Use Amazon S3 to store event files and allow consumers to poll and fetch updated inventory data on a scheduled basis.
    e. Use Amazon DynamoDB Streams directly to update inventory data across services in real-time.

    Answers: b. and c.

    Explanation:

    a. Incorrect. SQS (especially FIFO) ensures that only one consumer processes a message, not multiple, so it is not ideal for broadcasting.
    b. **Correct**. SNS perfectly fits pub/sub models for multiple consumers.
    c. **Correct**. EventBridge provides event buses that allow events to fan out automatically to multiple targets with filtering rules.
    d. Incorrect. S3 polling adds latency; it's not event-driven.
    e. Incorrect. DynamoDB Streams help capture database changes, but are not designed for event broadcasting to multiple unrelated systems.

3. A financial services company is transitioning from a monolithic architecture to a microservices-based architecture hosted entirely on AWS. Each microservice is aligned with specific business capabilities, such as customer management, transactions, and risk analysis. The CTO wants complete independence between teams, including freedom in the technology stack (some use Python, some use Java), independent database choices, and isolated deployments. Which AWS architectural decision best supports this goal?

a. Host all microservices on a large EC2 cluster and share a common Amazon Aurora database for faster management.
b. Deploy microservices individually on AWS Lambda and Amazon DynamoDB, ensuring each service has its own execution environment and database.
c. Consolidate all microservices into a single ECS cluster and use common S3 buckets for shared storage across services.
d. Use AWS Elastic Beanstalk to deploy all microservices in one environment, simplifying operational management for the DevOps team.

Answer: b.

Explanation:

a. Incorrect. A shared database increases coupling, defeating the purpose of microservices.
b. **Correct**. Deploying each microservice separately with Lambda and DynamoDB supports independence in deployment, technology, and scaling.
c. Incorrect. A single ECS cluster might cause resource contention if services aren't isolated correctly.
d. Incorrect. Elastic Beanstalk manages environments together, which is not ideal for independently evolving services.

4. Your e-commerce platform plans to implement DDD using AWS services, based on recommendations from *Chapter 13*. You have created domain models such as `Product`, `Customer`, and `Order`. You want to ensure that each entity is stored and retrieved reliably while maintaining clear aggregate boundaries. Which AWS services would you primarily use to implement DDD components such as aggregates, repositories, and factories? (Choose two.)

a. Use Amazon DynamoDB to store entities and aggregates as individual tables and enforce consistency through application logic.
b. Use AWS Lambda functions to implement factories that create domain objects consistently and on demand.
c. Use Amazon SNS topics to store entity attributes directly and notify consumers.
d. Use an Amazon RDS/Aurora shared schema for all aggregates to simplify entity management across domains.
e. Use AWS Fargate containers to batch-process entity creation at periodic intervals.

Answers: a. and b.

Explanation:

a. **Correct**. DynamoDB is highly recommended for storing aggregates and maintaining domain model consistency due to its scalability and speed.

b. **Correct**. Lambda functions fit perfectly to implement factories that create domain objects dynamically.

c. Incorrect. SNS is used for messaging, not entity storage.

d. Incorrect. Shared schemas contradict DDD's goal of bounded contexts and separation.

e. Incorrect. Fargate is good for container orchestration but inefficient for real-time domain object creation.

5. Due to synchronous dependency calls between services, your product development team faces long testing cycles when integrating multiple microservices. If one service is slow or unavailable, all related services get blocked, causing slow system performance and longer time-to-market. Based on *Chapter 13* guidelines, what approach would you recommend to minimize dependencies, enhance reliability, and promote service autonomy?

    a. Continue with synchronous APIs but increase service timeouts and retries to handle temporary failures better.

    b. Redesign services to communicate asynchronously using queues such as Amazon SQS or event buses such as EventBridge for better decoupling.

    c. Implement multi-Region replication so that if one service fails in one Region, another Region can take over immediately.

    d. Use Elastic Load Balancing with health checks to automatically reroute traffic from failed services to other healthy services.

Answer: b.

Explanation:

a. Incorrect. Increasing timeouts increases user-facing delays without solving the root cause.

b. **Correct**. Asynchronous communication using SQS/EventBridge is the AWS-recommended method for decoupling services.

c. Incorrect. Multi-Region replication solves disaster recovery issues, but not service-to-service dependency blocking.

d. Incorrect. Load balancers help distribute load, but don't decouple microservices communications.

Summary

In this chapter, you explored microservice architecture and learned about popular patterns such as layered architecture, EDA, and DDD. You learned about the advantages and disadvantages of EDA, when to use it, and how to troubleshoot if things go wrong.

Next, you went through the recommended best practices in developing microservices. You can now leverage and benefit from the list of tried-and-true best practices in your next project.

Not using architectures such as EDA in a modern-day enterprise is no longer an option. If you continue to use legacy patterns, it is a surefire way for your project and your company to stay stuck in the past and lag behind your competition. A microservice architecture will make your application more scalable, maintainable, and relevant.

Finally, you further explored how DDD has evolved and can address complex industry use cases to solve business problems. You learned about the principles and components of DDD and used them to design a domain-heavy e-commerce app using AWS services.

So far, you've learned about various AWS services and how to integrate them into your architecture, along with strategies for selecting the right service based on your workload requirements. In the next chapter, you'll put this knowledge into action by building an application through a guided, hands-on exercise.

Part 6

Hands-On Labs

In the final part, you'll apply everything you've learned by building a complete AWS application from the ground up. You'll configure IAM, create serverless functions, connect to databases, expose APIs, and monitor your system, all while following the AWS Well-Architected Framework. This hands-on project will prepare you for real-world implementation and give you the confidence to design, deploy, and manage cloud-native apps.

This part of the book includes the following chapter:

- *Chapter 14, Hands-On Guide to Building an App in AWS*

14

Hands-On Guide to Building an App in AWS

In this chapter, you will combine many of the concepts you learned about in previous chapters to build a practical, e-commerce serverless architecture for a fictional online store called *AWSome Store*. After reading this chapter, you should be able to build your own application using some or all of the components you will review.

For many of the services, you can plug and play and pick and choose the services that will be used in the application you develop. For example, your application may be more user-centric and may not require any asynchronous services such as Amazon SQS/SNS or Step Functions. In this case, you can pull the asynchronous component out of your architecture. However, including some of the services in your architecture is highly advisable. For example, suppose your application is going to have a frontend. In that case, you will want to ensure that you have an authentication component so that every user is authenticated before using other application services.

In this chapter, you will first review the use case and build the architecture upon your previous learning of the domain-driven architecture in *Chapter 13*. You will develop and implement an architecture using AWS services and the **command-line interface** (**CLI**). You will cover the following topics:

- Understanding the use case
- Building the architecture for a fictional e-commerce website called *AWSome Store*
- Deciding on your programming language
- Implementing *AWSome Store* in AWS
- Optimizing with the Well-Architected Framework

Let's start building in AWS now.

An introduction to the use case

This chapter will allow you to combine and practice many of the concepts we have covered throughout this book. You'll need to design your system's architecture to scale without impacting application performance. You can use a serverless architecture, which involves building small, independent functions triggered by events, such as changes in a database or the arrival of a new message. This allows you to scale your system as needed, paying only for the resources you use.

To build upon your existing knowledge, let's go into more detail about implementing **domain-driven design** (**DDD**) for a retail e-commerce application use case that you learned about in *Chapter 13, Building Microservices and Event-Driven Architecture in AWS,* under the *Domain-driven design* section. Let's take a trip down memory lane to understand the use case.

To make it a fun learning experience, we'll give the retail store a name that we will use to learn AWS. Let's name it *AWSome Store.* Our imaginary online store provides AWS merchandise, such as stickers, books, water bottles, and so on. You first need to identify the core business concepts, or entities, that make up the *AWSome Store* system to build a DDD. In the context of a retail e-commerce app, these entities include products, orders, customers, and payments. Next, you'll need to identify the different contexts in which these entities exist. For example, the product context might include product details, availability, and pricing, while the order context might include information about order status, shipping, and billing.

Once you've identified the bounded contexts, you'll need to define the relationships between the entities within each context. For example, an ordered aggregate might include an order, the customer who placed the order, and the purchased products. You may also identify services within each context that perform specific operations, such as calculating the total price of an order or processing a payment. Finally, you'll need to identify domain events that trigger actions within the system, such as a new order being placed or a product becoming unavailable.

Figure 14.1 shows a context map diagram for *AWSome Store* for identified bounded contexts in the different business areas or contexts comprising the *AWSome Store* system, such as order management, payment processing, order fulfillment, shipping, and customer management.

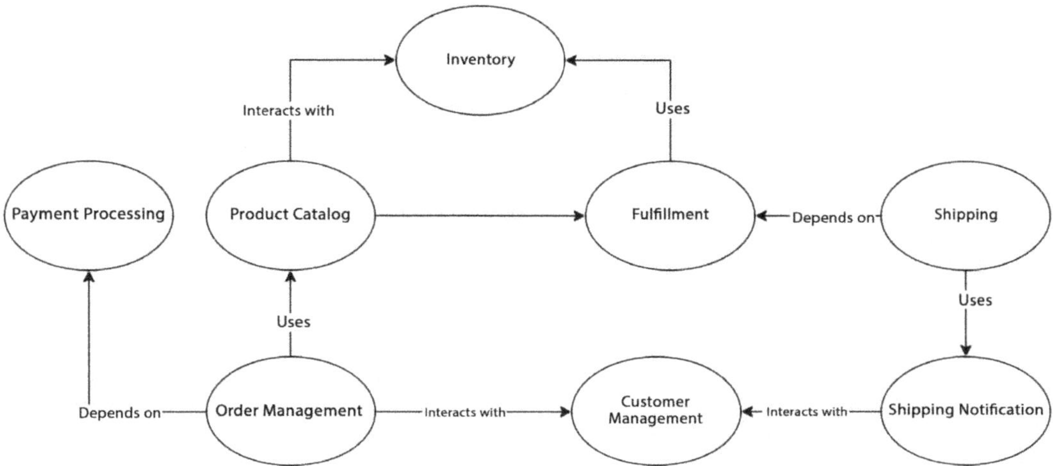

Figure 14.1: DDD context map diagram for AWSome Store

The preceding diagram defines the relationships between the different bounded contexts. For example, the *payment processing* context might be related to the *order management* context because products are ordered and sold. We have represented each bounded context as a separate oval on the diagram, and we labeled each oval with the name of the context and the main entities within that context. The lines between the ovals represent the relationships between the bounded contexts and the type of relationship, such as *uses*, *depends on*, or *interacts with*. You can further refine the diagram as needed and review it with stakeholders to ensure that it accurately represents the relationships and dependencies between the bounded contexts.

By creating a context map diagram, you can understand the relationships between the business areas of the *AWSome Store* e-commerce retail app, helping you make informed decisions about architecture, design, and implementation.

Let's start looking at the design for our serverless microservice application. First, we'll present the high-level architecture, and afterward, we'll analyze each component or **domain** independently in detail:

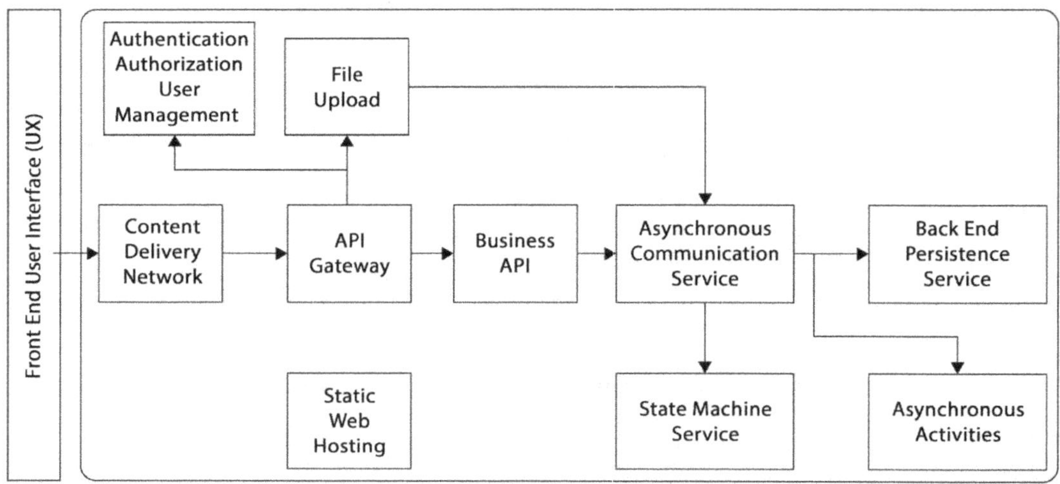

Figure 14.2: Serverless web-application architecture

As you can see, the architecture provides services for static web hosting, business services, an asynchronous service, a state machine service, and file uploads, among other components. In the following sections, you will look at each component in detail.

In *Figure 14.2*, each block represents delimited domains and technical functionality in many serverless implementations. Each block will represent one or more microservices, depending on the methodology and whether you use a microservice architecture. For example, the business API should be broken down into a series of microservices and not just one. You might have a microservice to handle *accounts* and another microservice to manage *companies*.

Building architecture in AWS

Now that you understand different domains and relationships, let's build an architecture diagram using AWS services. AWS offers several services that you can use to build a robust, scalable, and resilient system. For example, you can use Amazon Lambda to build serverless functions, Amazon DynamoDB to store data, Amazon S3 to store files, and Amazon API Gateway to create APIs. Also, implementing proper error handling and retry logic is crucial for building a resilient and robust system with AWS Lambda. Finally, you can use Amazon Q Developer to generate code for all components and bind them together. You can learn more about Amazon Q here: `https://docs.aws.amazon.com/amazonq/latest/qdeveloper-ug/command-line.html`.

To quickly implement new features, you'll need to implement a CI/CD pipeline that automatically builds, tests, and deploys new code to production. Let's look at *AWSome Store*'s proposed architecture using AWS cloud-native services:

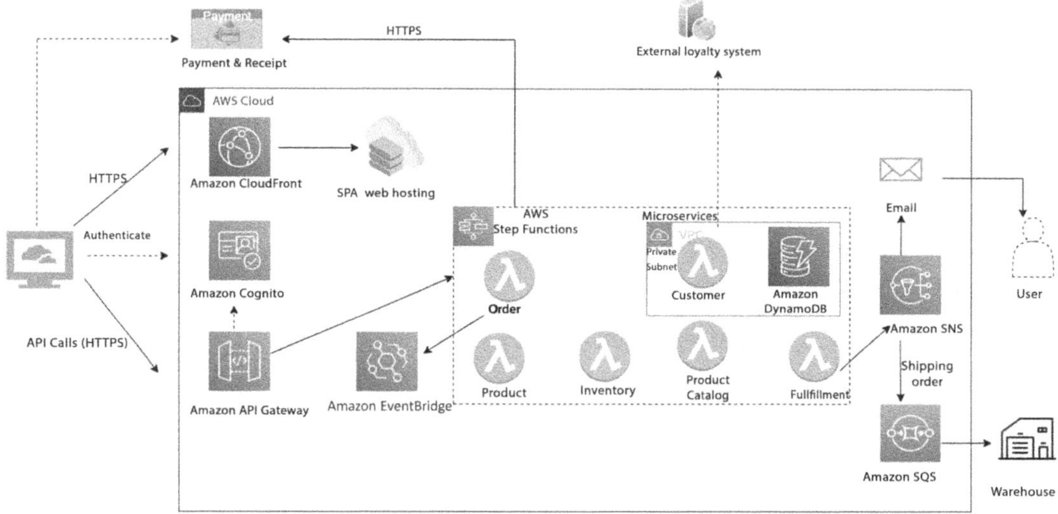

Figure 14.3: AWS cloud-native architecture to build AWSome Store

As shown in *Figure 14.3*, AWS provides various cloud-native serverless technologies to implement a scalable and resilient e-commerce retail app, such as AWS Lambda, Amazon API Gateway, Amazon DynamoDB, Amazon S3, and Amazon EventBridge. These services could be used to implement a cloud-native serverless architecture for the following key components of *AWSome Store*:

- **Frontend**: The frontend of *AWSome Store* could be built using a JavaScript framework such as React and hosted on Amazon S3. Amazon CloudFront is used as a **content delivery network (CDN)** to ensure that website content is available to global users close to their location.
- **Authentication and authorization**: Amazon Cognito authenticates end customers and authorizes them to use the application for creating profiles and placing orders.
- **API Gateway**: Amazon API Gateway creates RESTful APIs for the frontend to access the backend services and securely call them. API Gateway provides several features to help protect your API calls, including authentication and authorization mechanisms such as OAuth 2.0, API keys, and Amazon Cognito user pools. You can also use API Gateway to implement throttling, rate limiting, and caching to help prevent abuse and improve performance.

- **Lambda functions**: AWS Lambda is used to build the backend functionality of *AWSome Store*. The application logic could be broken down into multiple Lambda functions, each handling a specific aspect of the app, such as product catalog management, order management, and payment processing.
- **DynamoDB**: Amazon DynamoDB is the primary data store for *AWSome Store*, providing a scalable and managed NoSQL database for storing customer information, the product catalog, and order information.
- **EventBridge**: Amazon EventBridge builds event-driven architectures, enabling the application to respond to events such as new orders and payment transactions.
- **S3**: Amazon S3 could store and retrieve product images and other static assets, such as a PDF file for a product manual.

Other AWS services can be used with the preceding key services to ensure security, build deployment pipelines, carry out log monitoring, raise system alerts, and so on. For example, AWS IAM helps you control access to AWS resources. You can use IAM to create and manage user accounts, roles, and permissions, which can help you ensure that only authorized users can access your serverless app services. You can use CloudFormation to define and manage your infrastructure as code. AWS CloudTrail records API calls and events for your AWS account. You can use CloudTrail to monitor activity in your serverless app services and to troubleshoot issues by reviewing the history of API calls and events. You can also use CloudWatch to collect and track metrics, collect and monitor log files, and set alarms. You can use AWS Config to provide a detailed inventory of your resources, including configurations and relationships between resources.

You will learn about them as we move forward with the implementation details.

Deciding which is the best language

An important question is what language is best for you, your project, and your company. Generally, if you have a greenfield project with a wide choice of languages, it may be best to go with one of the newer languages. It also makes sense to pick a popular language such as Go, Java, or Python.

This choice is not always straightforward and clear-cut. A language's popularity is not static. As an example, Perl was one of the most popular languages in the 1990s, but its popularity has severely waned. So, it's not enough to consider the popularity of a language, but also how fast it's growing or fading away. Similarly, JavaScript was the most popular, but it was overtaken by Python in 2024. You can refer to this article published by GitHub to see the current trends in programming language popularity: `https://github.blog/news-insights/octoverse/octoverse-2024/`.

If a language is popular, you will easily find resources for your project. Some other considerations to keep in mind are shown in the following list:

- **Compiled versus interpreted**: If you don't expect your project to become the next Airbnb and know that the number of users or the workload will be capped, you might be better off using an interpreted language rather than a compiled language. Interpreted languages allow you to prototype and ramp up your application quickly. Being able to fail fast is key to succeeding fast eventually. Fast development cycles will enable us to test our ideas quickly and discard the ones that don't perform as expected. Usually, the development life cycle is quicker with an interpreted language because the code doesn't need to be compiled every time there is a code change. A compiled language may be better if your application has strict security requirements.
- **Problem domain**: If you have a small project and you are not working in the context of a company, the better choice may hinge on what other people have already done. You may be a highly experienced Java developer, but perhaps someone has already solved 90% of the requirements you are trying to cover. In this case, you may be better off teaching yourself Python to save on replicating a lot of work.
- **Staff availability**: After researching, you may conclude that Ruby is the best language and has everything you need. But if you expect the application to require a sizable team to complete it and Ruby developers are in short supply (and therefore command high rates), it may be best to settle for second best and not be a language purist.

Regardless of your language selection, if you design your application correctly and leverage the advantages of a microservice architecture, you will be well on your way to a successful implementation. The combined microservice architecture with serverless deployment in AWS or a similar environment has been the recipe for many recent hits, some so successful that billion-dollar companies have been created around these products and services.

It is time to start putting some components together using the microservice architecture we learned about in *Chapter 13, Building Microservices and Event-Driven Architectures in AWS.*

Setting up services

The first step in developing an application is establishing the essential infrastructure services. Since you have chosen to utilize AWS services extensively, these services can be configured via various means, such as the AWS console, AWS **Cloud Development Kit** (**CDK**), AWS CloudFormation, the CLI, or third-party tools such as Chef, Puppet, Ansible, Terraform, and so on.

In this section, the main emphasis is on how to use these services while building cloud-native applications rather than constructing the infrastructure itself. Therefore, this chapter will focus on setting up services utilizing the CLI. You will go through the following steps to implement *AWSome Store* in AWS:

1. Set up an AWS account.
2. Install the AWS CLI.
3. Set up IAM users, roles, and groups.
4. Create the AWS infrastructure.
5. Implement authentication and authorization for end customers.
6. Define database attributes.
7. Write the code for *AWSome Store* using Lambda functions.
8. Deploy and test your code.
9. Implement logging and monitoring.

Let's look at each of the preceding steps in detail.

Setting up an AWS account with a billing alert

The first step is to set up an AWS account. By now, you have likely already set up an account, but here are the steps to set up an AWS account in case you haven't:

1. Open a web browser and navigate to the AWS home page at `https://aws.amazon.com/`.
2. Click on the **Create Account** button in the page's top-right corner.
3. Fill in your account information, including your email address, password, and account name.
4. Provide your contact information, including your name, company name, and phone number.
5. Enter your payment information, including your credit card details.
6. You can choose a support plan that meets your needs: Basic, Developer, Business, or Enterprise.
7. Read and accept the AWS Customer Agreement and the AWS Service Terms.
8. Click the **Create Account and Continue** button.
9. AWS will send a verification code to your email address or phone number. Enter the code to verify your account.
10. Once your account is verified, you can start using AWS services.

11. To find your AWS account number, click on your name or account ID in the navigation bar in the top-right corner of the console. Your 12-digit AWS account number is displayed in the **Account Identifiers** section under **Account Number** on the **My Account** page.

After completing the verification process, you can access the AWS Management Console and start using AWS services. However, you may need to provide additional information or documentation to fully activate your AWS account, especially if you plan to use AWS services that involve payment or access to sensitive data.

Additionally, it's a good idea to set up billing alerts to ensure you know the costs incurred while using AWS services. The costs can add up fast if you are not careful.

Here are the steps to set up billing alerts in AWS:

1. In the AWS console, navigate to **AWS Budget** by clicking the **Services** drop-down menu and selecting **AWS Cost Management.**
2. On the **Budgets** screen, click on the **Create budget** button.
3. You can use a template to create a budget, such as a monthly cost budget.
4. Provide a name for your budget, the budgeted amount, and the email recipients, and select the **Create Budget** button to create the budget and complete the setup process. For example, it should alert you when forecasted spending reaches 80% of the budgeted amount.

Your final billing alert will look like *Figure 14.4*.

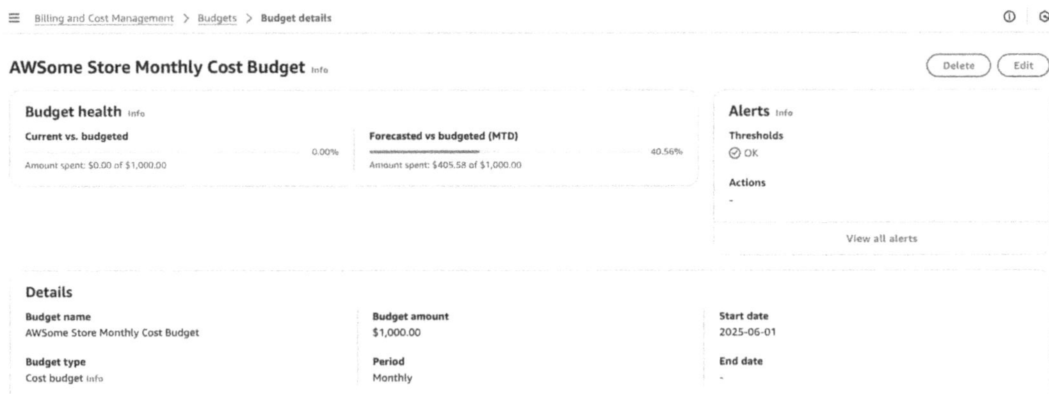

Figure 14.4: AWS billing alert dashboard

After setting up a budget, you will receive an email alert when the budget threshold is exceeded. It's a good idea to review your budgets regularly and make adjustments as needed to ensure that you are always aware of your AWS spending.

After creating an AWS account and setting up your billing alert, install the CLI to build the rest of the AWS services.

Installing the AWS CLI

The AWS CLI is available for Windows, macOS, and Linux. You can install it using the bundled installer, pip, or Homebrew. You can download the CLI installer and get started with it by visiting the AWS user docs here: `https://aws.amazon.com/cli/`.

The root account has unrestricted access to all AWS services and resources in the account, which makes it a valuable target for attackers. If the root account is compromised, an attacker could gain complete control of your AWS resources and data, potentially causing significant harm to your business.

Creating an IAM account with least privilege in AWS is a best practice. It is important to have separate accounts with appropriate permissions to help ensure the security of your AWS resources and data. Creating an account with limited permissions reduces the risk of unauthorized access and the impact of a potential security breach. You can create an admin account and give permissions to manage specific AWS services and resources, without granting them full access to the root account.

By creating an admin account, you can better control and monitor the use of AWS services and resources and reduce the risk of security breaches or accidental changes that can impact your data's availability, integrity, and confidentiality.

For simplicity in demonstrations or during initial app setup, you may occasionally see **Resource: "*" used in IAM policies**. This grants access to *all resources*, which simplifies policy creation while learning or testing. However, in practice, always apply the principle of least privilege. This means you should define access only to the specific AWS resources that the user or role needs—*nothing more*.

To configure the CLI, you need an IAM user with an access key ID and secret access key, so let's create an admin user by following these steps:

1. Log in to the AWS Management Console and go to the IAM dashboard.
2. Click on **Users** in the navigation menu.
3. Click on the **Add user** button.
4. Enter a username for the new user; in this case, you can give the name `store admin`, and click the **Next** button to land on the **Set permissions** screen.

5. Select the **Attach policies directly** option and tick the **AdministratorAccess** checkbox, as shown in the following figure. To keep things simple, we have defined an admin user. As a best practice, always follow least-privilege permissions; when you set permissions with IAM policies, only grant the permissions required to perform a task. You can learn more here: `https://docs.aws.amazon.com/IAM/latest/UserGuide/best-practices.html`.

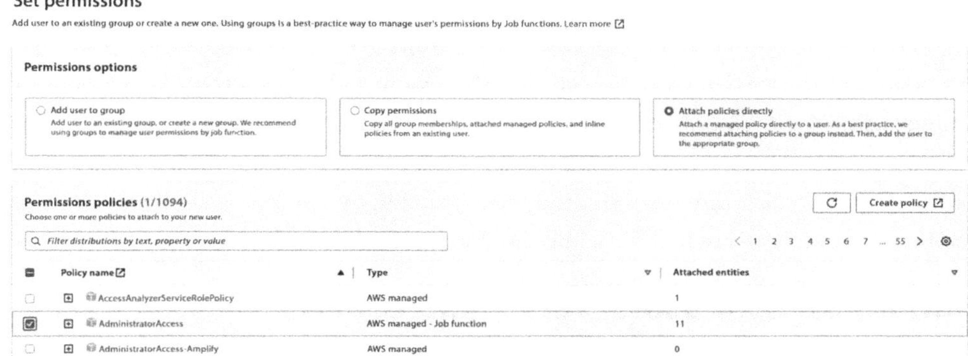

Figure 14.5: AWS IAM policy attachment

6. Review the user details and click on the **Create user** button.
7. Now, go to the newly created `store admin` user by navigating to **Users**.
8. Select the **Security credentials** tab and click **Create access key** in the **Access Key** section.
9. Retrieve the CSV file containing the access key ID and secret access key and ensure that it is stored securely. It will only be accessible once and cannot be retrieved later.

Now, the new user has been created and has administrative permissions. You can now use the access key ID and secret access key to access AWS services using the CLI programmatically.

To configure the CLI, run the `aws configure` command and provide your AWS access key ID, secret access key, default region name, and output format.

Here is an example of the configuration process:

```
$ aws configure
AWS Access Key ID [None]: AKIAIOSFODNN7EXAMPLE
AWS Secret Access Key [None]: wialrXUtnFEMI/K7MDENG/bPxRfiCYEXAMPLEKEY
Default region name [None]: us-west-2
Default output format [None]: json
```

Figure 14.6: Sample configuration code

The AWS CLI will prompt you for the following information:

- **`AWS Access Key ID`**: Your AWS access key ID allows you to access AWS services
- **`AWS Secret Access Key`**: Your secret access key provides secure access to your AWS account
- **`Default region name`**: The region where your AWS resources will be created, such as `us-west-2` for Oregon or `us-east-1` for North Virginia
- **`Default output format`**: The output from the AWS CLI commands, such as JSON or text

It's important to note that you will need an AWS account and the necessary permissions to perform actions using the AWS CLI. When creating an IAM user, role, or group in AWS, it's important to follow the principle of **zero trust**. This means that, by default, you should assume that any user or entity is untrusted until proven otherwise. You don't want anyone to have admin access, so let's create some IAM credentials using the CLI.

Setting up IAM users, roles, and groups

Following the **zero trust principle**, let's create a `dev` user with read/write access to S3, Lambda, and API Gateway using the AWS CLI. You can follow these steps:

1. Open the command line or terminal on your system and run the following command to create a `dev` user:

```
aws iam create-user --user-name dev-user
```

2. Next, create an IAM policy for read/write access to S3:

```
aws iam create-policy \
--policy-name S3-ReadWriteAccess \
--policy-document file://s3-readwrite-policy.json
```

Here, the `s3-readwrite-policy.json` file contains the following policy:

```
{
    "Version": "2012-10-17",
    "Statement": [
        {
            "Effect": "Allow",
            "Action": "s3:ListBucket",
```

```
            "Resource": "arn:aws:s3:::<bucket-name>"
        },
        {
            "Effect": "Allow",
            "Action": [
                "s3:GetObject",
                "s3:PutObject"
            ],
            "Resource": "arn:aws:s3:::<bucket-name>/*"
        }
    ]
}
```

Quick tip: Enhance your coding experience with the **AI Code Explainer** and **Quick Copy** features. Open this book in the next-gen Packt Reader. Click the **Copy** button

(1) to quickly copy code into your coding environment, or click the **Explain** button

(2) to get the AI assistant to explain a block of code to you.

```
function calculate(a, b) {
  return {sum: a + b};
};
```

Copy (1) Explain (2)

The next-gen Packt Reader is included for free with the purchase of this book. Scan the QR code OR visit `packtpub.com/unlock`, then use the search bar to find this book by name. Double-check the edition shown to make sure you get the right one.

The <bucket-name> placeholder text should be replaced with a unique name of your choice for the S3 bucket. For instance, you could use a name such as `aws-for-sa-book-s3-app`. It's important to ensure that the S3 bucket name is available and not already used by another AWS account. Additionally, it's recommended to follow AWS naming conventions for S3 bucket names, which include using lowercase letters, numbers, and hyphens, and not using underscores or uppercase letters.

3. Similarly, create a policy for read/write access to Lambda:

```
aws iam create-policy \
--policy-name Lambda-ReadWriteAccess \
--policy-document file://lambda-readwrite-policy.json
```

Here, the `lambda-readwrite-policy.json` file contains the following policy:

```
{
    "Version": "2012-10-17",
    "Statement": [
        {
            "Effect": "Allow",
            "Action": [
                "lambda:ListFunctions",
                "lambda:GetFunction",
                "lambda:CreateFunction",
                "lambda:UpdateFunctionCode",
                "lambda:DeleteFunction"
            ],
            "Resource": "*"
        }
]
}
```

4. And similarly, create a policy for read/write access to API Gateway:

```
aws iam create-policy \
--policy-name API-Gateway-ReadWriteAccess \
--policy-document file://apigateway-readwrite-policy.json
```

Here, the `apigateway-readwrite-policy.json` file contains the following policy:

```
{
    "Version": "2012-10-17",
    "Statement": [
        {
            "Effect": "Allow",
            "Action": [
                "apigateway:GET",
                "apigateway:POST",
                "apigateway:PUT",
                "apigateway:DELETE",
                "apigateway:PATCH"
            ],
            "Resource": "arn:aws:apigateway:<region-id>:<api-id>/*"
        }
    ]
}
```

When creating an API gateway in AWS, you need to replace the `<region-id>` and `<api-id>` placeholders with the actual values for your environment. The `<region-id>` placeholder should be replaced with the AWS region identifier where you want to create the API gateway, such as `us-east-1` for the US East (N. Virginia) region.

The `<api-id>` placeholder should be replaced with a unique identifier for your API gateway. This identifier is used to generate the API Gateway endpoint URL, so it's important to choose a unique name that reflects the purpose of your API, such as `my-api-gateway` or `ecommerce-api`. Make sure to select appropriate values for both placeholders, as they will affect the configuration and functionality of your API gateway.

5. Attach the policies to the dev user:

```
aws iam attach-user-policy --user-name dev-user --policy-arn
arn:aws:iam::<account-id>:policy/S3-ReadWriteAccess
aws iam attach-user-policy --user-name dev-user --policy-arn
arn:aws:iam::<account-id>:policy/lambda-ReadWriteAccess
aws iam attach-user-policy --user-name dev-user --policy-arn
arn:aws:iam::<account-id>:policy/apigateway-ReadWriteAccess
```

When you create a new AWS account, it is assigned a unique 12-digit account number. When executing commands in AWS that require specifying the account number, you will need to replace the placeholder text with the actual account number for your account. For example, if a command specifies the account number as `<account-number>`, you should replace this placeholder with your 12-digit account number, such as `123456789012`. Using the correct account number is important to ensure that the command is executed in the correct AWS account, especially if you have multiple AWS accounts.

6. Finally, verify that the policies have been attached to the `dev` user:

```
aws iam list-attached-user-policies --user-name dev-user
```

Similarly, you should create policies for other users as needed. You can use a policy generator to build the right policy for each user by referring to this link: `https://awspolicygen.s3.amazonaws.com/policygen.html`. Alternatively, you can use the AWS Q Developer CLI to generate the desired policy using GenAI.

Best practices

Security is most important for your application, so make sure to use the following best practices when creating IAM entities with zero-trust principles in mind:

- **Least privilege**: Assign the minimum permissions necessary to accomplish a task. For example, if a user only needs to access a specific S3 bucket, grant them access only.
- **Role-based access control**: Use IAM roles instead of long-term access keys. Roles are more secure because they are limited to a specific permissions set and can be revoked at any time.
- **Multi-factor authentication (MFA)**: Require MFA for all IAM entities, including root, users, roles, and groups. MFA provides an extra layer of security and helps prevent unauthorized access.
- **Use policies and conditions**: Define policies and conditions that limit access to AWS resources based on factors such as the time of day, IP address, and user agent.
- **Monitor and audit**: Regularly monitor and audit your AWS environment to detect potential security issues and ensure that users only access resources as intended.

- **Use managed policies**: Use managed policies instead of custom policies whenever possible. Managed policies are prebuilt policies reviewed and approved by AWS security experts.
- **Rotate credentials regularly**: Rotate access keys, passwords, and other credentials regularly to ensure that only authorized users can access your AWS resources.

By following these best practices, you can ensure that your AWS environment is secure and that only authorized users can access your resources.

Let's move on to the next step of creating cloud infrastructure for architecture.

Creating the AWS infrastructure

After creating IAM credentials, let's make the app infrastructure. For simplicity and to explain the concept, you will use the CLI to bring up various AWS services; however, as a best practice, you should choose the route of writing a CloudFormation template and using that to bring up your AWS infrastructure. Here is an example of how to create API Gateway, S3, DynamoDB, CloudFront, and Lambda instances using the AWS CLI:

1. Create an S3 bucket:

```
aws s3 mb s3://<bucket-name>
```

The `<bucket-name>` placeholder text should be replaced with a unique name of your choice for the S3 bucket.

2. Create a DynamoDB table:

```
aws dynamodb create-table --table-name awsome-store-table
--attribute-definitions AttributeName=id,AttributeType=S --key-
schema AttributeName=id,KeyType=HASH --provisioned-throughput
ReadCapacityUnits=1,WriteCapacityUnits=1
```

3. Create a CloudFront distribution:

```
aws cloudfront create-distribution --distribution-config file://
cloudfront-config.json
```

Here is some example code for a CloudFront configuration file in the YAML format. The `cloudfront-config.yaml` file should contain the CloudFront distribution configuration:

```
Comment: "My CloudFront Distribution Configuration"
Logging:
  Bucket: "<my-logs-bucket>"
  IncludeCookies: true
  Prefix: "my-cloudfront-logs/"
Origins:
  Quantity: 1
  Items:
    - Id: "my-origin"
      DomainName: "<my-origin-domain>"
      CustomOriginConfig:
        HTTPPort: 80
        HTTPSPort: 443
        OriginProtocolPolicy: "https-only"
        OriginSslProtocols:
          Quantity: 1
          Items:
            - "TLSv1.2"
DefaultCacheBehavior:
  TargetOriginId: "my-origin"
  ForwardedValues:
    QueryString: false
    Cookies:
      Forward: "none"
  TrustedSigners:
    Enabled: false
    Quantity: 0
  ViewerProtocolPolicy: "redirect-to-https"
  MinTTL: 0
  MaxTTL: 86400
  DefaultTTL: 3600
Enabled: true
PriceClass: "PriceClass_All"
DefaultRootObject: "index.html"
Aliases:
```

```
    Quantity: 2
    Items:
      - "<www.mydomain.com>"
      - "<mydomain.com>"
  ViewerCertificate:
    ACMCertificateArn: "<my-acm-certificate-arn>"
    SSLSupportMethod: "sni-only"
```

This configuration file defines a CloudFront distribution that uses one origin, enables logging to an S3 bucket, and specifies cache behavior settings. Note that some values, such as `<my-logs-bucket>` and `<my-origin-domain>`, need to be replaced with actual values specific to your environment. For example, `<my-logs-bucket>` should be replaced with the name of an existing S3 bucket where CloudFront can store log files, such as `my-cloudfront-logs-bucket`. In the same line, `<my-origin-domain>` should be replaced with the domain name of an existing origin server for your CloudFront distribution, such as `www.example.com`.

When creating an API Gateway API and a Lambda function in AWS, you can use any valid name of your choice for these resources, as long as the name is unique within your AWS account and follows the naming rules and restrictions for AWS resource names. In the following examples, `awsome-store-api` and `awsome-store-lambda` are just example names that could be replaced with others of your choosing. Use the same names consistently throughout your code and configurations when referring to these resources.

4. Create an API Gateway REST API:

```
aws apigateway create-rest-api --name awsome-store-api --description
"Awsome Store API"
```

5. Create a Lambda function:

```
aws lambda create-function \
--function-name awsome-store-lambda \
  --runtime nodejs22.x \
  --handler index.handler \
  --zip-file fileb://lambda.zip \
  --role arn:aws:iam::<your-account-id>:role/<your-lambda-role>
```

The `lambda.zip` file typically contains the code for the AWS Lambda function you want to deploy. In the example command you provided, the code in `lambda.zip` is for a Node.js 22.x runtime environment. However, AWS Lambda supports various other programming languages and runtime environments, including Python, Java, C#, Go, and Ruby. To deploy code for a different runtime environment, you would need to make sure that the code is compatible with that specific runtime environment, and then package it into a new ZIP file with the appropriate file extension for that language (such as `.py` for Python or `.jar` for Java). Once you have the latest ZIP file with your code for the desired runtime environment, you can use a similar command to the one you provided, but specify the appropriate runtime flag and other parameters as needed for the specific language and environment.

Creating the AWS infrastructure using CloudFormation

The previous step is a basic example of creating these AWS resources using the CLI. Here's an example CloudFormation template to deploy the necessary resources for an *AWSome Store* e-commerce website:

```
---
AWSTemplateFormatVersion: '2010-09-09'
Description: CloudFormation template to deploy resources needed for an
AWSome Store e-commerce website
Resources:
  S3Bucket:
    Type: AWS::S3::Bucket
    Properties:
      BucketName: awsome-store-bucket
      WebsiteConfiguration:
        IndexDocument: index.html
  DynamoDBTable:
    Type: AWS::DynamoDB::Table
    Properties:
      TableName: awsome-store-table
      AttributeDefinitions:
        - AttributeName: id
          AttributeType: S
      KeySchema:
```

```
        - AttributeName: id
          KeyType: HASH
      ProvisionedThroughput:
        ReadCapacityUnits: 1
        WriteCapacityUnits: 1
  CloudFrontDistribution:
    Type: AWS::CloudFront::Distribution
    Properties:
      DistributionConfig:
        Origins:
          - Id: awsome-store-origin
            DomainName: !Join ['.', [!Ref S3Bucket, 's3.amazonaws.com']]
            S3OriginConfig:
              OriginAccessIdentity: !Join ['/', ['origin-access-identity/
cloudfront', !Ref AWS::AccountId]]
        DefaultCacheBehavior:
          TargetOriginId: awsome-store-origin
          ViewerProtocolPolicy: redirect-to-https
        Enabled: true
  APIGateway:
    Type: AWS::ApiGateway::RestApi
    Properties:
      Name: awsome-store-api
      Description: Awsome Store API

  LambdaFunction:
    Type: AWS::Lambda::Function
    Properties:
      FunctionName: awsome-store-lambda
      Runtime: nodejs22.x
      Handler: index.handler
      Code:
        S3Bucket: !Ref S3Bucket
        S3Key: lambda.zip
```

The preceding is just an example; you may need to modify it to meet your requirements. Additionally, you may need to add additional resources, such as IAM roles and policies, to fully implement the *AWSome Store* e-commerce website. Later in this chapter, you will learn more about writing Lambda code and putting it in `lambda.zip`. For the time being, you can copy the preceding code in `awsome-store-app.yaml` and run the following command to deploy the CloudFormation template:

```
aws cloudformation create-stack --stack-name <stack-name> --template-body
file://<template-file>
```

Replace `<stack-name>` with the desired name of your CloudFormation stack and `<template-file>` with the name of your CloudFormation template file, as in this example:

```
aws cloudformation create-stack --stack-name awsome-store --template-body
file://awsome-store-app.yaml
```

To monitor the progress of the CloudFormation stack creation, you can use the following command:

```
aws cloudformation describe-stacks --stack-name <stack-name>
```

Once the CloudFormation stack is created successfully, it will return a status of `CREATE_COMPLETE`.

Creating an EventBridge instance and a queue

You can use Amazon EventBridge and SQS to build a loosely coupled architecture and send asynchronous messages, such as emails, for customer notifications. Here are the high-level steps to set up Amazon EventBridge and SQS for *AWSome Store* using the AWS CLI:

1. Create an SQS queue. You can use the following AWS CLI command to create a new SQS queue:

   ```
   aws sqs create-queue --queue-name awsome-store-queue
   ```

2. Get the ARN of the SQS queue. You can use the following AWS CLI command to get the ARN of the SQS queue:

   ```
   aws sqs get-queue-attributes --queue-url <queue-url> --attribute-
   names QueueArn
   ```

To use the preceding command, you need to replace `<queue-url>` with the actual URL of the SQS queue for which you want to retrieve the attribute. For example, if the URL of your SQS queue is `https://sqs.us-west-2.amazonaws.com/123456789012/my-queue`, you would replace `<queue-url>` with that URL, like this:

```
aws sqs get-queue-attributes --queue-url https://
sqs.us-west-2.amazonaws.com/123456789012/my-queue
--attribute-names QueueArn
```

This command would retrieve the `QueueArn` attribute for the `my-queue` SQS queue in the `us-west-2` region.

3. Create a new Amazon EventBridge rule. You can use the following AWS CLI command to create a new Amazon EventBridge rule using the `QueueArn` attribure retrieved from the previous command:

```
aws events put-rule \
--name awsome-store-rule \
  --event-pattern '{
    "source": ["aws.sqs"],
    "detail-type": ["SQS Message Notification"],
    "resources": ["<queue-arn>"]
  }'
```

4. Add a target to the EventBridge rule. You can use the following AWS CLI command to add a target to the EventBridge rule:

```
aws events put-targets --rule awsome-store-rule --targets
Id=1,Arn=<lambda-function-arn>
```

The `aws events put-targets` command adds one or more targets to an Amazon EventBridge rule, specified by the `--rule` parameter. In this case, the target being added is an AWS Lambda function, specified by its ARN using the `--targets` parameter. To use this command, you need to replace `awsome-store-rule` with the name of the EventBridge rule to which you want to add the target. You also need to replace `<lambda-function-arn>` with the ARN of the AWS Lambda function that you want to use as the target.

For example, if you have an EventBridge rule called `my-event-rule` and an AWS Lambda function with an ARN of `arn:aws:lambda:us-west-2:123456789012:function:my-lambda-function`, you would replace `awsome-store-rule` with `my-event-rule`, and replace <lambda-function-arn> with arn:aws:lambda:us-west-2:123456789012:function:<your-lambda-function>, as follows. In this case, suppose your Lambda function name is `my-lambda-function`:

```
aws events put-targets --rule my-event-rule --targets
Id=1,Arn=arn:aws:lambda:us-west-2:123456789012:function:my-lambda-
function
```

This command would add the `my-lambda-function` AWS Lambda function as a target to the `my-event-rule` EventBridge rule in the `us-west-2` region.

5. Next, send a message to the SQS queue. You can use the following AWS CLI command to send a message to the SQS queue by using the queue URL you captured earlier:

```
aws sqs send-message --queue-url <queue-url> --message-body "Hello,
this is a test message."
```

Once these steps are completed, you have successfully set up AWS EventBridge and SQS for *AWSome Store* using the AWS CLI. You will learn about best practices to set up AWS infrastructure later, in the *Optimization with a well-architected review* section of this chapter.

Implementing authentication and authorization for end users

Earlier, you set up IAM credentials for the internal development team, but what about end users who will access *AWSome Store* and build their profiles? You need to give them a way to create their account securely and give them the required access. You can use Amazon Cognito to simplify user authentication and authorization for cloud-based applications. It can help you with the following scenarios:

- **User sign-up and sign-in**: Cognito provides secure user authentication, with features such as MFA, forgot password, and social identity sign-up.
- **Mobile and web app authentication**: Cognito supports users' authentication in mobile and web applications and integrates with the AWS Mobile SDK.
- **Unauthenticated and authenticated access to APIs**: Cognito integrates with Amazon API Gateway and AWS AppSync to authorize API access.
- **User data storage**: Cognito provides user profile storage, which can be used to store user information such as preferences, custom data, and more.

Here is an example of how you can use the AWS CLI to implement authentication and authorization for end users for the *AWSome Store* website using Amazon Cognito:

1. Create a Cognito user pool:

   ```
   aws cognito-idp create-user-pool --pool-name awsomestore-pool
   ```

   Using the default settings, the `aws cognito-idp create-user-pool` command creates a new Amazon Cognito user pool with the specified pool name. To use this command, you need to replace `awsomestore-pool` with the name you want to give to your user pool. For example, if you're going to create a user pool called `my-user-pool`, you would replace `awsomestore-pool` with `my-user-pool`, like this:

   ```
   aws cognito-idp create-user-pool --pool-name my-user-pool
   ```

   This command would create a new Amazon Cognito user pool named `my-user-pool`. Using additional parameters and options, you can customize the settings of your user pool.

2. Next, create a group for the user pool:

   ```
   aws cognito-idp create-group --user-pool-id awsomestore-pool-id
   --group-name awsomestore-group
   ```

   The `aws cognito-idp create-group` command creates a new group in the specified Amazon Cognito user pool with the specified group name. To use this command, you need to replace `awsomestore-pool-id` with the ID of the Amazon Cognito user pool in which you want to create the group. You also need to replace `awsomestore-group` with the name of the group that you want to create.

   For example, if you have an Amazon Cognito user pool with an ID of `us-west-2_abc123xyz`, and you want to create a new group called `my-group`, you would replace `awsomestore-pool-id` with `us-west-2_abc123xyz`, and replace `awsomestore-group` with `my-group`, like this:

   ```
   aws cognito-idp create-group --user-pool-id us-west-2_abc123xyz
   --group-name my-group
   ```

   This command would create a new group called `my-group` in the `us-west-2_abc123xyz` Amazon Cognito user pool.

3. Next, attach policies to the group:

   ```
   aws cognito-idp add-user-to-group --user-pool-id awsomestore-pool-id
   --username <username> --group-name awsomestore-group
   ```

The aws cognito-idp add-user-to-group command adds a user to a specified group in an Amazon Cognito user pool. To use this command, you need to replace awsomestore-pool-id with the ID of the Amazon Cognito user pool in which the group exists.

You also need to replace <username> with the username of the user you want to add to the group. Finally, you need to replace awsomestore-group with the group name to which you want to add the user.

For example, if you have an Amazon Cognito user pool with an ID of us-west-2_abc123xyz, and you want to add a user with the username myuser to a group called my-group, you would replace awsomestore-pool-id with us-west-2_abc123xyz, replace <username> with myuser, and replace awsomestore-group with my-group, like this:

```
aws cognito-idp add-user-to-group --user-pool-id us-west-2_abc123xyz
--username myuser --group-name my-group
```

This command would add the user with the username myuser to the my-group group in the us-west-2_abc123xyz Amazon Cognito user pool.

4. Next, create a Cognito user pool client:

```
aws cognito-idp create-user-pool-client --user-pool-id awsomestore-
pool-id --client-name awsomestore-client
```

The aws cognito-idp create-user-pool-client command creates a new app client in an Amazon Cognito user pool. To use this command, you need to replace awsomestore-pool-id with the ID of the Amazon Cognito user pool in which you want to create the app client. You also need to replace awsomestore-client with a name of your choice for the app client. For example, if you have an Amazon Cognito user pool with an ID of us-west-2_abc123xyz, and you want to create a new app client called my-app-client, you would run the following command:

```
aws cognito-idp create-user-pool-client --user-pool-id us-west-2_
abc123xyz --client-name my-app-client
```

This command would create a new app client called my-app-client in the us-west-2_abc123xyz Amazon Cognito user pool. The command will return the newly created app client's ClientId value, which will be required to authenticate the users.

5. Next, create a Cognito identity pool:

```
aws cognito-identity create-identity-pool --identity-pool-name
awsomestore-identity-pool --allow-unauthenticated-identities
--cognito-identity-providers ProviderName=cognito-idp.us-east-1.
amazonaws.com/awsomestore-pool-id,ClientId=awsomestore-client-id
```

The `aws cognito-identity create-identity-pool` command creates a new Amazon Cognito identity pool. To use this command, you need to replace `awsomestore-identity-pool` with a name of your choice for the identity pool. You also need to replace the `awsomestore-pool-id` with the Amazon Cognito user pool ID that you created earlier. Additionally, you need to replace `awsomestore-client-id` with the `ClientId` value of the Amazon Cognito user pool client you created earlier. For example, if you want to create a new Amazon Cognito identity pool called `my-identity-pool`, and you have an Amazon Cognito user pool with an ID of `us-west-2_abc123xyz` and a client ID of `1234567890abcdef`, you would use these.

6. Finally, grant permissions to the identity pool:

```
aws cognito-identity set-identity-pool-roles --identity-
pool-id awsomestore-identity-pool-id --roles
authenticated=arn:aws:iam::<aws_account_id>:role/awsomestore-auth-ro
le,unauthenticated=arn:aws:iam::<aws_account_id>:role/awsomestore-
unauth-role
```

The `aws cognito-identity set-identity-pool-roles` command sets the roles for the authenticated and unauthenticated identities in an Amazon Cognito identity pool.

To use this command, you need to replace `awsomestore-identity-pool-id` with the ID of the Amazon Cognito identity pool that you created earlier. You also need to replace `<aws_account_id>` with your actual AWS account ID and replace `awsomestore-auth-role` and `awsomestore-unauth-role` with the names of the IAM roles that you want to use for authenticated and unauthenticated identities, respectively.

For example, if you want to set the roles for an Amazon Cognito identity pool with an ID of `us-west-2_abc123xyz` and have two IAM roles named `my-auth-role` and `my-unauth-role` that you want to use for authenticated and unauthenticated identities, you would replace the relevant fields with these labels.

With the preceding steps, you can use Amazon Cognito to implement authentication and authorization for end customers for the *AWSome Store* website. When using Amazon Cognito for authentication and authorization, it is best to follow these best practices:

- Use MFA to enhance the security of your user pool.
- Implement a password policy requiring strong passwords with letters, numbers, and special characters.
- Monitor the security of your Cognito user pool regularly, such as tracking sign-in attempts and detecting suspicious activity.
- Use Amazon Cognito's built-in user sign-up and sign-in process for a smooth and secure experience for your users.
- Use the appropriate user pool attributes to store user data, such as email addresses and phone numbers.
- To reduce the risk of data breaches, use Amazon Cognito's built-in features for storing user data, such as custom attributes and user pools.
- Store encrypted sensitive information, such as passwords, in the Amazon Cognito user pool.
- Enable logging and monitoring for Amazon Cognito to help detect security issues and respond to them quickly.
- Consider using Amazon Cognito federated identities for secure **single sign-on** (**SSO**) across multiple AWS services and applications.

Finally, regularly review and update your Amazon Cognito user pool's security policies to ensure they comply with the latest security standards. To explore more best practices, refer to AWS's user documentation here: `https://docs.aws.amazon.com/cognito/latest/developerguide/multi-tenant-application-best-practices.html`.

Now, let's jump into building your app, starting with the database.

Defining database attributes

To define database tables and attributes for your *AWSome Store* e-commerce website, you can start by considering the data you need to store in your e-commerce website:

- **Products**: This table can store information about each product available in the store, such as product name, product ID, description, price, image URL, and so on.
- **Customers**: This table can store information about each customer, such as customer name, email address, password, billing address, and so on.

- **Orders**: This table can store information about each customer order, such as the order ID, customer ID, product ID, order date, shipping address, and so on.
- **Categories**: This table can store information about product categories, such as category name and ID.
- **Inventory**: This table can store information about each product's inventory, such as its product ID, the quantity available, and so on.
- **Promotions**: This table can store information about promotions and discounts available for products, such as promotion ID, product ID, discount amount, and so on.

When creating these tables, you can set the primary key as the unique identifier for each table, such as product ID, customer ID, and order ID. You can also define secondary indexes to support querying data in your application.

Amazon DynamoDB is a good choice for *AWSome Store* as you require fast and flexible data storage. DynamoDB is optimized for low latency and high throughput, making it ideal for storing large amounts of data that need to be retrieved quickly. It automatically scales with the growth of your data, allowing you to store and retrieve any amount without worrying about capacity planning. DynamoDB is a cost-effective solution, as you only pay for the read and write capacity that you use, and there are no upfront costs and minimum fees. It integrates seamlessly with other AWS services, making it easy to build complex, scalable, and highly available applications.

Here is a sample CLI command to create DynamoDB tables and their attributes for *AWSome Store*:

```
aws dynamodb create-table \
--table-name awsome_store_products \
--attribute-definitions \
AttributeName=product_id,AttributeType=S \
AttributeName=product_name,AttributeType=S \
--key-schema \
AttributeName=product_id,KeyType=HASH \
AttributeName=product_name,KeyType=RANGE \
--provisioned-throughput \
ReadCapacityUnits=5,WriteCapacityUnits=5

aws dynamodb create-table \
--table-name awsome_store_orders \
--attribute-definitions \
AttributeName=order_id,AttributeType=S \
```

```
AttributeName=order_date,AttributeType=S \
--key-schema \
AttributeName=order_id,KeyType=HASH \
AttributeName=order_date,KeyType=RANGE \
--provisioned-throughput \
ReadCapacityUnits=5,WriteCapacityUnits=5
```

You can create more tables and customize the table names, attributes, and provisioned throughput per your requirements. The following are some best practices to follow when using DynamoDB:

- **Use partition keys wisely**: Selecting a good partition key that distributes your data evenly is crucial for performance.
- **Consider provisioned throughput**: Ensure you set the right amount of throughput to ensure the required performance.
- **Use secondary indexes**: Secondary indexes can optimize queries based on different attributes.
- **Batch operations**: Use batch operations such as `BatchGetItem` and `BatchWriteItem` for efficient data retrieval and modification.
- **Use the time to live (TTL) attribute**: The TTL attribute automatically deletes old or expired items from your table.
- **Store data in a denormalized form**: Storing data in a denormalized form in DynamoDB can simplify and speed up queries.
- **Use automated backups**: Use DynamoDB's automatic backups to ensure data durability and reduce the risk of data loss.
- **Monitor and troubleshoot**: Monitor your DynamoDB usage and performance regularly to identify potential issues and optimize accordingly.
- **Use DynamoDB Streams**: DynamoDB Streams allow you to capture changes made to your DynamoDB tables and process them in real time.

You should use a serverless architecture and AWS Lambda functions to integrate with DynamoDB and offload compute-intensive tasks. You can explore more best practices here: `https://docs.aws.amazon.com/amazondynamodb/latest/developerguide/best-practices.html`. After putting your database together, let's define Lambda functions to know how to use them.

Defining order context and writing AWS Lambda functions

In the previous section on use cases, we defined the order-bound context in an e-commerce retail application as follows:

- **Order class**: Start by defining the `Order` class, which represents a customer's request to purchase one or more products. The `Order` class could have attributes such as order number, date, customer information, and a list of order items.
- **Order Item class**: Next, define the `Order Item` class, which represents a single product in an order. The class could have attributes such as product ID, name, quantity, and price.
- **Customer class**: Also define the `Customer` class, which represents the person placing the order. The `Customer` class could have customer ID, name, address, and email attributes.
- **Payment class**: Define the `Payment` class, which represents the payment information for an order. The `Payment` class could have attributes such as payment method, card number, and expiration date.

Add methods to the classes to represent the actions that can be performed on them. For example, an `Order` class could have a method for calculating the total cost of the order. Also, an `Order` class could have a one-to-many relationship with the `Order Item` class, indicating that an order can have multiple order items, as shown here:

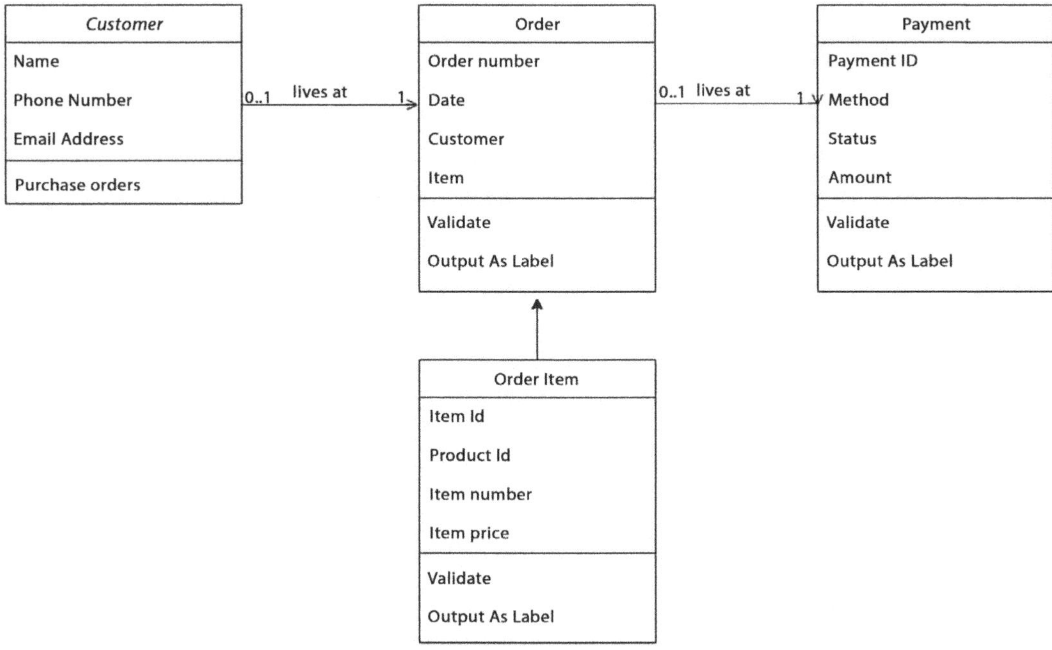

Figure 14.7: Order context class diagram

Here is an example of how you could implement the `Order`, `OrderItem`, `Payment`, and `Customer` classes in Node.js using AWS Lambda functions:

```
const AWS = require('aws-sdk');
class Order {
  constructor(orderId, customerId, orderDate, items, payment) {
    this.orderId = orderId;
    this.customerId = customerId;
    this.orderDate = orderDate;
    this.items = items;
    this.payment = payment;
  }
  save() {
    const dynamoDB = new AWS.DynamoDB.DocumentClient();
    const params = {
      TableName: 'AwsomeStoreOrders',
      Item: {
        orderId: this.orderId,
        customerId: this.customerId,
        orderDate: this.orderDate,
        items: this.items,
        payment: this.payment
      }
    };
    return dynamoDB.put(params).promise();
  }
}
class OrderItem {
  constructor(productId, quantity) {
    this.productId = productId;
    this.quantity = quantity;
  }
}
class Payment {
  constructor(paymentId, amount, paymentDate, paymentMethod) {
    this.paymentId = paymentId;
    this.amount = amount;
    this.paymentDate = paymentDate;
```

```
    this.paymentMethod = paymentMethod;
  }
}
class Customer {
  constructor(customerId, firstName, lastName, email) {
    this.customerId = customerId;
    this.firstName = firstName;
    this.lastName = lastName;
    this.email = email;
  }
  save() {
    const dynamoDB = new AWS.DynamoDB.DocumentClient();
    const params = {
      TableName: 'AwsomeStoreCustomers',
      Item: {
        customerId: this.customerId,
        firstName: this.firstName,
        lastName: this.lastName,
        email: this.email
      }
    };
    return dynamoDB.put(params).promise();
  }
}
```

This code defines the `Order`, `OrderItem`, `Payment`, and `Customer` classes with their respective properties. The save method in each class uses the AWS SDK for JavaScript to interact with Amazon DynamoDB and store instances of the class as items in a DynamoDB table. Each save method defines the table's name in the `TableName` parameter. You can modify this code to fit your needs and add more functionality. Here are some best practices for AWS Lambda:

- **Keep functions small and focused**: Minimize the code in each function and make it perform a single, specific task.
- **Use environment variables for configuration**: Store configuration values as environment variables to avoid hardcoding values in code. Parameter Store is better suited for managing application configuration data that needs to be shared across multiple hosts or environments, requires encryption, and needs versioning and auditing capabilities. On the other hand, environment variables are simpler to use. They can be useful for storing smaller configuration data that only needs to be available to a single process or host.

- **Design for statelessness**: Lambda functions should be stateless, meaning they do not persist data between invocations.
- **Optimize cold start time**: Minimize the initialization code and the size of the deployment package to reduce the time it takes for your function to start.
- **Use VPC for network isolation**: If your function needs to access resources in a VPC, use VPC connectivity to provide network isolation.
- **Use versioning and aliases**: Versioning and aliases allow you to manage multiple versions of your functions and deploy changes incrementally.
- **Secure secrets and sensitive data**: Store encryption keys and sensitive data in AWS **Key Management Service** (**KMS**) or **AWS Secrets Manager**, rather than in the function code.
- **Monitor function performance**: Use CloudWatch metrics and X-Ray to monitor performance and track requests and errors.
- **Automate deployment**: Use AWS CloudFormation, AWS CodeDeploy, or other tools to automate deployment and reduce manual errors.

Finally, you should regularly test and validate development and production functions to ensure they are functioning as intended. You can refer to more Lambda best practices here: `https://docs.aws.amazon.com/lambda/latest/dg/best-practices.html`. Now that you've written your code and built your table, let's deploy and test your code.

Deploying and testing

Here are the steps to deploy a Lambda function for *AWSome Store* and connect it with API Gateway:

1. Compress your Lambda function code and any required dependencies into a `.zip` file.
2. Use the AWS CLI `aws lambda create-function` command to create a new Lambda function in your AWS account. In this command, you need to specify the name of the function, the runtime environment (Node.js), the path to the `.zip` file, the name of the handler function, and the IAM role that your function will use to execute. Here is some example code:

```
aws lambda create-function \
--function-name my-nodejs-function \
--runtime nodejs22.x \
--handler index.handler \
--memory-size 128 \
--timeout 30 \
--zip-file fileb://lambda.zip \
--role arn:aws:iam::<aws_account_id>:role/my-lambda-role
```

This command creates a new Lambda function named `my-nodejs-function` using the Node.js 22.x runtime. The `index.handler` handler specifies the entry point to the function code within the `lambda.zip` file, which is uploaded as the function's code. Next, `memory-size` specifies the amount of memory in megabytes allocated to the function. The `role` parameter specifies the IAM role that the function uses to access other AWS resources.

3. Use the `aws apigateway create-rest-api` command to create a new REST API in API Gateway. In this command, you need to specify the name of the API, the description, and the endpoint type (regional). Here is an example code:

```
aws apigateway create-rest-api --name MyRestApi --description "My new REST API"
```

   In this example, the command creates a new REST API named `MyRestApi`, with the description `My new REST API`. You can then use other API Gateway commands to add resources, methods, and integrations to this API.

4. Use the `aws apigateway create-resource` command to create a new resource in the REST API. In this command, you need to specify the parent resource, the path, and the REST API ID. Here is the syntax:

```
aws apigateway create-resource --rest-api-id <rest-api-id> --parent-id <parent-resource-id> --path-part <path-part>
```

   In this command, you need to replace `<rest-api-id>` with the ID of the REST API that the resource belongs to. You also need to replace `<parent-resource-id>` with the ID of the parent resource of the new resource you're creating. The `<path-part>` parameter specifies the last part of the resource's path. For example, if you wanted to create a new resource with the path of `/products`, and its parent resource had an ID of `abc123`, the command would look like this:

```
aws apigateway create-resource \
--rest-api-id abcd1234 \
--parent-id abc123 \
--path-part products
```

   This would create a new resource with the `/products` path under the parent resource with an ID of `abc123`.

5. Use the `aws apigateway put-method` command to create a new method (such as `GET` or `POST`) for the resource. In this command, you need to specify the REST API ID, the resource ID, and the HTTP method. Here is an example code:

```
aws apigateway put-method \
--rest-api-id <rest-api-id> \
--resource-id <resource-id> \
--http-method <http-method> \
--authorization-type <authorization-type> \
--request-parameters <request-parameters>
```

   In this command, you need to replace `<rest-api-id>` with the ID of the REST API that the resource belongs to. You also need to replace `<resource-id>` with the ID of the resource that the method belongs to. The `<http-method>` parameter specifies the HTTP method (e.g., `GET`, `POST`, `PUT`, or `DELETE`). The `<authorization-type>` parameter specifies the type of authorization used for the method (e.g., `NONE`, `AWS_IAM`, `CUSTOM`). The `<request-parameters>` parameter is a JSON object that defines the request parameters accepted by the method.

   For example, if you wanted to create a new method for a resource with the ID of `abc123` that responds to HTTP `GET` requests and uses AWS IAM authorization, the command would look like this:

```
aws apigateway put-method \
--rest-api-id abcd1234 \
--resource-id abc123 \
--http-method GET \
--authorization-type AWS_IAM \
--request-parameters '{"method.request.querystring.foo": true,
"method.request.querystring.bar": true}'
```

   This would create a new method for the `GET` HTTP method that accepts two query string parameters (`foo` and `bar`) and uses AWS IAM authorization.

6. Use the `aws apigateway put-integration` command to integrate the API method with your Lambda function. In this command, you need to specify the REST API ID, the resource ID, the HTTP method, the type of integration, and the ARN of the Lambda function:

```
aws apigateway put-integration \
--rest-api-id <rest-api-id> \
--resource-id <resource-id> \
```

```
--http-method <http-method> \
--type <type> \
--integration-http-method <integration-http-method> \
--uri <uri> \
--credentials <arn-of-iam-role>
```

Here's a brief description of the parameters used:

- `rest-api-id`: The ID of the REST API in API Gateway to which you want to add the integration.
- `resource-id`: The ID of the resource you want to add the integration to.
- `http-method`: The HTTP method for which you want to create an integration.
- `type`: The type of the integration. This can be `HTTP` for integrating with an HTTP backend or `AWS` for integrating with an AWS service.
- `integration-http-method`: The HTTP method used to call the backend. This is typically `POST`, `GET`, `PUT`, `DELETE`, or `PATCH`.
- `uri`: The **Uniform Resource Identifier** (**URI**) of the backend service or resource. For example, if you're integrating with an HTTP backend, this would be the URL of the HTTP endpoint.
- `credentials`: The ARN of an IAM role that API Gateway assumes when calling the backend service or resource.

Here is a sample code:

```
aws apigateway put-integration \
--rest-api-id abcdef1234 \
--resource-id abc123 \
--http-method POST \
--type AWS_PROXY \
--integration-http-method POST \
--uri arn:aws:apigateway:us-east-1:lambda:path/2015-03-31/functions/
arn:aws:lambda:us-east-1:123456789012:function:myLambdaFunction/
invocations \
--passthrough-behavior WHEN_NO_MATCH \
--content-handling CONVERT_TO_TEXT
```

This command creates an AWS Lambda proxy integration for a `POST` method on a specific API Gateway resource. The `--rest-api-id` parameter specifies the ID of the API Gateway REST API, while the `--resource-id` parameter specifies the ID of the resource to which the method is attached. The `--http-method` parameter specifies the `HTTP` method for the method.

The `--type` parameter specifies the type of integration. In this case, it is set to `AWS_PROXY`, which means that the Lambda function is invoked directly from the API Gateway. The `--integration-http-method` parameter specifies the HTTP method used to invoke the Lambda function. In this case, it is set to `POST`.

The `--uri` parameter specifies the ARN of the Lambda function to integrate with.

The `--passthrough-behavior` parameter specifies the passthrough behavior for unmapped requests. In this case, it is set to `WHEN_NO_MATCH`. The `--content-handling` parameter specifies how to handle the request payload. In this case, it is set to `CONVERT_TO_TEXT`.

7. Use the `aws apigateway create-deployment` command to deploy the API to a stage, such as `prod` or `test`. In this command, you need to specify the REST API ID and the stage's name:

```
aws apigateway create-deployment --rest-api-id <rest-api-id>
--stage-name <stage-name>
```

Replace `<rest-api-id>` with the ID of the REST API you want to deploy, and `<stage-name>` with the name of the deployment stage you wish to create.

You can also include additional parameters to customize the deployment, such as the deployment description, stage variables, and tags. For more information on the available parameters, refer to the AWS CLI documentation for this command.

Here's an example:

```
aws apigateway create-deployment --rest-api-id abc123 --stage-name
prod --description "Production deployment"
```

This command creates a new API deployment with ID of `abc123` to the `prod` stage with the description `Production deployment`.

8. Finally, use the CLI `aws apigateway get-invoke-url` CLI command to get the URL of the deployed API. You can then test the API using this URL. Here is the syntax:

```
aws apigateway get-invoke-url --region <region> --rest-api-id <rest-
api-id> --stage-name <stage-name>
```

Let's break this down:

- `<region>` is the AWS region where the API is deployed
- `<rest-api-id>` is the ID of the REST API for which to retrieve the endpoint URL
- `<stage-name>` is the name of the API deployment stage for which to retrieve the endpoint URL

The command returns the public URL of the API endpoint, which clients can use to access the API by making HTTP requests.

DevOps is an important step toward automating the entire software delivery pipeline and improving efficiency. Let's learn about DevOps in detail.

DevOps in AWS

DevOps is a methodology that integrates cultural philosophies, practices, and tools to enhance an organization's capacity to deliver applications and services quickly. It helps the organization evolve and improve products faster than traditional software development and infrastructure management processes. This speed allows organizations to serve their customers better and compete in the market more effectively.

To build a **continuous integration/continuous deployment** (**CI/CD**) pipeline for the *AWSome Store* app, follow these steps:

1. **Code repository**: Store the *AWSome Store* app's source code in a version control system such as AWS CodeCommit or GitHub/GitLab. Ensure that your code is stored in a branch suitable for production deployment. You can choose a repository of your choice to check in code.
2. **Build and test**: Use a tool such as AWS CodeBuild to compile the source code and run tests. This step ensures that the code is stable and working as expected.
3. **Continuous integration**: Integrate the build and test process with the code repository to trigger the pipeline automatically when code changes are pushed to the repository. AWS provides several tools for continuous integration and delivery, including AWS CodePipeline, AWS CodeBuild, and AWS CodeDeploy. These tools enable teams to automate the building, testing, and deployment of their applications.
4. **Monitoring**: Use Amazon CloudWatch to monitor the app's health and detect and alert on any issues. AWS provides various monitoring and logging services, including Amazon CloudWatch, AWS X-Ray, and AWS CloudTrail. These services enable teams to monitor the performance and health of their applications, diagnose issues, and troubleshoot problems.

5. **Continuous deployment**: Automate the deployment of new releases to the production environment whenever the code is integrated and tested successfully.
6. **Roll back**: If you encounter any issues with the new release, plan to roll back to the previous version of the app.

By implementing a CI/CD pipeline, you can ensure that the *AWSome Store* app is continuously integrated, tested, deployed, and monitored, which helps improve the reliability and speed of software delivery.

After setting up your code repository, the following are the steps to build a CI/CD pipeline using AWS CodePipeline:

1. **Create a build stage**: The build stage will compile your code and create the artifacts that will be deployed. You can use AWS CodeBuild to create the build stage. You will need to define a `buildspec.yml` file that specifies the commands to build your code. The artifacts should be stored in an S3 bucket.
2. **Create a deployment stage**: The deployment stage will deploy your code to your production environment. You can use AWS CodeDeploy to create the deployment stage. You will need to define an `AppSpec` file that specifies how the deployment will be done.
3. **Create a pipeline**: Create a new pipeline in AWS CodePipeline and specify the source code repository, build, and deployment stages. You can configure triggers to start the pipeline automatically when code changes are committed to the repository.
4. **Test the pipeline**: Test your pipeline by committing code changes to the repository, verifying that the pipeline is triggered, building your code, and deploying it to your production environment.
5. **Configure pipeline notifications**: Configure pipeline notifications to receive notifications when pipeline stages succeed or fail. This will help you monitor your pipeline and respond quickly to any issues.
6. **Fine-tune the pipeline**: As you use the pipeline, you may find areas for improvement. You can fine-tune the pipeline by adjusting the settings or by adding new stages.

As you can see, building a CI/CD pipeline using AWS CodePipeline requires some initial setup and configuration. However, once the pipeline is set up, it can automate the process of building, testing, and deploying your code, which can save you time and help you deliver software more quickly and reliably.

Rollback planning is essential to any deployment process, as it allows you to revert changes if something goes wrong. Here are some steps you can follow to plan a rollback:

1. **Define the criteria for a rollback**: Identify the conditions that warrant a rollback, such as a critical error affecting your application's functionality or a significant decrease in performance. Make sure the criteria are well defined and communicated to all stakeholders.
2. **Identify the rollback process**: Determine the steps needed to perform a rollback. This should include backing up your data, rolling back to a previous version of your application or code, and ensuring that all changes made during the deployment are appropriately rolled back.
3. **Prepare the rollback plan**: Document the rollback plan, including all the steps you need to take, the timeline for each step, and the roles and responsibilities of everyone involved. Make sure the plan is easily accessible to all stakeholders and that everyone is aware of their duties.
4. **Test the rollback plan**: Before deploying your application, test it to ensure it works as expected. This will help you identify any issues or gaps in the plan before using it in a real-world scenario.
5. **Communicate the rollback plan**: Communicate the rollback plan to all stakeholders, including developers, QA, operations, and management. Ensure everyone knows the plan and what to do if a rollback is required.
6. **Monitor the deployment**: During the deployment, monitor the performance of your application and keep an eye out for any signs that a rollback may be necessary. This will help you identify issues early and take action before they become critical.

By following these steps, you can ensure that you have a well-defined and tested rollback plan in place. This plan will help you minimize downtime and avoid potential losses in case something goes wrong during the deployment.

AWS offers various adaptable services to help businesses develop and distribute products more quickly and consistently using AWS and DevOps methodologies. These services streamline the processes of setting up and maintaining infrastructure, releasing application code, automating software updates, and overseeing the performance of both applications and infrastructure.

Logging and monitoring

Setting up logging and monitoring helps organizations better understand their systems, improve their performance and reliability, meet compliance requirements, and enhance their systems' security. It provides insights into the system's behavior and performance, which can be used to identify and troubleshoot issues more quickly. Monitoring the system for potential issues and triggering alerts makes identifying and resolving problems easier before they become critical.

Logging and monitoring provide detailed performance data that can be used to identify and resolve bottlenecks, leading to improved system performance. They help ensure that the system is meeting compliance requirements and provide evidence in the event of an audit. Monitoring also helps detect and respond to security incidents, protecting sensitive data and maintaining the system's integrity. Here are the high-level steps to set up logging and monitoring for the *AWSome Store* app in AWS using the CLI:

1. Create a CloudWatch Logs group for your Lambda function:

   ```
   aws logs create-log-group --log-group-name awsomestore-log-group
   ```

2. Enable AWS X-Ray for your Lambda function. To enable AWS X-Ray for a Lambda function, you can use the following command:

   ```
   aws lambda update-function-configuration --function-name <function-
   name> --tracing-config Mode=Active
   ```

   Replace `<function-name>` with the name of your Lambda function. This command enables active tracing for the Lambda function using AWS X-Ray.

3. Create a CloudWatch alarm to monitor the error rate of your Lambda function:

   ```
   aws cloudwatch put-metric-alarm
   --alarm-name awsomestore-error-rate   # The name of the alarm
   --comparison-operator GreaterThanThreshold   # The comparison
   operator
   --evaluation-periods 1   # The number of periods to evaluate the
   alarm
   --metric-name Errors   # The metric to evaluate
   --namespace AWS/Lambda   # The namespace of the metric
   --period 300   # The period of the metric in seconds
   --statistic SampleCount   # The statistic to apply to the metric
   --threshold 1   # The threshold for the alarm
   --alarm-actions arn:aws:sns:us-east-1:123456789012:awsomestore-
   alerts   # The ARN of the SNS topic to send notifications
   --dimensions FunctionName=awsomestore   # The dimensions to apply to
   the metric
   --treat-missing-data breaching   # The action to take if data is
   missing
   ```

In this command, you need to replace awsomestore with the name of your Lambda function and 123456789012 with your AWS account ID. You also need to replace arn:aws:sns:us-east-1:123456789012:awsomestore-alerts with the ARN of the SNS topic to which you want to send notifications.

4. View and analyze your logs and metrics in the CloudWatch console. Configure your Lambda function to send logs and metrics to CloudWatch. You can use the following AWS CLI command:

```
aws lambda update-function-configuration --function-name <function-
name> --handler <handler> --role <role-arn> --environment
Variables={LOG_GROUP_NAME=/aws/lambda/<function-name>,METRICS_
NAMESPACE=<namespace>}
```

Here, you need to replace <function-name> with the name of your Lambda function, <handler> with the name of your function's handler, <role-arn> with the ARN of the execution role for your Lambda function, and <namespace> with the namespace for your CloudWatch metrics.

You can also replace the LOG_GROUP_NAME environment variable with the name of the CloudWatch Logs group where you want to send your function's logs.

To view logs and metrics in the CloudWatch console, here are the steps:

1. Open the AWS Management Console and navigate to the CloudWatch service.
2. In the left sidebar, click on **Logs** to view logs or **Metrics** to view metrics.
3. To view logs, click on the log group associated with your Lambda function, then select a log stream to view the logs.
4. To view metrics, select **Lambda** as the namespace, then select your function name and the metric you want to view (such as **Errors**).
5. You can adjust the time range using the drop-down menu in the top-right corner of the page.

Here are some best practices for logging and monitoring in AWS:

- **Centralized logging**: Centralize logs from multiple services and resources in a single location, such as Amazon CloudWatch Logs.
- **Automated alerting**: Set up alerts to notify you of real-time potential issues and failures.

- **Real-time monitoring:** Use real-time monitoring tools such as Amazon CloudWatch metrics, Amazon CloudWatch alarms, and Amazon CloudWatch dashboards to track key performance indicators.
- **Log retention policy:** Define a log retention policy to ensure that logs are stored for a sufficient time to meet compliance and business requirements.
- **Security logging:** Enable security logging for all critical resources to detect and respond to security incidents. You can enable AWS CloudTrail to log API calls made to the resource, enable Amazon S3 server access logging to log requests made to an S3 bucket, and enable VPC Flow Logs to log network traffic to and from an EC2 instance.
- **Monitoring of third-party services:** Monitor the performance and health of third-party services and dependencies to ensure a smooth end-to-end experience.
- **Error logging and debugging:** Ensure that detailed error logs are captured and stored for debugging purposes.
- **Log analysis tools:** Log analysis tools such as CloudWatch Log Insights, Amazon Athena, and Amazon QuickSight can be used to analyze log data and identify trends and patterns.
- **Monitoring of resource utilization:** Monitor resource utilization of critical services to ensure they are running optimally and within budget.

You can explore more logging and monitoring best practices here: `https://docs.aws.amazon.com/prescriptive-guidance/latest/logging-monitoring-for-application-owners/logging-best-practices.html`.

This section took you through the high-level steps to build an app. You can extend the provided AWS infrastructure and code based on your needs. You can refer to the AWS Builder library to learn about implementing a different pattern: `https://aws.amazon.com/builders-library`. Also, multiple cloud solutions are available to explore from AWS as per your industry use case here: `https://aws.amazon.com/industries/`.

Optimization with a well-architected review

You learned about the well-architected review in *Chapter 2, Understanding the AWS Well-Architected Framework and Getting Certified*. A well-architected review report is a comprehensive review of your AWS infrastructure and applications, designed to help you improve your solutions' robustness, security, and performance.

A typical well-architected review report would include a summary of your current architecture and recommendations for improvement in each of the six pillars. The report would also include a list of best practices and guidelines for ensuring that your solutions are well-architected. Here are some best practices to consider when setting up the AWS infrastructure for your use case:

- Use AWS Organizations to manage multiple AWS accounts for production, testing, and development purposes. In this chapter, you deployed your app in a single dev account. Still, you should have separate accounts and manage them using AWS Organizations for production and test environments.
- Use IAM policies and roles to control access to AWS resources and limit the permissions of users and services.
- Use **virtual private clouds (VPCs)** to create a virtual network with a logically isolated section of the AWS cloud where you can launch AWS resources. You learned about AWS networking in *Chapter 4, Networking in AWS*. In this chapter, we have not covered networking to keep things simple, but you can build VPCs and put Lambda inside them for security, especially for customer management functions.
- Use Amazon S3 to store user data, application backups, and website hosting.
- Use Amazon DynamoDB for NoSQL data storage to store information such as customer profiles, orders, and products.
- Use Amazon API Gateway to create, deploy, and manage APIs for your application.
- Use AWS Lambda to run your application code and to execute business logic.
- Use Amazon CloudWatch to monitor, troubleshoot, and alert on the performance of your AWS resources.
- Use Amazon CloudFront for content delivery and to distribute your application to multiple locations for low latency and high performance.
- Use AWS Certificate Manager to secure your website using SSL/TLS certificates.
- Use Amazon Route 53 for domain name registration and routing users to your application.
- Implement disaster recovery strategies, such as backups and multiple availability zones.
- Monitor and manage costs with the AWS Cost Explorer and monitor security with AWS Security Hub.

Finally, adhere to the AWS Well-Architected Framework and perform regular reviews to ensure your infrastructure is secure, reliable, and cost-effective.

Knowledge check

It's time for your final knowledge check. The following questions will not only help test your knowledge but also give an idea of the AWS SA Pro certification questions standard:

1. A multinational e-commerce company operates its primary application in the `us-east-1` region. The application consists of multiple microservices deployed on Amazon ECS Fargate, utilizes Amazon Aurora PostgreSQL for its database, and stores static assets in Amazon S3.

   To ensure business continuity and meet regulatory requirements, the company plans to implement a **disaster recovery** (**DR**) strategy that allows for failover to the `eu-west-1` region in the event of a regional outage. The DR strategy must meet the following objectives:

   - **Recovery time objective** (**RTO**): Less than 15 minutes
   - **Recovery point objective** (**RPO**): Less than 5 minutes
   - **Cost efficiency**: Minimize operational costs in the standby region
   - **Automation**: Failover processes should be automated to reduce manual intervention

   The company has already established a VPC in `eu-west-1` with the necessary networking configurations.

   Which combination of actions should the solutions architect recommend to meet these requirements? (Choose two.)

   a. Implement Amazon Aurora Global Databases to enable cross-region replication of the Aurora PostgreSQL database, allowing for fast recovery with minimal data loss.

   b. Set up **AWS Elastic Disaster Recovery** (**AWS DRS**) for the ECS Fargate services to replicate the application stack to `eu-west-1`, ensuring rapid failover.

   c. Configure S3 **cross-region replication** (**CRR**) to automatically replicate static assets from `us-east-1` to `eu-west-1`, ensuring data availability in both regions.

   d. Use AWS CloudFormation StackSets to deploy and manage infrastructure changes across both regions, facilitating consistent environments.

   e. Implement Amazon Route 53 with health checks and failover routing policies to automatically redirect traffic to `eu-west-1` in case of a regional failure.

   Answers: a. and e.

Explanation:

a. **Correct**. Amazon Aurora Global Databases are designed for applications with a global footprint, providing CRR with typical lag times of less than a second. This setup supports an RPO of less than 5 minutes and enables fast failover, meeting the RTO requirement.
b. Incorrect. AWS DRS is primarily used for EC2 instances and does not support ECS Fargate services. Therefore, it cannot be used to replicate Fargate-based applications.
c. Incorrect. S3 CRR ensures that static assets are available in both regions, supporting data availability and contributing to the RPO objective.
d. Incorrect. While AWS CloudFormation StackSets can help maintain consistent infrastructure across regions, they do not provide real-time replication or automated failover capabilities required for this DR strategy.
e. **Correct**. Amazon Route 53 with health checks and failover routing can automatically detect regional outages and redirect traffic to the standby region, supporting the RTO requirement of less than 15 minutes.

2. A healthcare analytics company is developing a data lake on AWS to store and analyze large volumes of structured and unstructured patient data. The data lake must comply with HIPAA regulations, ensuring strict data security and privacy. The solution should support various analytics tools and provide fine-grained access controls to different user groups, such as data scientists, analysts, and external partners.

   The company has the following requirements:

   - **Security**: Encrypt data at rest and in transit, and implement fine-grained access controls
   - **Scalability**: Handle petabytes of data with varying access patterns
   - **Integration**: Support integration with AWS analytics services such as Amazon Athena and Amazon Redshift
   - **Auditing**: Maintain detailed audit logs for data access and modifications

   Which combination of actions should the solutions architect recommend to meet these requirements? (Choose two.)

   a. Store data in Amazon S3 with server-side encryption using AWS KMS-managed keys (SSE-KMS) to ensure that data at rest is encrypted.

b. Use AWS Lake Formation to centrally manage data access permissions and provide fine-grained access control across various AWS analytics services.

c. Implement Amazon Macie to automatically discover, classify, and protect sensitive data stored in Amazon S3.

d. Use Amazon S3 Access Points to manage access for different user groups, simplifying permission management.

e. Enable AWS CloudTrail to log all data access and modification events for auditing purposes.

Answers: a. and b.

Explanation:

a. **Correct.** Using SSE-KMS for Amazon S3 ensures that data at rest is encrypted with keys managed by AWS KMS, meeting HIPAA encryption requirements.

b. **Correct.** AWS Lake Formation simplifies the process of setting up a secure data lake by providing centralized access control, fine-grained permissions, and integration with AWS analytics services, aligning with the company's requirements.

c. Incorrect. While Amazon Macie helps discover and classify sensitive data, it does not provide access control or auditing capabilities required for this solution.

d. Incorrect. Amazon S3 Access Points simplify managing application access, but they do not offer the centralized, fine-grained access control needed across various analytics services.

e. Incorrect. AWS CloudTrail logs API calls and actions taken within the AWS environment, but does not provide detailed auditing of data access and modifications within the data lake.

3. A **software-as-a-service (SaaS)** provider is developing a multi-tenant analytics platform on AWS. The platform will onboard customers from different industries with data segregation and compliance requirements. The application must scale dynamically to handle unpredictable workloads, support tenant isolation, and enable cost control mechanisms. The solution must also provide high availability, disaster recovery, and compliance with data residency rules (e.g., customers in the EU want data stored only within the EU).

   The company has adopted a microservices-based architecture and will use Amazon ECS with Fargate, Amazon RDS (PostgreSQL), and Amazon S3 for data storage. They want to automate infrastructure provisioning and manage environments through CI/CD pipelines.

Which combination of design choices should the solutions architect recommend to address these requirements effectively? (Choose two.)

a. Implement separate VPCs and ECS clusters per region to isolate tenant workloads and comply with regional data residency requirements. Use AWS CodePipeline to automate deployment across all environments.
b. Use a single multi-AZ Amazon RDS instance shared by all tenants, and isolate tenant data at the application level by assigning tenant-specific schemas within the same database.
c. Design the application to use AWS Organizations and **service control policies (SCPs)** for each tenant to provide strict isolation and billing separation across environments.
d. Enable S3 bucket-level access control using IAM policies and Amazon Cognito identity pools to enforce per-tenant data isolation and user-level authorization.
e. Use AWS CloudFormation StackSets to standardize and deploy tenant-specific infrastructure templates across multiple AWS Regions and accounts, ensuring consistency and compliance.

Answers: a. and e.

Explanation:

a. **Correct**. Deploying separate VPCs and ECS clusters by region addresses data residency and isolation concerns. AWS CodePipeline supports automated CI/CD deployment, aligning with scalability and cost control goals.
b. Incorrect. While tenant-specific schemas can be used for basic isolation, sharing a single RDS instance across all tenants introduces performance, security, and compliance risks, especially for regulated industries.
c. Incorrect. AWS Organizations and SCPs are designed for account-level management, not individual tenant isolation within a SaaS environment. They're not suited for micro-level tenant access control.
d. Incorrect. While Cognito and IAM can handle user authorization, S3 bucket-level controls do not adequately handle complex multi-tenant data isolation, especially with regional compliance needs.
e. **Correct**. AWS CloudFormation StackSets help maintain consistent tenant infrastructure across regions/accounts, supporting automated provisioning and compliance enforcement—key for scalable SaaS environments.

4. A global media and entertainment company wants to build an analytics platform on AWS to process and analyze user interaction data from its mobile app, web streaming services, and social media campaigns. The data is semi-structured and arrives in real time, with traffic peaks during major live events. The company needs to securely ingest and store this data, process it for near-real-time insights, and provide dashboards for business analysts and data scientists.

   The platform must meet the following goals:

   - Optimize for cost while maintaining scalability and availability
   - Support querying with Amazon Athena and Amazon Redshift Spectrum
   - Ensure that all data is encrypted at rest and in transit
   - Allow fine-grained access control for different user personas
   - Retain raw and processed data for at least 12 months to meet compliance

   Which combination of solutions should the solutions architect recommend to meet these requirements? (Choose two.)

   a. Use Amazon Kinesis Data Firehose to ingest and deliver streaming data into Amazon S3 in Parquet format with server-side encryption using AWS KMS. Configure S3 lifecycle policies to manage data retention.
   b. Stream all incoming data to Amazon DynamoDB and use Amazon DAX for in-memory acceleration to enable fast real-time analytics and compliance-level durability.
   c. Use AWS Lake Formation to manage table access controls, metadata, and integration with Amazon Athena and Redshift Spectrum for secure querying.
   d. Store raw data in Amazon S3 Glacier and retrieve it on demand for reporting to reduce storage costs and enable long-term archiving.
   e. Use Amazon EMR with Apache Hive to batch process all data hourly, write results back to S3, and use S3 Select for querying instead of Athena or Redshift.

   Answers: a. and c.

   Explanation:

   a. **Correct**. Amazon Kinesis Data Firehose simplifies the ingestion of real-time data into S3. It supports automatic conversion to formats such as Parquet and enables encryption with AWS KMS. Combined with S3 lifecycle policies, it supports compliance and cost-effective data retention.

   b. Incorrect. DynamoDB is not optimized for storing large volumes of semi-structured streaming data, and it lacks native support for SQL-based analytics across services such as Athena or Redshift.
   c. **Correct**. AWS Lake Formation provides a centralized framework for managing access to data stored in S3 across analytics services. It supports fine-grained access control and integrates with both Athena and Redshift Spectrum.
   d. Incorrect. S3 Glacier is intended for archival data and has high retrieval latency, which does not meet near-real-time analytics needs.
   e. Incorrect. While EMR is powerful for processing, using S3 Select is limited in querying capability. Athena and Redshift Spectrum are more suited for the SQL-based querying that analysts and data scientists need.

5. A **financial technology (fintech)** company must implement a real-time fraud detection system on AWS for its digital payments platform. The platform receives transaction data from multiple sources, including mobile devices, APIs, and partner services. The fraud detection system must analyze incoming transactions in real time using machine learning, flag suspicious activity, and trigger downstream alerts via messaging systems.

   The platform must meet the following business and technical requirements:

   - Process thousands of transactions per second with sub-second latency
   - Run inference using a pretrained machine learning model hosted on AWS
   - Automatically scale to handle traffic spikes without preprovisioning capacity
   - Store flagged and unflagged transactions for later batch analysis
   - Secure all data in transit and at rest, and comply with PCI DSS regulations

   Which combination of services and architectural patterns should the solutions architect recommend? (Choose two.)

   a. Use Amazon Kinesis Data Streams to ingest transactions and invoke AWS Lambda for lightweight stream processing. Lambda calls the Amazon SageMaker endpoint for fraud inference and stores results in Amazon DynamoDB.
   b. Ingest data through Amazon API Gateway, store transactions directly in Amazon RDS, and periodically run stored procedures to identify anomalies based on business rules.
   c. Deploy the ML model in a container on Amazon ECS Fargate and invoke it using synchronous API calls from a Node.js backend hosted on AWS Elastic Beanstalk.

d. Use Amazon EventBridge to trigger AWS Step Functions for each transaction, call a SageMaker model, and route the output to Amazon SQS for alerting and Amazon S3 for storage.

e. Stream data through Amazon MSK (Managed Kafka), perform real-time processing with Apache Flink on Amazon Kinesis Data Analytics, and send results to Amazon Redshift for dashboarding and historical analysis.

Answers: a. and e.

Explanation:

a. **Correct.** Amazon Kinesis Data Streams with AWS Lambda allows real-time ingestion and processing of high-throughput transaction data. Lambda can invoke a SageMaker endpoint for ML inference and write results to DynamoDB or S3. This setup is serverless, scalable, and PCI-compliant when encrypted properly.

b. Incorrect. RDS is not ideal for handling real-time streaming workloads or sub-second processing. It introduces latency and lacks the horizontal scalability needed for spikes in transaction volume.

c. Incorrect. Although ECS Fargate can host a model, invoking it through Elastic Beanstalk does not scale effectively for sub-second real-time processing. This pattern is more suited to low-frequency or batch inference workloads.

d. Incorrect. While Step Functions provide workflow orchestration, invoking it per transaction introduces additional latency and overhead, contradicting the sub-second latency requirement.

e. **Correct.** Amazon MSK with Apache Flink (via Kinesis Data Analytics) is a robust solution for streaming analytics. It supports complex event processing at scale and can stream results to Redshift for visualization or S3 for compliance logging, satisfying real-time and historical analysis needs.

Summary

In this chapter, you have put together many of the technologies, best practices, and AWS services we have covered in this book. You weaved it together into an e-commerce website architecture that you should be able to leverage and use for your future projects.

You built architecture using AWS services following DDD. You learned about implementing various AWS services, including IAM, S3, DynamoDB, Lambda, and API Gateway, and using the AWS CLI. You learned about several best practices and a well-architected framework to optimize your architecture.

As fully featured as AWS has become, it will continue providing more services to help large and small enterprises simplify their information technology infrastructure. You can rest assured that AWS is creating new services and improving the existing services by making them better, faster, easier, more flexible, and more powerful, as well as by adding more features.

As of 2025, AWS offers more than 200 services, a big jump from its 2 services in 2004. AWS's progress in the last 20 years has been monumental. I cannot wait to see what the next 20 years will bring for AWS and what kind of solutions we can deliver with their new offerings.

I hope you are as excited as I am about the possibilities these new services will bring.

Happy learning! Always learn, and always be curious.

Join us on Discord

For discussions around the book and to connect with your peers, join us on Discord at `https://discord.gg/kbFRRSB2Qs` or scan the QR code below:

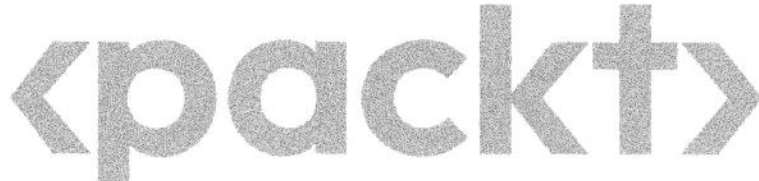

Other Books You May Enjoy

If you enjoyed this book, you may be interested in these other books by Packt:

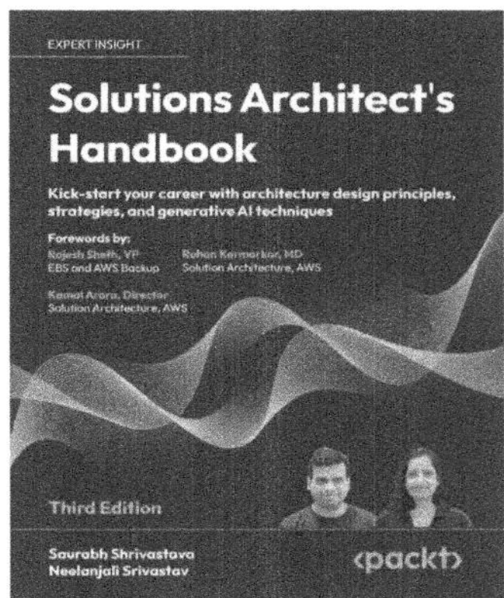

Solutions Architect's Handbook - Third Edition

Saurabh Shrivastava, Neelanjali Srivastav

ISBN: 978-1-83508-423-6

- Explore various roles of a solutions architect in the enterprise
- Apply design principles for high-performance, cost-effective solutions
- Choose the best strategies to secure your architectures and boost availability
- Develop a DevOps and CloudOps mindset for collaboration, operational efficiency, and streamlined production

- Apply machine learning, data engineering, LLMs, and generative AI for improved security and performance
- Modernize legacy systems into cloud-native architectures with proven real-world strategies
- Master key solutions architect soft skills

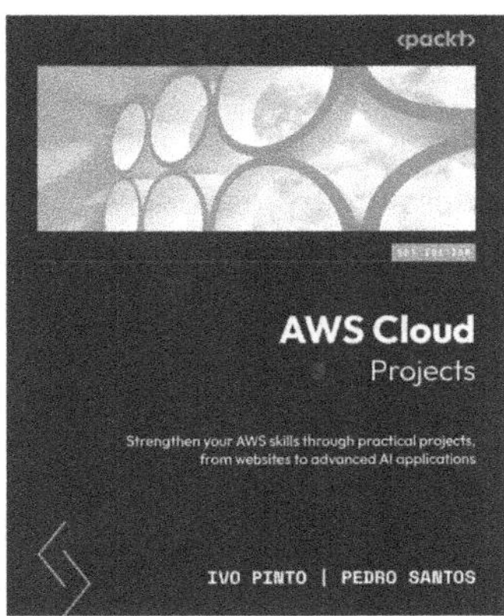

AWS Cloud Projects

Ivo Pinto, Pedro Santos

ISBN: 978-1-83588-928-2

- Develop a professional CV website while learning AWS fundamentals
- Build a recipe-sharing application using AWS's serverless toolkit
- Leverage AWS AI services to create a photo friendliness analyzer for professional profiles
- Implement a CI/CD pipeline to automate content translation across languages
- Develop an AI-powered Q chatbot using Amazon Lex and cutting-edge LLMs
- Build a business intelligence application to analyze website clickstream data and understand user behavior with AWS

Packt is searching for authors like you

If you're interested in becoming an author for Packt, please visit `authors.packt.com` and apply today. We have worked with thousands of developers and tech professionals, just like you, to help them share their insight with the global tech community. You can make a general application, apply for a specific hot topic that we are recruiting an author for, or submit your own idea.

Share your thoughts

Now you've finished *AWS for Solutions Architects, Third Edition*, we'd love to hear your thoughts! Scan the QR code below to go straight to the Amazon review page for this book and share your feedback or leave a review on the site that you purchased it from.

`https://packt.link/r/1836641931`

Your review is important to us and the tech community and will help us make sure we're delivering excellent quality content.

Index

A

E

I

J

K

L

M

N

O

P

Q

R

S

www.ingramcontent.com/pod-product-compliance
Lightning Source LLC
Chambersburg PA
CBHW081207220326
41598CB00037B/6705

* 9 7 8 1 8 3 6 6 4 1 9 3 3 *